'Holbrooke in all his capacious brilliance and arrogance has been captured by George Packer... [*Our Man*] is, I strongly feel, a classic'

Richard Cohen, *Washington Post*

'You may ask yourself, is it worth one of the best American non-fiction writers producing a book of just under 600 pages on an arrogant and abrasive egotist whose highest sustained rank in the State Department was that of a lowly assistant secretary? The answer is unabashedly yes. This is a remarkable work about a remarkable, if deeply flawed, statesman whose career was intimately intertwined with the 50 years of American decline from Vietnam to Afghanistan. Nearly all biographies have long, boring stretches you want to skip. This one has none... A fascinating and compulsive read'

Jonathan Powell, *Spectator*

'*Our Man* is a great, exuberant read, gossipy and thoughtful, about a remarkable American diplomat who tried to place himself at the heart of some of the bloodiest, most intractable wars of our age: Vietnam, Bosnia and Afghanistan... Packer displays his talents as a master of narrative reconstruction'

Roger Boyes, *The Times*

'Dazzling   decline that's
heartfelt,   at the same
time   l with
grea   ookian

C334518381

'Deeply researched, compelling... *Our Man* is not just a portrait of a fascinating historical figure, it is a contemplation of a half-century of US foreign and security policy and its most intractable challenges'

Julian Borger, *Observer*

'[Packer] is such a masterful narrator – and Holbrooke such a vexing subject to portray – that this story is both gripping and surprisingly pacey, its wheels greased by revealing excerpts from Holbrooke's personal letters and the private reflections he recorded to tape. Added to this is Packer's arresting thesis: that his brash but erudite and driven subject symbolises something about America's engagement with the world following the Second World War that will never be recovered after Trump'

John Bew, *New Statesman*

'A brazen book, one that buttonholes the reader...in just the way that its subject did... So perfectly has Packer captured his [Holbrooke's] style that there is no sense of discontinuity when the subject himself takes over as author... Enthralling... *Our Man* is unputdownable'

Niall Ferguson, *Sunday Times*

'Brilliant reporting...brave and intellectually honest... This is the kind of biography (massive, detailed) by the kind of author (respected, experienced) reserved for great books on great men'

Adam B. Kushner, *Washington Post*

'Packer's portrait is so full because he...[is] a first-rate reporter and writer who understands the history of the big conflicts at the centre of his story: Vietnam, Bosnia and Afghanistan... A vivid biography'

Lawrence Freedman, *Literary Review*

'The story has been told many times…but it has never been told as George Packer tells it… *Our Man* is a nuanced portrait of a driven man whose brilliance was held back by his almost comical insecurities… Packer is an accomplished reporter and careful writer, and he manages to sketch out the three conflicts at the heart of Holbrooke's career – Vietnam, Bosnia, Afghanistan – with subtlety and texture'

Toby Vogel, *Times Literary Supplement*

'A brilliant, abrasive diplomat struggles to resolve foreign conflicts while fighting bureaucratic wars at home in this scintillating biography… Packer makes him a Shakespearean character – egomaniacal, devious, sloppy enough to make presidents deny him the prize of becoming secretary of state, yet charismatic and inspiring – in a larger-than-life portrait brimming with vivid novelistic impressions… In Holbrooke's thwarted ambitions, Packer finds both a riveting tale of diplomatic adventure – part high drama, part low pettiness – and a captivating metaphor for America's waning power'

Publishers Weekly (starred review)

'By the end of the second page, maybe the third, you will be hooked… There never was a diplomat-activist quite like [Holbrooke], and there seldom has been a book quite like this – sweeping and sentimental, beguiling and brutal, catty and critical, much like the man himself'

David M. Shribman, *Boston Globe*

'The riveting life of a deeply flawed diplomat whose chief shortcoming seems to have been the need to be more recognized than he was… Students of recent world history and of American power, hard and soft, will find this an endlessly fascinating study of character and events'

Kirkus Reviews (starred review)

'It is impossible to read George Packer's new biography of Richard Holbrooke without a piercing sense of melancholy, not only that a man so supremely alive should be dead, but also because such people – *Our Man*, in Packer's title, the incarnation of vanished glory, imperial hubris, exceptional Americanism – no longer walk the earth... Extraordinary'

James Traub, *Foreign Policy*

'Stunning... If you're one of the dozens of people running for president, the book is probably the best guide you can find to navigating a transitional moment in American leadership and foreign policy. For the rest of us, it's a gripping read, and a sad one'

Ben Smith, *BuzzFeed News*

'Through a depiction that may be likened to Robert Caro's *The Power Broker*, Packer analyzes the forces of character that led us from a commitment to unity to the chaotic division in which we find ourselves today'

Lauren LeBlanc, *Observer*

'Best appreciated like a novel, consumed whole... Charming, brilliant, cocksure'

Jennifer Szalai, *New York Times*

'Like Holbrooke, Packer's account barrels along, brimming with mischief, verve and a sense of history. Unlike Holbrooke, it is tender and self-aware'

Tom Fletcher, *Prospect*

GEORGE PACKER

George Packer is a staff writer for *The Atlantic* and a former staff writer for *The New Yorker*. He is the author of *The Unwinding: Thirty Years of American Decline*, which was a *New York Times* bestseller and won a National Book Award. His other nonfiction books include *The Assassins' Gate: America in Iraq*, and *Blood of the Liberals*, which won the 2001 Robert F. Kennedy Book Award; and two novels, *The Half Man* and *Central Square*. Packer's writing has also appeared in *The New York Times Magazine*, *Mother Jones*, *Harper's*, and other publications. He lives in Brooklyn, New York.

ALSO BY GEORGE PACKER

Nonfiction

The Village of Waiting
Blood of the Liberals
The Assassins' Gate: America in Iraq
*Interesting Times: Writings from a
Turbulent Decade*
*The Unwinding: Thirty Years of
American Decline*

Novels

The Half Man
Central Square

Plays

Betrayed

GEORGE PACKER

Our Man

Richard Holbrooke and the End of the
American Century

VINTAGE

1 3 5 7 9 10 8 6 4 2

Vintage
20 Vauxhall Bridge Road
London SW1V 2SA

Vintage is part of the Penguin Random House group of companies
whose addresses can be found at global.penguinrandomhouse.com

Copyright © George Packer 2019

George Packer has asserted his right to be identified as
the author of this Work in accordance with the Copyright,
Designs and Patents Act 1988

First published by Jonathan Cape in 2019
First published in Vintage in 2020

penguin.co.uk/vintage

A CIP catalogue record for this book is available from the
British Library

ISBN 9781784704216

Printed and bound in Great Britain by Clays Ltd, Elcograf S.p.A.

Penguin Random House is committed to a sustainable future for our
business, our readers and our planet. This book is made from Forest
Stewardship Council® certified paper.

For Les and Judy Gelb
and for Frank Wisner

Contents

Our Man

H olbrooke? Yes, I knew him. I can't get his voice out of my head. I still hear it saying, "You haven't read that book? You really need to read it." Saying, "I feel, and I hope this doesn't sound too self-satisfied, that in a very difficult situation where nobody has the answer, I at least know what the overall questions and moving parts are." Saying, "Gotta go, Hillary's on the line." That voice! Calm, nasal, a trace of older New York, a singsong cadence when he was being playful, but always *doing* something to you, cajoling, flattering, bullying, seducing, needling, analyzing, one-upping you—applying continuous pressure like a strong underwater current, so that by the end of a conversation, even two minutes on the phone, you found yourself far out from where you'd started, unsure how you got there, and mysteriously exhausted.

He was six feet one but seemed bigger. He had long skinny limbs and a barrel chest and broad square shoulder bones, on top of which sat his strangely small head and, encased within it, the sleepless brain. His feet were so far from his trunk that, as his body wore down and the blood stopped circulating properly, they swelled up and became marbled red and white like steak. He had special shoes made and carried extra socks in his leather attaché case, sweating through half a dozen pairs a day, stripping them off on long flights and draping them over his seat pocket in first class, or else cramming used socks next to the classified documents in his briefcase. He wrote his book about ending the war in Bosnia—the place in history that he always craved, though it was never enough—with his feet planted in a Brookstone shiatsu foot massager. One morning he showed up late for a meeting in the secretary of state's suite at the Waldorf Astoria in his stocking feet, shirt untucked and fly half zipped, padding around the room and picking grapes off a fruit basket, while Madeleine Albright's furious stare tracked his every move. During a videoconference call from the U.N. mission in New York his feet were propped up on a chair, while down in the White House Situation Room their giant distortion completely filled the wall screen and so disrupted the meeting that President Clinton's national security advisor finally ordered a military aide to turn off the video feed. Holbrooke put his feet up anywhere, in the White House, on other people's desks and coffee tables—for relief, and for advantage.

Near the end, it seemed as if all his troubles were collecting in his feet—atrial fibrillation, marital tension, thwarted ambition, conspiring colleagues, hundreds of thousands of air miles, corrupt foreign leaders, a war that would not yield to the relentless force of his will.

But at the other extreme from his feet, the ice-blue eyes were on perpetual alert. Their light told you that his intelligence was always awake and working. They captured nearly everything and gave almost nothing away. Like one-way mirrors, they looked outward, not inward. I never knew anyone quicker to size up a room, an adversary, a newspaper article, a set of variables in a complex situation—even his own imminent death. The ceaseless appraising told of a manic spirit churning somewhere within the low voice and languid limbs. Once, in the 1980s, he was walking down Madison Avenue when an acquaintance passed him and called out, "Hi, Dick." Holbrooke watched the man go by, then turned to his companion: "I wonder what he meant by that." Yes, his curly hair never obeyed the comb, and his suit always looked rumpled, and he couldn't stay off the phone or TV, and he kept losing things, and he ate as much food as fast as he could, once slicing open the tip of his nose on a clamshell and bleeding through a pair of cloth napkins—yes, he was in almost every way a disorderly presence. But his eyes never lost focus.

So much thought, so little inwardness. He could not be alone—he might have had to think about himself. Maybe that was something he couldn't afford to do. Leslie Gelb, Holbrooke's friend of forty-five years and recipient of multiple daily phone calls, would butt into a monologue and ask, "What's Obama like?" Holbrooke would give a brilliant analysis of the president. "How do you think you affect Obama?" Holbrooke had nothing to say. Where did it come from, that blind spot behind his eyes that masked his inner life? It was a great advantage over the rest of us, because the propulsion from idea to action was never broken by self-scrutiny. It was also a great vulnerability, and finally, it was fatal.

I can hear the voice saying, "It's your problem now, not mine."

He loved speed. Franz Klammer's fearless downhill run for the gold in 1976 was a feat Holbrooke never finished admiring, until you almost believed that he had been the one throwing himself into those dangerous turns at Innsbruck. He pedaled his bike straight into a swarming Saigon intersection while talking about the war to a terrified blond journalist just arrived from Manhattan; he zipped through Paris traffic while lecturing his State Department boss on the status of the Vietnam peace talks; his Humvee careered down the dirt switchbacks of the Mount Igman road above besieged Sarajevo, chased by the armored personnel carrier with his doomed colleagues.

He loved mischief. It made him endless fun to be with and got him into unnecessary trouble. In 1967, he was standing outside Robert McNamara's office on the second floor of the Pentagon, a twenty-six-year-old junior official hoping to catch the secretary of defense on his way in or out, for no reason other than self-advancement. A famous colonel was waiting, too—a decorated paratrooper back from Vietnam, where Holbrooke had known him. Everything about the colonel was pressed and creased, his uniform shirt, his face, his pants carefully tucked into his boots and delicately bloused around the calves. He must have spent the whole morning on them. "That looks really beautiful," Holbrooke said, and he reached down and yanked a pants leg all the way out of its boot. The colonel started yelling. Holbrooke laughed.

Back in the Kennedy and Johnson years, when he was elbowing his way into public life, the phrase "action intellectuals" was hot, until Vietnam caught up with it and intellectuals got burned. But that was Holbrooke. Ideas mattered to him, but never for their own sake, only if they produced solutions to problems. The only problems worth his time were the biggest, hardest ones. Three fiendish wars—that's what his career came down to. He was almost singular in his eagerness to keep risking it. Having solved Bosnia, he wanted Cyprus, Kosovo, Congo,

the Horn of Africa, Tibet, Iran, India, Pakistan, and finally Afghanistan. Only the Middle East couldn't tempt him. As the Washington
bureaucracy got more cautious, his appetite for conquests grew. Right
after his death, Hillary Clinton said, "I picture him like Gulliver tied
down by Lilliputians."

He loved history—so much that he wanted to make it. The phrase
"great man" now sounds anachronistic, but as an inspiration for human
striving maybe we shouldn't throw out the whole idea. He came of age
when there was still a place for it and that place could only be filled by
an American. This was just after the war, when the ruined world lay
prone and open to the visionary action of figures like Acheson, Kennan,
Marshall, and Harriman. They didn't just grab for land and gold like the
great men of earlier empires. They built the structures of international
order that would endure for three generations, longer than anything
ever lasts, and that are only now turning to rubble. These were unsentimental, supremely self-assured white Protestant men—privileged,
you could say—born around the turn of the century, who all knew
one another and knew how to get things done. They didn't take a piss
without a strategy. Holbrooke revered them all and adopted a few as
replacement fathers. He wanted to join them at the top, and he clawed
his way up the slope of an establishment that was crumbling under his
crampons. He reached the highest base camp possible, but every assault
on the summit failed. He loved books about mountaineers, and in his
teens he climbed the Swiss Alps. He was a romantic. He never realized
that he had come too late.

You will have heard that he was a monstrous egotist. It's true. It's
even worse than you've heard—I'll explain as we go on. He offended
countless people, and they didn't forget, and since so many of them
swallowed their hurt, after he was gone it was usually the first thing
out of their mouth if his name came up, as it invariably did. How he
once told a colleague, "I lost more money in the market today than you
make in a year." How he bumped an elderly survivor couple from the
official American bus to Auschwitz on the fiftieth anniversary of its
liberation, added himself to the delegation alongside Elie Wiesel and
left the weeping couple to beg Polish guards to let them into the camp so
they wouldn't miss the ceremony. How he lobbied for the Nobel Peace

Prize—that kind of thing, all the time, as if he needed to discharge a surplus of self every few hours to maintain his equilibrium.

And the price he paid was very high. He destroyed his first marriage and his closest friendship. His defects of character cost him his dream job as secretary of state, the position for which his strengths of character eminently qualified him. You can't untangle these things. I used to think that if Holbrooke could just be fixed—a dose of self-restraint, a flash of inward light—he could have done anything. But that's an illusion. We are wholly ourselves. If you cut out the destructive element, you would kill the thing that made him almost great.

As a member of the class of lesser beings who aspire to a good life but not a great one—who find the very notion both daunting and distasteful—I can barely fathom the agony of that "almost." Think about it: the nonstop schedule, the calculation of every dinner table, the brain that burned all day and night—and the knowledge, buried so deep he might have only sensed it as a physical ache, that he had come up short of his own impossible exaltation. I admired him for that readiness to suffer. His life was full of pleasures, but I never envied it.

We had few things in common, but one that comes to mind is a love of Conrad's novels. In one of his letters, Conrad wrote that "these two contradictory instincts"—egotism and idealism—"cannot serve us unless in the incomprehensible alliance of their irreconcilable antagonism. Each alone would be fatal to our ambition." I think this means that they need each other to do any good. Idealism without egotism is feckless; egotism without idealism is destructive. It was never truer of anyone than Holbrooke. Sometimes the two instincts got out of whack. Certain people—his younger brother, Andrew, for example—couldn't see his idealism for the mountain of his egotism. Andrew thought his brother was missing the section of his brain that would have made him care about anyone other than himself. But Holbrooke's friends, the handful he kept for life, absorbed the pokes and laughed off the gargantuan faults without illusion. They wanted to protect him, because his appetites and insecurities were so naked. Now and then they had to hurt him, tear him to pieces. Then they could go on loving him. They knew that, of them all, he had the most promise, and they wanted to see him fulfill it—as a way to affirm them, their generation, their idea of public service, and their country. If Holbrooke could do it, then America might still be an adventure, with great things ahead. He always wanted more, and they wanted more for him, and when he died they mourned not just their friend but the lost promise.

He loved America. Not in a chest-beating way—he didn't wear a flag pin on his lapel—but without having to try, because he was the child of parents who had given everything to become American, and he grew up after the war amid the overwhelming evidence that this was a great and generous country. In the late summer of 2010, he went with his wife—his third wife and widow, Kati—to see a revival of *South Pacific* at Lincoln Center. Lifelong friends can't remember Holbrooke ever shedding tears, but he wept at *South Pacific,* and other men his age were weeping, too, and he tried to understand why. That was around the time he began speaking his thoughts into a tape recorder for some future use—maybe his memoirs—and here's what he said: "For me it was the combination of the beauty of the show and its music, and the capturing in that show of so many moments in American history, the show itself opening in New York at the height of New York's greatness, 1949, the theme—Americans at war in a distant land or islands in the South Pacific—the sense of loss of American optimism and our feeling that we could do anything. The contrast with today—" At this point his voice breaks, and I find it hard to keep listening. He had only a few months to live. "—it was very powerful, and I kept thinking of where we were today, our nation, our lack of confidence in our own ability to lead compared to where we were in 1949 when it came out, evoking an era only five years or seven years earlier, when we had gone to the most distant corners of the globe and saved civilization."

I'm trying to think what to tell you, now that you have me talking. There's too much to say and it all comes crowding in at once. His ambition, his loyalty, his cruelty, his fragility, his betrayals, his wounds, his wives, his girlfriends, his sons, his lunches. By dying he stood up a hundred people, including me. He could not be alone.

If you're still interested, I can tell you what I know, from the beginning. I wasn't one of his close friends, but over the years I made a study of him. You ask why? Not because he was extraordinary, though he was, and might have rivaled the record of his heroes if he and America had been in their prime together. Not because he was fascinating, though he was, and right this minute somewhere in the world fourteen people are talking about him. Now and then I might let him speak for himself— that was something he knew how to do. But I won't relate this story for his sake. No: we want to see and feel what happened to America during Holbrooke's life, and we can see and feel more clearly by following someone who was almost great, because his quest leads us deeper down the alleyways of power than the usual famous subjects (whom he knew, all of them), and his boisterous struggling lays open more human truths than the composed annals of the great. This was what Les Gelb must have meant when he said, just after his friend's death, "Far better to write a novel about Richard C. Holbrooke than a biography, let alone an obituary."

What's called the American century was really just a little more than half a century, and that was the span of Holbrooke's life. It began with the Second World War and the creative burst that followed—the United Nations, the Atlantic alliance, containment, the free world—and it went through dizzying lows and highs, until it expired the day before yesterday. The thing that brings on doom to great powers, and great men—is it simple hubris, or decadence and squander, a kind of inattention, loss of faith, or just the passage of years?—at some point that thing set in, and so we are talking about an age gone by. It wasn't a golden age, there was plenty of folly and wrong, but I already miss it. The best about us was inseparable from the worst. Our feeling that we could do anything gave us the Marshall Plan and Vietnam, the peace at Dayton and the endless Afghan war. Our confidence and energy, our reach and grasp, our excess and blindness—they were not so different from Holbrooke's. He was our man. That's the reason to tell you this story. That's why I can't get his voice out of my head.

Dreams So Far Away

D o you mind if we hurry through the early years? There are no mysteries here that can be unlocked by nursery school. Why Holbrooke was Holbrooke is not even the question to which we need an answer. I wonder if there's an answer for anyone, least of all him. You really need to know just one thing, and it has to do with Holbrooke's father.

His name was Abraham Dan Golbraich. He was born in 1912 in Warsaw, where he once saw a crowd of young Poles knife off the beards of Hasidic Jews. During World War I, Abraham and his mother, Agnes, a nurse, fled the German army east to her Russian hometown, Vitebsk. After the revolution in 1917, Agnes was accused of having czarist sympathies, and she and her son fled west, across Europe all the way to France. Golbraich grew up tall and good-looking, poor, serious, with gray-green eyes and wavy blond hair—a Jewish Paul Henreid. He studied at the Sorbonne in Paris and took a medical degree in Bologna. In the spring of 1939, on the eve of war, Golbraich sailed alone from Rome to New York. That summer, he opened the Manhattan phone book and found a name that sounded close to his: "Holbrook." He added an "e" for good measure, went before a judge, and, on July 6, 1939, became Dan A. Holbrooke, M.D. What a great country!

Gertrud Moos was dark haired, dark eyed, high-spirited. She was born in 1920 into Germany's leading hide-trading family. Her father, Samuel, served in the kaiser's army in World War I, posing in a pickle helmet and winning the Iron Cross. He fought in Poland, in Serbia, and on the western front in France, where he wrote to his brother-in-law in 1916: "After the war the Americans will discover that they have lost the sympathy of the Germans; perhaps they will yet rue their conduct, for in the future Europe such a vital and strong power like Germany, which is undefeatable, will weigh heavily in the scales, far more than before." That was how assimilated German Jews sounded before Hitler. Later, Sami Moos had the foresight to read *Mein Kampf,* and when the Nazis came to power he informed his children that they were Jewish and that the family was leaving Hamburg and Germany forever. They sailed to Buenos Aires, where Moos Hide had its export office. In January 1939, Trudi swapped her German passport, stamped in swastikas, for an Argentine one and immigrated to New York.

Dan and Trudi met the next year over dinner at International House, a haven for foreign students on the Upper West Side of Manhattan, and fell in love. On the night of April 24, 1941, twenty-year-old Trudi gave birth to a baby boy. They named him Richard Charles Albert Holbrooke—as if by piling up all these names on the foundation of an invented surname they could bury once and for all the pogroms and Bolsheviks and Nazis and Golbraichs from which the young couple had escaped. Dan and Trudi never used their many continental languages around the house. They didn't breathe a word of the ancestral religion to Dick, or to Andy, who came along in 1946. Later, the boys were sent to Quaker Sunday school—for the high-minded culture, not the theology (this was an atheist household). Trudi only told them the secret of their past in adolescence, and Dick didn't know his father's original name until late in his own life. The Old World had been nothing but trouble on both sides. The Holbrookes were no longer Jews. They were Americans.

And they did what Americans do. Trudi bought a pink nylon-bound logbook titled "Life Begins," illustrated with drawings of baby-blue birds and a cherub-cheeked WASP infant, in which she recorded Dickie's meteoric rise: his first smile after twenty-three days, his weight doubling in four months, standing unaided at eight months, walking at fourteen months. I frankly cannot imagine Holbrooke diapered. By three he would have been saying, "You haven't read that book? You really need to read it."

After the war, the Holbrookes, like other Americans, moved to the suburbs—Scarsdale, New York. Dan and Trudi became Democrats. They got interested in art. Lipchitz and de Kooning were patients of Dr. Holbrooke, as were scores of poorer refugees who sometimes paid in wine or salami. On Saturdays, cars lined up outside the two-story yellow stucco house at 2 Obry Drive—far from the nicest house on the Holbrookes' dead-end street—where Dan received patients at home and was locally admired.

He pushed his older son to study hard—"Why would you go to a baseball game when you can read a book?" He wanted Dick to win a Nobel Prize in the sciences, and he gave him a sense of history. In 1949, he took the eight-year-old boy to the East River to see the construction site of the future United Nations headquarters. He told his son—in a voice like a Hollywood character of vaguely European origin, a Slavic accent riding on Latin cadences—about this new body that would prevent wars like the ones of Dan's and Trudi's youth.

In the summer of 1956, at fifteen, Dick traveled alone to Europe to visit relatives on Trudi's side. He kept his father informed and impressed with letters that read like early diplomatic cables. The Suez Crisis was just beginning. "Is Nasser another Hitler? The British papers are asking themselves. If he is, now is the time to act. Britain is up in arms over what is their lifeline. For 80 years this has been one of their most important assets, keeping G.B. in top command. The British are ready to act. The French also. But Ike hesitates." In all other areas, he found America to be ahead of Europe—music, movies, architecture, science. But not statesmanship. Dick wanted America in the lead. "I think of Truman, who with snap decisions stopped a Russian advance in Korea. Now [Ike] must, as leader of the West, act, not hesitate. The world waits."

With his mother, the correspondence was as minimal and stilted as a third grader's: "I am going to send Andy some chocolates. They will arrive in a few days. Today it is raining. I met a girl from my class in Scarsdale here." The son was withheld, the mother preoccupied. Ever since 1950, Trudi had been taking care of a sick man.

That year, Dan had received a letter from his good friend, the sculptor Isamu Noguchi, who was in Asia: "I had a dream that you were seriously ill. I would have written to ask if there was anything to it, but I thought it was just too silly considering your vitality, profession—

dreams so far away in Bali half way across the world could have no basis in telepathic fact. So I dismissed it."

But Noguchi's dream was true: Dan was suffering from colon cancer, initially misdiagnosed. For seven years, the years of Dick's youth, his father was in and out of hospitals and surgeries.

One day in January 1957, Dick came home from Scarsdale High to find Andy in the kitchen. "You know Daddy died," Andy said.

"I know," Dick said. That was all he ever said. Andy never heard him speak about their father again. Hardly anyone did.

Forty-one years later, in 1998, at the Rose Garden ceremony announcing his appointment by President Bill Clinton as the American ambassador to the United Nations, Holbrooke recalled the construction site on the East River: "These buildings, my father said, would become the most important in the world. They would prevent future wars." Something was happening inside Holbrooke, and he swallowed. "My father did not live to see how his dream for the U.N. dissolved in the face of the harsh realities of the Cold War"—the thing was causing his voice to tremble; he paused to rub his nose—"and the inadequacies of the U.N. system itself." He swallowed again. He took a breath. "But I never forgot the initial visit and my father's noble if overly idealistic dream." His voice was breaking. He rubbed his nose again. He turned to Clinton at his side and murmured, "Excuse me. I'm sorry, I don't normally talk about my father in public." Clinton smiled and patted his back.

A lifelong repression briefly gave way on the evening news. Holbrooke had invoked his father and it nearly undid him. If those few words were enough to break his formidable public control, imagine what else lay breathing in his depths. Throughout his life, the person whose approval he needed most was no longer there to be impressed. If you want analysis, that's the best I can give you. But Holbrooke lived through action, and it's through action that we can know him. The smothering silence that settled over his early years and the family tragedy—that was an action. The self-creation that begins in self-erasure was another, maybe more radical than opening a phone book and taking a new name. He became the son of no one and nowhere—of himself, of America.

AFTER HIS FATHER'S DEATH, he immigrated to the family of a classmate named David Rusk. David became his best friend at Scarsdale High, fellow editor at the student paper, and tennis partner on the clay courts in town, where one summer they hit balls while keeping a radio tuned to news of an American military intervention in Lebanon. Holbrooke began spending more time at the Rusk house than at his own, often sleeping over. For Trudi, who soon found another man, he substituted gracious, dowdy Virginia Rusk. In place of his late father there was bald, round-faced, pouchy-eyed Dean Rusk. He was barely aware that Mr. Rusk was president of the Rockefeller Foundation and utterly ignorant of his past as assistant secretary of state for Far Eastern affairs under Dean Acheson in the Truman administration, or of Rusk's role in advocating a hard line after North Korea invaded the South in 1950.

Rusk was a dirt-poor son of Cherokee County, Georgia, diffident and aloof—unpromising material for a surrogate father. But when, in the spring of 1958, he came to a breakfast at Scarsdale High and told the senior class, "When you're thinking of careers, think of the Foreign Service." Holbrooke, who had never heard of it, paid attention.

In December 1960, President-elect Kennedy nominated Rusk (not his first choice) as secretary of state, after being assured by Dean Acheson and Robert Lovett, titans of the previous generation, that Rusk was so loyal and discreet, such a thoroughly reliable soldier of the Cold War—an Asia hand who had somehow emerged untainted from the loss of China and the stalemate in Korea—that Kennedy would get to be his own secretary of state.

Nineteen-year-old Dick Holbrooke was thrilled. He had never known anyone famous—suddenly, his reluctant surrogate father was someone of international importance, a step away from the young president himself. Holbrooke was a junior at Brown University and the new editor of the *Brown Daily Herald*. The previous May, he had contrived to have himself sent to Paris as the paper's correspondent at the four-power summit meeting on the Berlin crisis, and, once there, had talked his way into a ten-dollar-a-day job as a gofer for the *New York Times*, holding down conference room seats for *Times* reporters at the Palais

de Chaillot and fetching Carlsberg beer—until news that a CIA U-2 spy plane had been shot down while overflying the Soviet Union sent Khrushchev into a two-and-a-half-hour tirade before the assembled press, bringing the Paris summit to an abrupt end.

It had lasted long enough for Holbrooke to impress Clifton Daniel, the *Times*'s assistant managing editor and President Truman's son-in-law, and to wangle an internship in New York for the summer of 1961. He spent it living in a Greenwich Village walk-up and riding the Eighth Avenue subway to the *Times*, where he performed the chores of a copy boy on the national desk, grabbing any chance to write short unsigned pieces, and befriend famous Timesmen like Gay Talese. Back at Brown, he was becoming "*the* Dick Holbrooke." He told friends—they didn't know how seriously to take it—that his ambition was to be managing editor of the *Times* or else secretary of state.

Journalism, diplomacy: one operated on the outside of power, the other on the inside, but both put you at the center of historic events. For the rest of his life Holbrooke compressed the gap between them as much as possible. Diplomats envied and distrusted him for preferring the company of journalists; journalists pursued and suspected him for being a diplomat.

On trips to Washington he stayed with the Rusks. Once, the col-

lege student went to the secretary of state's office to interview him for
a senior history paper comparing Dean Rusk and Woodrow Wilson.
The First World War obsessed Holbrooke all his life. At nineteen, he
had hitchhiked through Europe to Sarajevo and stood in the concrete footprints—later destroyed by Muslims at the start of the Bosnian civil war in 1992—marking the spot where, on June 28, 1914, the
Bosnian Serb nationalist Gavrilo Princip stood by the Miljacka River
and fired the shots that started the Great War. He read the diaries of
Harold Nicolson, the junior diplomat who, later that summer, handed
the British declaration of war to the German ambassador in London.
After the war, Nicolson served on the British delegation at the Paris
Peace Conference, where the four victorious powers drew up the map
of the modern world, including the creation of Yugoslavia, and where a
kitchen assistant at the Ritz Hotel named Ho Chi Minh sent President
Wilson a petition on behalf of Vietnamese self-determination that was
ignored. Everything from the fate of Dan and Trudi to the wars of Holbrooke's professional life came out of what his friend the historian Fritz
Stern called "the first calamity" of the twentieth century, "from which
all other calamities sprang."

The end of that war was the first moment in history when an American stood at the center of the world. In Holbrooke's paper, Wilson was
a great and tragic figure. He "had a beautiful dream" of universal peace
and freedom, "and it shone in the skies for all the world to see and—for
a while—believe." It was the same as Dan Holbrooke's dream. But Wilson was too moralistic and rigid to carry it out. The failure of Wilson's
vision, which destroyed him, would be redeemed forty years later by
the new president and his secretary of state. Kennedy and Rusk were
tougher, more sophisticated, more pragmatic than their predecessor—
the harshness of intervening events had made them so. But they would
act on the same democratic faith as Wilson, which put America on the
side of right, and without which America would be just another big
country. Everything depended on that.

HE TOOK the Foreign Service exam, passed, and was offered a place
in the class of 1962. Meanwhile, the other path unexpectedly closed
down. James Reston, the *Times*'s Washington columnist and bureau

chief, didn't offer Holbrooke an entry-level job. A young reporter would need to spend a few years learning the trade at a lesser paper first. That wasn't in Holbrooke's career plan. So he would be the protagonist, not the chronicler.

He was sworn in at the Foreign Service Institute in July 1962—three months before the Cuban missile crisis—by Secretary of State Rusk, who, to Holbrooke's delight, inscribed a copy of *Satow's Guide to Diplomatic Practice,* fourth edition: "With warm congratulations to my friend Dick Holbrooke as he enters upon the greatest profession." Holbrooke got himself and his classmates invited to the secretary's office. Rusk lectured them to report the truth no matter how unpopular with their superiors. Then he said, "This is probably the closest any of you will ever get to a secretary of state."

Holbrooke had other ideas. He was twenty-one, the youngest member of his class. Today it's impossible to imagine someone his age, aglow with molten ambition, choosing the Foreign Service. But in those days it was different. Business wasn't entrepreneurial and heroic—it was corporate and dull. If you didn't have what it took to be a writer or athlete or movie star, or president of the United States, the other way to be great was as a statesman. In later years, after he became a personage, Holbrooke would attribute his choice of career to Kennedy's generational call to service—"Ask not what your country can do for you . . ."—which made an attractive story, but an apocryphal one. If any call inspired him, it was history.

I can see him: so old so young, tall and dorkish, the conservative suit and narrow tie of the early sixties, thick black-framed glasses and a faint smile that conveyed a shade of mischievous irony and all the optimism of an American going out into a world where Americans could do anything. There was a girl at Brown to whom he was or was not engaged; it didn't really matter. He was going to play his part in a great struggle—an actual war, rumor had it. His first assignment was two years in South Vietnam. He was ecstatic.

VIETNAM

How Can We Lose
When We're So Sincere?

I

Holbrooke landed in Saigon on a hot, dense night at the start of the summer monsoon. He walked down the gangway onto the tarmac and everything became more vivid—the noise of the Pan Am engines, the smell of jet fuel and wet asphalt, the close crowded air. As long as he remained in Vietnam, this heightened sensation never left him.

He was wearing a brand-new tropical suit that he had bought in Hong Kong. So was Vladimir Lehovich, his friend and Foreign Service classmate, who had arrived with him to begin their tour. As they waited on the tarmac for their luggage, the American official who had come out to greet their plane looked them over. "Boys, take off those suits," he said. "When you come into work tomorrow, remember—we're a shirtsleeves outfit."

In those years before the American buildup, Tan Son Nhut was just a small civilian airport. U.S. Army H-21 helicopters and Air America light craft were parked a ways off from the commercial jets. The terminal was a spare two-story building on which the rain beat a deafening noise. The Vietnamese officials looked indifferent and withdrawn in their crisp white uniforms.

There were two other people in the little welcoming party at the airport: Anthony and Antonia Lake, Tony and Toni. To distinguish one half of the couple from the other, their friends called them He Tony and She Toni. He Tony was another member of the Foreign Service class of

1962, now assigned to the Saigon embassy. She Toni had studied Vietnamese at the Foreign Service Institute and learned the language better than any of the men. The Lakes had already been in Saigon for two months. Of all the young men among Holbrooke's peers, it was Lake's friendship that he craved. Of all the American wives in Saigon, it was Toni's company that he sought. The Lakes were part of the excitement of being in Vietnam.

They drove south from the airport, past roadside night markets, down empty boulevards lined with tamarind and flame trees, into the center of the city, to the official guesthouse where Holbrooke spent the night of June 26, 1963.

Saigon was still a pretty little backwater along French colonial lines—the whitewashed villas, the parks, the bakeries, the nightclubs—except that most of the French had left after 1954, when they lost their Vietnam war. The American war was coming, and within two years the destruction of Saigon would begin in a crush of jeeps and barbed wire and GIs cruising the bars on Tu Do Street, the shade trees cut down, and then the flood of refugees and war maimed pouring in from the countryside. But in the summer of 1963 the bargirls still spoke French. The diplomatic wives hadn't been evacuated yet, and they gave social teas where they handed out calling cards embossed with their husband's title. Everyone went home for noon siesta, when the streets filled with pedicabs and blue-and-yellow Renault taxis, and at six the American embassy was locked for the night. The war was somewhere else. The Associated Press handbook informed correspondents: "Private clubs in Saigon include Le Cercle Sportif (for swimming and tennis), Le Cercle Hippique (for riding), and Le Club Nautique (for boating; but don't take boats too far up the river. Several members have been shot and killed by the Viet Cong doing this)."

Part of Saigon's allure was the distant possibility of being killed. You could drive down to My Tho at the head of the Mekong Delta first thing in the morning, sit for a briefing, go out on a South Vietnamese army operation, and get back in time for a few sets of tennis at the Cercle, then talk about the war over cracked crab and French wine at Le Diamant or a Chinese dinner out in Cholon. The terrace of the Continental Hotel was covered by a steel screen to prevent a VC terrorist from tossing a grenade at foreigners enjoying their coffee, but the croissants

were Paris quality, and, although *The Quiet American* had come out in 1955, you could still imagine Graham Greene sitting there with his acute eyebrows, taking notes for his savage and prophetic portrait of murderous American innocence.

Holbrooke had asked for Southeast Asia. He had read Hemingway and Crane and he wanted to see a war, to find out what war was and who he would be in it. But all the major ones were over. The only war on offer in 1963 was Vietnam. David Halberstam's reports in the *New York Times* about the deteriorating military situation in the Delta had given him pause before his departure, but his greatest concern, based on the briefing he received in Washington, was that he wouldn't get to Saigon quickly enough—that the war would already be won. There were around fifteen thousand Americans in South Vietnam, most of them military advisors. Within a few years the number would be half a million, but fifteen thousand was far too many for Holbrooke, as if their presence would dilute the experience. Around fifty Americans had been killed. That number also struck him as enormous.

Officially, Holbrooke knew almost nothing about Vietnam. That's always been the weak spot of our Foreign Service—other countries. It's hard to get Americans interested in them, and the more interested you get, the worse your career prospects. Strange for a country of immigrants from everywhere. But to become American the new arrivals have to erase the past. We wipe out this immense store of knowledge about the rest of the world and lose ourselves in the endless drama of America the Exceptional. So other countries are never quite real to us.

For training the State Department had sent Holbrooke and Lehovich to Berkeley, where they were instructed in the dialect of the North instead of the Vietnamese spoken around Saigon and the Delta. (On arrival in South Vietnam he realized that his proficiency was at idiot level, and it didn't get better.) His Area Studies course was taught by experts on Thailand and Malaya. Community Development was even worse—a lot of abstract social science jargon instead of practical information about agriculture or public health, along with the absurd warning to stay away from politics in Vietnam. Holbrooke found most of his colleagues and instructors intellectually mediocre, and they knew it. On his final exam, a "personality inventory," he answered most of the 575 questions without bothering to read them. His evaluator bemoaned his negative influence on Lehovich and predicted that Holbrooke would have a subpar career.

At the same time, he was reading everything he could find on the subject of counterinsurgency—Bernard Fall's *Street Without Joy*; Larteguy's *The Centurions*; *Communist Revolutionary Warfare*; *The Guerrilla and How to Fight Him*. He declared his intention to become "the State Department's leading expert (perhaps the leading lay expert in the whole goddamn free world)." Counterinsurgency was very big at the White House. The Kennedys loved the image of Green Berets fighting guerrillas in the jungles of Laos and the Congo—beating the Communists at their own game on the borderlands of the free world and doing it with style. It was a lot more Kennedyesque than the dull, static nuclear deterrence of the Eisenhower years. JFK gave speeches on "limited wars" and budgeted extra millions for Special Forces and CIA paramilitaries, and Robert Kennedy, whose regular job was attorney general, chaired the top-level Special Group for Counter-Insurgency, and it was all very promising, except that they forgot to take into account the government of South Vietnam. This would be a recurring American oversight. Before shipping out to Vietnam, Holbrooke and a few classmates at the Foreign Service Institute had put on a counterinsurgency training skit called "Modernizing at the Mekong," with Tony Lake as the U.S. ambassador and Holbrooke as his political officer, featuring Vietcong guerrillas, Chinese Communists, and "a slinky, silk-clad, slant eyed wench"—but not one character from the government the Americans were there to save. If they hadn't been so young and confident, the class of 1962 might have taken it as a bad sign.

The State Department detailed Holbrooke to the Agency for International Development, and AID assigned him to its office in Saigon, the United States Operations Mission, or USOM. (Military advisors belonged to MAAG, the army command was MACV, information officers worked for USIS—the buildup of acronyms was several years ahead of the arrival of ground troops.) Within USOM was a small, unconventional entity called Rural Affairs. This was the "shirtsleeves outfit."

Rural Affairs was an odd place for a young diplomat to land— unheard of, really. Holbrooke and Lehovich were going to be the first Foreign Service officers sent into the field as aid workers. Put them out among peasants in Vietcong strongholds where the war was being fought, have them hand out bulgur wheat, cement, fertilizer, and barbed wire. As bachelors, they were considered relatively expendable. It was an early experiment in counterinsurgency.

Rural Affairs was led by a long-legged Virginian named Rufus Phillips—Yale, CIA, Army PSYOP. Phillips was just thirty-three and already shrouded in mystique, not least because he was a protégé of the great man in American counterinsurgency, Colonel Edward Lansdale. Holbrooke didn't know much about Lansdale, either. He went to Vietnam thinking that the name was spelled Landsdale, that he was the original for a character in a famous novel, and that he "is somehow involved in our efforts out there." But from the morning Holbrooke started at Rural Affairs, Lansdale's ghost was everywhere.

This is a particular story of the war. I'm not going to tell you the whole history—how the French lost colonial Indochina, how we took over the fight as a war against communism, how every president from Truman to Ford made it American policy to keep South Vietnam non-Communist, how every failed American effort required an even greater American effort, because we never bothered to learn the history and never understood what we had gotten into. That story isn't my concern here, and if you don't already know it I can recommend half a dozen excellent books. My concern is to understand what young Dick Holbrooke had gotten into, and why at first it all seemed promising.

LANSDALE WAS an advertising man from Detroit by way of California, with a brush mustache and a low-key manner. He served in the OSS during World War II, then became an air force intelligence officer, working with the CIA. His expertise was psychological warfare. He was an original figure in the American century, and he emerged in answer to a basic need of the Cold War. While great strategists like Kennan were inventing the policy of containment in Washington, someone had to carry it out in strange and dangerous places—and so this friendly fellow with a flat middle-American voice and a knack for the American art of public relations became our homely version of T. E. Lawrence. Lansdale had a talent for attaching himself to foreign leaders, winning their trust with epic feats of listening, and patiently guiding them in the desired direction: a sort of strongman whisperer. He was the opposite of the loud, brash American who stomps into someone else's country, tries to straighten things out with a few whacks of his stick, and leaves behind an even bigger mess. No—Lansdale's messes were much more sophisticated.

In the early fifties, he had success helping the Philippine army defeat a Communist insurgency. Lansdale would play his harmonica with the locals in the countryside and sing their folk songs. His next stop was Saigon, just after the French defeat at Dien Bien Phu, in 1954. "Do what you did in the Philippines," Lansdale was instructed. The Geneva Accords that ended the First Indochina War divided Vietnam along the seventeenth parallel. In the North, Ho Chi Minh's Communists won the mantle of nationalism by defeating the French. But South Vietnam was a colonial remnant, ruled by a playboy emperor who spent most of his time at his château on the Riviera. It was hardly a country at all. Lansdale set about to make it one.

He created his own clandestine intelligence team of around ten men, including Rufus Phillips. They conducted black ops across the seventeenth parallel to sabotage the North—hidden weapons caches, forged documents, sugar in gas tanks, fortune-telling propaganda leaflets—

while Lansdale got to know the emperor's chosen prime minister in Saigon: Ngo Dinh Diem. The Ngos were a family of Catholic mandarins from Hue. With partition, almost a million northern Catholics fled south—a vast exodus that remade the social structure of South Vietnam. They became Diem's urban base of support and his loyalists in the military and civil service. Most of them regarded the majority of Buddhist peasants under their authority with contempt. At the same time, fifty thousand Communist troops withdrew to the North, leaving behind a network of cadres throughout the southern countryside, the seeds of the insurgency that was coming.

Diem was untainted by collaboration with the French, but otherwise he wasn't an obvious choice for the George Washington of South Vietnam. He was chaste by vow, short and plump and ballooning out in white double-breasted sharkskin suits as he walked penguin-like, his thick hair slicked back and parted. But the struggle against the Communist North needed a leader and a cause, and Lansdale would sit in the palace and listen for hours, sometimes half the night, while Diem chain-smoked, putting out each cigarette as soon as he'd lit it, and delivered monologues from his encyclopedic knowledge of Vietnamese history and culture that no foreigner other than Lansdale could endure. They talked in an alcove off Diem's bedroom that was so small their knees touched. Lansdale, with his sensitivity to character, picked up the gleam of dry humor in Diem's eyes. Diem was a passionate photographer—Lansdale helped him set up a darkroom. So Diem came to trust Lansdale as he trusted no one else outside his family, even inviting him to live at the palace. Lansdale declined, preferring to remain behind the scenes, where he headed off coups and co-opted rivals to the government, while Diem crushed the religious sects and gangsters arrayed against him. In 1955, Diem won election as chief of state over the emperor with 98 percent of the vote, thanks to massive rigging, and South Vietnam became a republic. America had its anti-Communist partner in Vietnam.

And the cause? Democracy and self-determination, of course. Lansdale believed that South Vietnam couldn't withstand the appeal of communism without a positive ideal. The only way to win was by giving the rural population a different version of people's war—a war for freedom. He urged Diem to spend nights in mosquito-ridden hamlets and look peasants in the eye and enact land reform and put the army to work building schools, and as long as Lansdale was around, Diem took the advice. Lansdale came up with the idea of commissioning a Vietnamese version of Thomas Paine's *Common Sense*. He believed in the universality of the Declaration of Independence and the Bill of Rights, and now and then he had his staff reread them just to refresh their inspiration. At the bottom of Lansdale's sympathy for Asians was his belief that they and we were brothers.

There's a short line from having local friends and caring about their problems to thinking up American solutions for them. And here you find the essential contradiction, right there at the start of our long entanglement and never to be resolved because it was lodged in the very heart of the project: Americans were pushing Vietnamese to build a new country (modeled loosely after ours, since they and we were brothers). But as long as we pushed, it wouldn't be their country. But if we stopped pushing, it would collapse.

Nobody else could make the cause sound real and noble like Lansdale. After leaving Asia in 1956, he became a Cold War legend. He was the thinly disguised model for Colonel Edwin Hillandale, one of the good-guy officials in a fictitious Southeast Asian country in *The Ugly American*, a best-selling novel published in 1958 and made into a movie starring Marlon Brando. The novel's message was, Less lecturing, more listening, and we can beat the Communists. *The Ugly American* was a favorite book of Senator John F. Kennedy, who bought a copy for every one of his colleagues. Kennedy called Lansdale "our answer to James Bond"—the highest praise he had to offer. In the first month of his presidency, he summoned Lansdale to the White House and asked him to return to Saigon as the American ambassador.

But Lansdale didn't get the job. Holbrooke heard a rumor that Dean Rusk so disliked Lansdale's unconventional ways that he had threatened to resign over the appointment. Lansdale also had detractors at the Pentagon, where his approach to the war was too soft for the data crunchers working under Robert McNamara. McNamara thought only body counts were real, while what Lansdale called "the X factor"—the feelings of the Vietnamese people—was unquantifiable and therefore irrelevant. So Kennedy had to withdraw the offer, and instead he put

Lansdale in charge of Operation Mongoose, the devious and futile campaign to assassinate Fidel Castro.

There were Americans who believed that, if only Lansdale's appointment had gone through in 1961, the war might have turned out differently. Rufus Phillips believed it. He had been at Lansdale's side in Saigon in the fifties as a young army lieutenant, big and blond and earnestly committed, and then he had tried to apply Lansdale's principles in Laos with the CIA. In 1962, Phillips was sent back to Vietnam as a stand-in for his mentor, who had recommended him to Kennedy. He arrived that September to run an outfit of his own invention, the Office of Rural Affairs and Counterinsurgency.

The Vietcong insurgency was entering its fourth year and gaining ground all over the South, especially in the lower Mekong Delta. The South Vietnamese army and its American advisors were trying to fight a conventional war—helicopter-borne troop movements, big-unit sweeps through hamlets, air and artillery barrages—against a guerrilla force that disappeared into the population by day and owned the countryside at night. Diem's regime had grown deeply unpopular—insular and corrupt, keeping all power in the palace, locking up opponents. Diem's intelligent and paranoid brother, Ngo Dinh Nhu, stoked Diem's authoritarianism and cut him off from outsiders, while Nhu's secret police force terrorized the population. The Americans pressured Diem to carry out reforms, but when he resisted they backed off. Instead, Washington sent shiploads of helicopters and jet fighters and thousands of military advisors, hoping for the best. Kennedy's policy was to keep South Vietnam non-Communist and off the front page until he was re-elected.

Rufus Phillips knew more Vietnamese politicians and generals than any other American. He came with the Lansdale mantle and ten million dollars cash, authorized personally by Kennedy, converted into piastres. The idea was to bypass U.S. bureaucracy and Vietnamese corruption by putting an American civilian out in each province, where he would live among the locals, find out what they wanted, and sign off on ready money for projects like wells and new strains of rice. It was the Lansdale method of fighting communism. Phillips and his crew were waiting for the day when the great man himself would come back and save South Vietnam.

RURAL AFFAIRS WAS the heart of American can-do. That was the meaning of "shirtsleeves." Morale was high and rules were ignored. The staff and field reps were all volunteers, a pickup team from around the government and outside it, many of them remnants of Lansdale's old group—ex-spooks, retired army officers, rural development experts, Peace Corps types. There was a Filipino colonel who had made his name hunting guerrillas in Luzon. Some of the older men had bounced around the Far East for so many years they'd become incapable of living in the States. They were anti-Communists of the right kind—they had Vietnamese friends, spoke a bit of the language, and liked to travel to remote villages. They were all devoted to their blandly smiling, shrewd, charismatic boss Phillips, whose CIA past and entrée with Diem gave him the air of a man who knew more than he let on. They *believed* in the mission and worked day and night in the humid heat to carry it out. The Rural Affairs handbook declared that the goal was "to give the Vietnamese people something worth risking their lives to defend" and "to help the Vietnamese make their aspirations for a better life come true." It was the only way to win a revolutionary war. The catchwords were "self-help," "civic action," "people-first approach," "hearts and minds," "the other war"—all under the banner of "pacification."

You can't hear these words today without shaking your head. Some of them have acquired a sinister ring. And perhaps by now you're also shaking your head over Edward Lansdale and Rufus Phillips—the high-mindedness, the illusions. They're an American type. Perhaps they make you think of that line in *The Quiet American:* "I never knew a man who had better motives for all the trouble he caused." Greene had already completed the novel when Lansdale first showed up in Saigon in 1954, but Lansdale is often mistaken for the original of Alden Pyle, the naïve and ruthless American of the title, who comes to Vietnam full of noble ideas about democracy and a "third force" and ends up getting a lot of people killed. My god, Greene loathed Americans. Our bathrooms were air-conditioned and our women deodorized and we were too shallow to know good and evil. It was a left-wing Catholic's version of the usual British upper-class snobbery. I always thought Orwell had Greene's number when he called it "this cult of the sanctified sinner" in which "there is something rather distingué in being damned; Hell is a sort of high-class nightclub." But I have to admit Greene was onto something in Vietnam. The intensity of his animus made him clairvoyant.

In the early sixties, all the Americans in Saigon read *The Quiet American,* admired its style, wished they had a Vietnamese girlfriend like Phuong to fill their opium pipe, and dismissed the warning. "We used to sit in the small French cafés and talk about Greene's book," David Halberstam later said, "the best novel about Vietnam . . . It was only his portrait of the sinister innocence of the American that caused some doubt, that made us a little uneasy." Lake read it on the flight over and never wondered if he might actually be Alden Pyle—a fellow New Englander and Harvard grad. Pyle was a ridiculous character mouthing absurdities, and Lake thought it was all cynical colonialist bullshit. The Americans didn't want to run the place—they were here to help the South Vietnamese people defend themselves against Communist aggression so that the war didn't have to be fought in Bangkok or Honolulu. Holbrooke disposed of the novel in one evening before coming to Vietnam: "Not too bad—not too good. Not me, either."

It's easy to see the self-deception. But try to unwind everything that came after: marines setting Zippo lighters to thatch roofs, free-fire zones, napalm, Tet, the ditches at My Lai, peace with honor, the Khmer Rouge, *Apocalypse Now* and *Platoon* and the final black granite of the Wall, the fact that today you can sit in the pleasant rooftop bar of the Rex Hotel in downtown Ho Chi Minh City at sunset and sip a Saigon Export beer and gaze out past Ho's statue to the rooftop of the decrepit apartment building where Vietnamese climbed on to one of the last helicopters on April 29, 1975, and notice that "Seasons in the Sun," released a year before the fall of Saigon, is playing over the bar's sound system as if to remind you that the war was an insane mirage, that none of it needed to happen.

Unwind it all and go back to 1963. There was hardly a soul in the U.S. government who didn't believe that communism had to be stopped in Vietnam. Even the American reporters in Saigon, who were daily exposing the failures and lies of the war, believed it. Years later, Holbrooke asked one of the best of them, "Do you ever remember any of us sitting around and discussing whether the war's basic objectives were right or wrong?" And Neil Sheehan answered, "No."

In the summer of 1963, the most important place for a young person to be was in either South Vietnam or the American South—fighting for freedom overseas or at home. From Saigon Holbrooke wrote to his brother, Andy, who was finishing high school:

> The fight that the Negro is fighting for is really a fight for the United States, for the principles which we learned in school and so on. If you can help in this fight just a little bit, just being one more picketer or one more innocent man in jail, then you will always be able to feel that you took part—did your part—in the great struggle. I don't know whether or not you realize, Andy, but if I were home now I am certain that I would be involved in it somehow.

You could support the schoolchildren in Birmingham and the war in the rice paddies and believe you were being true to America. Vietnam was still a place for idealists. They were unlike the desk-bound diplomats at the embassy, or the military advisors flying Vietnamese units on pointless operations that chewed up whole villages. They thought of themselves as the ones who knew how to fight this war right, disciples of the great Lansdale. Holbrooke fit right in.

II

En route to Vietnam, on a stopover in Tokyo, he had seen a news photo that appeared on front pages all over the world: an elderly Buddhist monk, seated in the lotus position on a Saigon street, hands together in prayer, consumed in fire. The halo of flames surrounded his shaved head and robed body like an aura of divinity. Holbrooke had no idea what it meant.

The previous month, Buddhists in the ancient imperial city of Hue had demonstrated against an official ban on flying their flag on the Buddha's birthday. Government forces had fired into the crowd and killed nine people. Diem's brother, Ngo Dinh Nhu, controlled the secret police force that killed the protesters, but Diem blamed the Vietcong and continued to crack down on Buddhist protest, which spread to Saigon.

On June 11, a procession of several hundred bonzes—monks—and nuns, chanting and carrying signs in Vietnamese and English, made its way to the busy corner in front of the Cambodian embassy, a few blocks from the presidential palace. An old monk named Thich Quang Duc got out of the pale-blue Austin Westminster sedan that had been leading the procession and seated himself on a small cushion in the middle of the intersection. Two younger monks brought over a five-gallon canister from the car. They splashed gasoline on the old monk's head and robe. Then Thich Quang Duc put a match to himself and burst into flames.

His face tightened with agony but his body held still in prayer. The poise of his posture was miraculous. The monks and nuns around the intersection began moaning, weeping, and many prostrated themselves on the pavement, and a monk with a loudspeaker chanted in English, "A Buddhist priest burns himself to death, a Buddhist priest becomes a martyr," and oily black smoke filled the air with the smell of burning human flesh, and Malcolm Browne of the AP, who had been tipped off in advance that something big would happen, kept snapping pictures to steel himself against his own horror, until finally, after four or five minutes, the charred corpse of the old monk toppled over.

Browne's photograph of the moment of ignition immediately flew around the world and found President Kennedy in bed in the White House that same morning. "Jesus Christ!" he exclaimed.

At the end of Holbrooke's first day in Saigon, as he was leaving Rural Affairs to walk back to his temporary quarters, he noticed a crowd streaming into a pagoda across the garden wall from his office, right around the corner from the immolation site. The Xa Loi Pagoda, a tall new building of red-and-yellow pebbled concrete, was the most important pagoda in Saigon. Holbrooke decided to see what it was all about. He followed the line of pilgrims to the back of the sanctuary. On the altar there was a glass chalice, and in the chalice there was a dried and blackened object that looked to him like a piece of burnt liver, but in fact was Thich Quang Duc's heart. It had survived intact his ritual suicide and subsequent cremation, and now, two weeks later, it was a holy relic, the object of religious devotion.

Joining the throng at the pagoda was something a journalist was more likely to do than a young diplomat just arrived at his first overseas post. But Holbrooke's curiosity led him right, and he saw at once that the pilgrims in Xa Loi, by worshipping the monk's heart, were expressing a political opinion. They were protesting a repressive regime. Though Holbrooke didn't yet understand it, he had witnessed the first signs that the regime was about to collapse.

On his second day, Holbrooke drove out of Saigon with one of Phillips's deputies at Rural Affairs, a gnarled and intense man named George Melvin.

Melvin controlled aid money for the provinces in III Corps, the region between Saigon and the Central Highlands. He was a Lansdale holdover, a retired army lieutenant colonel—supposedly Signal Corps but probably intelligence, like most of the Lansdale team. He was tall and lean, with a pitted face, and fanatically dedicated. Though he was around fifty, Melvin seemed old to Holbrooke. He had been in the East for years and he had seen a lot of war, and as they headed north on Route 13—"Bloody Route 13," because of VC attacks on American vehicles—and passed roadside wrecks from accidents and land mines, and miles of newly planted rice paddies, which Holbrooke was seeing for the first time, Melvin began to undertake his education in the twilight struggle against communism.

In the course of their work, Melvin said, Holbrooke would hear, maybe even do, certain things that he should never tell anyone. There were other things that he wouldn't understand and shouldn't know or ask about, things on the dark side of the fight that it was wise to keep from higher-ups. Melvin's ideal American ambassador would be "a nearly dead body, with just enough strength to sign the papers we put in front of him." Melvin hated bureaucrats almost as much as he hated Communists. He had retired from the army because he couldn't stand headquarters staff work. The war had to be won out in the field, with land reform and the things that shouldn't be spoken of. "We have to take the revolution away from the VC," he said, again and again. There was no alternative to victory.

One night, in a town on the Cambodian border, Melvin talked about his first encounter with communism. It was in Chicago in the 1930s, when he was working for a man who turned out to belong to a front organization. Melvin found a plan of the Chicago sewer system in the man's desk and realized that the Communists were planning to destroy the city. On another field trip, driving to the airstrip of another province, Melvin explained to the local authority, a certain Major Minh, that the supposed split between Red China and the Soviet Union was phony—Moscow gave the orders, Peking carried them out, and Hanoi was a puppet of both. Major Minh, whose funds depended on Melvin's signature, completely agreed.

Holbrooke hadn't met anyone like George Melvin at Brown or the *Times* or the State Department. Melvin's zeal intimidated Holbrooke a little, and his politics appalled him, but not enough to keep him from enjoying the older man's company, or from asking the kind of questions that Melvin had warned against.

For the rest of the summer Holbrooke never stopped moving. He and Melvin visited dozens of Rural Affairs projects around the countryside. They rode in gunboats and dugout canoes through the marshes. They flew in unmarked Air America six-seaters through the mountains, circling an airfield until an armed escort showed up, then landing on a grass strip cut out of the jungle. In bad weather they stayed below two hundred feet and followed the contours of the terrain to avoid crashing into a mountainside. Over heavy VC areas they flew at fifty feet to evade ground fire. A few times they were shot at and later found bullet holes in the aircraft. Once, Holbrooke was given the controls and piloted the plane from Cambodia to the South China Sea. He felt invulnerable, like a great downhill skier. "The terrible truth that people do not like to admit," he later wrote, "was that the war was fun for young men, at least it was fun if they were civilians or journalists, or if they were assigned almost anywhere other than a combat unit or helicopter duty, so that the odds of getting seriously hurt were fairly low, unless you took stupid chances."

In Nha Trang, on the coast, Holbrooke saw Montagnard tribal people who had been forced from their homes in the VC-infested mountains by the South Vietnamese army, their animals and houses burned, and herded into impoverished settlements where they were dying of dysentery. This was called the Strategic Hamlet Program. The idea was to separate the population from the guerrillas and thereby drain the sea where the guerrillas swam. In the marshes south of Saigon, Holbrooke ran into the father of the idea, the British counterinsurgency expert Sir Robert Thompson. In the fifties, Thompson had used fortified hamlets to help defeat an ethnic Chinese Communist insurgency in Malaya. With Thompson's advice and CIA money, the Diem regime was building them as quickly as possible, defended by moats, barbed wire, and sharpened bamboo stakes, and guarded by local self-defense groups—thousands of hamlets all around the South, requiring the forced dislocation of hundreds of thousands of peasants from their ancestral lands. The program was run by Diem's brother Nhu.

The mission of Rural Affairs was to bring aid and turn the hamlets into outposts of local democracy. But the VC kept overrunning them at night, shooting the elected chiefs, burning the houses—137 of them in just one hamlet in Binh Duong province the same week in August when Holbrooke met Thompson.

Holbrooke wanted to be assigned to an embattled province like Binh Duong. He didn't know whether the Strategic Hamlet Program was working or not—he doubted the misery among the Montagnards in Nha Trang had won friends for the government, but he thought the brutality in Binh Duong might backfire on the VC. He didn't know whether the war was being won or lost. It wouldn't end before he had a chance to taste it, of that he was now certain. Vietnam wasn't beautiful to him as it was to other Americans—he found the country cruel and sad. But it swallowed him whole.

ONE DAY in early July, Holbrooke showed up at the door of a flat off Tu Do Street in downtown Saigon, two blocks from the river. Inside, David Halberstam and Neil Sheehan sat at their typewriters on opposite sides of a cluttered kitchen table. On the wall was a plastic-overlay map of Southeast Asia, where Sheehan kept track of battles with a grease pencil. The flat belonged to his employer, United Press International, and Sheehan slept—when he could sleep—in a windowless back room. The wall facing the street was glass and practically invited a drive-by delivery of *plastique* from either the VC or the Diem regime, more likely the latter.

Halberstam, the *Times* man in Saigon, had teamed up with Sheehan in January, after a major battle south of Saigon on the edge of the Plain of Reeds, in a hamlet called Ap Bac—the biggest defeat of the war for the South Vietnamese army, and a big scoop for Sheehan. These ferociously competitive reporters, in their late twenties, were cooperating because, in Saigon in 1963, they needed each other. Halberstam—a couple of years older, an inch taller, a few decibels louder—needed a friend and a telephone. Sheehan—working alone for a stingy wire service that was always playing catch-up with Browne's fully staffed AP bureau, six blocks uptown on Rue Pasteur—needed a journalistic buddy. So they joined forces, sharing tips and stiffening each other's spines.

The reporters in Saigon were doing something dangerous and new in the history of American journalism. They found themselves in the middle of not one but two wars—the one they were covering, the obscure and confusing shooting war with the Vietcong in the countryside, and the starker, riskier confrontation in Saigon with the high command of the United States military, which was declaring success after success when the reporters knew the war to be slipping toward failure. They hadn't come to Vietnam looking to challenge authority, and they didn't set out to remake American journalism in an adversarial role—though that was what they ended up doing. Sheehan was just out of the army; Halberstam wore his black hair in a military flattop. They were products of the fifties, Harvard grads, Cold War patriots, and they wanted to help the war effort by reporting accurate facts so that the right decisions could be made. Reporters in their twenties were not supposed to challenge generals twice their age, all decorated veterans of the big one. General Paul Harkins, the four-star commander of MACV, had been Patton's staff aide in North Africa, Sicily, and France. In Vietnam, Harkins wore dress whites and carried a silver-tipped swagger stick and smoked through an ivory cigarette holder. He never walked along a rice paddy or toured the muddy remains of a battlefield. "I'm not that kind of general," he said. Instead, Harkins escorted high-level visitors—McNamara, Rusk, the military brass—to sanguine briefings and sent them back to Washington with statistics that showed the war was being won.

At Ap Bac, the Vietcong—vastly outnumbered and outgunned—had stood their ground, killed scores of South Vietnamese soldiers and three Americans, shot down five helicopters, lost just eighteen of their own men, and then gotten away. With American advisors screaming in their faces, the South Vietnamese army had refused to fight. But afterward, when Admiral Harry Felt, the commander in the Pacific, paid a visit from Honolulu to look into Ap Bac, Harkins pronounced the battle a victory. He didn't give a moment's thought to how this rice paddy war might be different from the Battle of the Bulge. He kept predicting that it would be over in a year.

The official press strategy was deception. The Kennedy administration didn't want the American public to know that their men in uniform—supposedly noncombatant advisors—were fighting and dying in an undeclared war in Southeast Asia. In late 1961, Rusk cabled the Saigon embassy: DO NOT GIVE OTHER THAN ROUTINE COOP-

ERATION TO CORRESPONDENTS ON COVERAGE CURRENT MILITARY
ACTIVITIES IN VIETNAM. Two weeks later, the press wasn't supposed
to notice when the aircraft carrier *Core*, loaded with a fleet of forty helicopters, appeared among the sampans on the Saigon River, in full view
of the Majestic Hotel's rooftop bar. So the reporters demanded more
information, and when it didn't come they left Saigon to find the truth
for themselves by going into battle and talking to unafraid field-grade
advisors—none less afraid than Lieutenant Colonel John Paul Vann,
Halberstam's and Sheehan's tutor in the Delta. The reporters concluded
that the generals and diplomats were concealing the truth from them.

The reality was worse: the officials were deluded. The habit of deception slipped into self-deception. At the high noon of American power,
the generals were too arrogant and complacent to believe that peasants
in black pajamas could stand and fight against regular South Vietnamese battalions and U.S. technology. Ambassador Frederick Nolting,
Kennedy's man in Saigon, clung to the illusion that President Diem
was popular with his people (his portrait was all over South Vietnam).
Nolting once asked François Sully, the *Newsweek* correspondent, "Why,
Monsieur Sully, do you always see the hole in the doughnut?" Sully, soon
to be expelled by Diem, replied, "Because, Monsieur l'Ambassadeur,
there is a hole in the doughnut."

In Washington, the president and his advisors maintained their public optimism. Privately, Kennedy demanded a line-by-line analysis of
every one of Halberstam's stories. The CIA acknowledged their accu-
racy without accepting the pessimistic conclusions that should have
followed. Kennedy finally tried to have the *Times* ship Halberstam elsewhere, without success.

The mutual suspicion between the officials and the reporters in Saigon had no precedent—in World War II the press was practically a tool
of military propaganda. After Ap Bac, this suspicion hardened into deep
hostility. Each side imagined the other was damaging the war effort;
each side was trying to get the other removed from the country. Nolting threw Halberstam out of his office. At Tan Son Nhut Admiral Felt
exchanged words with Sheehan. At the American mission's Fourth of
July party, Halberstam refused to shake Harkins's hand.

IT WASN'T LONG after the embassy party that Holbrooke appeared at
the flat off Tu Do Street. He didn't notice or else ignored Nhu's leather-
jacketed spies hanging around outside. He was carrying a letter of
introduction from Clifton Daniel, number two at the *Times,* whom
he'd sought out in his brief career as a foreign correspondent in Paris
back in 1960. The letter earned him derision from the enfant terrible
Halberstam, who was fighting on yet another front, with his cautious
editors back in New York, and who despised "E. Clifton Daniel" for his
courtly oiliness, and perhaps for being Truman's son-in-law.

Holbrooke's visit surprised the reporters. This eager twenty-two-
year-old, a junior diplomat from the other side, the official side—what
was he doing showing up unannounced? Didn't he know that the
embassy and the press were at war? Official Americans kept a wary
distance, unless they were foolish or brave enough to talk, and then
they did it under deep cover. One of Halberstam's best anonymous
sources was Rufus Phillips, who remained close to old friends at the
CIA station. Nonetheless, Halberstam and Sheehan took young Holbrooke under their wing. Their outsider rawness—Halberstam, Jewish and middle-class, with thick-framed glasses and big hairy hands
and violent gestures and moral certainties, with his gift for dramatizing
everything, including himself; Sheehan, Irish and working-class, more
the real underdog, less aggressive but at least as driven, given to dark
spells, with an alcoholic past and an insomniac's facial tics and bursts of
temper—found a kindred spirit in the audacious young Foreign Service
officer at their door.

Holbrooke, just arrived in Saigon, was too new to be of use to the
reporters, though that would change. He looked them up for the same
reason that he ventured inside Xa Loi and followed Melvin all over
III Corps. He wanted to learn. And what better instructors than these
two—"the young commandos at the vortex of the battle of the Saigon
correspondents," he called them. They were doing a job he had once
dreamed of doing, and in the most dramatic circumstances.

They took Holbrooke to dinner at one of their favorite haunts.
L'Amiral was a fine white-tablecloth restaurant near the riverfront,
owned by a Corsican. The Corsicans had stayed on after the French left
Saigon, running guns and trafficking in opium from Laos. Holbrooke
was devouring the conversation along with his cannelloni when Hal-

berstam began working himself into one of his thunderous rages at American officialdom in Saigon. "Don't trust anything those bastards tell you," he instructed Holbrooke. Over a bottle of wine the reporters court-martialed General Harkins for incompetence and dereliction of duty. With each charge Halberstam brought his big fist down on the table, rattling the dishes, and found Harkins guilty, guilty, guilty, and then Sheehan sentenced the commanding general to death by firing squad, providing sound effects of machine-gun fire and laughter loud enough to silence the diners at the other tables.

Holbrooke glanced around the restaurant to see if anyone recognized him. He suddenly wondered what he was doing in the company of these two wild men. He didn't want his career to end in his first week in Vietnam.

He intensely admired both reporters, but he was too much like Halberstam to be a docile pupil. Did they figure out that they were both sons of Jewish New York doctors who had died young? No—these men didn't talk that way, Holbrooke never mentioned his past, they talked only about the war. That summer Halberstam was incandescent with righteous fury, naked to the waist in the swelter of the office and clattering out thousands of words a day on his Olivetti. He didn't disguise his satisfaction with the course of events and it bothered Holbrooke, who needed to be right every bit as much, but who was, after all, on the government team and had not yet pursued his education in Vietnam far enough to know how to assess the state of the war. The embassy had sources the press didn't—how could the reporters know more than the officials?

Holbrooke's taste for Halberstam wasn't shared by Tony Lake. He couldn't stand the reporter's sense of superiority, and he was too good a soldier to become a source. As for Toni Lake, one day she and Holbrooke were walking together on a downtown street when they ran into Halberstam, and Holbrooke made introductions. Halberstam's lack of interest in Toni was so complete that, after saying goodbye, Holbrooke turned and called out: "Dave, she went to *Radcliffe.*"

LAKE WAS DIFFERENT. Where these other men seemed bigger than their height, he seemed smaller, was subtle where they were demonstrative, ironic where they were self-serious. He would snap off puns and disarming one-liners, often against himself—his oversized ears, his New England uptightness—then stretch his cheeks into a grin and his dark blue eyes would gleam with an enigma. When angry, he turned polite and ice-cold. His fate was tied to Holbrooke's from beginning to end. Hamilton and Burr come to mind, but don't ask me which was which.

William Anthony Kirsopp Lake was born into the kind of name that the Holbrookes had to invent. Lake's paternal grandfather was an unorthodox Anglican theologian who immigrated to America and taught a wildly popular Bible studies class at Harvard. Lake's father, a naturalized American, dropped out of Harvard and went to work at a textile mill, rising to management, but he remained such a passionate New Dealer that Adolf Berle, FDR's economic advisor, became Tony's godfather. Lake's grandfather on his mother's side was an editor at the early *New Republic* and advised President Hoover in his medicine ball cabinet. Lake's mother grew up in Georgetown and was briefly engaged to the great Kennan. She edited books at *Reader's Digest* and read Dickens to Tony when he was a boy. For the bipartisan WASP ascendancy this was a pretty solid pedigree, even if, by mid-century, it was fading toward shabby gentility. The Lakes belonged to the upper class of accomplishment, not money. While Holbrooke fought his way into this world, Lake kept looking for a way out.

He was raised in the gray-flannel belt of Fairfield County, Connecticut, and summered with his family in Sharon, not far from Winsted, where Halberstam grew up, but on the other side of the line separating the rising postwar middle class from the WASP establishment. Lake rebelled, of course—if not he'd have lived out his life as a well-bred stiff who could turn his manners on or off depending on the stage of his drinking. Being small for his age and a year ahead of his grade, he was bullied at school, so he picked up a tough-guy act and started shoplifting. He was kicked out of the New Canaan public schools and sent to a fancy prep school outside Boston, where he got serious and even considered a career as an Episcopal clergyman like his grandfather.

Inevitably he ended up at Harvard. He was president of the freshman Democrats and captain of the nation's number-one squash team. His senior year, against Yale, he lost his match and the team's national title by two points in the fifth game—his opponent made four fantastic corner shots that Lake vividly remembered almost sixty years later. He walked off the court laughing at himself.

And that was Tony Lake: so competitive that he knew winning required detachment. Focus hard, but don't care so much that you can't stand to lose, because then you will lose. Years later, when his students at Georgetown would ask him how to become secretary of state, he would answer: "If you eat turds for the rest of your life to become someone, either 1) you'll achieve it and discover you're not happy, or 2) because you're eating turds and your ambition is so obvious, you won't get it." Maybe he had Holbrooke in mind. Lake kept his ambition more tightly wrapped, his relation to it was more ambivalent, but you would have been badly mistaken to believe him when he sometimes denied it was there at all, and the mistake would end with you losing to him.

He had ready entrée to the best clubs—the Fly at Harvard, the Century in New York, the Council on Foreign Relations—and so he felt free to quit them on principle and without regret when, for example, they solicited his money to hire lawyers to keep women out. He hated the rich. This was sociologically necessary for someone of his background, since new money pissed on the values of Lake's class, possessed the power his class thought it was due, and aroused the material envy it pretended not to feel. No one inspired this class's lust for power like Jack Kennedy (and no one again until Barack Obama). The intellectual upper class accepted the Kennedy wealth because of the Kennedy wit and brains. On Election Eve in 1960, Lake's senior year at Harvard, he was leaving a restaurant with friends in downtown Boston when Senator Kennedy's motorcade drove by. Lake was propelled to the front of the ecstatic crowd, right next to the open window through which the smiling candidate was waving. Lake felt a surge of power—he would follow Kennedy anywhere. Being a descendant of Puritans, he interpreted this rush as a call to service, and he became one of the twenty-two-thousand young Americans to take the Foreign Service exam in the first year of the Kennedy administration. Yes, there was idealism—but there was also the smell of power. They're hard to tell apart, and the mix can be dangerous.

One of Lake's fantasies was to be a professor of colonial American history. Another was to live the retiring life of an ambassador in a small West African country like a nineteenth-century British diplomat and become the world's leading expert on some obscure tribe. And another was to serve Kennedy's America by alleviating human suffering in Asia. That was the kind of dilemma that made Lake's mind an interesting place. He resolved it while on a fellowship year at Cambridge and returned home to become a rising star in the Foreign Service class of 1962. He ranked second, to his annoyance, in the A-100 course that all new officers take. And, being a rising star, and liking sports, and having a sense of fun, Lake captured the attention of his slightly younger, less refined, but equally promising classmate Dick Holbrooke.

That summer in Washington they became each other's first friend in government. They spent their evenings talking about world politics and inventing a game called fan ball—throw a tennis ball into a ceiling fan on high speed and, when the ball ricocheted out, scramble to catch it for a point. Friendly competition, of course.

By then Lake had married his college girlfriend. Antonia Plehn was the daughter of German immigrants and the granddaughter of wealthy industrialists. She grew up in Litchfield, Connecticut, near Sharon, and was educated at Miss Hall's in Pittsfield, then Radcliffe. She was small and fine-boned, with warm brown eyes and a radiant smile and brown hair that she wore unstylishly short. She met Lake on New Year's Eve in 1960 at a charades party—a nice guy from a similar background. Six weeks later he called her up: "This is Tony Lake, do you remember me?"

Toni had no great expectations for a career—she loved children, animals, and music, and she wanted to teach, to lead a good and useful life. But she shared Tony's lofty goals, and she imagined the Foreign Service as a partnership. She was the only spouse in the class of 1962 to study Vietnamese. Together they would make the world a better place.

During evenings at the Lakes' in Washington, Holbrooke didn't much like She Toni. He thought she was a New England prude. He was focused on He Tony.

Lake volunteered for Vietnam. Not to experience war—he was different from Holbrooke in that way, too—but to save democracy. He packed a white sharkskin suit like the ones worn by Diem and the Saigon diplomatic corps. He thought the suit would identify him with Vietnamese tradition against the radical Communists. He didn't understand yet (it would take a few years) that the VC in their black pajamas were restoring the traditional order of village society, which the French and their successors in sharkskin suits, Diem and the Americans, had uprooted. In this sense the Lakes were just like all the other Americans who went to Vietnam. They went as innocents.

Upon landing at Tan Son Nhut, Lake wanted to get on the next plane home. In the humid darkness imagination took over and filled the shadows with VC terrorists and he was scared shitless. At the same time he didn't want to be anywhere else in the world. He would learn to conceal his fear in Vietnam, especially around Holbrooke, who didn't seem to feel any. The next morning, Lake left Toni in their room at the Majestic Hotel on the river and reported for work in the consular section of the embassy two blocks away. (He wanted to follow the traditional diplomatic path, to be posted as consul to a provincial city and send deeply informed reports up the chain.) Toni sat alone on the bed and spent most of the day watching the glare of the tropical sun filter through the window shutters, until she finally worked up the courage to go out of the hotel into the busy afternoon streets.

They settled into their quarters on the ground floor of a French villa, with high ceilings, checkered terrazzo floors, and servant quarters at the back of the tropical garden. The villa was in the city center, across the street from the presidential guard barracks and a few blocks from

Diem's palace. The Lakes acquired a puppy and an interest in Buddhist culture. In the evenings they went down to the river and watched the dockworkers unload the ships amid the smell of fish sauce and charcoal and diesel. Vietnam began to get under their skins.

Lake plunged into his work in the consular section, visiting American citizens in the Saigon jails, scouring the bars for drunken servicemen who believed they'd met their soul mate in the person of a Vietnamese club singer and refused to listen when Lake tried to explain that she would never get an American visa because of her police record as a prostitute. When Holbrooke was in town he liked to accompany Lake on his official rounds. He thought the job was perfect material for a Conrad novel. He and the Lakes would go out for dinner in Cholon, the Chinese quarter, or they'd have him over to the villa and Holbrooke and Lake would play fan ball in the living room. Or the two men would get up a game of touch football with friends in the field behind the Lakes' house, or go bowling, or play tennis under the big shade trees on the clay courts at the Cercle Sportif until they collapsed in the heat. They were pretty evenly matched, but Lake would psych Holbrooke out by hitting high topspin shots to his weaker backhand side, and Holbrooke, knowing that Lake had his number, would lose his temper and the set.

That summer Toni got pregnant. In August she went into the hospital with a miscarriage scare that turned out to be dengue fever. Holbrooke visited her there with Lake. His view of her began to improve.

III

All through the summer, monks set themselves on fire, and Diem and Nhu met student protests with riot police, and Nhu's beautiful and wicked wife, Madame Nhu, called for more human "barbecues." The Buddhist crisis demonstrated on the political front what Ap Bac had shown militarily: the South Vietnamese government was a hollow thing and starting to collapse. In the Delta the VC were beefing up troop numbers and weapons, operating for the first time at battalion strength. And in that strange Saigon atmosphere of ritual suicide and tennis, the tension gathered like the saturating air before the afternoon rain.

On the night of August 20, Holbrooke passed up dinner with Halberstam to see Toni in the hospital. At six the next morning, he woke up in his two-room apartment at 498 Phan Dinh Phuong—air-conditioned and equipped with a maid who also cooked—and switched on the radio. The Vietnamese national anthem was playing. When it ended there was an announcement of martial law.

Holbrooke jumped in a taxi and reached the neighborhood around the office by six-thirty. The streets were swarming with Vietnamese troops and he had to walk the last few blocks with his ID out.

Shortly after midnight, truckloads of Nhu's Special Forces dressed in regular army uniforms had smashed down the gate of the Xa Loi Pagoda, fired live ammunition and teargas grenades, hauled away bloodied monks and nuns by the hundreds, and seized the charred heart of Thich Quang Duc. The Diem regime arrested almost fifteen hundred monks around the country in a shocking crackdown on the protests. As a pretext, Nhu's forces planted weapons in the pagodas. During the raid, two monks escaped Xa Loi with the urn containing Thich Quang Duc's ashes and scaled USOM's garden wall. They took refuge under marine guard in the room next to Holbrooke's office, while Vietnamese troops ringed the building. Sheehan and Halberstam had been tipped off in advance, and they had reached the pagoda shortly after midnight, fought their way through the trucks and troops, and ended up watching the whole spectacle from USOM's roof. Meanwhile, no American official knew a thing in advance—not even the CIA station, which funded the Special Forces.

Holbrooke left USOM again around seven-fifteen that morning. He was the last one out. Immediately afterward, the troops laid barbed wire around the building and blocked entry and exit for the next seven hours.

He was supposed to travel north to see some hamlets that the Communists had recently hit hard, but he couldn't get out of Saigon by air—all flights from Tan Son Nhut were canceled. He drove through the city streets, now filled with paratroopers and jeeps mounted with .30-caliber machine guns, to the embassy, where he read cable traffic. But there was very little official information. At nine that night a curfew closed the city down. People fled the streets and an utterly unfamiliar silence fell over Saigon.

Back in his apartment, Holbrooke felt what he would always feel in dramatic moments—happy to be there for it. If he'd only gone to dinner with Halberstam instead of visiting Toni, he might have witnessed the raid on Xa Loi; if he'd only stayed at USOM, he could have experienced the seven-hour siege.

With the pagoda raids, the regime completed its isolation from the South Vietnamese people. The American mission started to realize that the press had been right all along. Halberstam told Holbrooke that Diem was finished and the war lost. "Dave is really high on this thing now, and riding an emotional wave so wild he is literally livid and incomprehensible when he talks about the Embassy," Holbrooke wrote home. He was a little upset that the reporters hadn't let anyone at the embassy know about the raids. "I like Dave, and we had another one of our good tough fights over the state of the world. In this case, however, he had a powerful ally, events. He is rather right now when he claims superior sources to State and CIA; after all, he was at the pagoda, wasn't he? And we did mess things up with our over-optimistic reporting, didn't we? Well, there is some truth in all this, but I wish there could come some balance . . . We may well be losing this war—I don't know—and we may be misreporting—there is some evidence—but Dave goes at the whole thing in such a way as to create a situation in which he cannot be part of a constructive dialogue."

Ambassador Nolting, Diem's steadfast supporter, had been recalled to Washington after a lengthy Mediterranean vacation. Diem and Nhu had chosen this vacuum of American leadership to act and present Nolting's successor with a done deal. On the morning of August 23, Holbrooke was on his way to the embassy when he saw a limousine approaching USOM. He guessed that it contained the new ambassador.

Henry Cabot Lodge Jr. had arrived the night before and was on his way to pay a visit to the two fugitive monks, with instructions for them to be given vegetarian meals—letting Diem know that the old game was over, that the Americans were no longer his unquestioning supporters.

Later, while Holbrooke was reading cable traffic on the embassy's second floor, Lodge appeared, trailed by a cameraman. He was tall and lean and cold-eyed, with an upper lip that disappeared when he smiled and a lower jaw that snapped shut on his consonants. He was a Republican politician from an illustrious Massachusetts family—a two-time loser to President Kennedy, whom he hated, and who had gotten him out of the United States ahead of the 1964 election. "Now let's do some play-acting," Lodge murmured to the cameraman, and he grinned and reached for the hands of embassy secretaries. Holbrooke waited as he approached, but Lodge stopped short and turned away. Holbrooke would have to hope for another chance to introduce himself to the new man in charge.

IT WAS ONE of those moments when no one really knows what the hell is going on. History works that way more often than we'd like to think. It's comforting to believe that a group of powerful people sit around a table in secret and lay out the options, weigh the facts, and decide on a course of action, which then unfolds according to their design. If only history were a sinister conspiracy! More often, we can't say why events of the most momentous consequence even happened. "Foreign policy makes no sense," Holbrooke's friend Les Gelb liked to say (he's still a few years off in this story). The people in charge make decisions based on the politics of the moment, or on an ideology that bears little relation to human reality, or on sheer ignorance compounded by wishful thinking—on anything but solid information. Or they don't make a decision at all—events gallop ahead and the decision makers stumble to keep up. Then they spend the rest of their lives pretending that they knew what they were doing all along and justifying something that made no sense in the first place.

Lodge didn't know what was going on—he had just arrived, with ambiguous instructions to improve relations with the American press and get Diem to yield to American demands. The top officials in Washington didn't know what was going on—they were at odds with one another and waiting to hear from Lodge. Diem didn't know—his generals were starting to plot against him, but he believed himself the only man who could save his country. He might have been an American puppet, as the Communists charged, but he was, in the words of one American in Saigon, "a puppet who pulled his own strings." The Vietnamese generals didn't know—they were grouped in factions with no obvious leader, each waiting for one of the others to make a move. The reporters didn't know—they were so close that they always had a lead on events, but this kept them from taking in the big view that they would later achieve in their books. Dick Holbrooke, two months in-country and as young as anyone in the American mission, sure as hell didn't know. But he tried to find out.

Three days after the pagoda raids, on Saturday, August 24, he played tennis with Rufus Phillips and beat his boss, 6–2 ("the very best I have played in several years"). Afterward, they talked. Phillips told Holbrooke that he'd been summoned by an embassy official named Lieutenant Colonel Mike Dunn, whom Lodge had brought to Saigon as his personal assistant and hatchet man. Dunn told Phillips, "Lodge wants to know what the hell is going on." So Phillips canvassed his friends among the Vietnamese generals and found they'd all turned bitterly against Nhu, who had tricked the army into taking the fall for raids that Nhu had ordered. Phillips thought that Diem should remain in power if he could be convinced to get rid of Nhu and his wife. Holbrooke disagreed with his boss—he thought that Diem was beyond redemption, that he had to go as well as the Nhus (Halberstam and Sheehan thought so, too). Without Diem, he believed the war could be won. Not interfering was out of the question. "We are in this thing as deep as the Vietnamese are," he wrote.

Something crucial was going on in Washington that Holbrooke didn't learn until years later, when the documents were leaked by his friend Daniel Ellsberg. And here is where foreign policy truly makes no sense. That same night of Saturday, August 24—with Kennedy mourning his dead infant son and nursing his afflicted back in Hyannis Port, Rusk attending a Yankees game in New York, McNamara mountain-climbing on Grand Teton, and late-summer Washington mostly empty—a group of top people at the State Department, led by the undersecretary for political affairs, W. Averell Harriman, and Harriman's successor as assistant secretary for Far Eastern affairs, Roger Hilsman, drafted an "Eyes Only" cable to the embassy in Saigon. Its bureaucratic name was DEPTEL 243. The cable told Lodge: "US Government cannot tolerate situation in which power lies in Nhu's hands. Diem must be given chance to rid himself of Nhu and his coterie and replace them with best military and political personalities available. If, in spite of all your efforts, Diem remains obdurate and refuses, then we must face the possibility that Diem himself cannot be preserved."

Kennedy was wary of the message, but he approved it because he thought it had Rusk's support. Rusk gave the green light because he thought Kennedy approved. McNamara never heard about the cable, but his deputy signed off because it had Kennedy's and Rusk's support. Deputies at the Joint Chiefs and the CIA therefore approved without informing their bosses. So DEPTEL 243 went out to Saigon from the State Department at 9:36 that Saturday night with no discussion and no consensus. That thing we now call the interagency process—the hashing out of differing views across the government toward the formation of a policy, the thing that in later years would foil Holbrooke at crucial moments when he was among those sitting around the table in the Situation Room—failed.

The next day, Lodge wrote back: "Believe that chances of Diem's meeting our demands are virtually nil. At the same time, by making them we give Nhu chance to forestall or block action by military. Risk, we believe, is not worth taking, with Nhu in control combat forces Saigon. Therefore, propose we go straight to Generals with our demands, without informing Diem. Would tell them we prepared have Diem without Nhus but it is in effect up to them whether to keep him."

On Monday morning, August 26, with thousands of police and troops filling the streets two days in advance of the March on Washington for Jobs and Freedom, Kennedy's top officials convened around the long table of the Cabinet Room in an uproar. The principals—particularly McNamara and General Maxwell Taylor, chairman of the Joint Chiefs of Staff—claimed that they'd never approved DEPTEL 243. Hilsman insisted that they had. "My god! My government's coming apart," the president said, and when the officials kept arguing, he yelled, "This shit has got to stop!" But it was too late. When Kennedy went around the table, no one was willing to reverse the cable's instructions. "It is difficult indeed to tell a President to his face that something he has approved is wrong," William Colby of the CIA later said, "and to do so without anything positive to offer in its place."

And so this was how the United States abandoned its eight-year policy, going back to Lansdale, of supporting Ngo Dinh Diem as the Vietnamese leader who could defeat communism. Diem was no longer working out, so the United States was going to get in even deeper, without any idea what would come next—as if South Vietnamese politics could be controlled by a group of Americans with backgrounds in politics, law, academia, the military, and automobile manufacturing, sitting in a room eleven time zones away. Kennedy, Hilsman, and Rusk had served in the Pacific theater during the war; Hilsman had spent ten days in Vietnam on a fact-finding tour at the start of the year; McNamara and Taylor had done shorter stints, always coming back with optimistic reports. That was the regional expertise around the table. And Lodge—who had been in the country less than a week and admitted that he barely knew Vietnam at all, suggesting to Phillips over lunch at the ambassador's residence that the primitive superstitions of the Vietnamese people made them hard to understand and their politics unworthy of serious respect, a plaything compared to the high-level American politics that had been the stuff of his long and notable career as a U.S. senator, ambassador to the United Nations, vice-presidential nominee in 1960, and possible presidential candidate in 1964—Henry Cabot Lodge now took charge of the new policy. On August 28 he cabled to Washington: "We are launched on a course from which there is no respectable turning back: the overthrow of the Diem government."

Holbrooke was aware of none of this. He was still operating under the assumption that the U.S. government knew what it was doing, that it certainly knew more than he did (though the assumption wouldn't last much longer). But he felt that the Diem regime was finished—all his Vietnamese acquaintances were speaking openly against it for the first time—and boy, was he excited. "It is coming to a critical moment in our history here—how critical of course cannot yet be known. We must begin the task of showing that our position and Diem's cannot be reconciled. In this regard the presence of the monks in USOM is extremely lucky for it lets us show daily where we stand. Without those two bewildered people, we might be in a much more ambiguous position . . . I wish I knew more of what was going on."

Everyone in Saigon was waiting for a coup. But August ended and the coup didn't come. The generals weren't unified enough to turn their guns against the regime. There was lightning in the sky but no rain, and the Saigon air kept getting heavier.

THE END OF AUGUST answered Holbrooke's most fervent hope. He was going to be sent to a province in the lower Delta that was infested with Vietcong.

Down in Ba Xuyen, the Rural Affairs man, a guy named Bob Friedman, was having trouble with the province chief, Colonel Chieu. Chieu had ties through his wife to the Ngo family and was believed to be smuggling charcoal from the Delta to Saigon, with the money going to Nhu's secret political organization. When Phillips went down to talk to Chieu in Soc Trang, the provincial capital, Chieu stiffed him. Phillips conveyed his anger by pulling Friedman out of Ba Xuyen.

Holbrooke saw his chance. "I'd like to have a province," he told Phillips, who laughed, because Holbrooke was twenty-two years old. "Send me down there—there's nobody there."

"I don't want to send anybody down there," Phillips said in his soft Virginia drawl.

"Send me. I'm as good as nobody."

His chutzpah interested Phillips, and so did the thought of insulting Chieu by assigning this brash kid to be the provincial representative, the top American civilian, with sign-off authority on AID funds. It was an outrageous notion, impossible to imagine in the diplomatic corps, but Rural Affairs was a shirtsleeves outfit and Phillips instructed Friedman to brief his replacement.

But there was an obstacle: old George Melvin told Holbrooke that he wanted him to stay on as his staff aide. Instead of yielding, Holbrooke mentioned that he was going to be briefed on Ba Xuyen the next day. It was a way of not quite saying that he didn't want to be Melvin's staff aide while putting an obstacle in Melvin's way, and it angered Melvin, who took him upstairs to Phillips's office. "Which is it?" Melvin said. "Me or Ba Xuyen?"

How many twenty-two-year-olds would have told their boss in front of his boss, "Ba Xuyen"? But that was what happened when something came between Holbrooke and an object of his desire.

Ba Xuyen was the end of the earth. It was almost all the way to Ca Mau, and Ca Mau was the terminal point of the Asian continent, "the southernmost province of North Vietnam," Halberstam once called it, because Ca Mau and the lower Delta were the heartland of the Vietcong, who had been lurking for years among the hamlets and canals and rice paddies and mangrove forests. Ba Xuyen was a province of more than half a million, eight or nine hours' drive from Saigon down Route 4, across the interminable wet flatness of the Delta, nothing but flooded paddy fields mile after mile all the way to the horizon—in mid-September, when Holbrooke arrived in Soc Trang, the rice shoots were still golden, not yet the emerald green of the harvest—though more often he would fly, since there was a daily milk run on an Air America Caribou between Tan Son Nhut and airstrips around the Delta, and driving was risky by day and out of the question after dark.

His room was on the second floor of a clay-colored colonial guest-house, with a balcony overlooking the town square, across from Colonel Chieu's provincial headquarters and its tennis court. Next door to the guesthouse was a dance club called the Bungalow, except that Madame Nhu had banned dancing in order to protect the honor of Vietnamese women, so the Bungalow was now just a bar where local soldiers could go drink and pick up girls. Holbrooke's neighbors, also newly arrived, were a young Christian couple from Rhode Island, George and Renee McDowell. George was an aggie with International Voluntary Services—he was introducing local farmers to a strain of enormous watermelons from Georgia. Holbrooke made it known that he wasn't interested. He and McDowell once went to the Soc Trang airstrip to meet some officials visiting from Saigon, and Holbrooke introduced himself: "I'm Richard Holbrooke, the AID man here in Ba Xuyen." He gestured to McDowell, who was three years older. "This is George McDowell, the IVS boy."

Holbrooke's thing was strategic hamlets. There were 324 of them in Ba Xuyen—at least, that was what he arrived believing. When he asked to visit a few of the farther-flung hamlets he was told that it was too dangerous. He went anyway, in his white short-sleeve button-up shirt, with his sunglasses case clipped to the breast pocket, and found that the strategic hamlets consisted of punji sticks stuck in a moat and a barely armed local militia. The VC were overrunning and destroying them at will. There were three thousand hard-core cadres in the province, according to the intel reports. Saigon had permanently conceded half the provincial territory to the guerrillas, who had their own district chiefs, tax collectors, and schools. At night only the towns belonged to the government. Nonetheless, in Saigon and Washington there were 324 strategic hamlets in Ba Xuyen, putting 61 percent of the population under the government's theoretical control.

In Soc Trang the war was very close. The airstrip was often hit by mortar fire.

Holbrooke lost fifteen pounds in the heat. His room had no air-conditioning or fan, no working toilet or shower, and he could never get away from the mosquitoes, so he spent a good deal of time at the MAAG compound a block toward the canal. The American military advisors had a small projector and showed movies like *Seven Brides for Seven Brothers* and *Satan Never Sleeps,* for which Holbrooke had a bottomless appetite. On weekends he tried to get back to Saigon, to see the Lakes and the reporters, and to keep up with the bigger game.

Holbrooke was a good writer, never better than in his youth. I'll let him tell it.

IV

I wish I could tell it all to you—the poorly lit room and bar that I am now sitting in, where the MAAG men sit and wait their tours out; the playmates from *Playboy* on the walls here, somehow very much out of place; the stacks of old magazines and paperbacks, the other hints of home that the US Army flies into the Vietcong's homeland to make us feel a little less lost; the water everywhere, rising, raining, so that literally this province, even the ground around our building, is under water; the waiting; the ugliness, the cruelty, the tragedy. And in Saigon a regime so totally bankrupt and disgusting it is hard to describe. Events of the last 2 weeks have ended the dying hopes of some Americans that Diem and the family he is captive of will be able to lead this country anywhere but towards more death and dissension. So now we wait—for many things; above all, the end of this regime.

105 mm cannon have begun firing from somewhere to our rear, over the house, and towards the north. Small arms fire is audible, but not within 300 yards.—I am going to sleep.

There is something different about the Delta. Flying over it begins to give you some idea of the problems. It is completely flat, and ⅔ of it is under water right now. Yet it is the great VC stronghold, which may be the last to fall. How is it possible? Where can they possibly be? Many are in the marshes and inaccessible swamps of the far south, but the fact is that for most, this day means being sheltered in someone's house and in one of the hamlets right below us. To reduce the Delta:

what is going to be needed is a new approach, perhaps a recognition
that the hamlet program is not suited to the present situation. In this
regard last week's attacks may prove helpful; as the statistics roll in,
we begin to see already that there may have been several hundred
incidents in one night!

The province chief is not one of the nicest I have met, unfortunate
since I will work more with him than anyone else. His wife is very
beautiful, the best woman tennis player in Vietnam, and very very
brittle. She is apparently a bosom friend of Madame Nhu's, and she
let us all know this at lunch by showing around a tinted photograph
sealed into a plate and embroidered with ribbons—Madame Nhu
and Madame Chieu arm in arm. Behind her in the dining room were
about 10 tennis trophies. She said I should bring my racket, and the
acting chief of RA (Rufus is back in Washington, kicking up a storm)
Bert Fraleigh (a good player himself) says I will get beaten badly, but
should try to beat her if possible, for policy reasons.

I hand out money, Bulgar wheat (that brilliant way of unloading
our colossal surpluses—only a few people here like the stuff, since it
is not white and doesn't taste like rice), cooking oil, cement, roofing,
various goodies. We train and arm the hamlet militia, pay relocated
families (3950 in this province alone—a huge number which would
have been even bigger if we hadn't ordered a stop to it), try to start the
well-intentioned but difficult to implement self-help programs, train
hamlet officials, theoretically elected (for the first time in Vietnamese
history), and build schools, paying the first year's salary. This is foreign
aid at its very best—direct aid to the people, with no opportunity
for Saigon to get cut in on the gravy. Even in province, while some
corruption must exist, it probably is not too bad. I am quite impressed
with the program and wonder only why it is such a revolutionary
thing—somehow in my misguided way I had always pictured much of
our aid as working this way.

Soon, I am told, it will stop raining and get slightly hotter, but
otherwise, no change. The country is so sad, and I feel it more and
more. Today a Vietnamese came to us and said that some of his
friends have been killed by the police. True or not, I am sure that some
students have been. We work hard and often well here, but so much
is beyond our power, and winning the war will in the end depend on

factors we may not be able to control. But we are here now, and there is of course no other choice.

ONE STRANGE THING here; the more one drives a road the more nervous one becomes, rather than the reverse. One just knows too much about its past history. I was to drive down to Bac Lieu with Chieu and Major Butcher this morning, but somehow Chieu left ahead of us, while I was loading the CARE school kits into my jeep. This got Butcher so mad that he refused to go, without escort and so on. I really did not want to drive the road without escort today (there was an ambush on it last night), but since Butcher refused to go, and the time for the ceremony was approaching, I really had no choice. With a Lt who had to return to Bac Lieu (division headquarters), I drove it at a very fast speed, getting there in exactly 30 minutes, about 10 faster than any earlier trip for me.

At a pagoda, to which we had to walk 4 kms each way through a rich rice paddy, the bonzes had built a school, a nice big school of 5 classrooms, but they had run out of money and now asked for 30,000 piasters more (about $400US) to finish the job. I intend to give them the money, of course, although I would not have been able to put up the entire original amount. This brings me up against a variant of the problem faced daily in this most frustrating of situations; how much should one demand from the recipient of your aid? I would much prefer to give aid to people who know exactly what they want to do with it, as with these people, who come to me (indirectly) and ask for an exact amount for something, rather than give the Vietnamese some money and tell them what to do with it. I find that when this is done the results are usually not as hoped, since you have just given the people something you wanted to give them rather than something they wanted. On one hand, they may not ask for what we consider their prime need; on the other hand, they will at least be pleased with the requested item. With limitations, I lean towards giving them what they want. The limitations occur when the war effort becomes too directly involved, and we must at all times try to direct our aid so that it hurts the VC the most.

We hiked to another hamlet to look at a self-help request for

money and materials for a bridge; after changing some of the
demands, I accepted it. Then after lunch on to two more hamlets to
approve six more projects, making this a big day for self-help in Ba
Xuyen. We travelled by boat and jeep over bad and terrible roads
and small and terrifying canals, in an area which I am convinced is
VC underneath it all. In one hamlet the old women, who really run
things, started in on the district chief about how poor they were, and
asked for everything they could think of—rice, clothing, etc. I can give
them clothing and Bulgar wheat, but not rice, and they didn't seem
too enthralled with the possibility of Bulgar. Tough. Then we passed
another old lady, and she suddenly let loose with wails and cries. It
seems her cow had just, two hours before, brushed up against a mine
and been killed by a grenade. The cow was dead all right, although
there was only a tiny bruise behind its ear. I think the cow really was
killed by the grenade, although I wasn't sure, but her wailing was
something. The district chief at first seemed to consider paying her
for it out of his pocket, then changed his mind, and as we were leaving
later I saw that the villagers were carrying off pieces of the cow to eat,
at 40 piasters a kilogram.

The McDowells now live in a new house right behind mine. Mrs.
McDowell seems to be feeling the strain already, she is always writing
or reading, and looking for conversation. Her husband, a good man,
is unfortunately pretty dull, and I am afraid that in the life she now
leads (with not another western woman in town, and the Vietnamese
women unapproachable for her, since they speak no common language
and anyway they could not possibly communicate even if they did
speak a common language) she must by necessity find out so much
about her husband. Of course it is more than possible that she is also
pretty dull—probable, in fact. But George will do some good work
for USOM, and that is the important thing. Only it really is too bad
they are not more interesting. The MAAG people are really one of
the less appealing groups in Vietnam. They are big bitchers, that is,
day-counters, and they do not have anyone really too intelligent. But I
spend a lot of time there, eating most of my meals there, and trying to
get along with them. I also have to go there for my showers and for my
toilet, which here is not wholly adequate for what it be needed for.

My job as civilian advisor to the province chief and overseer of the aid program here puts me continually in the position of advocate of plans and projects which would seek to make a reality out of the clichés that everyone pays lip service to. I don't mind this (actually enjoy it) but it is sometimes tiring to try to get the Vietnamese to do something which is, after all, for their own good (or so we think . . .). On the other hand, when I step back just a little to look at everything, it seems to me that the Vietnamese have taken our overbearing presence rather well over the last few years. We arrive here with no knowledge of the country or of the situation and immediately start giving advice, some of which we can really turn almost into orders because of the materials and money and transportation that we fully control. I think that no American would stand for such a deep and continuing interference in our affairs, even if it appeared that survival was at stake. Yet the Vietnamese accept it, and with rather good grace.

TWO DAYS AGO I went out on my first operation. We left at about 5 A.M., travelling by boat to the starting point. We walked about 8 kms, through some very dense mangroves deep in VC territory, and never saw a VC. 3 grenades, set as traps on a trail, were the limit of our contact with the elusive enemy. The unit I was with was a Civil Guard company. This is called a "search and clear" operation, and for limited returns, it is unparalleled. For one thing, we move slowly and noisily; firing warning shots (presumably to warn the VC we are coming) was a favorite device. The VC, with good intelligence, have the option of either melting away before us, as they did Wednesday, or massing for a local numerical superiority and ambushing us. (At most times they could have been 10 yards away and we wouldn't have been able to see them.) Most of the time they fade away before us, but occasionally they clobber us.

I am fast deciding that the Mekong Delta is perhaps the most supremely unlivable place I have ever seen—yet 50% of Vietnam's 15 million live here. I am really relatively close right now to the most important thing happening strategically in the war on our side for some time: the consolidation plans for the Delta. Anyway, as always, I feel myself on the edge of a terrible precipice, and I hope I do not do anything to fall in. I know Mr. Melvin was impressed with my early success here, and to be frank, so am I. It is a deadly situation, where I will have to say no nicely and keep us moving, and I am likely to fall flat on my face. I am facing the most complex and subtle situation of my life, and have no idea how I am doing. We will see. Big big BIG things are flying around over my head these days. McNamara and Taylor are in now; Rufus is back; basic decisions must be made, by Kennedy, about our future military policy in the Delta and our political policy in Saigon.

McNamara and Taylor were in Phan Rang for 30 minutes today. The schedule the visitors are following is sad and annoying. For example, in Phan Rang they stopped for only 30 minutes and heard a briefing by the Province Chief. Now they asked the PC questions like "how are things, what are your problems?" etc. And all this was done in front of reporters. This is worse than trying to find out America's problems by interviewing governors in front of reporters. (Tell me, Governor Wallace, what is wrong with Alabama?) The only way to do it would be to sit down along with the sector advisors and get the true facts—none of this crap. They are being told some highly false slants, and even if they are also hearing some more accurate statements, it does us and our position here no good when the accurate is balanced off by the manure. I feel more and more strongly about this, because if the opportunity is lost on this visit, we have lost a great deal. What to do? What to do? I am tired and a little discouraged right now at the thought of those brilliant men returning to Washington thinking the bland thoughts produced in an intelligent listener when he hears directly conflicting interpretations and does not know which is right.

I CAME BACK to Saigon from Soc Trang today after a week in the field. It is good to get back after the provinces, where for me, to be honest, living is a little difficult—no place to dry from the wetness, no place to sit down and relax, or even work in peace, and right now—no toilet or water, but they will be fixed soon, I am sure. I just took a look in the mirror, maybe for the first time in months, and I honestly (no literary metaphor) couldn't figure out who I was. This sort of scared me, and never happened before. I have lost a lot of weight, but it must be more than that. The weight loss is large enough so that whoever knows me here comments on it. I am glad to lose it, but it is keeping up and up. I guess I perspire a lot. Still amazingly enough, no stomach troubles, which is the quick way to really lose. But why I couldn't recognize myself I don't know. I looked so goddamn mean and serious, and didn't look like I would ever smile again. But that is not wholly true, since I think I smiled yesterday (after losing a tennis match in Soc Trang in front of 150 gaping Vietnamese, and I played fairly lousily, while being eaten alive by bugs and sweating so much that I dropped the racket twice while serving to the crowd's delight). It was a brave smile. Sort of the kind I am trained to give to any people who might just happen along and ambush me.

When I came in this evening I immediately got 3 dinner invitations, which made me feel more socially accepted than ever before in my life. All for tonight, and I went, of course, to Tonys', who are really my favorite people here. He is getting a little fed up with the consular section, and it is understandable. With all this whirling around above us I think that Lodge and Lodge's very important assistant, Mr. Dunn, will pick Tony out fairly soon for a key inside job. Tony laughs at this, but I really think it is possible.

And Saigon—before 1954 it was, according to the old hands, a wonderful French city, un peu de Paris et tous ca. Today it is increasingly one of the least interesting cities I have ever been in. There is a total lack of real art or artifacts, for one thing. What passes for them—little cellophane fishes, porcelain dragons, and so on—is avidly seized on by the Americans here. The lack of anything to do also makes things tough. Without dancing or night-clubs as we think of them, Saigon is reduced to a few charming singers (always the same ones, every night in every club) and bars. No big sports events, no museums, and one fair zoo. (Zoos, however, lose a lot of appeal when instead of looking at a weird bird from the other side of the world you are looking at a weird bird found 30 miles away.) At first the tenseness created by the soldiers helps distract one from a realization of just how grim this city is, but I feel it more and more. Myself, when I am in Saigon, I play tennis, bowl, eat out (at one of a handful of restaurants), visit a few friends, and sit in front of my airconditioner to dry out. When I am in the provinces I dream about that airconditioner. Tony

has food poisoning today. I hope it is not serious. Toni and I get on
better and better.

I see them every time I am in Saigon, and they are really the only
people I really like up there. I call Tony first thing when I arrive, and
we always have one or two or more meals together, and go bowling
and play tennis together and so on. They are always ready to have
me barge in, and I like to. Toni is the only American wife out here
who I find at all bearable, and to me all the others are either bitches,
dull, overtalkative, or all three. I think there are some reasons for
this, and it is not just coincidence. For one thing, the men work very
hard and very well, and that leaves the wives spending a lot of time
fighting the little trials of life in Saigon. While they do no housework
at all—any of them—and this is a major contributing factor to their
awfulness, they also fight the servants, and talk endlessly about the
servants, and worry about their children, who may be growing up
(in my opinion) in the worst possible way, alienated from everything
that is real, both in their homeland and in Vietnam. The women worry
about their husbands' careers, in the wrong and worst way; they gossip
endlessly; they dislike the natives more than their husbands (this is a
commonplace from the days of British imperialism—the men were
quite equalitarian until they brought their wives out after them, and
they set up the exclusive clubs etc.).

So anyway, I do not like the American women of Saigon at all, and
I emphasize this point. The Exception, as we call her here, is Toni
Lake, who increasingly impresses me. In a way, she has changed since
Washington, and in a way, perhaps I misjudged her in Washington—
a quite surprisingly strong person. She really handles old Tony in
a great way, since she always sort of deflates him gently when he
starts out on one of his "I made a mistake today which will get
me transferred" bits, a very common and annoying thing he does
(annoying since we all know he is doing a great job in a terrible slot—
vice-consul—and will be the first of us to be promoted). "Oh no," he
says, "I will be the last. Really"—and that gets me mad, because he is
sort of begging you to tell him how good he is. But Toni handles him
well always.

———

IT IS SATURDAY in Soc Trang, without a doubt as the song goes, the loneliest night of the week. I know a good bar where all the Americans go and the girls all are friendly and even more so to me cause I speak the Vietnamese but NO. One of the main reasons I return to Saigon on weekends and when possible is that the MAAG and McDowell here are about as sad a group of Americans as one could find. Hating the country (not McDowell, but the MAAG), counting the days, swearing without stop, they just sit around when not in their office. Few if any understand the situation, and all see it as a merely military one— "one division of Americans would clean this place up" is a common statement, and nothing could be more wrong: a division of Marines would be bled to death in the swamps and paddies here, and never make a dent against the VC. It is what I am convinced the VC want us to do, it would be a ghastly mistake. These are guys who pride themselves on their toughness and skill, but they show so little perception.

The Army, about which I am learning enough to dislike it, makes of men complainers who respect only rank, and consider their own rank as a mark of their intelligence. The attitude here toward civilians is one which I of course do not like. They feel that I am a "Bulgar wheat salesman" and that my job has nothing to do with the war. They resent and actually fear the possibility that a goddamn civilian might be

doing things that influence the war effort. These things are not true
of the best we have out here, men like the assistant senior advisor at
Division, Col Montague, who has said that a well hurts the VC much
more and more permanently than any number of sweep operations.
But he is too rare, and our effort is too full of people who would kill
at sight in the Delta, since "they're all VC anyway."

I do not know the solution for our present difficulties in South
Vietnam. But I think I do know the nature and scope of the problem
now, and I am constantly amazed that so many military men who
have been here for many months can miss the facts in front of their
eyes. The cliché is now so hoary and reused that I thought everyone
knew that it was virtually policy and dangerous to disagree with: This
is a war for the minds and hearts of the people. I think this becomes a
major role for USOM and the Embassy, to push at all levels and at all
times the idea that this war cannot be solved merely by a series of big
defeats for the VC.

For the third night in a row the biggest guns we have over here,
the 155 howitzers, are firing to the east of Soc Trang, onto the island
in the Bassac River that forms the province's northern border. A large
operation—objective: destruction of rice, since the island is all VC—
has been going on, with some ground contact and a great deal of air
and artillery support. This is how ARVN fights this war: if the enemy
is possibly around, ahead of the advancing troops, stop all movement,
and call for a smothering air strike or an artillery barrage. Never go
in after them on the ground. The huge casualty figures you always see,
then, are in large part based on the sum of these two types of warfare,
and they are estimates based on the guess of an observer whizzing
over an area at 150 mph, or the reports of intelligence agents who vie
with each other to send in the most pleasing reports to their superiors.
Worse still, a sizeable percentage of all casualties in air and cannon
fire certainly are non-combatants, the peasant forever trapped in the
middle of the war.

Some things I enjoy about Vietnam, not necessarily related to our
mission but to my disposition: I enjoy the fast pace of the people who
are good, the men who are doing the best job for us. While there are
many people here who should be ejected, the good ones are very very
good. It is in a way thrilling to return to Camau or Bac Lieu or Saigon,

and meet these people, with whom you may have shared a tough day
in the field somewhere. It is wonderful to meet someone you know and
respect suddenly on an airstrip somewhere in the Delta. I enjoy the
drama of the helicopters, even the much-disliked H-21s, which keep
going down all over the place—if I keep riding them I will I suppose
eventually go down in some rice paddy like everyone else does. With
the air being slapped at by the rotor blades and driving hard against
you, we jump out of the choppers, and move quickly to the waiting
people. The noise is great, and you can never hear anyone. Those
scenes, so common to me now, are still thrilling moments, although
I would not dare admit it to anyone here.

AT 0500 THIS MORNING the news came in that the VC had attacked
and possibly overrun the furthest out outpost in the southeastern
district of Ba Xuyen. It is a Cambodian post, located just three
kilometers from a mangrove forest which forms the point where
the lower branch of the Mekong meets the South China Sea. The
mangrove forest is a VC haven, as almost all mangrove forests are.
The post protects a huge and critical hamlet, also Cambodian, which
was originally scheduled to be visited by McNamara today before the
schedule was cut. Anyway, by helicopter we flew out over the area
for about an hour, circling at around 1500 feet, and from that height
it could be clearly seen that the post had been destroyed. What the
situation was on the ground could not yet be known—we did not go
any lower, since we were getting shot at from time to time as we moved
over the area. We refueled at Soc Trang, and joined an Eagle Flight
moving out over the area now. An Eagle is a group of about 6 to 10
choppers, which fly very low over bad areas, hoping to draw fire, after
which they pounce. We were above the main force choppers, which
carry Vietnamese army. Finally, after the infantry had reached the
hamlet and post, we went in.

On the ground was one of the worst sights I ever hope to see. The
VC had apparently dug in with recoilless 75mm fire only 50 yards away,
and leveled the post before moving a man against it. (Such a weapon
is definitely from China—they never were used here by either US,
French or VN.) Unlike most posts which fall here, it was apparently

not an inside job. This may in part be due to the fact that these were Cambodians, and they are the best fighters around.

The fort was a shambles, of the 31 men in it 10 were dead, as were 7 children and 4 women, who live with their men in these terrible traps. The bodies were being assembled as we came in, and the noise of the women wailing, plus the horrible air and stench that overlay everything, was . . . One sees pictures of people picking their way through the war-torn rubble of Europe and Japan, and we have seen this sort of thing often in the histories of our times, but going in on the ground like this is still something new. One doesn't know quite what his reactions will be. Mine were not as bad as I was afraid they might be; perhaps little by little I have been working up to this anyway. (There have been so many similar to this, and Vietnam is such a cruel country to begin with, but this was the worst I have yet been in immediately afterwards.)

But afterwards it has been harder to put away the pictures of Can Nganh post. In a way, so unreal, since the birds still flew around, and the children in the nearest houses, less than 50 yards away, played games and seemed normal. But there were the women crying over the torn bodies of their husbands, and legs sticking out here and there grotesquely. In one corner of the post, near where a shell had exploded, a brain was all splattered on the ground.

McNamara was supposed to visit the hamlet and post today. There is so little one can do, but of course I told the province chief that if he wanted additional funds to give to those who lost part of their family, or to those in that hamlet, who have been attacked so often, and are now really under the gun worse than ever, it was all right with me. But it really doesn't seem to mean much on a day like today.

For the McNamara visit, the province chief asked for all the American flags around, and found out there were none. He ordered all the tailors in Soc Trang to sew them all night the night before, and when 40 were done, they were loaded on a truck and sent down to Bac Lieu. Half-way there the truck hit a mine, and both drivers were wounded, the flags destroyed, and the next day there were no US flags in sight. Except one, with 25 stars on it. I asked about it and was told that there were, after all, 25 stars on each side.

Yesterday I went down to MAAG and saw the new report, the

result of the McNamara-Taylor trip, that MAAG-USOM have to
submit jointly 4 times a year, starting in two weeks. This is the report
that the dreamers in Saigon and Washington think will eliminate the
gap between facts in the field and reports received in headquarters.
It will presumably be compiled, rebutted, analyzed and on the basis of
it and similar information decisions should be taken. The only trouble
is that somehow I doubt it will work. True, it may help, but it won't
solve the basic problem, which is that the information written by one
person on this crazy situation cannot be properly used by someone
12,000 miles away to arrive at decisions. And much more, which I
cannot scarcely put down on paper, because it is all so confused and
discouraging. Reports lie, they lie.

MY PICTURES CAME back from Honolulu, the ones in color of the
destroyed post. They are remarkable, perhaps great pictures, but very
gruesome. One, of a mother nursing her child next to her husband's
body, is the best—the worst.

I have my doubts, getting deeper and deeper, about our basic
approach here. Recent discussions and hints I have got from various
sources would indicate that out of the McNamara visits came added
weight for the exponents of Victory through Air Power—the Air
Force, and the armed helicopters. I feel that this is a terrible step, both
morally and tactically. Of course, it would never do to actually attack
policy on moral grounds in the American community here, which is a
basically tough and getting tougher community ("War is hell," justifies
any horror among vast numbers, including, I am sorry to say, Jim
Rosenthal, who is one of my closest friends). However, the decision
to fight the VC from the air can be quite easily attacked on the simple
grounds of stupidity (or as Talleyrand once said, "Sir, it is worse
than a crime, it is a blunder"). The VC, I am convinced, often fire on
our planes merely to draw artillery and air destruction down upon
hamlets. This may sound amazing, but it is a generally accepted fact,
and the reason for it that once we have committed such an act, the VC
can make great propaganda hay out of it.

The French lost Indochina by killing the enemy; one shot from a
hamlet would bring down the full fury of the air force, and the next

day the Viet Minh would have dozens of new recruits, both out of
the wreckage of that hamlet, and from relatives. This, I think, is the
basic point, the key difference between indiscriminate terror, such as
air strikes, and selective terror, as practiced by the VC. They will kill
one man, and one man only, to show the rest that it is unwise for you
individually to stick your neck out and show how good you are against
the communists. (Last week they killed the best district chief in one
province, and one of the best province chiefs in Vietnam.)

So, anyway, if by air power we mean to win this war, thousands of
Vietnamese will die and the enemy will resist far longer; we will be
making a grave mistake and I am not happy about it. Of course the
irony of the whole thing is overwhelming, if one is ever stupid enough
to stop and think about it. Today, in Vietnam, we are using by far
worse weapons and worse—less humane tactics—than the enemy. I
have no doubt at all that we kill more civilians than the VC, and with
what might generally be admitted are less selective, less "right" tactics.
I suppose that we are on the right side in the long run here. There is
no doubt in my mind that if we lose here we will be fighting this war
in other countries in Latin America and Asia within a few years. But
right now, we are fighting wrong, and it hurts. In the short run terms,
we really should be on the other side. Take away the ties to Hanoi and
Peking and the VC are fighting for the things we should always be
fighting for in the world. Instead we continue to defend a class of haves
which has not yet shown its real ability to understand that the have-
nots must be brought into the nation. Let that be shown, and perhaps
there will be an improvement in the situation, not of our making, but
to our benefit.

The whole damn thing makes me slightly ill. (Or is it my throat?)
This is the most exciting assignment in the world, and I will always
be grateful for having it. But I do not think I will be sorry to leave.
One friend of mine just got his next assignment: Luxembourg. It
seems almost a joke, but it is true. There are such places. I think I am
beginning to see war, which goddamn it this really is, in the least
glorified of lights. That is when the fight sometimes doesn't even seem
worth it, so bloody is the cost. But there is no choice, really, is there?

V

October 26 was National Day—the date in 1955 when Ngo Dinh Diem proclaimed himself president of the Republic of Vietnam. Holbrooke was an honored guest on the reviewing stand in Soc Trang. The Lakes were supposed to come down and join him, but Toni got sick again and had to go back to the hospital. There was a military parade, and rifle-carrying girls in the blue uniforms of Madame Nhu's paramilitary corps kept fainting in the midday sun. An L-19 observation plane flew overhead and dropped pieces of paper saying "All Hail to the Republic and its President." Afterward, at the province chief's house, Holbrooke and other dignitaries ate slices of a cake in the form of a strategic hamlet.

Holbrooke was too junior to know that the coup was coming. But Rufus Phillips knew.

He had been called back to Washington in September by his father's terminal illness, and on the morning of September 10 he was summoned to the White House. Around the table in the Cabinet Room Phillips recognized McNamara, Taylor, Rusk, Harriman, Hilsman, John McCone of the CIA, the national security advisor McGeorge Bundy—all the big names in Vietnam policy. Kennedy was being briefed by yet another two-man fact-finding delegation just returned from South Vietnam. Marine General Victor Krulak, from McNamara's staff, informed the president that, during his two-day tour of the country, he had spoken with eighty-seven American advisors, twenty-seven Vietnamese officers, and General Harkins, and he reported with great confidence that the crisis in Saigon was having very little effect on the shooting war, which was going impressively well. Then Krulak's civilian counterpart on the trip, a State Department official named Joseph Mendenhall, reported that the war against the Vietcong had become secondary to the battle over the South Vietnamese government, which was close to collapse.

"You two did visit the same country, didn't you?" Kennedy asked.

Phillips was sitting against the wall in one of the chairs designated for lesser officials who were present to listen, not speak. That he was even there was an accident—on a swing through Saigon the columnist Joseph Alsop had given Phillips a sealed envelope to hand to a Kennedy aide in Washington, with a note inside saying "He knows more about this show and judges it better than anyone I know," and the aide had shown the note to Kennedy, who had scribbled, "You should ask Phillips to report." People with the deepest knowledge are almost never in the room when an important issue is debated at the highest level. Only the inner circle can be trusted not to leak.

Phillips was thinking how abstract and irrelevant the discussion seemed, how little it had to do with the Vietnam he knew, when his presence was suddenly mentioned to the president. He was invited to come forward and sit at the principals' table. Kennedy asked him to explain the vast difference in the accounts they'd all just heard. Phillips said that no Vietnamese army officer would tell a hard truth to a visiting American like Krulak, a complete stranger, in front of his superiors— lying was professionally required. The truth was reserved for longtime American friends over a private dinner.

In that moment, with his keen mind, Kennedy might have realized that Phillips had just shone a light powerful enough to expose in all their falsity the many high-level missions the president had been sending out on lightning tours of Vietnam since 1961.

Kennedy asked Phillips about the war. "I'm sorry to have to tell you, Mr. President," Phillips said, "but we are not winning the war, particularly in the Delta." The VC had recently destroyed sixty strategic hamlets in the province just south of Saigon, cutting the barbed-wire fences, taking down the iron roofing, and sending the farmers back to their home villages, while the Vietnamese troops responsible for their defense had been confined to quarters because Diem feared they might join a coup attempt. It was nearly unthinkable to confess a failure in one's own program to the president, but Phillips had just done it.

"You don't know anything about the military," General Krulak said. "This is a war."

"This is a political war, and we are losing it," Phillips replied. Krulak was fuming, McNamara was shaking his head, and Kennedy was taking notes. "Most Vietnamese would like to see Diem remain but are unalterably opposed to the Nhus," Phillips went on. "What is needed is a campaign to isolate Nhu and get him out of the country. The campaign needs a campaign manager. That man is General Lansdale."

"I want to thank you for your remarks," Kennedy said when Phillips finished, "particularly for your recommendation about General Lansdale." But separating the Ngo brothers was beyond even Lansdale's power, and Diem had lost touch with his country, and perhaps Lansdale no longer had the old magic, and perhaps Phillips was indulging in wishful thinking of his own.

Lansdale wasn't sent back to Saigon—McNamara still stood in the way. Instead, Kennedy ordered McNamara and Taylor on yet another fact-finding mission, as if the glimmer of light from Rufus Phillips was quickly doused by bureaucratic pressure or Kennedy's reluctance to see by it.

Phillips returned to Saigon to find the Diem regime and the American mission in open hostilities. Lodge canceled economic and military aid programs. The black market rate for dollars surged from 90 to 140 piastres in one week. The regime's paper, the *Times of Viet Nam,* accused Phillips of being the CIA's number two in Saigon. Then, at the end of October, Diem summoned Phillips to the palace and apologized for the story.

"Do you think there will be a coup?" Diem asked softly, looking Phillips in the eye and drawing on a cigarette.

"I am afraid so, Mr. President," Phillips said. Lodge had already signaled to the dissident generals through his liaison and bagman, a French-born operative named Lucien Conein, that the time had come and the Americans were on board.

———

ON FRIDAY, November 1, Holbrooke was supposed to fly to Saigon for the weekend on the mid-afternoon milk run from Soc Trang. After lunch, he and George McDowell drove out of town to see the proposed site for the Rural Life Demonstration Center. It was to be a training school where farmers from outlying hamlets would take classes in agriculture and animal husbandry, and it was to be built by soldiers of the South Vietnamese army—who had so far done no civic action projects in Ba Xuyen, because they didn't want to, and because their American military advisors didn't see the point, either—in order to contradict the VC propaganda line that the government didn't care about the people. The slogan Holbrooke devised was "The Army and the hamlet people work together for their common good against the common enemy, the Viet Cong." The project excited him. It was hearts and minds, pure Lansdale.

Near the site, the jeep's right wheels slipped off a narrow dirt path and into a canal. The situation looked hopeless, until Holbrooke enlisted a dozen farmers who were staring at this minor American quagmire to get in the water and help push the jeep out. He would have still made his plane, except that the plane wasn't coming. At the airfield in Soc Trang an announcement told all Americans to stay in quarters due to a civil disturbance.

Holbrooke reached Lake by phone at his house. Lake calmly reported that he and Toni were trapped by small-arms fire.

Something big was happening in Saigon. There was a better chance of catching a flight out of Can Tho, a large town on the lower branch of the Mekong sixty kilometers north. Holbrooke drove to the MAAG compound and the military advisors told him that the road to Can Tho was very bad, a VC battalion was operating in the vicinity. But he had to get to Saigon—he would go crazy stuck in Soc Trang—and he jumped in his waterlogged jeep, with his .45 on the passenger seat, and drove alone up the two-lane road toward Can Tho. He kept passing obvious ambush spots in the elephant grass along the canals and a quarter of the way there he decided that it was foolish to keep going. Just as he was about to turn around, a South Vietnamese army truck raced past, and he continued to Can Tho trailing the truck as his escort.

On arrival, he removed the clip from his gun and started to clear the barrel, aiming down as he was supposed to—but the .45 was cocked, and it fired off a round into the floor between the clutch and four-wheel-drive shift with a tremendous blast and heavy recoil. It was the kind of thing that happens in a crisis and the most shameful thing he ever did in Vietnam. From then on he decided to take his chances unarmed.

There were no flights from Can Tho. Holbrooke reached Lake again, and Lake said, "I can't talk to you now," and hung up.

The Lakes had just finished lunch at their villa, and Tony was getting ready to go back to the embassy, when the shooting started. A machine gun was firing from their yard at the presidential guard barracks across the street. Lake pushed a mattress against the window and immediately felt like a fool. It was the long-awaited coup and they were right in the middle of it. He Tony, She Toni, their poodle Kim Chi, their maid Tiba, and their upstairs neighbors the Kinneys took shelter in a storage closet with cans of PX pineapple juice, where they remained for the next thirteen hours. Toni was five months pregnant and Ann Kinney was due in a week. Shells tore through the tree branches and shrapnel whacked against the outside walls as rebel artillery found the range of the barracks. Lake occasionally crawled out of the closet to answer the phone, peer through the shutters, and report on the fighting to the military attaché at the embassy. When the barracks fell, the rebel tanks turned toward the presidential palace several blocks away.

And after Lodge, upon finishing his lunch that day, went up to the roof of the residence to watch with detached interest the shooting and shelling down in the streets; and after Diem, under siege in the palace in the late afternoon, reached Lodge by phone and asked for the United States government's view of the matter (for Diem was finally ready to be a good puppet, now that it was too late), and Lodge (who, with his wife, had been Diem's overnight guest at the president's mountain villa up in Dalat four days earlier, all the while knowing and encouraging what was about to happen) told the South Vietnamese president that it was too early in the morning in Washington for the United States government to have any view of the matter, but offered Diem safe passage out of the country, which Diem refused ("I would like you to know that you are talking to a president of an independent and sovereign country"); and after Diem and Nhu escaped from the surrounded palace that night through a network of secret tunnels to a car waiting near the Cercle Sportif and were conveyed to the house of a Chinese merchant in Cholon, where they spent the rest of that long night; and after the brothers were discovered and arrested by army troops the next morning in a nearby Catholic church, shoved into the back of an armored personnel carrier, bound at the hands, and shot and bayoneted to death on orders of the coup leader, General Duong Van "Big" Minh, who took over as head of the military junta; and after Lodge, now a hero to the citizens of Saigon, received this news with a chilling sangfroid, asking Halberstam, "What would we have done with them had they lived?"—after all this, Rufus Phillips fell into a state of gloom.

He had known Diem for almost a decade. He had seen the best of Diem, when Diem kept the new country together while few others gave it a chance. He had watched Diem deteriorate under the pressure of the war and his insidious brother and the Americans and his own autocratic character. Phillips still considered Diem a friend. For his overthrow to end in murder cast a shadow across the whole enterprise, past and future. His blood was on American hands.

Phillips had also lost his father, and with no one else to run the family business he would have to leave Rural Affairs before the end of the month.

Kennedy had a sense of ill omen, too. When the deed was done, he spoke into a private tape recorder in the Oval Office. "I feel we must bear a good deal of responsibility for it, beginning with our cable . . . in which we suggested the coup," he said. "It should never have been sent on a Saturday. I should not have given my consent to it without a roundtable conference."

John-John entered the room and briefly distracted his father: "Naughty, naughty daddy."

"I was shocked by the death of Diem and Nhu," Kennedy went on. "The way he was killed made it particularly abhorrent. The question now is whether the generals can stay together and build a stable government." Kennedy had less than three weeks to live.

By the time Holbrooke reached Saigon the day after the coup, it was all over. At the Lakes' house he overstayed the seven p.m. curfew two nights running, hearing their tales and admiring their collection of shrapnel and spent casings, and ended up sleeping on the tile floor. Their neighborhood was a shambles of broken trees and burned houses.

The tense air in Saigon had cleared overnight and everyone's mood lifted, the city turned into a street festival, civilians climbing on tanks to give food to soldiers, monks and students sprung from jail, Americans greeted and thanked by random locals. At the Tu Do nightclub workers were already hammering the dance floor back in place. Lodge and the reporters—who considered him a vast improvement on his predecessor—saw the end of Diem as a problem solved.

Holbrooke wrote, "I think things are looking up in Vietnam."

THE RAINY SEASON WAS ending. Back in Soc Trang, Colonel Chieu was suddenly cooperative, but he had been close to the Nhus through his tennis-playing wife and didn't last two weeks after the coup. There were changes in command all across South Vietnam, with Diem's loyalists out and the junta's cronies in, and the resulting chaos paralyzed the army. The coup had meant a new regime, nothing more. Big Minh turned out to be a passive leader, and Lodge was no strongman whisperer like Lansdale—he had accomplished his mission and quickly lost what little interest he'd had in Vietnamese politics. The war was in

the countryside, where the peasants had no more love for the French-trained generals in Saigon than they'd had for the Catholic mandarins.

After the coup, the biggest VC offensive of the war began, and everything in the Delta went to pieces. The guerrillas were now using anti-aircraft weapons and 75-millimeter recoilless rifles and Chinese mortars. The roads around Ba Xuyen became too dangerous to drive. The whole province outside Soc Trang was poised to fall. The strategic hamlets were left undefended, they were overrun or abandoned, and the program disintegrated.

Halberstam's tour was ending in December, and he wanted to spend a few days with Holbrooke in the Delta before going home, a visit that Holbrooke dreaded because it could hurt him with the Saigon office and because he knew that Halberstam was coming to see one last time how right he'd been, which he had. Holbrooke agreed to the visit anyway—he couldn't resist the company of a journalist as brilliant and important as Halberstam—and they flew down together from Tan Son Nhut. Holbrooke tried to interest Halberstam in his civic-action projects like the Rural Life Demonstration Center, but Halberstam quickly grew bored and kept asking where the real war was, since the VC were all around them, which, again, Holbrooke couldn't deny.

Years later, Holbrooke would describe an almost inevitable sequence of doubt and disillusionment that took place in the minds of certain Americans in Vietnam. By now he had gone through the first stage, which was to question the assessments. Were there really 324 strategic hamlets in Ba Xuyen? On paper, maybe; in reality most of them were flimsy death traps. But the Vietnamese told the Americans what they wanted to hear, and the Americans in the field, especially the military, told their superiors in Saigon what they wanted to hear, and Saigon told Washington what it wanted to hear, and by the time reports reached the president they were useless. The lies and self-deceptions made it harder to reach the right policy, and this shocked and angered Holbrooke.

The second stage of doubt was to question the tactics. By the end of 1963 he was already at this stage and would remain there for most of his time in Vietnam. He knew that Hueys and heavy artillery were wasting ammunition and killing more civilians than guerrillas and turning the survivors into VC sympathizers. Whether or not the tactics were immoral, they were inefficient and counterproductive. He knew that in a war for the people you needed different tactics, and though killing was necessary, so were rural life demonstration centers, which meant that his civilian job was fundamental to the war.

Seventy kilometers south of Soc Trang, at the farther reaches of the Delta, the town of Bac Lieu was headquarters of the South Vietnamese army's Twenty-first Division and its American advisory group, led by Colonel Jack Cushman and his brilliant deputy, Lieutenant Colonel Bob Montague, who became Holbrooke's closest friend in the military, not coincidentally because he was one of its fiercest critics. Holbrooke began spending time with the advisors in Bac Lieu. The Strategic Hamlet Program had failed and they were looking for another approach to counterinsurgency.

There was an aging Vietnamese officer at Division named Major Yi, who spoke good French and passable English. Major Yi had fought with the French in the Delta, and he told the Americans about a concept of pacification that the French had used in the First Indochina War, though it went back earlier, to the turn of the century and Marshal Hubert Lyautey, the French commander who colonized Morocco. The concept was called *tache d'huile,* or "oil spot." Instead of the massive relocations and grandiose failures of the strategic hamlets, start where the people lived, use regular army platoons and self-defense forces to secure the population of a limited area, set up local government, provide services, and then slowly expand the zone of control outward into VC areas, like a spreading drop of oil.

Holbrooke and the advisors set up a training center in Bac Lieu, wrote up lesson plans in Vietnamese and English, and began to teach the oil-spot technique to officers of the Twenty-first Division. Holbrooke's job was to get support from the American civilians in Saigon.

But they had other worries. The conspirators who had overthrown Diem were indecisive and prone to infighting, and by early 1964 the war was going so badly that Big Minh talked openly of negotiations with Hanoi. Negotiating was one line that the new American president, Lyndon Johnson, like the president he'd replaced, would not cross. On January 30, Big Minh was overthrown in a bloodless coup by another general, Nguyen Khanh. After meeting the new leader, Lodge returned to the embassy full of excitement: "He's going to kick ass!" he told Lake. But soon coups and countercoups became routine in Saigon. The state itself was falling apart.

Holbrooke's optimism of November was gone. "While <u>Diem definitely had to go</u>, with his departure we learned that many problems and difficulties we had blamed on his regime went far deeper, into the history and tradition and situation of the tragic country," he wrote home. "Secondly, we saw even more clearly than before—when so much was blamed on Ngo Dinh Diem—the absolute limitations of our ability to advise, to try to get a country (one cannot say 'nation') to save itself."

Cushman was scheduled to rotate out in April, and before leaving he wanted to sell the oil spot to General William Westmoreland, who had arrived as Harkins's deputy and eventual replacement (Harkins still believed victory was at hand). Westmoreland gave Cushman the fifteen minutes it took to drive from MACV headquarters to Tan Son Nhut, where the general was scheduled to welcome a group of students from the National War College. On the way, Cushman told Westmoreland that the path to success wasn't just military operations but pacification of the hamlets, and he described his experiment in Bac Lieu. With a dozen of the right American advisors in place, who understood the concept and extended their tours to two years, they could win back the countryside. Cushman didn't know how he'd answer if Westmoreland asked *him* to stay for a second year, but Westmoreland didn't ask that question, or any question. He gave no reaction at all. His mind was elsewhere. Three weeks later Cushman was gone.

And by the time the first American combat divisions arrived a year later under Westmoreland's command, the oil spot was collecting dust on a shelf at MACV. Westmoreland needed just one word to sum up his strategy for victory: "attrition."

AS HOLBROOKE PREDICTED, Lake was promoted first. A top official at State named U. Alexis Johnson—the one who had proposed that bachelor diplomats be sent out as aid workers to Vietnam's dangerous provinces—looked at Lake's personnel record and said, "No Foreign Service officer that young is that good." After the coup Lake was transferred to a new assignment as Lodge's staff assistant. He immediately fell under the ambassador's thrall—they'd attended the same prep school outside Boston, belonged to related New England tribes, Lodge's wit was delivered in Lake's native dialect. But sitting at the right hand of power could be humiliating. Lake answered the ambassador's mountainous mail (the end of Diem had burnished Lodge's name back home and there was a movement to draft him for the 1964 Republican presidential nomination), and was summoned to the Majestic Hotel to pick up Joe Alsop's laundry, and scurried along the edge of the pool at the Cercle Sportif with a notepad and pen, sweating in his suit, while Lodge swam laps and occasionally barked out an instruction, until Emily Lodge called to her husband, "Cabot! Cabot! You let that boy go home now!"

At Christmas 1963 the Lakes and Holbrooke went to Cambodia and visited Angkor Wat. As they crossed a footbridge to the temple, they looked down in a moat and saw a beautiful Cambodian village. It was a replica set up by a crew that was shooting a film of Conrad's *Lord Jim*. A few weeks later, Lake flew down to Soc Trang to see what Holbrooke was doing and they spent a few days traveling around hamlets in Ba Xuyen together. This was real counterinsurgency, the kind Lake had read up on during his Foreign Service training, and he returned to Saigon deeply impressed by Holbrooke's dedication.

There was a *Peanuts* cartoon strip of the time that circulated among Holbrooke and his friends in Vietnam. Charlie Brown's baseball team has just gotten slaughtered, 184–0. "I don't understand it," Charlie Brown says. "How can we lose when we're so sincere?"

Why do Americans keep falling in love with counterinsurgency? I ask because we're obviously no good at it. Except for Lansdale in the Philippines I can't think of a real win, while there are too many losses to remember, though none bigger or more complete than Vietnam, including the ones that came at the end of Holbrooke's life—Iraq, which he stayed away from, and Afghanistan, which pulled him in so deep that his ice-blue eyes began to seem ghosted by shadows of the far-off war of his youth.

We're no good at it because we don't have the knowledge or patience, few of our people are willing to learn the history and language and spend the years out there necessary to understand the nature of the conflict. There are always exceptions, like Holbrooke's friend Frank Scotton. He was an information officer who spent the better part of thirteen

years in Vietnam. He got to know the jungle trails and mastered the language and organized Vietnamese commandos into armed propaganda units that mirrored the VC right down to the black pajamas. He figured out that the war wasn't in villages or towns, let alone provincial capitals or Saigon, but in hamlets, the essential unit of Vietnamese society. He spoke his mind and was considered unreliable by higher-ups, and he failed to influence their policies or win promotions. Holbrooke had great respect for Scotton, while Scotton regarded Holbrooke as one of the few Americans who understood about hamlets. But even Holbrooke, who would devote the rest of the decade to the war, never learned to speak the language or made Vietnamese friends.

We prefer our wars quick and decisive, concluding with a surrender ceremony, and we like firepower more than we want to admit, while counterinsurgency requires supreme restraint (its apostles in Vietnam used to say, "The best weapon for killing is a knife. If you can't use a knife, then a gun. The worst weapon is airpower") and is, according to the experts, 80 percent political. We spend our time on American charts and plans and tasks, as if the solution to another country's internal conflict is to get our own bureaucracy right. And maybe we don't take the politics of other people seriously. That has to do with the innocence that disgusted Graham Greene—Lansdale's conviction that we're all brothers and sisters who want the same things. But that very conviction explains why we keep fighting this kind of war. It comes down to the power of our belief in ourselves. If we are good—and are we not good?—then we won't need to force other people to do what we want. They will know us by our deeds, and they will want for themselves what we want for them.

So Holbrooke and Cushman and Montague didn't pause to consider that the idea of the oil spot, *tache d'huile,* came out of a French colonial campaign of subjugation in Morocco by way of a disastrous French colonial defeat in Vietnam. This should have at least called into question its utility for fighting the same revolutionary movement that had beaten the French. Instead, the Americans saw the chance to turn our goodness into a practical, teachable technique.

Counterinsurgency isn't for everyone—it's a sophisticated taste. In Vietnam it attracted the idealists. This attraction wasn't what got us into the war. We fell into Vietnam and kept on sinking out of a mistaken belief that Kennan's policy of containment required us to stake our security and credibility on not losing another square mile of Asia to communism even though the enemy were nationalists. But counterinsurgency was part of the lure. It was what kept Holbrooke and Americans like him there.

Lake's parents owned a collection of *New Yorker* cartoons that included a James Thurber from 1938. A girl seated in a living room is staring intently ahead, while one woman confides to another, riffing on a famous line of Walter Pater's: "She says she's burning with a hard, gemlike flame. It's something they learn in school, I think." That was how Lake, with irony and admiration, saw Holbrooke.

I sometimes think this first year in Vietnam was the best of Richard Holbrooke. I've lingered long enough for you to see him clearly—if you can see anyone clearly at this distance—because the Delta explains a lot that came later. He plunged so fast and deep into the war, yet through all the action he kept his head clear. By the start of 1964 he knew that the war was being fought wrong—he would never know anything with such certainty again. He knew that clichés were making it impossible to think of a better approach. He believed that he knew more than any American official in Vietnam, at least any official above him, and he might have been right. But he was too fresh for the hide of a personage to have grown on him and irritate half the people it scraped against. Almost everyone liked him, except disregarded lesser mortals like George McDowell, who would never forget being called "the IVS boy."

His ambition still had a clean smell, and youth was working in his favor—physical courage, moral passion, the boundless energy and enthusiasm and sheer sense of fun, the skepticism, the readiness to talk straight to ambassadors and generals. Lodge gave him forty-five minutes one-on-one and was so impressed by Holbrooke's account of Ba Xuyen that he invited him back for a two-hour lunch. Lodge was cold and cruel to anyone who gave off a whiff of weakness or fear, but he liked holding forth in the company of martinis and bright young men. Holbrooke wanted the attention of someone like Lodge, wanted it badly, and his way of winning over his betters was to combine personal flattery with policy candor. He was exceptional from the start, not just because he was brilliant and curious and widely read, but because he was unafraid to face the truth, cared enough to act on it, and was willing to take the consequences.

He wasn't questioning the war itself, not yet, not by a long shot. That would be psychologically just about impossible for someone serving the U.S. government in Vietnam and living the war every minute of the day, and as soon as such a question began to germinate it would be time to ship quietly out to some other port of call—you'd have no business staying. Instead, he put his whole effort into fighting it better. That was the watchword of Holbrooke and Lake and their friends. A better war.

VI

I haven't told you about Holbrooke and women. There's a lot to say, for he was the kind of man who needed women and the need cracked him open, exposing tenderness and vulnerability and bad judgment. Since women were rarely his competitors, he allowed them to see him more clearly than men. In their company the hard, gemlike flame adjusted to a soft, illuminating glow. But in this first year in Vietnam they didn't figure much. His world there was a man's world, except for the Exception, and his sexism was as unthinking as it was blatant.

The Vietnamese women noticed by American men rode around Saigon on the back of motorbikes, with their long lustrous hair perfectly combed, the tailored silk tops of their traditional ao dais slit to the hips and floating behind them like colorful flags. These women, Holbrooke later confessed, were "a white man's dream." Most of the unmarried Americans had local girlfriends, and some of the married ones, too. Husbands would send their wives and kids to the beach resort at Nha Trang on weekends and holidays and stay behind in Saigon to get some work done. Sheehan's girlfriend was called Blue Lotus, and he was going to marry her until Halberstam, who also had a Vietnamese girl but was more practical about the whole thing, argued Sheehan out of it. The older Asia hands at Rural Affairs shocked Holbrooke with their hard-edged advice: be realistic about the financial nature of the liaison, and afterward wash with Physicians' and Surgeons' Soap.

After the evacuation of dependents and the arrival of ground troops in 1965, South Vietnam became a vast brothel. But even before there were half a million Americans, sex was an elemental part of the war. "I have the theory that if the women of Vietnam had big copper spoons through their noses and looked like Ubangis," a reporter once said, "this war wouldn't have lasted half as long, and maybe wouldn't have even started." The whole scene repelled the Boston Puritan Henry Cabot Lodge. "I not only don't wanna," he said, "I don't even wanna wanna."

Holbrooke might have wanted to, but he didn't. He was too inexperienced, too geeky, too consumed with the war. And he was the kind of man who required more after sex than Physicians' and Surgeons' Soap—who needed the intimacy that talk brings. And then, there was the possible fiancée I mentioned.

Her name was Larrine Sullivan but people called her Litty. He had met her on a blind date at Brown and hired her to write for the campus paper when female reporters were rare. She was tall and attractive and she wore her hair short like those girls in early Beatles pictures. She was a better student than Holbrooke but much less worldly. She came from a small town in Maryland, where her father owned a diner, a dry cleaner, and the local Republican newspaper. He was an alcoholic and Litty's childhood home was a battlefield. She survived by developing a character of cheerful solidity and a capacity for avoidance. Holbrooke found in her an intellectual match and a woman with few demands or complaints. As for Litty, Dick Holbrooke was the most interesting man she'd ever met, with the most interesting life ahead of him, and she was ready to wait out their long separations in order to be together. From 1962 to 1964, while he was in Washington, Berkeley, Saigon, and Soc Trang, and she was at Brown and then in Holland studying art history on a Fulbright, they exchanged hundreds of letters. The letters are worth our consideration. Unlike letters written by most of us as very young adults, they can stand it.

Hers—handwritten in the rounded feminine cursive of the Jackie Kennedy/Sylvia Plath period—are upbeat, loving, sometimes banal recitations of events and longings. His—typed, or scrawled in slanted longhand—are playful and pushy and didactic, discussing civil rights ("the greatest crisis since the Civil War") and *Catch-22* and *Dr. No*, cajoling "darlingbabyhoneylambpiesweetiepoopsiecutieohyoudollsugarmine" to visit him, scolding her for not writing more, analyzing her strengths and weaknesses, counting on her steadiness while trying to rattle it, dropping references to other girls (she refused to be provoked). He was the one who wanted everything on the table, more feelings expressed—not the usual stance of an ambitious young man in the Jack Kennedy/Sean Connery period.

And so, a week before the Cuban missile crisis, while he was at Berkeley and she in her dorm room, Litty overcame her aversion to negative things and confessed that she had lied about not having posed nude for an older painter they both knew. She quoted an essay she'd been reading by Lewis Mumford on the subject of male and female sexual dissatisfaction in modern urban life. She thought it applied to them; she wanted to know if he agreed. She knew that she kept difficult things like these from him, and that telling him now might be a terrible mistake, but if they were to spend their lives together she had to try.

He read her letter and then lay down and decided not to answer immediately, since he was angry. He read the entire *New York Times* and calmed down. He reread the letter and was struck by phrases that he hadn't noticed the first time, that showed she had been trying to get closer to him, not just hurt him. Then he answered.

DICK: It seems to me that you should have more sense than to write such a letter when we are 3000 miles apart and unable to even see each other's faces, let alone touch each other . . . I know damn well what sometimes annoys you about me, and your friend Lewis Mumford says it for you, doesn't he: "bothersome insistence instead of really persuasive aggression." On the other hand, you know equally damn well, or at least you had better, that the quality Mumford misses and you desire was what brought you to this stage of a letter-writing contest with me; that is, well, you know what I mean. It is just that I cannot, or will never be, what you want every second, if you always desire that. I can try, but I would not succeed. Why? Because, quite simply, I do not always enjoy that role. When I do, I do it. But I also like to on occasion be loved by you (not necessarily physically) in a more relaxed and less aggressive way. I like to lie down and read the paper, knowing that you are in the same room with me. I like to eat your breakfasts, which somehow taste better, even when the bacon is a little too crisp, than any

other food in the world. I like to watch you at a party, impressing
people you don't know you are impressing. I like to take you to
an expensive restaurant, where I never would go under any other
circumstances, just to enjoy the meal, and the shine in your eyes. I
like to run down a hill with you, or watch you refuse to run down
a hill with me, knowing that either way you are mine, and you
love me. I like to know that you know me well, very well, and you
care about everything about me. I like your interest in my dull dull
stories, and your sometimes sage advice. And the way you put me
to bed when I was feeling so sick last year, and the way you would
tiptoe into the bedroom last year, trying not to wake me, when
I was already awake and watching and waiting with my eyes not
really closed . . . You know, I really hate this letter, and your letter,
and everything about it. I should be studying now, and nothing
should be allowed to distract me from that now. With the secure
knowledge that you love me and wait for me, I can do anything I
want to do. With a letter like the one I got this morning from you,
I am confused and distracted, and of course distance prevents any
resolution . . . I am not really as mad as I might be. But certainly
not happy. Why don't you get smart once and do the right thing? I
mean, <u>do</u>, DO, that is, do. Remember, what is true in foreign policy
is also in this case true in love: Inaction, inactivity is as much an
action as action itself; it is as much of a decision to do nothing as
it is to do something. And the results are often so-o-o poor. Well,
I think I shall close for awhile. Meanwhile, I await your next word,
which had better be better than the last. NOT LESS HONEST, but
better.

LITTY: It's fine for you to say that I would have told you all these things
when we were together again in a few months, but I'm pretty sure
I could never have told you face to face. I wish this weren't so
but I know that I just would have never been able to. These were
all things that I pretty much always push away and repress and
if I hadn't told you last week I might never have. And, rightly or
wrongly, I felt that it was important to do this. I probably did this
only to ease my own conscience, which is selfish, I suppose. In the
midst of what are probably the nastiest things you have ever written
or said to me, are also the nicest, the most lovingest thoughts you

have written to me. Revealing, and reassuring, I think, when in the midst of a hurt and mad paragraph you write of bacon and running down hills. This meant a lot to me. And aside from the context, the thoughts were beautiful, and I think I'll always remember them.

DICK: Either never never lie to me, or else lie like hell but never never never never let me know about it. Obviously the first course is infinitely wiser, and the only honest one which can let us head to our respective roles in still uncertain relationship (wow) with a high chance of success. But I think in some ways, especially if you do not want to marry me, the second course is better than the method you used yesterday, when a letter, unanswerable, unavailable for clarification or holding or forgetting or understanding, comes out of the blue with the simple news: I lied to you. I am glad, actually very glad that you can write me deep feelings, and I appreciate the thought, effort, and emotion that must have gone into that letter. Don't hold back deep thoughts from me in letters.

LITTY: I'm afraid that letter was primarily selfish and egoistic—I was concerned not with your faults, but with my own; not with your feelings so much as with my own; not with your problems except insofar as they touched upon mine. Of course, you have faults (I'm sure you must, altho, for the life of me, I can't think of any of them right now), and you make mistakes. But always, they're only minor ones, and your wonderful points overwhelm the flaws. Funny— it seems that the longer and better you know a person, the more faults would become apparent. I'm sure this has been your experience with me. But it's just the reverse with you—Things that I first thought were faults have turned out not to be so, and you turn out to be a far more perfect person than anyone has a right to be.

DICK: Thank you for saying that you think I am perfect. It's lucky you are right, otherwise it might go to my head! Seriously, though, I am touched by such blindness; I feel so inadequate compared to your image of me. I feel so corrupt often, + you think I am good. I think I am too imaginative, thus I always think both the good thought + its fearsome corrupt opposite at same time. Usually only the better thought comes out, but I am horrified at the kinds of thoughts a la Dostoyevsky, which I find cropping in my mind. On no subject any more do I find any certainty, nothing in politics, religion, morals, etc. No, wait—there is one thing on which I remain certain—the essential evil of intolerance on racial or ethnic grounds. Outside of that, I find no certainty on anything—yet on surface I am too dogmatic. This in itself is an example of what I mean. So there's your "perfect man"! He really is pretty weak, but he thinks highly of himself.

Except in fiction, the only inner life you can ever really know is your own. With others we might get flickers, intimations of the continuous parallel hidden experience that's just as alive and rich in contours as the visible, audible person. Some of us have a talent for projecting it outward—detailed dreams and memories, Tourette's-like eruptions, self-analysis. Holbrooke was not among these translucent souls. For most of his life, in almost every situation, he kept the parallel experience under heavy guard. If you can catch a glimpse anywhere of the inner life of Richard Holbrooke, before it began to disappear, even from his own view, under the pressure of his drive to be a great man, it's in these early letters to Litty.

When Holbrooke went off to Vietnam and Litty to Europe, their understanding was to make a go of it, insisting, with the earnestness of young adults, that nothing was promised and anything could happen. From Vietnam the letters kept coming, sometimes two or more a day. She was his mainstay at every turn in that crucial year. As her Fulbright neared an end, they prepared for a reunion in Saigon in June 1964. He expected to get married but was hedging his bets. The closer the date, the edgier he got.

February 19: By the time this letter reaches you it will be only 3 months until you are ready to come out here. I think of all this often (on helicopters, in sampans, on planes, etc.) and I just hope that you understand how difficult I might be when you get here. This is not to say that I will be difficult, merely that I might be. I want you to come out here, but I am just sometimes afraid that I may not be quite up to your expectations. Whether or not this year has changed me in any way I cannot know, really. But I do know that I am sometimes quite—

well, frightened—at the prospect of really settling down. At other times I think that is what I most need, namely, You . . . It <u>might</u> be a life with a guy who just can't be home on time for dinner every night, and who does sort of unexpected things, and who sometimes just won't pay attention when he should, and other times gets all tangled up in some point which is not of any interest to you, and sometimes is just inconsiderate. But he also (what's this he business. You know it's me.) would need you very much, and ask a hell of a lot of you, and expect miracles and understanding and sympathy and also a little firmness when he needs to really be put down. All that <u>and</u> sex, too. I've never thought of anyone else for the position really, except you, Larrine E. Sullivan (alias Mrs Thin Man; alias the Mythical Nam; alias a combination of Delcia, The Exception, a long-lost high school disaster, and Lee Remick).

March 16: I got a nice letter from you today, full of plans about weddings and things. You certainly are taking a hell of a risk, talking about things like that. I would suggest that you do not sell your typewriter, since there is nothing more wonderful than a two-typewriter family, and also that if you go ahead and buy anything like the goddamn things you named in your letter—I recall towels and plates among others—don't tell me about it, because I don't think I could take it yet . . . I am pretty tired right now. And I miss you. I am not yet making any of the plans which I suppose must be made for when you arrive. I am not even sure what must be done. Someday I will ask Tony. It is really all beyond me. Write more often, but not about dinner service for eight. That is depressing. And I do love you.

April 20: Oh darling, I am always tired and worried and a little confused these days, but I AM ALSO VERY MEAN SO WATCH OUT. WHEN ARE YOU COMING OUT HERE TO FIND OUT HOW MEAN IS MEAN?

May 18: Well, darling, if you want to try all this just tell me which plane and what day, and a magic US government vehicle will whisk you off to a Southeast Asian paradise.

May 24: If I figure right, darling, you will be here within three weeks—
it does seem hard to believe. I hope you won't find me other than what
you remember, I am sometimes afraid that you are not really prepared for the worst of me, which can be pretty bad . . . see you soon.

Litty came anyway. She was game for Holbrooke and for Vietnam.
Reunited in Saigon, they set a wedding date.

The Lakes got involved in every aspect of welcoming their friend
Dick into their ranks. Toni helped Litty plan a civil ceremony and hand-
write invitations to the reception at the Lakes' villa. The ceremony took
place in downtown Saigon's white colonial city hall, on the morning of
Saturday, June 27, a year and a day after Holbrooke arrived. It took place
in Vietnamese, performed by an official in a sash, with Tony translat-
ing and witnessing for the U.S. government in his white sharkskin suit.
The other witness was Toni, along with Vlad Lehovich, Jim and Britta
Rosenthal, and Holbrooke's mother and brother, Trudi and Andy, who
had flown in from New York. Litty had no friends or relatives on hand,
no one to give her away or be privy to her secret thoughts, but she
smiled calmly throughout, in the long-sleeved, scallop-necked, knee-
length white wedding dress that she'd had made by a Saigon tailor.

That afternoon in the Lakes' tropical garden a hundred guests drank

champagne and ate cake, including most of Rural Affairs and, briefly, Henry Cabot Lodge, who was ending his tour the next day and returning home to try to prevent the Republican Party from nominating Barry Goldwater. Trudi, taking to Saigon with the exuberance that mortified her son, whom she persisted in calling "Dickie," had bought seventy-three small birds in the animal market, and Dick and Litty released them from wooden cages, good luck in Vietnamese tradition. The next morning, Dick stood in for Toni's brother as godfather at the Episcopal christening of the Lakes' baby boy.

In later years, forgetting his hundreds of letters to Litty, Holbrooke claimed that he had stumbled into his first marriage by accident. He blamed the Lakes.

THE WEDDING BROUGHT an end to his year in the Delta. He had learned what he could and wanted to play the bigger game in Saigon. Without Rufus Phillips to keep it alive, Rural Affairs was dissolved into USOM and the bureaucracy took over. The days of twenty-two-year-old Foreign Service officers with responsibility for whole provinces were over. Holbrooke was reassigned to the Saigon headquarters where, a year before, the monks had taken refuge. Dick and Litty moved into a small apartment north of downtown on the boulevard going to the airport. In the mornings he took a taxi to the office and she took another to the shops, and except for the fact of Vietnam they acted like any other newlywed couple of the early sixties, still basically the 1950s. There were fewer nights out at restaurants because of VC bombings and violent student protests, but the social whirl of Saigon went on in endless rounds of private dinner parties. The Holbrookes bought a new reel-to-reel tape recorder in Hong Kong and their guests danced to the Beatles.

Litty taught English to the monks at a pagoda to relieve the boredom. But, like the other American wives, she had no role to play. Their views on the only subject that mattered—the war—were never sought at parties and diplomatic receptions. Litty and Toni put aside their Ivy League educations for their husbands' careers, but more than Toni, Litty gave up herself. The Lakes had entered marriage with a sense of shared ideals, of going through the adventure of life side by side, and even when the reality of the Foreign Service intruded they didn't completely abandon the idea. At a dinner party with embassy people, when Toni mentioned a piece of sensitive information that Tony shouldn't have told her and he kicked her under the table, she said in a loud voice, "Are you kicking me?"

The Holbrookes' marriage was different. Dick's world determined everything.

VII

I n Saigon he got to know powerful people and learned the savage art of bureaucratic politics.

In the summer of 1964 President Johnson replaced Harkins with Westmoreland and Lodge with Maxwell Taylor. Taylor wasn't a politician like Lodge (who treated South Vietnam like a Massachusetts party boss), but he was a hero of D-Day, the Kennedys' favorite general, and a true believer, particularly in airpower. His appointment would mute criticism from the right wing, which Johnson feared more than the growing anti-war critics. Taylor would suit a new stage of the war in which the generals were taking over.

It was never clear who was running the American war in Vietnam. In 1961, Kennedy had signed an obscure document that placed all U.S. agencies in a theater of war under the control of the American ambassador—except for the military, which reported to the president through the Pentagon, not through the embassy. So from the start, authority in Vietnam was divided, while counterinsurgency doctrine called for unity of command. Lodge had tried to get around the difficulty by cutting Harkins out of his communications with the White House. But even an ambassador as strong as Lodge was eventually outmatched by the U.S. Army, which had the airplanes and the men. The militarization of American foreign policy was getting into gear. "To one brought up on the theory and statements that the foreign service was the base of foreign policy, and the embassy ran and coordinated

American efforts overseas, it has been sad to see all this," Holbrooke wrote to David Rusk in the summer of 1964.

Taylor and Westmoreland were not natural mentors for Holbrooke— modern military types, straight, corporate, enamored of technology and statistics—but soon he was playing tennis at Cercle Sportif with both men. When the Rusks came through Saigon, he joined them to watch a Davis Cup match between South Vietnam and India. He took McNamara shopping to buy a Vietnamese antique for Mrs. McNamara (the secretary was nicer than expected). Being in Saigon meant face time with important visitors and, if necessary, fetching chocolate ice cream for them. So began Holbrooke's ascent as a public man. It happened younger and faster because of the war.

Nineteen sixty-four, McGeorge Bundy once said, was a "year off" in Vietnam. Johnson followed Kennedy's example and delayed making crucial decisions until after the election. The only question was whether South Vietnam, with its revolving-door coups, would survive until November. It barely did. By then, the choice had come down to lose the war or Americanize it, and since losing—even negotiating a withdrawal—was intolerable to Johnson, escalating was inevitable. Official views in both Saigon and Washington turned deeply pessimistic in 1964, but that proved no more clarifying than the self-deceiving optimism of 1963. Having failed at managing South Vietnam's politics, America opted for militarization, and the Gulf of Tonkin resolution passed by Congress in August gave Johnson the means to use it. Imagine a man trying to drive a nail into a wall and finally realizing that the nail won't sink because what he believed to be a wooden stud is actually a cast-iron waste pipe. So he exchanges his hammer for a sledgehammer and keeps pounding away.

Holbrooke's tour was supposed to end in June 1965. After that he would be posted to Vienna. Vienna sounded as improbable as Luxembourg. One day in late 1964, he ran into U. Alexis Johnson, who had arrived in Saigon to serve as Taylor's deputy ambassador. Johnson asked if Holbrooke would be willing to stay on for a third year in Vietnam. Holbrooke was more than willing. Johnson had him reassigned to the embassy, where, on Lake's recommendation, he took Lake's old job as the ambassador's staff aide, with a desk just outside Taylor's fifth-floor office.

The Lakes were no longer in Saigon. In August, Tony was posted as vice-consul to the old imperial capital of Hue, up near the demilitarized zone. At twenty-five he was the number-two American in the entire central coast. Hue was a lovely, quiet town, with schoolchildren riding bicycles in the wide empty streets and monks in single file carrying alms bowls and ringing bells. The Perfume River flowed down out of the Annamite Range and made its tranquil way past the walled citadel where the Nguyen emperors lay in their tombs.

At first, Hue gave the Lakes the life they both wanted—a little like Tony's dream of being an ambassador in an obscure West African country. They lived in a bungalow along a canal off the river. Toni would push the baby through town in a rattan stroller and explore the beautifully decaying citadel, where she took lessons on the sixteen-string *dan tranh* at the Hue Conservatory of Music. She taught English to medical students and Montagnard children, and Lake taught a class in international relations at the university. He had made lightweight crew at Harvard, and he found an old single scull and practiced his strokes on the Perfume River, and sometimes he rowed to a monastery outside town where Thich Tri Quang, the dissident monk who had led the uprising against the Ngo Dinhs, ate flowers one petal at a time and gave enigmatic answers to Lake's questions. Back in the consulate, Lake would try to turn their conversations into diplomatic cables. The Lakes invited musicians and student leaders to their house and listened to their criticisms of the Saigon generals.

The higher up you sat in Vietnam, the less you knew. Having spent his first year and a half at the embassy instead of the provinces, Lake was ahead of Holbrooke on the career ladder but slightly behind in the stages of doubt. As Lodge's staff aide he would read an optimistic after-action report about a battle, and then Neil Sheehan would come into the embassy and give the ambassador an eyewitness account that totally contradicted the official version. This was how Lake began to realize that reports lied. In Hue, the process of disillusionment accelerated.

There was the time he was invited to tour a battlefield south of town and view the results of a government victory over a VC platoon. Locals were milling around the muddy fields, enjoying the sight of enemy corpses—a lighted cigarette stuck between a dead man's lips, a carrot where a penis should have been, a charred body beside which an old woman squatted, rocking back and forth. Lake forced himself to continue the tour—he was the American vice-consul and this was war. In a ditch by the Perfume River a .50-caliber machine gun had shredded half a dozen VC. The last guerrilla had almost made it to the safety of the river when a round cut his body in two. He was about Lake's age, glasses askew, his thin scholarly face filled with terror. It was strange to see such a face amid the blood and mud of the ditch. Lake stared at the face for a long time, not even hearing the Vietnamese army briefer. The face reminded him of his students, and then he wondered if in different circumstances it could have been his face, and what that might mean. It was a question he wouldn't share with anyone, not even Toni. The question would make him seem weak, and it met strong inward resistance because to pursue it might lead to the conclusion that we were wrong to be here at all, and that was still unthinkable.

AT CHRISTMAS the Holbrookes came up for a visit. In January 1965 all hell broke loose in Hue.

Students and Buddhists who were protesting the latest South Vietnamese government closed the university. Lake sympathized with them. Like Greene's Alden Pyle, he hoped that the Buddhists represented a third way between the VC and the generals. The protests put an end to Toni's music lessons, because her teacher was afraid to be seen with an American. A Vietnamese soldier was posted to guard the Lakes' house, and every time Toni left home she took their son and dog with her for fear of never seeing them again.

On January 23, a mob attacked the American library two blocks from the consulate. Tony walked over and saw, amid hundreds of rioters, some of his students setting fire to the books. The sight made him angry, and anger gave him the courage he always looked for and doubted he had in Vietnam, just as Toni's terror of a VC grenade through their window shored up her wavering commitment to the American cause. It isn't ideas like Communist aggression or self-determination or containment that keep you loyal in a war—it's anger and fear and wild impulse. Lake pushed through the crowd into the library. For some reason he was thinking of a book he'd read as a boy in which a British bagpiper faces down an uprising of Malayans, and this absurd Victorian image inspired him to try single-handedly to put out the fire. Lake was pelted with rocks. Still under the influence of the bagpiper, he turned and glared at the mob. The rocks stopped coming, and soon the fire died out, after burning thousands of books. That evening, some of the students came to the Lakes' house to discuss their grievances, and Tony pointed out that their signs had misspelled numerous English words.

The demonstrations grew. Hue was the center of a national rebellion—after years of war, the South Vietnamese people were turning against the Americans and demanding a negotiated peace. Thousands of Buddhists marched on the consulate, and Lake received an intelligence report that the Vietcong had infiltrated the protest. He instructed the army guards not to shoot, sent his staff home, and locked himself behind the metal door of the code room. This was far worse than sitting through the coup in a closet in Saigon for thirteen hours—this time he was the target. He listened to the mob and waited for the explosions, weeping with fear. After ninety minutes the protesters moved on.

Lake was given authority by Taylor to order the evacuation of all American families from central Vietnam. The danger was no longer just from the VC and the North Vietnamese regiments moving south across the demilitarized zone. The threat now came from the South Vietnamese people.

The American war was reaching its point of no return. In the first week of February, Johnson sent his most hawkish advisor, McGeorge Bundy, to Vietnam for four days. Not to assess the war, for the die was already cast and Bundy's trip report was drafted shortly after his arrival, but to prepare the U.S. mission for escalation. Bundy was making his first visit to Saigon, where yet another coup had just taken place, and if he had been as wise as he was smart he would have looked and listened and understood that the uprising of monks and students that had driven Tony Lake into a secure hiding place and Toni Lake out of Hue represented a social revolution in the South, that popular support for the war was evaporating, that no number of U.S. ground troops or bombing tonnage could create a South Vietnamese government capable of winning over its people, and that a negotiated withdrawal was therefore the only sane policy. But that would have been a different McGeorge Bundy, not the one who served as national security advisor to two presidents.

On February 6, his last night in Saigon, Bundy assembled a group of Americans at the house of the deputy ambassador, U. Alexis Johnson. Holbrooke was there, and for several hours he watched Bundy fire questions at the people seated around the dining room table. Some of them had been in the country for years and had things to teach Bundy. But they were not used to cross-examination by a man as sharp and fluent as the youngest-ever dean of the Harvard faculty, and as soon as they hesitated, or spoke with less than quicksilver confidence, Bundy stopped listening or cut them off and moved on. Holbrooke had revered Bundy as exactly the kind of successful public figure—the "action intellectual"—he hoped to be, and he would continue to relish the chance to meet top officials like Bundy, but after that night he didn't want to emulate Bundy. He was no longer so dazzled by Bundy's intelligence as disturbed by his cool detachment from the war and the deaths and the reality of Vietnam.

In the middle of that night, a few hours before Bundy's scheduled departure, a company of VC attacked an American helicopter base near Pleiku, in the Central Highlands. Eight American soldiers were killed, 126 injured, and ten aircraft destroyed. Bundy rushed up to Pleiku with Westmoreland to survey the damage. The sight of the destruction upset this man who had seen nothing of the war. He got on a secure line to the White House and urged immediate reprisal bombing of the North. Johnson had already picked out the targets well before Pleiku. Since the United States had been hoping for a provocation in order to initiate air strikes, the attack could be seen as fortuitous, and when, back in Washington, a reporter asked why America had retaliated after Pleiku but not earlier VC attacks, Bundy replied, "Pleikus are streetcars." There would always be another and you could board any of your choosing.

On February 8, the Johnson administration gave the twenty-three hundred U.S. dependents in Vietnam one week to leave. American schools closed, villas emptied, servants were let go, families prepared to separate. Toni Lake and her baby were the first to reach the United States, and she was interviewed at Kennedy Airport in New York by the *Today* show. "I'm just sorry I had to leave my husband over there," Toni said. What was going on in Vietnam? "The problem in Vietnam is the Vietcong," she replied, like a good Foreign Service wife, making her husband proud—though in truth she was less and less sure. After the violence in Hue, the evacuation came as a relief to both Lakes. Within a few months Tony was back at the State Department, his two-year tour in Vietnam over.

The Holbrookes didn't welcome the order. The danger in Saigon hadn't noticeably increased, and leaving was a huge disruption in their lives. They decided that Litty would settle in Bangkok for Dick's last year in Vietnam so that he could make monthly visits. Boarding a C-130 transport plane at Tan Son Nhut with other American women, Litty wept. She had just found out that she was three months pregnant.

The evacuation, in the works for weeks, was justified to the American people in the tortured and deceptive terms that were standard operating procedure for the Johnson White House: since 1965 would bring added U.S. personnel to support increases in the South Vietnamese military, dependents were being withdrawn to avoid a disproportionate number of Americans in-country. But in a classified cable, Taylor explained the real and politically explosive reasons: growing mob violence in the South and the "need to clear the deck as a preliminary to any extension of military actions." They had to get the women and children out of the way to prepare for the escalation that Johnson kept publicly denying.

Bundy's trip report urged the president to begin sustained bombing of North Vietnam before South Vietnam fell. Operation Rolling Thunder began on March 2 and continued for more than three and a half years, until the eve of the presidential election in 1968, with three times as much ordnance dropped on North Vietnam as in all of World War II. On March 8, two marine battalions came ashore in Da Nang, south of Hue, to protect the U.S. air base—the first American ground troops in Vietnam. Soon the marines were conducting search-and-destroy operations in the hamlets and paddy fields of the central coast. Taylor, who as a White House advisor in 1961 had advocated sending combat troops, opposed them now that he was ambassador and well acquainted with the chaos of Saigon—they would take the initiative away from the Vietnamese and turn the Americans into colonizers. But Johnson was listening to Westmoreland, not Taylor, who would be gone by midsummer—replaced by the man he had succeeded, Henry Cabot Lodge. When bombing of the North didn't produce the desired results—supplies continued to flow down the Ho Chi Minh trail, North Vietnamese army units kept infiltrating across the DMZ, Hanoi refused to back down—Johnson ordered up another fifty thousand troops in July. By the end of the year there were nearly two hundred thousand Americans in Vietnam.

THE EVACUATION ORDER of February 1965 rates a footnote in any history of the war, but in my mind it marks the before and after. It was the end of the pretty colonial town of Saigon and the small civilian airport of Tan Son Nhut and the fishing village of Da Nang. It was the end of the afternoon siesta and the French-speaking nightclub girls and the diplomatic teas and American children at the Saigon Zoo. It was the beginning of sprawling U.S. bases and B-52s and black-market Marlboros and industrial-scale prostitution. It was the end of the old embassy near the river, an office building where security was so loose that on March 30, 1965, two VC pushed a car right up to the ground-floor windows and detonated three hundred pounds of explosives, killing twenty-two people, almost all Vietnamese bystanders. It was the end of opium and the beginning of heroin. It was the end of the civilians and the beginning of Westmoreland's killing machine.

When Rufus Phillips came back to Vietnam in September, for the first time since 1963, and drove out of Saigon, he was astonished to see ten miles of U.S. military vehicles and equipment jamming the Bien Hoa Highway, as if they had come to fight Soviet armored divisions in Europe, not the Vietcong in the jungle. Holbrooke's friend John Negroponte said that Tu Do Street was Forty-second Street on New Year's Eve all the time. "The atmosphere in Saigon was deteriorating," Holbrooke later wrote. "The Americans were becoming corrupted by the Vietnamese—a corruption which was turning Americans into the very things which we said we were fighting against in the world." The Americans had the run of the city and everything was for sale.

He came to dislike the evacuation order intensely, because it forced officials to choose between the war and their families, and some of the best refused to extend their tours. Just when America most needed knowledgeable people in Vietnam, the quality of personnel dropped sharply. The U.S. mission accumulated the ruins of broken marriages, the Physicians' and Surgeons' Soap brigade, and although some of the men had talent many were refugees from normal life, salted war junkies rather than the cream of the government. There was a new saying in Saigon: "You can't be a good counterinsurgent unless you've wrecked your marriage." When Litty gave birth to their son David in Bangkok that August, she was all alone.

The big-unit war crushed what was left of the fragile shoots of pacification that Rural Affairs had planted in the provinces. American pilots were told to return to base with their bomb bays empty. Holbrooke once flew out on an inspection trip with Lodge and Westmoreland. "These planes are allowed to dump their bombs if they see anything moving," the twenty-four-year-old staff aide complained to the proconsul and the four-star commander on the way back to Saigon. "There are people living down there." Holbrooke argued vehemently that "free-fire zones" and "harassment-and-interdiction fire" were self-defeating—the blind killing only created more VC sympathizers. He had first learned it in the Mekong Delta two years ago and now he was seeing it all over South Vietnam. Told that the areas were Communist controlled, he insisted: "No, this is crazy."

Few officials, let alone junior ones, spoke to the top Americans in Vietnam that way, but by now Holbrooke regarded the likes of Lodge and Westmoreland not as his superiors but as well-intentioned, ill-informed men who could correct bad tactics with advice from someone who knew more than they did. Lodge finally cut him off: "You should listen to your fears, my boy, but not be governed by them."

But Holbrooke was already moving into the third stage of doubt. After assessments and tactics, he was beginning to question the American strategy. Westmoreland's war of attrition depended on reaching what the commander called the "crossover point"—the hypothetical moment when the North would no longer be able to replace its fighters at the rate they were being killed. The American strategy was to bleed the enemy into submission.

In the fall of 1965 Holbrooke joined the embassy's political section as a provincial reporter, gathering information around the country on this new phase of the war. On one trip he went up to the central coast and spent a week with the Ninth Marine Regiment in Quang Nam province, south of Da Nang. He was briefed by a general named Lewis Walt, a giant of a man who had fought valiantly in the South Pacific and was every inch a marine. Walt seemed to understand the little seaside hamlet where he met Holbrooke as if it were Iwo Jima—a beachhead to be secured. While a crowd of children looked on, Walt knelt and swept his big arm across the sand in a semicircle to show how the marines would move outward from the hamlet to the surrounding area, clearing it of VC and then handing it over to the South Vietnamese army, with the objective of linking up with a cleared area farther south—like the oil spot. "But the VC will just move in behind you," said Holbrooke, who had been in Vietnam two years longer than the hero of Guadalcanal. But Walt kept pushing the sand with his arm. He had full confidence in the plan.

The marines had built a schoolhouse in a nearby hamlet. Holbrooke was taken to see it, only to find a charred shell. A local boy had burned the school down a few hours before—no one knew why. Some of the Vietnamese hated the marines for the destruction they brought, the fact that they didn't belong here; others wanted them to stay forever because they were kinder and more generous to children than the South Vietnamese troops. In either case the marines were trapped, but they didn't seem to know it.

A few months later, Holbrooke went back to Quang Nam. What he saw moved him deeply: the marines had done an extraordinary job of building schools, handing out fertilizer, vaccinating children. But they had been unable to clear out the VC. In spite of all the marines' efforts, the guerrillas kept infiltrating, mining, and ambushing from the rear. The marines didn't speak the language, they had no interest in the local history, they barely knew where they were—but these were essential to making the strategy work. "They were beginning to realize—but slowly, and expensively—that the area they were trying to clean up was not just another beachhead left over from World War II, when all that was necessary was to move onto the beach, hold it against the Japanese counterattacks, and then build out gradually from it into the hinterlands," Holbrooke later wrote. "No, this time the beachhead was more than a beachhead, it contained living people, some of whom had for years, even decades, lived under communist control, and they were not going to switch sides in return for some free soap."

The strategy wouldn't work, he concluded, while costing numerous lives, because what the Americans considered pacification was actually occupation. They had taken the place of the French.

Holbrooke's report on the marines so shocked Lodge that he refused to send it on to Washington.

ONE DAY in early December 1965, while Holbrooke was dealing with the usual dire cable traffic between Saigon and Washington, Lodge approached him with an important issue.

"My boy," the ambassador said, "I have been giving some thought to the problem of the holiday season. Here we are, surrounded by war, and everyone thinks that we are scared silly of the guerrillas. We must find a way to show them that we are not worried by them in the least. Do you have any suggestions?"

"No, Mr. Ambassador," Holbrooke said.

Lodge had an idea: a New Year's Eve party. "A huge party," he said, "in which we can all forget for one night that we are living in this horrible place."

Lodge had lost some of the command of his first time around. He often seemed checked out, working just four or five hours a day, while infighting among Vietnamese generals and politicians swirled around him. But when it came to the New Year's Eve party, the ambassador was single-minded. He immersed himself in the details of decorations, music (an ensemble of U.S. airmen called the Blue Notes), and, above all, the guest list. A guest list was an important political document, he instructed Holbrooke, with the potential to create enemies for life. Losing his puritanical reserve on his second tour, Lodge made it clear that above all he wanted young people at the party, people who were "really alive," who would dance the war away. Since the evacuation order had stripped the American community of almost all its women, these bon vivants would need to bring what Lodge called "flowers," meaning nightclub girls. And the guest list kept growing—the unforgiving Philippine ambassador had to be invited, as did the Italian ambassador, since his beautiful Vietnamese secretary was already on the list—until it passed three hundred.

There was a problem: Saigon was under an eleven p.m. curfew. The embassy couldn't be seen to flout the rule, even for a New Year's Eve party, so, as a formality, the invitation said eight till eleven. The diplomats arrived at Lodge's residence at eight sharp, and the "really alive" people showed up a bit later, and by ten-thirty both groups began to leave—to the dismay of the ambassador's aides, who had thought that no one would observe the eleven o'clock formality and were desperate to make good on their boss's desire for an unforgettable bash. Holbrooke begged, berated, and threatened his colleagues, but all the revelers, especially the "really alive" ones, had somewhere else to go, except for Lodge, who was dancing with the Italian ambassador's secretary, and some of the "flowers," and of course Lodge's aides, who couldn't leave. By midnight the residence was almost empty, but the ambassador was happily oblivious, still dancing with the secretary and singing to the band's rendition of "Georgia on My Mind," and Holbrooke suddenly realized that, if for no one else, the party had been a success for Lodge.

At the stroke of twelve a musician called out, "Happy New Year, ya mothers," and with that the Blue Notes departed, but the ambassador broke out his own record collection to entertain his captive aides, and that was how the American mission in Saigon rang out 1965—the year of Operation Rolling Thunder, 175,000 U.S. combat troops, nearly two thousand American deaths, and the total Americanization of the war—and rang in the new year 1966, in which more than six thousand Americans and tens of thousands of Vietnamese would die and a million people would become refugees.

As Holbrooke made a quiet exit with the last guests, Lodge called from his gate into the warm fragrant darkness, "Well, we really showed them tonight!" Holbrooke didn't get it. "Those guerrillas," Lodge said. "We showed them that we aren't afraid of them. We can be just as crude and drunken and sloppy over here as we are at home."

IT WAS a strange twist of fate that at this point in the story, with the United States committed to fighting a war of attrition, which meant destruction on a mind-boggling scale, Edward Lansdale finally returned to Vietnam.

Around the beginning of 1966 Johnson suddenly remembered the war for hearts and minds. He tried to revive it, with the blind frenzy that marked his every move in Vietnam. Johnson saw pacification as an extension of his Great Society—the war on poverty carried to the hamlets of Quang Ngai and Long An. (He had already failed to buy off Ho Chi Minh with a Tennessee Valley Authority on the Mekong River.) Holbrooke's final assignment in Vietnam had him working on pacification at the embassy. "The pressure on people to produce has been increased beyond any previous measure," he wrote to David Rusk. "There are serious resulting dangers that reporting will once again revert to the kind of misleading think positive type which plagued the mission in 1963 under Harkins."

Vice President Hubert Humphrey wanted Lansdale in Saigon, and Lodge agreed. Lansdale moved into a white stucco villa with a team of his old hands from the fifties, like Lou Conein and George Melvin, and a gung-ho new hand, a brilliant reserve marine officer on loan from the Pentagon named Daniel Ellsberg. Lansdale was named a "special advisor" to Lodge, with a mission to breathe energy and coherence into the calamitous Saigon government. The villa became an open house for Vietnamese leaders to drop by, talk late into the night, and sing folk songs. But Lansdale had no money and no authority, while the embassy had become a giant organization, with hundreds of officials to support all the programs that came with Americanization. Lansdale's method struck the officials as quaint if not absurd. He had been away from Vietnam for almost a decade. His friend Diem was long dead. He no longer knew the country—he didn't even speak Vietnamese.

One of Lansdale's biggest detractors was Holbrooke. Strange, since they saw the war the same way. But governments are composed of human beings, not policy positions, and a place as intense as Vietnam made them even more prone than usual to petty rivalries and debilitating hatreds. If you look close enough and are in a bad mood, public service seems to be composed of paperwork and personal feuds. Holbrooke disliked bureaucracy, but he disliked losing to a competitor even more, and his team was in direct competition with Lansdale's for the ear of prominent South Vietnamese, including the latest rulers, Air Marshal Nguyen Cao Ky and General Nguyen Van Thieu. They were also fighting for the attention of Lyndon Johnson. "EL has made one bad mistake," Holbrooke wrote to the Lakes in Washington, "and that was bringing back with him so many people who once could blow up bridges in the River Kwai but now are a little too old and a little too exposed."

Holbrooke spread the word that Lansdale was past his expiration date. The *Washington Post*'s Stanley Karnow wrote a front-page piece called "Legend of Lansdale's Miracles Badly Tarnished in Vietnam." It ended with an anonymous quote from "a seasoned American official": "We are up against a superb Communist organization that must be uprooted by a better organization. This simply cannot be done by a few men of goodwill."

Enraged, Lansdale tried to track down the source. Holbrooke reminded colleagues that whenever Karnow came to Saigon, he stayed at the house of another young embassy official named Frank Wisner. Anyone looking for Karnow's source should start there.

Wisner wasn't just another junior Foreign Service officer. He was a prince of the establishment. His father, Frank Wisner Sr., was a legendary intelligence operative and, throughout the 1950s, head of the CIA's clandestine operations section—chief conspirator in the overthrow of elected governments in Iran and Guatemala and many other dubious, tragic covert actions carried out in the prosecution of the Cold War. Frank Sr. was also given to manic depression, and in October 1965, at the family farm on Maryland's Eastern Shore, he ended his life with one of his hunting shotguns. Frank Jr. went home from Vietnam for his father's funeral and then immediately returned to the war.

He was short and straight-backed, handsome and rakish. He spoke in a slightly old-fashioned diction that was only half jest, using phrases like "in due course" and "well in hand," and he believed in old-fashioned concepts like having a good war, which meant seeing one's share of action. He accompanied South Vietnamese soldiers on night patrol and he once got in trouble for driving with a pair of friends in a Triumph sports car to the Cambodian border. His house at 47 Phan Thanh Gian, near the Bien Hoa Bridge over the Saigon River, had been built by the emperor for one of his mistresses, with a high wall and a lovely garden, and it was staffed with a cook and a maid and decorated with Wisner's collection of Chinese porcelain. He presided over elegantly debauched evenings, carving the meat and procuring the cognac and proposing the elaborate toasts.

The house became the center of an elite social scene that took the connections formed in Georgetown and the Upper East Side, Princeton and Harvard, and neatly reproduced them in Saigon. Holbrooke had not been born or educated in this world—Scarsdale and Brown didn't quite qualify—but the war had introduced him to it and he was a frequent guest at Wisner's table. Among the others was a willowy blond big-eyed young journalist named Frances FitzGerald, whom everyone called Frankie. Her father, Desmond FitzGerald, had been one of Frank Sr.'s top recruits to the agency, and her mother, Marietta Peabody, was a liberal activist, socialite, and lover of John Huston and Adlai Stevenson. There was a lieutenant in the Special Forces named Tobias Wolff, whose brother Geoffrey, the book critic for the *Washington Post*, was a friend of Wisner's from Princeton, his regular supplier of new books, and husband of one of Frankie FitzGerald's friends from Radcliffe. There was John Negroponte, a future U.N. ambassador, who became Holbrooke's roommate in Saigon after a drunken, knife-wielding American sailor chased him out of his own apartment in the mistaken belief that Negroponte was messing around with the sailor's Vietnamese girlfriend. There was Ward Just, the *Post* correspondent, who would go on to write acclaimed books, like Frankie FitzGerald, like the brothers Wolff. And so on. I hope by now you can see that there were many Vietnams for the Americans there and not all of them looked like *The Deer Hunter* and *Platoon*.

Wisner didn't think much of Lansdale. He compared Lansdale's team to the group of aging British double agents trying to stay relevant in *The Looking-Glass War*, a new John le Carré novel that Geoffrey Wolff had sent him. But Wisner wasn't the sort to give anonymous quotes to journalists, not even his houseguests. No, Wisner wasn't Karnow's source. It was Holbrooke—who liked journalists, enjoyed playing the leaking game to advance his goals, met Karnow at Wisner's house, and covered his tracks by fingering their host.

An army captain named Pete Dawkins once told Holbrooke about his idea to reverse the military's battle rhythm and turn American troops into a night army like the Vietcong, capable of fighting when the enemy was on the move. Dawkins—class president and star halfback at West Point, 1958 Heisman Trophy winner, subject of a *Life* magazine cover—was preparing to brief the idea to Westmoreland. Intrigued, Holbrooke asked to see the classified paper. Dawkins gave it up reluctantly and on the condition that it be returned within twenty-four hours and shown to no one. A few days later, the night army was the subject of an article by R. W. Apple Jr. in the *New York Times*. Dawkins, who thought it was the end of his career, eventually forgave Holbrooke, who had liked Dawkins's idea enough to push for it. As for the deception—that was just Holbrooke.

Still, I've never understood why, on learning of Holbrooke's treachery over Lansdale, Wisner kept silent. Why, instead of cutting Holbrooke's balls off, Wisner became his best friend for life. Perhaps Wisner accepted the betrayal as an entry fee for the pleasure of such a friendship. Perhaps it was Wisner's gallantry—perhaps Holbrooke knew that he could count on it. Frank, he thought, carried himself with the gorgeous grace of a character in a novel by his fellow Princeton grad F. Scott Fitzgerald.

But episodes like these began to crop up—the early worms in the apple. Acquaintances noticed that the feverish air of American Saigon was going to Holbrooke's head. Ward Just found him too ambitious to be trusted and avoided using him as a source. "You have a brilliant future ahead of you," an administrator at the embassy told Holbrooke, "but you will move faster if you slow down."

He had reached the end of his years in Vietnam. In the spring of 1966, Litty and the baby sailed from Bangkok halfway around the world to Rome, where Holbrooke met them on his way back to Washington. A job was waiting for him at the White House. Just as important, a meal ticket was waiting for him in Georgetown. Wisner had sent word to his mother, the newly widowed Polly Wisner, whose salon would introduce Holbrooke to the great men of the American century.

VIII

I 've been reading a report that they cut Route Four between Saigon and Can Tho," Lyndon Johnson announced to the eight men around the mahogany table in the Cabinet Room. "You know, in Texas, if the price of pigs goes up, you get thrown out of power. You lose elections. The price of pigs is power in Texas." The president saw the cutting of Route 4 in terms of its effect on the Saigon pork market. Rocking back in a leather armchair, he turned to the man seated to his right, Robert Komer, bow-tied and with a pipe clamped in his mouth. Komer was Johnson's pacification czar and Holbrooke's new boss. "Komer, I want you to get the price of pigs down by fifty percent in twenty-four hours and get that road open."

"Yes, Mr. President," replied Komer, a former CIA officer, and such a fierce and volatile bureaucratic operator that Henry Cabot Lodge gave him the permanent nickname "Blowtorch."

Across the table, Holbrooke was thinking that Johnson sounded like Hitler at the end of the war, imagining himself in command of divisions that didn't exist. No American could get Route 4 open—not even Blowtorch Bob Komer.

Johnson went on. "I have another idea, Bob. You know at the end of World War Two we had all these civil affairs advisors who ran occupied Germany and occupied Japan. We ought to reactivate them and get them out there to run Vietnam."

It was the late summer of 1966. Holbrooke had never spoken to a president, but he had already concluded that he knew more about the war than anyone in Washington. Vietnam was the flimsiest of notions at the White House and the Pentagon and the State Department, while the belief that America could do whatever it wanted remained strong as iron, as if Washington was stuck in the year 1945. He raised his hand. "Mr. President?"

Johnson peered over his glasses and across the table at the junior aide.

"Mr. President, I've just come back from Vietnam and, you know, I'm a little worried about this. I'm not sure American advisors of that sort would be qualified. There are some limitations to what Americans can do in the civilian field in Vietnam."

Johnson removed his glasses and fixed Holbrooke with his sad-eyed, heavy-jowled look. "Well, son, your job is to get rid of those limitations."

The Holbrookes bought a two-story house on Nebraska Avenue in northwest Washington, by the wooded towpath over the Potomac River. The Lakes lived five minutes' drive up the hill, in a slightly fancier neighborhood off Foxhall Road. Every morning, Litty and the baby drove Dick in their red VW Bug downtown to the Old Executive Office Building—the giant pile of Beaux Arts ostentation that Truman called "the greatest monstrosity in America," right next to the small decorous White House—and every evening they picked him up. Holbrooke and the six other members of Komer's team, including Lieutenant Colonel Bob Montague, Holbrooke's army friend from Bac Lieu, shared offices on the first floor. They were fighting "the other war" from Washington.

Johnson wanted quick results—"coonskins on the wall"—which is why he placed responsibility for pacification in the White House, not the State Department, which had asked for it. But in Vietnam results never came right away, if at all, except for the kind that counted 324 strategic hamlets in Ba Xuyen. Nothing had really changed since 1963. The South Vietnamese army had little interest in the welfare of the rural population, the peasants had little attachment to their government, the politicians and generals in Saigon were divided into factions, corruption was rampant. Year after year the problems remained the same, while the American will to solve them with more money, more programs, more people, more guns, more words remained mysteriously, almost admirably, inexhaustible.

If you can't win the war, you can at least get the bureaucracy right. I've learned that when terms like "manage," "coordinate," "reorganize," and "backstop" start popping up, it means a policy isn't working. Changing the structure of the American government wasn't easy, but it was a lot easier than changing the behavior of the South Vietnamese. So Komer spent a year on the organizational chart. The question was how to force all the agencies involved in pacification to work together across the divides between provinces and Saigon, Saigon and Washington, military and civilian, Americans and Vietnamese. In early 1967, Johnson created Civil Operations and Revolutionary Development Support (CORDS), which took control of pacification away from the civilians and gave it to Westmoreland. The huge military apparatus had absorbed the entire American presence in Vietnam. In May 1967, Komer went out to Saigon to be Westmoreland's deputy for pacification, the DEP-COMUSMACV CORDS (acronyms were reaching full strength), with four thousand military and civilian personnel under his command, the rank of ambassador, and—on his explosive insistence, after a guard at headquarters had refused entry to Komer's chauffeur-driven Chrysler Imperial—the prerogatives of a four-star general.

"It's the end of the independent civilian mission," Holbrooke, in Saigon with Komer that month, wrote Litty. "Everything I worked for here is lost, and so is Komer."

After six years in Vietnam, after strategic hamlets and oil spots and black pajamas, the Americans thought they had finally figured out pacification. The answer turned out to be better management. They were also dropping more bombs and using more firepower than ever. By the end of 1967, Johnson, Westmoreland, and Komer were convinced that the war was being won.

Meanwhile, Holbrooke became Komer's Komer. He traveled back and forth between D.C. and Saigon, hammering the bureaucrats on both ends to move faster. He compiled lists of newly sworn Foreign Service officers to serve mandatory one-year tours in Vietnam (it was no longer a post anyone asked for). He made himself unpopular with colleagues. He even blowtorched Komer. Once, on a flight to Manila for one of the periodic summits between LBJ and South Vietnam's leaders, Holbrooke was sitting at the back of the plane with Tony Lake when Komer approached. "Dick, take a letter," he ordered Holbrooke, trying to humiliate one of them in front of the other, as if he could smell the competition between them. Komer began to dictate. Holbrooke opened a notebook and wrote furiously as Lake watched.

"I didn't know you took shorthand," Komer said.

"I don't," Holbrooke said, closing the notebook. It was full of meaningless squiggles.

One night, over dinner at the Lakes', Tony introduced him to a man named John Helble, a personnel counselor at the State Department. Lake and Holbrooke had both reached the level of FSO-5 in very fast time—Vietnam helped—and Lake had just gone in for a session of official career advice. "Dick, you have to go in," Lake told Holbrooke. "It was terrific—I really learned a lot."

"I don't think that's necessary for me," Holbrooke said. He had begun to think of most Foreign Service officers as unimaginative timeservers. He was on a faster climb.

But Lake persisted, and out of regard for his friend or competitiveness with him (these were inextricable), a week later Holbrooke went in to see Helble. His personnel file showed, in addition to high marks for performance, a recurring problem of getting along with others. There was a pattern of abrasiveness the likes of which Helble had not seen in the scores of other files he'd read.

Helble started to discuss the problem, but Holbrooke cut him off. "I'm not here for that. I'm not interested in that. I just want to know what my promotion rate is going to be."

Helble insisted that Holbrooke's advancement would depend on changes in his behavior. The man's inability to grasp his talents only made Holbrooke angrier.

"I want to know at what age I can expect to be an FSO-1."

FSO-1 was the rank just short of career ambassador. "At what age do you think you should be an FSO-1?" Helble asked.

"Thirty-five," Holbrooke said, adding that by then he also expected to be an assistant secretary of state. Helble stifled a laugh and pointed out that the youngest FSO-1 in the history of the Foreign Service had been forty. At thirty-five Holbrooke would also be the second-youngest assistant secretary ever. If he wanted to be a senior foreign policy figure, Helble advised, he should resign from the Foreign Service and take the path of politics, business, or academia. Inside the department he stood no chance of rapid promotion, or much promotion at all, unless his behavior improved. Holbrooke walked out unhappy.

HE DRIFTED AWAY from old friends like David Rusk and Vlad Lehovich to new ones like Frank Wisner. At parties he looked over shoulders for someone more interesting to talk to. In a way, all the acronyms and reorgs of these early Washington years, all the trips and reports, mattered less than what he was doing in off-hours. He was making himself attractive to powerful people and thereby becoming "Holbrooke." That was how Polly Wisner referred to him after he became a regular in the dining room of her four-story townhouse on P Street. She would talk affectionately about "that Holbrooke," as if he were the raffish young hero of a nineteenth-century picaresque.

Dick and Litty thought they were paying a courtesy call on a lonely widow, but Polly, with her bright mid-Atlantic accent, welcomed them into the world of Washington power. Dinner was at eight, a dozen or so guests, the list calibrated for status, variety, and age, well-known personages mixed with rising youth, the ranking guest seated to the right of the hostess, Negro servants attending, the meal prepared by Polly's French cook. Senators, diplomats, journalists, spies—that was the mix, in the seamless Washington blend of careerism and social life. Polly's friend Katharine Graham—another suicide widow, now owner of the *Post*—was often there, and the Alsop brothers Joe and Stewart, the country's premier Sovietologist Charles Bohlen, Sir Isaiah Berlin, and Frankie FitzGerald. Guests rolled with the roast—talked to the person on their right for the first course, on their left for the main course. His first time there, when the women stood up at the end of the meal, Holbrooke stood with them to be polite. "Sit down," Joe Alsop growled. "Now we're going to have a real conversation." It was customary for the men to stay at the table for brandy, cigars, and political talk while the women retired to the drawing room.

Holbrooke made Polly's list as a friend of Frank's, but he stayed on it because he was a rising star who had spent years in Vietnam. Few people in Washington had any real knowledge of the war and could also hold their own at a Georgetown dinner table in a language the elder statesmen understood. Holbrooke charmed the great men and their hostesses by speaking to them naturally, as an equal, gossiping and flirting with them, sensing their loneliness and sparing them the burden of awe. Alsop, who lived like a Georgetown pasha, pursued Holbrooke so aggressively that he invited himself to dinner one Sunday at the barely furnished house on Nebraska Avenue; the next day Alsop sent over a lacquered black Korean end table. He wanted Holbrooke's support for his hard-line position on Vietnam, and soon the Holbrookes were guests at Alsop's legendary salon on Dumbarton Street, where Dean Acheson showed Dick how to knot the tie of his cheap tuxedo properly, and Ethel Kennedy kept forgetting Litty's name.

This was Washington before restaurants. The WASP ascendancy still ruled in Georgetown. The dinners rotated among a few prestige townhouses all within a few blocks of one another like neighboring castles of an extended royal family. But the Cold War consensus was cracking up over Vietnam, and with it the establishment itself. The argument split mainly along age lines. Alsop raged at FitzGerald, the daughter of his friend Desmond, for denouncing the war—this was generational betrayal within the clan and the feelings were quite bitter. As for Holbrooke, an outsider who wanted in, his doubts were deepening, but in 1966 he was still trying to find a way to fight a better war. And he had to be careful about his reputation inside the government.

One night at Polly Wisner's, Geoffrey Wolff, the *Post* book critic, was seated across from Holbrooke, who was talking about having seen captured enemy documents.

"Not those goddam captured enemy documents," said Wolff, twenty-eight and anti-war. "You sound like Joe Alsop. Give me a break."

Holbrooke flared up. "What do you know? You don't know anything."

"How can you be so sure?"

"Because I'm not a fool."

"And I am a fool."

"You be the judge. I'd call it case closed."

"You're a jackass."

They went on to become good friends.

Playing tennis with Maxwell Taylor acquainted Holbrooke with Bobby Kennedy, and from Georgetown the Holbrookes ascended to Hickory Hill in McLean, Virginia, the Kennedy estate and government-in-exile. Litty read by the pool and Dick played tennis with Bobby or, if Bobby was swimming, with Ethel, a better player than her husband. Litty thought there was something strange about the Kennedys. Ethel wasn't friendly, and Bobby kept climbing out of the pool in front of Litty with his swim trunks hanging far too low. As for Dick, he was pretty dazzled by the Kennedys, though it was a high-risk act for a young official in the Johnson White House to be drawn into the orbit of the president's mortal enemy. Of these two Democratic Party giants, Johnson was the one Holbrooke resembled more—the appetites, the insecurities, the will—but by this point in his presidency Johnson was being destroyed by paranoia and the war. Bobby became Holbrooke's political hero, and he would have gone to work for Kennedy's election in 1968 if the senator had asked him. Bobby didn't, out of concern for Holbrooke's career prospects. After RFK's assassination, Holbrooke wrote Ethel a condolence letter: "There is nothing to say, really. Except that I will always remember Senator Kennedy. For me, he was a mediocre tennis player and a great man."

Four blocks from Polly Wisner's, on N Street, was Averell and Marie Harriman's mansion. Averell was seventy-four and nearly deaf. Everyone made a point of addressing him as "Governor," since he had served one term in Albany in the 1950s, but out of earshot he was known as "the Crocodile" for his prominent teeth and the dangerous carnivore still lurking beneath the senescent manner. He was a living link to FDR, Churchill, and Stalin, Lend-Lease, Yalta, and the Marshall Plan, as well as to his railroad baron father. He had always longed to be secretary of state, and it had seemed possible whenever Kennedy grew tired of Rusk, but Harriman lost JFK's favor when DEPTEL 243 led to the bloody overthrow of Diem. After LBJ took charge, Harriman sent the president long letters citing his illustrious past and pleading to be put to significant use, but he was fatally tainted as a close friend of Bobby Kennedy. In 1966, Harriman was an ambassador at large without much to do.

There's something poignant about a restless old man who can't settle into the role of Wise Man, a distinguished Wall Street banker or Washington lawyer who occasionally advises presidents. The Wise Men created the architecture of containment, and Dean Acheson persuaded Truman to fund the French war in Indochina, the beginning of America's involvement in Vietnam. At key moments of the Vietnam War they were summoned to the White House to assure Johnson, on the basis of nothing except heavily slanted briefings, an unexamined attachment to the domino theory, and their own code of resoluteness, that this distant country they didn't understand was a necessary battlefield of the Cold War, before returning to their stately offices and sterling reputations. The war in Vietnam was a consequence of their ideas, but the blame fell on younger men who revered them.

Alone among the Wise Men, Harriman could not get free of the demon urge to remain a player, as if withdrawal from the game would mean a rapid descent into profound deafness and then death. The urge was humiliating, but also maybe a sign of being serious about the one thing that really counted. Publicly, Harriman was obsequious in his support of Johnson's Vietnam policy. Privately, he had growing doubts and began to search for a way out. In the summer of 1966, he heard that there was a small group of Foreign Service officers in Washington who had served in Vietnam, and he sent for Holbrooke and Lake to visit him on N Street. They sat in the Harrimans' grand living room, the walls hung with Matisse and Renoir, van Gogh's *Roses* over the fireplace, and talked about the war. Harriman, half a century older than his guests, kept losing the thread and slipping into silence. But Holbrooke came away with the sense that this was the only senior person in the administration who was looking for a way to talk to Hanoi. Negotiating a peace deal with North Vietnam would be the crown on a great man's life. Maybe then Harriman could let go.

He became Holbrooke's most important patron in Washington. The young man offered the old man knowledge and advice on the issue that consumed everyone. The old man offered the young man a thrilling connection to the years of greatness before Vietnam came along and rattled American confidence.

HOLBROOKE TRIED to bring Lake into the Georgetown world with him. Polly set up a dinner for the two of them with Walt Rostow, the uber-hawkish national security advisor who had replaced Bundy. But Lake found the scene distasteful. He disliked the social climbing and the old-money customs. I don't know if this made him more honorable or less honest, but it's easier when you're a descendant of Georgetown and your mother was engaged to Kennan.

He was beginning to find Holbrooke a little distasteful, too. They were still close friends and tennis partners. The two couples often socialized, smoked pot one night as a foursome at the Lakes' house, and Dick became godfather to their second child. But friendship with Holbrooke had acquired a whiff of the instrumental. He talked about the two of them, along with Wisner and John Campbell, another leading member of the Foreign Service class of 1962, as the elites of the Vietnam generation, heirs to Kennan and Acheson and Harriman, the next great figures in American foreign policy. In Vietnam, Holbrooke and Lake had jokingly asked friends which of them would make ambassador first. Now, in Washington, friends debated which of them would make secretary of state first, judging Lake to have the inside track. But Holbrooke wasn't the kind of friend Lake could count on if he needed someone to meet him at the bus station at two in the morning. He was beginning to feel used.

Something else was happening to Lake. The war was making him sick. He was working extreme hours at the State Department, first in the East Asia bureau, then as staff aide to Rusk's deputy, Undersecretary Nicholas Katzenbach. Buried in the daily paperwork from Saigon, Lake was occasionally seized by a report that wouldn't let him go. One day he read an account of American soldiers blowing up the entrance to a cave and entombing, along with enemy soldiers, a large number of civilians. He and some of his colleagues were disturbed enough to question the Pentagon about the incident. But to push even harder—to ask whether such incidents were compatible with morality, whether they indicated that America could not go on fighting this war without losing its national soul—that would sound hysterical.

At the beginning of 1967, Lake was incautious enough to ask Jim Rosenthal, his and Holbrooke's friend from Saigon, who was now on the State Department's Vietnam desk, why the United States should put troops in Vietnam and not elsewhere. Why not fight communism all over the world? Rosenthal, a hard-liner, replied brutally. The question was frivolous and the answers so obvious that they made Lake look naïve. Vietnam was the front line of the free world, the place where the Communists had chosen to fight "our side," and the most favorable place for America to take a stand. "If you have time," Rosenthal wrote to Lake, "I suggest you read the reams of position papers produced in EA every few months for the benefit of the Secretary or the President explaining why a posture of strength is necessary and why the entire complexion of the Far East has markedly improved since the U.S. took such a posture, starting in 1965." In government, foolish certainty usually beats fragile wisdom.

Lake didn't think America should withdraw from Vietnam in defeat. But he was coming to realize that we couldn't win there. The North Vietnamese wouldn't yield under bombing. The South Vietnamese government was incapable of reform—the notion of the "clean colonel" was an illusion. There was no better war. The only way out was to negotiate with Hanoi. Over the years there had been plenty of useless attempts. The standing American position called for the North to stop the infiltration before talks could begin. North Vietnam insisted that the United States end the bombing first. The leaders of both countries believed they could win and wanted to use negotiations to advance their goals. But Lake knew that real negotiations would end with the departure of the Americans and ultimately a Communist victory. So he was trapped.

An honorable man could live with himself by dissenting on the inside, not the outside. One week, Lake said something at a departmental meeting that made a colleague, a captain in the navy, accuse him of sounding like Senator William Fulbright, who was holding critical hearings on the war. Two weeks later, over dinner with his wife and parents, after carefully avoiding the subject of Vietnam, Lake finally ventured a comment that made his father yell, "You sound just like Dean Rusk!"

Toni had become a dove. It was easier to be a dove in Washington than in Saigon or Hue, where threats from the VC were personal and the pressure of American cohesion was intense and she had to confront the fears of Vietnamese who were counting on the Americans. It's easier to see the clear truth of a lost cause once you're far away and undistracted by daily complexities and human faces. Toni began arguing, often in front of Tony's colleagues, that the war was wrong. She banned TV news at home and started attending peace demonstrations. She disliked the violent certainties of the anti-war protesters—she knew Vietnam and nothing there was simple, including the motives of Americans. But she was sure that America had no business interfering in a country— destroying a country—that was not our enemy.

Lake encouraged her to express her views. Perhaps she was saying things that he could not. But Toni was no longer the good Foreign Service wife, and her resentment of the war extended to the crushing workload it imposed on Tony, and even to his willingness to privilege his career over his family. He was gone from home so much that she wondered if he cared more about the prestige of his position than about his wife and young children. The less she saw of him, the harder it became to defend him when friends criticized his part in a war government. Searching for her own vocation, she now refused the notion that her husband's work mattered more than hers.

Imagine an official, still young, thought brilliant by his peers and superiors, a great career ahead of him. Imagine he begins to have doubts about the most important problem facing his government, a problem he's been working on day in, day out for five years—and the doubts turn grave. You wonder why he doesn't quit. But look what you're asking: that he give up not just his ambitions but also his illusions. For he can still find a hundred reasons to believe that he can do more good by staying inside. An Asia hand during the Vietnam years named James Thomson once wrote about "the effectiveness trap"—the notion that staying connected to power is the only way for an official to do good and prevent harm, which of course becomes a reason never to stick his neck out too far or quit on principle. "The most important asset that a man brings to bureaucratic life is his 'effectiveness,' a mysterious combination of training, style, and connections," Thomson wrote in 1968, once he was out. "The most ominous complaint that can be whispered of a bureaucrat is: 'I'm afraid Charlie's beginning to lose his effectiveness.'" Losing your effectiveness is like dying. And what or whom would quitting save anyway, except your self-respect, which is partly your vanity? Quitting is the easy, selfish thing. True sacrifice is to stay. And staying raises your sense of your own value. If people like Lake quit, who would be left to know anything? Who would take the side of the angels?

But Lake was so discouraged that by the middle of 1967 he was thinking seriously of resigning. To keep him in the Foreign Service, Katzenbach got him a two-year leave and a scholarship to Princeton for a doctorate in international relations. As in Saigon, Lake recommended that he be replaced by Holbrooke. So the Lakes went to Princeton and Holbrooke went to the State Department.

IX

Nineteen sixty-seven was the year Holbrooke entered the fourth and final stage of doubt. He began to question the American commitment in Vietnam. From nine thousand miles away he could see that the true threat was on the home front, that Vietnam was tearing America apart. His crisis of faith was more intellectual and less tormenting than Lake's, but he was reaching the same conclusion: the United States could never win, at least not on terms that Americans would accept. But you have to understand what this meant for the few doves in government. It didn't mean, Let's get the hell out of Vietnam. It meant, What the hell do we do now? That was about as far as skepticism could take you while you were still inside. The process of disenchantment was excruciatingly slow. Later on, people would backdate their moment of truth, their long-deferred encounter with the glaringly obvious. This was often inadvertent—they honestly couldn't believe that they were so wrong for so many years. And when they finally did begin to lose faith, they kept it to themselves and a few sympathetic friends, or else someone like Jim Rosenthal would take their head off. No one wanted to be called a dove.

Katzenbach, number two in the State Department and Holbrooke's boss, was having his own doubts. He began to meet with a dozen senior people from around the government every Thursday afternoon at five o'clock in his office on the seventh floor. For ninety minutes they would sit in a circle of chairs and have drinks and talk about Vietnam. Katzen-bach called it the Non-Group because there was no agenda, no paper trail, and no one was allowed to quote anyone to outsiders. The Non-Group became a safe place to explore alternative policies—that was how deep the lying and fear ran throughout the Johnson administration. Dean Rusk knew but never attended so that he wouldn't be tainted by talk of peace. Holbrooke walked uninvited into Katzenbach's office and badgered him so many times that Katzenbach, who found his boyish enthusiasm refreshing, finally agreed to let him join the Non-Group. Holbrooke's neckties were too loud and his manner too flip for some of his colleagues, but he kept quiet unless one of his superiors asked him a question. Thus he was allowed priceless time with the likes of Harriman, Rostow, and McNamara's deputy, Cyrus Vance. Holbrooke was the only one of them with any experience in Vietnam.

In the summer of 1967, he got a call from Les Gelb, a friend he'd made the year before, who was working on the secretary of defense's staff. Gelb had just been handed a project that came straight down from McNamara: assemble a team of six analysts and take three months to answer one hundred questions about the war. Are the body counts accurate? Has the bombing worked? How will we know if pacification is succeeding? Could Ho Chi Minh have been an Asian Tito? In other words, did this have to happen? The project was top secret, but Gelb told Holbrooke about it, and Holbrooke was interested.

Gelb had never set foot in Vietnam. His ignorance was nearly complete—he'd read just one book on the subject, Bernard Fall's *The Two Viet-Nams*—and yet for two years he drafted regular memos on the war that went from the secretary of defense to the White House. As I've said, this is normal for officials doing foreign policy. What wasn't normal was Vietnam. Like Holbrooke and Lake and a few others, most of them still in their twenties, Gelb talked about nothing but the war, and his whole life, like theirs, would be marked by it—damaged, he would say.

In 1966, Gelb got a letter from a friend who was commanding an air cavalry battalion in the Central Highlands. His men were fighting with great skill, but the North Vietnamese were fighting even better. They were on either drugs or nationalism, the friend wrote, and if it was nationalism, we were in deep trouble. Thus was the seed of doubt planted by sheer chance in Gelb's unschooled mind, and there it grew. By the summer of 1967 he was reaching the dovish position. But there was nothing soft about Gelb.

Politically, he was a centrist and a realist. Personally, he was a poor boy with bad eyesight and a sly, full-lipped smile. Unlike Holbrooke, he was unmistakably Jewish and came from *somewhere*—New Rochelle. His parents owned a corner grocery store where they worked fourteen hours a day and only closed for Rosh Hashanah, Yom Kippur, and the week the family went to the Catskills to listen to Hungarian music. The Gelbs read no newspapers and owned two books—the Bible and *The Rothschilds*. They were loving parents with the worst lives of anyone Les knew. The store was their life and he worked in it every summer, even the summer he got married. He was so poor that his bride Judy's parents refused to bless the marriage, and so smart that he got into Harvard's graduate school in government, and so badly educated that he had no idea what his teachers were talking about. He was basically lazy, but he worked hard in order to keep away from the store. Then Professor Henry Kissinger picked him out and Gelb began to rise.

But the store never left him. It gave him a kind of immunity to the temptations and deceptions of power. He was never too impressed with anyone and never let bullshit go unremarked—usually by saying, "Bullshit." When, in the summer of 1966, twenty-five-year-old Dick Holbrooke, just back from Vietnam, barged into the Capitol Hill office of Jacob Javits in order to give the senator from New York his ideas about pacification, twenty-nine-year-old Les Gelb laughed and told him that the senator was unavailable and Holbrooke would have to unload his wisdom on the senator's executive assistant. Their first encounter set the pattern for the rest of their lives, through thousands of conversations brief and epic: Holbrooke advocating; Gelb interrupting, countering-proposing, and, if the bullshit got too heavy, holding the phone to the toilet and flushing. Holbrooke was usually the protagonist and Gelb the critic who kept his judgment free. Holbrooke held the floor with the drama of his life, but he could never hold Gelb. So it became a friendship of equals and lasted to the end.

Through the fall of 1967 Gelb's project kept expanding. McNamara's questions led to more questions, which led to the vast archive of documents spread across the U.S. government. Gelb's team grew from six analysts to three dozen, working anonymously on a massive study of America's involvement in Vietnam going back to the 1940s. No officials were interviewed so that the project wouldn't leak. It was so secret that not even Dean Rusk, Walt Rostow, or Lyndon Johnson himself knew the nature of it.

Holbrooke wanted a piece. This would be the first inside history of the war, and he convinced Gelb and Katzenbach to let him write a chapter about the pacification effort that he'd been involved in from 1965 to 1967. He performed his duties at the State Department early in the day, then he went across the river to the Pentagon and the rooms right behind McNamara's suite on the third-floor E Ring, where Gelb was running the project. Holbrooke began tunneling through the mountain of files, taking breaks to prowl the halls and look for senior officials to corner, staying late many evenings. Gelb's office took on the feel of a floating seminar, with writers coming in and out, including Daniel Ellsberg, still a hawk, who was working on the chapter about Kennedy's decisions in 1961.

One day, Gelb asked a handful of analysts for lessons they had learned from the war. His deputy, Paul Gorman, an army colonel just back from Vietnam, said, "I'll tell you the lesson I've learned from this war." Gorman went to the blackboard on the wall behind Gelb and wrote in chalk a single word: "*Don't.*"

As Holbrooke read through the documents, he had the strange experience of viewing from a great height and distance the history that he had lived and tasted and smelled just a few years earlier down on the ground. Strategic hamlets, pagoda raids, the Diem coup, the marines in Quang Nam, the bureaucratic reorgs. He was able to see how policies he had carried out in Vietnam were made in Washington, and by whom. The archive revealed private pessimism on the part of top officials who had been publicly sanguine. It was a record of voluminous lies.

Most of the study's authors summarized the documents, but Holbrooke wrote with a point of view. He focused on the Sisyphean irony of an American effort to get the Vietnamese to save their own country with American ideas, on an American schedule. "We have concentrated on the history of the United States bureaucracy in this study because that, in retrospect, seems to have been where the push for pacification came from—not the Vietnamese."

Why did McNamara order up the study? Some people—Dean Rusk, for example, when he found out about the project upon its publication in the *New York Times*—thought that McNamara intended to give it to his friend Bobby Kennedy if he ran against Johnson. McNamara later claimed it was for the sake of historical scholarship. Or maybe, after almost seven years in office, he wanted to understand his own immense failure. Maybe he wanted answers to the fundamental questions that he had never bothered to ask. For at least a year, McNamara had known, in private and in torment, that the war he was publicly advocating could not be won. On November 1, 1967, in a long memo, he finally gave the president his honest view. It wasn't welcome, and by the end of the month Johnson moved McNamara over to the presidency of the World Bank, where he remained in 1969 when Gelb showed up at his office carrying two boxes with forty-seven volumes of analysis and documents—one of just fifteen copies, still top secret. They sat down on the couch and Gelb took out one of the studies. McNamara glanced through it and handed it back. "I don't want them," he said. "Take them back to the Pentagon." McNamara refused to read the Pentagon Papers.

ON THAT EVENING of November 1, eleven elder statesmen of the Cold War assembled at the State Department for drinks, dinner, and a briefing on Vietnam. McNamara was there, having just finished his memo to Johnson, and he couldn't conceal his gloom, but Rusk remained a good soldier, and the briefing was upbeat—body counts and captured documents showed that the United States was winning. The next morning, the Wise Men filed into the Cabinet Room and, one by one, told Johnson what he wanted to hear—stay the course. Acheson invoked American resolve during the dark days of the Korean War and the inspiring work of the Citizens' Committee for the Marshall Plan. General Omar Bradley called for more patriotic slogans. McGeorge Bundy told Johnson to start talking about "the light at the end of the tunnel." The president was greatly reassured.

Katzenbach wasn't. He thought the briefing of the Wise Men had been misleading and their validation of Johnson all wrong. Holbrooke thought so, too, and he offered to write up a dissenting memo for his boss to give to the president. Government service tends to turn written prose to fog and mud because it's far better to say nothing intelligible than to make a mistake. Not in the case of Holbrooke. The memo filled seventeen pages, and if there's a better piece of writing on Vietnam by an American official, I haven't read it.

He laid out the strategic problem by turning to his first love, history: "Hanoi uses time the way the Russians used terrain before Napoleon's advance on Moscow, always retreating, losing every battle, but eventually creating conditions in which the enemy can no longer function. For Napoleon it was his long supply lines and the cold Russian winter; Hanoi hopes that for us it will be the mounting dissension, impatience, and frustration caused by a protracted war without fronts or other visible signs of success; a growing need to choose between guns and butter; and an increasing American repugnance at finding, for the first time, their own country cast as 'the heavy' with massive fire power brought to bear against a 'small Asian nation.'"

North Vietnam couldn't defeat half a million American troops, but it could drain the American public of the will to go on fighting. So Johnson had two choices. He could turn all of North and South Vietnam along with parts of Laos and Cambodia into a free-fire zone and try to knock out the enemy before dissent at home grew too strong. Or he could win back the center at home, and thus more time—not with patriotic slogans and false hopes, but by reducing America's commitment. The first option was unlikely to work, because Hanoi's will to fight was inexhaustible. The second option might work, but it would require several steps.

Johnson should restate America's objective—from victory over communism to a South Vietnamese government that could survive and deal with an ongoing Communist threat. The United States should demand more of the South Vietnamese, militarily and politically. It should look to its own moral values and stop using airpower and artillery that killed large numbers of civilians or turned them into refugees in order to eliminate a few Vietcong: "Too many people are appalled by the brutality of the war. They feel that to fight a war of insurgency with vastly superior fire power is immoral and counter-productive . . . Some feeling (more abroad than in the United States) is based on a feeling that the United States is calloused where non-whites are concerned." And Johnson should announce a bombing halt over most of North Vietnam, which could lead to negotiations.

"Time is the crucial element at this stage of our involvement in Viet-Nam," Holbrooke concluded. "If we can't speed up the tortoise of demonstrable success in the field we must concentrate on slowing down the hare of dissent at home."

The memo didn't call for unilateral withdrawal, or even negotiated withdrawal. It made an argument for a way to buy more time. The war in Vietnam would go on. But on the spectrum of official opinion, the view was far dovish. In vivid and uncompromising language, the twenty-six-year-old author said that America could not win the war. For this reason Katzenbach hesitated to put his name to the memo. But since he agreed with it and thought its analysis brilliant, he finally signed it on November 16. He didn't show the memo to his boss, Dean Rusk, until a copy had been sent to the White House. When Rusk read it, he told Katzenbach, "I always try to find out what the president thinks before I give my advice." No word came back from the White House. Johnson didn't want to hear it.

Holbrooke was working just down the hall from his onetime surrogate father, but he seldom saw the secretary of state. Bundy was gone, McNamara was on his way out, but Rusk kept soldiering on into his eighth year of Vietnam. For Rusk, it was always the early spring of 1942, with Hitler's troops overrunning Russia and the American fleet in ruins at Pearl Harbor; or the late summer of 1950, with North Korea sending division after division against the U.S. Eighth Army trapped in the Pusan Perimeter; or the summer of 1961, when the Soviets cut off West Berlin from the NATO allies. Rusk would talk about the strength of American democracy, about something always giving if the United States just put its shoulder to the wheel. The only enemy that could beat America was defeatism. It was the faith of a generation that had seen the country come to greatness young, almost by accident, without ever knowing utter failure.

Rusk was more pessimistic about Vietnam than he let on, but he saw his job as supporting his president, not thinking for himself. There was a principle in this, even a principle Holbrooke respected, just as he respected Rusk for never showing him any favoritism. But Rusk was the kind of Foreign Service officer Holbrooke never wanted to become.

Things hadn't been the same between them since a Sunday afternoon in 1965 when Holbrooke was in Washington on home leave and Rusk called him into the department. They sat in the secretary's office overlooking the Lincoln Memorial, where Holbrooke had interviewed Rusk for his senior history paper on Woodrow Wilson. Holbrooke tried to tell Rusk, who was wearing his off-hours Hawaiian shirt, that the situation in Vietnam was more serious than Washington heard and believed from reports. When Rusk brought up the need to stop North Vietnamese units from infiltrating across the DMZ, Holbrooke countered that even then South Vietnam would not be pacified, because this was a civil war in the South, not just aggression from the North. Rusk wasn't happy with Holbrooke. "Dick, the North Vietnamese are not ten feet tall," he said. "They are not men from Mars. They are not supermen."

Rusk began to feel betrayed by his protégé. He suspected Holbrooke of leaking negative news to friends in the press, and he wasn't wrong. Holbrooke was an important source for Philip Geyelin, the editor of the *Post*'s editorial page, who used the leaks to move the paper away from its pro-war position. In December 1967, Geyelin wrote to the *Post*'s owner, Katharine Graham, that Holbrooke "belongs to this strange, unofficial, shadow government of very young officers . . . Because they are very junior, it is not easy for them to get a hearing . . . there is a kind of genteel terror in the air, and in this atmosphere, careers can be so easily destroyed." In early March 1968, Holbrooke had lunch with Neil Sheehan at Martin's Tavern in Georgetown. Holbrooke chose it as their regular meeting place because department officials never went there (he didn't know that it was a CIA hangout). Sheehan told him that the *Times,* where he now worked, was about to publish an explosive scoop on the administration's internal argument over the Pentagon's request for mobilization of the reserves and 206,000 more troops for the war. He wanted to know who had asked for that number.

"Westy," Holbrooke said, giving Sheehan the confirmation he needed to go to press.

Years later, Holbrooke and Rusk exchanged letters over their rift, and Rusk voiced his suspicion that the *Times* source had been Holbrooke. "I absolutely refused to confirm or deny the story," Holbrooke replied. The lie was self-serving, but the leak wasn't. He wanted the story to force a debate over the war. He wanted to head off the military. He knew that Tet had made Westmoreland's request untenable.

X

On January 30, 1968, the first day of the Vietnamese Lunar New Year truce, Vietcong and North Vietnamese troops attacked cities all over South Vietnam. Sappers penetrated the walled compound of the brand-new, heavily fortified U.S. embassy, built on the field next to the Lakes' villa where Holbrooke and his friends used to play touch football. Trudi Holbrooke happened to be in Saigon for Tet. She was visiting her son Andy, who had enlisted in the army after dropping out of Kent State and was serving in a pacification unit in the Delta (he still worshipped his big brother). Trudi was, everyone said, "a piece of work," the kind of woman who would go on vacation to Vietnam in 1968. Her loud enthusiasms were such an embarrassment to Holbrooke that he seldom admitted he even had a mother. Nonetheless, he called a friend in Saigon to check up on her. Trudi was fine—she was watching the fireworks from her room in the Continental Hotel and having the time of her life. She was up for anything: chatting with celebrities, traveling around the world, the Tet Offensive.

For most other Americans, Tet was an earthquake. It shook the officials in Washington to the core. There was panic at the State Department, and Rusk and Katzenbach sent Holbrooke to Vietnam in early February to assess the Communist offensive while it was still going on. In Saigon he found the Americans, including Westmoreland and Komer, in shock. They had believed their own talk of a demoralized enemy—the embassy's New Year's Eve bash had been called, without irony, the "light at the end of the tunnel" party—and utterly failed to see the offensive coming. Holbrooke found Westmoreland almost a broken man. Saigon was never the same after Tet. You could no longer tell yourself that the war was somewhere else.

Wisner, now a provincial rep in Dalat up in the Central Highlands, had used his own weapon to defend his compound from being over-run by the VC. He found that his friend Holbrooke, experiencing the war from Washington, had turned against it. Wisner, still in the fight in Vietnam, still believed in the better war. So did Holbrooke's friend John Vann, who had retired from the army and was serving under Komer as a senior civilian in CORDS. Ten days after Tet, Vann and Holbrooke flew by helicopter to Hau Nghia, a dangerous province of rice paddies between Saigon and the Cambodian border that fell under Vann's area of responsibility. South Vietnamese army positions had been reduced to the provincial capitals, and the atmosphere at the base was tense. After dinner Vann asked an American lieutenant colonel where the defensive perimeter was. Four hundred yards out, he was told. Vann suggested that they go make sure it was there. Holbrooke thought the idea crazy, but he couldn't say no to Vann. At ten o'clock they set out into the dark-ness, walking almost a quarter mile along the narrow paths between paddy fields before coming upon a forward position of two lonely South Vietnamese soldiers. It was one of the riskiest things Holbrooke ever did in Vietnam, but for Vann, who couldn't be happy if he was away for any length of time, it was just another night of the war. Holbrooke saw him as Henry V, disguised among his troops at Agincourt in order to gauge their resolve.

A lot of Americans in Vietnam claimed that Tet was a massive defeat for the enemy—and it was, if you figure the staggering count of VC dead, and the failure of South Vietnam's urban population to rise up. This was Vann's thinking. In Washington, Holbrooke had been one of his ardent supporters, trying to get Vann high-level audiences when no one wanted to hear his clear-eyed pessimism about the state of the war and his passionate ideas for fighting counterinsurgency. Vann now saw Tet as a great opportunity to turn the war around. Yet it was Vann, a legend of physical and intellectual courage, who had taught Halberstam and Sheehan to see Vietnam as a political war. The politics that now mattered most, as Holbrooke wrote in his Napoleon-in-Russia memo, was American. Tet broke the will of the American people to go on believing the lies of their leaders. It broke the leaders' will to go on asking for patience and sacrifice. So the tactical Communist defeat of Tet became the crucial strategic victory of the war.

Back in Washington, Holbrooke found everything changing with fantastic speed, as if Tet had suddenly jerked into motion a train stalled on a steep downhill. McNamara was out. His replacement was Clark Clifford, a Washington lawyer and junior Wise Man who had worked for Truman and advised Kennedy and Johnson. Clifford was the establishment personified—the perfect suits and hair, the soothing voice like bourbon poured over ice. In 1965 he had privately advised Johnson against escalation, but then he became one of the war's strongest public supporters, which is why Johnson made him secretary of defense. At the Pentagon, Clifford began a complete review of Vietnam policy, including the new troop request. As a newcomer he put the most basic questions to the military, questions about the war that no one had asked from the beginning, including "What is the plan for victory?" The generals had no answer. The war would just go on and on.

Clifford realized that the only way ahead was to negotiate. By late March he had moved his friends the Wise Men toward the same view. They met with Johnson at the White House one last time on March 26 and urged an end to the war. The Wise Men had been wrong all along.

Johnson pulled Clifford and Rusk out of the Cabinet Room. "Who poisoned the well?" he growled.

The president planned to give a major televised speech on the night of March 31. Holbrooke helped Katzenbach and Johnson's chief speechwriter, Harry McPherson, to draft it. But there were two versions—a belligerent speech expressing resolve to fight on, and a second speech, one that Clifford, in despair at the first version, urged on the writers, and that talked about peace. No one knew which speech Johnson was going to give until two days in advance, when he called McPherson to complain about a line on page five, and McPherson, scrambling to find the passage, realized that Johnson was working off the peace draft. The president planned to announce a halt to the bombing of North Vietnam above the infiltration routes near the DMZ. It was the end of three years of escalation.

The authors of the speech thought they were taking political pressure off a beleaguered candidate, with the Wisconsin primary just two days away. They doubted that Hanoi would react—the audience was American. They didn't know that the president planned to conclude the speech with a passage of his own, announcing the end of his candidacy for re-election. If they'd known, if he had told them, they would have pushed him to enlarge the offer of a partial bombing halt and make it a complete end to the bombing of North Vietnam. That would have allowed for real peace talks to begin. Later, Holbrooke imagined telling Johnson, "Look, Mr. President. If you are going to end your public career tonight over this issue, stop all the bombing and see what you can get for the next ten months. Don't make a halfway gesture, which is either going to get no response or at best a limited response." But Johnson didn't tell them. He didn't want to end his career with a peace that meant defeat.

ON APRIL 3, Radio Hanoi announced North Vietnam's willingness to meet with American negotiators to discuss "the unconditional cessation of bombing and all other war acts against the Democratic Republic of Vietnam so that talks could begin." Holbrooke became a junior member of the American delegation. His presence at Georgetown dinners and Katzenbach's Non-Group won him the confidence of the delegation's leader, Harriman, and his deputy, Cy Vance, a mild-mannered New York lawyer and former Pentagon official who was supposed to keep an eye on Harriman for Rusk. Three generations of the establishment got ready to go to Paris. Rusk, still loyal to Johnson, instructed the team to stick with the official line—that North Vietnam must stop infiltrating the South—and not even consider other objectives without approval from Washington. "Of course we have to consider other objectives," Les Gelb said at a meeting of Pentagon planners, thinking he was stating the obvious. "Otherwise, how are we ever going to have negotiations?" When word got back to Rusk, he tried to have Gelb removed from the planning group.

In May, the delegates took rooms at the Hôtel de Crillon—they were thinking in terms of weeks. But there were no deadlines, and Paris was beautiful, and nothing happened. Holbrooke attended the French Open and watched the huge student protests against de Gaulle in the Latin

Quarter. He played tennis and drank whiskey with leading American journalists in spite of a ban on talking with them. There was almost nothing to tell them anyway. Neither side was willing to budge from its starting position. Holbrooke settled in for the long haul, rented an apartment, and summoned Litty and David to Paris. Spring turned to summer, and Bobby Kennedy was killed in Los Angeles, following the murder of Martin Luther King Jr. in Memphis, but at the Paris talks nothing happened.

Harriman told Holbrooke that when FDR sent him to accompany Churchill to Moscow in the summer of 1942, his only instructions were to explain to Stalin why the Allies couldn't yet open a second front in Europe. Now here he was in Paris, handcuffed with rigid instructions from Dean Rusk, whom Harriman despised for having the job that he had always sought and using it to prevent him from negotiating an end to the war, which would have helped elect Hubert Humphrey and defeat Richard Nixon. Soviet tanks rolled into Prague, and the Democratic convention in Chicago exploded, and Humphrey was nominated by a party at war with itself over Vietnam, and the Holbrookes toured the Romanesque architecture of northern France. Summer turned to fall, and in the absence of progress Humphrey's poll numbers collapsed. Harriman and Clifford agreed that the president must want his vice president to lose the election, and nothing happened.

In mid-October, Johnson finally decided to declare the total bombing halt that Holbrooke and others had hoped for in March. The United States and North Vietnam agreed to begin negotiations, with South Vietnam and the National Liberation Front—the Vietcong—joining them in Paris. But before anything could happen, Richard Nixon sabotaged the chance for peace. The only outsider with access to the secrets of the American delegation was Henry Kissinger, a White House consultant on Vietnam and an acquaintance of Holbrooke. Kissinger was also secretly advising both campaigns. He traveled to Paris that September and met with Holbrooke and another junior member. Upon his return, Kissinger warned John Mitchell at Nixon headquarters that a bombing halt might be coming in mid-October. "We trusted him," Holbrooke later admitted. "It is not stretching the truth to say that the Nixon campaign had a secret source within the U.S. negotiating team." On Nixon's orders, the campaign opened a back channel to Saigon and convinced President Thieu to drag his feet with the promise of a better deal for South Vietnam from a Republican administration.

Was it treason? I can't think of any other word. Johnson found out about Nixon's scheme through FBI wiretaps. He called to warn Nixon, who swore, "My god, I would never do anything to encourage them not to come to the table." Lacking absolute proof, Johnson decided to keep it quiet. So did Humphrey, even in his memoirs. In those days politicians colluded with foreign countries to win American elections, and sitting presidents said nothing about it, but there were still limits.

Because of obstruction in Saigon, and perhaps because of his own ambivalence toward Humphrey and toward ending the war, Johnson only announced the bombing halt on October 31, five days before the election. Humphrey surged in the polls, but it was too late. Vietnam would become the problem of the Nixon administration.

In mid-November the South Vietnamese and the Vietcong arrived in Paris, and nothing happened. Neither accepted the legitimacy of the other, and for two months the parties argued over nameplates, flags, and the shape of the negotiating table. Square, round, rectangular? Critical principles must have been at stake. At one point Holbrooke drew up his own design—a long table with a single row of chairs facing a mirror curved in such a way that the images of the North Vietnamese and the Vietcong would merge into a single delegation that could only see that of South Vietnam. A Soviet diplomat finally solved the problem with a round table separating two rectangles.

Two days before the inauguration of President Richard Nixon, the Paris peace talks finally began, with Harriman replaced by Henry Cabot Lodge. Nothing happened. Americans would go on killing and dying in Vietnam for four more years.

"Henry, I don't want a job in the Nixon Administration," Holbrooke told Kissinger when they met at the Nixon campaign's transition offices in New York.

"Why?" Kissinger had just been named Nixon's national security advisor and assumed that everyone who came to see him wanted a job.

"Because I don't think I can work for Richard Nixon."

Holbrooke stayed on in Paris, where he learned things about negotiating, negative lessons that would be useful to him in coming years. But by the summer of 1969 he'd had enough and returned with his family to Washington.

He was at loose ends. For seven years he had worked on nothing but Vietnam. He couldn't stay in the Nixon administration, but he wasn't ready to leave the Foreign Service. Then the State Department found him a one-year fellowship at Princeton. For the third or fourth time, he was following Tony Lake.

Lake was going back in. Kissinger hired him to be his special assistant on the National Security Council. At Princeton he had finally read the history of Vietnamese nationalism and now he saw the war's futility. The stakes were artificial, made in America. It was wrong to keep shedding blood. The human cost was too high. After two years on the outside, he agreed to return in order to try to get America out of Vietnam. When Kissinger was vetting Lake, Bundy told him, "Tony opposes the war, but he's a good soldier." The line got back to Lake and stung him. He was determined to challenge every premise of the war. He put his hopes in his brilliant, charming, witty new boss, and Kissinger encouraged Lake to argue. So did Toni, though at times she was among the chanting protesters outside the cordon of buses that circled the White House.

Holbrooke, on his way out, sent Lake two long letters of advice. It all came down to one thing. "We have to get out of Vietnam," he wrote. "The war has already spread a poison through our nation which will take years to neutralize."

Holbrooke confessed to being depressed, professionally and personally. Seven years and no end in sight. He was finished with Vietnam.

"In any case, it is your problem again and not mine anymore."

How Does He Do It?

I have something to tell you." Holbrooke put his suitcase down in the large marble entry hall of their house in Morocco. It was just before Thanksgiving 1971. Litty was listening. "I've fallen in love with someone else. But she's married and doesn't want to leave her marriage. So it's over." Litty was still listening. "I thought I ought to tell you."

They had two boys now. Anthony—they chose the name in part because it didn't have to be spelled, but Holbrooke gave people to think that their second son was named after his best friend—was born in Princeton on the morning of December 16, 1969, the day after the baby's father got back from a ski trip to the Poconos. Holbrooke had lunch with George Kennan, then went to the hospital to meet Anthony. New Jersey had a public health law dating back to the twenties that kept husbands out of delivery rooms, but neither of the Holbrookes wanted Dick there anyway.

On Christmas Dick felt like seeing the new Bond film, *On Her Majesty's Secret Service*. Litty wasn't up to it, and besides she had a nine-day-old and a four-year-old to take care of. She told Dick to go anyway—she would be all right. That was how it went with them: he didn't hesitate to go, or she to let him. While Dick was at the movie, Litty hemorrhaged. A friend came up from Washington to help her out for a few days. In January, the new father went to Vermont for another five-day ski trip.

Even by the standards of this last, end-of-the-sixties moment before the feminist revolt changed middle-class American family life, he was

an absent husband and an indifferent father. He was also restless, restless. The fickle goddess history had temporarily put him on the bench. So he read Vonnegut's *Cat's Cradle* one day and Acheson's memoirs the next and then all the other Vonnegut novels, saw *True Grit* and *Oh! Calcutta!* one week and *They Shoot Horses, Don't They?* and *Z* another, watched every game of the NBA finals as Willis Reed limped triumphantly onto the court and the Knicks beat the Lakers in seven, dinner parties four nights a week, up to New York for John Campbell's birthday, down to Washington the next day to stay with the Lakes for a few nights, dinner and the movie *Cactus Flower* with Toni (Tony was working inhuman hours again), lunch the next day with Joe Kraft and Art Buchwald, black-tie dinner that night at Polly Wisner's with Harriman, Alsop, and other grandees, dinner with the Lakes the next night, and with the Lakes and Frank and Genevieve Wisner the night after that following a Harriman lunch and five other meetings in one day including a visit to Tony's office in the White House basement.

This was the normal Holbrooke energy gone berserk for want of occupation. How did he find time? When you took away the daily stuff of living that he always left to others—the cleaning, shopping, raising children—it made a lot of room for his favorite pursuits.

History had called Lake back onto the field, as Kissinger's favorite bleeding heart. Lake spoke to the Harvard in Kissinger who respected expertise and wit. He took Lake to Paris for his secret meetings with North Vietnam's Le Duc Tho, which made the State Department's official peace talks even more meaningless than usual.

Lake spent the summer of 1969 with Kissinger in San Clemente, California, while Nixon was at the Western White House. Toni and their two kids joined him for a week, staying in a high-rise hotel wedged between the powerful Pacific surf and a four-lane highway. One night, the Lakes went out for drinks with Kissinger and his blond date. Tony left early to return to work, and Kissinger took Toni back to the hotel. He was shit-faced and driving erratically while pelting his date with increasingly nasty comments. "Toni, this is the way I gain my objectives," he said. "I keep pushing them under until they yell for help."

Toni was the kind of quiet woman men like Kissinger underestimated. "It depends on what your objectives are," she said.

During the massive October Moratorium, Lake and two colleagues went out on the South Lawn of the White House and wondered where their wives were in the crowd on the Ellipse and asked themselves whether they should be on the other side of the buses and M16s. Lake and Kissinger both wanted to end the war, but Kissinger thought we couldn't just leave without losing credibility, and credibility meant heavier bombing, a wider war as American troops were withdrawn. Lake argued that slow withdrawals would only weaken the U.S. negotiating position later. Once, Kissinger chided Lake for writing memos that were less than "manly," and afterward, when he thought he was alone, Lake slammed his fist into the Coke machine outside the White House mess.

The Nixon in Kissinger suspected his liberal aides of leaking state secrets to undermine policy. As the venomous atmosphere in the Nixon White House spread to the National Security Council, Kissinger approved FBI wiretaps on members of his own staff, at work and at home. Lake discovered that the transcripts were under twenty-four-hour guard in a safe in the Situation Room, right around the corner from his desk. But he never raised the wiretapping with Kissinger. It was enough to argue Vietnam.

One Saturday in late April 1970, Kissinger called Lake and his colleagues in for a meeting and informed them that the United States was going to invade Cambodia. Lake argued passionately against it— Cambodia would be destroyed, America further torn apart, the war in Vietnam would go on. "Tony, I knew what you were going to say," Kissinger told him with disdain. If Kissinger could dismiss his argument so easily, Lake was already finished. The invasion of Cambodia finally sprang him from the effectiveness trap, and he decided to do what he had long contemplated, what a lot of people in government contemplate but hardly anyone, in the face of monstrous lies and crimes, ever does— resign on principle.

Along with two colleagues, Roger Morris and William Watts, he did it quietly, without telling the press. They thought they could be more influential that way. (The illusions of the effectiveness trap were slow to fade.) Later, when the investigative reporter Seymour Hersh came to Lake's house to try to get him to talk about Nixon and Cambodia, Lake refused. "Do it, just do it!" Toni said. "I want to, but I can't," Lake said. Though he believed his career in government was over, he hoped that he might come up for another job someday.

After his resignation, an FBI tap went up on the Lakes' home phone and stayed there for nine months. Kissinger justified it with the fear that Lake would leak the secret Paris peace talks to the Democrats. When Lake became the top foreign policy advisor to Senator Edmund Muskie, the Democratic front-runner in the 1972 presidential race, the Nixon administration was able to eavesdrop on the opposition. "Just gobs and gobs of material, gossip and bullshitting," Nixon complained on his own tapes. "The tapping was a very, very unproductive thing."

Lake learned about the wiretap through the Watergate hearings and sued his former boss until, years later, he finally got the apology that was all he'd wanted from Kissinger.

AT PRINCETON, even preppie Princeton, Holbrooke saw that the war was turning young people against America and against the establishment he still prized. To the best students, a career at General Motors seemed better, less hypocritical, than government service. "Their country in the world outside means Vietnam, Vietnam, Vietnam," he wrote to Charles Bohlen, the Soviet expert and architect of the Cold War. "The fight against Fascism and Nazism, the defense of Korea and Berlin and indeed all of Western Europe during the height of the Cold War, the terrible struggle over McCarthyism and bigotry at home, and even the Cuban missile crisis (!)—all of these are events from another age, and the kids are barely aware of them."

The Nixon poison—it made Holbrooke want to leave the country. After working on staffs for five years, he also wanted to be in charge of something. That was impossible for an FSO-4, which he had just become, on the normal unimaginative embassy career path. So he looked into the Peace Corps, asked for a country program to run, and when Morocco was offered, he accepted it. In the summer of 1970 he studied Arabic at the Foreign Service Institute and played intense tennis with Lake, as if it were Saigon 1963, recording each score in his calendar: 2-6, 2-6; 6-2, 3-6. The Holbrookes saw the Lakes every week, sometimes two or three times a week. In September, he flew with Litty and the boys to Rabat.

Just before Christmas 1970, Daniel Ellsberg visited with his new wife, his second wife. At dinner they sat on the restaurant banquette and couldn't keep their hands off each other. "Get a hotel room," Holbrooke muttered. He wasn't very fond of Ellsberg, who had turned against the war as ostentatiously as he was once for it. Holbrooke considered Ellsberg analytically talented but lacking in judgment and an emotional exhibitionist.

"Don't you think something should be done about the war?" Ellsberg asked Holbrooke.

"Well, what are you talking about?"

"I don't know," Ellsberg said. "Don't you think something should be done with the study?"

He meant the Pentagon project they had both worked on. Holbrooke had the uneasy feeling that Ellsberg was trying to pull him into something. "No, I certainly don't," Holbrooke said.

He didn't understand the conversation until six months later, on June 13, 1971, when he went to get the *International Herald Tribune* at his local tobacco shop and saw, over Neil Sheehan's byline, the headline "Vietnam Archive: Pentagon Study Traces 3 Decades of Growing U.S. Involvement." He immediately knew what it was, and who had given the Pentagon Papers to Sheehan.

Holbrooke came to see Ellsberg as one of those accidental characters of history who show the pattern of a whole era. The leak of the Pentagon Papers was the hinge between two decades. It plunged Nixon into the deeper reaches of paranoia and drove him to create the Plumbers, the off-the-books gang of spies and dirty tricksters whose first black-bag job was to break in to the Santa Monica office of Ellsberg's psychiatrist in search of embarrassing information. The Plumbers next turned to the Kennedys and tried to prove that JFK was behind the assassination of Diem and Nhu. Finally, a year after the leak, they bugged the Democratic National Committee in Washington. Nixon always justified his crimes in terms of national security. To Holbrooke, Watergate was "a domestic Vietnam" and Ellsberg was "the triggering mechanism for events which would link Vietnam and Watergate in one continuous 1961-to-1975 story."

There isn't much to tell you about the Peace Corps years. Holbrooke had 176 people and a half-million-dollar budget to supervise. He traveled around the country and was popular with the volunteers. "I wish I had half a dozen Holbrookes working for me," the rating officer wrote in his evaluation. Holbrooke would call it the best job he ever had. But Morocco never got under his skin. He was waiting out the Nixon administration.

Litty had followed her husband to another foreign country. She was a mother of two and nearing thirty. She wore her hair long, straight, and parted in the middle, like Judy Collins. She still had the placid pretty looks of a decade ago. Her days were spent swimming with the boys and framing pictures and hosting guests like Polly Wisner or John and Brenda Campbell in their vast house and throwing buffets for fifty volunteers and cleaning the carcass of a sacrificial lamb for the feast of Eid al-Kabir. She was often bored, and she filled her letters to her parents with the trivia of daily life: "Please send me several potholders! Mine are worn out and I keep burning my fingers." Holbrooke once said that he had given them a pretty interesting life, and when she told him that it depressed her to hear it, he didn't understand why.

In October 1971 Holbrooke left for a month-long trip on Peace Corps business to Thailand, India, and Nepal. (He had done the same thing the year before in Afghanistan and found it the most beguiling country he'd ever seen. Zahir Shah still sat on his throne. Kabul was a city of modern people surrounded by a stony and ancient land. Foreigners on the hippie trail fell under its spell. Holbrooke, who loved mountains, loved the sublime Hindu Kush.) On November 8 he was sitting in the Kathmandu living room of the Nepal country director, hiking boots and backpack on, about to set off for a five-day trek, when the phone rang. It was Tony Lake. "John just died."

John Campbell was one of the stars of their Foreign Service class, though not a member of the Vietnam circle. He was the irreverent managing editor of the upstart new quarterly *Foreign Policy*—Holbrooke had turned the job down in 1969 when it was offered by one of the founding editors, Samuel Huntington, and recommended Campbell instead—and the author of a new book on the stupidity of State Department bureaucracy called *The Foreign Affairs Fudge Factory.* He was also a heavy smoker and drinker. An undetected thyroid cancer that was blocking his air passage killed him at thirty-one.

While Holbrooke was still absorbing the news, Brenda Campbell called on a bad line and asked Holbrooke to come to New York for the funeral.

En route, he wrote to Litty on TWA stationery. It was a confused letter, almost desperate. He was in a fog and asking for her help. "Right now I am so depressed and so dazed that I don't think I could go right back to Rabat. Maybe I should take a few days of leave + stay in New York. What do you think? What should I do? . . . Maybe I will go to Washington. I wonder if I can make the Christmas trip as planned . . . At this time I have no idea what to do or what to say. <u>What can you say?</u> Are you going to New York? Did you speak to anyone in Washington or NY? Will I see you again?" He squeezed the word "When" into the start of that last sentence, but it was as if he was contemplating sailing out to sea forever and asking Litty for permission.

He persuaded Brenda to let him speak at the funeral. On the day of the service, while Tony worked at the New York offices of the Carnegie Endowment, which had given him a fellowship, Holbrooke walked around Manhattan with Toni. At the funeral Holbrooke remembered Campbell's sense of the absurd. "He loved the Foreign Service, but in some ways John was too bold for it," Holbrooke said. "He found it almost impossible to exist in the narrow bounds now defined by the Department of State." Afterward, he met with the second founding editor of *Foreign Policy,* Warren Manshel, who offered him Campbell's job. This time Holbrooke accepted it. He went to Washington and stayed, as always on trips home, with the Lakes. Then he flew back to Rabat, walked into the house, and said, "I have something to tell you."

LITTY DIDN'T ASK whom he'd fallen in love with. She thought, strangely enough, that it was none of her business, though that wouldn't keep her from asking herself the question again and again, for weeks, torturing herself with the who and what and why. The worst thing wasn't that he might have slept with someone else. It was that he loved someone else and found it, he told her, one of the most powerful experiences of his life—and she was utterly excluded from it. Jealousy was part of the storm raging inside her, but even more intense was the feeling of being erased. This feeling grew stronger over time, and eventually it became a mortal danger.

She packed her bags and flew home with the boys to her parents in Maryland for the Christmas holidays, while Holbrooke stayed in Morocco to wrap things up. Then she wrote to him that she would not be coming back to Rabat. She'd known this when she left without telling him. Her mother was terminally ill, but the real reason was that she couldn't bear the thought of sharing a house with her husband during their final months in Morocco while he made up his mind whether or not to stay married. "I thought I ought to tell you"—why, if it was over? Because he was thinking of leaving her, even suggested that they live apart when they returned to Washington. She was seizing the initiative and her self-respect. After New Year's she would look for a job—even waitressing. Staying in Washington would also spare her the need to explain herself to anyone. She could say that she was home to arrange a school for David, while Dick would return in March, a year early, to start at *Foreign Policy*—and no one would think twice. So she didn't tell a soul. Just as she hadn't asked him the obvious questions. She kept everything to herself, while buying the boys' Christmas presents and finding that Anthony had broken both her pairs of glasses as she lay in bed with the flu.

The marriage might or might not be over—she found that she didn't much care. The shock had woken her up to herself. She surveyed her life and the first thing she noticed was that she was all alone and had been alone for a long time. She had no close friends, had stopped seeing the last one ten years ago when it became clear that the girl detested Dick Holbrooke. In Holland she had felt sorry for the Fulbright wives and even a bit smug since she had earned the right to be there on her own. Then she gave up her graduate studies and professional ambitions to follow him around the world, not for the status of being Mrs. Richard Holbrooke, but to be with him—only to find herself in a much worse position than those pitiable Fulbright wives, because her husband was hardly ever there.

When the U.S. government deemed her a superfluous nuisance in Vietnam, instead of forcing him to choose between her and Saigon she had gone off meekly to Bangkok, pregnant before she wanted to be. She vowed never to get in the way of his career, knowing what it meant to him. His life was her life. So she waited all alone in Bangkok, and then she followed him to Washington, to Paris, to Princeton, to Rabat, unpacking crates and shelving books and then doing it all in reverse, and in each place she was lonely. She felt invisible to his friends—they could never spell her name right—and even to him. She was an intelligent woman, Phi Beta Kappa at Brown, but his brilliance sapped her self-confidence. There was nothing in her life she could be proud of, except the boys and the occasional *canard à l'orange*. She felt that she bored her husband when she tried to confide in him, and so she was lonely even when they were together.

While she slept, there had been a revolution in the lives of American women. In 1964 she was expected to be her husband's helpmeet. In 1971 she was a loser for having no career of her own. She had been a fool to let herself be erased. But that was what she had done.

Her instinct was not to save her marriage—she doubted that it could survive or that he wanted it to, and she would never go back to what it had been these past eight years, a parasitic marriage in which an interesting life had been given to her secondhand—but to save herself. "Since my life depends on yours in a way which yours does not on mine, I find myself shattered that you have fallen in love with someone else," she wrote to him. "This threatens my whole life in a way which would not be true for you if the situation was reversed. So I'm determined now, really determined, since I'm so frightened, to build a life of my own."

A new woman seemed to be speaking in the letters Litty wrote. Anger and fear tore away her instinct for evasion; she was alive and acute and spoke the truth with bitter clarity. Holbrooke wrote back with the sudden interest of a man who finds himself separated from his wife and pummeled by her eloquence. He wondered why she had never said these things to him before, and he asked her to come back for a few weeks so they could talk it all over. She saw little reason. She didn't spare him the news that the boys hardly noticed his absence. "When Daddy comes, we can buy a TV," was all David said, and Anthony said, "Daddy all gone."

She always seemed to get the short end of the stick in their marriage, she told him, and yet she didn't drop it. She still managed the logistics of balancing the checkbook, instructing him how to pack the house in Rabat, and reclaiming the house on Nebraska Avenue, which was occupied by a tenant until the end of January. Meanwhile, she and the boys stayed with the Lakes.

Tony was away at his parents' house in Connecticut, finishing his doctoral thesis on Rhodesia. He had found Muskie a disappointment— volatile, lazy, unwilling to hear advice. Toni was taking classes on urban education and making plans to have a farmhouse built on land they had bought in the remote hills of West Virginia, near the Sheehans' farm. Litty wanted to confide in Toni—she couldn't think of anyone else to talk to—but Toni was so busy around the house, so occupied with her three small kids and her dogs and cat, that Litty never had the chance and began to sense that this wasn't the person to tell. The Lakes gave her their old black-and-white TV so that Litty could watch Nixon's trip to China when she moved back to Nebraska Avenue in February.

Holbrooke didn't tell anyone, either. He didn't tell Frank Wisner on a New Year's trip to Fès and Tangier, and he didn't tell Geoffrey Wolff on a January ski trip in Spain. He had every chance to tell Wolff. They drove for four hours through the night from the Wolffs' house on the Mediterranean up into the bald lunar Sierra Nevada mountains to the slopes around Granada. Wolff was in the middle of his own crisis. He had quit his professorship at Princeton and his job reviewing books for *Newsweek* in order to write novels, but his first hadn't sold well, his publisher had refused his second, and he feared the same fate for his third, which he had just completed. Holbrooke read the manuscript in Spain and was enthusiastic. Wolff knew plenty of people who couldn't stand Holbrooke, but he found him to be an exuberant and loyal friend. It helped to be playing an entirely different game. When Holbrooke once tried his hand at fiction—a Graham Greene–ish novel set in Washington—Wolff read it and gently said that creative writing was not his métier. Afterward, Holbrooke told people, "Wolff said I'm the worst novelist he ever read." If Holbrooke found you interesting but not threatening, he could be the best company in the world.

On that night drive to Granada, Holbrooke told Wolff that he knew how people saw him—ruthlessly ambitious. But he was beyond that now; he didn't care about getting to the top: "That's not who I am." It wasn't true, of course, but Holbrooke thought it was true because he didn't want to be that man, least of all now that he was about to break up his family, and because he couldn't see himself clear, which would cause him to return to this illusion throughout his life. He and Wolff spent four days together and Holbrooke never said a word about the woman he'd fallen in love with.

He got back to Washington on March 14 and joined his family in the house on Nebraska Avenue. The next day, he was mustered out of the State Department on a two-year unpaid leave. He came home with a briefcase full of mail that had been forwarded from Morocco. Litty was sorting through it when she noticed a letter from Tony Lake. Something made her open it.

You'll be back soon and we're bound to see each other, Lake wrote to Holbrooke. *I hope we can get past this and go on being friends.* The tone was calm and thoughtful.

Litty's body started to tremble. She couldn't get herself under control. She had never felt like this in her life. She was practically frothing at the mouth. She took the black-and-white TV and put it in her car and drove the mile from Nebraska Avenue up to Lowell Street and carried the TV from her car. She could have thrown it at the house—but she was a woman who had kept herself on an even keel her whole life, and so she set the TV down at the Lakes' front door. "I can't believe you did this," she told Toni.

———

WHAT WAS "THIS"? I don't know. Two people fell in love. For how long? I don't know. Whenever he returned to Washington from Rabat and stayed with the Lakes, Dick and Toni would sit in the kitchen and talk for hours while Tony was off at work as usual. She was lonely and overwhelmed with motherhood, and she found herself drawn to this friend who listened so well, who was available to her when her husband wasn't.

The day he came back for Campbell's funeral and they walked around Manhattan, the feeling between them grew dangerously intense. He asked Toni to run away with him. That was the thing that he'd known he was going to do when he wrote to Litty from his TWA flight. He would have shattered two families on a fleeting dream. Why? I don't know. "The power it gave him over Tony was irresistible," said one of their close friends—a dark view with a certain psychological force, but there must have been other things he couldn't resist as well. Perhaps he saw in Toni a rare woman with the strength to check his egotism and the warmth to elicit his idealism. And perhaps, after following Tony to Saigon, to the State Department, to Princeton, he felt that he could only become what he wanted to be by taking Lake's place.

But Toni still loved her husband, and so she told him about "this"—a warning flare that got his full attention. She decided to stay in her marriage, while Holbrooke headed down the big American highway and tried to swallow the world whole. That was the end of it.

So there's a mystery. And maybe there should be. We like to think that truth lies in details, the more details the clearer the truth, like the cumulative pages of a trial transcript, but this piling up of facts only gives us the false assurance that we've gotten to the heart of the matter when in fact we understand almost nothing. There's a kind of injustice that goes by the name of thoroughness. Who could hold up under trial by biography? None of us. I'll try to stay clear of testimony, verdict, and sentence. I said at the start that I'm not telling you Holbrooke's story for his sake. "This" wouldn't even concern us if it didn't carry consequences far into the future.

"Dick has been seeing my wife," Lake told Gelb, who had become his friend. "This has totally destroyed me."

Gelb didn't want to talk to Holbrooke about it because it was too horrible and would forever color his feelings. But Holbrooke brought it up when he got back from Morocco. "Has Tony told you about us?"

"Are you having some sort of problem?"

"Our relations are difficult." Something had happened between him and Toni. "It's over."

Toni tried to apologize to Litty, but they never really spoke again. Dick apologized to Tony, and later he apologized again, and again, and then he said, "I'm not going to keep apologizing to you," and eventually he came to feel that Tony was the one who had wronged him, which was how he could live with it.

Since Litty and Tony were in the same position, they decided to commiserate. One day they went for a walk in the woods along the towpath below the Holbrookes' house. Toni's feelings for Dick had infuriated Tony, deeply wounded him. As with Litty, the feelings mattered more to him than whether they had slept together, which Toni told him they had not. But he quickly locked his emotions in a box and moved on. People fell in love all the time. It was no reason to stop being friends—and now he could see that there had never been all that much to the friendship anyway. Lake could afford to be a gentleman. The result had been a lot better for him than for Holbrooke—not 6-1, 6-1, but at least 5-7, 6-0. He Tony and She Toni were both determined to keep the marriage alive. Litty now understood why the Lakes had gone to see just about every movie in Washington together that winter.

Litty, the gaslit woman, the last to find out, thought that none of the others grasped the seriousness. Dick never faced the depth of the wrong he had done. Tony never faced the depth of his own feelings. Litty couldn't imagine how the two of them would go on being friends.

And they wouldn't. Holbrooke's betrayal would stay secret from almost everyone, while the acid it released would take years to eat silently at the bonds of youthful ambition and Vietnam and tennis and American greatness that had held the two men together until, by the end, there would be nothing left between them except hatred and the ineradicable past.

THE DEATH THROES of the Holbrookes' marriage lasted a few more months. One day near the end of the summer of 1972, the family visited the home of Johnny Apple, the *Times* reporter, and his wife Edie Smith, a former Foreign Service officer, who had been hurt by flying glass in the 1965 Saigon embassy bombing. The Apples were part of the Vietnam circle to which Holbrooke remained loyal all his life. While the men sat and talked, Litty and Edie and the boys went for a walk. As they were coming back inside, Holbrooke suddenly looked up in panic, as if he had misplaced something: "Where's my family?"

Soon after, he moved out of the house on Nebraska Avenue.

His first stop was Georgetown, where he would always wash up when adrift in Washington. He became a resident of the brick town-house that Harriman had acquired to hold his archives, next door to his mansion on N Street. Holbrooke was taken in like a wayward boy in need of an adopted home, as the Rusks had done in Scarsdale in 1957, the last time he had lost something of great value.

There was a new Mrs. Harriman. Averell's wife of four decades, Marie, had died in 1970. The next year, when Pamela Digby Churchill Hayward's second husband, a wealthy Broadway producer, met the same fate, the new widow made sure that his obituary was placed in front of the grieving Harriman. Averell and Pamela had a history.

In 1941, Harriman, almost fifty, was sent to London by FDR to oversee the Lend-Lease program, and in his first week, on the night they met at a dinner party, he took the prime minister's twenty-one-year-old daughter-in-law as his lover while they sheltered from a German air raid in his hotel suite. Pamela wasn't quite beautiful—her face was too square and the baby fat became a permanent double chin, until corrected—but she more than made up for it, she later explained, with enthusiasm. Far from being scandalized, Churchill and his cabinet regarded the affair as a diplomatic coup in their effort to woo the Americans deeper into the British war effort. In 1943, Harriman left London to serve as ambassador to Moscow and became the American closest to Stalin. Pamela's wartime lovers after Averell included a U.S. Air Force general, a Royal Air Force marshal, the newsman Edward R. Murrow—the only one she really loved, because his farm-boy moralism led him to resist her—and Murrow's boss at CBS, William Paley. But none of them, starting with Harriman, would leave his wife for her.

So at the end of the war she divorced Randolph Churchill and embarked on a life as the consort of rich, good-looking, often much older men—international playboys, polo players, the head of Fiat, Paki-stani royalty, Frank Sinatra, a banker named Rothschild—as if she were scripting an over-the-top movie about such a woman as herself. She did it with the focus of a serious career woman, jotting down their personal preferences on a silver notepad. After all her men had left or died on her, in the summer of 1971 she ran into Harriman at a dinner party at Katharine Graham's mansion on R Street. Pam was fifty-one; Averell was a few months short of eighty and practically deaf, but he remained as alive to women as he was to power. Within a week they were back in bed. Just before their wedding in September, one of his financial advi-sors asked Harriman, "Governor, do you want to continue the allow-ance for Mrs. Hayward?" "What allowance?" Harriman didn't realize that he'd been supporting his ex-mistress for thirty years.

There are two ways to feel about Pamela Harriman. She was British upper crust who'd had everything handed to her but always wanted more, forever maneuvering for her own benefit, bedding men whom the war had separated from their wives, eating steaks purchased by American taxpayers for American servicemen, stealing and pawning one set of stepchildren's heirlooms, squandering another set's trust fund as debt collateral, all without a twinge of conscience. Or she was a woman of intelligence and charm dedicated to pleasure and power in a man's world, and as long as you had something she wanted she was great fun.

Polly Wisner warned Holbrooke that Pam could be dangerous, but he didn't want to choose between his patronesses. He adored Pam and they flirted shamelessly. He loved being the Harrimans' nonpaying ten-ant. He would sit on his bed in his underwear and eat caviar straight out of a jar that they'd brought back from Moscow. His appetite was more than large enough for a salon full of Pamela Harrimans—millionaires, movie stars, society fixtures. He would seek them out for the rest of his life. He was a star-fucker, and the star could be Averell or Pamela or Dikembe Mutombo or Angelina Jolie.

If you're not paying much attention, ambition looks like a politician's sober memoir of triumphs and setbacks; a determined woman rising to the top of an important organization; a diplomat working around the clock for peace while keeping his hands to himself. But ambition is not a pretty thing up close. It's wild and crass, and mortifying in the details. It brings a noticeable smell into the room. It's a man cajoling a bereaved widow to include him among her late husband's eulogists, then rearranging name cards so that he can chat up the right dinner guest after the service. Because of Holbrooke's psychological mutation of not being able to see himself, and maybe not giving a shit anyway, he lets us ogle ambition in the nude.

If you follow him closely, especially at this moment after springing himself from family life, you can draw a nice map of Washington's circles within circles and see the interplay between social connection and power and publicity and money and sex. He had accomplished nothing of importance, yet people began to talk about him as someone destined for great things. And if, while following him, you ever feel a disapproving cluck rise to your palate, as I sometimes do, don't forget that inside most people you read about in history books is a child who fiercely resisted toilet training. Suppose the mess they leave is inseparable from their reach and grasp? Then our judgment depends on what they're ambitious *for*—the saving glimmer of wanting something worthy.

THE FOREIGN SERVICE GAVE Holbrooke two years of unpaid leave to edit *Foreign Policy,* but he would never get back in line as a career officer and crawl his way up the ladder. When the leave ended in 1974, he would resign. "I may come back one day," he told Wisner, "but I'll be explicitly political. It would have to be with the Democrats, and I'll try for a senior policy position." The institution had a way of hemorrhaging talent and promoting mediocrity. Holbrooke and Lake, brightest lights of the class of 1962, were both out.

The war was not done and they were not done with the war. They would never be done with it. Holbrooke, Lake, and their generation entered government in what seemed like the late morning of American power. Then the dark came down early and they spent a decade trying to find their way through. They went in as true believers, and Vietnam upset every one of their assumptions about what it meant to serve the United States. How could there be a next Acheson and Kennan if

America was going into decline? They were still insiders, and neither conviction nor ambition would let them walk away from their chosen profession. But Vietnam was too big for them just to move on.

They carried the stigma of being on the scene at America's first lost war. The peril came not from the doves, who never gained much power, but from the hawks, who would blame them for stabbing America in the back. Holbrooke and his friends gained nothing in Washington from having faced the truth of the war. Vietnam fixed them with the dreaded label "soft," and it didn't matter that the hawks were dead wrong—in government that label could destroy you. The Vietnam civilians were spooked, marked by their primal experience—some of them were crippled by it. Holbrooke spent the rest of his life pointing out that the Vietnam War was not lost by the reporters, the Democrats in Congress, the anti-war movement, or insiders like him: "It was lost in the rice paddies of Indochina."

He tried to write his way through the war. At Princeton he composed sketches of his time in Vietnam, vivid essays with inconclusive endings. In Morocco he jotted down chapter headings for a book on key themes of the war ("Lying on the Outside," "Lying on the Inside," "Pacification—theory vs. practice," "American types in Asia: Lansdale—Ugly American—Quiet American") that he never wrote. He published pieces in the *Times*, the *Post*, and his own magazine, with titles like "The Machine That Fails," "A Little Lying Goes a Long Way," and "Relentless Patterns to Our Vietnam Nightmare," focusing on the destructive effects of official mendacity and overgrown bureaucracy—on the way his generation of Foreign Service officers was subtly corrupted by years of work on Vietnam. "Dissent took unusual courage," he wrote, "and so gradually it was suppressed except among the rare men of strength."

You can sense his aversion to sounding moralistic or panicky. He was thinking with crystal clarity but the feeling was muted. Vietnam threatened the heart of his mission in life, which was inextricable from the whole project of an American-led order. The task of restoring both to strength required great care.

Gelb, who had gone to work at the *Times*, wrote a long essay for *Foreign Policy*, later extended into a book called *The Irony of Vietnam: The System Worked*. He argued that the disaster was not an accident or perversion of American foreign policy, but the result of a quarter century of official consensus that South Vietnam must not fall to communism. America had believed its way into a needless war. The task was to understand the original failure to think critically about the country's real strategic interests. John Negroponte, who remained in the Foreign Service and replaced Lake as Kissinger's aide on Vietnam, wasn't free to write openly, but he gave the details of Kissinger's negotiations with Hanoi before the 1972 elections—how the peace deal secretly sold out the South Vietnamese—to the reporter Tad Szulc, who wrote an account that was the longest and most important article published during Holbrooke's time at *Foreign Policy.* Kissinger punished Negroponte with a post as consul general in Thessaloniki.

Of all Holbrooke's friends, Lake—the good soldier, the staff assistant who avoided the press—was the one most driven to reconsider American power. Vietnam left him grieving, and his reflections on the war were personal and anguished. In *Foreign Policy,* he and Roger Morris, who had resigned with him over Cambodia, described foreign policymaking as bloodless and indifferent to the consequences for human beings. They argued for the importance of the human factor in statecraft. Inside government, any mention of the appalling suffering in Vietnam meant that you were losing your "effectiveness," even your grip. "We remember, more clearly than we care to," the authors wrote, "the well carpeted stillness of those government offices where some of the Pentagon Papers were first written. The efficient staccato of the typewriter, the antiseptic whiteness of nicely margined memoranda, the affable, authoritative and always urbane men who wrote them—all of it is a spiritual as well as geographic world apart from piles of decomposing bodies in a ditch outside Hue or a village bombed in Laos, the burn ward of a children's hospital in Saigon, or even a cemetery or veteran's hospital here."

Holbrooke never let himself sound like that. He didn't gaze inward. As always, he was looking ahead.

JOHN CAMPBELL'S DEATH changed Holbrooke's life. *Foreign Policy's* offices at the Carnegie Endowment for International Peace, off Dupont Circle, gave him a high perch to wait out Republican rule in Washington while making himself an arbiter of policy views—soliciting pieces from Harriman and Zbigniew Brzezinski, turning down George McGovern. He had the power to advance or set back the professional hopes of younger writers who couldn't get their work into the stodgier *Foreign Affairs,* a mouthpiece of the establishment that had grown dull and irrelevant during the Vietnam years, once publishing back-to-back articles on "Japan: Eye on 1970" and "Japan Beyond 1970." *Foreign Policy,* designed to slip into a breast pocket rather than sit on a coffee table, was serious, but it wasn't dull. It began with the premise that the postwar era in American foreign policy was over, broken by Vietnam.

In May 1972, as if to show that there were no hard feelings, Holbrooke and Lake coauthored an op-ed in the *Post* criticizing Nixon's decision to bomb Hanoi and mine Haiphong harbor during a North Vietnamese offensive. Their tennis matches ended, their lunches grew rare, and when they appeared together at public events friends noticed a lot of tension. But the professional relationship continued. Lake wrote pieces on the war for Holbrooke's *Foreign Policy,* and Holbrooke wrote a chapter for a book Lake edited on the legacy of Vietnam, and he helped Lake to become the director of International Voluntary Services after the Muskie campaign imploded, and no one was the wiser.

Holbrooke was a single man in Washington. Nineteen seventy-two was a low, raunchy year, the year of *Deep Throat* and Deep Throat. At the Democratic National Convention in Miami Beach, Jack Nicholson and Julie Christie did nitrous oxide with journalists and movie agents, and everyone was sleeping with everyone else. The Harrimans were there, but unofficially, out of pride. After the backroom fiasco of Chicago, the party rules had been rewritten, and this time Averell had to campaign with Pamela door-to-door in upstate New York for a spot as a Democratic delegate. The great man lost to the George McGovern slate anyway. The Democrats were in such disarray that McGovern gave his acceptance speech at two-thirty in the morning, after rushing the nomination of a vice presidential candidate who had been treated for depression with electroshock therapy.

Holbrooke was in Miami Beach, too—keeping his distance from the far-left McGovern campaign—and so was a young couple named George and Anne Crile.

Anne was the twenty-two-year-old daughter of Joe Alsop's wife,

Susan Mary. Green eyes, tulip lips, luminous smile, fuck-you manner. Her best friend was Frank Wisner's sister. George Crile III was a reporter from a family of Cleveland medical royalty, a gorgeous philanderer who could steal your girl from under your nose with no hard feelings because he made everyone think they were the most interesting person he had ever met. That was how Crile met Tobias Wolff, who became his best friend. In 1972, George and Anne were living on the bad side of Dupont Circle with Wolff, who was out of the army and working the night shift on the police beat at the *Post*. The Criles were having the expected problems.

Anne knew of Holbrooke from Joe Alsop's salon in Georgetown and tennis doubles at Stewart Alsop's weekend house in Maryland. One day Holbrooke saw Anne breeze through Joe and Susan Mary's living room, and one glimpse was enough. He made a play for her that summer, when they were both on the verge of separations. To put George off the scent Holbrooke insinuated that Wolff was the one moving in on Anne. It wasn't true, but it nearly ended Wolff's friendship with Crile.

Holbrooke and Anne fell into an affair. Her attraction for him was obvious, including the Alsop connection. She was even a descendant of John Jay. What was his—a decade older, with two small boys—for her? His body had filled out since Vietnam, his broad face lacked definition, and his curly hair grew wild. In 1962 he had been an old-man boy; in 1972 he was a boyish man. There was an air of carelessness about him, but when he looked straight at them with the full power of his ice-blue eyes, his frank and playful intelligence, women felt seen and known and were drawn to him. That was something he discovered in the year 1972—that and the mind-boggling possibilities of sex. If you've been a geek for thirty-one years, it's an important discovery. He was an attentive lover, without kinks. He liked women and allowed them to see what his closest friends never did.

"I fell in love with my best friend's wife," he once confessed to Anne, and another time he spoke wistfully of his sons. His guilt was a wound he occasionally licked and it made him vulnerable. Anne had no interest in tending to the insecurities of a man in his thirties, so she kept herself back.

In the early spring of 1973 they went away for the weekend to a cabin outside Harper's Ferry. Over a picnic lunch he proposed to her. Anne was completely taken aback—for one thing, they were both married. This was how a man who had messed up his life behaved.

She stalled. "Where do you see yourself in five years?"

"I'm going to be the next Henry Kissinger."

Anne knew Kissinger from her parents' dining room and found him to be a pompous asshole. That was the end of her fling with Holbrooke. She returned to George Crile, though the marriage didn't last.

THERE WERE OTHER GIRLFRIENDS, but the important one after Anne was a British photographer, not quite thirty, named Gail Malcolm. She was brown haired and freckled and she wore floppy hats and her heart on her sleeve, going without makeup or other defenses. Holbrooke saw her across the room one night at a party and headed straight over to introduce himself.

"Oh, I just met your wife." Gail had run into Litty the week before at a brunch where much of the talk had been about Dick.

"That's not a very good way to start," he said. "Why don't you try again?"

Before leaving the party he slipped a note into her hand:

Dick Holbrooke
797–8405
Pls call

Later that night they ran into each other at another party. Gail was in the bathroom, lying in the bathtub fully dressed, when Holbrooke walked in. "Can I join you?" he asked. They danced, and it felt to Gail like slipping her hand into a glove. He drove her to the Capitol Hill apartment where she was house-sitting for the British journalist William Shawcross. Gail had nowhere of her own to live, she moved from friend to friend, everything in her life was up in the air.

A few nights later he took her out to dinner. They compared pasts and it turned out that she'd just broken up with George Crile. I sometimes think of Washington in these years as a sticky web of relations spun out by desire, with Holbrooke's long limbs spread-eagle at the center.

Back at the Shawcross apartment he made a move.

"This isn't the time or the place," Gail said.

"Would upstairs in ten minutes suit you?"

Just as seductive as his confidence was the warning of a friend of Gail's who had been at the brunch where she met Litty: "Whatever you do, do not get involved. He's fun, but stay away." They slipped into one of those 1970s relationships with no strings attached and hurt feelings inevitable.

She found a two-story townhouse for him on Corcoran Street near Dupont Circle and kept her stuff there. He would stay in bed till around ten and then walk over to *Foreign Policy*'s offices. He was taking a break from the climb—it wouldn't last forever, he warned her, but meanwhile they went to see *American Graffiti* and afterward danced like sock-hoppers up Wisconsin Avenue, and he spent an hour explaining the Yom Kippur War, and he read *Fear of Flying* because Gail said it captured how she felt. When she claimed to be able to spot an Englishman anywhere, he approached total strangers whom she IDed for him and posed random questions to hear their accent.

He told her that sex was a bonus for him, extra credit, cream on top of the other wonderful flavors of life. She said that for her it was a string of disastrous men. He knew how to make her laugh, and in her presence he didn't hesitate to cry. He never mentioned his parents, Litty was someone he hardly seemed to have known, and even Vietnam had vanished. He didn't look back, and she didn't push him to. She was the perfect companion for a slack season. "I just want to be beside you," he told her. "You make me feel tranquillized."

They once walked into a party together and Holbrooke immediately spotted Clark Clifford across the room. Gail had no idea who the silver-haired man on the sofa was, but from Holbrooke's hushed excitement she knew that he must be important. Holbrooke brought her over to be introduced, and as they chatted Clifford drew her out, expressing real interest in what she had to say, never once peering over her shoulder. Maybe that was Clifford's own style of ambition—part of how he became an advisor to four presidents. Afterward, Gail told Holbrooke how impressed she was by "Mr. Clark."

Holbrooke looked at her. "How does he do it? *How does he do it?*"

They had no future. His career didn't interest her. She wanted children, but she could never have his after seeing what kind of father he was, even if he wanted more, which he adamantly did not. Litty, who had her hands full with sole custody of the boys, a job at the Federal Trade Commission, and law school at night, found it easier to make arrangements with Gail than negotiate the terms of a handoff with Holbrooke. A weekend with his sons would compress to a day, always at his convenience, and then he would dump them on friends with kids like the Gelbs and the Wolffs, or else take them to swim at the Harrimans' and spend the whole visit talking with Averell, or absorb himself in *Time* while the boys tried more and more frantically to get his attention. "Just give them an hour," Gail told him. "Thirty minutes. Then you'll be fine." She took beautiful pictures of David and Anthony, and they clung to her instead of him.

Dick and Gail would drift apart and back together while he saw other women. On a trip to Berlin toward the end of 1975 he wrote to her: "Right now, and for at least one more year, I am apparently living a free-flowing life, travelling constantly, meeting astounding numbers of attractive women, and in general having a good time." He mentioned a few of them and told Gail that he couldn't promise her anything. "Maybe all this adds up to a creeping case of someone who wants his cake and eats it too. Am I too greedy for my own good? Perhaps so; that is a value judgment I leave to others. A phase? Perhaps so: time will tell. Something I must proceed with? Pour le moment. In any case, I try not to hurt anyone, and especially never you."

His friends thought he treated her shamelessly. "Why do you put up with it?" Genevieve Wisner asked, and Gail replied, "Because it doesn't impose anything on me." Even Holbrooke once asked her, "Why don't you protect yourself more?" Gail tried to break up a few times, but he always begged her to stay. Rejection was intolerable to him. If they were going to split, he would be the one to do it.

THE END MATERIALIZED in the fall of 1975, in the golden-brown skin and small curvy shape and smart hustle of a foreign policy news producer for public television named Blythe Babyak. She was twenty-three and just out of Yale, where she had excelled in one of the first classes to include women. Blythe approached him for an interview and he converted it into a date, during which they competed to show off who knew Kissinger's decade-old book on the Atlantic alliance better. Can you imagine a bigger turn-on for Holbrooke? Blythe mixed intelligence, ambition, and sex in a dish that was simply too much for him. At a Harriman dinner she flirted with Clark Clifford from her seat on the arm of his chair. At picnics she wore bikinis whose skimpiness infuriated the wives of his friends. On a ski trip to Vermont, Holbrooke pined for her so abjectly—"Oh Blythe, she's so good in bed, why won't she answer the phone? Do you think I should write her a letter?"—that Geoffrey Wolff and Pete Dawkins nearly threw him off a chairlift.

Blythe lived in New York, coming to Washington to see Holbrooke and employ his connections to scout career prospects in TV journalism. That attracted him, too. The great era of American newspapers was beginning to end, and the senior columnists of his youth, like Reston and Alsop, and the reporter heroes of his twenties, like Halberstam and Sheehan, were being displaced by TV stars—Barbara Walters, Mike Wallace—who covered politics as a spectacle akin to entertainment. Holbrooke wanted to learn how to ride the wave. He and Blythe looked at each other and saw appealing opportunities.

She was too savvy to tolerate his semi-live-in girlfriend. On a weekend visit to Corcoran Street, Blythe told Gail to disappear, then wrote

Holbrooke demanding that he do something about this other woman. By the summer of 1976, Holbrooke and Gail were through. In a post-breakup letter she told him that she loved him, and it made him cry—"Why didn't you say this before?"—as if Gail had been the one to drive him off to Blythe. But he was gearing up for the next stage, waiting for a break in the weather to resume the ascent, and an apolitical English-woman with a gift for photography, whose kindness tapped his deepest feelings, would not be the ideal climbing partner.

In the late fall, he asked Gail to come see him on Corcoran Street. By then she was engaged to an ACLU lawyer and civilian Vietnam hand named Mark Lynch, who was representing Lake in his lawsuit against Kissinger. Holbrooke was a mess—his hands were shaking. He had something to tell her but he couldn't bring himself to say it.

Holbrooke and Blythe were married in New York on New Year's Day 1977, in a chapel at the Cathedral of Saint John the Divine, where a Jewish Quaker could imagine that he had ascended to the WASP estab-lishment. Bishop Paul Moore, the husband of John Campbell's widow, Brenda, performed the ceremony in miter and cassock. He warned the couple that marriage was not to be entered into lightly. Four or five people attended, including Frank Wisner. "You're my WASP Episco-palian friend," Holbrooke had told him. "Will you be my best man?" Wisner thought Holbrooke should have married Gail, but after losing his wife, Genevieve, to brain cancer, Frank had turned to Holbrooke for support, and it was Holbrooke who had been there for him, and concern for their friendship prevented Wisner from replying that mar-rying Blythe was a terrible idea.

Holbrooke wouldn't have listened anyway. His new boss, Jimmy Carter, had made it clear that none of his top hires could live in sin.

Swallow Hard

How did a thirty-five-year-old semi-unknown get to be a high officer of the American imperium, assistant secretary of state for East Asian and Pacific affairs, the job Harriman had at seventy, and Rusk before him, claiming a hunk of the vast geography from Korea to Australia, from the teak forests of Burma to the island states of Polynesia out in the middle of the ocean, with the shadow of China sprawling over it all? How did he win a seat at the grown-ups' table in the Situation Room and become a big enough deal that the president's top advisor set out to destroy him? I don't know what you were doing in your mid-thirties, but I wasn't trying to establish diplomatic relations with two of America's former enemies simultaneously. For the first time Holbrooke was in a position to shape his country's policies. He had the chance to relieve human suffering, or ignore it, or make it worse, all in the national interest. That's the meaning of statecraft.

At times it drove him to frenzy, and he suffered lasting wounds. The story is worth telling, because if we watch him closely we can see what power looks like just below the treetops, where the animals are still fully exposed, hindquarters and all, but have climbed so close to the highest branches that their behavior in the fight for advantage gets wild.

Start on April 30, 1975. Holbrooke had lunch that day with Halberstam and Gelb. It was the last day of the Vietnam War. In the State Department Operations Center, Wisner and others were manning an emergency task force to rescue the Vietnamese who had staked their lives on America. Some of them made it onto the last helicopters out of Saigon; most didn't. The end of South Vietnam came with such violent swiftness that it shocked even people like Holbrooke who had long expected it. He sat down with a yellow legal pad and tried to sum up the war that had made him: "It was the most curious mixture of high idealism and stupidity, of deceit and self-deceit, of moving heroism and inexcusable cruelty. For a long time I tried to separate out these contradictory strains, to understand why some things seemed right and some others seemed wrong, to see also if there was any way that some good could come out of the whole mess. But then finally it all seemed to come down to one simple, horrible truth: we didn't belong there, we had no business doing what we were doing, even the good parts of it."

In the spring of 1975, the guilt-ridden left and the Manichean right converged on the same conclusion—the war had fatally weakened America. Henry Kissinger, Gerald Ford's secretary of state, went around saying that the fall of Saigon was a terrible blow to American credibility. The loss of Indochina turned Kissinger into a prophet of American decline.

Holbrooke was obsessed with Kissinger. He wasn't a strategic thinker on Kissinger's level, and he admired Kissinger's brilliance and envied his power and fame, and he also despised him. In public Holbrooke said, "He is the most successful diplomat and negotiator in American history, but he is one of the most devious men ever to serve in high office . . . Here is a man placed in a position to do something which might reduce suffering, and he has often either done nothing or done something which increased the human problem."

In private he called Kissinger a liar, an amoral and deeply cynical man with an overblown reputation, who, even if he committed no crimes, contributed to the culture of Watergate by bugging his own aides. The 1973 Paris Accords, for which Kissinger received the Nobel Peace Prize, was basically the same deal that Holbrooke and his colleagues in Paris could have had in 1968—five years and hundreds of thousands of deaths later, with the fire spread to the whole of Indochina. After the signing ceremony, Kissinger lost interest in Vietnam. "We want a decent interval," he once scribbled in a briefing book—a two- or three-year grace period between American withdrawal and Communist victory that would disguise the abandonment of South Vietnam. "Obviously there's nothing decent about the interval at all," Holbrooke told Neil Sheehan after the war. "It's an indecent interval. He probably didn't think much about it, and he certainly couldn't imagine the dimensions of the catastrophe."

Kissinger's view of Holbrooke was just as jaundiced. "I am an expert on Holbrooke," he told his top aides at the State Department. "He was my chief source of information on the department when I was designated assistant to the president. During the last transition period he was leaking stuff to me all the time." He added, "You have to admit that at least Holbrooke has reached some minimum level of intelligence. But he is the most viperous character I know around this town." That's something, coming from Kissinger.

Holbrooke didn't see the fall of Saigon as a giant step in American decline. The end of the war almost came as a relief, and it opened a path for him to take his own place in administering the Pax Americana. Economically, culturally, politically, militarily, the United States was still the most powerful country in the world. What ailed it was a loss of faith—bad leaders and the decade and a half of Vietnam and Watergate that degraded American values. In the new era, with new and better leadership, the United States could set aside its "demicolonial" role in Asia and restore its position without resorting to B-52s.

He commissioned articles for *Foreign Policy* on natural resources, global economics, human rights, and the environment—soft transnational issues that held no interest for a student of power politics like Kissinger. The domino theory was dead, containment passé, and the Cold War itself hardly figured into Holbrooke's thinking. In the *New York Times Magazine,* he even suggested withdrawing American troops from South Korea. In his own magazine he wrote, "We still possess, in addition to the sheer measurable elements of power already mentioned, an enormous force that we cannot use these days, but that I hope will once again, someday, be part of our 'arsenal'—the basic moral force that exists in the principles of our system of government—a force eroded in recent years under leaders who apparently did not really believe in them."

Vietnam sorted most foreign policy types into extreme hawks and doves. Few came out of the war, as Holbrooke did, speaking the liberal internationalism of his heroes from the Truman years.

PUBLISHING THINK PIECES was one way to position himself to get
back into the game. Another was to accompany Senator Walter Mondale of Minnesota on a high-profile trip to the Middle East and Europe.
And another was to join the kind of elite global groups for world peace
and free markets—the Trilateral Commission, the Bilderberg Group,
the Council on Foreign Relations—that give insiders a chance to meet
the right people and swell their reputations while filling outsiders with
resentful paranoid fantasies. Everyone in these groups knows what
everyone else is up to, and everyone accepts the charade.

A month after the fall of Saigon, the Trilateral held its annual conference in Kyoto. The commission was run by a starchy, sharp-featured
Polish immigrant and Columbia political scientist named Zbigniew
Brzezinski. He was on the board of *Foreign Policy* and had pissed
Holbrooke off by giving an article promised for the magazine to its
rival *Foreign Affairs* instead. Brzezinski was frantically networking the
whole time in Kyoto. Among those present was the governor of Georgia, whom Brzezinski and David Rockefeller had selected as a member,
and who was about to take Brzezinski as his own personal Kissinger.

It was in Kyoto that Holbrooke met Jimmy Carter for the first time.
He was running as a long shot for president and used the Trilateral
to burnish his foreign policy credentials. Holbrooke had a loose commitment to Sargent Shriver, a placeholder for a stronger commitment
to Shriver's brother-in-law Ted Kennedy, but in January 1976 he was
invited to join Carter at a dinner of about ten people in Washington.
Among these policy bigs, Carter was unintimidated, thoughtful, determined. His views were close enough to Holbrooke's, but the attraction
was more instinctual—as a moderate white southerner Carter spanned
the divisions of the Democratic Party and seemed capable of uniting
them. He offered the moral leadership that Holbrooke believed necessary to cleanse the smell of the Johnson-Nixon-Kissinger years. He was
practically a Vietnam virgin, had barely taken a position on the war. He
was the new man the country needed, and he could win. When Carter
asked for the backing of the dinner guests, Holbrooke was in.

At that point Carter had the support of around 4 percent of Democratic voters. Gelb, who joined him once on a flight from Indiana to

Georgia and found him to be an exceedingly thin reed, thought Holbrooke was crazy. But Holbrooke's political nose was one of his gifts. Two months later, he helped Polly Wisner arrange a larger, glitzier dinner for Carter on P Street. Carter was practically running against Georgetown, and Polly's new husband, a journalist named Clayton Fritchey, toasted him: "Governor, you're going to find this is not such a bad town." Holbrooke became one of Carter's main conduits to Washington and the biggest big in Georgetown, Averell Harriman, who was indignant that the Democratic candidate was someone he had never even met.

The other thing to do was write campaign memos, and starting in March Holbrooke sent Carter a steady stream of advice. He wrote that presidential advisors from Bundy to Kissinger had amassed outsized power in the White House. The State Department should have the central role in running foreign policy, and the president should choose people for their ability to play well together, like the Bill Russell Celtics, not for their individual brilliance. After getting one of these memos, Carter wrote back to thank Holbrooke in his cloying confessional style, a perfect fit with the mellow populism of the mid-seventies: "PS. I feel at ease with you! J."

By May Holbrooke was on Carter's foreign policy task force, and in late July, after the convention in New York—around the time Holbrooke finally dropped Gail for Blythe—he flew to campaign headquarters in Atlanta and became the nominee's foreign policy coordinator. Lake came down after Labor Day to put together the campaign's transition papers. Holbrooke claimed to have landed him the spot, but it turned out to have been Cyrus Vance.

And then one last pre-election memo to the candidate, thanking Carter for the opportunity, reminding Carter of his early support, repeating the advice to choose team players, and summing up his own career in Vietnam, Washington, Paris, and Morocco: "If there is anything of value to you from this experience, which I believe is greater than that of almost anyone else in the foreign and defense fields today, it is entirely at your disposal at any time." On November 15, President-elect Carter wrote back and said what Holbrooke longed to hear: "Your performance was impeccable. I want your direct & personal recommendations about major appointments in my administration."

On Thanksgiving, Carter called from Plains. Holbrooke was sitting by the fireplace at the Wisner farm in eastern Maryland. And that was when he made the biggest mistake of his short career.

Carter listed possible cabinet choices and asked for Holbrooke's views, and Holbrooke enthused over them all, especially Vance. He knew Vance well as Harriman's deputy in Paris in 1968—a gentleman of the dying WASP establishment who learned almost genetically how to whisper into the ear of power, so self-effacing and committed to fair play that Joe Alsop compared him to a piece of bread dunked in milk. The catastrophe of Vietnam had edged Vance from the respectable center toward the liberal left—he was sympathetic to Third World grievances, took negotiation as his first principle, and wanted more than anything to resume the thaw in U.S.-Soviet relations. He was the kind of establishment figure who would mesh well with Carter's post-Vietnam worldview.

"You haven't said anything about national security advisor," Carter prodded, almost teasingly, "or yourself."

"There are a lot of people who could do the NSC job," Holbrooke said. He named a few, including Tony Lake. "I'll serve you in any capacity you want—I'll be honored. But the job that would really excite me would be Asia," he went on. "The Far East is where America has had its great problem over the past thirty years. Our last three wars have started out there, and we've had the greatest domestic battles over who lost China and Korea, Vietnam and Cambodia. And I think that your administration could be the turning point. We could put back together a coherent policy that ended this and built a logical position in Asia."

Carter listened, and then he asked, "What about Zbig and the NSC?"

Holbrooke paused. Brzezinski—the son of a Polish diplomat who had been a refugee from both Nazism and communism—was a hawk on the Soviet Union. He saw the world hard and clear through the Cold War lens that Holbrooke found too narrow. He reminded Holbrooke too much of Kissinger—a famous academic with an abstract mind who spoke the language of realpolitik in a European accent and was possessed of an ego so large that he would try to pull foreign policy into his office at the White House, if only to compete with Kissinger's legacy. The State Department would be further diminished, and Vance eaten alive.

In personal terms, Brzezinski could never become a benevolent patron like Harriman or Clifford or Vance, nor could Holbrooke ever be his flattering acolyte. They were already rivals, and during the campaign Holbrooke had shot down more than one of his proposals. Brzezinski was a different creature from the old Georgetown establishment. He belonged to a new generation of foreign policy professionals—academic experts, products of universities and think tanks, more partisan, less secure, given to perpetual feuding. They were good at self-publicity, and they came to power by attaching themselves to a politician and riding him as far as he could take them, as Kissinger had done with Nelson Rockefeller and then Nixon, as Brzezinski had done with Carter.

Holbrooke didn't say any of this to Carter. Instead, he gently suggested that Vance and Brzezinski would be more like the runner-up Lakers than the championship Celtics. "Governor, I don't think that Vance and Brzezinski will make a good team. I think Brzezinski is too combative and has too strong a personal agenda for that job."

Carter was silent, and his silence nearly froze the phone in Holbrooke's hand. This was not what the president-elect had called to hear. Holbrooke had assumed an intimacy ("I feel at ease with you!"), an openness to frank talk that didn't exist. Abruptly Carter thanked him and hung up. That was the end of any warmth between them, and any chance for Holbrooke to maintain a détente with Brzezinski, who became one of the two or three most powerful men in the new administration and Holbrooke's dedicated enemy.

Vance called Holbrooke the next week to tell him that Carter had offered him secretary of state and Holbrooke assistant secretary for Asia, making him the youngest in department history.

"That's great news, Cy," Holbrooke said. "What about Brzezinski?"

"I told the president-elect that I can work with anyone," Vance replied, true to his code.

You might not recall the hope that came with Jimmy Carter. You probably think of the gas lines, blindfolded hostages, double-digit inflation, 20 percent interest rates, Carter wrapped in his cardigan in the Oval Office solemnly preaching low thermostats, collapsing from heat stroke during a six-mile road race, delivering the nationally televised "malaise" speech, which was actually the "crisis of confidence" speech. In the late seventies everything kept getting uglier and shabbier—cities, cars, AM music. Carter swore that unlike his predecessors he'd always tell the truth to the American people, and he was pretty much as good as his word, and the American people turned him out for it. He was the last president to make that mistake.

But he came in with hope and a long-toothed smile and hair over his ears. He ran against Washington, as everyone since him has done. He was a blank slate, and he promised the renewal that Americans perpetually seek in a republic founded by the grandchildren of Puritans—a renewal through politics that transcends politics and is therefore doomed by politics. In 1980, after everything had gone wrong, Holbrooke wrote in a notebook: "1976—I did not see JC clearly. I was too dazzled by the proximity, its opportunity, his intelligence—overlooking the problems, + minimized them."

AFTER THEIR NEW YEAR'S DAY wedding, Holbrooke and Blythe went off to Palm Beach for a week. They spent much of the time with the Harrimans at their estate in Hobe Sound. Holbrooke told his new special assistant, Kenneth Quinn—a Foreign Service officer who had spent six years in the Mekong Delta—to handle all matters in his absence. Blythe didn't want to be disturbed by Washington business on their honeymoon.

Holbrooke was officially sworn in by Vance on March 31 in the John Quincy Adams State Drawing Room on the eighth floor of the State Department. This was before the top floors were renovated like a museum of eighteenth-century Americana, with period brass hardware and furniture and chandeliers and portrait paintings, as if no actual work is going on in the foreign ministry of the global superpower. The room where Holbrooke took the oath still had the brutal drabness of the building's functional mid-century origin, with wall-to-wall carpeting and an acoustical-tile ceiling. His mother was there, and his sons, Averell and Pamela Harriman, Clark Clifford, Polly and Frank Wisner, Tony Lake, Holbrooke's Vietnam circle, his journalist friends—and John Helble, the personnel counselor who, at their session in 1967, had suppressed a snicker when Holbrooke said that he expected to be an assistant secretary by thirty-five. As country director for Thailand and Burma, Helble was required to witness the fulfillment of his new boss's prediction.

Holbrooke was so grateful for Helble's decade-old advice to quit the Foreign Service that he offered to make him an ambassador. But Helble was an organization man who didn't believe in promotion above his rank and preferred to remain at the proper level, which dumbfounded Holbrooke. He had no time for plodding, unimaginative career types— foreign policy was drama and adventure! As Helble watched Holbrooke sweep out the old staff and hire his own without regard to protocol (he made it a priority to hire black civil servants), tell the deputy assistant secretaries that their offices needed painting and could they please vacate temporarily, then replace them—as Helble watched Holbrooke blow through the East Asia bureau, he decided to transfer out to the Inspector General's Office, and he never saw Holbrooke again.

So he bruised people on his way in, and we barely know their names. Maybe they deserved it. Maybe he could do what he wanted to Foreign Service officers whose next assignment would be in the Procurement Office of the Bureau of Administration. He gave it no thought; he was acting on instinct in the name of excellence. A colleague in Saigon was "that guy who sold bidets in France"; a colleague during Bosnia was "the best note-taker in the history of the State Department." His central nervous system required losers. There's something heedless and needless about these scattered cruelties, as if none of them mattered—but in the end they would all count.

The bureau was in the southwest corner of the sixth floor. A key measure of status in Washington is proximity to power, and in the State Department your status drops one floor at a time. Officials refer to "the seventh floor," meaning the secretary's mahogany-paneled suite, as if it's the Palace of Heavenly Purity in the Forbidden City. Being a floor down was a constant source of aggravation to Holbrooke, worsened by the fact that all his friends had landed offices above him. Lake was director of policy planning, the job originated by his mother's onetime fiancé George Kennan in 1947—first door outside the secretary's suite. (Toni overcame her misgivings about losing her husband to government again, but she made him promise to refuse weeknight invitations, and Lake complied.) Gelb was next door to Lake, director of politico-military affairs. Peter Tarnoff, a close friend of Holbrooke and Lake from Saigon days and a consummately elegant diplomat, was in

the heart of the secretary's suite as Vance's executive assistant. Wisner, who declined an offer to work for Holbrooke in order to preserve the friendship, was Tarnoff's deputy. Lake's closeness to Vance unnerved Holbrooke, who frequently visited Gelb's office in search of intelligence that Lake might be undermining him with their boss. Gelb saw no evidence of it, but he did notice that his two friends no longer talked unless required to by work.

Holbrooke invented any reason he could think of to go upstairs and chat with Tarnoff and Wisner outside Vance's office, or hang around the secretary's private elevator, or invite himself into the secretary's limousine as it waited outside the building. Vance was too polite to object, so it fell to his personal secretary, Elva Morgan, to send Holbrooke a memo:

> This office exclusively schedules appropriate individuals to ride with the Secretary to and from various meetings. Your office and other bureaus of the Department cannot be constantly apprised of the Secretary's frequently-changing schedule or other personal arrangements made in his behalf. Henceforth, you may not insert yourself as a passenger in the Secretary's car unless this office has specifically approved your request to accompany him. The Secretary's security

detail has been instructed to permit you to ride in the automobile only when it has received prior authorization from this office.

Holbrooke, undeterred, had the memo framed.

A new administration whirls into power bent on changing everything its predecessor did, and Carter's was no different, and nowhere did the disturbance register more sharply than in Holbrooke's corner at East Asia. He acted less like an assistant secretary of state (hardly a glamorous job—how many can you name?) than a young politician whose star was rising fast. He tended feverishly to his various constituencies. He was constantly on the Hill or calling members of Congress, buddying up with Tip O'Neill, Ted Kennedy, and John Glenn. He offered himself as a source to important reporters, none more valuable than *Time* magazine's diplomatic correspondent Strobe Talbott, who became a close friend. Since the Republican administration had neglected the U.S.-Japan relationship, he organized a softball game near the Lincoln Memorial between the bureau and the Japanese embassy, and he smashed the Japanese ambassador's first pitch far over the parked cars for a home run, laughing all the way around the bases as the ambassador, who had just lost face with his U.S. allies, looked on. He gave his staff, not personal warmth—during conversations he was always on a phone call and shuffling paperwork—but intellectual stimulation, openness to dissent, and a sense of collective mission. In return they gave him their best.

His larger purpose was to restore our influence in the region by freeing the United States from its overlord role. This vision was in sync with Carter, who gave an early speech warning against a foreign policy that abandoned American values and bidding goodbye to "that inordinate fear of communism which once led us to embrace any dictator who joined us in that fear." The superpower standoff—the central foreign policy issue of the postwar era—didn't much interest Holbrooke. The prospect of World War III was too abstract and static, too *boring*. But countries interested him, and none more than Vietnam.

IN MARCH 1977, Carter sent a delegation to Hanoi, led by the autoworkers chief Leonard Woodcock, to find out about missing American servicemen. Unofficially, the purpose of the mission was to be able to say that no American was left alive in Indochina. The POW/MIA question was the issue that still made Vietnam dangerous for politicians, because it embodied the grief and humiliation and rage of the American defeat, and so it became a potent myth of betrayal, a weapon in the hands of the stab-in-the-back right wing. This is why, decades past any chance of finding Americans alive or dead in Indochina, black POW/MIA flags still fly all over the country. Because we still can't accept that we lost the war.

But in 1977 there were Americans missing in Vietnam. Kissinger had refused to even talk to the Vietnamese until they accounted for them all. Holbrooke tore up that policy—he had bigger things in mind.

Quinn, Holbrooke's special assistant, was on the Woodcock delegation, along with, among others, Jim Rosenthal from Saigon days, now working for Holbrooke at East Asia. Quinn was shocked to find central Hanoi relatively unscathed by the war—the old colonial quarter was intact, the big trees around Hoan Kiem Lake still standing. For all the thousands of tons of American bombs, the heart of the enemy capital was spared.

The Americans were courteously received by the Vietnamese in a series of meetings and dinners. Then they were driven to a cemetery outside Hanoi and taken into a dark, cramped room where they were shown a collection of small metal boxes, two feet by three. The boxes contained the bones of American airmen shot down over North Vietnam.

On the last day Quinn joined his colleagues in an honor guard at the airport. The boxes, a folded American flag placed on each one, were carried up the ramp onto the plane, and as he stood at attention with his hand over his heart, Quinn, who had spent his six years in South Vietnam accompanying Special Forces troops on combat operations, felt that he was fulfilling the commitment he had learned from those soldiers: to leave no Americans behind, however hard the effort, whether you knew them or not.

The Woodcock delegation returned to Washington with the remains and a sense that Vietnamese leaders were ready to move on. This was what Carter wanted as well—to be the president who healed the wounds of the war. Vance believed that, with a presence in Hanoi, the United

States could moderate Soviet influence in Southeast Asia by diplomacy rather than military might. In early May, he sent his assistant secretary to Paris to negotiate the terms of normalization with the Socialist Republic of Vietnam.

Holbrooke and his aides stayed at the Hôtel de Crillon, where the Harriman-Vance delegation had stayed in 1968. The two sides met in Vietnam's unfinished new embassy, with emergency plants and pictures installed but not much furniture. Holbrooke's opposite number was Phan Hien, Vietnam's deputy foreign minister, who had also been in Paris in '68 as roughly Holbrooke's counterpart—they'd had an authorized dinner one evening in the Bois de Vincennes. Now Phan Hien, smiling, hair slicked carefully back, fluent in French, was in Paris again to represent a unified and victorious Vietnam. As Holbrooke sat across from the Vietnamese, he remembered being the junior American at the end of the table while the great Harriman represented the United States, and now he felt with a heavy jolt what it meant to be the one speaking for his country.

He didn't look like a diplomat. His hair was a tangled thicket, his glasses dwarfed his face, his tie was off-kilter, his shirttail kept coming untucked. Once, on an official trip to Japan, he had to borrow a pair of suit pants from a colleague after forgetting to pack his own; on another trip, a pair of socks. But for the first time in his life the TV cameras were focused on him; he was front-page news. Everything seemed aligned for Holbrooke to be the American who would bring a final end to the war of his youth.

It didn't take long for him to be reminded what tough, disciplined negotiators the Vietnamese Communists were. When he offered to drop the U.S. veto of Vietnam's seat at the United Nations, Phan Hien produced a secret letter from Richard Nixon to North Vietnam's prime minister, Pham Van Dong, a side agreement to the 1973 Paris Accords, promising almost five billion dollars in American reconstruction aid. Now Vietnam wanted the money as a condition for relations. The Carter people were vaguely aware of the letter and considered it null and void. North Vietnam had violated the accords with its final invasion of the South, and anyway, the American people and Congress were in no mood to pay what amounted to war reparations (though Phan Hien avoided the term). Holbrooke considered the secret letter a typical Nixon-Kissinger deception—they wrote it as a sweetener for North Vietnam, didn't bother telling the American people about it, and never had any intention of honoring it.

Holbrooke told Phan Hien that aid could be discussed only after normalization. But the Vietnamese wouldn't let it go. They had won the war, and winners dictated terms. And they desperately needed the money. Victory had bankrupted the country.

At the second meeting the next day, faced with a stalemate, Holbrooke leaned across the table, looked Phan Hien in the eye, and said, "Mr. Minister, let's leave aside the issues that divide us. Let us go outside and jointly declare to the press that we have decided to normalize relations."

The room was silent. Holbrooke had no written instructions to make such an offer. He had gone completely off script. Over the years this would be his diplomatic technique—seize the moment, create drama, try to push something loose when everything was jammed. He cared far less about the process than the result.

In a voice so quiet it was barely audible, Phan Hien said, in English, "Not without aid."

Holbrooke, on the verge of making history, was utterly deflated.

After the meeting, Phan Hien held a press conference and made Nixon's letter public. Holbrooke called him afterward. "You understand, Mr. Minister, that you have now done immense damage to these negotiations."

"Why?"

"Because the Congress is going to react very, very badly to this." Holbrooke reminded Phan Hien that it took sixteen years for the United States to recognize the USSR, twenty-three to establish a liaison office in the People's Republic of China. "Do you want to wait twenty-three years before we have relations?"

He overshot it by just five.

Holbrooke sensed that the Vietnamese had lost their political touch with the Americans. They didn't understand that Congress was no longer a dovish counterweight to a hawkish presidency as it had been during the war. Now that Americans were no longer destroying Vietnam, the years of guilt were over. These were the years of sour memories. Congress, like the rest of the country, wanted to forget about Vietnam.

And in fact, right after Phan Hien's press conference, Congress took up and soon passed legislation banning aid to Vietnam and imposing a trade embargo. Diplomacy depends on political support at home—that was a lesson Holbrooke had learned in 1968.

He didn't give up. But there was another obstacle, and it was right in the White House.

AT FIRST ZBIGNIEW BRZEZINSKI had no strong feelings about normalization one way or the other. To him Vietnam symbolized something larger: a fatal loss of confidence among Democrats. He considered the State Department a convalescent home for wounded Vietnam veterans. Holbrooke, Lake, Gelb, Tarnoff, even Vance, who had been McNamara's deputy—all crippled by the Vietnam syndrome and reluctant to use American power. "I cannot help suspecting that guilt feelings over the Vietnamese war have something to do with the evident desire of Cy and Holbrooke to move on this issue rapidly," he wrote in a memo to Carter, who snapped back in the margin, "I don't have guilt feelings & I want to move re VNam."

Brzezinski considered Vance a member of the dying WASP elite, with its outdated values and rules. The seventies was a decade of nonstop upheaval around what we used to call the Third World, and in the age of Qaddafi and Castro U.S. foreign policy could not be made by a New York litigator who saw international relations as a protracted negotiation between parties to a dispute. Both American politics and geopolitics had grown too rough for the discreet bipartisan institution builders of the postwar years. The times required someone younger, brasher, and more ideological. Brzezinski's nose and pompadour were shaped like an axe-head. Vance could do the talking with other countries, but Brzezinski saw the White House, not the State Department, as the center of policymaking. It took him about a week in office to throw his first punch inside the government. It was aimed at Holbrooke.

In late January, Vice President Mondale was scheduled to visit Tokyo on a tour of allied capitals, and Holbrooke was to accompany him. Brzezinski's deputy, David Aaron, told the NSC member on the trip, Michael Armacost, that his main job was to keep Holbrooke out of the meeting with the Japanese prime minister.

"But the purpose of the NSC is to coordinate policy with the inter-agency," Armacost protested.

"*Do it*," Aaron told him.

Aaron had worked for Mondale in the Senate, which put him in a position to make sure the blow hit home. It wasn't as if Holbrooke's presence would matter. Not even Mondale would be free to speak his mind—he had instructions from Carter to tell the prime minister that Japan was an important ally, and that human rights in neighboring countries like South Korea and the Philippines would have a major effect on the new administration's policies. But keeping someone out of a meeting is about the rawest form of bureaucratic power. Whenever it happened to Holbrooke—and it would happen a lot—he fought and clawed as if his oxygen supply had been cut off.

Armacost and Holbrooke shared a commercial flight to Paris. As they talked into the night, and Holbrooke glanced through top-secret cables, ripped them up, and stuffed the pieces into his seat pocket, Armacost decided that he didn't want to start the new administration by reigniting the war between the NSC and State that Kissinger had launched in 1969. Before they reached Tokyo he found a way to get Holbrooke into the meeting with the Japanese prime minister. (Three years later, Armacost went to work for Holbrooke at East Asia.)

Back in Washington, Holbrooke, Lake, Gelb, and Tarnoff warned Vance that Brzezinski was already trying to get at him through his subordinates—planting news stories that portrayed them as hopeless left-wingers, cutting State out of policy memos that went straight to Carter for approval. They urged Vance to fight back. Vance didn't want to hear it, and he ended the discussion by slamming his hand on his desk and asserting that he knew how to work with Brzezinski. Holbrooke and Gelb joined the battle anyway, using their many friends in the press. When a story in *Time* attacking Brzezinski quoted an unnamed State Department official, Vance called Gelb into his office: "Did you do it?" Gelb admitted to being the source. "Don't do it again," Vance told him. "That's the wrong way. It will only spread the poison and make it worse. I'll take the issues up with the president, but I'm not going to talk to him about Zbig or any bureaucratic nonsense. I'll talk to him about the issues. That's the way to do it."

That was the old way to do it. It worked for a little while. But Carter didn't belong to Vance's world, and it was Brzezinski who had the president's ear first thing in the morning, in the holy hush of the Oval Office. His aggressiveness appealed to Carter. And, like all modern presidents, Carter preferred to go around his own bureaucracy. Interagency war was inevitable.

Brzezinski's China expert at the NSC was a Michigan political scientist named Michel Oksenberg. Holbrooke and Oksenberg shared the goal of establishing diplomatic relations with the People's Republic, an issue they would need to work on together, and so at the start of the administration he invited Oksenberg to breakfast. "I want to make one commitment with you—one promise," Holbrooke said. "We will not keep secrets from each other. We will tell each other everything we know so that there is no rivalry between us." He was trying to reduce his exposure to the coming bureaucratic storm. "Let's shake on it," Holbrooke said, and they shook.

But Oksenberg was Brzezinski's guy, and Holbrooke was Vance's guy, and in Washington whose guy you were mattered more than whether you agreed on policy or shook hands over breakfast. Foreign policy is given to heavy internal bleeding, for reasons I've never really understood—perhaps they'll become clear as we go along. And yet, in the sorry tale of the Carter battles, Brzezinski and Holbrooke belonged to the same species. They were political animals, street fighters with sky-high self-opinions who craved publicity and saw government service as a zero-sum struggle. They also agreed on China. They both wanted to push ahead quickly with normalization—more quickly than Vance, who didn't want the issue to upset delicate talks with the Soviet Union over the SALT II arms treaty limiting nuclear missiles, not to mention the Panama Canal treaty, which was facing an intense debate in Congress. Vance had the whole world to juggle but Holbrooke had just the countries of East Asia, none as important as China. The key geopolitical fact of the seventies was that relations between the two Communist giants had grown much worse than relations between either of them and the capitalist superpower, and Chinese fear of Soviet expansion gave the United States a strategic opportunity. By the mid-seventies, Nixon and Kissinger's opening to Beijing had stalled because of Watergate, conservative backlash, and the radical Gang of Four that took power near the end of Mao's life. Now Mao was dead, the Gang of Four under arrest, the reformer Deng Xiaoping rehabilitated and back in power, and America had a new president who wanted peaceful relations with the entire world.

Vance flew to Beijing in August 1977, along with Holbrooke, Oksenberg, and Holbrooke's deputy William Gleysteen, a veteran Asia hand, to begin talks about normalization. The Communist Party had just finished choosing the Eleventh Central Committee, and the streets of Beijing were lined with hundreds of thousands of people, chanting slogans and joylessly celebrating in the revolutionary Maoist way for the very last time.

The Americans were lodged at the same guesthouse where Nixon had stayed in 1972. Holbrooke soon noticed the ritual pattern of talks with the Chinese. They seemed to replicate the ancient and arduous path of petitioners trying to gain an audience with the emperor in the Forbidden City, who were made to wait for days, then to pay bribes to officials of various levels in the outer courtyards, before they were finally granted entry to the Celestial Throne and, having already given everything away, approached the emperor empty-handed as beggars. So the American diplomats were first brought to meet the foreign minister, Huang Hua, who waited to see if the visitors were foolish enough to change their position unilaterally. Vance avoided the trap, and only after two meetings with Huang Hua were the Americans told that they would be allowed to see Deng.

He received them in the Great Hall of the People, with its towering two-story entrance. Deng was a tiny figure, five feet tall, in a blue-gray Mao suit, standing at the end of a long corridor and seeming to grow even smaller as the Americans approached. He was smiling, and the smile gave an impression of adorableness. (When Blythe first laid eyes on Deng, as he descended the ramp of his plane at Andrews Air Force Base on his historic visit to the United States in January 1979, she cried, "He's so cute!") But Deng was all business. At the age of seventy-three he was enjoying his third political life after two deaths by purge. "You know I am the only man who was twice resurrected," he quipped to Vance. Now he was in a hurry to begin the modernization of China's economy.

As Deng and Vance exchanged remarks, Holbrooke became fascinated with Deng's eyes. They gleamed from deep pouches of leathery skin. They seemed not to look at the person he was talking to but to gaze at something in the far distance—backward to the blood-soaked history of the People's Republic, or ahead to the rich and powerful future Deng wanted for his country. Holbrooke had never met any leader so unsentimental, ruthless, quick to brush aside obstacles—so ready to smash the clay pot of history and seize the gems stored inside.

The only topic that disturbed Deng's calm was Vietnam. He complained bitterly about Vietnam's ingratitude for China's help during the two Indochinese wars, and his voice rose in anger, his hands gestured wildly, his words grew intemperate. In Deng's eyes, Vietnam was becoming a Soviet satellite, an "Asian Cuba." China's antagonism was so great that it had in effect switched sides on the Vietnam War. Deng regarded American doves as naïve—he preferred to deal with the hawks. Holbrooke couldn't tell where this put him, but Deng knew something of his history, and when the subject of Vietnam came up, Deng kept looking at Holbrooke sideways.

The talks on normalization didn't go well. With the Panama Canal debate about to begin, Carter wasn't ready to antagonize Congress, and so Vance, stiff and ill at ease, didn't move away from an American commitment to keep some official presence on Taiwan. This crossed the Chinese red line, and Deng argued sharply that the Carter administration was taking a step back from the discussions he'd had with Ford and Kissinger. The Americans went home with the burden of an unsuccessful trip.

HISTORY LOOKS INEVITABLE afterward, but the failures to launch with both Vietnam and China were the kind of missed chances that come from bad timing, or when one side misreads the other, or an official on the spot doesn't have the freedom or character to seize a fleeting moment. "Policy is not a dry, airless product that emerges full-blown from the heads of people," Holbrooke later wrote. "It is often the product of accidents, egos and ambitions in conflict, misunderstandings, and deception, as well as careful plans." To succeed, diplomacy requires political support at home and something even harder to gain—a knowledgeable read of the other country's politics, which is like mastering a foreign language with an impossible orthography. Diplomacy also needs momentum, and the rest of 1977 and the first months of 1978 passed without movement on either front. By the time talks resumed, the terrain had changed dramatically.

In Vance's failure Brzezinski saw an opening. At the end of 1977, he wangled an invitation from the Chinese to visit Beijing, and then, over several months of maneuver and subterfuge, he secured Carter's agreement to let him go, which meant in effect that China policy was taken away from State and given to the NSC. Vance was stunned, resisted, gave in, and then insisted that Holbrooke and Gleysteen join the trip, which was scheduled for the middle of May 1978. During preparations Brzezinski singled out Holbrooke for treatment so nasty that it violated his role as the coordinator of policy. He refused to let Holbrooke read the talking points for key meetings. When Holbrooke pushed for a larger role for State, Brzezinski called him at home at six-thirty in the morning and screamed that he would keep Holbrooke off the plane. "I have never heard such a vile, profane man," Holbrooke complained to Oksenberg. "Zbig yelled at me over the phone so loud that it woke up my wife!"

The humiliation continued all through the trip. On the flight over, Brzezinski showed his talking points to Gleysteen on the condition that he not give them to Holbrooke. Brzezinski planned to keep Holbrooke and the rest of State's contingent out of the crucial encounter with Deng, and when Holbrooke found out, he was enraged. Unable to fight his own cause, he enlisted Leonard Woodcock, now Carter's envoy in Beijing. At dinner on the first night Woodcock tried to talk Brzezinski out of such a naked slight. Wouldn't it seem strange to the Chinese for the State Department to be missing from the most important session of the talks?

"You represent the State Department, don't you?" Brzezinski said.

"Frankly, I think of myself as representing the president," Woodcock replied.

Brzezinski wouldn't budge. The next day, on a tour of the Forbidden City, Gleysteen begged him: "Zbig, this is totally wrong, you are destroying the processes of government, you have to have Holbrooke in the meeting."

"Screw you," Brzezinski snapped. "I'm not going to."

Brzezinski and Deng saw the world in light of the Soviet threat, and

the shared adversary brought the two sides closer. On a visit to the Great Wall, within earshot of reporters, Brzezinski challenged his Chinese escorts to a race to the top—whoever lost had to fight the Russians in Ethiopia. He flattered his hosts, teased them with offers of technology transfers and intelligence sharing. He made it clear that Taiwan would not stand in the way of mutual recognition between two great nations.

No one, including the Chinese, was spared the spectacle of Brzezinski desecrating the corpse of his fallen foe. He stuck Holbrooke at the back of every American motorcade until, frantic with frustration, Holbrooke would jump out of his car and run ahead to ask Woodcock for a ride. At a formal dinner, Brzezinski's wife, Muska, mocked Holbrooke for his unkempt appearance. One morning, Brzezinski glided by the table where Muska and Sharon Woodcock were having breakfast and, holding an imaginary plate over his head, boasted, "I have Richard Holbrooke's head on my platter and I am going to serve it to the Chinese."

Holbrooke sulked and stormed. Imagine this ferocious infighter, in the thick of a truly historic mission—his role was to discuss economic and cultural ties with the Chinese—reduced to begging rides. On the air force plane home everything exploded into the open. Brzezinski wanted transcripts of his talks with Deng kept secret from Holbrooke and the rest of State until he had met with Carter. "He is not to see them," Brzezinski instructed Oksenberg, who, not quite as committed to the fight as his boss, got permission to show them to Gleysteen.

This was more than Holbrooke could bear. He rushed up the aisle and grabbed hold of Oksenberg's shirt collar. "If you don't give me those memcons after we get back," he shouted, "I will destroy you!"

Oksenberg, who had broken their breakfast promise not to keep secrets many times over, grabbed Holbrooke's collar right back and offered to destroy *him*. Everyone was yelling, including Gleysteen, who had never seen anything like it in a quarter century of government service. Before they came to blows, Holbrooke let go of Oksenberg's shirt.

"Are you trying to threaten me?" he demanded.

CHINA BECAME Brzezinski's wedge to take over all of foreign policy. He and Vance were now in a race to achieve Carter's two most important goals by the end of 1978—normalization with China and arms control with Russia. Because of Sino-Soviet hostility, each effort threatened to derail the other before the finish. Vance wanted separate and independent relationships with the two Communist powers, refusing to allow the United States to be pulled into their rivalry. Brzezinski was coming to see the world more and more from the Chinese point of view. He wanted to use a tilt toward China to isolate the Soviets and contain their adventurism in Africa and elsewhere. He regarded Vietnam as a Soviet proxy in Southeast Asia and a threat to regional peace, but otherwise peripheral to America's global strategy.

"You need to choose: Vietnam or China," Brzezinski wrote to Carter in July, "and China is incomparably more important to us." Refusing to make a choice, Carter wrote in the margin: "I should think that a U.S.-VNam relationship would be better for P.R.C., worse for U.S.S.R."

Holbrooke was still trying to make headway with Vietnam. Suddenly, in the summer of 1978, the Vietnamese responded as if they were in a hurry. Their strategic situation had changed. On their northern border China was growing increasingly hostile, and China's genocidal ally, the Khmer Rouge government of Cambodia, had been staging cross-border attacks into the Mekong Delta. Vietnam wanted to disrupt the chance of a Chinese-American deal that could strengthen the region's most threatening power.

On September 22, with world leaders in New York for the annual opening of the United Nations General Assembly, Holbrooke met with a senior Vietnamese official named Nguyen Co Thach. They sat down at Vietnam's new UN mission, a sparsely furnished apartment in a development of brutalist brick towers on the East River called Waterside Plaza. Thach acknowledged that the American objection to aid as a precondition for recognition still stood. "So the ball is in our court," he said in French. They agreed to meet again on September 27 in the same place.

Holbrooke called Oksenberg right away to fill him in on the talks so that Brzezinski couldn't accuse him of operating secretly. Oksenberg let his boss know what Holbrooke was up to. "His adrenaline obviously flowing, Dick Holbrooke called me immediately after his three-hour meeting with the Vietnamese today," he wrote Brzezinski. "I believe the Vietnamese are going to drop their demand for aid, and we are going to be in the unpleasant position of having little bargaining room left. We may find ourselves, by pushing these negotiations forward, normalizing relations with Vietnam before we do so with China and complicating our normalization process with China immeasurably."

Oksenberg reluctantly came to New York for the second round. Holbrooke's deputy, a Vietnam hand named Robert Oakley, was there, and so was Wisner. A year and a half after the failed talks in Paris, Thach was giving every sign of wanting to move ahead, and yet he still didn't drop the demand for aid. After an hour of pointless exchanges, Holbrooke collected his papers and put them in his folder as if to leave. "Let me ask you a very frank question," he said to his counterpart. "When I return to our offices after this meeting and the secretary of state asks me if Vietnam was responsive to our position, what should I say to him?"

Thach didn't answer directly. Instead, he suggested that they break for tea. Tea breaks between the Americans and the Vietnamese always meant that one side was going to say something real. Thach and Holbrooke walked over to the corner of the room and chatted by a table with pots of tea and freshly fried spring rolls. When they sat down again, Thach said, "We will tell you what you want to hear. We can agree that we do not see American aid as a prior condition to normalization. I can verify that."

The stamina of these diplomats! After a bluff that lasted five hours through two meetings, Thach was so eager to get down to business that he suggested writing up an agreement then and there. Holbrooke said that he needed higher approval. In the meantime, each side would set up a working group to scout a future embassy in the other's capital. The Socialist Republic of Vietnam would get the former South Vietnamese embassy in Washington. At the State Department a few old Saigon hands would submit applications for the first assignments in Hanoi.

"Wasn't that amazing?" Holbrooke exclaimed as he and Wisner drove away from Waterside Plaza in a taxi. "We were there all those years ago, and now here we are, this close to normalization!" He squeezed his friend's arm.

THE INDOCHINESE WARS were not over. In the last weeks of 1978 history began to move very fast. Half a dozen things were happening at once.

Ten days before Holbrooke reached his understanding with Thach, Carter secured the Camp David peace agreement between Egypt and Israel. He wanted to add more notches to his belt, but the Vietnam deal was too sensitive to announce just before the midterm elections. For domestic political reasons, Holbrooke would have to stall the Vietnamese until November.

Throughout the month of September, unseaworthy vessels began to appear on the South China Sea, loaded with thousands of desperate Vietnamese refugees, many of Chinese origin, fleeing persecution. The drama of the boat people made the timing of normalization awkward. So did new intelligence reports of Vietnamese troop movements along the Cambodian border. All of this put the final deal on a slower American schedule. But the Vietnamese were in a hurry, for they knew two things that the Americans did not. They were about to sign a treaty of friendship—a mutual defense pact—with the Soviet Union as a hedge against Chinese aggression. They were also preparing to invade Cambodia. They wanted diplomatic relations with the United States in their pocket before either happened.

On October 11, Carter met at the White House with Leonard Woodcock, who was doing the day-to-day negotiating in Beijing, and Brzezinski, who added himself to the meeting while keeping Vance out. Brzezinski and Woodcock persuaded the president to put off Vietnam until after China was done. Carter set a target date for normalization with Beijing: New Year's Day 1979. For the time being it was to be kept secret from everyone, including the assistant secretary of state for East Asia.

In late October Holbrooke took off on a trip to Southeast Asia. In Laos he met the Vietnamese ambassador at a diplomatic reception in Vientiane. From there he went on to Burma, one of the most isolated countries on earth, traveling by helicopter beyond Mandalay north to Lashio, where the Burma Road, built by the British in the 1930s and used by the Allies in the war, began its winding path through the mountains into China. He was drawn by the history, the names of far-flung places—he was a romantic. "I am tormented with an everlasting itch for things remote," says Ishmael at the start of *Moby-Dick* in a favorite passage of Holbrooke's. "I love to sail forbidden seas, and land on barbarous coasts."

Then he heard some very bad news. According to a report by the Vietnam News Agency, a "U.S. dignitary" had "warmly" greeted the Vietnamese ambassador at a social gathering in Vientiane. The American dignitary was quoted as saying that, after the American elections, diplomatic relations with both Vietnam and China would happen simultaneously, but that an American official (it sounded like Brzezinski) was "pressing the Southeast Asian policymakers of the U.S. State Department into continuing to woo China and contain Vietnam." The report was monitored by the CIA and passed on to the NSC, where it landed on Michel Oksenberg's desk as part of the daily intelligence haul. Oksenberg showed the story to Brzezinski, who marched straight into the Oval Office and demanded that the president recall the insubordinate dignitary from Asia and fire him.

A radio message reached Holbrooke in Mandalay with a sketchy account of the brewing crisis. Vance wanted an explanation.

While Holbrooke was away at the ends of the earth, his enemies in Washington were preparing his execution. The everlasting itch suddenly stopped tormenting him, and he hurried back to Rangoon. There a piece of good luck was waiting. Frank Scotton, his old Vietnam buddy who had trained South Vietnamese cadres to fight like guerrillas, happened to be the U.S. Information Service's man in Burma. And Scotton had a brilliant idea—an idea that might well occur to someone who had spent a decade of his youth fighting a propaganda war against a canny insurgency. Why not attribute the report to an act of Soviet disinformation?

By now it was the middle of the night in Rangoon, and Scotton had to wake up the CIA communicator. They gathered in the embassy's secure room, where Holbrooke dictated a cable that the agency man typed out and Scotton reviewed for plausibility. Then the cable was transmitted as a piece of CIA intelligence to the State Department, where it was received by another Vietnam friend of Holbrooke's, Peter Tarnoff.

Scotton's idea saved Holbrooke's career. The cover story worked so well that Holbrooke took the game to a level where no bureaucrat who'd just survived a brush with death would dare to play. Back in Washington, he leaked the story to the conservative writers Rowland Evans and Robert Novak. In their syndicated column they reported that, according to CIA analysts, Brzezinski had been duped by his archnemesis the Soviet Union in an effort to undermine Sino-American relations and turn members of the administration against one another. Brzezinski was furious but, for once, outplayed. Holbrooke stuck by the lie to the end of his days.

EVERYTHING IN EAST ASIA was coming to a head. On November 2, Leonard Woodcock gave the Chinese Carter's communiqué proposing the establishment of full diplomatic relations on January 1. The next day, Hanoi and Moscow signed a friendship treaty. Holbrooke returned from Southeast Asia on November 6, a day before congressional elections brought good news for the Republican Party (an omen of what was to come in 1980). That same week, the State Department's intelligence bureau concluded that Vietnam was getting ready to invade Cambodia. Normalization with Vietnam was losing speed. Normalization with China went into high gear.

Formal relations with the People's Republic meant that the United

States would end relations with the Republic of China, close down all its offices in Taipei, and allow a mutual defense treaty to expire. The last sticking point between Washington and Beijing was whether the United States would continue to sell weapons to Taiwan so that the Nationalists could defend themselves in the event of a Communist attack. With negotiations in the exclusive hands of Brzezinski and Woodcock, Holbrooke's role as State's member of the China team was to talk to Congress and mitigate the reaction to the abandonment of Taiwan.

Woodcock and Deng were to have their decisive conversation on Wednesday, December 13. The night before, Holbrooke went to dinner with Strobe Talbott and his wife at a new Vietnamese restaurant in Georgetown. Talbott had received a tip that Carter was about to recognize the People's Republic, and he asked Holbrooke if it was true. Holbrooke looked straight at him and lied: "There's no truth to it." The next day, Woodcock and Deng sat down in the Great Hall of the People. When the cables came into the Situation Room early that morning in Washington, Brzezinski kept even his close aide Oksenberg from seeing them. Finally, around ten-thirty a.m. he called Oksenberg into his office. "The deal has been made. Normalization is going to occur. The president wants to announce it Friday evening and I want you to draft a statement that the president will read on television."

As the day wore on, Holbrooke kept calling Oksenberg to find out what had happened in Beijing, and Oksenberg kept lying to put him off. Everyone at State still thought that the public announcement on China would be made on January 1—*after* Vance completed the strategic arms talks in Moscow. Brzezinski had outmaneuvered him again: China would come first, and Vance, away in Jerusalem, wasn't there to argue his case. In his absence, the State Department was being run by his deputy, Warren Christopher. Holbrooke told Christopher that the White House was sitting on crucial information from Beijing. Christopher phoned Brzezinski, who told him to come to the White House in the late afternoon. Christopher, a white-shoe lawyer with a frozen face who found Holbrooke distastefully pushy, slipped out of the building without a word to the assistant secretary.

At the White House Brzezinski filled Christopher in on the good news. Finally Christopher asked, "When will Dick Holbrooke learn about this?"

"Well," Brzezinski said with a smirk, "maybe Friday evening"—
two days away, when the rest of the world would learn. Holbrooke
was a known leaker, he said, and Carter didn't want him involved. But
Christopher feared that his assistant secretary would quit over being
excluded. Finally, around ten-thirty that night, he was allowed to call
Holbrooke, who was home in bed, stewing.

"I am sitting here in Zbig's office and we've got a message from Beijing," Christopher said. "Would you like to come down and see it?"

When Holbrooke read Woodcock's cable and Brzezinski's draft reply
to Deng, he immediately saw a problem. It was clear that the Chinese
neither accepted nor even understood that the United States would
reserve the right to sell arms to Taiwan. The critical issue had been left
deliberately ambiguous. But without a clear statement on the defense of
Taiwan, Holbrooke argued, the administration's political support would
evaporate. "Zbig, Chris, if you send that message out, we're never going
to be able to get Congress to approve what we have done."

Brzezinski dismissed Holbrooke's concern. This was his show. But
Holbrooke was right—the Chinese assumed there would be no more
arms sales, and the assumption threatened to kill the deal just before
Carter was scheduled to announce it. Only after two more meetings
in the Great Hall of the People, in which Woodcock and Deng essentially agreed to ignore the disagreement in order to conclude a deal that
both sides badly wanted, could Carter go on national TV on December
15 with the shocking announcement that, on the first day of 1979, the
world's most powerful country would establish diplomatic relations
with the world's most populous.

A week later, in Moscow, the Soviets told Vance that the timing of
normalization with China cast a pall over arms talks just as the two
sides were about to reach an agreement. SALT II wasn't signed for
another six months, and it came into the world stillborn.

Ten days after Carter's announcement, on Christmas, thirteen
Vietnamese divisions, 150,000 troops, crossed the Cambodian border
and attacked the army of the Khmer Rouge. By January 7 they were in
Phnom Penh.

————

BRZEZINSKI TURNED OUT to be right about many things. He was right to see normalization with China as the most consequential goal of the Carter years. He was right to be skeptical of normalization with Vietnam. He was right to regard the Soviet Union as a human rights abuser at home and an expansionist power in Africa and Asia. His hard-line view of the Cold War was amply borne out by the time Carter left office.

But he also helped to smash up the last pieces of the postwar consensus, bringing viciousness and deception into the heart of government, making trust among people working for the same president impossible. Holbrooke was young and strong and similar enough to survive, though his wounds would be evident in his lifelong silence about what Brzezinski had done to him. But Holbrooke thought that Vance never recovered from the events of that week. At the end of 1980, out of office and dropping the code of the establishment, Vance told Holbrooke, "I still cannot understand how the president was so taken in by Zbig. He is evil, a liar, dangerous."

Brzezinski, like Kissinger, loved the spectacle of power wielded for its own sake. When Deng Xiaoping arrived for a state visit in January 1979, and was the dinner guest of honor at the Brzezinski home in Virginia, he let the Americans know that China was planning to teach the Vietnamese "a lesson" for overthrowing its friends the Khmer Rouge. Brzezinski could hardly restrain his enthusiasm. Deng had America's implied blessing to start a war. Brzezinski later called Deng's attitude "the single most impressive demonstration of raw power politics that I encountered in my four years in the White House . . . I secretly wished that Deng's appreciation of the uses of power would also rub off on some of the key U.S. decision makers."

Deng's sixteen-day "lesson" in February 1979 killed twenty thousand people—ten thousand Vietnamese soldiers and civilians and an equal number of Chinese soldiers—while destroying a large swath of northern Vietnam that had been spared American bombing. This was what raw power politics looked like. The war gained China nothing—if anyone delivered a lesson, it was the Vietnamese. Ten years later, Deng again demonstrated his appreciation of the uses of power when he sent the People's Liberation Army into Tiananmen Square to mow down twenty-five hundred peaceful demonstrators and crush China's democracy movement for at least two generations.

Brzezinski, unlike Kissinger, didn't revel in his own indifference to the human suffering exacted by statecraft. But, like Kissinger, he saw the world as a contest of great powers. The catastrophe of a little country like Cambodia was doomed to be an afterthought.

IN 1973, Ken Quinn was a Foreign Service officer stationed in the Mekong Delta on the Cambodian border. One day, he hiked up a mountain, looked across the border, and saw flames and smoke coming from every village for miles around. Nixon and Kissinger's decision to bring the Vietnam War to Cambodia had accelerated the growth of the Communist Khmer Rouge, and this was an area under its control. Quinn interviewed refugees who fled into South Vietnam and began to develop a picture of life under the Khmer Rouge. In early 1974, he sent a forty-page classified airgram back to the State Department. It described a party system of totalitarian terror, reminiscent of Nazi Germany and Stalinist Russia, whose goal was to reconstruct Cambodian society and the minds of the Khmer people from zero. The Cambodian Communists, far from being under the control of Hanoi, as Kissinger and other U.S. officials believed, had increasingly hostile relations with the Vietnamese Communists.

Quinn's report was the first American analysis of the Khmer Rouge. It was completely ignored in Washington. The next year, in April 1975, the Khmer Rouge took power, renamed the country Democratic Kampuchea, sealed it off from the world, and began to carry out their radical vision along just the lines that Quinn had described. Reports of forced labor, starvation, and mass killings came out of Cambodia slowly, from the few refugees able to escape. The stories sounded incredible—genocide always does at first—and American politics worked against the truth. Washington wasn't eager to denounce China's ally; many leftists, like Noam Chomsky, defended the Khmer Rouge; and the public didn't want to think about Indochina anymore. In its first year the Carter administration had nothing to say about Cambodia, with one exception.

In July 1977, Holbrooke was summoned to testify before a House subcommittee chaired by a congressman from Brooklyn named Stephen Solarz, who had more Holocaust survivors in his district than anyone else in Congress and wanted to call attention to Cambodia. On his way out of the office to Capitol Hill, Holbrooke passed Quinn's desk. He knew of the classified report, and he asked Quinn what he should say to Congress. Quinn was Holbrooke's kind of Foreign Service officer. In the Mekong Delta he had served face-to-face with the war, and his account of the Khmer Rouge contradicted higher official views—it had the ring of truth from the ground. In five minutes, with Holbrooke standing at his desk, Quinn summarized his findings.

"The new government seeks a radical restructuring of Cambodian personality and society," Holbrooke told the Solarz subcommittee, echoing Quinn. "Coercion is their instrument to effect rapid change. Individual political liberties have been eradicated or subordinated to collective goals." The Khmer Rouge had been in power for more than two years, and Holbrooke estimated the number of dead "in the tens if not hundreds of thousands." Some journalists put the figure at more than a million. "We have said that our human rights policy applies to Cambodia, and I must reemphasize that here today. We cannot let it be said that by our silence we acquiesce in the tragic events in Cambodia. I wish to say in the strongest possible terms that we deplore what has taken place there." He was leading up to the bad news. "I cannot tell you, however, that anything we can realistically do would improve the lot of the Khmer people in the foreseeable future." The only tool available to the United States was aid for refugees.

Back in the office, Holbrooke stopped by Quinn's desk. "It was exactly the right thing to do," he said.

Holbrooke was the first American official to denounce the crimes of the Khmer Rouge. His remarks had no effect on policy. The United States had no leverage over Cambodia. Was it a higher form of political morality to point out an ongoing crime and do nothing to stop it than to stay silent? The only real solution—organizing an international force to rescue the Khmer people from what a French writer called history's first "auto-genocide"—was so extreme that its only proponent in government was George McGovern, the anti-war senator who had been crushed by Nixon in 1972. "Do we sit on the sidelines and watch a population slaughtered," McGovern asked at a hearing of the Senate

Foreign Relations Committee, "or do we marshal military force and put an end to it?"

That was in 1978, when estimates of Cambodian dead ranged from one to three million. America bore some responsibility for the genocide, and out of sheer moral anguish McGovern was raising the prospect of what came to be called humanitarian intervention. The idea appalled the left and right alike and had no takers in the Carter administration. Fifteen years later, and closer to home, it would become Holbrooke's signature. But in 1978, in Southeast Asia, it was a nonstarter.

Human rights was Jimmy Carter's main contribution to American foreign policy. He put it at the center of his campaign—Holbrooke wrote many of those passages in his speeches—and he created the position of assistant secretary of state for human rights and humanitarian affairs, which he filled with an uncompromising civil rights activist named Patricia Derian. Tony Lake set up monthly meetings of a working group, chaired by Warren Christopher, where Derian would get to weigh in on the human rights implications of all aid programs and weapons sales. Carter and his officials mentioned human rights in speeches throughout his presidency.

But it was one thing to write a speech and another to put it into practice. Human rights struggled for air from the first weeks of the Carter administration. That thing called the national interest always came first, and Holbrooke, whose overriding goal was to re-establish the United States as a Pacific power, was particularly energetic in pushing it. He wanted to sell F-5 aircraft to an Indonesian regime that was carrying out massive repression in East Timor. He wanted to renew leases on two major American bases in the Philippines with the dictator Ferdinand Marcos. Derian argued that these deals should be conditioned on improved human rights, and she traveled around Asia lecturing heads of state as if they were southern governors. Holbrooke regarded Derian as a naïve and reckless intruder on his territory.

In April 1977 he spent twenty-four hours with Blythe on Ferdinand and Imelda Marcos's enormous presidential yacht, eating, drinking, dancing, water-skiing, and warning Marcos that human rights was a top concern of President Carter. In the end Holbrooke got the bases renewed, while Marcos released the opposition leader Benigno Aquino from prison and sent him into exile. Holbrooke considered that a suc-

cess; Derian considered it a sellout. They fell into shouting matches. The Philippines remained an American ally and a corrupt dictatorship.

Another example: Carter came into power determined to withdraw American troops from South Korea. Where did the idea come from? Of course, from Holbrooke's 1975 piece in the *New York Times Magazine*. Once in office, Holbrooke immediately backed away from it—all but denied the article's existence, made Gelb promise not to mention it to anyone, and was so touchy about it that Gelb had to stop kidding him. Holbrooke and others maneuvered Carter into reversing his position, though the price of success was a severe presidential tongue-lashing on a trip to Seoul in 1979. In May 1980, when South Korean soldiers massacred hundreds of protesters in Kwangju, Holbrooke supported the American position of saying nothing. A few months later, he quietly intervened to prevent the execution of the dissident leader Kim Dae Jung.

These were all classic cases of national interest coming up against universal principles. Holbrooke favored the former while making gestures toward the latter. But Cambodia was something else. The scale of the killing was so vast. Five years of civil war and American bombing. Four years of terror and massacre that eliminated a quarter of the country's people. And now, with Vietnam's invasion and occupation, another war—the Third Indochina War—brought famine and a massive flow of refugees to the Thai border. American policy was not to acknowledge that Vietnam had liberated the Cambodian people from a genocidal regime, or to make sure that aid poured into the starving country, but to prolong the conflict on this new battleground of the Cold War for however many years it would take until Vietnam sued for peace. Over Holbrooke's objections, Brzezinski encouraged the Thais to funnel Chinese weapons to Khmer Rouge fighters in the refugee camps. The U.S. government refused to apply the word "genocide" to Cambodia.

In September 1979, the United Nations debated whether to give Cambodia's seat to Democratic Kampuchea—that is, Pol Pot and the remnants of his regime of killers in the jungles of western Cambodia. The night before the vote, Vance summoned Holbrooke to his office to go over the pros and cons. Holbrooke pointed out that a no vote would cost the United States far more than it would gain, while rewarding Vietnamese aggression. America's allies in Southeast Asia, especially Thailand, feared Vietnam and wanted to isolate its puppet government in Phnom Penh. There was no thought of leaving the seat empty. The next day, the United States voted with the majority of the General Assembly to give Cambodia's seat to the Khmer Rouge.

Holbrooke called the decision the "single most difficult thing" he'd ever done. "It ran counter to my private views. But, as a public official, I had to swallow hard."

Public officials take an oath to swallow hard. Whatever statesmen say in their speeches or their memoirs, public service is seldom about saving lives or reducing suffering. It's about swallowing hard. Even Jimmy Carter, who held Henry Kissinger in contempt—even Carter couldn't escape the cold logic of siding with Pol Pot. Statecraft is about national interests, and quite often the equivalent of a few million traumatized Cambodians have to be sacrificed, and the sacrifice becomes a little easier because they're hard to see and easy to forget from the treetops.

If Holbrooke had succeeded in his talks with the Vietnamese in 1977 or 1978, things might have been different for Cambodia. The United States might have assumed the role of mediator in Southeast Asia and prevented the Third Indochina War from continuing the torment of the Khmer people for another decade. Holbrooke lost that battle, and he went along with a policy of punishing Cambodians in the name of our national interest.

This was the central lesson of Holbrooke's first taste of power. I've gone on longer than I meant to about these years because they say something important about our story. Good people imagine that their government should also be good and do good in the world—especially Americans. It's in our idea of ourselves going back to the Declaration of Independence. It was Carter's campaign slogan in 1976. We don't take naturally to realpolitik, and insofar as Carter resisted it he achieved some worthy goals, none bigger than making human rights a permanent part of our foreign policy language—even as lip service. Without that, anything can be justified by the national interest. So let's never give up the idea, but it's not what governments are for. Be unhappy when high officials fail to live up to it—just don't be surprised.

BLYTHE MOVED to Washington on the assumption that she would find the right job and they would live the right way. Holbrooke, utterly smitten with his quick, spiky, much younger wife, went to great lengths to please her. They moved into a large apartment near Embassy Row that he couldn't afford, and he took her on official trips around Europe and the Pacific, staying in the guesthouse of the U.S. ambassador to Rome and the private quarters of the U.S. Pacific Command on the beach in Honolulu. It's not easy to live the right way when you have no money.

Working in the treetops introduces you to world leaders while reducing you to mooching. Holbrooke's salary was around $36,000 after taxes. He withdrew all $9,000 from his Foreign Service retirement fund, received a $13,000 loan from Harriman, and chased down reimbursements for expenditures of $4.43. His child support checks grew erratic, then stopped altogether, and only resumed after Litty got a lawyer friend to send him a letter. His boys didn't interest Blythe. Despite fitful efforts, he saw less of them than ever.

Blythe's ambition was to be a writer—she had a flair for tart Didion-esque sentences—and Holbrooke introduced her to all the editors he knew (Wisner considered it a gross conflict of interest), but the right job didn't come her way. Holbrooke's friends didn't care for her or she for them. He was oblivious and made sure Blythe spent a lot of time in the company of Gelb and the Harrimans and his colleagues at State. She dressed far too provocatively for the department. Once, when Holbrooke went out to Andrews Air Force Base to greet the Japanese prime minister, she accompanied him in jeans and a sheer blouse. The Japanese were scandalized and never got over it—from that point on they considered Holbrooke, a careless dresser himself, insufficiently respectful.

Blythe couldn't stand Washington. Her reasons weren't original—it was full of self-important bores who made no distinction between work and personal life—but you can imagine her particular frustration as a young woman. She was smarter than most of the mediocre minds that ran the U.S. government, but they didn't take her seriously. Her bosses in public television resented the invitations that came with being Holbrooke's wife. Attaching herself to him was the obvious move of an operator, but she still wanted to be recognized on her own terms. Like Pamela Harriman, she was using what she had to get the things men felt entitled to, and they derided her for it.

One night, when Blythe had been in Washington for a year, the man seated next to her at a Katharine Graham dinner party asked, "What's it like here?" She told him. "That's marvelous," he said. "Write it for me." He was the editor of *Newsweek*. The next day Blythe sat down and began, à la Didion: "On bad days when asked how I am, I answer, 'In Washington.'" The key line came partway down: "Sure there is sex, but the only romance in town is the one with power."

She showed the piece to Holbrooke, aware of the trouble it could cause him. "I won't print it if you don't want me to." But he loved it and told her she could be the next Tom Wolfe. They were partners in crime—her success would be part of his own. When the column came out, under the title "Why I Hate Washington," he made dozens of copies and proudly handed them out to his bemused staff and colleagues, who considered the piece a subtle attack on the author's husband. For a short time, Blythe was the buzz of Washington. Bob Woodward's soon-to-be ex-wife made him carry around a folded copy in his pocket. The political women were on Blythe's side, but the hostesses were out to get her. When Pam chided Holbrooke for his wife's indiscretion, he suddenly cooled on the whole thing. If he had to choose between Blythe and the

Harrimans, that was easy. He began to work longer hours than ever. Blythe, still in her mid-twenties, felt abandoned.

Toward the end of 1979 she returned to New York. Holbrooke wanted her back and shut himself in his office to talk by phone for an hour at a time, but the marriage was heading toward its inevitable conclusion. One day, a staff aide named Jeff Bader was going through Holbrooke's mail when he opened a legal document from Blythe's lawyer demanding that the recipient show cause why the marriage should not be dissolved. Bader assumed that his boss was expecting the letter, but when Holbrooke saw it his face turned red: "Where did this come from?"

He moved back into the Harriman guesthouse on N Street, like an injured animal returning to its familiar habitat. He wept openly with his friend Sally Quinn, the wife of the *Post*'s editor Ben Bradlee, and turned for solace to various ex-girlfriends, including Gail. By then she was married with children and after two lunches refused to see him again.

In advance of the court hearing, Holbrooke asked Gelb to testify that he and Blythe hadn't had sex in more than a year. "I don't know that that's true," Gelb couldn't resist saying. "If they put me under oath I don't think I can lie."

"Just say I told you," Holbrooke said. "I'm sorry I'm making you do this."

Gelb would have lied for his friend, but Blythe failed to show up at the hearing, and the no-fault divorce went through. By then she had changed her name to Blythe Holbrooke. It appears on the jacket of both books that she went on to write.

The last time Holbrooke saw Blythe was in the fall of 1980, when he was in New York to finalize the divorce and reaffirm the American vote for the Khmer Rouge seat at the United Nations. "Pol Pot, Dick?" Blythe said after they signed the papers. "How could you?"

THIS PART OF THE STORY isn't quite over. There's one more turn, and it shows what made Holbrooke different from the others in the treetops.

After the fall of Saigon, President Ford had let 130,000 South Vietnamese into the United States. Then the gates closed. Americans wanted to be done with the region. In Carter's first two years hardly anyone paid attention to the plight of Southeast Asians uprooted by war and repression. The United States had no clear stance on refugees—they weren't even considered a foreign policy issue, and the State Department's refugee office consisted of just two people. Vance, who saw foreign policy as relations between states, believed that refugees were an internal matter for a "host country" like Thailand and the humanitarian concern of the United Nations. Brzezinski gave them no thought at all.

But because they occupied the narrow space between various national interests—in terms of statecraft they were neutral, almost invisible—and because they were from Indochina, and because they were desperate, the refugees became Holbrooke's concern. For four years he never lost sight of them. In August 1977 he appeared before Congress and argued for admitting an additional fifteen thousand Vietnamese refugees. "The motivation is simple," he said: "the deep humanitarian concern which has for so long been a descriptive part of our national character." In 1978 and 1979, when Vietnamese by the tens of thousands were forced to take to the South China Sea, he pushed for a stronger American response, such as using navy ships to pick up those turned away by neighboring countries. But the navy didn't see rescuing refugees as a military mission.

Holbrooke recruited an ally in Vice President Mondale, who called a meeting in the spring of 1979 in the Situation Room, where national security emergencies were debated. Holbrooke found this airless, windowless room in the basement of the White House, sealed off by design from the outside world, to be a place where even drowning refugees became a bureaucratic abstraction. Every agency found a reason to oppose his idea, especially the Pentagon. After two hours of discussion, Mondale, chairing the meeting from the head of the table, turned to the admiral in the room. "Are you telling me that we have thousands of people drowning in the open sea, and we have the Seventh Fleet right there, and we can't help them?" The vice president told the admiral to carry out the mission or find another job.

A couple of months later, Mondale flew by helicopter over Manila Bay to an aircraft carrier involved in the rescue operation. "I didn't like the mission when I got those orders," the ship's commander told Mondale. "I thought it would demoralize my sailors . . . I was dead wrong." The sailors reveled in saving the lives of boat people. "It's going to make a difference to the way those people think about America," the commander said. "Because when their life was at risk, they saw this ship with an American flag come up and these young guys go down and pick them up. They felt safe for the first time in months. The world looked better to them. It's hard to stay mad at a policy like that."

But it wasn't enough to rescue people at sea—they had to be given permanent homes somewhere. Neighboring countries announced that they were full up, tugging boats back out to sea and even threatening to shoot the desperate passengers. In June 1979, Holbrooke flew on Air Force One to Japan for the G7 summit meeting, and during the flight across the Pacific he badgered first Vance and then Carter to double the number of Southeast Asian refugees admitted into the United States from seven to fourteen thousand. It was not a priority issue. The SALT II treaty was losing support in the Senate, there was a revolution in Iran, and the world was in turmoil. But when Carter reached Tokyo, he announced that the monthly quota would go up to fourteen thousand.

The next month, Carter abruptly canceled his trip to a conference in Geneva on the refugee crisis—he had withdrawn to Camp David to prepare his "malaise" speech—and sent Mondale in his place. No one expected much from the conference. A previous one had produced little, and while thousands of Southeast Asians faced death, the U.N. refugee office was stuck in its own bureaucratic inertia. The vice president's speechwriter had to pull together an address en route. Among his briefing papers was a document provided by Holbrooke that described another conference on refugees—the one on the fate of Germany's Jews held in 1938 at Évian, France, just up the lake from Geneva. Not a single country at Évian offered to increase its refugee quota except the Dominican Republic. President Roosevelt did everything he could to keep the American number low. When Mondale's speechwriter saw Holbrooke's paper, he knew that he had his hook.

In Geneva Mondale urged the delegates not to repeat the tragedy of Évian: "Let us renounce that legacy of shame. Let us honor the moral principles we inherit. Let us do something meaningful—something profound—to stem this misery. We face a world problem. Let us fashion a world solution. History will not forgive us if we fail. History will not forget us if we succeed." Mondale's speech prompted a standing ovation and large increases in refugee quotas and aid money on the part of the governments present in Geneva.

Holbrooke must have known of Évian from his family origins. But I don't think being the child of refugees explains his passion on this subject. That past was buried by his parents, and their son didn't want to dig it up. No, it wasn't the Jews—it was Vietnam. That was where he had seen a mother nursing her child next to her husband's corpse. Afterward he couldn't get her out of his mind. He was not a bleeding heart—he had taken her picture, and even admired it. He didn't wring his hands over the refugees, or express any deep feeling. Human suffering didn't plunge him into psychological paralysis or philosophical despair. It drove him to furious action.

Most of the American officials who made the refugees their concern had Vietnam in common. Maybe it was guilt, or maybe it was just the memory of human faces, but their government service had kept the issue from being an abstraction. Holbrooke's friend Lionel Rosenblatt worked for Komer on pacification in the late sixties and, defying orders, helped evacuate South Vietnamese from Saigon in 1975. In 1979 he was at the U.S. embassy in Bangkok when tens of thousands of Cambodians began to stagger across the border into Thailand.

They were starving ghosts. Many had been force-marched by Khmer Rouge soldiers. Some collapsed at the border and died in place. Thailand considered the refugees "illegal immigrants," and in June Thai soldiers began to force them back over the steep border cliffs and down into minefields. Reluctant to offend the Thais, the office of the U.N. High Commissioner for Refugees said nothing. The protests of the American ambassador Morton Abramowitz, another Holbrooke friend, failed to move the Thai prime minister. Abramowitz and Rosenblatt signaled to Holbrooke that a crisis on the scale of the boat people was unfolding on the border. Holbrooke gave them political cover to push hard on the Thais, and he rallied interest among his contacts on the Hill and in the media, and then he traveled to Thailand in October and visited the primitive camps that aid groups were belatedly constructing.

A young British U.N. worker named Mark Malloch-Brown was given three days to bulldoze roads and dig latrines and build a camp for sixty thousand "illegal immigrants" on a muddy field outside a small town forty miles from the border. Malloch-Brown was working in a world of international do-gooders who seemed more concerned with correct procedures than solving problems. Many of them were skeptical about the Khmer Rouge genocide and believed that the U.S. resettlement effort was intended to destabilize Communist Indochina.

Holbrooke descended on the camp by helicopter—this big, sweaty-haired American in a tan safari suit and enormous glasses, dwarfing the refugees, denouncing the U.N. bureaucracy, asking Malloch-Brown what he needed from Geneva and who was blocking it, enlisting his friends at the embassy to break the impasse. If this was an American imperialist, Malloch-Brown was happy to see him. Because the Washington treetops didn't much care about refugees, Holbrooke was free to be relentless. It's the first glimpse you get of his egotism and idealism in perfect balance to achieve something good.

Toward the end of 1979 a Vietnamese offensive against the Khmer Rouge created a new flood of refugees. Carter was under pressure from Ted Kennedy, who was challenging him in the Democratic primary and criticizing the weak American response to the Southeast Asian disaster. In early November, Carter sent his wife Rosalynn to Thailand with Holbrooke. Mrs. Carter toured the camp that Malloch-Brown had helped build. She wasn't told that it was controlled by the Khmer Rouge, whose young soldiers stared sullenly at the visitor. Holbrooke trailed behind the First Lady as she walked among the refugees, and knelt like Leonardo's Madonna to hold a wisp of a child in her arms, and spoke to the child's mother lying exhausted at her feet, and kissed the forehead of a young woman, murmuring, "Give me a smile," while 150 reporters and photographers fought for position, and one of Mrs. Carter's aides yelled at Malloch-Brown, "Create a photo opportunity!"

"It's like nothing I've ever seen," the First Lady told the press. "As a wife, as a mother, as a human being, it's devastating."

After that, the world paid attention to Cambodia. The next year—the last of his presidency—Carter signed the Refugee Act of 1980, which tripled the annual number of refugees allowed into the country. By 1982 the United States had admitted half a million Indochinese, by far the most of any country in the world. The number eventually reached one and a half million. Holbrooke had a lot to do with it.

It shames us today.

Since I Am Now Hopeless

Twelve years. His forties and then some. Three presidential elections. Wars in Cambodia, El Salvador, Nicaragua, Ethiopia, Mozambique, Lebanon, Iran, and Iraq burned on until they burned out. The war in Afghanistan never ended. Democracy came to the Pacific Rim. Saddam Hussein swallowed Kuwait and had to spit it out. The Berlin Wall fell and the Cold War, with its millions of nameless dead, was over. The Soviet Union disappeared and the United States became the superpower and Yugoslavia crumbled. Holbrooke put on ten pounds and his boys grew to manhood while he waited for another turn of the wheel.

The scene shifted to New York, just as the Wall Street carnival was getting started. He made money for the first time and acquired a new roster of friends, more chiefs than Indians because that's how it goes when you rise with age. Girlfriends—of course! For all the hot lights of Manhattan, you'll find that during stretches of the eighties he grows indistinct—the very glare of the camera starts to blur the man. But the interior light in the sleepless brain never dimmed. The whole time he was positioning, connecting, learning, expanding, surveying, getting ready for the only thing that really counted.

Twelve years was a long time to wait. By the end he would be gnawing the bars of his cage.

HOLBROOKE KNEW THAT Carter would lose in 1980. The seizure of American hostages in Tehran and the Soviet invasion of Afghanistan allowed Ronald Reagan to claim that the peace president, the human rights president, had made America weak. At home, in the cities, at the gas stations, in the economy, things looked even worse. Carter finished his term like a man staring under the hood of his car in the middle of a mudslide. On some things he was a generation ahead of his time, but he couldn't lead and that's what voters want, even if it means being lied to.

Clark Clifford, who had been stage-whispering in the ear of power since Truman, saw an epic political shift, the kind that lasted longer than an election cycle. Holbrooke jotted in his notebook: "<u>Clifford</u>— Dems coasting for 40 years on FDR coalition. But it is disintegrating."

Within days of the election Holbrooke was looking for his next move. By the second week of November he had a proposal for a book on America and the future of Asia in the hands of New York agents and editors. Every time he left government he made plans to write a book, but he followed through on only one occasion and this wasn't it. A. M. Rosenthal, executive editor of the *Times*, offered him a job at the paper that had turned him down in 1962. It came at the wrong time. Holbrooke was in debt, and friends such as Clifford on the other side of the wealth gap counseled him to find a more lucrative second career. Holbrooke didn't need much pushing. "In journalism I was regarded as a bureaucrat, in government as a journalist, so I have felt an outsider in both," he wrote at the start of 1981, "so now I will try for something really outside—business." In his notebook he jotted down a line from Robert Frost: "Work is play for mortal stakes."

In Georgetown in the early seventies Holbrooke had gotten to know Peter Peterson, the son of a Greek diner owner in Nebraska, who was Nixon's secretary of commerce for a year and then took over the old Wall Street firm Lehman Brothers. Holbrooke had hired Peterson's son to work at *Foreign Policy,* and Peterson made his house available to Holbrooke on trips to Manhattan. Two weeks after Carter's defeat, they had breakfast at the Carlyle Hotel on the Upper East Side. Holbrooke listed the businesses that he'd assisted in their efforts to enter Asian markets— Chase Manhattan, Pan Am, Weyerhaeuser, many others. He said that he knew all the senior leaders in East Asia. His references included David Rockefeller, Cyrus Vance, even Henry Kissinger.

There was a long tradition of Wall Street firms hiring big names from government and the other way around. Lehman Brothers had the elderly George Ball, Kennedy's and Johnson's undersecretary of state, who had helped engineer the overthrow of Diem and then became the in-house dissenter on Vietnam. Holbrooke had a name, but it wasn't George Ball. With the eclipse of the WASP establishment, the Washington–Wall Street passage had narrowed. Investment firms were hiring top MBAs who knew something about banking. Holbrooke knew nothing about banking, and Lehman didn't have a full-time job for him.

But in January a senior banker suggested a different arrangement: Lehman would hire Holbrooke as a private consultant on the firm's business in Washington and Beijing, taking about a quarter of his time and paying him $40,000 plus a bonus. The idea was appealing. He had no other prospects.

Then his friend Jim Johnson called with a proposal. They had first met at Princeton in 1969, and since then Johnson, a Minnesotan, had become Walter Mondale's closest aide (and Holbrooke's only friend in the hostile terrain of the Carter White House). Mondale was the party's likely presidential nominee in 1984, and Johnson guarded the door to Mondale. Every rich Democrat in the country would want to know him. So why not go into business together as consultants, offering their services to companies that needed help navigating public policy?

It was a relatively new niche in Washington—not outright lobbying, but strategic advice, a mix of door opening and opinion peddling. Holbrooke's biggest calling card was China. After normalization, he had handled the negotiation of economic and cultural ties, joining Mondale on a high-profile trip to Beijing in the summer of 1979 that was the first step in hammering out the new relationship. Johnson offered Holbrooke the title of vice president for international affairs and a 40 percent stake in the partnership. In case anyone missed the political point, they would share a floor in a building on M Street with Mondale's law offices. They would be called Public Strategies. Holbrooke accepted over the phone.

He began beating the bushes for gigs with companies that wanted to expand their business across the Pacific—Seagram's, John Deere, Levi Strauss. He wrote to Lester Crown, the largest shareholder in General Dynamics and an old Harvard Business School classmate of Jack Valenti, head of the Motion Picture Association of America, whom Holbrooke knew from the Johnson White House (this is now called social capital): "Dear Mr. Crown: At the suggestion of Jack Valenti, I am writing to suggest a relationship between General Dynamics and myself which I believe would be of mutual benefit and would also serve American foreign policy and strategic interests. My interest is in discussing with you the possibility of developing a comprehensive and successful marketing strategy to sell the FX aircraft to the five nations of ASEAN."

Mr. Crown didn't bite, but Edgar Bronfman of Seagram's did, for $50,000 a year, and so did Hyundai ($30,000 plus $6,000 in expenses), and Nike, which wanted to open factories in the People's Republic. Holbrooke advised Philip Knight, Nike's president, to remove the initials from the "Made in Taiwan R.O.C." labels on his shoes, to avoid offending Beijing.

On foreign business trips, including many to Beijing, Holbrooke was received by top leaders as if he still represented the U.S. government. He wasn't the first official to trade on his public service for private gain—in 1981 there were nearly seven thousand lobbying groups in Washington, and the number was growing astronomically. He would be far from the last. But the work smelled enough like corruption to leave him uneasy. He was always trying to make it rhyme with the greater good of America.

He bought a townhouse on the edge of Georgetown and moved out of the guest quarters on N Street where he'd been squatting for two years. Harriman, ninety years old, insisted on walking three blocks with Pam to inspect Holbrooke's acquisition. He looked it over upstairs and downstairs, even the bathrooms.

"Nice house," Harriman said. "How much did you pay for it?" He already knew the answer, having loaned Holbrooke $57,000 toward the purchase.

"Two hundred fifty thousand dollars."

"Why, that's the same amount I paid for my house up the street."

"Averell, that was over twenty years ago," Pam said.

The Crocodile, who was not only deaf and half blind but pretty much humorless, nonetheless grinned.

Holbrooke had never had money before. He remained a cheapskate— never broke the habit of sticking friends with the lunch bill—but money allowed him to live more like the people whose company he kept. It was like discovering at age thirty-one that women wanted to sleep with him. He never really got over it. "Money doesn't interest me," he once wrote; "it's what you can *do* with money that does." This was a high-minded way of saying that the intricacies of finance bored him, that he didn't care about keeping score, that he was in it for the things money could buy. They included power, and proximity to people who could be helpful to his other career, the one that mattered.

DURING THE EIGHTIES it sometimes felt like there would never be another Democratic president. Reagan found the perfect formula for Republican supremacy: wave the flag and ask nothing of the American people. Swell the defense budget while cutting taxes. Make America number one again at the Summer Olympics. Roll back communism through dirty little wars that didn't cost American lives. If you wanted to send troops into combat, do it in a country the size of Grenada. If almost three hundred Americans got blown up by Iran-backed suicide bombers in Beirut, quietly withdraw the marines and change the subject—but for God's sake, don't dramatize your own impotence like Carter with the hostages. And this was enough to keep winning.

Holbrooke's generation of Democrats couldn't shake the image of weakness. It had started with Vietnam—the name the Republicans hung around the necks of Democrats was McGovern's, not McNamara's, as if dragging us into that unwinnable war was forgivable but opposing it wasn't—and now there was no end to it. Carter was an accident of Watergate, a feckless time-out during twenty-four years of Republican rule after 1968. Holbrooke thought that Democratic activists were pulling the party too far to the left. Liberals needed to get off the defensive, start sounding strong, take on the right wing's own failings. He supported arming anti-Communist rebels in Afghanistan and Nicaragua. "A liberal foreign policy should not be equated with a weak foreign policy," he wrote to Senator Gary Hart, a rising Democratic star. "But more than the simple assertion that we know about the evils of Communism is necessary. We must be prepared, for example, to show that we understand the strategic importance of Central America better than Reagan, and we would have better policies to protect that interest."

He called for human rights in foreign policy, but not too much. He wanted America to be true to itself by example and quiet pressure, not by hectoring and interfering. He was an American exceptionalist, but he wished the State Department would stop publishing its annual report on human rights around the world. He didn't like the moral arrogance of the isolationist left or the jingoist right. Human rights should be a beacon, not a bludgeon. He was trying to position himself somewhere between the hawks and the doves.

The great thing about foreign policy is that you can arrange abstract terms in whatever combination you like: "values and interests," "peace through strength," "Wilsonian pragmatism," "realistic idealism." Whole conferences and books and party platforms are steeped in this meaningless language, especially when your party is out of power, but none of it solved Holbrooke's and the Democrats' problem, which was finding a way to get back in. It would take the end of the Cold War to do that.

He knew that it didn't matter if the public agreed with Democrats on specific issues like arms control. What mattered was the sense of a leader's character. "As Commander-in-Chief they want somebody they can trust to go eyeball-to-eyeball with the Soviet leadership," Holbrooke wrote to Mondale in late 1982—"someone who will make America feel strong and proud, protect our national honor and security without leading us into wars or foreign entanglements. The details of almost every foreign policy issue are too complicated for most Americans to follow, and we are thus willing to leave them to the President as long as we trust him. Thus symbolism becomes considerably more important in foreign policy issues than in bread-and-butter domestic issues where the voter can measure promises and rhetoric against performance and reality."

Reagan was unbeatable at symbols. In 1984, Mondale lost every state except his own Minnesota. It was worse than Reagan's devastating defeat of Carter. It was also the end of the business model for Public Strategies. So much for guarding the door to the White House!

After the election, the real estate billionaire Larry Tisch asked Jim Johnson, "What are you going to do now?" Johnson had no idea. The partners were making a few hundred thousand a year, but by the mid-eighties that barely counted. Johnson was sitting in Tisch's Manhattan office only because Tisch liked him and the Mondale name still meant something. "I've got it," Tisch said. "Sell your company to Saatchi and

Saatchi." He yelled at his secretary to get Goldman Sachs on the phone, and then he yelled at the Goldman guy to tell Maurice Saatchi in London to buy Public Strategies and have Goldman underwrite the deal.

But Holbrooke objected: if they were going to sell, they had to give Lehman the first shot. Pete Peterson had been driven out in a putsch in 1983 and Lehman had been acquired by Shearson/American Express. The new boss, Peter Cohen, told Holbrooke, "If you're selling the firm, you're selling it to me." The next day Lehman offered five million dollars for Public Strategies. Johnson and Holbrooke would get a million-dollar payout. So in 1985 they became managing directors at Lehman and went to work as investment bankers in the brand-new World Financial Center, next to the Twin Towers in Lower Manhattan. Holbrooke never even pretended to care about the business.

By then he had already moved to New York. His girlfriend, Diane Sawyer, had a job there.

THEY MET IN WASHINGTON in 1979. She was in her mid-thirties, a new correspondent in the CBS Washington bureau. She had to work overtime to beat several raps against her. One was that, having been crowned America's Junior Miss as a high school senior from Louisville in 1963, she still carried herself with a ladylike grace that was almost provocatively at odds with the louche style of the seventies. Second: she was stunning, glamorous—long legs, sensuous mouth, opaque blue eyes, hair so silky blond and lustrous that you could use it as a high-end comforter and reading light. Worst of all, she had just spent six years working for Richard Nixon—two in the White House press office under Ron Ziegler, building flimsy walls to hold back Watergate, and then four in San Clemente, helping the disgraced ex-president write his memoirs. Only a true Nixon loyalist would do that. It struck CBS veterans like Dan Rather as incomprehensible and disqualifying. Sawyer had to prove herself by taking any shitty little assignment the bureau gave her. And she was so diligent, so smart, so *nice*, that she soon won them over.

Sawyer was promoted to cover the State Department. In the early days of the Iran hostage crisis she staked out offices and slept on chairs for an entire week. She called up every official on the phone chart, and when she got to Holbrooke he offered himself as a source and took her on for instruction. His leaks raised her status at CBS. With Blythe out of the picture they began to date. A pattern with women he felt to be above his station set in. His friend Sally Quinn watched him turn so insecure and frantic to please them that it made him, at least to her, simultaneously lovable and unfuckable.

Anxiety sparked by women he cared for lit brief fires of inwardness. It happened with Litty, with Toni, and now with Diane. From his notebook, early 1981: "DS—calm? or controlled/she is controlled but I'm not sure calm—I think I am calm, but appear not controlled . . . draining—because takes, but is unable to give—can't accept love as real, bec. sees herself as inferior, unworthy of love, yet able to get it. Groucho Marx line about club applies—Must be more honest about where relationship stands—"

He showed her the world as she would never have seen it. They roughed it through Tibet and she endured dirty toilets at bus stations and altitude headaches at eighteen thousand feet with a spectacular view of Everest. In their joint travel diary his entries are long discursions on Buddhist monasteries, people and history and culture, his keen traveler's curiosity alongside his playfulness, teasing Diane for overtipping out of "conservative guilt," the prose always glancing sideways in the expectation of being read. Hers are short observations with little imprint of personality. As they drive on the road to Lhasa and a truck passes, you get the sense of a woman who's allowed herself to settle in the hands of a man she's bound one day to leave.

"Did you observe the people in the truck?" he asks.

"No," she says. "I was looking the other way."

"Be observant! Look inside trucks at the people. That's how you learn about a country."

Everyone liked Diane—his friends, his colleagues—and she was wonderful with his boys, even as her star ascended to the *CBS Morning News*. He pushed her to go for the cohost job, and when she got it he negotiated her contract, then followed her to New York. They lived like squatters in her apartment, in a luxury building on Central Park West called the Beresford, with mattresses on the floor and no dinner in the fridge, the lodging of two busy people. She woke up before two in the morning to be driven to the studio, and some mornings Holbrooke rode with her through the dark streets, proposing questions to challenge McGeorge Bundy or corner Zbigniew Brzezinski, then badgered her producer to give her a bigger share of that morning's show, and afterward critiqued her performance down to posture and clothes and hair. He once called Larry Tisch, who owned CBS, to complain that Howard Stringer, who ran CBS News, had failed to compliment Diane on something or other, when in fact he had. Stringer couldn't understand why a woman as capable as Sawyer let her boyfriend interfere in her work. "You can't do this," he reproached her. "Why don't you come directly to me?"

But she allowed it. Holbrooke was doing the dirty but necessary job that she would rather avoid in order to remain enigmatically gracious. No one could really unlock Diane, at least not this man, and the inability drove him to work even harder at it. On a visit to Peter Tarnoff's vacation home in Nova Scotia, Holbrooke told her, "You've had everything come easily. I've had to fight like hell for everything I have, because for some reason people don't like me."

They were a Manhattan power couple in a decade of televised glitz. It's strange to remember that there were no bigger celebrities in the eighties than the men and women who read news scripts on TV. Everything about them—their seven-figure salaries, their rivalries, their

haircuts—was a story, often bigger than the news itself, as when ABC and NBC tried to steal Sawyer away from CBS (ABC finally got her). The networks were beginning the long evisceration of their news divisions. This was the last moment when Americans viewed the bringers of the world into their living rooms (some of them actual journalists) as unifying authorities on reality. It was a halfway point between Cold War sobriety and the celebrity shitbox, between Walter Cronkite and Laura Ingraham. The nation still thought it needed the news but it wanted entertainment, so the networks showered glitter and fairy dust on their anchors and turned them into movie stars. The whole thing attracted Holbrooke, who finagled his way onto *Nightline* every time a foreign news story made booking him thinkable.

Once, around 1985, a neighbor in the Beresford saw Dick and Diane standing out on Central Park West, waiting for a car, and paused to admire them. Holbrooke looked sleek and handsome in a navy-blue cashmere coat with the collar turned up. Sawyer was a vision in tall blond. The neighbor, whose name was Kati Marton, and who was married to another TV news personality, Peter Jennings, thought: *What a glamorous couple. They look as if they belong right here.*

Holbrooke asked Diane to marry him, have children with him. She declined. Friends detected no heat between them. They were affectionate, useful to each other; she depended on his counsel and protection, he basked in her light as she rose from *CBS Morning News* to *60 Minutes.* But she complained to Judy Gelb that Holbrooke was exhausting—he filled his Connecticut vacation house with guests when Diane wanted to read in peace, never had the cash ready when the cabbie arrived at their destination. Her complaints got back to Holbrooke, as she intended, but he dismissed them.

In the fall of 1987, a friend said to Diane in Dick's presence, "Time's passing—when are you going to get married?"

"When the right guy comes along."

He had already arrived. He was Mike Nichols, the film and stage director. Diane had met him at the end of 1986, in the first-class Concorde lounge at Charles de Gaulle Airport in Paris, as they were both waiting for the supersonic flight to New York. Nichols approached her from behind a potted palm. "You're my hero," he said. "And you're mine," she said back. Nichols was freshly divorced from his third wife and involved with another woman who was involved with another man; Sawyer was living with Holbrooke. But the real obstacle was Nichols's addiction to the sleeping pill Halcion, which made him delusional. Once he kicked the drug and regained his sanity, he and Diane began to meet for lunch.

One day in September 1987, when she was abroad on a working trip, Holbrooke suggested that they have dinner out the night she got back. No, she said, she was seeing Mike Nichols that night, and could Dick please move out of her apartment. The next day he did.

To make it official, Diane planted a story with her friend the gossip columnist Liz Smith. Before it ran, she found Holbrooke where he was temporarily holed up, in Pete Peterson's apartment on the East River, and told him what was coming in the *Daily News*. The item read: "Now that he is divorced, Mike Nichols seems awfully smitten with Diane Sawyer, it's true. But on the other hand, she is still going around with her long-time steady, that onetime tall and handsome hope of the State Department, Richard Holbrooke."

Holbrooke picked himself up—he always did—and scrawled a note to Liz Smith: "My friends (all three of them) have asked me whether, in your October 1 column, the word 'onetime' refers to 'tall,' 'handsome,' or 'hope.' I am taking the position that, since I am now hopeless, I must still be tall and handsome, but my friends (both of them) said this is self-evidently absurd."

It was a gallant effort, for Holbrooke's friends had never seen him so low. He had tried like hell to be big enough game for Diane Sawyer and lost her to a German Jewish refugee who made her laugh. After seven years, she could relax. One despondent night, over a plate of squid-ink pasta, Wisner was moved to ask Holbrooke which was the more bruised, his heart or his ego. Who could tell the difference? It's hard enough for those of us who conduct our romantic lives outside the glare of the glossies, but the distinction blurs to nothing when your girlfriend leaves you the month she's on the cover of *Vanity Fair* in a black off-the-shoulder dress whose risks and benefits you calculated together.

Sawyer and Nichols married in the spring of 1988 and stayed married till his death in 2014, though she continued to turn to Holbrooke for professional advice, while in his office he continued to display a framed magazine cover bearing the imperishable image of her face.

———

IN JULY 1986, Averell Harriman finally died at the age of ninety-four.

Holbrooke wrote Pam a pained, loving, grateful letter, ten pages long. He told her that Averell had lived "the life of the century." He tried to describe what it was like to work for this man, Harriman's impatience with abstract thought, his lifelong trust in his own instincts. "He was like someone who could solve very complex equations in his head but couldn't explain how he did it." He pondered why Harriman had failed to achieve his highest ambitions—to be a successful politician and secretary of state—and concluded that it was his unease with self-advancement in the absence of a particular mission. (He didn't mention Averell's stiff humorlessness.) "He was most effective when, as a troubleshooter or Special Envoy, he dealt with a specific crisis," Holbrooke wrote. "Yet he, and not the men who gained the prizes he sought, will be remembered for historic achievements and, in the end, for a towering personality."

There was more than a little aspiration in this praise. Could you be a great man without a great title? Leave a mark on history while never rising above assistant secretary of state? Watch in disappointment as your career petered out, then have such a letter written about you posthumously by your chief disciple? Maybe—if the crisis was big enough, and the achievements lasting, and the personality suited to the moment.

Holbrooke was among seven or eight hundred mourners who attended the funeral in an Episcopal church on Fifth Avenue, and among the smaller group of sixty friends and family who followed the hearse, escorted by New York City police and state troopers, across the George Washington Bridge and up the Hudson to the Harriman estate. Bishop Paul Moore—who had married Holbrooke and Blythe—led prayers over the coffin at an open grave next to Marie Harriman's. The guests withdrew for a lunch reception at the mansion while the grave was filled in. Only two or three family members knew (though the story would appear two months later in the *Washington Post*, despite Holbrooke's best effort on Pam's behalf to have it killed) that Harriman's grave was empty. His corpse was being kept refrigerated in a funeral home in a New York suburb until the completion of the final resting place that Pam had secretly chosen by the shore of a lake three miles away from the Harriman family plot, on a piece of ground where there would be room someday for a second grave, her own, under a stone monument inscribed with the words PATRIOT, PUBLIC SERVANT, STATESMAN.

During the eighties, as Pam was nursing her aged husband, and even more after his death, she became the Democratic Party's biggest fund-raiser. She started her own political action committee—PamPAC—with office and staff in the Harriman guesthouse, hosting "issues evenings" next door in the grand salon of the main house, serving creamed lobster and champagne before a discussion of energy policy, matching big names—John Glenn, Mario Cuomo, Gary Hart—with big money at a thousand dollars a head, tending to the ailing party, anticipating its every need as she had done with the Fiat heir and the Broadway producer and the great man himself. She helped return the Democrats to a majority in the Senate in 1986. By the end of the decade she had raised twelve million dollars.

Holbrooke became a core member of Pam's brain trust—his calls to her office were always answered on the first ring, and she sometimes taped them for future study—advising her on issues and guest lists, helping her get a coveted spot on the Council on Foreign Relations. The regular introducer at PamPAC's fund-raisers was the silver-maned, silky-voiced, courtly mannered Clark Clifford, who was also a co-trustee of Harriman's hundred-million-dollar estate (nearly all of it went to Pam, with trusts for his heirs). Clifford was Holbrooke's last surviving link to the dawn of the American century and Harry Truman's poker table. Harriman was a greater god to Holbrooke than Clifford, who had served just six years in government during his four-decade career in Washington, but the high windows of Clifford's wood-paneled law office looked directly across Lafayette Square at the White House, and his biography and style conveyed an insider so deeply connected and widely respected, so *knowing* (lawyer to Jack Kennedy, board member of Phillips Petroleum and Knight Ridder, the only senior Johnson official to come out of Vietnam with his reputation enhanced), that he still commanded authority just by rising from his desk chair or picking up the phone.

Once, when Clifford was representing DuPont, the company came under investigation for antitrust violations. Clifford spoke to people he knew at the Justice Department and managed to convince them that the charges were unfounded. He sent DuPont a bill for $750,000, which prompted an outraged letter from its chairman, Irving Shapiro. Clifford got on the phone with Shapiro and explained that he had saved the company ten million dollars in legal fees by preventing the case from going further. "Now you can do one of two things," Clifford told his client. "You can pay the amount on the bill—it won't go down—or don't pay me anything. If you don't, we'll go on being friends, we'll play golf together, but never ask me to do any work for you again." DuPont paid.

Harriman had the achievements Holbrooke revered (his proudest was negotiating the 1963 Test Ban Treaty with the Soviets), but Clifford had the persona he admired and could never hope to emulate. "You and I will never be that," he once said to Peter Duchin, a Jewish-born bandleader who was Averell and Marie's surrogate son. They would always be on the outside of the old WASP world looking in. But Holbrooke couldn't resist the warm glow in the window. "There is, at times, a quality of magic around Clark Clifford," he wrote in a notebook. "You may know that it is based, at least in part, on illusion, but if it is powerful enough, you still may find yourself believing in it, or wanting to believe in it." So when, in 1987, eighty-year-old Clifford approached him for help in writing his memoirs—the crown of a legendary career—

Holbrooke immediately signed on. Hadn't McGeorge Bundy ghostwritten the memoirs of Henry Stimson, an earlier titan of the American century? Holbrooke would receive half of the million dollars that Mort Janklow, his and Clifford's literary agent, had gotten out of Random House, and he would help one of his idols while he waited for the wheel to spin around again.

But first he had to check with Lehman.

Holbrooke had lost his sponsor there when Peterson was ousted in 1983, but he was still well liked at the firm. Not because he ever closed a deal—he didn't—but because bankers who knew their own deficiencies were as dazzled by his political intelligence and worldliness as he was by their money. No matter how rich and successful, bankers tend to be narrow and gray, and Holbrooke was polychromatic company. The firm's head of government affairs had never even worked in Washington, and Holbrooke schooled him. Executives liked to go back to the office and report that they'd had lunch with Holbrooke. He explained China and Korea to Lehman's top people, brought the likes of Phil Knight and John Glenn to the table, gained entry for colleagues to the Council on Foreign Relations, and made his own rules because finance plainly bored him.

Still, you had to bring in kill to survive. The atmosphere at Lehman was cigar-smoking, back-stabbing greed. At the end of 1986, Holbrooke went to the eighteenth-floor offices of the heads of investment banking, Sherman Lewis and the enfant terrible Peter Solomon, to make his case for his annual bonus. This was the one aspect of finance that engaged his full attention. Ever since the acquisition of Lehman by Shearson/American Express, Holbrooke had been star-fucking the CEO of AmEx, James Robinson (in spite of finding him intellectually incurious and self-absorbed), to the point of neglecting the department that paid his salary. So his bosses decided to have some fun.

> SOLOMON: Nice to meet you, Dick, how are you? Sherman, this is Dick Holbrooke.
> HOLBROOKE: What do you mean, "meet me"?
> LEWIS: Dick, I haven't seen you all year. Why are you here?
> HOLBROOKE: Peter asked me to come in and talk about my bonus.

LEWIS: Why us? I thought you were spending all your time with Jim
    Robinson. I don't think we can pay your bonus.

This went on for ten minutes. Holbrooke left in disarray.

The next day he caught up with Solomon outside his office. "Peter,
have you ever thought of joining CFR?"

"No, what is it?"

Holbrooke explained the Council on Foreign Relations. "Somebody
like you really should be in it."

The blatancy struck Solomon as irresistible. Holbrooke actually
imagined he was getting away with something. It was the kind of move
that made you put up with him, if your skin was thick enough. He got
his bonus, around a quarter of a million dollars that year, on top of his
half-million-dollar salary.

But by the fall of 1987—around the time Diane was getting ready to
leave him—the terrain had shifted. It was a bearish year, culminating in
the worst stock market crash since 1929. Shearson Lehman was going
all-out into trading and leveraged finance in pursuit of its rival Drexel
Burnham and no longer had as much room for an underproducing
investment banker. In fact, at the moment when Holbrooke went in to
see Vincent Mai, a Lehman banker and South African native who was
Holbrooke's one true friend on Wall Street, and asked Mai how the firm
would react if he were to spend some time working with Clark Clifford,
he had no idea that he was about to be fired.

"I love it here, I think I have a great future," Holbrooke said. "If you
think it will hurt me, I won't do it."

Mai, a man of impeccable decency, saw the way to extricate Lehman
from an unpleasant incident and Holbrooke from disaster. He advised
Holbrooke to tell the firm about this exciting new offer, go on reduced
hours at lower pay, and help a great statesman write his memoirs.

IN LATE OCTOBER Holbrooke and Clifford sat down with their editor
from Random House, Peter Osnos, in Clifford's downtown Washington
office—not at his law firm, but three blocks away in the chairman's suite
at First American Bankshares. This was a new business that Clifford

had taken on as his law practice declined during the Reagan years. He once told Mort Janklow that he wanted to be the guy who got to tell a hostile congressman whether or not he would receive the big mortgage he needed. The bank's mahogany-paneled premises were decorated in the same early Americana style as the State Department's seventh floor, furnished with pieces from Mrs. Clifford's family collection, including a chair once owned by Daniel Webster, and a Currier and Ives series of twenty-seven American presidents on horseback lining the walls. So Peter Osnos was puzzled to notice that the owners pictured in the bank's brochures all appeared to be Arab.

Over lunch, Clifford confessed that he'd had trouble plowing through the autobiography of his old friend Dean Acheson, let alone Henry Kissinger's and George Ball's. He was worried about his ability to write an interesting book that would sell. And in fact the memoirs of great men are almost always disappointing—more on that later.

Osnos told Clifford and Holbrooke that they could write a successful book, but it "must have that sense of true verisimilitude. Readers must have a sense that this is what it really was like."

Holbrooke threw himself into the project. He spent hours and hours in Clifford's plush office at the bank, capturing his voice on a micro-cassette recorder—the same theatrical drawl as ever, the confiding cadences and whispered emphases that won the trust of Democratic presidents and deep-pocketed clients, though it had slowed and grown slurry—prodding Clifford's memory, prompting him with lost names. Here was Holbrooke, forty-six years old and in his prime, already an emblem of uncontrolled ambition, gladly subjugating his ego to the task of coaxing ancient tales out of an old man. Surprising, isn't it? The Clifford magic pulled him in, but what kept him plugging away for months if not the enchantment of history?

From his arrival in the summer of 1945 as an aide at the Truman White House, Clifford embodied the liberal internationalism that Holbrooke later made his own. On domestic issues, Clifford pushed Truman to the left. In foreign policy, he helped bring into being the Truman Doctrine, the Marshall Plan, American recognition of the state of Israel, and the National Security Act of 1947, which created the Defense Department, the CIA, and the National Security Council. Clifford was, in Acheson's phrase, present at the creation of the structures that made the United States a global power, when we turned away from a century and a half of looking inward and assumed the leadership of the free world.

You could say that he embodied the best and worst of the Wise Men. In July 1965, at Camp David, he tried as a private citizen to persuade Johnson not to send fifty thousand troops to Vietnam, arguing passionately against the president's advisors, especially McNamara, that the war was unwinnable, would go on for five years, cost fifty thousand American lives and hundreds of billions of dollars: "It will ruin us."

But after the president rejected his counsel, Clifford became an arch-hawk, making the same pro-war arguments that he'd dismantled at Camp David—out of personal loyalty to Johnson, misguided commitment to the policy, a need to maintain his access to the White House. Then, in January 1968, just before Tet, Johnson named him to replace McNamara at the Pentagon. For the first time, Clifford studied Vietnam carefully, and he came back to his original view that the war could not be won. He spent his year as secretary of defense trying to turn the ship around. For Holbrooke, who had worked on Vietnam at ground level, all of this was thrilling inside stuff.

Then he had to write the thing. Because that's what ghostwriters to the famous do—they write every damn sentence, for the honor of having their name on the cover qualified by a preposition and in diminished font (WITH RICHARD HOLBROOKE was required by contract to be exactly half the size of CLARK CLIFFORD). They hand over their hard-won words like surrogate mothers surrendering the baby before the hemorrhaging has stopped, and afterward they're considered midwives at best, if they're remembered at all. When Senator John F. Kennedy published *Profiles in Courage*, for which his father wangled him the 1957 Pulitzer Prize, and a reporter claimed that the book's real author was Kennedy's aide Ted Sorensen, who had gone entirely unacknowledged, it was Clark Clifford, Kennedy's lawyer, who forced ABC News to retract the charge by politely threatening a lawsuit. Ghostwriters are a tolerated literary scandal, but their presence lingers like the echo of another voice that confuses the sense of true verisimilitude. I'm getting to why the accounts of great men are disappointing.

In his Senate office, Kennedy employed a stunning receptionist named Pam Turnure. One day in 1958, with the presidential campaign on the horizon, Kennedy summoned Clifford to see him. Jack was in a terrible jam. He'd been enjoying regular trysts in his receptionist's apartment on the second floor of a house in Georgetown. The couple living on the first floor had observed the comings and goings of the famous senator, gained illegal entry into Turnure's apartment, installed a microphone in her bedroom, drilled a hole through the floorboards, run a wire down to their apartment, and connected it to a tape recorder. After gathering great material, they had gotten in touch with Kennedy and demanded payment in the form of a Modigliani painting that his father owned.

"I am not the right sort of lawyer for this," Clifford told his client, "but I know who is." He suggested that Joe Kennedy contact a former FBI agent named James McInerney, who knew how to navigate the lower depths of Washington. McInerney looked into the blackmailing couple's past—they had a history of embezzlement—and then paid a visit to their house. "You have got two weeks to get out of town," he told the couple. "If you don't get out of town within those two weeks, then you will deeply regret it. In fact, if you don't get out of town, and if we ever hear from you again, you will be dead."

Dead as in *dead*.

This was one of the things that powerful men hired Clifford to do—get them out of jams. But the story was allowed nowhere near his memoirs. Clifford didn't want to embarrass Jackie or himself. He didn't even let Holbrooke record him as he recounted it, but the ghostwriter later jotted the story down, with an exclamation mark.

You don't expect Clifford to tell the truth about Pam Turnure. But what about his own wife? When Holbrooke interviewed Marny Clifford, she told him how she had met her future husband. In 1929, in their early twenties, they happened to take the same boat cruise down the Rhine. Marny was playing bridge with her traveling companions from Wellesley when a good-looking young man walked up and said, "I haven't seen a good bridge game since I left the States." "You'll have to come up with something better than that," Marny said back. As they continued to flirt she kept drinking white wine, and in the heat of the day she started to get drunk and feel sick, and she thought: *Well, I'll never see him again*. But Clark and his friend followed Marny and her friends through Italy to Paris.

Not a totally dignified story, but a pretty good one. The translation into memoir wrecked it:

> Onboard was a group of six young American girls on a college tour. I noticed immediately a tall, slender blonde, and Lou picked a gorgeous redhead. After Lou and I had eyed them for a while from a distance, we approached them, and rather boldly asked if we might join them for the day so that we might speak English instead of our fractured French and German. Our offer was courteously accepted.

When Holbrooke finished the book, Clifford insisted on reading the whole thing aloud in his presence, pouring his bourbon-on-ice voice over every word as if to take ownership, an exercise of droit du seigneur that restored the relation of author to scribe.

Yet Clifford was right to worry. Verisimilitude was the last thing a great man wanted in his memoirs. Holbrooke had written that way when he was in the Mekong Delta and not important enough to be dishonest. Now he was a semi-famous person writing a book in the voice of a more famous person about historic events featuring even more famous people. At its heart a book like that had to be a fraud. I don't mean that it contained fabrications, or even that it was self-

serving—all autobiographies are. I mean that, pushed down beneath the self-sacrificing public servant and sober statesman whose favorite descriptors were "gracious," "charming," and "delightful," there was, there *had to be,* a monomaniac whose ambition was so insatiable that he took on the running of a bank in his eighth decade (First American got half a sentence in the book), a fixer so smoothly ruthless that he could make an antitrust suit or a pair of blackmailers go away, a man so consumed with power and money that he was at times estranged from two of his three grown daughters. That character, far more alive than any Wise Man, was scrubbed out as thoroughly as Pam Turnure. Clifford, like Acheson and Kissinger, managed to make himself boring.

Counsel to the President was a good book of its kind. In the spring of 1991 it was serialized in two parts in *The New Yorker* (Holbrooke was given a co-byline) and appeared near the top of the best-seller list. Pam Harriman threw a party on N Street for her friend the author, attended by four hundred Washington dignitaries. But at the very moment of his final crowning, everything went wrong for Clark Clifford.

The week of Pam's party, First American Bankshares was reported to be secretly and illegally owned by Bank of Credit and Commerce International, based in Pakistan. BCCI had used the Arab investors pictured in First American's brochure as front men to make the purchase and Clifford's sterling reputation to dupe U.S. regulators. BCCI was laundering money for drug cartels, terrorists, and dictators like Saddam Hussein and Manuel Noriega. Clifford was not just First American's chairman but also its lawyer, as well as BCCI's. He and his partner, Robert Altman (married to Lynda Carter of *Wonder Woman*), had received a sweetheart loan in the form of undervalued BCCI stock, which they sold for a shared profit of $9.8 million.

When BCCI's criminal activities came to light, Clifford claimed ignorance of First American's true owners. "I have a choice of either seeming stupid or venal," he said, and like everyone he chose the first. Senator John Kerry held highly publicized hearings, and bribery charges were filed in Manhattan. Altman was ultimately acquitted; Clifford was deemed too frail to stand trial, though he faced civil suits running to a hundred million dollars. The scandal dirtied his reputation, destroyed his law firm, and sank his book, which fell off the best-seller list as soon as its author turned into a symbol of Washington corruption. "I have become a pariah," he told Holbrooke. "Old friends don't return my calls."

There was more. In the six years after Harriman's death, his estate, with Clifford as one of its trustees, lost thirty million dollars from the trusts set up to provide for Averell's descendants—some of it gone in bad real estate investments, some to float Pam Harriman's expensive life. In 1994 the heirs sued her and Clifford. To settle, she had to sell a Matisse, a Picasso, a Renoir, and the two houses on N Street. She blamed her old friend Clark for refusing to pay more than a million dollars as his part of the settlement.

By then Clifford had receded from public view. He died in 1998 at age ninety-one. On his tombstone you won't find the words "Here lies someone who used to be a Washington titan, and you probably never heard of him." Clifford's ghostwriter never stopped believing in his magic. Holbrooke considered the scandals a late-life lapse that didn't lay a glove on the great man.

WHILE HOLBROOKE WAS getting down the facts of Clifford's life, he was living out his own version. The differences are instructive and, to me, a little poignant.

By the end of the eighties he was sharing an Upper East Side triplex with his younger son Anthony, who had been kicked out of boarding school for pot and was finishing high school in New York. Anthony's academic career had been continuously troubled and Litty had had enough. "I have spent too little time with him, in the late 1970's especially," Holbrooke admitted. So father and son lived together for several years like two disheveled bachelors, going to see WrestleMania IV at Trump Plaza in New Jersey, even dating a mother-daughter pair. David was around, too, working at NBC in a job his father helped him land. Holbrooke finally began to get to know his sons.

Girlfriends came and went. There was the fine-boned, elegant Dutch-born photography agent who spent weekends at his country house in the woods of Litchfield County, Connecticut, until he grew restless with her artistic and unworldly soul and moved on to the brash and naughty English-born magazine editor he was already seeing in the city, who introduced him to Mick Jagger. There was a socially prominent and emotionally fragile interior decorator, and the widow of the British theater critic Kenneth Tynan, and the future Republican lieutenant governor of New York, and a famous movie star, and the woman with whom a colleague saw him disappear into the lavatory on the Eastern Airlines shuttle, and someone named Stormy, and the wife of a shady New York City pol, which was when things turned to farce.

Holbrooke accompanied the pol's wife on a trip to Puerto Rico, where she owned a cellular business, taking separate flights and booking separate hotels. But the pol—who had recorded their phone calls and leaked the contents to the *New York Post,* before changing his mind and hiring a lawyer to get the story killed—followed the lovers down to San Juan. In the middle of the night he pounded on his wife's door: "I know you're in there, Holbrooke! Open the goddam door!" Holbrooke, who *was* in there, grabbed his clothes and hid out on the balcony, until the pol finally stopped screaming at his wife and left. Holbrooke decided to leave as well, prudently taking the elevator past the lobby floor straight down to the garage, where the pol was waiting on a bench, laughing.

When Holbrooke tried to end the affair, the wife, herself prone to jealous rages, came banging on his apartment door. He had to shush his boys, who were seeing their father in all his humanness, until the banging stopped and she went away. (She did fine. After her divorce from the shady pol she was introduced by Kissinger to a titled Rothschild and, outdoing Pam Harriman, married him.)

Holbrooke became a New York media target. After a prolonged struggle with his own better judgment, he couldn't resist stepping into the trap of a snide profile in *Spy,* as if to confirm the magazine's opinion of him as "the prototypical New Age political power networker." In the summer of 1988, *Time* magazine mocked him for trying to hustle his way into the Dukakis campaign after Holbrooke's candidate, Al Gore, dropped out. Furious and wounded, Holbrooke told the writer and editor that it was untrue and damaging. "'Ambitious'—maybe," he once complained to Les Gelb's wife Judy about another magazine profile. "But 'self-promoter'? *Me?*"

That July, *Vanity Fair* ran a profile of Pam Harriman, who was basking in her role as the Democratic Party's godmother. Holbrooke tried to help her cause and his own by using his influence with both the writer and one of the editors, his brash and naughty English girlfriend—only to end up in a nasty spat with the writer while getting no thanks from Pam, who disliked the piece because it failed to omit her prior life as a courtesan, and who left him off the guest list of her star-studded fund-raising dinner for Michael Dukakis. "In the long run it won't matter, but it just adds to my feeling of isolation right now," Holbrooke wrote to himself. "This despite my very real ambivalence about even going back into a Dukakis Administration." In November Dukakis got creamed, the Democrats' third straight rout, and Holbrooke didn't have to test his ambivalence.

He created a wake of disorder and indignity that Clifford couldn't have imagined even at the ignominious end of his life. Clifford perfected the art of discretion, seeming to want nothing while everything came to him—presidential job offers, big-money clients. That model of power exercised in private by a few of the right men with no need to justify themselves was long gone—one more casualty of Vietnam. Holbrooke was a creature of the post-WASP establishment where power was diffuse and you had to shout for attention to get great things done.

Yes—great things. By now you might think that nothing mattered to Holbrooke if a magazine writer or TV camera wasn't there to record it. He wanted them around, but he tried just as hard, and cared no less, when they weren't. I'll give you one example.

In 1991 he went back to Tibet—not to show off for a glamorous girlfriend, but to find out whether its traditional Buddhist culture was surviving China's iron-fisted growth. He traveled with a group of humanitarian types, closely questioned their official Chinese hosts, met political dissidents, and pushed hard to see the inside of Tibet's prisons along with its temples. On his last day, on the flight out, he wrote in a journal that he expected no one ever to read:

Ahead of us lies the normal pace of life—telephones, meetings, crises, dramas, peripheral contact with major events, personal problems, large or small. Behind us lies Tibet, still unique, still compelling. If one doesn't think about it, it doesn't exist really—a landlocked region of Inner Asia still with little outside contact, with its own peculiar problems so far away that they can drop immediately to the bottom of any list of priorities. When I return to New York, I know I will be told that no one cares, or should care, about the problems of Tibet, with its 2 million people, when New York City, four times Tibet's size, is deep in crisis. But I do not believe that New York's very real problems (and for that matter the rest of the nation's) means we must turn away from pressing human tragedies elsewhere. That process leads only one way—towards an ever-narrower definition of what is in one's interests—geographically, ethnically, and so on. Will we all end up so self-absorbed that we have room in our lives for only ourselves?

When I hear these attacks (and I know I will), I will remember Tashi, sitting in his living room off the Jokang, burst into sudden tears when talking of America, a land he hasn't seen since 1964, but whose ideals and values inspire him. I will remember that America is always best when it is true to its own values + ideals, not with government intervention that by its very nature denies the values it seeks to promote, but by steady articulation and skillful pressure.

He still burned with the hard, gemlike flame of the *New Yorker* cartoon on the Lakes' coffee table. But in the twelve-year absence of the only thing that really counted, during a corrupt, repellent decade—the eighties stank up even Clark Clifford—amid the money and the girlfriends and the TV gigs, it was hard to tell that he was orchestrating the scattered pieces of his life in order to seize some chance that he alone saw dimly in the future. His shameless hunger made him more vulnerable than his heroes, and, to me at least, more human.

But I wonder if I've really made you feel what he was like to be around, and I'm not sure I can. Jumping on a trampoline in Connecticut with Strobe Talbott as the canvas sagged and sprang under his boyish zeal. Lying in bed with the elegant photography agent, asking about her day, her children, intimate and funny, indulging his love of the art of conversation in that postcoital spell when the restlessness temporarily faded. Giving the Gelbs plot summary and analysis of all nine movies he saw last week. Playing *Donkey Kong* in a video arcade for hours on end, jamming quarters into the machine and cursing and laughing in his quest for the Epic Win that kept eluding him. What was he like? He didn't want to miss a minute of his life.

IN THE SPRING OF 1991, when he was about to turn fifty—eleven years out of government and no end in sight, with communism fallen and Iraq defeated in just the first two years of Bush's first term—Peter Tarnoff, who led the Council on Foreign Relations, planned to throw Holbrooke a birthday party with a dozen friends. But Holbrooke told Pete Peterson that he thought the milestone demanded something more. This was hubris, but Peterson and Tarnoff obliged with a dinner at the 21 Club in Midtown, where presidents dined and Frank Sinatra and Donald Trump had favorite tables. Around eighty or a hundred of New York's aristocracy of success—Tom Brokaw, Tina Brown and Harry Evans, the Halberstams, the Janklows, the others—gathered upstairs in the private dining room, along with Holbrooke's mother, brother, and sons. The speakers took turns on the podium making fun of Holbrooke's uncontrolled libido, his weakness for socially connected women, his habit of canceling plans if something better came along. The Chinese-American novelist Bette Bao Lord pointed out that he had been born in the Year of the Snake—appropriately enough, since the snake was devious. Jim Hoge, publisher of the *Daily News,* said, "You probably noticed that my left shoulder is lower than my right. That's from talking to Dick, who always looks over my shoulder to see if there's someone more worth talking to." David Holbrooke described what it was like to be the son of a man who forced his friends to throw him such a party.

Something went wrong. The speakers were improvising and trying to top one another, paying back the high cost of being in his life. They didn't know how to be witty, the jokes cut too deep and true, and the smell of blood turned the play savage. Holbrooke, who could never laugh at himself because he didn't know himself, was laughing now from his table by the podium because it was the only way to survive the disaster, and he kept looking around for others to join him. But no one else was laughing.

Then came Gelb, his best friend in the room. The comedian Jackie Mason, who was performing on Broadway, had recently been a dinner guest at the Gelbs' house, where he ran into Holbrooke in the kitchen. "Are you Jewish?" Mason demanded. Holbrooke allowed that he was. Judy Cohen Gelb, who had known him for twenty-five years, nearly dropped the plate she was carrying. Mason looked from Holbrooke to her. "He says he's Jewish, but he's spent his whole life denying it."

With this revelation Les Gelb had his routine for the birthday party. He played both sides of an interview with the guest of honor.

REPORTER: Are you Jewish?
HOLBROOKE: No.
REPORTER: Are you sure?
HOLBROOKE: Yes, I'm sure.
REPORTER: We have information.
HOLBROOKE: Actually, I had a Jewish great-grandmother.
REPORTER: We heard it was a more direct line.
HOLBROOKE: Well, maybe I'm half Jewish.
REPORTER [to the audience]: And that sounds half true.

Holbrooke gamely pretended to enjoy the whole thing, and at the end he rose to thank everyone. But Gelb saw the pain in his face. Afterward, his friends were appalled at one another and themselves. Years later they still couldn't get over the cruelty. "That was the worst day of my life," Holbrooke told his brother.

TONY LAKE STAYED far away from the birthday party.

In 1981 the Lakes left Washington—the war between Vance and Brzezinski had soured him on government—and moved to western Massachusetts. They bought an 80-acre farm on a winding road in the foothills of the Berkshires. She Toni bred horses while He Tony raised thirty head of beef cattle and hayed the fields and produced 150 gallons of maple syrup a year. He taught international relations at Amherst and Mount Holyoke and wrote books. Their teenagers became farm kids. This was the life Toni wanted—Tony, too, at first—and it was her turn, and it worked for a while.

Lake and Holbrooke hardly ever saw each other. Every four years they exchanged memos with ideas for the latest doomed Democratic presidential candidate. Once, Holbrooke invited the Lakes to his Connecticut country house, and they found him surrounded by moneyed people and didn't like what they saw. Another time, over lunch in New York, Holbrooke kept trying to tell Lake how much he was making at Lehman (ten times a professor's salary), and Lake kept waving him off, to Holbrooke's irritation: "I don't want to know, Dick." Lake the gentle-man farmer–scholar was a person Holbrooke neither understood nor liked—it smacked of false humility, just as, when Lake said he didn't want to be secretary of state, it actually meant that he did. With Wisner, Holbrooke gave Lake the nickname "Cincinnatus," after the reluctant Roman leader who had to be coaxed off his farm to save the republic.

After the drama of the early seventies, Toni and Dick went years without seeing each other—she put as much distance between them as she could—but the connection didn't die. In the early eighties, on a visit to the farm, Judy Gelb came upon them standing together in the kitchen doorway and locked in such an intense conversation that she left them alone. In 1984, Toni's mother took her own life while suffering from cancer, and Toni needed someone to talk to. Her husband was no help, so she called Holbrooke and asked to meet him for lunch. Tony didn't like it, but he didn't ask her not to. So she went down to New York and for three hours she once again had Holbrooke's complete attention.

By the end of the eighties Lake feared that he had been forgotten in Washington. Perhaps as a way to get back, he set out to write a book about the foreign policy of the Democratic Party. Every four years, Democrats refought Vietnam and engaged in the same futile civil war between hawks and doves, while the Republicans owned the presi-dency. With the end of the Cold War, those arguments were history, and Lake wanted to know if the new era would give Democrats a chance to develop a new vision that could win back a majority. His plan was to talk to the presidential contenders for 1992 and write a campaign nar-rative. But the Democratic candidates didn't want to talk about foreign policy—they had already ceded the subject to President Bush.

Sandy Berger, a Washington lawyer who had been Lake's deputy on the Carter policy planning staff, was advising Bill Clinton—Berger and Clinton were old friends from the McGovern campaign. In Novem-ber 1991, Berger arranged to have Lake tag along on a campaign trip. He caught up with Clinton at a fund-raising dinner outside Boston, where Hillary introduced herself and surprised Lake by saying that she admired him for quitting the White House over the invasion of Cambodia. After dinner, Lake got ten minutes with the candidate in the backseat of a car. Clinton asked Lake where he lived, and Lake, who had anticipated discussing theater missiles in Europe, began talking

about the economic troubles of family farmers in western Massachusetts. Clinton lit up—he wanted to know all about these hard-pressed
neighbors, and he seemed to care. Even though they hadn't talked about
foreign policy, Lake came away impressed.

A week later, George Stephanopoulos called Lake to ask him to work
on Clinton's first foreign policy speech. Lake flew down to Little Rock
and went over a draft line by line with the candidate. Clinton would
say, "Okay, I believe that," and they would go on to the next paragraph.
The speech blamed Bush for focusing so much on foreign affairs that
he was neglecting the economy and turning Americans dangerously
inward, just when the world was poised to embrace democracy and
free markets. Bush's foreign policy was stuck in the past and betrayed
American values: he refused to support democracy in China after the
Tiananmen Square massacre, abandoned the Kurds at the end of the
Gulf War, and did little to encourage the newly independent states of
the former Soviet Union. "Having won the Cold War," Clinton said, "we
must not now lose the peace."

This was Lake's answer to his own question. His party's foreign policy would reject isolation in the name of democracy. He dropped his
book idea and joined the campaign as Clinton's advisor with Berger.

On the last night of the Democratic convention in New York, Lake
was in his hotel room with Sandy and Susan Berger. Clinton was about
to go onstage in Madison Square Garden to give his acceptance speech.
The speech itself (which, as Gelb pointed out in a *Times* column, contained just 141 words on foreign policy) was less memorable than the
slick and touching film, *The Man from Hope,* that preceded it, and the
spectacle that followed, with the Clintons and the Gores hugging and
dancing to Fleetwood Mac's "Don't Stop." It was an ecstatic moment for
starving Democrats, but Lake was overcome with sadness.

"What's the matter?" Berger had noticed the expression on his face.

"I think it's going to work," Lake said. Clinton was going to win, and
Lake was going to return to Washington, and he knew what that would
mean to Toni.

In the long history of Holbrooke and Lake, Lake again had the pole
position. Holbrooke sent him his first campaign memo just before
Christmas 1991. After the New Hampshire primary, he began sending
one a month, and by the convention they were going out every week,

and in the run-up to the fall debates it was almost daily. The memos were about the defense budget, trade, Hillary, Bill's character problems, the debates, Japan (he traveled there in April), the former Soviet republics (May), Italy (June), China (July), the former Yugoslavia (August). His political advice was to go after Bush as backward looking on foreign affairs and fight him to a draw, then win on domestic issues. Holbrooke thought that Bush's passivity in the face of the growing civil war in Bosnia left him particularly vulnerable. Clinton called for air strikes against the Serb guns besieging Sarajevo.

Holbrooke suggested that he, Lake, and Berger form a triumvirate of advisors. Lake turned him down cold. He caught Holbrooke in some petty lie and called Gelb from a highway in Connecticut: "Why does he *lie* to me?" To which Gelb answered, "That's his nature." They had tolerated each other during the Carter years, but time and the acid released two decades ago had brought them to this point: they were becoming enemies.

The person running Clinton's debate preparations was a lawyer and Democratic operative named Tom Donilon, who had been a twenty-something Carter aide. Holbrooke knew him through their mutual friend Jim Johnson and the Mondale campaign. Debate prep gave the issue advisors precious hours with the candidate: Lake, Berger, and a full-time staff person named Nancy Soderberg prepared the briefing books, and Lake and Berger observed the rehearsals and fact-checked Clinton's answers. Holbrooke tried to break into the inner circle through Donilon. "Dick, it isn't going to happen," Donilon had to tell him. They were full up, and important people didn't want him. But he kept on writing memos, right up to Clinton's breakthrough win.

Several weeks after the election, Holbrooke took some notes to prepare for a meeting with Al Gore, the vice president–elect. After twelve years, the wheel had come around again. Last time he'd blown it with Carter, and he wanted to get his words right.

Great campaign—proud to be your friend—Your selection unquestionably the turning point of the campaign . . . Must manage the evolution from the Cold War to the post-CW world better: FSU; Yugoslavia; Cambodia; Somalia, etc . . . Personnel—TEAM—Basketball vs. baseball. NAT. SEC.: Top 5 jobs + second top 5 = TEAM . . . NSC—

Tony or Sandy—great campaign job. Also: Tarnoff . . . <u>Personal</u>—
I'm honored you ask. After 16 years in gov't + 12 on Wall Street—I
think that I have learned how to integrate econ + traditional foreign
policy—I would be honored to be considered for some of those top
posts we just discussed—Not DOD or CIA or Treasury—I would be
thrilled to serve as <u>Dep. Sec. State</u>—can run Dept—good administrator; know all regions of the world—know F.S.—believe in your
agenda. If not, might be useful in reassuring panicking Asians as
Amb. in Tokyo (no conflicts of interest)—USUN, if possible—but I
understand it unlikely—

The meeting gained Holbrooke nothing. The job as U.N. ambassador
was not only unlikely, it was out of the question—it went to Madeleine
Albright, who had worked for Brzezinski in the Carter White House
and, through the conferences and academic programs and campaigns
that determine a political party's experts, become a leading Democrat
on foreign policy.

Strobe Talbott, an old Clinton friend from Oxford, who was going
to leave *Time* to take an important job with the new administration,
met the president-elect at the Hay-Adams hotel in Washington just
before Thanksgiving. Talbott was Holbrooke's only loyal friend inside
the magic circle, and he raised Holbrooke's name. Why wasn't it on
any of the lists at transition headquarters? Clinton, who hardly knew
Holbrooke, said that he liked him and wanted to consider him for secretary of state, except that Holbrooke seemed to stir up so much con-
troversy and opposition. Clinton instead chose Warren Christopher, the
immaculately tailored and mannered lawyer who was the director of his
transition and proposed himself for the job. Choosing Christopher was
Clinton's way of trying to keep foreign affairs under dull, predictable,
buttoned-up control while he fixed the economy. Christopher knew
Holbrooke from their years together in the Carter State Department
and quite disliked him, more on stylistic than substantive grounds.
They were neat opposites—Christopher had no enemies and no foreign policy views, while Holbrooke had both in passionate numbers.
Christopher at State meant that the position of deputy secretary, and
every other type of secretary, was out.

As for Lake, he told Clinton that he didn't want a job unless the price of beef fell, which of course meant that he did. He was appointed national security advisor. Berger, who could have had the number-one job but yielded to Lake's greater knowledge and experience, became his deputy. Lake promised Toni that he would stay in Washington for only two years. So the top foreign policy jobs, at the White House and the State Department, went to two people who didn't want Holbrooke around.

His friend Les Aspin, a Wisconsin congressman and Pentagon whiz kid from Saigon days, was named secretary of defense. Wisner became Aspin's number three. Tarnoff got the number-three job at State. It seemed as if Holbrooke's entire Vietnam cohort, led by Lake, was ascending to the very treetops, bringing the wisdom and wounds of that war to the nineties, poised to reshape American foreign policy for the post–Cold War, while Holbrooke sat around his apartment going crazy, dashing off memos and then getting on the phone to Talbott: "Has the president-elect seen it? Whose desk is it on? Warren Christopher and I talked every month for twenty years and I can't reach him?"

Some instinct for action in the face of pain made him decide to get out of the country. He would spend Christmas in Cambodia. He would celebrate New Year's in Bosnia.

BOSNIA

They'll Come for Me

I

It was very cold but there was not yet snow on the ground. The refugee camp was in a barracks town called Karlovac, an hour outside Zagreb, the Croatian capital. Three thousand Bosnian Muslims, mostly men, lived in two concrete buildings. Between the buildings there was the shell of a Serbian Orthodox church damaged in fighting. "The damn thing could fall down any moment," a Danish relief worker told Holbrooke. "We should take it down, but the Serbs treasure it and want to rebuild it. It is very dangerous, but we can't get agreement on what to do."

The Bosnians were housed in metal bunk beds stacked three high on concrete floors, with clothing draped from the bed frames. In the musty air they waited and waited for word of a new home in another country. The internationals wanted them to return someday to Bosnia, but the men had no such desire.

Holbrooke leaned forward with his hands behind his back and stood listening to a young man in a group sprawled on bunks. He was a baker from Prijedor, a small town in northern Bosnia. The town had been majority Muslim until war broke out in the spring. Then Bosnian Serb paramilitaries came to Prijedor—and to Zvornik, Bijeljina, Omarska, Orasac, Biscani, Sanski Most, and other towns. Following careful plans, the gunmen would surround the town, block the exits, and go house to house while local Serbs pointed out the Muslim and, in fewer cases, Croat families. The paramilitaries would send the residents out into the street, then loot and destroy the houses. Women, children, and old people were driven out of town and forced to make their way to the relative safety of Croatia. Men were separated into groups. Those whose names appeared on lists of local notables were taken away and never seen again.

The others were sent to concentration camps, where they were starved and made to live in their own filth. The gunmen tormented their prisoners with tales of wives raped and children murdered. They ordered them to perform sexual acts on one another. They forced them to dig mass graves and fill them with the corpses of their friends, their kin. In some towns the paramilitaries were less discriminating and killed every last Muslim. But the goal was everywhere the same: to make the place purely Serb, to render it impossible for Bosnia's different groups to live together ever again.

When the gunmen came to Prijedor, the baker hid in the woods and watched the Serbs destroy his house. His neighbors—whom he'd known for years and considered friends—found him and turned him over to the paramilitaries. The neighbors did it without remorse. It was the first sign of hatred that the baker had ever seen in them, and the suddenness of it stunned him. When Holbrooke asked why the Serbs had done these things, the baker said simply, "I don't know." He was lucky to be a baker and not a notable. He was taken to the concentration camp at Manjaca, from which he escaped across the border to Croatia, where he became one of the war's two million refugees.

All of this was called by an ugly euphemism that reflected the thinking of the perpetrators: "ethnic cleansing." On an earlier trip to Bosnia, in August, Holbrooke had seen its immediate aftermath: the destroyed houses of Muslims alongside a lonely intact Serb house, the wrecked factories, the fields of rotting corn, the armed Serb bullies, the Muslims lined up to sign away all their property and then be crammed onto buses for Croatia. He had even passed through Prijedor. Now he was talking to the survivors of ethnic cleansing.

There was a factory worker from Sanski Most whose Serb foreman came to his house one night in a group of uniformed and armed Serbs. They ordered him to leave the house, and then they blew it up, and the whole time the foreman avoided looking him in the eye. There was a man whose seventy-year-old mother had been raped and was still trapped in Sanski Most. Could Holbrooke help get her out of Bosnia? There was an old man who had to drag himself across the bunks to show Holbrooke how the Serb guards had broken his leg. "These Serbs are so awful that they bring their little sons of ten years old to the camps to watch them beat us," the old man said.

"Not all the Serbs are so bad," a younger man said. "But those that refused to participate were killed by the other Serbs right at the beginning."

The stories were all the same. A savage and inexplicable fever had spread overnight through their friends and neighbors of many years, and now everything was finished.

As Holbrooke started to leave, the baker brought out a dirty plastic bag from under his mattress. Inside was a pair of small figures, three or four inches tall, in blond wood. Human figures, with nearly featureless faces and heads bowed and hands together behind their backs. The baker had carved them with a piece of broken glass while he was interned at the Manjaca camp, where the prisoners had stood bound for hours with their heads down to avoid being beaten. The mute simplicity of the figures evoked immense sorrow. As Holbrooke held them

they seemed to burn in his hand. He was too moved to do more than mumble a few words and return them.

"No," the baker said. "Please take them back to your country and show them to your people. Show the Americans how we have been treated. Tell America what is happening to us."

HOLBROOKE WAS in the Balkans on behalf of the International Rescue Committee, a refugee organization with a board of prominent men and women, including him. But really he went for no official reason at all. He went for the same reason that he had gone inside the pagoda where the monk's charred heart lay in a chalice. He wanted to see for himself. He was traveling alone, except for a guide and interpreter—a twenty-eight-year-old graduate student from Seattle named Stefanie Frease, who was working for the IRC in Zagreb. She had a Serb and a Croat grandparent, she had spent part of her childhood in Yugoslavia, and after the country began to disintegrate in 1991 she went back to see the war and help people if she could. She knew nothing about Holbrooke and was given just a couple days' notice of his arrival. Interpreting for him with the refugees in Karlovac, she had to fight her tears. She thought that he should have given one of the wooden figures to her.

On December 29 they flew from Zagreb to Split, on the Dalmatian coast. The next morning they got into a Nissan four-by-four and were driven up the Neretva valley to Mostar, in the Herzegovina region of southern Bosnia, which was dominated by Croats and strongly nationalistic. The war was about to become triangular, the Bosnian Croats and Muslims were a few months from turning their guns on each other, and at the Croat checkpoints the soldiers were tense and menacing. The drive took hours, with stops along the way to talk to refugees and relief workers, and in the backseat Holbrooke and Frease discussed the war. His ice-blue eyes were lit with strategic thoughts, and his words sounded detached from what he and Frease were hearing from the refugees. Traveling together through a war zone creates a temporary intimacy, and she had seen more of the war than he had. She told him that he didn't seem to have much empathy for the victims.

Holbrooke got upset. He said that he cared about Bosnia more than anyone in the U.S. government. "You don't understand what it's like to go into the White House and have to give a briefing and present very clear policy proposals that will be heard by a group of people who have less capacity for feeling and understanding of the situation than I do."

From Mostar they drove north over rocky highlands and steep ravines until they reached Vitez, a mostly Croat town within government territory in central Bosnia, where the IRC had an office. They arrived at dusk. Vitez was as far as they planned to go. After a day or two gathering information about refugees, they would drive back to Split. But at the office they learned that Holbrooke's old friend from Southeast Asia days, Lionel Rosenblatt, was just an hour away in Zenica. He was going to try to drive to Sarajevo first thing in the morning. The thought of Sarajevo was exciting.

Holbrooke reached Rosenblatt by phone. "Lionel, I've got to go with you into Sarajevo."

"There's no way you can get here in time." It was winter, night was falling, the roads were icy, but Rosenblatt was also thinking that Holbrooke should find his own way into Sarajevo. Without the proper ID he would only complicate the trip, which was already dangerous—the road passed through Serb checkpoints.

"I'm coming."

Rosenblatt was a modest and intense man with a thick black mus-

tache. He was one of those Vietnam officials who were driven by the war to step off the upward path of the U.S. government and devote themselves to humanitarian work. His passion was the Hmong refugees of Indochina and their endangered culture—but there were refugees in so many other places, more every year. By the time of Bosnia, forty million people around the world were homeless. The fall of communism had created messy new wars in places like Somalia and Nagorno-Karabakh with complicated local causes that Americans who grew up with the clarity of the Cold War had trouble understanding. The image of the post–Cold War era turned out to be not peace and prosperity but a child squatting in the mud, surrounded by tents bearing the logo "UNHCR." There were refugees now in the middle of Europe.

Rosenblatt, the president of Refugees International, had come to Bosnia to figure out the best way to spend fifty million dollars of aid money pledged by George Soros, the billionaire financier and humanitarian. Rosenblatt was staying at a brutal-looking concrete hotel in Zenica. Part of what made the Balkan wars so ugly was the Communist architecture they were destroying.

Over dinner in the cold, cavernous restaurant, Holbrooke filled Rosenblatt in on people they both knew in Washington. Lake had gotten the job of his dreams, and Berger too, while Holbrooke had gotten nothing—so he was in Bosnia instead. Throughout the trip he'd been unusually subdued, but the prospect of Sarajevo got his adrenaline running. He remembered the city from the hitchhiking trip he took across Europe at nineteen: the minarets and terra-cotta rooftops spread across a bowl surrounded by picturesque mountains; the commemorative footprints by the Miljacka River where Gavrilo Princip had stood and fired the two shots. Now Sarajevo was under siege. For a small city it kept making a lot of history.

There was room for Holbrooke and Frease in the U.N. armored personnel carriers, and her IRC card would probably get her through the Serb checkpoints, but he didn't even have that. He was a New York banker with no real business in Bosnia. In the morning, over breakfast, Rosenblatt left the table and went up to his room. He returned with a sack full of mug shots—part of his traveling kit for circumstances like this. (In April 1975, determined to rescue two hundred South Vietnamese, he'd arrived in Saigon disguised as a French businessman and forged a batch of exit visas.) He rummaged through the sack and picked out a photo of a friend with a wide smiling face and oversized glasses who looked like an Illinois insurance executive. The man bore a vague resemblance to Holbrooke. "This ought to do the trick."

Using a cigarette lighter, Rosenblatt laminated a piece of plastic, a blank U.N. pass, and the friend's photo into the ID card of a program officer for the U.N. refugee agency. Holbrooke was concerned that the face didn't look a bit like his, but Rosenblatt was more worried about the loose corner where he'd inserted the photo and the plastic had failed to seal. "When you show it to the Serbs, hold this corner," he said. If Holbrooke ran into trouble at a checkpoint, they would have to continue without him.

FROM ZENICA they drove south in their own cars through high pine forests to Kiseljak. Kiseljak was the beginning of Serb territory, but it was dominated by Croat militiamen, and the stranglehold on Sarajevo depended on both groups. Hardly anything got into the capital without going through Kiseljak. By the time a small sack of potatoes reached the streets of Sarajevo it cost seventy-five dollars, a liter of fuel a hundred.

After Kiseljak they rode in the APCs, with Holbrooke sitting up front in his oversized helmet and overstuffed, antiquated flak jacket. It was New Year's Eve, and the Serb fighters at the checkpoints had already started drinking, there was a woman wearing a lot of makeup, and in the holiday mood they allowed the foreigners through, including Holbrooke and his suspicious card. In the late afternoon the group reached the Sarajevo airport. The buildings were damaged, the runway littered with debris. The airport was under U.N. control, and the blue helmets had orders to let no unauthorized Bosnians leave, though the lucky few who scraped together a thousand German marks could bribe their way out. U.N. officials had to negotiate with Serb forces to let humanitarian supplies into Sarajevo—just enough got through to keep the city on life support and the outside world satisfied. The United Nations, too, was part of the siege.

The siege lines hardly ever changed. The point for the Serbs was not to take Sarajevo but to pound it and watch it die.

The group's plan was to transfer to private cars on the western end of the city, at the telephone building, where the U.N. Protection Force had its sandbagged headquarters. As the convoy arrived, the secretary-general, Boutros Boutros-Ghali—who was visiting Sarajevo for a few hours along with his special envoy, Cyrus Vance, both wearing identical blue flak jackets under identical beige fur-hooded parkas—was holding a press conference inside the building. The secretary-general told the people of Sarajevo that foreign intervention would only make matters worse, that a Bosnian army offensive to break the siege would be counterproductive, that they should give negotiation a chance.

"We think that you are guilty for our suffering," a young woman from a Sarajevo radio station told Boutros-Ghali. "What do you want before you will do something? How many victims are needed before you act? Aren't twelve thousand enough? Do you want fifteen or twenty thousand? Will that be enough?"

When Boutros-Ghali and Vance had been greeted outside the Presidency building by Sarajevans shouting, "Fascists!" "Ghali Hitler!" and signs saying "We Need Weapons," "Help Us or Go Home," and protesters had surrounded their car and started rocking it, Boutros-Ghali had kept his squint-eyed, loose-cheeked smile in place. But the radio reporter's questions rattled him.

"If I am guilty, then mea culpa," the secretary-general said. "I understand your suffering." Then, to the astonishment of everyone in the room, he added, "You have a situation which is better than ten other places all over the world. I can give you a list of ten places where you have more problems than in Sarajevo."

The reporter began to cry. "We are dying, Mr. Ghali, we are dying."

Boutros-Ghali and Vance left for the airport. As their old armored sedan was driven down the ramp, Holbrooke caught a glimpse of the white hair and furred parka of his former boss in the backseat.

When Holbrooke emerged from the APC, the sky was the color of dirty milk. All around were destroyed cars. Across the road stood the shelled and burned tower of the Sarajevo daily *Oslobodenje*, which continued to put out the paper in a basement bomb shelter. Children were picking through a garbage pile for scraps of wood.

Then Holbrooke saw someone he knew—someone tall, shaggy haired and shaggy bearded, with a sad, humorous face. It was John Burns, the *Times* correspondent in Sarajevo, leaving the press conference, a bit of a wreck himself. As casually as if they had run into each other in Times Square, Burns suggested that Holbrooke stay in his quarters at the Holiday Inn. It would be an interesting place to spend New Year's Eve.

The last stretch of the trip took Holbrooke down the wide boulevard called Sniper Alley into the center of Sarajevo. It was the 271st day of the siege.

Snow was falling over the city, over the blackened high-rises and the fresh graves and the Serb batteries in the mountains. They were quiet today because of the secretary-general's visit.

On a downtown street a man with the hood of his car propped open was rubbing his hands together in the fifteen-degree cold. An elegant woman walked past carrying a canister of water. Next to the Olympic stadium, in a park that had become a cemetery, a man was perched high up in a bare tree, sawing at a branch.

On Bosnian radio the announcer was saying, "The war criminal Radovan Karadzic has said he will not abandon sovereignty over territories which the Serbian people consider their own."

A classroom of elementary schoolchildren was receiving a lesson on land mines from Italian peacekeepers. Children with cardboard guns were running down a street. A man wiped away tears as he read a letter from his daughter who had reached safety in Split.

A reporter for *Oslobodenje* was burning his books in his fireplace to keep warm and writing in his diary, "Boutros Boutros-Ghali is here. When I hear his name, waves of hatred emerge from within me."

In a small, crowded apartment somewhere in the city, people were singing, clapping, hugging, kissing, raising plastic cups to toast the New Year by candlelight.

The Holiday Inn was a yellow-and-brown concrete cube missing most of its windows. In the months before the war, the hotel had been the headquarters of the political party of the Serb leader Radovan Karadzic. Now the upper rooms were occupied by Bosnian soldiers, and the hotel was run by a criminal gang with connections at the top of the government. The entrance faced Sniper Alley and Serb guns in the high-rises just across the river, so guests entered through the back, driving at high speed into the underground garage. There was no water, no heat, and rarely electricity. The room rate was $150 a night.

Burns slept and worked in room 305 and used room 306 for storage, stockpiling two thousand liters of fuel in the bathroom after he caught the garage attendant siphoning his supply to sell on the black market and replacing the stolen fuel with water. Holbrooke and Rosenblatt were billeted in room 306. Frease was given Karadzic's former suite.

After setting down his things, Holbrooke knocked on Burns's door. They sat and talked amid the maps and gear—two small generators, a word processor, and a satellite data transmitter. They had met before, in Beijing when Burns was a correspondent there, and again in Manila just after the fall of Marcos, when they explored the abandoned presidential palace together and rummaged through the Marcoses' closets and Holbrooke tied one of Imelda's bras around his head, with the size 32B cups as ears.

Holbrooke was enamored of John Burns: his good-humored courage, his foreign correspondent's savoir faire, the fact that, in order to file his story that evening on Boutros-Ghali's shameful remarks, Burns had to sit in his armored Land Rover out on the street, plug into the lighter, point his painfully slow data transmitter at the southern sky, and hope no sniper was taking aim at him in the blue light of the screen while he waited for questions to come back from New York. All of it spoke to the reporter Holbrooke had once wanted to be.

Burns had nearly died of lymphoma before coming, and his outlook remained poor. His editors tried to keep him away, but he had an instinct that Bosnia might save him—that running six hundred yards to the Presidency building to avoid sniper fire and falling from exhaustion and bleeding onto the pavement might restore him to life. The instinct was right. Burns went up the river in Sarajevo and lost himself in the story, in the city, in solidarity with its citizens—with the cellist who played Albinoni's Adagio every afternoon at four o'clock outside a bakery on a pedestrian mall in the spot where explosive rounds had killed twenty-two people lined up for bread. His dispatches were distress calls, increasingly grim and insistent, to the capitals of Europe, and above all to Washington.

Burns gave Holbrooke his view: this was no war of ancient hatreds in which all sides were equally guilty. There were aggressors and victims. Burns had interviewed the Serb gunners in the hills and seen how clear a view they had of the hospital locked in their artillery range, of the mother and child caught in their high-powered scopes. In the center of Sarajevo, a mosque, a Catholic cathedral, an Orthodox church, and a synagogue stood within a few steps of one another, and all of them were damaged. Sarajevo had been a mixed city forever, and now an army of fascists was destroying it. Nothing would stop the killing except intervention from outside. No one in Sarajevo expected anything from the United Nations or the Europeans. If there was any hope, it was the Americans.

Holbrooke in turn confided his frustration at getting no job in the new administration. "But they'll need me," he said. "They'll come for me."

THEY WENT DOWNSTAIRS to join other reporters in the cold smoky restaurant for a thirty-dollar-a-plate New Year's Eve dinner, served at room temperature by waiters who did their best to keep up appearances in black bow ties and green Holiday Inn jackets. Sarajevo appealed to the part of Holbrooke that had never stopped being a young adventurer with a sense of dark absurdity whose favorite novel was *Catch-22*.

After dinner, Holbrooke asked Burns to take him to the footprints of Gavrilo Princip, which he'd last seen in 1960.

"Impossible," Burns said. The footprints and the plaque, honoring an act of Serb nationalism—FROM THIS PLACE ON 28 JUNE 1914 GAVRILO PRINCIP EXPRESSED WITH HIS SHOTS THE PEOPLE'S PROTEST AGAINST TYRANNY AND THE ETERNAL STRIVING OF OUR PEOPLE FOR LIBERTY—had been ripped out by Bosnian soldiers at the start of the war. Instead, the reporters invited Holbrooke and his friends to a party in the Old Town. "You'll see something right out of Dante's *Inferno*," Burns said.

The party was in an art school on the Miljacka River, just past the spot where World War I began. It was called the Hole in the Wall Club because you entered by climbing over the rubble of a mortar round and through a gaping hole. Inside it was dark and noisy and thick with cigarette and pot smoke. A live band was playing Stones songs. Foreign do-gooders and reporters and Bosnian aesthetes were crowded next to the small stage, dancing, shouting, hugging, drinking local plum brandy and U.N. beer. At the stroke of midnight they all threw beer on one another. Everyone was young and beautiful and joyous, and Holbrooke danced in his flak jacket and flirted with Frease, but he never lost his detachment. He sensed the desperation beneath the wild spirits.

By one in the morning he was back in room 306. He requisitioned the bed, leaving the floor for his roommate, and fell asleep fully clothed in the cold. When Rosenblatt returned Holbrooke was snoring.

He woke up around seven-thirty. It was the first day of 1993. There was no water for washing. Breakfast was bad cheese, worse bologna, and tea. After breakfast, Burns took him on a guided tour—the hospital, the morgue, the cemetery.

Sarajevo lay under a crust of snow. Serb guns were ringing in the New Year. A man was climbing 344 stairs to bring a New Year's Day gift to his ex-wife. A pack of predatory dogs was patrolling a neighborhood. A group of friends was sharing a celebratory lunch of homemade pizza and red wine, debating whether the Serbs they'd known before the war had been misled by a handful of evil men or had always harbored this hatred, until the host finally said, "If America doesn't act, there is no hope for our salvation."

Cold fog was settling low over the city. A storm was coming, and so was a Bosnian army offensive.

Rosenblatt would stay on for a couple more days—he would advise George Soros that his fifty million dollars should go to keeping Sarajevo alive—but twenty-four hours was enough for Holbrooke. Around noon he and Frease got a ride in a soft-skin car on the exposed road to the airport. They waited all afternoon to find out if they could get out. Frease negotiated with the Danish peacekeepers but their credentials made them a low priority. Holbrooke sat on the floor reading, and he thought back to Vietnam—the heightened sensations, the endless waits, the exhaustion. Now Bosnia had the same hold on him. He took out his journal and wrote:

> If I don't make my views known to the new team, I will not have done enough to help the desperate people we have just seen; but if I push my views I will appear too aggressive. I feel trapped.

Suddenly there was room on a Canadian C-130. As darkness fell the plane climbed straight up into the sky and veered away from Sarajevo.

THE FORMER YUGOSLAVIA

II

The question in the Balkans was always how far back to go. Serb nationalists went back to 1389, the year the Serbs fought the Turks to a draw at the Field of Blackbirds in Kosovo and opened the way for the Ottoman Empire to conquer the lands of the South Slavs up to the gates of Vienna. The Croatian president Franjo Tudjman liked to start with the breakup of the Roman Empire. President Alija Izetbegovic of Bosnia began his autobiography by noting that Bosnia was first mentioned as a distinct territory in AD 958. Every few centuries some new foreign conqueror swept through the Balkan peninsula—Slavs, Ottomans, Austrians—crisscrossing the land and leaving a shifting pattern of identities and faiths. The Croats were Roman Catholics, the Serbs were Orthodox, the Muslims were converted to Islam by the Turks. Serbs used Cyrillic script, Croats and Muslims Latin, but they spoke pretty much the same language. They intermarried. You couldn't tell them apart by looking at them. They had a violent history, but they didn't have a genetic predisposition to exterminate one another.

Or you could go back to the start of the twentieth century, when two Balkan wars pushed the Ottomans out of Europe, expanded the Serb kingdom, and inflamed the nationalisms that burst out in Sarajevo on June 28, 1914, producing the First World War and, at the Versailles Peace Conference, the Kingdom of Serbs, Croats, and Slovenes, which became the Kingdom of Yugoslavia. Or, more to the point, you could go back to World War II—still a living memory decades later when Yugoslavia entered its death throes in the early nineties. Hitler and Mussolini attacked the country in April 1941. Serbs were targeted and slaughtered as an enemy race. Croatia became a nominally independent state under a puppet regime of homegrown fascists known as the Ustashe, who subscribed to a belief in their own Germanic origins and racial superiority. The Ustashe killed four hundred thousand Croatian Serbs, along with tens of thousands of Jews, Roma, and Communist Partisans. Bosnia was absorbed into Ustashe Croatia, which held Muslims to be Islamized Croats.

At the start of the war small numbers of Muslim notables in towns all over Bosnia issued declarations against the fascist persecution of their Serb neighbors, but many Muslims went on to join Ustashe civil and military organizations. In 1943 a Muslim-Croat division of the SS was formed, and one of its young supporters was Alija Izetbegovic. Resistance to the Nazis came mainly from Serb nationalists, known as Chetniks, who had murderous ethnic fantasies of their own, and from Communist Partisans, whose base was in the mountains of Bosnia. The Partisans and Chetniks fell to fighting each other. Toward the end of the war the Chetniks began to collaborate with the occupiers, while the Partisans became the most effective resistance army in Nazi-occupied Europe.

A million people were killed in Yugoslavia during World War II, the great majority Serbs. This was the collective memory, the buried ordnance dug up by ambitious politicians half a century later.

Or you could go back to 1987. This was the year when a Yugoslav Communist Party boss named Slobodan Milosevic realized that he could rise farther and faster if he picked up the forbidden flag of Serb nationalism. Josip Broz Tito, the half-Croat, half-Slovene Partisan leader who had ruled Yugoslavia from the end of the war until his death in 1980, held the country together through a skillful mix of repression, decentralization, and the balancing of tribes. He kept Serbs—the largest group in Yugoslavia, though not a majority—from gaining too much power, with the governing philosophy of "weak Serbia, strong Yugoslavia." But after Tito's death the whole thing began to come undone. Communism was now a bankrupt ideology that left the souls of Belgrade intellectuals empty. Some of them sat around in cafés over cigarettes and glasses of plum brandy and dreamed up an idea that was big and exciting enough to fill the place left by communism. It was the simplest idea in the world: I am what I am. We are Serbs, history's victims. Blood of our blood. This land is ours.

The idea is called nationalism. It turned out to be stronger than communism or democracy, stronger than religious belief, stronger than universal brotherhood and peace. It might be the strongest idea in the world. It took form in 1986 in a manifesto written by a group of Serb scholars—a pot of sweeping political grievances brought to a boil by a rumor that a gang of Albanians in Kosovo had sodomized a Serb farmer, though an examination showed that the farmer had tried to pleasure himself in his field by sitting on the wide end of a beer bottle.

The idea spread through the rest of Yugoslavia. It stirred among Slovenes, who considered themselves more Austrian than Slav, and among Croats, whose leader, the retired general Franjo Tudjman, seemed to style himself after Francisco Franco, right down to the all-white uniform—pompous, racist, entertaining fantasies of glory for his people and himself. It stirred among Albanians, 90 percent of the population of Kosovo, an autonomous region of Serbia, who wanted equal status with the other Yugoslav republics. It stirred among Bosnia's Muslims, who were barely even considered a nation. But by far the most aggressive strain was Serb. Someone once said that, for Serbs, nationalism was such addictive stuff that they couldn't even take one sip. It had the irresistible taste of bitterness, flavored with the sediment of ancient grievances, distilled to a dangerous potency that induced hallucinations of purification and revenge. It was the drink of political losers. Maybe that's true of nationalism everywhere.

IN APRIL 1987 Milosevic made a trip to the town of Kosovo Polje, where Turks and Serbs had fought their historic battle in 1389. He found himself surrounded by angry members of the local Serb minority, who were held off by police with clubs. Almost by accident, Milosevic began shouting what became the Serb battle cry: "No one shall dare to beat you again!" Thus did he go overnight from being a Communist Party hack in a decaying multiethnic state to a celebrated demagogue of a young and virulent fascism. He must have considered the chance miraculous.

In 1989 Milosevic became president of Serbia and quickly amassed more power than the Yugoslav prime minister, whose position dwindled into impotence. Milosevic revoked Kosovo's autonomy, cracked down on its Albanian population, began to turn the Yugoslav People's Army into a Serb fighting force, and used Belgrade TV to create an airless climate of fear and hatred among the Serbs spread across the other Yugoslav republics. He raised the ghosts of World War II. In June 1989, on the six hundredth anniversary of the battle of Kosovo Polje, Milosevic descended on the Field of Blackbirds by helicopter and told a crowd of two million Serbs that they must defend themselves against their ancient enemies. War might be necessary.

So it didn't quite happen overnight, as the baker from Prijedor told Holbrooke. It took a few years of diligent effort by a handful of power-hungry leaders to drive their people to genocide.

A Yugoslavia dominated by Serbia—"Serboslavia"—wasn't a country in which other groups believed they could live. In June 1991, Slovenia seceded. The war lasted ten days before the Yugoslav army withdrew. Slovenia was easy—it had hardly any Serbs. Milosevic didn't want to keep Slovenia. Croatia, which declared its independence at the same time, was different. Croatia had hundreds of thousands of Serbs, in the Krajina region on the Bosnian border, and in eastern Slavonia on the Serbian border. It wasn't hard for Milosevic's propaganda to convince these Serbs that Tudjman's regime was the second coming of the fascist Ustashe—Tudjman himself encouraged the idea—and that the catastrophe of World War II was about to befall them again. Serbs revived the insignia and long beards of the Chetniks.

In early 1991, Milosevic and Tudjman sat down together at one of Tito's hunting lodges and plotted, like Stalin and Hitler, to divide Bosnia between them. Since Bosnia had no identity of its own, it would disappear from the map. This fantasy proved so strong that not even the coming war between Serbia and Croatia could kill it.

Tudjman refused the Croatian Serbs both official recognition and the right to secede—his Croatia would be a Croat state within existing Croatian borders. When Croatia declared independence in the summer of 1991, the most extreme Croatian Serb leader, backed by Belgrade, chose to break away by force and remain in Yugoslavia, which was quickly becoming Greater Serbia. So war came to Croatia.

Serbia was readier for war than Croatia. It had the considerable weaponry and much of the officer corps of the Yugoslav People's Army. After three months of siege and shelling by Serb heavy weapons, the Croatian city of Vukovar, just across the Danube in eastern Slavonia, looked like Stalingrad. Vukovar finally fell in November 1991. Yugoslav soldiers and Serb paramilitaries took over the main hospital that was the last civilian shelter in the city. They separated out the women and children. Hundreds of men ended up in a mass grave. Croat atrocities were just as shocking as the Serb kind. By the end of the year half a million Croats and a quarter million Serbs had been forced from their homes. One third of Croatia was under Serb control. The United Nations sent twelve thousand blue helmets to keep the peace, which froze in place the lines of ethnic cleansing. The Security Council voted to impose an arms embargo on the whole region, which froze in place the Serbs' vast superiority in firepower.

Croatia showed how brutal this war of nationalisms would be. That the combatants had all belonged to the same Yugoslavia—that neighbors were turning on neighbors—made the cycles of violence and revenge more intimate and therefore more hateful. And the war would go on much longer than anyone on the outside understood. Foreign mediators—Britain's Lord Carrington, and after him Lord David Owen, both former foreign secretaries; Cyrus Vance; a litany of others—would visit the Balkans and chide the warring parties as if they were irrational children who needed to start behaving or else the world would leave them to it. The diplomats rarely bothered to learn enough to understand the causes of the conflict—the reasons why, from the point of view of those involved, war might not seem irrational at all.

In the summer of 1991, just before the shooting started, Secretary of State James Baker, on his way from somewhere to somewhere else, spent all of a day holding meetings in Belgrade. At times he hardly knew who he was talking to. He thought that a "rap on the knuckles" would be enough to keep Slovenia and Croatia inside Yugoslavia, as if the borders drawn seventy-two years before at Versailles were stronger than any local grievances. He didn't understand that those two republics were already on the verge of breaking away. Baker left and the war began. This was the extent of any attempt by the country that Baker's boss, President Bush, called the "undisputed, respected leader of the free world" to avert a terrible war in Europe.

After Croatia it was Bosnia's turn. Bosnia was the hardest case of all. Bosnians knew that war would be bloodier there than anywhere.

BOSNIA'S MUSLIMS DID NOT gain the status of a distinct national-ity until 1974, when Tito conferred it in his ongoing game of keeping the Serbs in check. But many Bosnian Muslims believed they belonged to a nation that was centuries old. They called themselves Bosniaks. Izetbegovic, an intellectual and political activist, wrote books calling for an Islamic revival among Bosniaks and spent most of the 1980s in prison as a threat to Yugoslav state security. The problem for a national-ist like Izetbegovic was that his people didn't have a republic they could call their own. Bosnia, with a Muslim plurality of 43 percent and large minorities of Serbs and Croats, was too mixed—the most mixed of all the Yugoslav republics. Sarajevo was the one truly cosmopolitan city in Yugoslavia. "Even though the Muslims are the most numerous nation in the republic, there are not enough of them," Izetbegovic wrote in 1990, after his release from prison. "They would have to comprise about seventy percent of the population" to form their own state.

Ethnic nationalism wasn't possible in Bosnia without massive kill-ing. So Bosnian nationality would have to be civic—open to all citizens regardless of ethnicity. But when the first free elections were held across Yugoslavia in 1990, the winners of the parliamentary election in Bosnia were the three parties formed along ethnic lines, with Izetbegovic lead-ing the Muslim party.

In 1989, an Englishman living in Sarajevo went to see a psychia-trist for treatment of depression. The psychiatrist, who also published poetry, was an excitable Bosnian Serb with a dimpled chin and a thicket of salt-and-pepper hair that fell over his forehead like a skunk's tail. Without asking a single question he prescribed some pills. Soon after the Englishman began taking them he felt ill. He went back to the psy-chiatrist and confessed that he had gone off the pills. The psychiatrist smiled and said, "I am so proud of you. At last you have shown an initiative." The Englishman never went back.

The psychiatrist-poet was Radovan Karadzic. In the mid-eighties he had spent eleven months in jail for writing fake medical reports in exchange for free building materials for his weekend home in Pale, a mountaintop ski resort outside Sarajevo. In 1990 he became head of the Bosnian Serb party. Its other leaders were a philosopher, a Shakespeare scholar, a biology professor, and a cement smuggler who had gone to prison with Karadzic for embezzlement. The dominance of intellectuals in the cast of Balkan war criminals shouldn't surprise you. The leader of the Shining Path was an ex-philosopher. Pol Pot became a Marxist while studying in Paris. Ideas can be killers.

In the fall of 1991, after the secession of Croatia and Slovenia, Karadzic stood up in the Bosnian assembly and warned the Muslims of what awaited them if they followed the same path: "Do not think that you will not lead Bosnia-Herzegovina into hell, and do not think that you will not perhaps make the Muslim people disappear, because the Muslims cannot defend themselves if there is war. How will you prevent everyone from being killed in Bosnia-Herzegovina?"

The Bosnian Serb parliamentary leader was threatening genocide. Izetbegovic rose to answer. "His words and manners illustrate why others refuse to stay in this Yugoslavia. Nobody else wants the kind of Yugoslavia that Mr. Karadzic wants anymore. Nobody except perhaps the Serbs . . . I solemnly state that the Muslims will not attack anyone. However, just as solemnly I state that the Muslims will defend themselves with great determination and survive. They will not disappear as Karadzic said. They cannot disappear."

The logic that drove Bosnia's Muslims and Croats to vote overwhelmingly for independence in early 1992 was defensive: the alternative was to remain under threat and humiliation in a dwindling Yugoslavia that was becoming Greater Serbia. Most Serbs boycotted the referendum. Milosevic secretly ordered the formation of a Bosnian Serb army, ninety thousand strong, and sent Serb officers from Bosnia home to take possession of the Yugoslav army's heavy weapons. He backed the new army with paramilitary terror squads from Serbia that were organized by his secret police chief, Jovica Stanisic, and sent across the border. Milosevic would finance and control the Serb fighters in Bosnia while keeping his fingerprints invisible. His master plan was to create a corridor across northern Bosnia that would connect the Serb statelet in Croatia with Mother Serbia, and to turn the Drina River valley along the Bosnia-Serbia border into a buffer zone. Both regions had Muslim majorities that needed to be eliminated.

The ethnic cleansing began in early April with massacres in the border towns of Bijeljina and Zvornik. Izetbegovic, even less prepared for war than Tudjman, issued a general mobilization order. Serbs set up barricades around Sarajevo and cut up the city into ethnic enclaves. On April 5, a hundred thousand citizens of all backgrounds gathered to march for a multiethnic Sarajevo. Snipers from a Serb neighborhood opened fire and killed a young medical student from Dubrovnik named Suada Dilberovic. The next day, the European Community recognized independent Bosnia, followed immediately by the United States. That night, Serb gunmen on an upper floor of the Holiday Inn fired down into a crowd in front of Parliament and killed six people. The Yugoslav army seized the airport, and within days the Serbs' heavy guns in the suburbs and hillsides around Sarajevo were raining shells down on the city. The siege began.

By summer Bosnian Serb forces, led by a brutal general named Ratko Mladic, controlled 70 percent of Bosnia. That wouldn't change for the next three years. They named their territory the Republika Srpska, with Karadzic as its president.

"We don't have a dog in that fight," James Baker said. Bush kept having to be reminded what the war was about. "Don't get bogged down in a guerrilla war where you don't know what the hell you're doing and you tie the hands of the military," he said—wasn't that the lesson of Vietnam? Bosnia wasn't America's problem. It was an age-old blood feud on another continent. "This is the hour of Europe," a diplomat from Luxembourg proclaimed. "It is not the hour of the Americans." But Europe talked and talked while night fell on Bosnia. The only hope was the new American president.

III

Holbrooke came back from Sarajevo seeing the war the way John Burns did. It was a terrible crime in the heart of Europe, and America could not stay out. Bosnia offended his lifelong horror of racism, it stirred his sympathy at the plight of helpless people, and it roused his belief in the need for American leadership. That was a potent mix. He was involved now in a way people at the top in government, the ones who have to be persuaded by clear policy proposals at White House briefings, usually don't allow themselves. Most of us would have returned from Sarajevo in a state of impotent outrage, full of self-congratulation or self-loathing, would have written our leaders and bored our friends and sent a hundred dollars to the IRC and lain awake thinking about the baker from Prijedor. But Holbrooke was a diplomat in search of a job, and you know him well enough by now to understand why the job ranked not an inch lower on his scale of values than the war. Egotism and idealism, incomprehensibly allied in their irreconcilable antagonism! To do something about Bosnia, he needed power.

Two nights after getting back, he went on the *Charlie Rose* show and laid out the options for the United States, from continuing to do nothing to military intervention, though he was careful to say, "The last option risks America getting involved in a Vietnam-type war in the Balkans, and nobody wants that, and I'm not advocating that." At the end of the interview he displayed the pair of wooden figures carved by the baker. "I hope they show up on television, Charlie."

Holbrooke drafted a memo and sent it to Lake and Warren Christopher on January 13, still a week ahead of Clinton's inauguration. He described the horrors of the siege of Sarajevo: "It is as though one negotiated with one's executioners over whether one's death will be slow or fast." But for the most part the memo was strategic, not a cry from the killing field, written in language policymakers understood—the kind of language that made Stefanie Frease assume Holbrooke lacked empathy for the victims. It proposed four objectives: to save lives, to contain the war, to punish the Serbs, and to strengthen the United Nations. But each of these required action, and the memo called for an aggressive Clinton policy: bomb the Bosnian Serbs and even targets inside Serbia, if necessary without U.N. approval; secretly allow weapons into Bosnia in spite of the U.N. embargo (small arms, along with religious fighters, were already coming in from Muslim countries, the memo pointed out, which might lead to an Islamic jihad in Europe); go after war criminals. Holbrooke urged qualified acceptance of the new Vance-Owen plan—the proposal by Vance and his co-mediator in Geneva, David Owen, to divide Bosnia into ten loosely federated ethnic cantons—but only as a placeholder. He did not think that diplomacy would end the war anytime soon. The United States should cut all ties with Belgrade and establish an embassy in Sarajevo. Bosnia required American leadership—that was the central message of the memo.

Holbrooke heard nothing back. The incoming president was focused on the economy. His foreign policy team was already riven with tensions. Instead of the Bill Russell Celtics, Clinton had assembled the Patrick Ewing Knicks, a team of mismatched players from around the league. Colin Powell, chairman of the Joint Chiefs and the only one with a celebrated reputation, wanted to keep the military's powder dry for the next conventional war like Desert Storm—anything else would be mission creep, quagmire, another Vietnam. Aspin at Defense was brilliant but disorganized, doomed to be overwhelmed by the massive bureaucracy and by Powell. Albright at the United Nations was a humanitarian hawk, and so was Vice President Al Gore. James Woolsey at the CIA was a hard-line conservative. Christopher had no strong views of any kind.

And Lake—Lake had to establish a relationship with the new president, whom he hardly knew, who didn't care about foreign policy, and who didn't want to talk about Bosnia at all, let alone in the aggressive

and moralistic terms that he'd used during the campaign to criticize
President Bush's passivity and to promise action if he got the chance,
in sentences crafted for him by Tony Lake. Those speeches turned out
to mean almost nothing.

A few weeks after sending the memo, Holbrooke called Lake at the
White House. Yes, Lake had received it. Yes, it had been useful—but
there were difficulties with the United Nations and the NATO allies.
Holbrooke offered himself as the president's special envoy on Bosnia.
Lake didn't answer, which meant no. Holbrooke wasn't getting a job,
not from Lake, and—given his impulse toward action—certainly not
Bosnia.

The national security advisor's office was in the northwest corner
of the West Wing, diagonally opposite the Oval Office. On Inauguration Day, January 20, Lake sat at his new desk and lit a cigar, a moment
of quiet satisfaction at having reached the place once held by his old
boss Kissinger. The smoke drifted down the hall to the Oval Office, and
afterward Hillary Clinton issued a ban on smoking in the White House.
Lake's vision of the job was the opposite of Kissinger's. He aspired to be a
trusted advisor and honest broker who avoided the limelight, like Brent
Scowcroft, not a master of the universe like Kissinger and Brzezinski
who nakedly pursued power and publicity. Lake decorated his office not
with the usual wall of pictures featuring himself alongside important
people, but with a large American primitive painting of a bull. Kissinger
told people that Lake was unsuited to the position and would fail at it.

In February, Holbrooke invited himself to lunch in Lake's office.
They'd had hundreds of lunches together. They'd had lunch in Saigon,
in the Delta, at Angkor Wat, in Hue, in Princeton, in northwest D.C.,
at the State Department, and now they were having lunch in the White
House, served by a navy steward.

Holbrooke pressed Lake hard. The Bosnian Serbs were rejecting
the Vance-Owen plan. Sarajevans were freezing as well as starving to
death. Muslim refugees crowded into a small town called Srebrenica, a
few miles from the Serbian border, were in even more desperate shape,
without the world's cameras to draw attention: sleeping in the frigid
open air, reduced to eating tree roots and wheat chaff, all humanitarian
relief blocked by the Serbs. Clinton's hesitation was allowing a catastrophe to unfold.

Lake argued back. He was working eighteen hours a day seven days a week and spending more time on Bosnia than everywhere else in the world put together, but he had any number of crises to deal with— North Korea, refugees streaming out of Haiti, an inherited humanitarian intervention in Somalia starting to go awry. Holbrooke didn't realize all that the new administration was doing on Bosnia. The National Security Council was working on a Presidential Review Directive of Bosnia policy, the administration's first. C-130s were being readied to drop food packages into besieged Muslim enclaves. Sanctions on Serbia were being tightened. "You don't know how many more people would now be dead if it were not for our efforts."

Holbrooke said that doing a little better than Bush wasn't much of a claim. He reminded Lake of the vigorous campaign rhetoric that he'd been proud to write for Clinton. Holbrooke pretty much called the lack of action immoral. He knew Lake's sensitivities and he was sticking a finger in and pushing deeper in revenge for having the door barred to him.

And Lake was doing the same, implying that Holbrooke didn't know the views of the principals in the Situation Room, or the gnarly scenarios raised by the military, or the arguments of the European allies. Holbrooke could take a strong position because he didn't have to answer for the consequences—he was still a banker who needed a visitor's badge to get into the White House.

Lake finally said that he was doing his best.

Over lunch in the White House they got closer to the hot core of what was between them than they ever had two decades earlier. Maybe because their subject—America, its role in the world, power and morality and ambition—was the really personal one. Lake came out of the meeting furious. An aide saw it on his pale, taut face.

THE TRUTH WAS that Lake viewed Bosnia about the same way as Holbrooke. Bosnia was Lake's kind of issue. It had intense human suffering with strategic consequences. This was genocide in southeastern Europe, not civil war in Southeast Asia. Lake believed that America had to intervene. But once he started his job nothing about Bosnia seemed clear-cut. Every proposal ran into a problem, every piece of bad Balkan news resisted a Washington solution. The longer you looked at the war, the more complicated it got. Yugoslavia was the post-Communist country that wouldn't behave, and without the Cold War as an organizing principle, no one could figure out where American interests lay or which ones were worth risking American lives. We wanted to take a break from history.

Lake chaired endless meetings in the Situation Room—endless, four or five hours at a time—down there in the basement just around the corner from where he'd once sat trying to find a way out of Vietnam. Sometimes Clinton and Gore came in at the end, Gore to pontificate, Clinton to ask worried questions and then reiterate the need for American leadership. Christopher and Aspin were trying to do just enough to keep Bosnia out of the headlines. Powell warned that any American involvement—opening a humanitarian corridor from the sea, enforcing a peace agreement—would require a couple hundred thousand troops, and what was the exit strategy? He'd roll his eyes at all the verbal circles that arrived at no decision—considered the meetings little more than think-tank seminars or, worse, group therapy sessions, and worst of all was how Clinton would walk in late and there would be no chair for him, as if he wasn't the president.

The civilians around the table were a little afraid of Powell, the hero of the Gulf War, with his erect bearing and chest full of medals. Aspin, Powell's civilian chief, a verbose intellectual in a baggy suit, had no desire to cross the general on Bosnia. When Albright once worked up the nerve to demand, "What's the point of having this superb military you're always talking about if we can't use it?" Powell nearly exploded, and Lake had to calm him down.

Even the president was intimidated by Powell, and in Clinton's deep craving for everyone's love he spent an inordinate amount of time trying to win the skeptical general over, and never did. Clinton had serious problems with the military. Some of them hated him as a Vietnam draft dodger, some of them didn't like his new policy of allowing gay Americans to serve, and his salute was so limp that Professor Tony Lake—the closest thing in the inner circle to a veteran because of his time in Vietnam—was brought in to give the president a quick lesson. The Democrats' long estrangement from the military had not ended with the Cold War, and neither had the aftereffects of Vietnam. All of this made it politically difficult and psychologically almost impossible for Clinton to order troops into harm's way in Bosnia.

While they talked in Washington, the siege of Sarajevo entered its second year. The Serbs closed in on Srebrenica and fifty-six civilians were killed in an artillery barrage, many of them children playing soccer. War broke out between Muslims and Croats in Mostar, and Tudjman's proxies followed the Serbs in the business of ethnic cleansing and setting up concentration camps. Muslim soldiers were so starved for weapons that they handed off guns at their shift changes and paid kids to collect brass bullet casings in the streets to be reloaded at an ammunition factory outside Sarajevo.

After three months of talking, the principals came up with a policy. It was called "lift and strike": lift the arms embargo, unilaterally if necessary, so that the Muslims could defend themselves, and hit the Bosnian Serbs with limited air strikes to prevent them from slaughtering the Muslims before weapons started flowing into Bosnia. The policy's main purpose was to keep the United States from getting pulled in deeper. The problem was that no one seemed to believe in it. Clinton's pollster told him that Americans were against unilateral action in Bosnia but public opinion was malleable. Clinton kept postponing a final decision, and Lake, sensing the president's aversion to the whole mess, refrained from pushing one on him. On May 1, Clinton finally sent Christopher to Europe to sound out the allies, who had thousands of U.N. peacekeeping troops in Bosnia and an official position of neutrality toward the warring sides.

It was a disastrous trip. Christopher read through the various options in his briefing book with his head down, no eye contact, like a lawyer arguing a case in which he'd lost all conviction, and by the time he got to lift and strike the British had practically tuned out. The same happened in Paris, Brussels, and Rome. "I'm here in a listening mode," Christopher said—words that never crossed Dean Acheson's lips, words the Europeans didn't expect or even want to hear from the American secretary of state, with the hour of Europe getting darker by the minute. But Christopher invited the Europeans to answer as they did: We have troops in Bosnia, you don't. Either put your men where your policy is or find another policy, because lift and strike is going to get our peace-keepers killed. Since Clinton had vowed never to send troops into the conflict, the U.N. mission became the prime reason to do nothing but stand by while the killing continued.

Britain and France saw the war in terms of European history: *We know those people—you don't.* The Serbs enjoyed residual sympathy for their sacrifices against the Nazis, especially from the French president François Mitterrand, who once told Bosnia's ambassador to Paris, who happened to be Serb, "You're a traitor to the Serb people." On another occasion, Mitterrand said to Alija Izetbegovic, "Not every village in Europe can become a state," by which he must have meant "Muslim state." That was the message of the British officials who told Clinton that the war was an unpleasant but unavoidable restoration of "Christian Europe." "Don't, don't, don't live under this dream that the West is going to come in and sort this problem out," Lord Owen warned Bosnians on a visit to Sarajevo. "Don't dream dreams."

No wonder they expected nothing from Europe. A genocide happened there every generation or two. Why did the Bosnians think they were special? With America it was different. Haris Silajdzic, the Bosnian prime minister (another university professor), retained enough faith in the decency of the American people—our innocence, Graham Greene would have said—that he made countless trips to Washington to appear on *Larry King Live* and testify on Capitol Hill. He denounced the arms embargo by telling a congressional committee that he and his family deserved the chance to decide how they would die. Enough interviews, enough testimony, and Silajdzic believed that Americans would do the right thing.

Clinton was reading a book that his wife had given him—*Balkan Ghosts,* by a journalist named Robert Kaplan. It portrayed the region as soaked in the blood of ancient tribal hatreds—they'd been fighting one another forever. Kaplan, in turn, had traveled around the Balkans avidly reading Rebecca West's enormous classic *Black Lamb and Grey Falcon,* about her journey through Yugoslavia just before World War II, a book with a strong pro-Serb and anti-Muslim bias. Where Europeans saw a war of civilizations, Americans threw up their hands at incomprehensible Old World trouble. We don't understand other people's nationalism—even though we have our own racial kind—because we made our republic out of a universal and very optimistic idea. Blood and soil are for history's losers.

We understand it better now that the American century is over and some of us sound more and more like Serbs. But in 1993 we had just won the Cold War, and we bestrode the world. Lake came up with a phrase to replace "containment" for the foreign policy of the new era: "democratic enlargement." American grand strategy would be to expand the circle of market democracies around the world by supporting free trade, helping economies to liberalize, enlarging NATO to the east, working through multilateral institutions. It was the foreign policy of globalization. What did a bloody little tribal war have to do with that?

In the Oval Office on May 6, Clinton told Powell and Aspin that *Balkan Ghosts* had made a deep impression on him. Aspin returned to the Pentagon and called Lake and Peter Tarnoff. "He's going south on this policy. His heart isn't in it." Christopher got the news in Europe and came home. A travel book based on a travel book fell into the young president's hands, and he changed his mind about Bosnia. I told you foreign policy makes no sense.

Lake wasn't ready to abandon the search for answers. He understood about the ancient hatreds, but he got emotional about a mother watching her child die. He didn't want to grow numb to the terrible suffering on CNN. That was the point of "The Human Reality of Realpolitik," the essay he'd written twenty years ago about Vietnam. That was why he'd resigned from Kissinger's staff over Cambodia. Foreign Service officers were resigning in protest over Bosnia—four of them in the course of a year—and Lake felt a sense of kinship with them. On the other hand, he was in a position of responsibility and couldn't let his emotions warp his judgment. He didn't lose his temper on the subject of Serb atrocities as Clinton sometimes did. He had to think through all the risks of action as well as inaction. He described his philosophy with the phrase "pragmatic neo-Wilsonian." It sounded like a paradox, if not an oxymoron. Holbrooke thought that it was in Lake's character to be conflicted.

Vietnam was the tiger in the forest, the ghost in the Situation Room. It haunted Clinton, who had demonstrated against the war and avoided serving in it. It haunted Aspin, who had seen the follies of the McNamara Pentagon as an army whiz kid and was elected to Congress in 1970 as an anti-war candidate. It haunted Powell, who had done two tours in Vietnam and spent the rest of his career developing a doctrine to ensure such a disaster was never again inflicted on American soldiers. And it haunted Lake.

Lake was tormented by Bosnia. If America decided to use force, people would die far outside the control of policymakers in the Situation Room. But people were already dying while America stood by and watched on TV. The lessons of Vietnam were complex and perhaps the wrong ones for Bosnia. Perhaps, just as getting into Vietnam had been the essential mistake of the Cold War, staying out of Bosnia would be the essential mistake of the post–Cold War. That was the view of the correspondents in Sarajevo—their stories and images carried the opposite message of the Vietnam reporting. Bosnia stood Vietnam on its head. Perhaps ongoing slaughter in a small far-off place could actually harm American interests. Perhaps the United States had to learn to use force in a limited way, and to rebuild broken countries. Perhaps *that* was being pragmatic.

Vietnam did not cast a shadow on Holbrooke. He loved history, but he didn't look back in anguish. It wasn't in his character to be conflicted, and he wasn't conflicted about Bosnia. Twenty-four hours in Sarajevo inoculated him against the uncertainty of his former colleagues. And Vietnam had given him, like Lake, a feel for the reality of other countries, of the people caught in the tragedies of history. "Must be engaged in Europe," he wrote on a scrap of paper. "Need and desire for US engagement (1947, not 1919)."

It was easier to write that when you didn't have to make decisions. Months went by and he still had no job.

BACK IN JANUARY, Holbrooke had let Tarnoff know that he was interested in becoming ambassador to Japan. Tarnoff ran the idea by Christopher and got little resistance. Then Walter Mondale, who had accepted Russia, changed his mind in favor of Japan—Joan Mondale, a potter, preferred Tokyo's art scene to Moscow's, and the ex–vice president didn't want to work under an ex-journalist, Strobe Talbott, who was Clinton's choice to be ambassador-at-large to the former Soviet Union. By then Holbrooke had spread rumors of his own imminent appointment and friends were writing to congratulate him. Holbrooke and Mondale had been allies during the Carter years—now they were competing for the same job. Four months passed and nothing happened.

In early June, Holbrooke was seated at a Manhattan dinner party next to the *New Yorker* writer David Remnick. "Do you know if there's a newsstand around here?" Holbrooke asked. They went outside and Remnick led him to a newsstand. Holbrooke grabbed the early edition of the *Times* and found what he was looking for: a front-page story, for which he'd been a source, about the Tokyo job. It didn't name the new ambassador, but he read between the lines and knew that he had lost to Mondale.

Early on the morning of June 8, Christopher called Holbrooke. "The bad news is that the president has asked Fritz Mondale to go to Tokyo. The good news is that he would like you to go to Germany." Christopher got off the phone in a hurry. He hadn't stood in Holbrooke's way, and neither had Lake, who was in the Oval Office with Clinton when the subject was discussed. Holbrooke had a job if he wanted one.

He didn't know if he wanted Germany. It was hardly a backwater, but it wasn't his area. He called Tarnoff to talk it over.

"One thing you have to realize if you go to Germany is that people will ask you if you're Jewish or not," Tarnoff said. "So are you Jewish?"

"Why is it important?"

Tarnoff explained why being Jewish was important in Germany.

"Yes, I am."

They had several conversations that day before Holbrooke accepted.

He set up meetings with American Jewish leaders. He received a private tour of the new Holocaust museum in Washington. At his swearing-in on the eighth floor of the State Department in September he introduced his mother, whom he hardly ever saw anymore. Her father, Holbrooke told the guests, had worn the Iron Cross in World War I, but with the coming of Hitler he knew that Jews had no place in Germany.

Holbrooke's friends looked at one another in astonishment. That was the moment when he became Jewish. It was an entirely public event.

I don't have much to tell you about his year in Bonn. Ambassadors in places like that have a nice deal. A beautiful old mansion on the Rhine with a pool and tennis court, a large and obsequious staff, nine-man personal security detail, armored Cadillac, honor guards, fancy dinners, high-level visitors (Nixon, one month before he died). Holbrooke even brought his own in-house expert, the historian Fritz Stern, who took a semester off from Columbia to sit at Holbrooke's elbow and explain German culture. In his living room, Holbrooke displayed the photograph of his grandfather with pickle helmet and Iron Cross. German visitors didn't care for it.

But the Germans loved Holbrooke. He knew their history, he valued the Atlantic alliance, and he didn't talk in Protocol. "Tell me what's wrong with the relationship," he said to German officials at dinner, "tell me what you'd like to see fixed." He even called Chancellor Kohl "Helmut." He hadn't wanted the job, but he poured himself into it. I don't know if Holbrooke ever once opened the Bible, but he lived by this verse from Ecclesiastes: "Whatsoever thy hand findeth to do, do it with thy might; for there is no work, nor device, nor knowledge, nor wisdom, in the grave, whither thou goest."

The Clintons came once. It was July 1994, and the Berlin Brigade—the last American troops in the once and future German capital—was leaving, and Clinton was scheduled to give a major speech on the eastern side of the Brandenburg Gate. These presidential trips are scripted to the minute and the inch: "2215: Upon arrival of Air Force One, Ambassador moves to end of red carpet leading to aircraft and waits at bottom of stairs with group to greet President." The arrival of the Clintons, with their giant retinue sweeping through and behaving like ugly Americans, alienated Holbrooke. But Clinton hardly knew who he was, and Holbrooke was frantic to get close to the president.

He hogged the press at the steps of Air Force One, loitered outside Clinton's hotel suite, inserted himself into high-level meetings, paged White House officials about last-minute changes in the menu for the state dinner with Kohl. He and Lake had a loud and public fight over who of the two was the senior official entitled to ride in the assassination seat, the right rear seat of the president's decoy limousine. Lake fought back and then—his manners overcoming his competitiveness—let Holbrooke have it. The White House staff was dumbstruck. It was Holbrooke at his worst. Another president would have cut him off (another president eventually did), but Clinton enjoyed big characters.

On the day of the Berlin Brigade's departure, Holbrooke attended a conference at Humboldt University. Over dinner he asked a small group of German and American businessmen to join him in a storage room next to the conference hall. They sat on folding chairs. "We need to do something," Holbrooke told them. "The United States has always had a special relationship with Berlin and we cannot let this die." He wanted to create an institution that would represent the best of America, not a monastery but an active place, not just in the arts and humanities but in public policy. The businessmen all nodded. "Can I count on you to be on the board?"

Before his year in Germany was over, Holbrooke set in motion the founding of the American Academy in Berlin. It's there today, in the far west of the city, in a grand villa on Lake Wannsee down the road from where the Final Solution was planned. The villa belonged to a wealthy Jewish family before the Nazis stole it; after the war it housed American officers, and then the family gave it to the academy. All year round the villa is filled with American artists and intellectuals and Germans who want to meet them. Holbrooke had the historical imagination to see that something of America must remain in the city of the Berlin Airlift and "*Ich bin ein Berliner*" and "Tear down this wall," and he was relentless. It was Holbrooke at his best. Try to separate the best from the worst—you can't.

He did other things as ambassador but you don't need to know about them. What mattered was that the war went on—passages of quiet, orgies of murder. Sarajevo was two hours away by plane, but in Bonn Holbrooke stopped thinking much about Bosnia.

IV

He invited himself to spend Christmas 1993 in Paris with Pam Harriman. Clinton had rewarded her fund-raising skill with the job of American ambassador. But Pam was a pretext—Holbrooke had another purpose.

The woman who had seen him waiting for a car with Diane Sawyer on Central Park West and thought, *What a glamorous couple*—she was in Paris. It's time you heard her part of Holbrooke's tale. She's essential.

Despite Kati Marton's marriage to Peter Jennings, Holbrooke had been pursuing her for a long time, if only in his own mind. He kept a list of their encounters, fifteen or twenty of them, going back to the early eighties: a couples dinner at Diane's barely furnished apartment, a chance sighting on the shuttle, a collision in the rain on Madison Avenue. By then Kati was trying to end her marriage.

Jennings was having an affair—he was usually having an affair—and Kati, who'd had a couple of her own, was miserable, and Holbrooke knew it. Jennings was a megastar and their problems were public. Kati even planted a breakup story with the same gossip columnist Diane had used, which is one way of untying bonds at a certain stratum. So in the summer of 1993 Holbrooke invited himself to be the Janklows' houseguest in the Hamptons and then—we're getting closer to Gatsby—prevailed on his hosts to invite Kati to dinner. He talked to her all evening, and as he escorted her outside he planted a kiss just above the upper-left corner of her mouth.

That fall he kept calling her from Bonn—"Hello, Katika," he said, in his teasing singsong way that assumed instant intimacy. She declined his offer to visit Germany, but when he suggested a three-day drive through the Loire Valley after Christmas, Kati accepted, against her lawyer's advice.

Holbrooke had unfinished business too—the wife of the shady New York pol invited herself to Bonn for Thanksgiving—but that was easy compared to Jennings, who refused to separate.

On Christmas Day Jennings arrived at Kati's sister's house outside Paris, in order to save their marriage and spend the holiday with their children, who were thirteen and eleven. Kati declined to sleep under the same roof with him, and she was also expecting Holbrooke the next day, so she moved to a nearby four-star hotel, across a park from the Palace of Versailles where Yugoslavia was created in 1919. In the morning Holbrooke pulled up in his official armored Cadillac, having left his security detail at the German border. He saw her slouching along a gravel path, head down, hands stuffed deep into the pockets of her camel-hair coat, too preoccupied to hear at first when he called, "Kati! Come on, let's go!"

She looked up, jumped in, and he took her away. That pleased them both—the idea of running off together, the theatricality of it.

He had planned out the whole trip. They drove first to Chartres, and as they strolled around the cathedral she slipped her arm through his. They sat in a pew and he said, "Just imagine the pilgrims' first reaction to the sight of these windows, the power of this place for medieval peasants." His role was to distract her from the thought of her family by reading aloud from an old guidebook about Chartres. From time to time she fell quiet and cried, then blew her nose, and he went on talking about Gothic and Romanesque—he liked Romanesque better, it was more earthbound—and she began to feel comforted.

On the way to Tours in the heart of the Loire Valley she described the weeks she'd spent there with a French family in the late sixties as a college student. She wanted to revisit those old places. She loved everything about France.

At the hotel in Tours they checked in to separate rooms and the desk clerk was right to be incredulous, because didn't both of them know what was going to happen? On the drive from Chartres hadn't she been telling him about her past lovers? Hadn't he kissed her in her favorite park near the Tours cathedral?

They went up to her room. They sat on her bed. They lay down and began kissing.

"Let's not make love tonight," she said.

"Okay."

They kissed some more.

"Wait a second," she said, "while I get this thing off."

He had trouble getting started. She said that he might be intimidated, which prolonged his difficulty because it was true. They laughed about it, and after a few minutes everything was all right.

Later, he went to his room and came back dragging his suitcase.

"You're not going to sleep in here tonight, are you?" she said.

"No, of course not."

They toured the Loire for two days before driving back to Paris. In his wallet, Holbrooke kept the scrap of pink embassy message paper on which he'd scribbled Kati's sister's phone number—kept it there for the rest of his life. In their various retellings this origin story had a fabled glow—French châteaux, his embassy car, the sadness that trailed her ("Do you know that I cried every time I was alone today?"), even an unwanted chance encounter at a Paris restaurant on their last night with Pam Harriman, who was annoyed at Holbrooke for running off with another woman. Pam had no time for other women, and later she spread the word that he'd been having dinner with some Swedish journalist, and what was the point of learning her name since he went through so many of them?

Holbrooke drove Kati to the airport with one hand on the wheel and the other feeling the warmth between her legs. Their goodbye was more abrupt than he wanted. He headed back to Germany, and upon reaching the residence he waited and timed his call to catch her just as she was walking into her apartment in New York. She picked up on the first ring. She sounded happy to hear from him.

———

WHAT WAS IT about Kati? You've never heard him use the tone of the letters he began to write.

Trenchant—

That was his nickname for her—or just "T."—because, when he told her how much he loved her name, she said, "It's so trenchant," and he said, "That's a ten-dollar word for a refugee girl."

Trenchant—

She did not like the name "Dick." She called him "Richard" and insisted that he call himself "Richard" and that everyone call him "Richard." "You're not a Dick," she told him. "You're a Richard. You're a man of great stature."

Trenchant—To me, the "miracle" part of it so far—the truly mysterious and mystical part—was the first three days *after* you returned to New York. I think it fair to assume that we both expected to have a good time together in France—I was probably more honest with myself as to what would happen—or else we would not have agreed to commit ourselves to spend so much time together. But what happened in those next three days—December 29, 30, 31—remains to me a fathomless and heartstopping thing . . .

So we were on our way, clearing away our tangled pasts to open the road to—to what? We don't know yet, but we each have our hopes. It can't always be as easy as it has been so far, because it has been, truly, a miracle. Will we take care of each other, comfort each other if we face setbacks? Will we care about each other in adversity as much as in triumph? It all lies ahead. To protect myself, I say: even if it ended tomorrow, it was wonderful, necessary, and good. But I am sure I would feel like shit, and forever wonder what spending our lives together would have been like.

He let her know that he was writing to her while scanning the daily intelligence summary; in the middle of a press conference; on stage waiting for his turn to speak, pretending to take notes while Kissinger talked about the German-American relationship, or Kohl droned on about NATO or Bosnia or something. Within a few weeks they were planning their future over a transatlantic phone line.

> I awoke this morning without an alarm clock after less than four hours of sleep. Did you propose to me, sort of, at about 3 in the morning? I want to capture the moment, just in case. Did my heart leap, instead of feeling crowded or ambivalent? Hey, is the Pope Polish? Do green eggs go with ham? . . .
>
> A few minor details. It would probably help if you divorced first— a technicality, perhaps, but worth considering. But the really important issue is your children (not my adult guys). They, and they alone, must matter. I would do it today—I really would! But only you can decide if, when, how—I'll be there, now and forever if you want me—
>
> Anyone who doesn't share our happiness is not our friend.

What was it about Kati? He was gone from beginning to end.

SHE WAS INDISPUTABLY BEAUTIFUL, with the middle coloring he liked. Magyar cheekbones. Brown eyes keenly, you could say acquisitively, fixed from earliest childhood photos on the object of their desire. European style of elegance—she could get away with a trench coat and foulard. Breasts larger than he expected—he liked that too. Her beauty wasn't the kind that sat back and waited to be unveiled. It was acutely conscious of its power, and when she walked into a room not only did every man think, *She looks great,* but they felt, in some subtle way that they didn't understand, compelled to tell her, as if the price of not doing so would be too high. She elicited admiration and fear, leading men and women alike to cast themselves as obliging extras in the drama she created. Her will was at least a match for Holbrooke's—at least.

They said what a remarkable character she was. And in fact you could easily imagine her as the passionate and calculating Comtesse de Marton in a novel by Stendhal—the quick wit, the love of books and talk, the shrewdness about other people, the machinations. Just being around her brought to mind the word "intrigue." Her family's story was full of it, overlapping with Holbrooke's obsessions as if he

had conjured her in a delicious daydream where history and eros were indistinguishable.

Her father and mother were Jews of the Budapest upper-middle class. They converted to Catholicism in their twenties, and when Eichmann began rounding up Hungarian Jews in 1944, Endre and Ilona escaped Auschwitz by hiding with Christian friends in Budapest and never wearing the yellow star. Ilona's parents perished in the death camps. When Julia and Katalin came along in 1946 and 1947, the Martons didn't just omit this history around their children, as in the Holbrooke household—they sealed it in an underground vault.

Endre Marton was a snob—a fencing champion who worshipped Fred Astaire and wore a seersucker suit and was always smoking a pipe. Ilona Marton played tennis and bridge as if Communist Budapest were Edwardian London. Glamor, concerned with surfaces, is a form of repression, and Kati's parents, who were conspicuously glamorous, had a terrible burden to repress. They were brave, too, even reckless. After the war, in the dark first decade of the Cold War, they became Budapest correspondents for the American wire services. Marton drove around in a big American convertible as if to announce his identification with the capitalist enemy, and some of his actions with the American embassy gave the secret police the evidence they needed to charge him with espionage in 1955. He served eighteen months, and his wife served almost a year, while the girls—Kati was eight—were sent to stay with a family of strangers.

The Martons were released during the brief period of reform in the summer of 1956, just in time to send the first gripping reports of the October Revolution to American newspapers. When it was crushed by Soviet tanks, the family's U.S. embassy connections secured their departure as political refugees to the United States. Their arrival in New York was a big deal—the Martons made the American papers again.

They lived outside Washington, where Kati's father covered the State Department for the AP and got to know Harriman, Rusk, and Kissinger. Kati loved America on principle, its freedoms and leadership in the Cold War, but she didn't much care for actual American life, didn't gorge on American food and movies. Her father's debonair style was her beau ideal, and she set her sights on his profession. When she became a TV journalist and went to work for ABC News in the late seventies, Endre urged her to get to know the network's London correspondent, Peter Jennings, who looked and sounded like an Anglo-Canadian version of a dashing Central European—he even smoked a pipe and wore a trench coat.

In 1979 Jennings became Kati's second husband. (The first, a Philadelphia banker, had given her instant WASP credentials but turned out to be less interesting than he seemed.) Their marriage was volatile from the start. They might have been able to survive the affairs—in the Stendhal novel they would have—but not the insecurities, which provoked constant fighting. Peter Jennings, insecure? Of course he was, and Kati too. All of them were. Just look at Kissinger. Their insecurity fueled their relentlessness.

Squeezed out of TV news by her husband, Kati decided to be a writer. In 1980, while researching her first book, on the Swedish diplomat Raoul Wallenberg, who shielded thousands of Hungarian Jews from deportation, she accidentally opened the family vault. "Of course, Wallenberg arrived too late to save your grandparents from the gas chambers," a woman in Budapest told her. Kati's parents greeted her discovery as if she had dug up a humiliating family scandal. They were not Jews—they were Hungarians. When she pressed to know more her father said, "You will never understand what it was like for us." The rift between them never really healed.

Kati was a disciplined worker with a talent for dramatizing episodes of recent history in nonfiction thrillers. But as she published more books while raising two children, her husband's attitude grew more caustic. He told her that she was "glib" and "ambitious."

Once, at a dinner party, when the marriage was coming undone, Jennings pulled aside Peter Duchin, the bandleader who was Averell Harriman's surrogate son. "What is Pam Harriman really like?"

"She only cares about power, money, and position," Duchin said, "only about herself, no one else." Jennings was nodding. "Why?"

"Because my wife models her life on Pam. She's Kati's idol."

Jennings underestimated Kati. She wasn't a woman to realize her desires through men. She had an independent will—she was ambitious for herself. She needed to be the equal partner of a great man while pursuing her own path with every resource at her command. Anyway, by then she was on her way out.

Holbrooke saw what she needed and it wasn't hard to see: attention, admiration, love. He celebrated her writing, he told her she could do anything. She could even cheat on him, he said, and he would have to forgive her. He discreetly vetted her with one of her lovers, who approved. Pam warned him that Kati—she pronounced the name "Katie"—wouldn't be loyal, but it didn't matter. He was already gone.

And because he wanted all of her, body and mind, Kati put up with the food stains on his tie and the fact that he was overweight and liked to spend hours watching TV sports and devoured the entire bowl of peanuts offered by a Central European head of state, or that her parents would never accept him because he wasn't Peter Jennings. Anyway, she could adjust certain things—she bought him new clothes, she changed his glasses and his name. (His more accommodating pre-Kati friends, like Wisner, went over to "Richard," but others, like Gelb, stuck pointedly with "Dick," as if to say, "I know you and I'm not playing.") They held hands at a screening of *Schindler's List* in Manhattan and felt an intense sexual current pass through their skin—that could have been *them*—and then went back to his hotel room to celebrate being alive. They fell in love in the consuming way that takes you out of the world, but both of them needed the world as audience and stage—the rhetorical note in his letters, her thrilling to "the idea of our couple" and immediately telling everyone they knew.

They soon unwound all other entanglements. With two failed marriages apiece they were going to get it right this time. They were going to be one of the great couples. They were going to take the world by storm. Some people would resent them for it—those people were not their friends. One friend who was their friend saw their coming together as a case of like drawn to like, "a chromosomal salute."

T.—I want you to know: if ever you feel that I am not putting you at the center—I mean, putting us at the center—you must tell me—warn me as soon as/if you feel it. I will always be there. I know you would never ask me to do so, but you must know that if you ever felt that I was drifting too far away, and if you asked me to choose, I would leave my job, I would leave Washington, I would quit to be with you.

How can I say this? Easy. You are for me more important than my career. If I never served again in the government, I would still feel fulfilled. But—if I didn't have our full allotted remaining time together—then I would not.

This is something astonishing to me. In January, when I first realized what was happening, I remember "warning" you that I was an ambitious man. I was trying to tell you that while I loved you then already, I had another agenda—a professional one—that was sufficiently important that it might affect us.

I don't feel that way anymore.

V

Clinton's foreign policy lay in ruins. During a single week in early October 1993 the United States was twice humiliated by mobs: in Somalia, where militiamen killed nineteen American soldiers and dragged several of the bodies through the streets of Mogadishu; and in Haiti, where a crowd on the docks of Port-au-Prince chanted "Somalia, Somalia" and turned away the USS *Harlan County* from carrying out a U.N. mission to remove Haiti's dictator and restore its elected president. In the face of thugs, the superpower looked helpless and feckless. Clinton fired Les Aspin over Somalia and replaced him with Aspin's deputy, William Perry.

A few months later Lake drafted a resignation letter that was more than pro forma. Lake suggested that he was too much of a pragmatic neo-Wilsonian, a believer in America as a force for good, and that the president should replace him with someone whose ideas were closer to his own: "While I have no doubt we agree on the importance of opening markets to American workers and reshaping our military forces, I do not sense the same depth of commitment on issues involving the spread of democracy and human rights or the carnage of foreign civil wars. These last are messy issues that require painful choices. But <u>once involved</u>, we can only resolve them through pragmatic but persistent and, when necessary, forceful action . . . (There is nothing wrong with a more 'realist' and economics-driven view of our interests abroad. It would probably make more sense in domestic political terms. It simply is not one that interests or compels me.)"

Clinton never saw the letter. But from Somalia he took the lesson that American casualties in faraway, badly understood conflicts were politically deadly, that foreign policy could only get him burned. All U.S. forces were soon withdrawn from Mogadishu. After that, Clinton paid attention to trade negotiations, global economics, the care and tending of Boris Yeltsin's Russia—but when the government of Rwanda undertook the swiftest genocide of the twentieth century, with nearly a million people slaughtered in a hundred days during the spring of 1994, Clinton steadily looked away. Lake, who had stayed on in the White House, didn't hold a single high-level meeting on Rwanda.

By then the Balkan wars were deep into their third year. Serbia was being choked by international sanctions and Milosevic wanted to cut a deal with the West that would bring relief. But the Bosnian Serbs were dreaming dreams of total conquest, and Radovan Karadzic, in alliance with ultranationalists in Serbia, was becoming a political threat to Milosevic, who neutralized the plot by arresting former comrades. For the first time the leaders in Belgrade and Pale were divided, and the flow of military supplies across the Drina River slowed, though it never stopped. Bosnian Serb forces were extended almost to the limit of territory they could hold against a numerically superior enemy. Tudjman, under threat of sanctions, had to defer his goal of carving up Bosnia with Milosevic and absorbing his piece into Greater Croatia. In March 1994, the Muslim-Croat war-within-the-war ended with an agreement brokered by diplomats in Washington—the first American achievement since the start of the war. The new federation became the first significant military threat to the Bosnian Serbs.

The configuration of forces in Bosnia now lent itself to a strong diplomatic push, backed by NATO jets.

But nothing changed. By the middle of the year the death toll in Sarajevo reached ten thousand, including fifteen hundred children. The lucky ones no longer expected to be rescued. They had no energy for anything but survival. Sarajevans dug a half-mile tunnel under the airport runway to the suburb of Butmir, using scavenged wooden supports and torn-up streetcar tracks, to smuggle in supplies on the backs of people bent double, wading in ankle-deep water. In their bombed-out rooms they raised rabbits for food. Meanwhile, the Serb stranglehold kept tightening on the other "safe areas" designated by the United Nations—Gorazde, Srebrenica, Zepa, Tuzla, Bihac. The international commitment to protect the enclaves was daily betrayed by the refusal of U.N. officials to approve NATO air strikes beyond targeting one Serb tank at a time. The Americans continued to reject sending troops. The Europeans continued to insist on the arms embargo. The war was tearing the Atlantic alliance apart. The great powers were paralyzed and nothing changed.

Lake once told a European visitor that his biggest problem was Bosnia and his second biggest was getting foreigners on the president's schedule. The first must have taken up two-thirds of his time. Just look at his note cards from NSC meetings—Bosnia was always the number-one topic, and the dilemmas in 1993 were the same dilemmas in 1994. "2/94. Little stomach for air strikes."

Jenonne Walker, Lake's director for Europe, saw his face turn whiter, his manner more taut, and his ability to laugh at himself—a saving grace that Lake had and Holbrooke lacked—disappear. He spoke too quickly and grew snappish and territorial, cutting other officials out of meetings, refusing to let them see Walker's options papers. She held Lake in the highest regard—he was the best foreign policy mind she'd ever met, and the least egotistical—but she wanted open-ended air strikes on Serb targets, while Lake had to serve a president who couldn't bear to overrule his advisors or risk political capital on Bosnia. Her constant prodding was straining their relationship—Lake's body language said, *That's enough.* In the summer of 1994 he moved her to another position. "I'm just a nagger," she told him.

The last time Lake had worked in the White House, the miasma of Vietnam hung over everything. Now the pall was Bosnia. It poisoned all of his important relationships.

Having allowed the secretary of state to be the chief foreign policy spokesman, Lake kept getting burned by Christopher's constant shifts in position—air strikes one day, stay out the next—most of them driven by the prevailing winds in the White House and the press. Christopher was a poor choice for the job—he had no concept of America's role in the world—but after sacking Aspin, Clinton, who didn't hesitate to blame others when things went wrong, had no stomach for firing more of his top advisors. The president was never comfortable with Lake. They had no history together. Lake was a professorial tutor, not Clinton's type, and Bosnia was always there between them. Lake would go into the Oval Office first thing every morning and exchange brief pleasantries with the president, and then he would have to bring up Bosnia and watch Clinton's mood cloud over. Lake began to feel as if the letter "B" was written on his forehead.

Berger, Lake's deputy, was not just one of Clinton's oldest friends but had been Clinton's original choice for the job Lake held, and this threatened Lake enough that he kept Berger out of the daily Oval Office briefings, and he drummed his fingers on the Situation Room table or looked at his watch when Berger spoke, and Berger was hurt.

One night the Gelbs attended a White House dinner. Clinton came up to Les and said, "You've really got to call Tony. He needs you, he needs help."

"I'll think about it."

Gelb was seated at Clinton's table, with Ethel Kennedy between them, and Clinton kept returning to the subject of Lake, until Gelb finally said, "A friend in power is a friend lost." Judy, who was reading the Roman philosopher Seneca, had recently quoted the line to Les. Not a very nice thing to repeat to Clinton, but it was true.

Gelb and Lake had been close for two decades—closer in the eighties than Gelb was to Holbrooke—but Gelb thought that the job was changing Lake for the worse. He had always expressed ambivalence about power, and now that he finally possessed it he seemed to be undergoing a functioning nervous breakdown. A single harmless word in one of Gelb's *Times* columns brought an early morning phone call from Lake that was answered by Judy because Les was still asleep. "How could you say that 'Anthony Lake, the president's national security advisor, *glides* over to Mr. Christopher's office'? What was that supposed to mean?"

Holbrooke told Gelb that Lake had always been this way—paranoid, secretive, cutting himself off from friends. "What are you talking about?" Gelb shot back. "You're the godfather of his child. You introduced me to him as your best friend." But Holbrooke had become totally irrational on the subject of Lake—obsessive, venomous—and he erased their long history with a summary judgment.

And Lake—under excruciating pressure, constantly attacked in the press, and his own friends pissing on him. He knew that Gelb and others were saying that Bosnia was a disgrace, that Clinton's foreign policy was a disaster, and sometimes they said it in print. He thought that the criticism was motivated partly by envy, but it hurt like hell. Lake once invited Gelb to see U Mass Amherst play in the NCAA basketball championships in New Jersey. During the game, Gelb made some critical comments about Bosnia, and on the drive back to New York neither of them spoke. Lake went up with Les to the Gelbs' apartment, and while Les got something to eat in the kitchen Tony spent half an hour bitterly venting to Judy, who was lying in bed with a book, though not Seneca.

When Tony first got the job, the Lakes bought a house in Washington near American University, even though the plan was to stay for just two years. Toni moved down from the farm and brought a horse with her to ride. But she never saw her husband. He even stopped coming home some nights. When they were together, he didn't talk to her. One morning as he was walking out the door she said, "What kind of marriage is this?"

"We'll talk about it."

Later that day he called Toni from the White House with the name of a restaurant. When she met him there, he told her that he wanted to stay on the job beyond two years, but not with her. Then he went back to work. The next day she drove north to the farm.

IN THE MIDDLE of May 1994, Holbrooke got a midnight phone call in Germany from Strobe Talbott, who had become the deputy secretary of state. The assistant secretary for Europe, a Wall Street lawyer named Stephen Oxman, was a flop. The Europe bureau was leaderless while Bosnia continued to deteriorate and the question of NATO enlargement loomed. Talbott and Tom Donilon, Christopher's chief of staff, were pushing Christopher to replace Oxman with Holbrooke.

"Look, Strobe," Holbrooke said, "you're asking me to go back to a rank I had seventeen years ago, in a situation where that job's been diminished." He said that he planned to leave government in a year for personal reasons—Kati—and until then he had unfinished business left in Germany.

"Well, one of the reasons we want you back is that even your detractors recognize you've done an extraordinary job in a short period of time." Talbott went on, "I would like you to consider it because Christopher himself proposed you, and this suggests to me that he realizes you're the best person available."

This wasn't true. Christopher was, as always, repelled by Holbrooke.

"Christopher and I can work fine," Holbrooke said. This wasn't true, either, but Holbrooke tried hard to conceal what he really thought—that Christopher was too vain to risk making any mistakes in the job. "We've never had a cross word. This whole thing about problems between us is one-sided. Strobe, he's not qualified to be secretary of state, but he is, and it's of national importance that we help him. The real problem is Tony, and you know it."

"Tony's relationships with you and everyone are a psychodrama that's still being played out."

"How are your relations with Tony?"

"They're not as bad as yours, but they're difficult. You know, Tony could last a long time or he could be gone in a couple of weeks."

"If he's likely to be gone, isn't it more in your interest and mine for me to wait here so that you and I can do what we always wanted to do, which is work in two of the top three jobs in some configuration?"

"I honestly think that your taking this job increases your chances of that."

"Strobe, I don't think the president has any clue who I really am—"

"I wish you'd stop saying that," Talbott broke in. "It pains me more than anything you can say."

"I'm sorry, Strobe, it pains you because it's true. And you know why—it's because Tony interposed himself between me and the president. I think if the president knew me better he would realize how valuable I can be to him."

Before they hung up, Talbott said, "This would also mean you'd have to solve the Bosnia problem."

Holbrooke didn't say what he wanted to say: "I can't solve the Bosnia problem because I wouldn't be in charge of it. *Nobody's* in charge of it— that's the problem with the Bosnia thing."

He hadn't said no to the job—that would be bad for him with Clinton. But on a conscious level he was trying to get Talbott to call it off, because Washington was a snake pit and the job was at least two rungs beneath him. On another level, utterly transparent to others but inaccessible to Holbrooke, he had already decided to accept the job, because it would put him back in the game where it mattered.

But the job hadn't been offered yet. At the beginning of June, Christopher, accompanying Clinton on a trip to Rome, was having breakfast on his hotel balcony with Donilon, who was going over to-do items on a yellow legal pad. "Chris, here's the deal—you need to make a decision on assistant secretary for Europe. Strobe and I strongly recommend Dick."

Christopher replied that he neither liked nor trusted Holbrooke. Then he relented. "Okay, I'll hire him. But he's *your* problem."

Holbrooke was summoned from Bonn to Rome. Donilon and Talbott poured their boss a third glass of Chardonnay to brace him for the meeting, but it went badly anyway. Christopher had the impression that Holbrooke didn't want the job and was demanding terms that put Christopher under some kind of obligation to him. Holbrooke thought that Christopher could sense his contempt, was afraid of being overshadowed, was right to fear it, worried Holbrooke wanted his position, wasn't wrong about that, either.

When Holbrooke left the secretary's hotel suite and a department official asked if he was going to take the job, Holbrooke replied, "What job?" Christopher had been unable to make himself offer it.

Holbrooke heard from Tarnoff that Lake was opposing his appointment, and he was certain this had something to do with Christopher's hesitation. It took another two weeks of maneuvering by Talbott, Donilon, and Tarnoff before Christopher was ready to cross the line, and even then Holbrooke had to give a push by leaking the story to the *Times*. The reporter covered for him: "Mr. Holbrooke, reached by telephone in Berlin, said, 'I do not have any comment at all.'"

Instead of offering the usual praise, Christopher's speech at Holbrooke's eighth-floor confirmation ceremony recycled some of the more withering lines from the fiftieth birthday party, details of which had just appeared in a snarky *Vanity Fair* profile that greeted Holbrooke's return to Washington.

Then Holbrooke went back to work on the sixth floor.

It's hard to understand if you've never been on the inside, but at the level where big decisions are made, government work can destroy people. It destroyed Les Aspin, who wept and begged Clinton not to let him go and was dead of a stroke within fifteen months. Officials work killingly hard under nonstop pressure for relatively low pay (Holbrooke's went from more than $1 million in 1992 to $123,000 the next year). They endure fourteen-hour days, endless meetings, mountains of paperwork, and a merciless press. But their egos, large by definition, find no objective standard to measure their performance—no annual bonus, popular vote, batting average, best-seller list—so they have to look for other ways, demeaning ones, to assure themselves that they're on top: office location, high-level meetings, presidential favor. The only way they can be sure of doing well is at the expense of others. If someone is winning the room, someone else is losing it. Everyone's stock is moving up or down every day, and if they ever lose track of their price, it's too late. So the nation's vital business is carried out amid humiliating pettiness.

This might be why foreign policy is the bloodiest field of all. Unlike domestic policy, which has jobs reports and public opinion to guide decisions, no one really understands what's going on out there in the world, and there's no time to learn by reading. Foreign policy comes down to naked human character.

And yet people in government feel—don't underestimate this—a profound sense of responsibility for matters that are ultimately uncontrollable. They spend their time failing to solve problems, or avoiding solving problems, because few problems lend themselves to bureaucratic solutions and few bureaucrats are willing to risk their careers to try. But most of them come into government with ideals, deeply felt ideals, and over time their inadequacy breaks them down. What else can they do except turn on one another?

Bosnia didn't poison Lake's relationship with Holbrooke—that had already happened. But when they began working together at the highest level on the biggest issue (and they agreed about Bosnia, in case you didn't realize—they *agreed*), everyone around these two men sensed that the fraught atmosphere couldn't just be Bosnia, that beneath Bosnia must be layers and layers of history. James Steinberg, Christopher's director of policy planning, returned to the State Department one evening from a particularly explosive White House meeting, sat down in Donilon's office, and said, "What the hell *happened* to those guys in Vietnam?"

Holbrooke took to recording his own story again. You'll hear a change in his voice from thirty years ago in the Mekong Delta. It no longer has that freshness and exuberance. Now greatness is looking over his shoulder while spite mutters in his ear. He is in his prime, his powers engaged to their fullest capacity, bringing out his very best and simultaneously reducing him to his very worst.

VI

This has been a very bad day for the administration, with Gorazde going down the drain and the administration looking impotent. The range of options they were considering all seemed inconsequential compared to the degree of the problem. These halfway measures, which remind me of the Rolling Thunder campaign against North Vietnam, are just not the right approach. Either we should attack hard—perhaps cutting all the bridges across the Drina—and make clear to the Serbs that it'll get worse until they stop, or else we should do nothing. The halfway house of small measures simply won't work, and yet that seemed to be the direction that people were headed today. It's a dangerous course, because it seems to me it's the one with the greatest chance of failure.

I told Strobe I thought the administration had never done a correct action on Bosnia. Having inherited a mess, they'd made it worse, and I suggested we shouldn't make tactical decisions on a day-to-day basis until we had a strategic objective, tried to figure out what it might cost, and whether it would be worth pursuing, and whether we could get public support for it. It sounds simple, but it is exactly what we did not do in Vietnam, and what we are not doing now in the ricocheting back and forth.

I talked to Les Gelb tonight, who said that he had had the worst conversation of his life with Tony Lake, a thirty-minute screaming match which had basically torn what was left of their friendship. I told

Les that it had taken him a long time but it was an inevitable event, but that nothing about it surprised me at all except that Les had been so loyal for so long. I told Les that after Sandy Berger, without whom Tony never would have had a chance to be national security advisor, Les had done more for Tony than anyone else, in 1992 coaching him privately and repositioning himself in public as a moderate tough guy rather than a Vietnam dove, and that I didn't think that Tony had ever done anything for Les in return, and now Les was going to have to confront the fact that this friendship had been very one-sided and that Tony was not his friend anymore. It's very bitter for Les, but Tony has had a progressive policy of cutting off all his friends one by one, because he cannot control his ambitiousness and his competitiveness. I'm sure when it's all over and Tony, who's a very smart person and still has considerable charm, realizes what he's done, he'll try to find ways to make amends, but by then it'll be awfully late in the game and the costs will have been very heavy.

I told Les that I didn't care anymore about any of this. That Tony's biggest mistake was to ever let me escape—not to block my appointment to anything in the administration—and by letting me get this job he'd lost control.

I have just finished talking to T., who had a difficult day but was more happy than ever, more loving than ever. Les, meanwhile, has said that while he thinks she's wonderful, he thinks also that he has to talk to me privately before I make some major commitment, and I assured him I would let him have his say, because I know that he means well.

I used to think, back in the sixties, that intelligence was far and away the most important factor you needed in government service. I still believe it's vitally important—no one wants idiots to serve in the government. But character is an equally important function. Under the pressure of events, one never knows more than five, ten percent at most of what one needs to know about a decision. Often one has to make decisions based on two percent of the information one ought to have in order to make important decisions. So one needs a set of guiding principles, a value system, and rock-hard integrity, or else one is buffeted by public opinion polls, pressure, and the confusion of the bureaucracy's competing claims. Without character one can lose one's way.

In this administration, the person who has shown the most character under pressure, without any question, is Strobe Talbott, who retains his value system and his innate decency. The persons who have shown that they have no character at all seem to be, first and foremost, Tony Lake, who remains the most intelligent person in the administration but has shown the least character and greatest personality change. And, to a lesser extent, Warren Christopher, who has not changed his personality and who does have some character, but it is weak and subordinated at all times to whatever pressures he feels. Christopher is quite intelligent, but his intellect, that of a lawyer, contains no framework, no conceptual values. I realized after our breakfast in Rome on June 1 that he literally had no idea what his job was in the classic sense. He doesn't know what the U.S.'s foreign policy goals are, and if you were to ask him he would probably say it's to promote American economic strength. Which is good rhetoric for public consumption but doesn't meet the actual needs of the job.

Obviously, Tony has been the greatest disappointment. He has had something amounting to a complete personality transplant since he took the job, becoming, one might say, Henry Brzezinski—all the things he swore he never would become: secretive, manipulative, dishonest, protective of his position with the president, and limiting everyone's access. Since he and Warren Christopher maintain a surface cordiality under which neither of them knows how to communicate with the other, the system is, at the top, dysfunctional. Whether the president understands this is not clear to me, but he is the big loser.

Before I joined the Clinton administration, I said there were two kinds of president. The ones with magic, like Reagan and Kennedy, could get away with huge mistakes, like the Bay of Pigs or Iran-Contra. The ones without the magic always had to perform well, and they rested and rose and fell on their own achievements. In those days I said that I thought Clinton had the chance to have the magic, and I believed it. Today I am reluctantly of the view that he will never achieve the magic. I hope he recovers, but the magic is unlikely to descend around him.

We cannot afford a one-term presidency or a failed administration. It would have great consequences, above all domestically. In foreign policy the margins are smaller, but Clinton is a far better domestic president than anyone the Republicans could ever produce. He wants to tackle domestic problems and do something about them—the kind of leadership we need. But he doesn't know how to conduct foreign policy and thereby jeopardizes his presidency.

I had a brief secret meeting with George Stephanopoulos, who wanted to meet outside the White House for various reasons, which weren't entirely clear to me. I spent most of the time briefing him on Bosnia, but I said at the end I wanted to make a personal comment. I could not be more deeply offended, I said, than I was by the blind quotes that came without question from young White House staffers that deliberately twisted my activities in Berlin during the president's visit. George, who knew exactly what I was talking about, apologized profusely, dissociating himself from them, though he did admit that he talked to Marjorie Williams about the *Vanity Fair* article.

Frank Wisner, who struggled manfully for a year and a half in the lunatic system of Les Aspin, is now going to New Delhi as ambassador, heaving a huge sigh of relief and telling me that I am heading into a nightmare situation. Les Aspin himself is another man who bent and broke under the pressure. Tendencies that were under control within him as a congressman erupted as a secretary of defense. He showed constant losses of self-control, temper tantrums, and childish behavior, which made it easy for Tony Lake and Warren Christopher to agree that he should be the sacrificial lamb to push over the side of the ship in order to save themselves in October, November of 1993. This they did, but it didn't solve their fundamental problems.

A late dinner between Frank and myself at our favorite Japanese restaurant, with him charmingly picking up the check. I asked him whether he thought that we had just gotten older or Washington had changed. He said he thought Washington really had changed and that there was not much joy left in it. Public service was no longer something one looked up to or respected. There was a sense in the public at large that people in the government were in it for themselves and themselves alone. There was no longer the respect for public service or the national interest, which, we now realized, was a legacy of the Second World War and the Cold War. For both of us, we agreed,

this was our last government job. We neither of us regretted the
careers that have been full of enjoyable and fascinating events, but
the pleasure, the payoff, was no longer there.

If I were to write the next year of my life today, I would say that
I would like to do the assistant secretary of state job for less than
a year, reorganize the bureau, try to articulate American policies
towards Europe publicly and set them into place privately, and then
get out of the government, go to New York, and be with Trenchant.
My enthusiasm for this is almost gone. If the president himself is not
ready to acknowledge my contribution to his administration, I see no
reason to make it anymore. I have lost, at least for the time being, my
zest and enthusiasm for public service unless it's highly productive,
and ambition—something which I have always had and which I think
is in itself neither admirable nor unadmirable, depends on to what it's
harnessed—is something which I feel in my case has been fulfilled.

Perhaps all this will change tomorrow. I put it down only to give a
snapshot of my weariness with the government race and my desire for
a different sort of life and a different city with Trenchant. I recognize,
of course, my own restless nature, and perhaps were I to be in New
York I would miss the very thing I'm now worn out with. Who knows.

YESTERDAY I HAD confirmation hearings in front of Senator Biden
and Senator Lugar, which lasted an hour and were rather pleasant,
the senators both being very complimentary. Biden, however,
sought to portray me as being in opposition to Christopher and the
administration on Bosnia and predicted that I would come to blows
with them over the policy. I tried to suggest that I was comfortable
with the policy, although in fact Biden knew that he was right. Earlier,
I had met with Biden privately in an attempt to create an intellectual
and moral base. This meeting took place in the vice president's
beautiful and ornate office off the Senate floor during the health debate
and was preceded by brief chats with about ten or fifteen senators,
most of whom were old friends like Sam Nunn, John Danforth, and
Paul Simon. My private conversation with Biden was difficult. His
ego and the difficulty he has in listening to other people made it
uncomfortable, but useful.

On Sunday afternoon President Clinton met with Izetbegovic. As Izetbegovic was speaking, I was seated in the semicircle next to Tony, and when Izzy made a point I nodded in agreement several times, catching his eye and hoping to encourage him when I thought it was appropriate. Suddenly, Tony whispered to me out of the corner of his mouth, "Don't nod."

"What?" I asked.

"Don't nod," Tony said in an insistent whisper.

"Why?" I asked.

"Because," Tony said, "your nod suggests that we're going to send eighty thousand troops to Bosnia."

I was so surprised I almost laughed in the middle of the meeting. "Well, I don't think it means quite that, Tony. I was nodding to encourage him," I whispered. All this going on while Izzy is talking in Bosnian between English-language translations. I thought about it afterwards, trying to figure out what was now possessing this once self-controlled, self-effacing WASP. On a piece of paper I wrote a note to myself: "A control freak who is now out of control."

Tom Donilon told me tonight that Warren Christopher was very pleased with the support he was getting from the European bureau and from me personally. I must say, I'm not terribly moved by that kind of praise, since I served him more than adequately in the Carter years in a job of similar rank and don't see anything particularly noteworthy in my being able to do the job again. I must say that EUR in the Clinton years is tougher than EA in the Carter years. One of the main reasons is Bosnia, of course—a problem much harder than anything we dealt with in Asia, including China and Vietnam. But in addition to that, there's a difference in the level of precision and support between Vance and Christopher. Vance, I was reminded the other day when I had lunch with him, was not terribly imaginative, but he was precise, quick, and had a substantial database. With Chris, it's slow, it's grudging, each thing has to be done inch by inch, and he is far more cautious than Cy ever was. The comparison between them is often made but is not accurate. If I had to choose, I would unavoidably choose Cy every time.

Tomorrow I leave for Sarajevo. It will be my third trip to the war zone in the last twenty-five months, but this one will be different—I'll be traveling with a large official contingent, which will certainly inhibit me greatly. Nonetheless, I'm awfully glad that my previous trips have prepared me for all this. Everything I'm hearing about the region and its problems, plus the political and bureaucratic binds that we're in, makes me increasingly depressed. Objectively, the correct thing to do is to put military pressure on the Serbs. They are the aggressors and their irredentist goals threaten the entire region. But I'm not sure the American public or its leadership has the will for it, the British and French are clearly opposed and say they will pull out of peacekeeping operations to protect their own troops, and the risks are enormous— even greater if we're not ready to follow through. It's an agonizing problem, and it's been much worse by its mishandling over the last year and a half.

Although I remain strongly of the view that the arms embargo is immoral and should be lifted so the Bosnian Muslims can defend themselves, getting there from here is extremely difficult in the present framework. Keeping the Bosnians alive through covert resupply strikes me as a better option, but I haven't had much luck with that one yet.

TUESDAY, NOVEMBER 8, Election Day. Clinton said a curious and memorable thing. Referring to Reagan's already famous note announcing to the world that he is suffering from Alzheimer's disease, Clinton said, "You know, they're so smart. I'll bet they released that note before the election just to gain sympathy and to get the attention away from us." I thought to myself at first, How absurd, but as I thought about it, it seemed right to me. Then he said something even more interesting. "You know," Clinton said, "Republicans really understand the symbolic use of the presidency. We Democrats don't. I'm just beginning to learn how to use it." I thought to myself, How strange, how touching and depressing at the same time, how insightful and yet revealing. Clinton is smart, and he does understand more about the symbolic presidency intellectually than his own behavior would suggest. But he's surrounded by teenagers and children who are not worthy of his own abilities. Yet he picked them and he stands by them. This is, of course, because in the final analysis the problems are attributable to him. His strengths got him to the White House, his weaknesses are hobbling him.

Watching the election results, one feels—I feel—deflated with the enormity of the Democratic setbacks. The next few months, the next two years are going to be additionally unpleasant in Washington, with Jesse Helms and Bob Dole in the majority and a whole slew of aggressive Republicans in town. It's not going to be much fun. What I already was not enjoying is going to be even less enjoyable.

I'm supposed to leave for London this afternoon with Kati for Thanksgiving, but I've been under pressure all of yesterday not to go because of the crisis in Bosnia and because of the general unease in the office. I'm intending to go anyway, but this will only further add to the enormous tensions that now exist. It looks like the last week has more or less laid the seeds for my early departure from the government and, I believe, my permanent exit from public service. This is a result of a series of events which have not only alienated me, but in turn alienated other people from me.

My attempt to control a chaotic policy over Bosnia had been reasonably successful, and Strobe and I had been working towards a U.N. resolution and a NATO decision to use airpower in the region, something which won't turn the tide but was at a minimum essential to show our ability to use force. In the middle of this situation, Tony played a small card with skill, and I in turn overreacted. The result was the most painful period I've experienced in the government in a long time. Tony's device was very simple. He excluded me from a meeting he was going to have with the NATO secretary-general, Willy Claes, a man with whom I've been working closely and with great effect on major issues. I called Strobe and Peter and said that this was wrong, and they did not back me up. On Sunday Strobe called me to inform me that Christopher would go to the meeting himself. I reacted very badly and very strongly, and Strobe reacted equally strongly, and we had the worst conversation we've had ever. I told Strobe that I'd been betrayed by him and Christopher—stronger words than I should've used—and he returned the fire. I told him this could only accelerate my departure from the government. There was no recovering from the damage, at least not for a while.

Meanwhile, the situation in Bosnia continued to get more dangerous. Working with great speed for once, the U.N. and NATO both approved new authorities authorizing NATO air strikes in Croatia in the period where the fighting was going on. I was centrally involved in every step of this difficult decision—an attempt to prevent the widening of the war by widening it. We had no choice in the face of Serb aircraft flying from Croatia across international borders and attacking the Bihac pocket. But the response, while constituting the largest NATO military action in history, was still not going to deter the Serbs. Within hours they had resumed their offensive against Bihac city.

The situation left everyone involved in it, or at least me, with a sick feeling in our stomachs. What will happen next is unclear, but I remain determined to go to London.

Last night's dinner was constantly interrupted by phone calls— Donilon pleading with me not to go to London, reports from the battlefront, other interruptions. It was the very kind of thing I least enjoy, although the other people there seemed to feel that it somehow connected them tangentially to great events—a Washington deformation if ever there was one. I found it intrusive and would have felt equally intruded upon if I had been a guest and somebody arrived an hour late, which I did, and then proceeded to take phone calls. But, Washington being Washington, they not only didn't mind, they seemed genuinely pleased at this touch with history.

The grim news continued late in the evening. My deputy Bob Frasure called me at dinner and said that Bihac was within one kilometer of falling.

At six-fifteen this morning the phone rang from London with a report that the British defense ministry thought that the situation was not as grim as we had heard. They may be right, but my first reaction was that this continued the ominous pattern in which the British always underreact in order to avoid putting pressure on themselves for action. The result is always too little, too late.

Off to the office now, and then—to London.

About four hours before departure, Strobe Talbott came to the office and, looking very hangdog and depressed, asked me again if I would not go. I said that Strobe was carrying water for Christopher, and if Christopher didn't have the nerve to ask me directly like a secretary of state should, he shouldn't get himself in the middle. I told him quite frankly and with considerable emotion, more than I'd intended, that not only was it an insult to my deputies to suggest they couldn't handle the problems while I was away, but in addition, if I didn't go, the personal consequences in my relationship with T. would be so enormous as to be unacceptable. I had lost two marriages to the Department of State and I was not going to lose this relationship. He got up looking absolutely stricken and started for the door. He called me about an hour later, saying that he'd taken care of everything and it was all right for me to go. I thanked him.

Meanwhile, Gelb called, stricken that Tony Lake had heard from Sandy Berger that I had been spreading the word that Tony couldn't stand to be in the same room with Sandy and wanted to get rid of him. I realized that my comments had gotten back to Sandy and Sandy had repeated them to Tony. I apologized to Les profusely and said quite honestly I did not know how it happened. Strobe was quite adamant in saying it hadn't come from him and, as far as I could remember, he was the only person I told. Les was very upset at this and I understood why, but there was nothing I could do about it except apologize for having mentioned it to Strobe.

THE TRIP TO LONDON clarified in ever starker terms the reality of the U.S. relationship with our European NATO allies. The Europeans will not use NATO force to help the Muslims, and the United States will not put ground troops into the region. The resulting stalemate is certain to doom the Muslims, except perhaps as a rump state. The Muslim offensive in Bihac triggered the Serbian counteroffensive, which as of this morning is on the brink of total success. Karadzic and Mladic, seeing an opportunity to break the will of their enemies before the winter breaks them in their isolation, have gone for broke, and the West is unable to figure out how to react. The allied response was pathetic. We therefore stand today on the edge of the end of our policy in the region. The search for a new policy is unavoidable, and that new policy will inevitably be at the expense of the Muslims.

I feel sick about being a part of such a policy. I don't feel responsible, however, as I inherited a terrible hand. But the American administrations' reactions have been as terrible as the Europeans', although in a different way. For example, during the week repeatedly my efforts to get quick responses were slowed down by indecision or disagreement or confusion between Christopher and Lake. The NSC's constant objections to anything we were trying to do slowed down even our pathetic reactions.

Nobody wants to say outright that the war is lost for the Muslims in its current mode and that we should salvage a rump state in the triangular wedge that runs from the Croatian coast up through Sarajevo to the Tuzla plain, to seek a cease-fire and preserve the international status of the state. No one wants to agree to that, and yet no one wants to put enough energy into the effort to make the Muslims win. The effort to save the Muslims now would require NATO airpower and American ground troops—something which is impossible to achieve. I had hoped to construct a policy that would get us through the winter with the status quo, but the Bihac offensive killed that opportunity.

Nixon and Kissinger, confronting the inevitable disaster in Vietnam, figured out a way to pretend that it was peace with honor to the America public, even though it was a sellout of the South Vietnamese. They blamed the Congress, they took some very muscular steps and said they'd done everything they could, and they misrepresented the nature of the deal with Saigon. I'm not suggesting we do the same thing. That level of cynicism is unacceptable, and in any case not something that this administration is capable of, since it lacks coherence and discipline. But the fact remains that we must confront our dilemma, we must confront the horrendous situation we're in, set up some priorities, and see if we can resurrect a strong American leadership role. It's going to be very hard to do.

Tony Lake prevents action and yet refuses to take any himself. Warren Christopher is willing to act but only uncertainly and with ambivalence, and only after checking with everyone else. The president seems totally uninvolved. I am under constant attack from Tony and lack support of the seventh floor, except from Strobe. That support is shaky because the price is so high for him, and because he doesn't like confrontation. Yet there's nothing more to be done except soldier on.

I feel like my government career is slowly coming to an end. I don't see how I can continue under the present circumstances, although I will try. I'm already trying to think of ways to leave with honor, dignity, and a reputation that isn't destroyed.

SATURDAY I JOINED the president and Christopher, Gore, and Sandy Berger for a lunch with the prime minister of Belgium. The lunch was a global *tour d'horizon* of no great consequence. Entering the Oval Office for the "pre-brief" with Christopher, Berger, and Gore, I was startled when the president looked up from his desk at me and said, "I didn't know that you were dating Peter Jennings's ex-wife." Then, looking right at me, he said, "She's lovely—*really* lovely." I said I agreed and thanked him, and he said, "Shows good taste on your part, but I don't know about the women." I wanted to say, "I'll tell you my secrets later, Mr. President," but looking at his watch Sandy pulled the discussion back to the reason for the meeting.

Tony Lake is increasingly assertive. For the first time in my presence he interrupted Christopher and disagreed with the president in front of foreigners. He made a rather surprising speech to the Dutch about democracy and grand themes. I suppose it was his way of trying to be Kissingerian, although it was not terribly impressive. Nonetheless, he, not Christopher, was the stronger force in the room in the presence of the foreigners. It is also clear that he continues to undercut Warren Christopher with journalists. Les Gelb says he will crack up after he leaves the job. I disagree. It's my view that by breaking up with his wife he has liberated part of himself—at least the part that wants to get laid—and now finally can admit it, and that it will bring him a little bit closer in touch with reality. But not too close—he remains the person in greatest denial of himself of anyone I've ever known.

Peter Tarnoff said that he and Mathea had dinner alone with Tony the other night, and Tony said to them that he feels completely liberated now, at peace with himself, he's overcome all the guilt in his life, guilt about his parents, and guilt about his wife, and he didn't screw around while he was with his wife, never, never in his whole thirty years, and so forth. To which Peter felt the correct answer should have been, "Well, you should've." Peter's impression was that Tony's really convinced himself with all this, and it's sort of my view, too—that Tony is going to be happier with himself, but he will now completely cut off himself from everyone he ever knew. I think he's a very, very sick person, in total denial, but he will be happier in his weird sickness, and he's come to terms with his power obsession. It's quite astonishing.

Dinner last night with Toni, who described with great passion and bitterness, and occasionally close to tears, the way her husband had walked out on her after thirty-three years of marriage. She said, "Why didn't he do this fifteen years ago?" And I said, "Because he needed you then." It was a sad evening. Mathea has given her a job working on drugs and that's giving her some focus and balance in her life, but her anger bursts out frequently. Still, she's not certain she wants to give up on saving the marriage after having invested thirty-three years on it. She's confused, but I think she'll do all right in the end. Her complaints about the coldness of her husband were astonishing—how he never talked to her—but, I reminded her, she had said similar things to me years ago.

BOB FRASURE, trying to get into Sarajevo to negotiate an extension of the cease-fire, was stopped at the airport by the Bosnian Serbs and unable to get into town. One of the most humiliating events we've yet experienced in Bosnia, illustrating our total weakness. Growing signs also that the Bosnian Serbs are thinking of what I call pulling a Saigon, going for broke.

I saw Hillary Clinton alone for thirty or forty minutes, a useful talk and good feedback. I got a chance to make some basic points about campaigning as an incumbent and campaigning as a challenger, and stressed the weakness of our presentation of our foreign policy. The next day, the president called Strobe and asked if he knew about my meeting with Hillary. Strobe said yes. Clinton said that Hillary understood me to be criticizing Tony Lake, whose name interestingly enough had never come up.

A week of the most intense negotiations with Milosevic by Bob Frasure collapsed, despite heroic and valiant efforts by Frasure, who negotiated with great skill. Frasure simply could not get Milosevic to agree to a very generous package. It's not clear tonight whether Milosevic never intended to agree and was just stringing us along (my view right now, but subject to revision), or whether we came close but just could not find solutions to some specific problems. In any case, the result is the same. Tomorrow the world will read of a failed negotiation, and we will begin getting more pressure from Paris and London to make more concessions. Still, it can't be said that we didn't try. Frasure spent over thirty hours with Milosevic in six brutal sessions, coming right up to the brink, making great progress, and then falling just short. It's going to be tough in the next phase.

I leave for Budapest Thursday to get married. It's an exciting prospect, and T. is definitely the woman for the rest of my life. But I wish I could spend more time focusing on this event instead of being dragged down by Bosnia, as I have been recently. Saturday I was in the office till one-thirty in the morning working on Bosnia. I had to cancel two tennis matches over the weekend because of Bosnia. I'm beginning to take this thing personally—especially when Milosevic told Frasure today, "The Russians tell me that Holbrooke is trying to become secretary of state by burying me."

VII

The wedding took place on May 28 in the garden of the American ambassador's residence in Budapest. Kati knew the place from her childhood. There were around sixty guests—most of Holbrooke's family, almost none of Kati's. Her divorce from Jennings was just a few weeks old. Holbrooke spent much of his wedding day on the phone to Washington.

This was the situation a few hundred miles south in the Balkans.

A four-month winter cease-fire negotiated by Jimmy Carter had ended in April. All the warring sides sensed that 1995 would be the last year of the war and began to maneuver for final advantage. In early May the Croatian army—by now the strongest of the three—staged an offensive in western Slavonia that killed or expelled the region's Serbs. This became the template for greater conquests to come.

The Bosnian government was still alive thanks to weapons from Islamic countries, which were smuggled through an abandoned Croatian airfield to a port on the coast between Split and Dubrovnik, and from there into Bosnia. The U.S. position on this violation of the U.N. arms embargo by Croatia was a wink and a nod from Lake, who replied to a request for instructions from Peter Galbraith, the American ambassador in Zagreb, by saying, "You are uninstructed." Don't ask, don't tell. Lake thought of Lord Nelson, who, when his commander in chief tried to signal him with the flag of retreat at the Battle of Copenhagen, put his telescope to his blind eye. Galbraith and Holbrooke turned this no-policy policy into a concerted effort, just about amounting to a covert action, to funnel small arms, mostly Iranian and Turkish, to the Bosnians. The Croatians took a cut on each shipment and refused to let heavy weapons through, since the Muslims might one day be their enemies again.

At the end of the winter cease-fire, the Bosnian army tried one more time to break the siege of Sarajevo, and failed. Karadzic and Mladic, the Bosnian Serb commander, decided to seize as much remaining territory as they could before the Muslim and Croat forces could turn the war around—what Holbrooke called "pulling a Saigon, going for broke." The Serbs cut the supply road from Kiseljak, shut down the Sarajevo airport, and resumed the strangulation of the city. Mladic's forces also moved on the isolated, overcrowded Muslim enclaves near the Serbian border that were under the supposed protection of the United Nations—Gorazde, Zepa, and Srebrenica.

For almost four years the Serbs had enjoyed unbroken battlefield victories. But corrupt and genocidal armies are lousy long-term fighting forces, and Milosevic knew that the game was nearly up. Serbia was selling artillery shells and small arms to Mladic's army at five times the black market rate in exchange for commodities like oak. Milosevic's objective had shifted from establishing Greater Serbia to preserving his own power by getting out from under sanctions and gaining international respectability, which could only be granted by America. "I think he is satisfied with his ill-gotten gains for at least a decent interval," Holbrooke told Galbraith.

That spring Robert Frasure, Holbrooke's deputy for the Balkans, got to know Milosevic well during weeks of talks in Belgrade over huge dinners of meat and potatoes. Their negotiation fell apart in late May over the mechanism for lifting sanctions. The United States insisted on being able to reimpose them without facing a Russian veto if Milosevic reneged on his promise to recognize Bosnia as an independent state. Milosevic refused to leave his fate in the hands of the Americans. By then Frasure had come to believe that nothing short of bombing the bridges over the Drina River between Serbia and Bosnia would break the stalemate, but he didn't think the U.S. government had the will to do it. "The lambs of Serbia will be delighted that I'm leaving," he wrote in a final cable before returning to Washington. "At the end of a long evening, Milosevic called all of this 'the edge of the knife blade.' I would call it a massive game of chicken. Milosevic clearly wants a deal, however . . . If we cannot get a deal, this diplomatic edifice will crumble quickly and Milosevic who told me he has a secret meeting in Slovakia with Tudjman next Saturday will look for another strategy, in that case possibly a Bosnia carve-up game."

In late May the renewed Serb shelling of Sarajevo brought a response from the internationals, and NATO warplanes blew up two Serb ammunition dumps. In retaliation the Serbs shelled the center of Tuzla, killing seventy civilians at a pair of outdoor cafés, then seized several hundred U.N. peacekeepers, handcuffed them to bridges and other targets as "human shields," and put them on television. The United Nations called off the air strikes.

Holbrooke, at the ambassador's house in Budapest, got on the phone to colleagues who were about to meet at the White House. "Give the Serbs forty-eight hours to release all the hostages unharmed, and tell them that if they don't, we will bomb Pale," he said. Send them a videotape of the bombing of Baghdad in the Gulf War, he added. "I am convinced that they will cave if the threat is credible. I'm serious," he said, "but now I have to get married."

To his colleagues it sounded as if he was saying all this for his memoirs (where it ended up). That afternoon in the Situation Room, the Principals Committee decided to suspend the bombing without making it public. The greatest military alliance in history backed down to hostage takers. Milosevic, embarrassed by his clients in Bosnia, sent his secret police chief, Jovica Stanisic, to Mladic's headquarters near Pale, in a bunker fifty meters underground. At the entry a guard disarmed Stanisic. "I could kill you now," the guard said. "Yes," Stanisic said, "but then you'd be killed too." Such was the love among brother Serbs. After two hours of negotiation, Mladic agreed to release the hostages.

The Europeans began to think seriously about withdrawing their peacekeepers from Bosnia. The Serbs now had a free hand to overrun the Muslim enclaves, starting with Srebrenica.

Holbrooke and Kati spent their ten-day honeymoon in the French Alps. She bought him a new wardrobe at a shop in Annecy. The war continued toward its climax.

THAT SPRING, Holbrooke published an essay in *Foreign Affairs* called "America, a European Power." It was the kind of strategic thinking that government rarely produces. When did he find time to write it? He looked back at the postwar order in Western Europe created by his heroes of the Truman era, Acheson and Kennan. He argued for a similar effort to make post-Soviet Europe whole, democratic, and free by expanding NATO to the former Eastern Bloc. I think this was the heart of his obsession with Bosnia—not the bloody doings among neighbors in unpronounceable villages, but the threat to the Atlantic alliance and America's role in Europe after the Cold War. That was a problem worthy of a statesman with an eye on history. Bosnia was destroying many things in Europe, among them American leadership. Every day of the war left NATO more impotent. One scathing half sentence from the essay got back to his busy colleagues: "Bosnia, the greatest collective security failure of the West since the 1930s."

His colleagues knew that he didn't respect most of them. He was on the inside pissing in—the melodramas of his diary might as well have been circulated through interagency mail and excerpted in the *Times*. At meetings in the Situation Room, he would start out seated against the wall with the other plus-ones, but soon his chair began to slide forward until it was wedged at the table between the cabinet officers, to their intense annoyance. Once he had to wait forty-five minutes at the White House gate for a security clearance because his name had been left off the list of participants, and when he complained bitterly about being kept out of important meetings, Christopher didn't back him up. Even his allies, Talbott and Donilon, were tired of defending him. He had used up his credit in Washington. He was looking for a new career in New York, and when the top job at the Doubleday publishing house opened up he made his interest clear, but nothing came of it.

WHILE HOLBROOKE WAS pushed out, Lake came forward. Rumors of his professional death—Holbrooke predicted it a hundred times—turned out to be premature.

Lake had hit bottom in the late fall of 1994, during Serb attacks on the northern "safe area" of Bihac. Just when the United States was about to call in serious air strikes, Lake pulled back in the face of European resistance. Saving NATO was more important than saving Bosnia. After Thanksgiving, he sent a memo to Clinton that declared defeat: "The 'stick' of military pressure seems no longer viable." The best the United States could hope to do was stop the war from spreading.

Benign neglect suited the top people at State and Defense, but Lake couldn't live with it for more than a few months. In the spring of 1995—around the time Holbrooke noticed a new, liberated Tony Lake— he decided to force the issue with Clinton and get the United States into Bosnia one way or the other.

Lake dropped the honest broker role that had led to nothing but failure for two and a half years and took over the policy himself. Working with his top aide for Europe, Alexander Vershbow, who had replaced Jenonne Walker, and with Madeleine Albright as an ally, he put together a new strategy to negotiate an end to the war or else allow Bosnia to defend itself and regain territory. It was called the "endgame strategy." If the warring parties couldn't reach an agreement by winter, the United States should help the blue helmets withdraw and then turn to arming and training the Bosnians and defending them with airpower. I won't go into the details—all the meetings and memoranda, the tedious gear turning of the National Security Council, which can't possibly keep up with the speed and volume of human beings killing one another somewhere far away. You can read about Lake's effort in a lot of books (just not Holbrooke's). The ideas weren't new—in one form or another they'd been lying around since Clinton took office. What had been missing was the political will of the president. Lake thought he might get it now.

One day in June he went into the Oval Office with the usual "B" imprinted on his forehead, plus a scar on his abdomen from a recent hernia operation that he imagined in the shape of Bosnia, like the famous cartoon of Lyndon Johnson displaying his gallbladder scar as the map of Vietnam. "Mr. President, tell me if you don't want to do this," Lake said after laying out his ideas. "Stop me now, because the risks are very clear." The risks included either a spectacular diplomatic failure with uncertain military involvement to follow, or else the deployment to

Bosnia of twenty thousand U.S. troops to enforce a diplomatic success, just as the 1996 election campaign was getting started.

Clinton told Lake to go ahead.

I would like to tell you that Clinton had finally seen enough death in Bosnia. I'm sure he had—but he was also hearing Republicans mock his fecklessness; and facing an upcoming vote in Congress to lift the arms embargo, which was sure to pass by a large and maybe veto-proof margin; and listening to the advice of Dick Morris, an amoral no-neck Rasputin of a pollster whom the president had installed in the West Wing and who told the president to "bomb the shit out of the Serbians to look strong"; and staring at the possibility of having to send thousands of American ground troops into Bosnia by prior agreement in order to aid the complex and dangerous withdrawal of U.N. peacekeepers if the allies decided to pull them out—the worst of all scenarios, because it would risk American lives in an ignominious defeat.

In a speech, Jacques Chirac, the energetic new president of France, goaded Clinton: "The position of leader of the free world is vacant." On June 14 Chirac met Clinton in the Oval Office and urged him to take action, and when Clinton made excuses, Holbrooke, the junior American in the room, stunned the French by speaking up: "Mr. President, you're wrong—President Chirac is right. We have to do something."

"I'm getting creamed," Clinton railed one day while practicing his putts on the White House green. "This has to stop. We've got to find some kind of policy and move ahead. Why aren't my people doing more for me?" He was always a maddeningly seductive blend of empathy and self-pity, clear thinking and evasion.

As usual, events outran the ability of American officials to come up with solutions.

ON THE AFTERNOON of July 11 Serb forces entered Srebrenica. The town was empty. Fifteen thousand Muslims—mostly men, with or without arms—had decided not to count on U.N. protection and slipped out of Srebrenica the night before, trying to escape through mountains and woods and minefields to Tuzla seventy miles north. Twenty-five thousand civilians and 370 Dutch peacekeepers remained behind, huddled together at the U.N. base in a roadside battery factory a few miles out-side town. NATO air strikes had come pitifully late and with no effect.

General Mladic, invoking an 1804 Serb rebellion against the Otto-man Empire, proclaimed victory over the "Turks," but he was enraged at the escape of so many men from Srebrenica. He summoned the Dutch battalion commander, Lieutenant Colonel Thom Karremans, to meet him at dusk at a decrepit hotel in town. Chin jutting out like a blackjack, powerful forearms flexed at his hips, psychopathic blue eyes fixed on his prey, Mladic demanded who had ordered air strikes on his troops. Karremans, lanky, with a nineteenth-century military mustache, his back to a wall, arms folded across his chest, mumbled in low accented English that he did not control the strikes. He wasn't in charge of the mechanism by which the United Nations and NATO had once again failed to use airpower against the Serbs.

"Do not fantasize, Lieutenant Colonel, sir, but answer my ques-tion," Mladic yelled in Serbian. "Did you order your troops to fire at my troops?"

Karremans unfolded his arms and clasped his hands in submission—they might as well have been bound behind his back like the baker's wooden figures. "I gave the order to defend themselves."

"Who were they defending themselves from when no one was attacking them?"

"I've been attacked by mortars and by tanks."

Mladic did more yelling. A Serb soldier opened a pack of cigarettes. "Light up," Mladic ordered the Dutchman. "It's not your last one in life." They shared a smoke and Karremans thanked Mladic for treating the Dutch soldiers well. "I want to help you," Mladic said, "although you don't deserve it, neither as a human being nor as an officer. That's why I want to ask you the following. Can you bring the representatives of the civilian population here, and when can you do that? I will work out an arrangement with them. From here you can all leave, all of you. Or all stay. Or all die here. I don't want you to die."

Karremans promised to cooperate. Mladic offered to care for the wounded among the Muslim population, and Karremans thanked him for his humanitarianism. Mladic toyed with Karremans for forty min-utes as the room grew dark. Over the Dutchman's objections he insisted that they share a drink. They toasted each other with wine spritzers. By then everyone was smiling.

The next day, July 12, Mladic and his men entered the battery factory outside town. While Serb troops passed out candy, Mladic patted children on the head and assured the Muslims that they would be allowed safe passage. Then his soldiers forcibly separated families—the men and older boys from the women, small children, and elderly. The latter were herded onto buses bound for Tuzla three hours north, though along the way some of the women were taken off to be raped, discarded, sometimes killed by Serb soldiers. The men and boys were brought to empty fields and abandoned buildings, where the Serbs mowed them down with Kalashnikovs, blew them to pieces with hand grenades, buried the bodies in deep pits dug by backhoes. The men who had fled into the woods were hunted down and killed one by one or else committed suicide.

If you go to Srebrenica today you can read their names, nearly seven thousand of them, carved into a large semicircle of speckled white granite, in the middle of a field covered with white Muslim gravestones, across the road from the battery factory. So many names from the same families—scores of Smajlovices and Delices.

Anthony Holbrooke was in Tuzla when the buses from Srebrenica reached the airfield and unloaded their desperate passengers. Anthony was working for Refugees International with Lionel Rosenblatt—his father had helped him get the job—and he heard the wails of women who knew that they would never see their husbands and fathers and sons again. An emaciated man wandered out of the woods, one of the few survivors of the slaughter.

Anthony got on a satellite phone with his father. "You've got to get your ass in gear!"

"I am. My paper is on the president's desk. They're not listening to me."

The world, as usual, neither anticipated the genocide nor wanted to believe it. Yasushi Akashi, the top U.N. civilian official in the Balkans, blamed Muslim "provocation" for the fall of Srebrenica. His boss in New York, Boutros Boutros-Ghali, said, "I don't believe this represents a failure. You have to see if the glass is half full or half empty. We are still offering assistance to refugees." In Washington, Lake imagined something awful, but he did not imagine something on the scale of Srebrenica, because nothing like it had happened before in this war, just as nothing as bad as the My Lai massacre had happened in Vietnam, until My Lai.

Holbrooke felt vindicated. He thought that bombing would have prevented the mass killing. If more officials got out of Washington and went to see refugee camps for themselves, he thought, the war would be less abstract and they wouldn't be surprised by something like Srebrenica.

Now the Clinton administration had to do *something*. "Our position is unsustainable," Clinton told his advisors. "It's killing the position of the U.S. in the world. This is larger than Bosnia." But he remained strangely detached and continued to allow the disaster to proceed—sitting in on a meeting for six minutes before getting up to leave, letting the Europeans make the hard decisions. Holbrooke thought that Clinton had utterly abdicated his responsibility—"an occasional visitor to the ship of which he is the captain." But at the beginning of August, with the whole of Bosnia in a violent cataclysm, Holbrooke left Washington with Kati for a three-week vacation in Colorado.

ZEPA FELL NEXT to Mladic's forces, and more Muslims were raped and killed and turned into refugees. The collapse of the enclaves along the Serbian border had the perverse effect of making the map of Bosnia more coherent. It removed the inconvenient green spots floating in the contiguous red of Serb-held territory. Some diplomats in Europe and the United States seemed to accept—maybe even welcome—the enclaves' fall, which would make negotiations easier.

On July 20, the allies met in London and finally agreed to draw a line. If Mladic attacked Gorazde, he'd be hit hard by NATO regardless of the danger to peacekeepers. From now on the decision would be left to the U.N. commanders on the ground—Boutros Boutros-Ghali wouldn't get a veto in New York. Though NATO and the United Nations were both postwar inventions of the United States, we had much more sway in the former than the latter.

But Mladic and Karadzic prepared to attack the remaining enclaves, with the final goal of taking Sarajevo and achieving all their war aims. They were delusional, drunk with nonstop victories. In fact, the Serbs were about to lose much of what they'd gained, and by the same brutal technique. Tudjman and his generals were preparing to ethnically cleanse Croatia, and on August 4 Tudjman's army staged a lightning offensive into the Krajina, the majority-Serb region of Croatia along the border with Bosnia, burning villages and driving the entire Serb population out. The United States gave a flashing green light to Operation Storm—this was ethnic cleansing we were willing to tolerate. Within three days, two hundred thousand Serbs whose families had lived in the Krajina for centuries had fled across northern Bosnia into Serbia itself. Milosevic, godfather of the Serbs, did nothing to stop the rout—he was interested in a peace deal, not a wider war—and sent the refugees to Kosovo. It was the Serbs' first military defeat since the start of the war, and it signaled a larger collapse. With Mladic's army preoccupied with genocide in the east, Croatian and Bosnian forces pushed Serbs out of areas in western and northern Bosnia that they'd conquered in 1992. The Serbs' 70 percent of Bosnia, a static figure for three years, suddenly fell toward 50, and it might have kept dropping much lower.

Clinton shook off his paralysis. After Srebrenica and Operation Storm, he knew that this was his last, best chance to dare to act in Bosnia. Better now than in the middle of the campaign. The churn of events in the Balkans coincided with the end of Lake's policy review. Every agency contributed a strategy, and Clinton had thirty pages of documents to read. Christopher at State and Perry at Defense remained skeptical of taking big risks. Clinton came down behind Lake's plan, which was the most ambitious, and which finally put together diplomacy and force in one strategy. It called for reaching a political deal in which Bosnia remained an intact state made up of two largely autonomous entities of roughly equal size, one Muslim-Croat, one Serb (this was the current international plan on the table), after which a large, American-led NATO force would deploy to Bosnia to enforce the peace. Or, failing that, the United States would arm and train the Bosnian army and use air strikes to reverse the Serbs' ethnic cleansing. Either scenario put American skin in the game for the first time.

"We should bust our ass to get a settlement within the next few months," Clinton told his top advisors in the Cabinet Room on Au-

gust 7. "We've got to exhaust every alternative, roll every die, take risks. If we let this moment slip away, we are history." He glanced across the table at Lake, who had been designated to inform the allies. "How quickly can you get your bags packed?"

"I've got a toothbrush in my office."

A LONG LINE of statesmen—Lord Carrington, Owen, Vance, even Jimmy Carter—had bruised their reputations in the unforgiving Balkans. The latest European negotiator, the Swedish politician Carl Bildt, would have to be nudged aside in talks with the warring parties. An American would take the lead.

The State Department insisted that the negotiator come from its ranks: this was a classic job of diplomacy. There was one obvious candidate, and Lake resisted him. Instead of Holbrooke, he floated the names of Frasure or Tarnoff. Albright suggested a White House special envoy like Charles Redman, Holbrooke's replacement as ambassador to Germany, who had negotiated the creation of the Muslim-Croat federation, and Lake supported the idea. In truth, he wanted the job for himself. He had recently finished successful negotiations in Haiti. He had led the process of finding a new policy for Bosnia and he wanted to see it through. The talks might well make or break the president's re-election. Kissinger would never have surrendered this high-wire act to anyone else. Yet Lake saw himself as a dutiful civil servant who avoided the limelight, the powerful figure just outside the picture frame. The national security advisor had too many demands on his time to devote several weeks or maybe even months to ending one small war.

During the first week of August, Warren Christopher was in Hanoi, concluding what Holbrooke had tried and failed to get done almost twenty years before—the normalization of relations between the United States and the Socialist Republic of Vietnam. On the homeward flight, Donilon, along with Talbott on the phone from Washington, argued for Holbrooke to lead the Bosnia talks. If he didn't get the job, Donilon said, he'd be gone by Labor Day. Holbrooke was already talking to a New York investment bank.

Christopher realized that Dick Holbrooke would be the perfect choice. The same traits of character that made the secretary of state shudder—the self-dramatization, the aggressiveness—would be more than a match for the Balkan warlords. People would pay money to see the show. On a stopover in Hawaii, Christopher called the White House to say that, at the end of Lake's trip to Europe, Holbrooke would go on to the Balkans. He assured Lake that Holbrooke would stick to instructions and report back every day.

Lake yielded. He knew Holbrooke's talents better than anyone. It might take that kind of shamelessness to push the ball over the line.

While the president and his advisors in Washington were making essential decisions about Bosnia, Holbrooke was away in Telluride like Achilles sulking in his tent. He wanted the mission—wanted it so badly that earlier in the summer he had invited himself into Donilon's office next to the secretary's suite on the seventh floor, stretched out on the sofa, and talked for an hour about how he had been preparing his whole career, ever since the Paris peace talks, for this one chance. But he had lost all faith in the Clinton administration.

On August 9, Lake and a few others flew to Europe to tell the allies and the Russians that the United States would lead a diplomatic initiative that could end in military action. Unlike Christopher in 1993, Lake asked for cooperation, not permission, and this time it readily came. The Europeans were relieved to hand over leadership to the United States. It had taken four years, but the sand in the hourglass of Europe had run out. The West was finally united on Bosnia. Lake called this exercise of American influence "the big dog barking." It was a sound that the world hadn't heard since Clinton became president. Lake's talks were so successful that people on his team tried to convince him that *he* should continue on as the negotiator.

On August 12, with Holbrooke en route from Colorado to meet Lake in London, the *Times* ran a piece called "Clinton's Balkan Envoy Finds Himself Shut Out." Holbrooke was quoted on the record pissing on his colleagues: "He says he is flailing against 'a gigantic stalemate machine' that produces 'watered-down policy,' a decision-making apparatus run by people incapable of making decisions, where 'bureaucrats of every stripe have their say.'" These were direct shots at Lake. "'What did we learn in Vietnam?' Mr. Holbrooke asks rhetorically. 'The only unambiguous lesson is this: if the national interest is engaged, you must succeed.' He pauses. 'You can see how brilliantly we've applied that lesson in Bosnia.'" When Christopher, who kept himself perpetually below room temperature, read these lines in Washington, he got angrier than Strobe Talbott had ever seen him.

Sandy Berger called Lake in London to warn him that Holbrooke's heart might not be in it—that he feared becoming the fall guy if the effort in the Balkans ended in failure. He would need some persuading.

On the morning of August 14, Holbrooke met Lake's team in a small conference room at the U.S. embassy. Lake gave Holbrooke his end-game plan. It included seven points: a comprehensive peace settlement throughout what had been Yugoslavia; a cease-fire and three-way recognition among the warring countries; two autonomous entities split roughly fifty-fifty—one Muslim-Croat, one Serb—inside one Bosnian state, under one constitution; the negotiation of borders based on ground-level reality in Bosnia, with the possibility of land swaps such as trading Gorazde, the last surviving eastern enclave, for Serb-held territory in central Bosnia; sanctions on Serbia lifted; the return to Croatia of the last piece of Serb-held land in eastern Slavonia; and economic reconstruction of the shattered region. Lake told Holbrooke that in his shuttle between the Balkan capitals he would need to stay close to these points.

Holbrooke replied that the plan was full of flaws. Giving up Gorazde and creating sixty thousand new refugees was unthinkable. The idea had been a bone thrown by the White House to skeptics at the Pentagon who wanted a militarily sound map, but Holbrooke used it to seize the moral high ground and set Lake straight about the realities of the war. Lake reminded him that Izetbegovic himself had called Gorazde indefensible, but Holbrooke dug in: "After Srebrenica we cannot propose such a thing." He wasn't out of his sour mood. He'd had nothing to do with the plan.

"We shouldn't let expectations outrun reality," Holbrooke said. "We'll give it our best, but it will be a very difficult process." He put the odds of success at 15 to 20 percent.

"Oh, at least fifty percent," Lake said.

Lake asked the others to leave the room. He and Holbrooke stayed behind. If you've kept up this far, you would want to have been a silent third in that room. Lake was fifty-six, Holbrooke was fifty-four. They had known each other for thirty-three years. They were around the peak of their careers. Lake had just handed off to Holbrooke his own plan and the role he wanted for himself. Holbrooke would take it and fly higher than either of them had ever flown, or come crashing down before the eyes of the world.

With all the self-restraint that Holbrooke lacked, Lake subdued his own competitive desire and everything else between them long enough to encourage his former friend. "I'm going to be with you all the way," Lake said. "If this thing fails, it's my ass more than yours." He suddenly thought back to their beginning, the days and nights in Saigon, their effort to find a better way to fight that war or else a way to end it, and in a quiet voice he said, "This is what we once dreamed of doing together."

His words moved both men. They shook hands.

VIII

Holbrooke flew on to the Balkans.

At last he had something to do, far from his agonies in Washington. A metabolic conversion was about to catalyze all his petty and destructive traits into single-minded purpose. The mission would focus the light in his ice-blue eyes and engage everything I told you he loved—speed, history, America, even a little mischief. Because it was true—he had been waiting all his life for this chance. By preparation and circumstance and luck his hand found the thing that it was meant to do.

When he started out he didn't know how he was going to do it. He barely knew the three Balkan leaders. He had Lake's talking points, nine single-spaced pages, already known in Washington as "the Lake-Holbrooke plan." He would come up with the rest as he went along.

I wish I could tell you what he was thinking. He would later write a highly readable account—finally joining, for the first and last time, his two dreams of diplomacy and journalism, by making himself the author of his own history—but it suffered from great man syndrome, which means it hid the true self behind a false one. It left out the broken plays and fakes, the hail Marys and sideline brawls—the craziness.

He started out with five people. They came along to advise, serve as extras in meetings, report back to their respective agencies, and make sure Holbrooke stuck to the script. When you travel on an official mission like this you have to bring the entire U.S. government.

From the military there was Lieutenant General Wesley Clark, along with his aide, Lieutenant Colonel Daniel Gerstein. Clark: Rhodes Scholar, company commander in Vietnam, shot four times in an ambush, Silver Star, silver hair, earnest handsome eyes, three stars, on a fast track, had to beat you at everything, widely disliked in the army. In 1994, Clark became head of planning at the Joint Staff, and he met Holbrooke early that fall during a discussion of NATO enlargement at the State Department.

"Is there anybody who doesn't agree that this is the policy of the United States?" Holbrooke demanded, patrolling the small room on foot while the other two dozen officials remained seated.

Clark represented the Pentagon, which opposed NATO enlargement. He raised his hand. "When did this become the policy? Did we get a chop at it?"

Holbrooke was standing over Clark. "Anybody who questions this is insubordinate to the president of the United States."

Clark's face reddened and he pounded the table. "You won't call me insubordinate." The room was hot, and he started to unzip his jacket.

Holbrooke took a quick step away as if a punch was about to land on his face. "I didn't mean insubordinate. But this is the policy."

You wanted to be Holbrooke's boss or his disciple. He doled out loyal flattery above and exacting patronage below, but anyone near his level was in his sights as a possible rival who had to be crushed, or at least subdued. On Holbrooke's team Clark came closest. That put him in a dangerous spot, and his excitable self-confidence sometimes outran his political skills, and Holbrooke exploited his mistakes. Clark once spent two hours in Banja Luka listening to Mladic recite the history of Serb grievances going back to 1389, and afterward the two generals were photographed swapping hats in a gesture of military bonhomie. Holbrooke was appalled, and he instituted an unwritten rule never to leave Clark alone with a Serb, Croat, or Muslim.

From the White House there was Colonel Nelson Drew, an air force officer detailed to the NSC staff and valued by Lake for his hard work on the endgame strategy. Drew was relatively junior and joined Holbrooke's group as a late addition after Vershbow, Drew's boss at the NSC, who shared a mutual dislike with Holbrooke, withdrew. From the Department of Defense there was Joe Kruzel, an air force intelligence officer in Vietnam (Vietnam ran like a muddy stream through the Americans working on Bosnia) and later a professor of international relations at Duke. He was a defense intellectual with a stocky build and a dry wit and skeptical dark eyebrows.

And from State there was Bob Frasure. A year younger than Holbrooke and his opposite—a career professional of the type that Foreign Service officers called "a classic diplomat," an imperturbable institution man, understated, balding, broad mustache, a bit stooped, a bit cynical. "Typical Foreign Service officer" was one of Holbrooke's favorite putdowns, but he valued certain members of the breed and none more than Frasure, who knew more about the Balkans than anyone in the government and had the clarity and guts to write, in a memo to colleagues, "Over the last three years, we have handled this extraordinarily difficult issue ineptly." He was sardonic by nature, and the combination of the war and the Clinton administration honed this trait to a fine edge.

One day, Frasure came back from another long, inconclusive White House meeting to his sixth-floor office at the State Department and stared out his window at the Lincoln Memorial with his hands in his pockets, as was his habit, lost in gloomy thought, when Christopher Hill, who worked for Frasure in the Balkan unit, walked in. "What happened, Bob?"

Frasure didn't answer at once. Without turning from the view, he said, "In the Civil War, troops in the field assembling for battle would always want to know the identity of the units in the battle formation on their sides to give a better sense of whether they could be expected to be flanked or not. So you can imagine you are out there, battle drums sounding, and you yell to your sergeant: 'Sarge, who's that yonder to our right?' And imagine the fear that must have swept through the lines when the answer came back, 'Don't worry, boys. That's the Clinton Brigade.'"

Frasure, Kruzel, Drew. Each middle-aged, with a wife and two kids, using vacation time to travel to the war. Shortly before they left, Gail Kruzel told a colleague of her husband's that she and their two small children hardly got to see him—the Pentagon's Balkan task force was taking all his time. Frasure had been going back and forth to the region for most of the year, and this would be his last trip—from now on he would stay behind in Washington, or at the Frasure farmhouse in the Shenandoah Valley with his wife, Katharina, and their two teenage daughters, painting the barn and doing carpentry projects.

Frasure, Kruzel, and Drew were the kind of career officials who commuted to their offices from the Virginia suburbs in suits and ties early every morning and worked long hours and might receive a department award now and then but were unknown outside their circle of colleagues. If they didn't make it to the treetops, it wasn't for lack of ability or dedication but want of that demon ambition. In other words, they were bureaucrats. We think of bureaucrats as colorless mediocrities performing meaningless tasks, but I'm using the word with high respect. Most of us have no idea how much talent and honor and toil lie buried in the mid-century concrete mausoleums of the federal government scattered around Washington. These three now seem like men from a bygone age of belief in—something.

The team spent the night of August 14 on the Croatian coast near Split, in a sixteenth-century stone tower converted to a hotel. On a dare from the others, Kruzel and Clark jumped from the third-floor balcony into the Adriatic Sea. Holbrooke sat at a picnic table in the outdoor restaurant and ate local shrimp and mussels with Peter Galbraith, the ambassador to Croatia. Galbraith was the son of the economist John Kenneth Galbraith, an action intellectual of the Kennedy era, which Holbrooke loved. He was also a Bosnia hawk, which made him an ally, and he had a good relationship with Tudjman and understood Croatia's crucial role as the swingman in the Balkan wars, which made him useful. But they were constantly throwing elbows. Galbraith's sense of his own importance rivaled Holbrooke's and made him just as unpopular with colleagues, and his cables took moral stands that Washington regarded as overly emotional. In November 1994, arguing for bombing the Croatian Serbs to defend Bihac, he goaded Holbrooke: "Does the 'C' in 'Richard C. Holbrooke' stand for 'Chamberlain'?" Holbrooke replied with a put-down of his own: "You're advocating a wider war and no one in D.C. wants that. I'm the only friend you've got here."

Over Croatian shellfish they went through Lake's talking points, which exasperated them both. "Washington" saw the war in abstract terms of maps and negotiating positions rather than aggression and genocide. Galbraith particularly objected to abandoning Gorazde, and he repeated the argument Holbrooke had made to Lake. Holbrooke then tried out the argument that Lake had made to him, but Galbraith insisted, just as Holbrooke had. Holbrooke decided that his instructions gave him enough flexibility to remove the proposal. With a thick felt-tip pen he drew a line through the sentence about Gorazde.

But that was not the end of Gorazde. He made one more move, and it tells you something important about how he negotiated. The next day, the Bosnian foreign minister Muhamed Sacirbey arrived in Split and spent an hour at the airport talking on Holbrooke's small plane. "We'd like you to consider exchanging Gorazde," Holbrooke began. Sacirbey was stunned, and he glanced at Frasure, who looked uneasy, as if Holbrooke shouldn't have asked. If Sacirbey had expressed any openness, Holbrooke would have learned something about the Bosnian negotiating position, but Sacirbey said that trading Gorazde was impossible, and Holbrooke didn't push. Reporters were waiting inside the terminal, and before ending the discussion Holbrooke asked Sacirbey not to tell the press that the Americans had pressured the Bosnians to give up Gorazde. Sacirbey thought that this was like saying, "Please tell the press that the sex was voluntary." So he got off the plane and approached the reporters: "Dick Holbrooke said to me, 'We're not asking you to give up Gorazde, and I want you to tell the press.'"

That took Gorazde off the table for good—but not before Holbrooke understood his options. Even though he believed that trading Gorazde was wrong, there were no moral absolutes. He wasn't going to give something up until he knew what cards the other players were holding.

HIS TASK WAS to present the American plan to the three warring parties and hear their responses. The team was scheduled to go first to Sarajevo, but rain and fog kept their helicopter circling for an hour and a half before they had to return to Split. So they flew instead to Zagreb.

Tudjman had installed his presidency in one of Tito's modernist palaces on several hundred acres of park above the city, furnished with gilded Hapsburg chairs and Persian rugs. The honor guard wore red capes and caps that gave the palace an air of comic opera. Croatia's greatness and his own were Tudjman's unwavering passions. He was punctual, stiff, impeccably dressed, his white hair combed back so neat and full in an old-time Yugoslav pompadour that it became the bodily symbol of his dignity.

Holbrooke, as usual, was a few minutes late. With Tudjman waiting at the far end of the grand reception room, he and Galbraith ducked into the men's room to talk last-minute strategy at side-by-side urinals where they wouldn't be bugged. (This became their practice until the Croatians finally switched off all the lights in the bathroom except one above the urinals, which illuminated a sign that said "Welcome, Mr. Ambassador.") Galbraith's advice was to build Tudjman up, treat him like the nineteenth-century leader he imagined himself to be— Garibaldi or Bismarck. In Tudjman's mind his country belonged to a civilization of sovereign European nation-states, each with its own language, folk costumes, freedom struggle, and glorious destiny. He regarded his two counterparts, Milosevic and Izetbegovic, as Balkan primitives.

The Americans and Croatians sat on opposite sides of a massive blond-wood conference table, as if this were a U.S.-USSR summit, with Tudjman at the head. He was flush with victory in the Krajina and annoyed at having to cool his heels. Ethnic cleansing brought out the Balkan primitive in him. He had once been a historian, and after listening patiently to Holbrooke's talking points, he lectured his guests on the history of Croatia from Ottoman times, the Muslim menace in southeastern Europe, the secret Bosnian plan to create a continuous Islamic state from the Adriatic to Macedonia that would be even more powerful than Serbia. The West was lucky to have Bosnia's Croats keeping the Muslims in check within the federation.

"Muslims are really Croats," Tudjman informed Holbrooke, "but religion did make a difference. People ask, 'How can we cooperate when they are not Christians?' Bosnia-Herzegovina should be kept as a country and U.N. member—for the time being." Eventually, its Serbs would turn to the Orthodox world and its Muslims would be Europeanized. Tudjman was a great fan of Samuel Huntington, Holbrooke's old boss at *Foreign Policy,* and he predicted that in the clash of civilizations Bosnia would dissolve into a fault line between East and West. It sounded like a postgraduate version of a carve-up.

"The United States will not be a party to the involuntary disappearance of a nation called Bosnia from the map," Holbrooke said.

Tudjman switched to English. "There is no future for Bosnia."

Galbraith, outraged, slipped Holbrooke a note: "Dick—These are all Tudjman's old prejudices, fully reemerged after 18 months of relative abeyance. This line needs to be responded to very harshly. It was the justification for the Croat-Muslim War. I always used to tell him that Americans were most sympathetic to the Muslims <u>precisely</u> because we saw them as the most Western of Bosnia's 3 peoples."

To which Holbrooke answered: "I agree—but NOT NOW, NOT HERE, NOT YET beyond what we already said. This is far too serious, if he proceeds on it, to deal with now."

The ethnic cleansing of the Krajina was a stain on the West, and Holbrooke was learning that Tudjman could sound like the World War II–era Ustashe. In the long run, Muslims and Croats would have a hard time maintaining their alliance. But for the moment, Tudjman was a useful nationalist with an effective army. The Lake-Holbrooke plan called for "all parties to suspend offensive military operations," but Operation Storm had changed the war more than anyone in Washington realized. The Muslim-Croat federation, with support from the Croatian army, was now pushing deep into Serb-held territory in western Bosnia. Before the map hardened, the Bosnians deserved a chance to recover towns lost to ethnic cleansing. Their military momentum could be used in the shuttle talks to apply pressure on the most recalcitrant faction, the Bosnian Serbs.

At lunch with Tudjman, Clark echoed the Washington view that the offensive needed to be stopped. Frasure wrote a note on his place card and passed it to Holbrooke. "Dick: We 'hired' these guys to be our junkyard dogs because we were desperate. We need to try to 'control' them. But this is not time to get squeamish about things. This is the first time the Serb wave has been reversed. That is essential for us to get stability, so we can get out."

Holbrooke had already drawn a line through the paragraphs in his talking points about military restraint. The insight was obvious and profound: war could be a tool of diplomacy.

THE NEXT DAY, August 17, the team flew from Zagreb to Belgrade. A Serbian police escort drove them downtown from the military airport at speeds that forced other drivers off the road. Along the streets men were selling black-market gas out of plastic containers. Serbia was a police state with a mafia economy.

Holbrooke had never met Milosevic, but he knew that Milosevic was the key to everything. When they sat down in the vast marble reception room of the Serbian presidential palace—a dingy building with high yellowish curtains and the smell of old carpet and the soulless decor of the Communist era, including a statue in one corner, in brown bronze, of a female nude with her left arm raised above her head and her nose pressed into her armpit—Holbrooke tried to break the diplomatic ice by describing his hitchhiking trip through Yugoslavia in 1960: how he was picked up by Tito's police as a suspected smuggler and talked his way out by saying, "*Autostop Americanski!*"

Milosevic was nervous with people he didn't know. He was wearing a boxy blue double-breasted suit that made him look like the state banker he'd once been. His skin was colorless and his earlobes pendulous and his emotions opaque. He did not strike foreign visitors as a cruel despot. He could be witty, charming, profane. Of the three presidents he was by far the most fun. It was hard to get any read on him at all.

There seemed to be no one else in the palace, other than the foreign minister and a notetaker, because Milosevic didn't trust anyone except his wife, Mira Markovic. He was uneasy in public and increasingly unpopular with his people, whom he ruled by fear. He shrouded everything in deception, leaving no trail, which was how he was able to conduct wars of aggression in Bosnia and Croatia while claiming ignorance. Carl Bildt, the Swedish diplomat who took over the negotiations after Frasure's talks fell apart, noticed that hours would go by and Milosevic never got a phone call except maybe once from his wife, was never called away on official business, his desk had no papers or any other sign of work—as if being the president of Serbia meant receiving the latest foreign guest and talking late into the night over an enormous dinner and a large quantity of alcohol about events in nearby countries. He seemed to have all the time in the world—it was the visitor who was racing against the clock.

Milosevic was just four months younger than Holbrooke. His family came from northern Montenegro, the Appalachia of Yugoslavia, but he was born in a provincial shithole an hour from Belgrade. His father abandoned him early and he grew up devoted to his mother, who didn't let him play sports. When he was seven, his uncle, a Partisan hero, shot himself in the head. When he was twenty his father committed suicide. When he was thirty his mother hanged herself. Milosevic never spoke of this morbid history. His rise through the Yugoslav Communist Party was skillful and ruthless, but his lifelong attachment was not to any ideology but to power itself, and to Mira, a true-believing Communist and a monster like her husband. She once wrote, "He would never say, 'I'll die for socialism, I'll die for internationalism' like I would." A Serb psychologist described Milosevic as a "cold Narcissus" who cauterized the wounds of his youth with a power lust that deadened any empathy. The empty palace and the traceless rule reflected the condition of his soul. If he had a suicidal tendency, it was his gambler's tactics that led him into strategic death traps.

By the time Holbrooke walked into the palace, Milosevic was trying to close out his depleted account in Bosnia. It was no easy thing and he needed American help—Holbrooke's help. Milosevic was a candidate for the war crimes tribunal in The Hague that had indicted Karadzic and Mladic after Srebrenica. But, for now, Holbrooke needed Milosevic to be a Serbian statesman.

A white-jacketed waiter served drinks from a silver tray—glasses of juice, Serbian wine, Scotch, the plum brandy called *slivovic.* The group repaired to the dining room for the usual heart-attack platters of lamb and potatoes. Milosevic drank like a functioning alcoholic and smoked cigarillos or Cuban cigars like a mafia boss, while trying to charm Holbrooke by dropping the names of American bankers he'd met in the seventies on trips to New York, though in fact he'd spent most of his time shopping at Bloomingdale's and Macy's. Holbrooke matched him banker for banker.

The talk went on for almost six hours—below average for Milosevic. He kept circling the subject, settling on minutiae or veering away into irrelevancies. He found Holbrooke less informed about the state of play in the Balkans than earlier visitors. Afterward, Frasure met Carl Bildt at the airport and told him wryly, "The two egos danced all night."

Holbrooke and Frasure stayed over at the residence of Rudy Perina, the senior American diplomat in Belgrade. Holbrooke asked Perina, who had sat through weeks of previous talks, if he thought Milosevic had said anything new this time.

"Frankly, no," Perina told him. "This was all stuff he went through with Bob."

It was just word games, with Holbrooke the latest partner. He went to bed early and woke up early and angry. He was pulling on his pants in the hallway when Perina and Frasure emerged from their rooms. "Get dressed," Holbrooke told them. "I want to talk to you out in the garden."

They walked together under the chestnut trees next to the tennis court, away from Milosevic's listening devices. "Listen, guys," Holbrooke said, "I'm going back to see Slobo this morning and I'm going to throw a goddam fit." He wanted to show that Milosevic wasn't dealing with one more polite diplomat. He wanted an intense encounter that would break the negotiating pattern, and for that he would keep the group small, bringing just Frasure and Nelson Drew. He was getting himself revved up for a fight. "I'm going to scare the shit out of him."

For two hours Holbrooke did most of the talking, much of it loud enough to be heard through the door. The time for endless discussion was over, he yelled, the West's patience had run out, Milosevic needed to produce results or face the consequences. Holbrooke was capable of uncontrolled rage, but this was entirely tactical. Milosevic—whose survival depended on concealing any sign of vulnerability—stared back. Holbrooke added that it was demeaning for President Clinton's peace mission, which was about to try for Sarajevo again, to have to drive the dangerous road that wound down into the city from Mount Igman. He asked that Milosevic secure them a safe flight from Belgrade to the Sarajevo airport.

Milosevic stared a moment longer. "You're right. I'll try."

He sent his notetaker out to call Mladic. Milosevic had spent the past year claiming to have no control over his murderous clients, and in fact he had begun to think that Mladic, who saw himself as a medieval crusader, was going mad—mad enough to shoot down an American plane. Twenty minutes later the reply came back.

"Mladic says the airport is too dangerous," Milosevic reported—as if the Americans' fate didn't lie squarely in the hands of Mladic's own troops and artillery around Sarajevo. "Mladic says you can fly to Kiseljak and go in by road from there." The checkpoints were under the control of Karadzic's police, not Mladic's army. "You will be completely safe."

That was the same road Holbrooke had taken into Sarajevo with Rosenblatt and Frease in 1992. Bildt had driven it without incident two days earlier, and he thought it was foolish bravado to take the other road, over Igman. But the choice wasn't Holbrooke's. The U.S. government refused to recognize the Republika Srpska, which made the Kiseljak road out of the question.

"We can only consider using Kiseljak," Holbrooke told Milosevic, "if you give us your personal guarantee that we will not be stopped." He was testing whether Milosevic would agree to speak for the Bosnian Serbs. Holbrooke had begun to see a solution in compelling Milosevic to deliver the entire Serb side.

"I can't give you that guarantee," Milosevic said, "but I'll ask Mladic for one."

"That's out of the question, Mr. President."

Frasure whispered to Holbrooke, "We have no choice except Igman."

Mount Igman loomed over Sarajevo from the southwest. In the 1984 Winter Olympics the ski jump track was in a bowl at one end of the plateau and the biathlon course at the other. During the summers Yugoslav families went up Mount Igman for all-day hikes and picnics. It was steep and densely wooded, mostly evergreens, and it gave dramatic views of the red-tile roofs and minarets of Sarajevo. Where the mountainside ended, the land suddenly flattened out into the airport. This became the siege line.

Throughout the war Mount Igman was in Bosnian government hands. To leave or enter Sarajevo by land, officials and diplomats and most foreigners had permission from the United Nations to drive across the airport, though they took their chances and anyone might open fire. But Bosnian civilians trying to escape the city had to scramble through the half-mile tunnel under the runway, emerging in the house of a Muslim family on the other side, and then find a way up the mountain.

Serbs controlled the neighborhoods just east and west of the airport. Their anti-aircraft guns had line of sight on the switchbacks above them where the woods thinned and the Igman road was completely exposed. It became a shooting gallery, and all along the lower road lay the shells of abandoned trucks and overturned cars. Bosnians usually drove at night with their lights off, using night-vision goggles if they had them. A woman named Aida Cerkez, who worked with foreign journalists, risked leaving and re-entering Sarajevo over Igman dozens of times. On her way back down to the city, whenever she approached the danger point on the lower road where drivers coming up in the opposite direction stopped to vomit or pass out in relief, she would start singing an American spiritual under her breath:

> *There will be peace in the valley for me someday*
> *There will be peace in the valley for me I pray*
> *No more sorrow no sadness no trouble I see*
> *There will be peace in the valley for me*

ON THE MORNING of August 19, Holbrooke and his team flew out of Split on a U.N. helicopter. There was a clearing in the heavy clouds over Igman and they touched down on the plateau at 9:40. The landing zone was a soccer field called Veliko Polje, which meant "Big Field." It had rained for four days and the ground was wet. The air was already warm and smelled fragrant and alpine.

They were met by two vehicles, an armored U.S. Humvee and a six-wheeled French armored personnel carrier. The Humvee was the escort vehicle. It contained Pete Hargraves, the embassy security officer; Lieutenant Colonel Randall Banky, the senior American liaison officer at U.N. headquarters, next door to the U.S. embassy in town; and Staff Sergeant David Respass, the driver. The APC, painted white and manned by three French peacekeepers, was to bring the visitors down the mountain.

Right away the seating arrangement changed.

"Hey, sir," Lieutenant Colonel Banky said to General Clark, "do you want to ride in the Hummer?"

"Yeah, sure," Clark said. He felt it was improper to have the delegation's leader confined to the APC, and he turned to Holbrooke. "Have you ever been in one of these?" Holbrooke had not. "Come on, we'll get you in the Hummer. It's a lot better than the jeeps you were used to in Vietnam." So Clark and Holbrooke switched vehicles with Hargraves.

As Frasure started toward the APC, Holbrooke told him to think about what they would say when they met Izetbegovic. Frasure, who knew better than anyone what a long shot the whole mission was, gave one of his sardonic laughs. Holbrooke and Clark got in the Humvee behind Respass and Banky, Holbrooke on the left in his suit and Clark on the right in his dress greens, both wearing helmets and flak jackets. Frasure, Drew, Kruzel, Clark's aide Gerstein, Hargraves, and a French sergeant squeezed into the back of the APC on opposing seats, with the two other French soldiers in front.

The APC was also carrying a jerry can of fuel and a lot of munitions—five boxes of bullets, fifteen hand grenades, half a dozen rocket-propelled grenades, a pair of anti-tank rockets. Banky had told the APC crew that, if they became separated on the way down, they would link up at the French observation post at the bottom. The APC should not stop at Bosnian army checkpoints. The Serbs hadn't been firing on vehicles lately and the delegation would be safe inside.

They started down the mountain with the Humvee in the lead.

The Igman road, dirt and limestone gravel, was narrower in those days—twelve or fifteen feet wide. About twelve miles from the landing zone, it rounded a bend to the left and straightened out for a hundred yards on a moderate downhill grade before curving to the right. The mountain was very steep here and the road passed between a cliff rising on the left and a ravine plunging on the right.

The Americans had been on the road for thirty minutes when, halfway down the straightaway, they met a French column of freight trucks and APCs headed up the mountain. The column had pulled to the side and stopped. As the Humvee approached the last French vehicle a soldier on the road began yelling and pointing. Sergeant Respass, the Humvee driver, couldn't make sense of what he was saying.

THERE ARE TWO WAYS to tell this story. Really there are hundreds, but only two that need to be told.

The first is the way that history remembers it, which is the way its most important characters have told it in their own published accounts and journalistic reconstructions. If you know anything about what happened that morning on Mount Igman, this is the story you've heard.

I'll let Holbrooke and Clark take over.

Holbrooke: "I jumped out of the Humvee to help, but I couldn't quite grasp what the French soldier was saying, something about a vehicle behind us going over the edge of the road. I thought I had misunderstood him. Behind us was—nothing. I signaled Clark to join me. The APC must be far behind us, I thought."

Clark: "We looked behind us. Nothing."

"Then it hit me."

"Then it hit us. They were talking about our armored personnel carrier!"

"Clark and I ran back about thirty yards. About six inches of red clay seemed to have broken off the edge of the roadbed."

"Holbrooke and I were frantic. That armored car had been filled with our team members! Finally, I could wait no longer, and I started down the mountain."

"Wearing the heavy flak jackets and helmets—mine over a business suit—we jumped off the edge of the road and started down the steep incline. We were less than ten feet below the roadbed when two enormous explosions went off. Small-arms fire broke out around us. From below and above people cried out in French, 'Mines! Get back on the road!' Grasping roots to pull ourselves up, we scrambled back onto the road."

Holbrooke ran back down the straightaway to the Humvee and told Respass to turn it around in case they had to evacuate under fire and return to the landing zone. "We tried to set up our portable satellite dish to establish communications with the outside world, but the vertical rise of the mountain made contact impossible. Colonel Banky had disappeared."

Clark: "At that moment, a Bosnian general appeared, but he spoke no English. Through my poor Russian and sign language, we learned that the road switched back. This meant that if we kept going down the road, we would find the fallen vehicle from below."

"Wes and I started running down the road, twenty pounds of extra weight cutting into our necks and chests. We rounded the hairpin turn and followed the road for almost a kilometer."

"The Bosnian was right, and a mile or so farther down the road, as it circled back in a horseshoe bend, we saw a cluster of halted vehicles. Someone spoke broken English, but no one could explain what had happened." Here the uphill slope just above the road was nearly vertical, a ten-foot ledge of rock. Clark hoisted himself into the thickets. "I scrambled hand over hand up the steep mountainside, and soon found a medic with a dead French soldier. Two more, he pointed. That's all. The dead soldier could have been from our vehicle, but I couldn't be sure. I slid back down to the road."

"The vehicles were grouped at the spot, we now realized, where the APC had *bounced over the road* and continued to somersault down the mountain. Below us trees had been flattened as if by a giant plow. The shooting died down and rain began to fall."

"Someone pointed down below, where a column of greasy black smoke was rising. I just started running, breaking through the brush as I stumbled and fell down the mountainside."

"Since I was the only person on the mountain who spoke both French and English, I stayed on the road to work with the French while Wes descended. We anchored a rope around a tree stump so that he could rappel toward the vehicle, which French and Bosnian soldiers had already reached. Huge plumes of smoke rose from somewhere below us."

"A couple of hundred meters down, I saw the vehicle, turned on its side and burning. A Bosnian fighter leaned against a tree nearby. Stay away, he cautioned with his hands. But my men might be in that vehicle, and I couldn't stay away. I used a log to pry open the hot metal door, and it was like looking into a furnace. Two of our men were there, clearly dead, the flames licking only inches from their still faces. I quickly looked around for something with which to put the fire out."

"We could hear Clark yelling through his walkie-talkie that he needed a fire extinguisher urgently. I looked around frantically; there was none. A French jeep drove up and stopped. A solitary figure was seated upright in the backseat, covered in blood and bandages. His face was unrecognizable. I asked him who he was. He mumbled something unintelligible. 'Who?' I asked again. 'Hargraves . . . your . . . security . . . officer . . . sir,' he said, very slowly, talking in a daze."

Holbrooke and a pair of French soldiers helped Hargraves out of the jeep and laid him on a stretcher on the road.

"I got down on my knees next to him. He was having great difficulty speaking. I understood him to be saying that he should have saved people, that it was his fault, that his back was broken. I tried to calm him down. Desperate for information, I started asking him, one by one, about our team. 'Frasure. Where is Ambassador Frasure?' I almost shouted. 'Died.' He could barely say the word. I stood up. Three years as a civilian in Vietnam had exposed me to occasional combat and its awful consequences, but this was different. This was *my* team, and my deputy was apparently dead. But there was no time to grieve. Wes Clark was still far below us on the mountainside, and the only thing that I knew was that Hargraves believed that Bob Frasure was dead. I got back on my knees. 'Joe Kruzel,' I said. 'What about Kruzel?' 'Don't know. Think he made it.' 'Nelson Drew?' 'Gone. Didn't make it.' Hargraves started to cry. 'I tried . . .' 'It's not your fault,' I said hopelessly. 'There was nothing you could have done.'"

"I ran back through the brush, scrambling up toward the road, hoping to find a fire extinguisher. Every soldier I'd ever lost, every accident I'd ever seen, every trace of guilt I'd ever felt, they all came back to me now. I would have done anything to rescue those men."

"Clark struggled up the hillside, using the ropes. He looked ten years older. 'It's the worst thing you've ever seen down there,' he said."

"We put the fire out and recovered the bodies of Ambassador Bob Frasure and Colonel Nelson Drew. Then we combed the area and learned that two of our team had crawled out of the vehicle before it exploded."

"By now, journalists in Sarajevo had picked up some conversations about the accident on the internal radio network of the French military and had begun to report a confused and inaccurate version of the accident around the world. It was time to talk to Washington."

THAT'S ONE STORY of the tragedy on Igman. It was the most dramatic story of Holbrooke's life. It opens the only book he ever wrote. But there's another story that you haven't heard and that never got a foothold on history, perhaps because it fails a basic demand of narrative and would ruin the climax of a good novel if this were fiction (though I believe the second story comes as close to the fleeting truth as we are likely to get). In this story the famous characters become bystanders, while the protagonists of the action have names the reader has never seen and slip out of the narrative as soon as they appear, for Igman—their momentary brush with great men and great events—left their course unchanged as they proceeded into the utter obscurity that history reserves for almost all of us.

Randall Banky was forty, lean and dark. He grew up in a working-class Baltimore row house and enlisted out of high school toward the end of Vietnam. When he and the other guys lowered their right hands, the enlisting officer said, "Suckers." Later Banky attended West Point for the free education and received a commission, but he was the kind of infantry officer who identified more with his soldiers. In his view you got ahead in the army by being a self-promoting yes-man.

Lieutenant Colonel Banky and Staff Sergeant Respass were among the few Americans in uniform in Bosnia. The mission on Igman fell to them because the U.S. embassy didn't have a working armored vehicle, and Hargraves asked Banky to take him up the mountain in the Humvee. Banky didn't know why such an important delegation wasn't coming by another route—Igman was the Wild West.

The delegation left the Veliko Polje landing zone at 9:52 a.m. As Respass drove, Holbrooke said to Clark in the backseat, "Looks like you'll get a star on your CIB." He meant that Bosnia would qualify the general for another combat decoration. Banky and Respass exchanged a look. "Won't happen here, sir," Respass said. Banky had tried without success to get combat-duty tax exclusions for U.S. soldiers in Bosnia. Holbrooke was indignant and told Clark that he knew a congressman back in Washington who would fix it.

At quarter past ten they drove through a Bosnian army checkpoint without stopping. In the woods nearby there was a French observation post. The French soldiers thought the Humvee was going fast—too fast—twenty-five or thirty miles an hour, twice the speed they used on the Igman road. The Humvee had already passed two other vehicles on the mountain, one French and one British, and both had signaled for it to slow down. And if the Humvee was going too fast, where did the responsibility lie? Respass was the driver. Banky was the vehicle commander. Clark was the senior military officer. Holbrooke was the mission leader, and he loved speed.

The APC, wider and heavier, was trying to catch up with the Humvee. As it approached the checkpoint, the senior French soldier at the observation post, Master Warrant Officer Eric Limousin, waved the

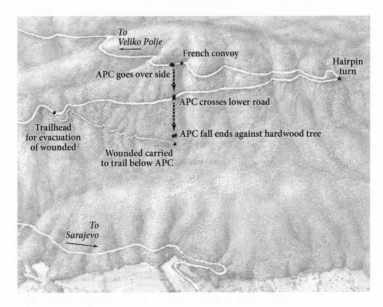

APC to stop. He told the vehicle commander in the passenger seat, Staff Sergeant Pause, that they would have trouble getting past a freight convoy moving uphill two or three kilometers ahead. Pause answered that they were escorting an important mission and had to get to Sarajevo. The APC's driver, Corporal Stéphane Raoult, sped off down the mountain.

Limousin got on the radio to the commander of the freight convoy, Staff Sergeant Jacques Duedal: "Be careful, Delta Unit, an APC is headed your way like a crazy man." Duedal got out of his armored jeep and walked back along the column, ordering the drivers to pull over against the cliff.

At around 10:20 the Humvee rounded the bend and drove past the armored jeep. Vehicles farther along the column hadn't pulled all the way over, making it impossible for the Humvee to pass even as it slowed to a crawl. Banky told Respass to stop, and they both got out. Banky walked ahead to speak to the driver of a truck blocking part of the road, and Respass went back to have the convoy tighten up so that the truck could move uphill and out of the way.

The driver of the armored jeep at the front of the column, Master Corporal Jean-Louis Jégou, saw the APC coming. As it approached it didn't seem to brake. It veered away from the jeep, toward the edge of the road, and hit a rough patch. The front end dipped and the rear wheels rose off the ground. On landing they bounced and skidded to the right. The APC's weight pulled it over the side.

HARGRAVES, the embassy security officer, was seated next to the rear doors, across from Sergeant Hervé Michel. In the interior darkness he felt the vehicle start to roll to the right. It rolled once and he thought it would stop, but it kept rolling and throwing its occupants around and someone landed on Hargraves. A piece of his seat broke loose and he put it to his face to protect himself from blows that felt like punches from his years as a young boxer. Gerstein did the same, instinctively pressing his face against the seat to reduce the impact that was fracturing the bones around his right eye and in his ribcage.

The front doors broke off. Forty meters into the plunge the APC commander, Staff Sergeant Pause, was thrown from the passenger seat onto the mountain. Another sixty meters and the driver, Corporal Raoult, was ejected, just before the APC sailed over the lower switchback road. Suddenly the rear doors were open and Sergeant Michel was gone and Hargraves was halfway out of the APC, feeling dirt against

his face, and he knew he had to get out or in. The doors closed on his hands and broke them. His ribs were broken and his nostril was ripped and part of his finger torn off.

The APC fell three hundred meters and rolled thirty or forty times. It might have kept rolling all the way to Sarajevo if it hadn't crashed against a big hardwood tree and come to a violent stop on its left side. The boxes of live ammunition scattered nearby were starting to explode. The munitions in the APC were hissing.

UP AT THE CONVOY, Respass rejoined Banky and told him that French soldiers were reporting gunfire down the mountain. Their position was exposed near the Serb fire zone and Banky hurried to move the column over. Respass came back—now the French were saying that an APC had gone over the side. Respass and Banky ran up the road a hundred meters to where French soldiers were yelling and pointing.

Down the mountainside every tree and shrub had been crushed to the earth as if by a giant lawn mower. The swath was the width of an APC. Several thousand feet below Sarajevo lay in full view. It was beginning to rain.

Holbrooke stayed with the Humvee while Clark joined Banky and Respass. Banky—it felt odd to give an order to a three-star—instructed the other two to set up radio contact with the embassy for medical assistance.

Then Colonel Banky disappeared. Over the side and down the mountain.

It was so steep that he had to slide on his rear. On the way down he didn't see Staff Sergeant Pause lying in the mash of vegetation. After a hundred meters, he came upon the APC driver, Corporal Raoult, who was moaning, while a soldier from the convoy, Warrant Officer Philippe Duplessy, gave him first aid. Raoult's left leg had been nearly torn off. Banky cut off part of his own bootlace and tied a tourniquet around Raoult's thigh. Raoult, who was twenty-two years old, stared at him. They both knew he was dying. A French soldier appeared from the road below, looked at Raoult, and ran away.

Shooting broke out a couple of hundred meters below Banky. He didn't know if it was gunfire or ammunition from the APC cooking off. There were larger explosions that sounded like Serb anti-aircraft rounds, or maybe rocket-propelled grenades. Banky thought of his friend Hargraves and the others in the APC. He did his best to dress Raoult's wound, then slid the remaining twenty-five meters and over the ten-foot ledge to the lower road.

Half a dozen French soldiers were on the road, staring at the continuation of the swath down the mountain. Banky took a few steps forward. "Mines, mines!" the French shouted. Banky stopped. No one else was going down. He had a bad moment of indecision. He was probably going to die right here, and he thought of his family. Then the moment was over and he grabbed a couple of aid bags from the French soldiers and continued down, with a French soldier following him.

Banky got about twenty meters when, farther down, one after the other, came two enormous explosions and a cloud of black smoke. Banky knew it was the APC, though he still couldn't see it. He started down again. A Bosnian soldier appeared from below shouting, "Mines!" The Bosnian motioned for Banky and the French soldier to follow him. They climbed back up to the lower road and ran half a kilometer down the road to where a narrow trail cut back to the left, almost parallel to the road. They followed the trail through thick green woods for a few hundred meters to a clearing where a group of Bosnian soldiers was giving first aid to three men.

Banky recognized Hargraves, propped up against a tree with a dressing on his head, and Gerstein, flat on his back. Both of them were coherent. The third man was lying on the ground moaning incomprehensibly. His head was injured beyond recognition. Gerstein told Banky that the man was Kruzel.

WHEN THE APC CAME to a stop on its side, Hargraves pulled himself out of the small roof hatch and fell on the ground. Gerstein was already out. The APC's fuel can had caught fire and the two anti-tank rockets in front were hissing in their canisters and shooting streams of white smoke. Hargraves heard someone screaming inside. He got the rear doors open and put his arms under Joe Kruzel's arms and braced his feet against the vehicle. He fell back on the ground with Kruzel on top of him. He started carrying Kruzel downhill until some Bosnian soldiers appeared and took Kruzel from him. Hargraves did not want to be next to Kruzel. He wanted to go home to his wife and he knew that the damage to Kruzel's head meant Kruzel would not go home.

Hargraves returned to the APC. The fire was burning and there were more screams. Frasure and Drew were still inside. Hargraves tried to yank open the rear doors but they had jammed shut and he burned his broken hands.

The rockets exploded, one after the other. The explosions threw Hargraves back ten or fifteen feet. A piece of shrapnel flew into his left knee and he thought how much that would hurt when he started feeling things. He propped himself up against a tree and sat down. If he lay on the ground, he wouldn't go home.

WITHIN A FEW MINUTES of the crash Bosnian soldiers reached the APC. They belonged to a five-man front-line unit in a wooden hut two hundred meters downhill. The commander of the unit was a thirty-year-old Muslim, six and a half feet tall, named Dervo Gadzo. Before the war he had been a mechanic in the Sarajevo Mercedes factory. He had spent most of the war on Igman, where he used to go hiking as a kid. Gadzo had no rank, no helmet or flak vest, and so little ammunition that he rarely used his rifle. That morning there was a brief truce because a diplomatic delegation was coming over Igman. Gadzo thought the noise of the crash was a truck bringing firewood to Sarajevo. The area wasn't mined—all the exploding ordnance came from the accident.

When Gadzo and his men arrived at the site, someone was trying to get the rear doors of the APC open. They ran to help him but the doors were stuck. The fire inside was so hot that the white paint was peeling off the metal. There was screaming from inside. Gadzo had never heard such screaming. He and another soldier ran around to the front and the other soldier started pulling a man out. There were two big explosions and the engine blew out and the man's head flew up the hill. The soldier, protected by the vehicle's armor, was covered in blood. The screaming stopped.

After that the roaring fire made it impossible to get close to the APC. The Bosnian soldiers tended to the three wounded men, joined by a second unit from nearby, including a Serb nurse named Biljana Rakic who had volunteered for the Bosnian army. Gadzo and a few others brought stretchers up from their hut. The day was getting warm and small flies were swarming around the wounded and the Bosnians had to wave them away.

HARGRAVES PASSED OUT against the tree, and he came to as a Bosnian was removing his G-Shock watch. The Bosnian seemed startled that Hargraves was alive.

"Watch, watch," the Bosnian said.

"Yeah, sure," Hargraves said. The Bosnian put his own broken watch into Hargraves's pocket.

BANKY ASSESSED the wounds of the three Americans. He gave an aid bag to the Bosnians and took the other bag fifty meters uphill to where the APC was burning. He was able to get within a few meters but couldn't find either of the two missing Americans, Frasure and Drew.

Since Kruzel was the most seriously wounded, Banky and several Bosnians carried him out first, several hundred meters up the narrow trail through the woods to the road. It was very hard going, with the steepness and the brush, and they had to pause once or twice. On the road they met a French armored jeep. A medical APC was on the way to take Kruzel to the nearest hospital. Banky wrote Kruzel's name on a piece of paper, left the dying man with French and Bosnian soldiers, and ran back down the trail with the stretcher. Along the way he met an armored jeep moving up toward the road. Hargraves was sitting upright in back—there was no room to lie down.

Gerstein, the least seriously injured, was the last to be evacuated. Banky and several Bosnians carried his stretcher up the trail. On the road, Kruzel and Hargraves were gone. Banky stayed with Gerstein—trying to keep him from losing consciousness by asking where he was from, whether he was married—until a medical APC arrived and took Gerstein away.

Banky went down the trail a third time to look for the two missing men. By the time he reached the APC, French soldiers were putting the fire out with extinguishers. There was too much smoke to see inside.

It had been almost an hour and a half since the accident. Banky's entire body was aching. He began climbing the swath up the mountain toward the road—looking for bodies and collecting pieces of paper on the way—to let General Clark know what he had found.

WHEN COLONEL BANKY DISAPPEARED, Holbrooke was upset at being abandoned by his escort officer in an exposed position near the sound of gunfire. After a delay, Clark started to follow Banky over the side. "Wait, don't leave me!" Holbrooke yelled. "Come back!" Clark scrambled back up onto the road.

Respass was directing the French convoy to make room for the Humvee against the cliff so that medical APCs could get by. Holbrooke told him to turn around and drive a hundred meters up the road toward the landing zone in case they needed to evacuate to safety. Eventually Holbrooke decided that there was no imminent danger, and he ordered Respass to turn around again and drive down around the switchback. The Humvee went a kilometer and a half and stopped at a cluster of French vehicles where the APC had bounced over the lower road.

There was a big fire below and Respass was concerned about Banky. He grabbed fire extinguishers from the Humvee and the French vehicles and scrambled down the swath, pausing to move scattered munitions out of the way. When he reached the APC he joined French soldiers who were trying to put out the fire. Respass could see the remains of one body inside, but the flames were still high. He helped carry a stretcher that held Sergeant Michel, the soldier who had flown out the rear doors just before the crash, the last to be evacuated. Then Respass climbed back up the swath to look for more fire extinguishers on the road.

Up at the Humvee Holbrooke and Clark were on the satellite phone.

DOWN AT THE EMBASSY, a voice was shouting through the radio. "Embassy Sarajevo, hello, is anybody there? It's an emergency, this is Holbrooke speaking! Fuck you, guys, answer me!"

The embassy was a two-story villa without amenities. The staff, including Ambassador John Menzies, slept in sleeping bags on cots. It was a quiet Saturday morning and a Bosnian staff woman was on duty at the reception desk. She was a Croat married to a Muslim, though until the war no one used the phrase "mixed marriage." Her son, born in the miserable winter of 1993, had hardly ever been outside the apartment.

The embassy radio was on an open channel and required an elaborate set of call signs. The caller was using none of them, which made the woman suspicious. She asked Menzies to come downstairs. Menzies had been at the embassy since April. He was a softhearted man who wept at the stories he heard from his Bosnian staff, and they loved him for sharing their dangers. He came down to the first floor to listen.

"Where are you fucking guys? This is Holbrooke, we had a tragedy on Mount Igman!"

Menzies confirmed that it was Holbrooke on the line. Two embassy vehicles raced toward the mountain while Menzies ran next door to alert the U.N. commander.

A LITTLE BEFORE NOON, Banky came up to the road and joined Holbrooke, Clark, and Respass at the Humvee. He hadn't seen any of them since going over the side. Banky was surprised to find that Hargraves hadn't yet been evacuated and was trying to tell Holbrooke about the others in the APC. Respass gave him a shot of morphine. Just before being taken away in a medical APC, Hargraves slipped off his wedding ring and asked Holbrooke to keep it for his wife if he didn't make it.

Banky briefed Clark on the situation below: Kruzel and Gerstein had been treated and evacuated, Frasure and Drew were still missing but almost certainly dead inside the APC. While Banky was giving his report, Holbrooke began relaying names and details over the embassy radio. Everyone in Sarajevo could listen in. Banky mentioned this to Clark, who snapped at Holbrooke: "Get the fuck off the radio."

The two embassy cars pulled up. "Get Ambassador Holbrooke off the site," Clark told one of the drivers, a former Bosnian army soldier.

"You're in charge, General Clark," Holbrooke snapped back. "I want all these fucking things sorted out."

All the way down to Sarajevo, Holbrooke was shouting over the radio: "I want every fucking political figure who's important in this country to get to the embassy, or get me them on the phone." He told Menzies to hold off confirming any deaths to Washington until Clark had checked out the site. But names were starting to be reported in the press, and Kruzel's family was initially told that he had walked away from the accident, and officials were already driving out to homes in the orderly Virginia suburbs. Katharina Frasure took Strobe Talbott into her husband's study to see the easy chair where he liked to work. It fell upon Tony Lake to give Sandy Drew the terrible news. After taking it in, she said, "You have to solve this, for Nelson."

ON MOUNT IGMAN there was nothing left to do but collect the remains. After hearing Banky's report, Clark told him to go back down, take pictures of the scene, then call him to come down. So Banky returned once more to the accident site, where the fire had gone out in the charred hulk. When Clark joined him, Banky pointed out what he'd been able to identify: a head and torso inside the APC, another head ten meters away. Clark ordered the remains placed in body bags. Respass arrived in the Humvee along the trail through the woods. Banky and Respass loaded the body bags into the Humvee and drove down to the military hospital at the airport.

A U.N. investigation found that the accident that took the lives of Robert Frasure, Joseph Kruzel, Nelson Drew, and Stéphane Raoult was unpreventable. But the report added, "This fatal traffic accident happened due to the excessive speed on Igman road. The responsibility is incumbent on the driver and the chief of APC even if the rhythm of the descent was imposed by a american [*sic*] armored vehicle." The report never saw the light of day.

The APC is still there, in a grove of fir trees, rusted and hollow, resting beside the big hardwood whose dead leaves fill it every fall. There is a memorial nearby. The woods feel haunted.

X

W e dream that, thrown into danger, we would act like Banky, and Hargraves, Respass, Gadzo, Duplessy, the Serb nurse Rakic. But we don't know—most of us will never know—whether we would run away at the sight of a dying man or start cursing at colleagues, and we should hesitate to judge anyone who's had to find out. The point of telling you all this in such absurd detail is that you've never heard these names and yet they were the heroes of Igman, while Holbrooke and Clark, who were famous and published accounts that made themselves the protagonists at every step of the tragedy, did almost nothing—saved no lives, carried no stretchers, dressed no wounds. I don't mean that they conducted themselves badly. Clark took physical risks, he was levelheaded and concerned for others, he could hardly bear to identify Kruzel's body at the French military hospital with Banky, and when he arrived somber faced at the embassy later that afternoon, his uniform was muddy and torn, and a staff woman washed and ironed his trousers. Afterward Banky gave Clark his highest praise: "That day he showed me he was a soldier. He showed he was one of us."

And Holbrooke? He did what the most important person on the mountain was supposed to do. He left the heroics to others. He had a peace mission to lead.

They didn't disgrace themselves. What I mean is that they were irrelevant. And this is intolerable for anyone who would be great. History can't be told that way. It's better for the main characters to be pariahs .

than beside the point. So before the day was over, a different story—the first story—began to take shape.

On the drive into Sarajevo, Holbrooke was in a rage. His colleagues had died on a dangerous mountain because of Serb pigheadedness, and in a larger sense because of the miserable failure of the West, including the United States, to end the war. They were the war's first American casualties. On arriving at the embassy, Holbrooke slammed open the door, threw down his helmet so hard that it bounced onto the reception desk, and stormed upstairs past Menzies. "Call Milosevic for me! I'm going to tell him what happened!"

When he phoned Kati that afternoon, so that she wouldn't hear the news from another source and worry about him, he sounded numb. "We lost Bob."

"What do you mean, you lost him?"

"He's gone. And so are Drew and Kruzel. I'm bringing them home and I'd like you to be there."

That night, in an interview at the embassy, Holbrooke looked pale and clammy and stricken. "We lost three great public servants," he said in the flat voice that protected him from his own deepest feelings. "These three people mattered. We can't afford to lose people like that . . . We will miss them unbelievably."

Along with rage there was grief and guilt. He was supposed to have been in the APC with the others. In losing three-fifths of his team, he had lost control of the mission, and it was necessary for him, psychologically and politically, to get it back. At the embassy he took over, brushing Menzies aside, yelling, storming, making demands: "Get Izetbegovic here! Get the press, I want a press conference now! We need a book of condolences!" Sarajevo bookstores closed at two o'clock on Saturday afternoon *in peacetime*. It didn't matter, they needed a book of condolences—and somehow someone procured one. The Bosnians at the embassy watched this performance with a mix of horror and admiration. Holbrooke didn't seem like a diplomat—he was more like a hooligan, rude, almost lunatic—but what had any diplomat achieved in Sarajevo? He acted just like the men who had brought the war. Watching him, one staff person thought that only this type of man would stand up to the warlords, including Bosnia's politicians, and force them to stop.

Holbrooke once said to the Bosnian driver who brought him to the embassy, "Do you know what carrots and sticks are? You can feed them or you can beat them. In your country negotiations are different."

"What do you mean?" the driver asked.

"You need a hammer or a sledgehammer. They know they're going to get beat up either way—the easy way or the hard way. It's up to them." And the driver told Holbrooke that he was right.

Holbrooke had kept Menzies from giving Washington more than basic information about the accident. He wanted to be the one. On the phone that afternoon with his colleagues at State and the White House he used phrases like "it is my sad duty" and "our fallen comrades" and "honor their deaths and continue the mission," until Sandy Berger urged him just to tell them what happened. But Holbrooke was already beginning to turn the accident into something larger than a mere tragedy. Igman had the power to bring Bosnia home to Americans, starting with the president, and get them irresistibly involved. Holbrooke would make it the origin myth of his effort to end the war.

Clinton, who was golfing in Jackson Hole, Wyoming, was eventually patched through to Sarajevo.

"Man, I'm sorry," Clinton began.

"We lost three good men," Holbrooke said. "I want to stress, this was not enemy action."

Clinton was thinking ahead to how the accident might give Holbrooke an advantage with Milosevic, Izetbegovic, and U.S. allies, who would no longer complain that the Americans had no troops in Bosnia. "What do you recommend doing?"

"We'd like, sir, with your authority, to keep our team intact and to bring the bodies home."

"My concern is what's the impact going to be on the peace process. How can we use this terrible tragedy to increase our leverage?"

Holbrooke described the accident at length. Clark was on the line with them, introduced by Holbrooke as "your fellow Arkansas Rhodes Scholar." Holbrooke told Clinton that Clark had gone down a four-hundred-meter precipice and was the first one to find the remains of Frasure and Drew.

Holbrooke had just given Banky's actions to Clark. It was the first hint of the great man story of Igman, and no less than the president of the United States now had it, so there was no going back. If Holbrooke had told Clinton that a certain Lieutenant Colonel Randall Banky—not a Rhodes Scholar, not on the call, not on the president's peace mission—had gone down the mountain, rescued the wounded, and found the remains of the dead, there would have been a subtle deflation over the line, and the origin myth might have never been born, and with it the American drive for peace. Holbrooke, who loved history, told the kind of story that history loves.

After that it wasn't so hard to jump over the edge of the road, bring the "mines" and "gunfire" much closer up the mountain, tie the rope around the tree, render the whole story in the rhetoric of leadership, and erase the minor characters. So by the time Holbrooke's book about Bosnia came out several years later, he must have been greatly surprised, during a stop on his tour in Minneapolis, to be confronted backstage by his military escort on Mount Igman, who had become a professor of military science at the University of Minnesota, read about the event in the *Star Tribune,* and showed up to inform Holbrooke that when he wrote "Colonel Banky had disappeared" on page 11 and *left it at that,* Banky's military friends assumed this meant that he'd been a coward and run away.

Distracted, Holbrooke introduced Banky to Walter Mondale, then did a phone interview. When he got off, he blamed Banky for abandoning him on the mountain. Then he admitted his mistake and said that he would correct it in the next edition.

Banky knew that this wouldn't happen, and it didn't happen, and in 2002, having been passed over for promotion, he retired as a lieutenant colonel, unable to lay to rest the suspicion that his army career ended because "Colonel Banky had disappeared."

AT THE SARAJEVO AIRPORT the wounded were put on board a British Sea King helicopter. The three coffins were loaded onto a French Puma helicopter. Clark offered to fly out with the coffins, and he turned to Holbrooke. "Will you go, too?"

Holbrooke didn't want to get on. Something about the Puma filled him with dread. He'd flown on hundreds of helicopters, but he felt sick and scared—unusually scared—as if the mission itself was doomed, the survivors of Igman were also going to die. "Do you think we ought to?"

Clark stared at him for a moment and then turned toward the Puma, and Holbrooke had no choice but to follow.

They crossed the Atlantic on a loud C-141 cargo plane with the flag-draped caskets. At Andrews Air Force Base, everyone noticed how Holbrooke's face was lined and his head was down and he leaned on others for support. When Frasure's sixteen-year-old daughter, Sarah, stood in the chapel at Fort Myer and said, "I took him for granted. I never told him I loved him. Now I will never wake again to hear him making pancakes on a Sunday morning," Holbrooke's tears flowed. For weeks he couldn't stop mentioning the three men, especially Frasure.

Bosnia was now the complete preoccupation of the U.S. government. After the funerals at Arlington National Cemetery, Holbrooke had to rebuild his team and head right back to Europe. Clark went with him, and a State Department lawyer named Roberts Owen was added to work on a new constitution for Bosnia. Colonel James Pardew, a retired army intelligence officer from Arkansas who had been hired by Kruzel for the Pentagon's Balkan unit, took Kruzel's place. The military remained opposed to ground troops in Bosnia even to enforce a peace agreement—Vietnam was still routinely invoked—but Pardew, another Vietnam vet, was a Pentagon outlier who saw the Bosnian war like Holbrooke, as genocide and failed American leadership.

General Don Kerrick, an army one-star at the NSC, replaced Drew as the White House's eyes and ears on Holbrooke. Holbrooke was so suspicious of anyone who reported to Lake that Chris Hill had to lie him into accepting Kerrick: "He's a great admirer of yours. Dick, he thinks you're the only person who really understands what to do in the Balkans." Holbrooke chose Hill to replace Hill's former boss and close friend Frasure. They were cut from similar Foreign Service cloth—cerebral and mordantly witty. Before leaving, Hill went out to visit Katharina Frasure. Her loss was still just a few days old, but she had found the strength to visit Hargraves in the hospital and tell him that he couldn't have saved her husband. She and Hill reminisced about Frasure. Then, as Hill started down the front steps, she suddenly asked, "How can you do this to your family?"

The team flew on Defense Secretary Perry's official plane, a ten-passenger C-20—a military Gulfstream—that announced "United States of America" on the side. It would become one of Holbrooke's instruments of power, impressive on arrival at dismal Balkan airports. There was a VIP compartment in front with a sleeping couch and easy chairs, but Holbrooke spent his time in the rear of the plane, shoes and socks off, feet up, huddling with his team. When he had time he read a book about the Camp David peace talks, but there was never much time. Everything had to be figured out on the fly. The key problems were to get Milosevic to stop temporizing and to isolate the Bosnian Serbs so that they would have to negotiate. Holbrooke thought the chances of success were slim, but he no longer hung his head and the lines were gone from his face. He had converted his emotions into high-energy fuel.

They landed in Paris on the morning of August 28. There was no real reason to stop over in Paris except that Holbrooke wanted to stay at Pam Harriman's. Izetbegovic was in town for a meeting with Chirac, along with his foreign minister Sacirbey, a dual U.S.-Bosnian citizen who spoke perfect English with a faint southern accent—he'd played defensive back at Tulane—and was as aggressive as Izetbegovic was withdrawn. Sacirbey always traveled with the president and made sure Izetbegovic didn't give too much away.

Of the three Balkan leaders, Izetbegovic was the hardest for Holbrooke to understand, or even like. He was seventy years old, physically slight, with a gloomy, remote nature. After seeing so much suffering, his eyes struck Holbrooke as dead to the pain of others—that was how they looked when Izetbegovic came to the embassy to pay his condolences after Igman. As for Izetbegovic, Clark was more his kind of American—solid, respectful. Holbrooke's intensity seemed to bring out the madness in Bosnian leaders, and Izetbegovic didn't trust him. He and Holbrooke talked by paying each other false compliments—"Mr. President, you are absolutely right, but . . ."—so they could never become partners like Holbrooke and Milosevic.

Izetbegovic was Milosevic's opposite, principled rather than cynical, which made him more difficult to deal with. Unlike Milosevic and Tudjman, Izetbegovic had no history in the Communist Party. He was a philosopher and activist who had been in and out of Yugoslav prisons. He had his own historical obsessions to match those of the Serb and Croat nationalists, who combed his writings for proof of Islamic fundamentalism. There were enough stray sentences to feed their anti-Muslim propaganda, but while Izetbegovic was not a cosmopolitan like other citizens of Sarajevo, including Sacirbey and Silajdzic, the prime minister, he wasn't an extremist either. He was a moderate Islamist who had come to symbolize Bosnian resistance to Serb aggression. He was an indecisive leader who had made grievous mistakes, none worse than declaring independence without preparing for war, but Bosnians respected him for staying in Sarajevo throughout the siege.

The Muslims were the war's main victims, but victimhood isn't elevating. Izetbegovic and his advisors were erratic and quarrelsome, among themselves and with others. Where Tudjman presided over meetings like a Hapsburg archduke, and Milosevic liked to bullshit mano a mano like a mafia boss, the Bosnians argued openly in front of their guests. They had put all their effort into surviving the war— few of them could look ahead to what they wanted to build. European diplomats barely concealed their dislike, while the Americans were torn between guilt and resentment at the Bosnian leaders' expectation that the United States would come to their rescue and support their most unrealistic aims. They wanted their whole country back, and Holbrooke worried that they would find the failure scenario in the Lake-Holbrooke strategy—U.S. air strikes, armaments, and military training—so appealing that they would deliberately sabotage the peace talks.

When Sacirbey met Izetbegovic's plane at Orly Airport on the afternoon of August 28, the president said, "Muhamed, have you heard what happened? I'm not sure I should have come to Paris." That morning in the center of Sarajevo, a mortar shell had landed in the same market where sixty-seven people had been killed in early 1994. This time the death toll was thirty-seven. Sacirbey told Izetbegovic that they should stay in Paris to pressure the West for a serious response, and he gave an ultimatum through the press: no bombs, no talks.

Sacirbey went to his room at the Hôtel de Crillon—where Holbrooke had stayed at the start of the Vietnam talks in 1968—and found Holbrooke waiting for him. "I heard you issued an ultimatum," he told Sacirbey. "You can't do that."

"We will." Sacirbey added that Izetbegovic refused to see Holbrooke until the bombing began.

Sacirbey later realized that Holbrooke had played him—that the Bosnian ultimatum helped Holbrooke's position. The American team spent the rest of the day on phone lines from the ambassador's residence to Washington, gathering support for air strikes.

THE MORTAR SHELL WAS the blunder that was worse than a crime. It was an accident of history that broke the years-long Western deadlock in Bosnia and set American foreign policy on a new, more muscular course. Where there had been no path to peace, the shell cleared one. Holbrooke saw the opening and took it. Clinton was finally ready to punish the Serbs—in part because of another accident, the three American deaths on Igman. This time he cut through any resistance from the allies, the United Nations, and his own military.

The Serbs, as usual, claimed that the Muslims had done it to win international sympathy. This had always been enough to keep the United Nations from taking decisive action, but the commander on the ground, General Rupert Smith, no longer needed permission from Boutros Boutros-Ghali in New York to call in NATO strikes. "I'm of the opinion that this is war," Smith told Menzies. "What's coming in is from the other fucker. Prove it isn't." After British peacekeepers were secretly withdrawn from Gorazde to avoid becoming the latest hostages, massive bombing of Serb positions around Sarajevo began shortly past midnight on August 30, just hours before Holbrooke's team was to fly to Belgrade.

Holbrooke always reacted to drama by taking a step back into the stream of history. In the middle of all the action, amid the Harriman Renoirs and van Gogh, he turned to Pam and pointed out how remarkable it was that the two of them were now working together in this crisis.

"And Averell would have been so proud of both of us," Pam said.

In Sarajevo, a woman went up on her roof to watch the NATO fireworks over Pale a few miles away. At the start of the war her parents had been caught behind Serb lines, forced to dig trenches in a labor camp, and she hadn't seen them for three years. The woman made a point of always wearing makeup outside the apartment, and always walking, never running, even on Sniper Alley—it was a risky way to hold on to pride. But she knew many Serbs who helped Muslims, including the man who dragged her sister over a bridge across the siege line to safety. When her neighbors on the rooftop cheered the air strikes, the woman pointed out that innocent people would also be killed.

Haris Silajdzic enjoyed the spectacle. The Serbs who had been casually murdering the people of Sarajevo now knew the feeling of terror and helplessness for the first time, and they deserved it. Neighbors of the embassy driver gave him thank-you cards and bouquets of flowers for Ambassador Menzies.

The U.S. Air Force thought it was too dangerous for Holbrooke's team to fly to Belgrade during the anti-Serb air campaign. Holbrooke thought there was no better moment. He didn't know how Milosevic would respond—if Milosevic would even see him—and his stomach tightened on the drive to the presidential palace, but he had an instinct that the bombs would strengthen his negotiating hand.

Milosevic greeted Holbrooke like an old drinking buddy. When the white-jacketed waiter offered glasses of mineral water and fruit drinks, Holbrooke asked, "May I take two?" and Milosevic replied, "Ambassador Holbrooke, please take three." He expressed sympathy for the loss of the three Americans, lingering on Frasure as if they had been close friends. Holbrooke introduced their replacements.

"I've been a busy man while you were away," Milosevic said. He reached one of his thick hands into the pocket of his blue blazer, took out a document written in Serbian, and gave it to Holbrooke. "This paper creates a joint Yugoslav–Republika Srpska delegation for all future peace talks." The delegation would have six members—three from Belgrade, three from Pale. Its leader, Milosevic himself, would break any tie. From now on he would negotiate for the Republika Srpska—removing the biggest obstacle to getting an agreement. "And this document has been witnessed by Patriarch Pavle, the leader of the Serb Orthodox Church. Look here."

Milosevic pointed to a signature next to an Orthodox cross. The patriarch's influence had made a difference with the devout Karadzic. As an insurance policy, Milosevic's secret police chief, Jovica Stanisic, had gathered a thick file on the criminal history of Karadzic's number

two, the Bosnian Serb assembly speaker and cement smuggler Momcilo Krajisnik. Perhaps Holbrooke's staged tantrum on his last trip to
Belgrade had also impressed Milosevic.

Hill, who knew a little Serbian, looked over the document and veri-
fied its contents. It seemed to offer the key to peace. "I wish Bob were
here to see this," Holbrooke said. Hill was thinking the same thing, but
he was too afraid of choking up to answer.

Milosevic lit a big Cuban. Holbrooke pressed him. "How do you
know that your friends from Pale will—"

"They are not my friends," Milosevic spat. "It is awful just to be in
the same room with them for so long. They are shit."

The talking and eating and drinking went on for eight hours. Milosevic drank steadily, getting high and then sobering up several times,
while Holbrooke lifted his glass of Scotch or *slivovic* to his lips and
barely sipped. He didn't stick to talking points—had no real talking
points—but let the conversation run its meandering course while looking for openings to run through. Milosevic digressed about Serbian
wine, the Ottoman Empire, World War II, his banking days in New
York, the economic future of Serbia, and Holbrooke let him go on,
enjoying the parley, and then always brought them back to the war. He
would step out to take calls—taking calls during meals was one of his
favorite shows of status—and come back to say that it was the White
House on the phone, though Hill and the others thought the calls were
probably from Kati.

When Milosevic finally brought up the bombing—two hours into
the talk, almost as an afterthought, without emotion—and asked that
it be stopped, Holbrooke said, "I can make no guarantees, but General
Clark may be able to stop it." It wasn't up to General Clark, but he was
the one with all the medals on his chest, and Holbrooke played him up,
just as he told Milosevic that Colonel Pardew spoke for the secretary
of defense and General Kerrick had a direct line to Clinton. Holbrooke
was playing a game, remaining ambiguous about how much say he had
over the NATO war machine, depending on his purposes, in just the
same way Milosevic spun an illusion of having little control over the
Bosnian Serbs—which made him the less odious negotiating partner
Holbrooke needed.

So a connection formed, with the tense familiarity of two card-playing rogues. Holbrooke didn't hesitate to deceive all three Balkan presidents, but he bluffed Milosevic more than the others. Clark and Pardew assembled an intelligence file on Serbian support for the Bosnian Serbs, making sure to include some true items and some false, and when Milosevic looked it over he didn't seem to know the difference. Once, in the middle of an endless session, Holbrooke phoned Les Gelb: "Hey, man. I'm here in Slobo's office. I told him that you were a Cuban cigar smoker, too, and I asked him if he'd give you some. He said he'd send you a box, but I wouldn't believe him because he lies all the time anyway. Don't you lie all the time, Slobo?" It was theater for the benefit of both the best friend in New York and the monster in Belgrade.

Milosevic was even more direct, sprinkling "fuck" all over his so-so English, needling Holbrooke: "Richard Charles Albert Holbrooke. Why do you have all those names?" Or: "Why is your collar always up? You're a politician—all you politicians have something like that. With Tudjman it's his hair, with you it's your collar." Actually, Holbrooke's collar was one of the few things he didn't have under control.

Thomas Mann called art "a very serious jest." Holbrooke's diplomacy was theater for mortal stakes. Large groups of reporters began to follow his team's every move, waiting in the lobby of the Hyatt Hotel across the Sava River from Milosevic's office, or outside Tudjman's palace above Zagreb, and Holbrooke would pause to give them a spontaneous and perfectly crafted paragraph of non-news, careful to keep expectations low because it did him no good to raise them. One of his rules for the team was no leaks, but he had his favorite journalists—Roger Cohen of the *Times,* Christiane Amanpour of CNN—whose prominence and sympathy with his views won them access to the inside story.

Holbrooke went without sleep for a day or two then crashed for a few hours. He gave the impression of being always in motion, sweeping with his entourage in and out of airports and hotels, crowding each day with meetings deep into the night, always pushing the pace, and this intensity created momentum for the next small breakthrough, and each breakthrough added more speed and power. The experience exhilarated him, and when he had to spend a whole day in Geneva conferring with European diplomats and got his first full night's sleep in a luxury hotel, he fell into exhaustion and wanted to get back to the Balkans, where the tense sleepless hours with warlords restored his energy. If he had a strategy, it was this: he set himself in motion and caused others to move, and things became possible that never happened with everyone at rest.

The Holbrooke skeptics on the team began to have confidence in him and the mission. Clark, who had to straddle the widest gap between the negotiating strategy and the views of his superiors in Washington, saw firsthand the results of diplomacy backed by force and became a Bosnia hawk. Pardew wondered if Holbrooke's ego would be his undoing and told colleagues at the Pentagon that, based on what he'd seen at the August 30 meeting with Milosevic, he wouldn't buy a car from either man. But on September 2 he wrote in his diary:

> We have no one else I've seen in the US government who could pull this off. He is tireless, intuitive, fearless of Washington and those he deals with in the area. He is charming all the snakes and moving them in the right direction. This is a big risk. RH has many enemies + detractors. If the mission goes under, they will let him take the fall. Lots of courage and skill. He works to keep us all engaged but manipulates the team as everyone else. A true character. Can't help but like him. He is something to watch.

XI

O ver Labor Day weekend the team flew between Belgrade, Bonn, Brussels, Geneva, Zagreb, Belgrade again, Athens, Skopje, Ankara, and Belgrade a third time. (Athens and Skopje because Holbrooke, Hill, and Pardew took time from Bosnia to resolve a volatile standoff between Greece and Macedonia over the latter's name.) Three and a half years after Bosnian independence, Milosevic finally agreed to recognize Bosnia and Herzegovina as an independent state within its international borders. But to keep Karadzic from rebelling, he refused to allow Bosnia to be called a "republic," which would give the central government too much power—it could be a "union" or a "confederation"— and he insisted that the Serb part of Bosnia go by "Republika Srpska," the name given it by the war criminals in Pale. In a military stalemate, names were proxies for victory and defeat.

On September 1, NATO suspended the bombing to test Mladic's readiness to end the siege of Sarajevo. Mladic gave the usual equivocal response, enough to weaken the will in the usual European and American offices. Holbrooke knew that it would help him sell Milosevic's demands to the Bosnians if the bombs started falling again.

On September 4, Labor Day in America, Holbrooke caught up with Izetbegovic in Turkey. They met late that night at the American ambassador's residence in Ankara. Izetbegovic had told Holbrooke—on the day of the Igman accident, and again at Pam Harriman's in Paris—that the Bosnians wanted a unitary state. They had not held on for three and a half years only to see part of their country annexed by Serbia. In the end it might have been better if the Bosnian Serbs had been allowed to leave—but that's getting ahead of the story. No one knew how the two entities in this single state—one Muslim-Croat, one Serb—would coexist under a constitutional framework. Would it be like Switzerland, with federated cantons, or like Cyprus, with a permanent hostile truce?

In the ambassador's living room, Izetbegovic and Sacirbey looked over the draft of principles that Milosevic had agreed to in Belgrade. The Bosnians didn't acknowledge the central fact that Milosevic was willing to recognize their country. They focused on the hateful name "Republika Srpska."

"That name is like the Nazi name," Izetbegovic said.

Roberts Owen, the team's legal expert, tried to argue that the name meant nothing. "In our country, some states call themselves 'republics' or 'commonwealths.'" He mentioned Texas. "It doesn't matter, as long as they acknowledge they are part of one country."

Izetbegovic replied that Yugoslavia had also been composed of republics—the difference was that the Republika Srpska was based on genocide. The argument went on well past midnight. Holbrooke kept stepping away to urge Washington to resume the bombing, which had been delayed all day by resistance from the U.N. generals Bernard Janvier in Zagreb and Rupert Smith in Sarajevo, the French, and the Pentagon. This was a moment when force and diplomacy had to be in perfect alignment. If Izetbegovic felt that the bombing would not resume, he would never accept Milosevic's offer. It helped for Izetbegovic to see how hard Holbrooke was trying.

"We understand your problems with this," Holbrooke finally told the president. "We can't get 'Republika Srpska' out of the draft. I'm sorry, but this is as much as we can do."

The Bosnians conferred. Izetbegovic retreated into gloom while Sacirbey said, "This is bad for my president, but we will try to accept it. It will be very difficult for him to explain to his people."

Afterward, in the early hours of September 5, Holbrooke got on the phone one more time with Berger and others in the Situation Room. "If we do not resume the bombing, it will have lasted less than forty-eight hours," Holbrooke told them. "It will be another catastrophe. NATO will again look like a paper tiger. The Bosnian Serbs will return to their blackmailing ways." What he said next might have sounded like another Churchillian message for his memoirs, but he meant it seriously, and they took it seriously in Washington. "History could well hang in the balance tonight. I truly believe that you may never take any decision as public officials more important than this one. Give us bombs for peace."

The bombing resumed in the morning.

Later, Holbrooke regretted pressuring Izetbegovic to accept the Nazi name. At that moment he might have had more leverage with Milosevic than he knew, and he wished he'd pushed harder for a change. "Republika Srpska" became a curse that the negotiators hung on Bosnia's neck into the future.

The episode in Ankara, and the entire experience of the two-month shuttle, showed that Holbrooke's reputation for bluster and bullying was overdone. Yes, he used F-16s and Tomahawk missiles to his advantage. Yes, he could be a bulldozer—the nickname was apparently coined by Tudjman—and in Serbia his last name became a verb: *holbrukciti,* to get your way through brute force. He could resort to yelling—that one time with Milosevic, once at Chris Hill when something went wrong, a couple of occasions with Sacirbey (they nearly came to blows in a New York hotel room). But his methods were diplomatic ones. His achievements came through persuasion, which is three-quarters persistence. The relentless undertow of that voice! I can hear it telling Milosevic, "Mr. President, we had an agreement. This behavior is clearly not consistent with it. If your 'friends' do not wish to have a serious discussion, we will leave now." Telling the press, "President Clinton has sent us here today on a mission of peace in a moment of war." Telling Izetbegovic, "Mr. President, you can end four years of fighting in your country with a single signature, and on your terms." Telling Pardew, "Jim, give me your tie. Kati said that I've been wearing the same tie on television for three days in a row and she wants me to change."

In his autobiography, Izetbegovic, who did not care for Holbrooke, wrote, "They say that diplomacy and power are two ends of the scale. The more power you have, the less diplomacy you need. In the extreme case—if you are a superpower—you don't need diplomacy of any kind. Holbrooke gave the lie to this theory. Although he represented the greatest superpower—in fact, the only true superpower in the world—he was to the fullest extent a diplomat, and used his persuasive skills like the most powerful of weapons."

And if Holbrooke's arsenal included an overblown reputation for brutality, he probably wanted it that way.

THE BOMBING WENT ON for days. The Russians were at the low ebb of their post-Soviet power under Boris Yeltsin, and their willingness to allow the Americans to take the lead had been surprisingly constant. But the bombing stirred Russian nationalism, and the Kremlin made noises about entering the war on the side of their fellow Orthodox Serbs. Bosnian and Croatian forces were exploiting the air strikes to push deep into Serb territory in western Bosnia, sending thousands of refugees to Belgrade. Holbrooke believed that military pressure made a final agreement more likely and he didn't want NATO to stop yet. But the U.S. Air Force claimed to be running out of targets.

On the afternoon of September 13, Holbrooke's team met Milosevic at one of Tito's hunting lodges by a duck pond in the woods outside Belgrade. Milosevic was chain-smoking cigarillos. There were no digressions into Ottoman history. "This bombing problem must be stopped immediately," he said. "Women and children are being killed. In Banja Luka, the missiles hit people who are opposed to Karadzic."

Holbrooke answered with his standard line: "General Mladic can stop the bombing anytime he wants." He didn't mention that in two or three days NATO would probably end the campaign of its own accord—that he was here to get the siege of Sarajevo lifted while he still had the leverage of bombs. Milosevic asked for a general cease-fire across Bosnia, but Holbrooke wasn't yet ready to call off the Muslim-Croat offensive in the west. The cease-fire had to start in Sarajevo.

For that, Milosevic said, he would need to bring the Bosnian Serbs into the talks. "And they are here."

Holbrooke was stunned. "Where?"

"Over there, in a villa." Milosevic gestured to a building two hundred yards from the lodge.

Holbrooke pulled his team aside. "Should we talk with them?"

Having refused to negotiate with the Bosnian Serbs in order to isolate them, Holbrooke knew that eventually they would have to be included—indicted war criminals and all. Everyone on the team thought the time had come.

"Should I shake their hand?"

They had come so far, Hill couldn't believe Holbrooke was even asking. "Dick, for Christ sake, do it, and let's get on with this and go home."

Holbrooke was afraid of being trapped into a meeting with monsters that wouldn't gain him anything. He warned Milosevic to remain in charge and put a stop to any harangues or other "historical bullshit."

"They will agree," Milosevic said. "No bullshit. Let me get them."

The Americans took a short walk in the woods while Milosevic summoned the Bosnian Serbs. A pair of black Mercedeses drove up to the lodge. Even from a distance the Americans could identify the two men who got out of the lead car in the late-afternoon light—the taller one with the skunk's tail on top of his head, the shorter one with the powerful physique and trudging swagger. There was something cartoonish about these two, like stock characters. An aide summoned the Americans to join the Serbs.

You don't often get to meet mass murderers while they're still at large. It comes with a little thrill of fear—not so much of what they might do as of what you might feel. As Holbrooke approached from the woods his nerves were raw. He didn't want to talk to Mladic, or even shake his hand. To give himself courage he thought of Raoul Wallenberg negotiating with Himmler for the lives of Hungarian Jews.

On the patio, Karadzic was smiling in a maroon suit, Mladic glowering in green fatigues. To Hill and Pardew they looked like a pair of Serb peasants. Karadzic was the image of banality, with his double chin and weak sloping eyes. Mladic actually looked evil, and he smelled to Pardew like a soldier who had been too long in the field.

Mladic held out a beefy hand. Holbrooke was determined not to touch it, but Mladic kept it extended for so long that Holbrooke gave the lightest shake before walking away. (He later claimed to have refused.)

There were other Serbs in the party, including Krajisnik, the cement smuggler who had done time with Karadzic and was now speaker of the Bosnian Serb assembly—a small, neatly dressed, slit-eyed man with a single bushy black eyebrow crawling across his forehead, who was the hardest-liner in the group. The two delegations faced each other across a patio table covered in green felt. The sun was beginning to set. Mladic stared down Pardew, and Pardew couldn't suppress a laugh.

Karadzic began in English, denouncing the NATO bombing, the crimes of the Muslims and Croats, and other humiliations inflicted on the Serbs. Holbrooke turned to Milosevic: if it continued, he said, they would leave.

Karadzic stood up. "I will call President Carter. I am in regular contact with him." Carter's freelance diplomacy had convinced the Bosnian Serbs that he was their friend.

"Let me tell you something," Holbrooke said with some heat. "President Carter appointed me as assistant secretary of state. I worked for him for four years. Like most Americans, I have great admiration for him. But he is now a private citizen. We work only for President Clinton. We take orders only from President Clinton."

Holbrooke's abbreviated résumé got Karadzic to sit down. Milosevic later told Holbrooke with contempt that the Bosnian Serbs thought Carter still ran American foreign policy. The news that Carter was no longer in charge put Karadzic in a more constructive frame of mind, though Mladic continued to simmer with rage. "No one can be allowed to give away a meter of our sacred Serb soil," he vowed.

Holbrooke spent the evening avoiding their company—describing the scene by phone to Washington, taking a walk with Milosevic—while Clark and the other Americans drafted a statement for the Serbs to sign. It said that they would stop the shelling, withdraw heavy weapons from the hills, and open the airport and the Kiseljak road to humanitarian traffic. They would end the siege of Sarajevo. In return, NATO would pause the bombing for three days to verify compliance, and the United States would restrain the Bosnians from taking advantage. Sometime after midnight, Clark stood by a lamp on the patio and read the statement aloud, while someone translated into Serbian and Mladic glared at Clark. When he was finished, the Serbs began picking over every word.

"Do we have an agreement or not?" Holbrooke asked. "If not, I see no reason to talk further."

No one else had ever called the Serbs' bluff, and he wasn't going to let up for a moment. Of his former bosses, he resembled Jimmy Carter less than he did Lyndon Johnson, who liked to say, "You've got to get 'em by the balls and you've got to squeeze 'em till they hurt."

The Serbs signed. It was two-thirty in the morning. Mladic scribbled his name and wouldn't even look at the document. He had a bandage on his left elbow and incipient kidney stones. He sank into a couch and a deep funk.

THREE DAYS LATER, on September 17, Holbrooke sat in the cockpit of a C-130 and gazed down at the gash of fallen trees on Mount Igman, just before landing at the newly opened Sarajevo airport. The air strikes had kept him out of the ruined city since the accident. At the presidential palace—bullet scarred, sandbagged, nylon sheeting over the windows, doorknobs falling off—Izetbegovic, Silajdzic, and Sacirbey (Holbrooke called them "Izzy, Silly, and Mo") were deeply unhappy with the bombing halt. They seemed to prefer the siege to continue as long as NATO was punishing the Serbs. "We are a small step from total success," Silajdzic fumed. Sacirbey told Holbrooke that his negotiations had contaminated him with the stench of the Serbs. The Bosnians were afraid that he had fallen for Milosevic's charm.

But when Holbrooke walked outside, a large crowd that had gathered across the street began to cheer. Hill told him to wave. Holbrooke normally used his broad shoulders and barrel chest to dominate a room or a street. His size and energy gave Bosnians an almost physical sense that here at last was a diplomat who intended to solve their problem. But this time he raised his hand slowly, awkwardly. He was close to tears. The siege had lasted forty-two months.

Even without air strikes, by mid-September the offensive in western Bosnia was close to a breakthrough. The Bosnian Serb army was collapsing, and Croatian and Bosnian forces were a dozen miles from Banja Luka, Bosnia's second city and a Serb stronghold throughout the war. Milosevic begged Holbrooke not to let Banja Luka fall. If it fell, another several hundred thousand refugees would pour into Serbia, possibly threatening Milosevic's regime. In Washington, Lake and Christopher wanted the offensive to stop. Holbrooke and Galbraith wanted it to continue *around* Banja Luka, and they urged the Croatians and Bosnians to take Prijedor, Omarska, Manjaca—towns with names that meant ethnic cleansing, that deserved to be taken back, and that would be easier to hold at the negotiating table if they were already in federation hands. But Tudjman, on a months-long roll, suggested to Holbrooke that in final negotiations Banja Luka could be swapped for Tuzla, allowing Croatia to dominate Bosnia, with the Muslim area shrinking to Sarajevo. Tudjman was still talking about the Islamic peril and the clash of civilizations.

And Izetbegovic—he saw in Banja Luka the Bosnian Serbs' Sarajevo. What justice to pay them back by raining shells on their biggest city! There had not been enough time to get used to seeing the Serbs in panic and defeat.

Each leader hated the other, each feared the other would one day betray their shotgun marriage, and this fear partly drove their hunger for conquest. Muslim and Croat troops were already starting to fight one another, which alarmed the Americans more than anything. To let Banja Luka fall would have been to roll the dice on human lives. One hundred thousand had already been lost.

So Holbrooke told both leaders a lie, the same lie, the only one that would force them to stand down. He said that he'd spoken by phone to President Clinton, who had warned that NATO jets would drop bombs on Bosnian and Croatian troops if they tried to take Banja Luka.

On October 11, a sixty-day cease-fire went into effect across Bosnia. By then the map had been transformed on the battlefield: from 70–30 in favor of the Serbs, the federation now had more than the 51 percent granted it by the Contact Group plan. The plan was largely an American product, and changing the terms now at the expense of the Serbs would have caused too many problems. The cease-fire ended the shooting, but other cease-fires had broken down. All the devilish questions that had started and sustained the war—who got what land, how Bosnia would function as a state—remained to be worked out at a peace conference scheduled for several weeks off. Having spent two months shuttling between the Balkan leaders, Holbrooke did not think the chances of success were good.

What if he had let Banja Luka fall? He wasn't given to regret, but this thought would trouble him in the years to come. It would have been the end of the Republika Srpska. Bosnia today would be a multi-ethnic state, messy but whole. The war would have had a winner. And there would have been no Dayton.

XII

The obvious place for a peace conference was Paris or Geneva. Holbrooke didn't want either. Those sparkling cities had seduced diplomats who spent years talking and talking about Vietnam, eating well and sightseeing, while the killing continued on the other side of the world. Holbrooke wanted the United States to host the conference, and on a military base, where there would be maximum American control, no distractions, and no temptation to linger. He wanted the success to be American and he was willing to risk an American failure, and although he was a mere assistant secretary of state, the success or failure would also be his own, because this was Holbrooke's show and he was going to gamble everything for his country and himself.

No one else liked the idea of an American venue, except for Lake. Why risk damaging the president just before an election year? But they deferred to Holbrooke, who had brought the talks this far.

The place turned out to be a few miles outside Dayton, Ohio— Wright-Patterson Air Force Base, one of the biggest in America, eight thousand acres sprawled across flat farm country, twenty-three thousand employees, an airstrip two and a half miles long. The delegations touched down on the night of October 31, and Holbrooke was the first on the red carpet to shake each arriving president's hand. Near the entrance to the base there were four two-story brick barracks around a rectangular parking lot—the Visiting Officers Quarters. These became the temporary home of the national delegations. The Bosnians and

Croatians faced each other from the north and south ends of the parking lot, the Serbians and Americans from the east and west, and the Europeans occupied a fifth barracks just outside the quadrangle. The housing blocks had long narrow corridors and cramped rooms, with vinyl trim and shabby furniture, like a forty-nine-dollar-a-night motel.

The base commander had workers knock down walls and install new carpeting and furniture to create a bigger, nicer suite on the first floor of each building for the three Balkan presidents, Holbrooke, and Carl Bildt, who led the European delegation. The only places to eat on base were the Officers' Club, a short drive away, and Packy's, a sports bar in the concrete-block Bob Hope Hotel and Conference Center, two hundred yards across a grassy field from the barracks. Workers laid a winding path over the grass and lined it with ground lights, a modest touch of elegance. But in the history of international diplomacy nothing was less elegant than Wright-Patterson.

And yet this mix of the outsized and drab—this American, specifically midwestern atmosphere, at once banal and imposing and earnest—it told the gilded palaces of Europe: you have the history and the beauty, but you failed to end this war on your continent. Nothing happened until the Americans got involved—until the uncouth, sleepless Holbrooke barged in.

He arrived nervous and exhausted. He had been crisscrossing the Atlantic and racing between Europe's capitals for two months, sleeping three hours a night and taking ten-minute catnaps, eating heavy food, grinding through nonstop meetings, and his face was pale and puffy. Now he had arranged for the entire Balkan cast to reassemble five thousand miles away inside the security fence of an American base.

I keep thinking of live theater—Holbrooke as a producer-director, an impresario. He refused to sell tickets—the enormous international press corps was confined to a featureless building at the far end of the base and fed a meager diet of daily briefings. (The no-interviews rule applied to everyone except Holbrooke, who took the *Times*'s Roger Cohen to dinner and steadily leaked to him, via Kati, for an in-depth profile of the man who would end the war.) He relegated the Europeans to minor players—their lengthy procedural discussions drove him crazy, and he soon handed off their morning meetings to his deputy,

John Kornblum. He also held Washington at bay, taking every question or objection from Lake as intolerable meddling.

There were hundreds of extras at Dayton, but the drama was stripped down to half a dozen characters. The set was so intimate that they could see the lights in barracks windows and know who was awake. The plot advanced in random encounters on the parking lot asphalt. Holbrooke created this claustrophobic stage as if its emptiness might force the characters to face the truths that he would show them.

There was no fixed closing date, though he didn't think they could last longer than two weeks at Wright-Patterson. He came without a schedule or script—this was an improv piece that could shut down at any moment.

He thought he would probably fail. And yet here he was, thrusting himself into every scene.

Tudjman came to Dayton the winner of the Balkan wars. All of Croatia was now ethnically cleansed, except for eastern Slavonia, the region across the Danube River from Serbia where the war had begun. Eastern Slavonia was all Tudjman wanted from Dayton—he would go back to war for it if necessary—so he was able to come and go from Zagreb with his obsequious retinue, playing the other two sides off against each other for his own gain.

Milosevic wanted peace at Dayton. He wanted the Americans to help get him out of what he had started years ago. In Holbrooke he'd found his redeemer, and just setting foot in the United States, where harsh coverage greeted Milosevic as the evil mastermind of the war, was a sort of victory. He wanted to hold on to power in Serbia, and he wanted sanctions lifted. Holbrooke had tried to suspend them before the talks began as an incentive for a deal, but Lake and Albright blocked him. The ongoing stranglehold made Milosevic vulnerable—he left Belgrade fearing that a military coup might occur in his absence or assassination await his return—and at Dayton he started out in no mood to negotiate. But he was ready to go further than anyone for peace. Karadzic and Mladic, indicted war criminals, would have been arrested by U.S. authorities, and they were not among the Bosnian Serbs at Dayton. Milosevic kept the others completely in the dark, cloistered on the second floor of the Serb barracks.

The Bosnian Muslims were the wild card. Izetbegovic hated to negotiate because it required him to make decisions, and any decision would
either plunge his people back into war or ratify Serb atrocities. He saw
the peace talks as a kind of blackmail, and he found the false niceties of
diplomatic chat over meals with people who wanted to destroy him so
unpleasant that he withdrew to his quarters. He slept badly at Dayton
and woke up in the middle of the night with his heart pounding as if he
were about to have a heart attack. "I felt crucified," he later wrote. His
two top advisors, Silajdzic and Sacirbey, hated each other. They were
fighting for their political futures—there would not be room in postwar
Bosnia for all three leaders.

No one could be sure of a final position from the Bosnians. They
wanted an undivided Sarajevo, and they also wanted the other enclaves,
including Srebrenica and Zepa, now held by the Serbs, and they wanted
the land they and the Croatians had recently taken, and they wanted
war criminals prosecuted at The Hague. The Bosnians were like an
assault victim too traumatized and embittered to watch the perpetra-
tor cop a plea.

The three sides were so hostile that after the first day of the conference they held no formal meetings until the very last. This was not
the United States and North Vietnam arguing about the shape of the
table and then repeating their official positions year after year. It wasn't
chess between two grand masters like Kissinger and Chou En-lai. It
was diplomacy in its most human form, the bruising collisions of raw
psyches.

ON THE FIRST NIGHT, Holbrooke took Milosevic to Packy's Sports
Bar & Grill in the Hope Hotel. Haris Silajdzic and Chris Hill were sitting at a table near a wall of wide-screen TVs. Silajdzic, the Bosnian
prime minister, was a Sarajevo academic, just turned fifty, with a modern vision of multi-ethnic Bosnia, but he was moody, given to sullen
glooms, rages, and vengeful hard-line stands. Holbrooke, always formal
with Izetbegovic, could deal with Silajdzic as an equal. Since Izetbegovic
was an unwilling negotiator, Holbrooke knew that Dayton would come
down to getting these two men, Silajdzic and Milosevic, to talk.

But at Packy's they ignored each other, barely shaking hands. Milosevic was in a foul temper over sanctions. He said that Holbrooke's whole approach to the negotiations was stupid. "You don't understand the Balkans."

"I'm sure I don't, Mr. President, but we're here to make peace and I hope you'll help us."

The bar food, Milosevic declared, was "*sheet*." After that first night he reserved a table at the slightly more upscale Officers' Club and held forth over Scotch and lobsters flown in from Maine by an American sympathizer. He went shopping at a mall across from the base and bought a pair of Timberland shoes for his evil wife, and seemed prepared to stay in Dayton forever.

It didn't go any better on the second day when Milosevic and Tudjman sat down with Holbrooke and Warren Christopher to talk about eastern Slavonia. The two presidents began yelling at each other in a mix of English and Serbian. "Franjo!" "Slobo!" Holbrooke kept pushing for an immediate agreement so that they could move on to other issues, but Milosevic resisted: "Mr. Holbrooke, you are too unrealistic. This issue must be settled in the field. I cannot control those people in eastern Slavonia." Milosevic turned to Christopher. "Tudjman is going back to Zagreb for a few days, but I am a prisoner of this dictator Holbrooke."

That night Holbrooke told his diary, "The attitudes were really frozen, and I don't see how the hell we're going to do this."

On the third night Holbrooke hosted a formal dinner at the National Museum of the United States Air Force, which filled several enormous hangars with aircraft from every American war of the twentieth century. Holbrooke staged the dinner for the Balkan leaders as an unsubtle display of U.S. military might. The Bosnian Serbs were seated beneath a Tomahawk cruise missile of the kind that had been fired from American submarines in the Adriatic at Banja Luka less than two months ago.

Kati was in Dayton to host the dinner with her husband. He had learned from Henry Cabot Lodge that parties were essential tools of diplomacy, and he loved to tinker with the minutest details of seating arrangements. He placed her, in her red silk Yves Saint Laurent jacket, at the head table between Izetbegovic and Milosevic. "You're going to sit between them and make peace," he told her. She tried to get them talking to each other, using her childhood in the Eastern Bloc and invoking the Hungarians who had taken refuge in Yugoslavia after the 1956 uprising: "We always admired Yugoslavia so much. What happened to you?" Izetbegovic was virtually uncharmable, but under Kati's prompting he and Milosevic reminisced about meeting each other when Yugoslavia still existed. They said that the war had surprised them, its duration and brutality—as if they had nothing to do with it.

"You goddam bastards," Holbrooke wanted to shout, "you're the ones who started this thing and kept it going!" But the band played Glenn Miller and the dinner guests turned to other subjects beneath the wing of a gigantic B-52 Stratofortress of the kind that had rained destruction on Vietnam.

THEY SPENT THE FIRST WEEK at Dayton getting nothing done. Isolation made the whole world, including the crumbling morsel of it called Bosnia, seem unreal. It was as if the warring parties were taking an extended breather in the American Midwest.

Sacirbey drove with Izetbegovic to Kentucky for a college football game and saw Sacirbey's alma mater, Tulane, get beat by Louisville. Silajdzic jogged around the base. The French representative received a shipment of Beaujolais nouveau from the French embassy and discovered a decent restaurant in Dayton called L'Auberge, which made his confinement just bearable. Holbrooke and Hill lost in straight sets to Tudjman, who was back from Zagreb, and a doctor on the Croatian delegation who happened to be an excellent tennis player.

"The most difficult thing here now is to gauge the psychological moments to put pressure on and to take pressure off," Holbrooke told his diary. "How do we bring them to discuss their core issues? I do not yet know, but I know that it is like a psychological group session and it will take a lot of effort."

Holbrooke scored one win that first week. A young reporter from the *Christian Science Monitor,* David Rohde, who first exposed the Srebrenica massacres, had received an intelligence tip at the end of October, driven a rental car into Bosnian Serb territory without papers or permission, and begun searching for human remains north of Srebrenica at a mud dam where a mass execution had taken place. He was seized by Bosnian Serb militiamen, who threatened to try him as a spy. Rohde's family flew to Dayton to appeal for his release. Holbrooke told

Milosevic that there would be no final agreement until Rohde was free, prompting Milosevic to ask, "You would do all this for a journalist?" One of the Bosnian Serbs at Dayton, a Shakespeare scholar and Milosevic toady named Nikola Koljevic, saw a chance to score points with the Americans and offered himself as a mediator. The Rohdes didn't realize that Koljevic had no pull with the gunmen holding their son. John Menzies, the American ambassador to Sarajevo, spent hours on the phone from Dayton to secure access for an American diplomat to visit Rohde's jail cell. Kati, who was chair of the Committee to Protect Journalists, threatened Milosevic with pressure from the world's media.

But the person at Dayton who sprang Rohde was Milosevic's hench-man Jovica Stanisic, and he did it in the traditional way—got on the phone with Karadzic and yelled, "Hand him over or I'll fuck your mother."

HOLBROOKE WAS MORE and more tense. Warren Christopher, who had opened the conference, was about to return, and there was noth-ing to show for the days between. Whenever the hard issues came up—the Bosnian constitution, the fate of Sarajevo, the final boundary lines between the sides—the parties dug in. The bitterness grew more concentrated in this strange place, in the dull silence, under the low November sky.

"It's increasingly unlikely we will have a peace agreement here, although it's not impossible. There's too much work to be done and too little time left. We don't have enough support from Washington, and the Europeans are whining and moaning the whole time that they're not being adequately consulted. But above all, the Bosnians are refusing to give us serious positions on any of the major issues. Without those positions, it's impossible to negotiate."

On Friday, November 10, Christopher came back to Dayton in time to announce two achievements. The Bosnian Muslims and Croats were ready to sign an agreement to strengthen their federation, which had practically stopped existing; and the Serbians and Croatians had reached a deal on the handover of eastern Slavonia to Croatia. With these two issues resolved, the parties could address the main conflict in Bosnia.

"Saturday, Sunday, Monday will be all map," Holbrooke told his diary. "Christopher will come back Monday night and he leaves for Asia Tuesday. He will extend his stay and delay Asia if we're close. If we're not, he'll leave for Asia, and we'll start to figure out how to get out of here in one piece by the end of the week, announcing interim agreements and suspending this and saying that in a few weeks we will return to the shuttle after we digest. Well, this is all a ploy, I hope. I don't want to return to the shuttle, but I don't want to spend the rest of my life in Dayton, so we're going to go for broke now. We're going to be out of here in a week. That's our plan, and I think it's a very good one. If these guys want to make peace, they can do it in a week."

ON SATURDAY, November 11, Holbrooke went to see Silajdzic in his room in the Bosnian barracks. The prime minister, distrusted by Izetbegovic and boxed out by Sacirbey, was in a state of furious despair.

"What's going on here?" Holbrooke demanded. "We've started the map discussions and you're not even in the room."

"You see what I'm up against? I don't know what's going on in there! You see what a terrible mess they are making of this?"

"You have to get back into this thing, Haris." Holbrooke added that if there was no progress by Christopher's return, he would advise that they close the conference.

"Suspend it, or end it?"

"I think suspend. Maybe resume the shuttle. I'm not sure."

"That's wrong. Threaten to end the conference once and for all."

Holbrooke crossed the parking lot to the Serbian barracks. A bitter sleety wind was blowing through the base. He went into Milosevic's suite and made the same speech he'd given Silajdzic about closing down the conference.

"It's the fault of the Muslims," Milosevic said. "They are pigheaded and stupid."

"That's not the issue." Holbrooke asked Milosevic if he would speak to Silajdzic right away. Milosevic said, "Sure."

Holbrooke went back to the Bosnian barracks. "Haris, this is the most important meeting of your life," he told Silajdzic as they walked out to the freezing parking lot. This was one of his tricks, pumping people up with grand appeals to history—invoking Mandela to Silajdzic, Sadat to Milosevic. He was shameless. But Silajdzic merely nodded. "Don't lose your temper. Hang in there. With Milosevic the meeting may only be starting just when you think it's ending."

He left Silajdzic at the door to the Serbian barracks.

"Look, I don't know why I'm here," Milosevic said to Silajdzic in his suite. "I'm trying to help you guys—you had a war. I want to go back to Belgrade and do my job."

"So you have no role?" Silajdzic asked, suppressing his outrage.

"Of course not. It's these stupid Serbs of yours. They're like you. They're your Serbs, not mine."

"What about the arms? And the troops coming in?"

"Haris, you're a smart guy—you know everybody in the Balkans has a gun."

"And the satellite pictures of tanks crossing the Drina?"

"Haris, a guy starts a tank and goes—what can you do?" Milosevic went on: "My godfather is a Muslim, so I don't hate you. This guy Tudjman hates you. I don't."

They talked for two hours. Silajdzic found Milosevic jovial and easygoing. Even Izetbegovic couldn't square the tipsy schmoozer at Dayton with the despot who started the Balkan wars.

BUT SATURDAY AND SUNDAY and Monday went by, and there was no progress.

Milosevic presented the Serb map and it was so unreasonable, with important cities suddenly showing up on their side of the line, that when Silajdzic saw it he exploded, waving his arms, eyes moving around the room so frantically that Holbrooke and Hill thought he might be on drugs. The Bosnian map was even worse—it added the new cease-fire line to the old Contact Group boundary, leaving the Serb entity with just one-third of Bosnia. The Bosnians now deeply regretted the 51–49 split that they had agreed to in 1994, when their military position was much worse—but that had been the basis for Holbrooke's deal with Milosevic, and the Americans would not go back on it.

The Frasure, Kruzel, and Drew families came for a day, on Holbrooke's invitation. He had them meet separately with each of the presidents so that they could better understand what their husbands and fathers had died trying to achieve, and so that the Balkan leaders might be moved to try harder, and when Holbrooke stood up at the end of the visit and said, "We would not be here today if it were not for Bob, Joe, and Nelson. They will always be with us," he could hardly finish his remarks.

Christopher barely touched down before flying on to Asia. Tuesday came, and Wednesday, and there was no progress.

The weather turned colder. Holbrooke was getting desperate. They had been confined here for two weeks and everyone was exhausted and angry. The Europeans in particular seemed to find the base and its food unendurable, and they were ready to leave. Over dinner one night at the Officers' Club, Holbrooke watched the Balkan presidents bicker about the map and felt that he was sitting with three terrible people. They could end the war that they had started and help millions of people who longed for peace, but it wasn't in them.

Christopher was due back on Friday, November 17. He would give the sides twenty-four hours to reach a deal before shutting Dayton down.

Kati was back. Holbrooke wanted to show her off and show off for her. Her presence was the only thing keeping him calm, and his tireless performance on this stage of his own design made her love him all the more. She was thinking of writing a book about Dayton and she sat in on meetings, sometimes in her husband's lap, privy to classified information, and he scripted roles for her to play, cornering Milosevic on humanitarian issues, taking Silajdzic for a tactical walk. Her involvement was against all protocol and it pissed off Holbrooke's colleagues. When Chris Hill, underslept at a morning meeting like the rest of the team, made a crack about some issue having to do with Gorazde—"We'll put it in Kati's talking points"—Holbrooke glared at him: "See me after the meeting." He pulled Hill into his suite and got in his face: "Don't you ever say anything like that again." Holbrooke was so frayed that he had started taking off people's heads. Hill bit the inside of his cheek and walked away. Kati was untouchable.

On Wednesday night, Holbrooke and Kati took Silajdzic to dinner in Dayton at L'Auberge. They asked him about his youth in Sarajevo, his family, his hopes for Bosnia. But Silajdzic could not be pulled out of his gloom. It was as if Dayton and the prospect of peace had brought the full tragedy of the war to him—as if he couldn't bear to let it go, for that would be to accept its injustice and betray the dead. "You don't understand," he said. "You don't understand what we have been through."

"Perhaps we don't," Holbrooke said, "but it was your request that we create a single country. Why are we trying if you don't think it can work?"

"What you want would have been easier in 1992, or even 1993," Silajdzic said. "Where was the world then? Where was the United States?"

Holbrooke knew the answer. What could he say except that more killing wouldn't honor the dead?

THE NEXT DAY, Thursday, November 16, Holbrooke and Hill had a steak lunch with Milosevic at the Officers' Club. Two Americans were taking a walk around the base with Silajdzic, and Holbrooke arranged for them to bring him to the club. Silajdzic sat down alone at the other end of the room from the corner where Milosevic had his reserved table. With its dim light and shabby elegance, the Officers' Club looked like the kind of dining establishment that might have been familiar to both men in Yugoslavia.

Holbrooke crossed the floor to Silajdzic. "Milosevic is willing to talk about Gorazde," he said. But Silajdzic refused to join their table. Undeterred, Holbrooke returned to Milosevic: "Silajdzic is ready to discuss Gorazde." Milosevic took a paper napkin and sketched a map showing Sarajevo, Gorazde, and the roads that connected them through Serb territory. "We can offer safe conduct along these two roads." The Bosnians could never trust such an offer, Holbrooke said. "Okay, then I will give them a kilometer on each side of the road."

Holbrooke carried Milosevic's napkin across the room to Silajdzic, who looked at the sketch, took out a napkin of his own, and drew a map with a much thicker land corridor connecting Gorazde to Sarajevo and the rest of federation territory. Holbrooke went back and forth half a dozen times between the two tables with the pair of napkins as Milosevic and Silajdzic watched each other's reactions from across the room.

Finally Holbrooke told Silajdzic, "Milosevic is ready to come to your table."

"No, I will come to his."

"Why?"

"Because I am the prime minister and he is the president. This is the protocol."

"Cut the crap. Why, really? I want to know."

"If he comes to my table, it's like he's conceding something already. 'I'm a good guy, a humble guy—and now, what will you do for *me*?'"

"I'll never understand you guys."

Silajdzic thought that Holbrooke understood them pretty well. He wasn't one of the wide-eyed American innocents whose generosity and trust endeared them to Silajdzic. When these disappeared, Silajdzic thought, America would still be a big power, but no longer a great one.

"Haris, what do you want?" Milosevic asked when Silajdzic sat down at his table.

Silajdzic said that he wanted security for Gorazde, the last small circle of Muslims in eastern Bosnia. After all they'd been through in the enclaves, the Muslims required a defensible link between Gorazde and the rest of the country.

"Why do you need a corridor?"

"Because you want to divide Bosnia."

"Enough is enough," Milosevic said. "I'll connect it."

They sat through the afternoon at Milosevic's table and argued about every mosque and village on the road from Gorazde to Sarajevo as the corridor grew thicker, while Holbrooke and Hill witnessed the first face-to-face negotiation over territory after sixteen days at Dayton.

HOLBROOKE HAD BEEN holding off Lake in D.C., but that Thursday he paid a visit. He told Holbrooke that back in Washington there was resistance to success. The Republican Congress wanted to deny Clinton a victory, the military still had no appetite for sending troops to enforce peace, and some of the president's political advisors thought a deployment to Bosnia would be a loser in 1996. Dayton would therefore be the end of the hundred-day American peace effort. If it failed, the Europeans would have to take over. Lake spent just a few hours with the Balkan leaders. "I hear you are the most anti-Serb in Washington," Milosevic told him, to which Lake replied, "No, I'm the most anti-aggression."

KEY TERRITORIAL ISSUES AT DAYTON

SLOV.

HUNGARY

SERBIA

Sava R.

Drava R.

EASTERN SLAVONIA

Danube R.

CROATIA

•Karlovac

Sava R.

•Prijedor

Sava R.

Sanski Most•

•Banja Luka

•Brcko

Drina R.

LIVNO VALLEY

BOSNIA-HERZEGOVINA

Srebrenica•

Zepa•

Sarajevo• •Pale
Mt. Igman ▲

•Gorazde

•Split

Mostar•

Drina R.

MONTE-NEGRO

0   20 miles
0   20 kilometers

| | Bosnian Serb–controlled area, November 1, 1995 | | Croat-Muslim Federation–controlled area, November 1, 1995 | ••••• Dayton Agreement inter-entity boundary line, November 21, 1995 |

As Lake and Holbrooke walked through the parking lot, Lake said, "This is the craziest zoo I've ever seen."

The next day, November 17, Don Kerrick, the White House official on Holbrooke's team, wrote in his daily memo to Washington: "Endgame personal dynamics taking downward spiral. Milosevic and Pale Serbs never seen together—rarely speak. Izetbegovic, Mo, Haris continue to amaze us all with their desire to torpedo one another—and possibly even peace."

Christopher returned that night to close the deal in twenty-four hours or close the conference. If it worked, there would be another day to tie things together, then Clinton would come on Monday for the signing ceremony.

Now Holbrooke truly needed Christopher, for Holbrooke was near the end of his rope. Something had changed in their relationship. Christopher still found Holbrooke distasteful, and Holbrooke still wanted to claim all the credit, but the secretary trusted him and let him take the lead. "Even when I am not sure why you are doing something," he said, "I have come to realize that you have always seemed to have a reason."

They had twenty-four hours to do almost everything. Other than Gorazde, the map was still a disaster—there was no agreement over Sarajevo, or Brcko in the northeast, or the boundary line between the two entities. The Americans, who had drafted the constitution, abandoned those negotiations to the Europeans, and essential matters—whether Bosnia would have nine or three presidents, one or two houses of parliament, a prime minister, whether refugees would vote in their original hometowns—were hammered out on the fly. Bildt thought that the American emphasis on the map and military issues, which were all about the division of Bosnia, got everything backward: Bosnia could only survive and heal as a united country through politics. This looked like partition, not reunification. As for how to implement the whole thing, it was almost an afterthought.

The symbol of the war was Sarajevo. The Bosnian Serbs wanted to carve up Yugoslavia's most mixed city into ethnic districts, like Cold War Berlin or East and West Jerusalem—Karadzic even proposed a wall. The Muslims wanted it as Bosnia's undivided capital, in federation territory. Holbrooke was adamant that there could not be another

Berlin Wall at the end of the twentieth century in Sarajevo, and the Americans proposed a third, federal model, like the District of Columbia. The discussions went in circles.

On Saturday, Holbrooke took a walk around the parking lot with Milosevic and threatened again to shut everything down. "Sarajevo must be settled at Dayton," he said.

"Okay." Milosevic laughed. "I won't eat today until we solve Sarajevo."

A little later, Milosevic came into Holbrooke's suite. "Okay, okay. The hell with your D.C. model. It's too complicated, it won't work. I'll solve Sarajevo."

Holbrooke was stunned. Milosevic was going to give up the Bosnian capital. That was how much he had come to despise his clients who had destroyed Sarajevo for three and a half years. *"They are shit."* Milosevic told Holbrooke not to breathe a word to the Bosnian Serbs on his delegation—Milosevic had completely shut them out, refused to show them a single map. Krajisnik, the cement smuggler with the unibrow, considered his twelve-acre farm near the airport sacred Serb ground—for Krajisnik the war came down to Sarajevo. The crucial lines remained to be drawn on the map, but the whole city, including its Serb-held districts, would go to the besieged. "You deserve Sarajevo because you dug a tunnel and went in and out like foxes," Milosevic later told Silajdzic. "But you fought for it and those cowards killed you from the hills."

SUNDAY DAWNED COLD. The deadline passed. Christopher extended it to Monday morning. But in spite of Sarajevo no one believed there was time and will to resolve everything, and a sense of imminent failure set in. Holbrooke, who was going through cycles of collapse and recovery, told the Americans to pack their bags and take them out to the parking lot, in full view of the other delegations, for transport to the airstrip. It was a bluff, and it failed miserably. By evening the bags were back in the rooms.

John Menzies had put together a pair of charts on poster board to show the Bosnians all they had gained thus far at Dayton. Holbrooke let the Bosnians keep them, and when Milosevic came to talk to Izetbegovic in his suite on Sunday afternoon, one chart was propped up between the couch and lamp table, with a single line visible at the top: "Federation Gets 58% of the Territory." The Gorazde corridor and other concessions had taken away 7 percent from the Serbs' allotted 49. Milosevic hadn't realized how much he had given up, and whenever he tried to find out, Holbrooke—who had access to a computerized military map in a secure room across the hall from his suite—avoided telling him.

Milosevic hurried out of the Bosnian barracks to the American quarters and found Holbrooke in his room. "You tricked me!" he yelled. "How can I trust you?"

Milosevic was willing to give up just about anything for a deal— even a Serb cemetery in the hills above Sarajevo left him cold—but he wouldn't back down from 51–49, and the Americans couldn't ask him to.

So Milosevic and Silajdzic stared at maps in a small conference room of the American barracks and argued over where the 7 percent would come from all evening, past midnight, into the early morning hours. Silajdzic wasn't yielding—he demanded Grbavica, the Sarajevo neighborhood from which Serb gunners had clear line of sight on Sniper Alley, and he wanted a reservoir outside Sarajevo that had fallen on the Republika Srpska side, and he claimed a village just outside the

Gorazde corridor where the Serbs had destroyed an ancient mosque. "You're going to take away my pants, too," Milosevic moaned, but he gave Grbavica and the reservoir and the destroyed mosque to Silajdzic, and he kept looking for his 7 percent. Dayton had come down to carving up slices of land.

In the map room across the hall from Holbrooke's suite, computer engineers had transformed aerial footage of Bosnia shot by NATO bombing planners into a 3-D video game. Viewers using a joystick could fly over the entire country and see its features in fine detail. When Holbrooke brought Milosevic and his sidekick, President Momir Bulatovic of Montenegro, to experience this wonder of American technology, he suddenly realized that there was hardly anything on the screen to see—no houses or villages, just mountains and rocks. He pointed this out to the two leaders.

"That's right," Bulatovic said, "but that is Bosnia."

Holbrooke put his head in his hands. "This is going to ruin my marriage, ruin my life. Look at what you're fighting for. There's nothing there."

Around three-thirty a.m., Silajdzic came up with an idea: give the Serbs a hunk of the terrain in western Bosnia that Muslim and Croat forces had seized just before the cease-fire. Silajdzic considered most of it worthless, and Milosevic just wanted to get to 49 percent, and suddenly they were shaking hands. It was four in the morning. Christopher called for a bottle of his favorite California Chardonnay. They toasted one another around a small circular table.

Since Tudjman was fast asleep, Foreign Minister Mate Granic was summoned to give the Croatian blessing. Izetbegovic was also roused, and he arrived wearing his pajamas under an overcoat, looking unhappy. Granic, bald and mild-mannered, studied the map and flew into a rage. All the land that Silajdzic had given to the Serbs was Bosnian Croat. Granic pounded the map and shouted, "Impossible! Zero point zero percent chance that my president will accept this!" He stormed out. Milosevic and Silajdzic sat in silence. The peace had lasted just over half an hour.

Izetbegovic was staring at the northeastern corner of the map. The town of Brcko, where Bosnia, Croatia, and Serbia converged along the Sava River, had been in Serb hands since the ethnic cleansing of 1992.

It occupied the narrow chokepoint between the two chunks of Bosnian Serb territory, joining them to each other and to Serbia. For this reason the Serbs considered Brcko strategically vital. Every diplomatic map, including the Contact Group's, had given Brcko to them. Milosevic kept pushing for a wider ten-mile corridor through Brcko, while Silajdzic wanted to narrow it down to a thirty-yard underpass beneath a railroad bridge, trying to squeeze the Republika Srpska in two.

Earlier that night, Izetbegovic had urged Silajdzic to claim Brcko outright. The prime minister had replied that this would end the talks. Now Izetbegovic was staring at Brcko on the map. Silajdzic had left it to the Serbs.

Holbrooke knew that something was wrong. "What do you think, Mr. President? Can we finish the negotiation right now?"

Izetbegovic always took a long time to answer difficult questions. "I cannot accept this agreement," he said quietly in English.

"What did you say?" Christopher demanded.

Izetbegovic repeated himself, louder this time.

Silajdzic threw his papers on the table. "I can't take this anymore!" he shouted as he rushed from the room.

Sunday had been the longest day at Dayton, and it ended in dismal failure.

ON MONDAY the sun shone and the exhausted delegates wandered outside, running into one another in the parking lot, stopping to talk as if in a daze. That night Christopher went to see Izetbegovic. The Bosnian president spent ten minutes reciting the history of Muslim grievances against Serbs and Croats, until Christopher finally lost his immaculate temper. Almost trembling, his voice rising, he scolded the Bosnians for their irrational behavior and gave Izetbegovic one hour to change his mind, or else the conference would end. The hour went by, and Izetbegovic answered the ultimatum. In order to bring the Croatians back on board he would yield 1 percent of Muslim land in Bosnia to the Serbs—but now he also wanted Brcko. This was a new demand, and the Americans rejected it out of hand.

With the knowledge that the conference would close down in the morning, Izetbegovic went to bed and enjoyed his first good night of sleep in a long time. He would not have to be the Bosnian president who acquiesced in the results of genocide.

And Holbrooke? It was the worst day of his diplomatic life. He had hardly slept in three nights. He had no more moves, no more lines. His incomprehensible stamina was spent. The show had collapsed, and much of the blame would fall on him. At a meeting with the Europeans he slumped in his chair, shoes and socks off, shirt open, trousers rumpled, and said, "That's it, we're leaving."

It wasn't a bluff. The delegations were asked to review a press release announcing the failure of the peace conference. President Clinton's visit was canceled, and the next day, Tuesday, November 21, everyone would go home. Holbrooke looked so shattered that even Pauline Neville-Jones, the British diplomat with whom he had a notably testy relationship, felt sorry for him. The Balkan leaders were all crazy, he told Bildt, but the Bosnians—the war's victims, for whom the Americans had gone so far and done so much—the Bosnians enraged him more than anyone. He suspected they wanted the talks to fail so they could go back to fighting and win the war. If so, they would no longer have the Americans behind them.

THERE WAS ONE PERSON who would not let Dayton fail.

Milosevic ran into Bildt in the parking lot and begged him to keep trying to get the Serbs their 49 percent: "Give me something—hills, rocks, swamps—anything will do, it doesn't matter anymore." He berated Holbrooke's deputy, John Kornblum, as if Izetbegovic was the Americans' Karadzic: "You can't let this happen. You're the United States. You can't let the Bosnians push you around this way. Just tell them what to do."

On Tuesday morning it snowed. Milosevic, the man most responsible for millions of individual tragedies during the past four years in the Balkans, was standing in the parking lot. He was waiting for Holbrooke to come out of an early staff meeting at which he was thanking his American colleagues for their valiant effort to end the war. Kati spotted Milosevic outside in the snow and rushed him into Holbrooke's crowded and unspeakably messy room.

Milosevic announced that he wanted to leave Dayton with an agreement signed by just Tudjman and himself—at least that was *something*. Holbrooke was desperate enough to do it, but Christopher refused: "It is not a viable contract."

"Okay, okay," Milosevic told the Americans. "I will walk the final mile for peace." He would agree to submit the status of Brcko to international arbitration a year from now. It was the last card he had to play.

Holbrooke instantly recovered his strength. "Chris," he told the secretary of state when they were alone and he'd locked the door for privacy, "the next meeting may be the most important of your entire tenure as secretary." Christopher wasn't rolling his eyes—he was listening hard. "We can get this agreement—or we can lose it. Forget Washington. It's entirely in our hands. We must go into the meeting with an absolute determination to succeed."

They went next door to the Bosnian barracks. They refused to sit down. From the doorway Holbrooke presented Milosevic's offer. Izetbegovic, Silajdzic, and Sacirbey listened. Holbrooke repeated it.

"Do you accept the Brcko arbitration?"

Izetbegovic experienced a moment of confusion. He hadn't expected Milosevic to give in. The pause seemed to last forever. Then he said, "It is not a just peace." Another eon of silence. "But my people need peace."

"Then it's all right," Holbrooke said. To Silajdzic he looked like a man who had just been pulled back from the gas chamber. He murmured to Christopher, "Let's get out of here fast."

We Are Close to Our Dreams

L et's give him his due. He ended a war. Well, he and others—but without Holbrooke I don't know who would have stepped forward to cajole and bully and outlast the Balkan warlords until they sat down together for the initialing ceremony in the B-29 conference room at the Hope Hotel that Tuesday afternoon, and the signing ceremony the next month in Paris. He was once asked what tactics he had used. "Persistence," he said. "A kind of relentless harassment of the parties into concessions that they were not ready to make unless pressured by the United States with the credible threat of the use of force."

The end of the war came much too late for the living and the dead. The peace was as Izetbegovic said—unjust. What the Serbs gained by murder they were allowed to keep by agreement. You can't blame Holbrooke for that. By the time he took over, the Republika Srpska was a stubborn fact. The time to reverse it was in 1992 or '93—Silajdzic said that over dinner at L'Auberge—and back then Holbrooke wanted to intervene on the side of the victims. You can blame it on Bush and Baker, on the British and the French, on Boutros-Ghali, on Clinton, on Powell and Christopher and maybe, though I think it's unfair, on Lake. But by 1995 Holbrooke's only purpose was to end the war. That was what Bosnians needed more than anything. Izetbegovic felt crucified at Dayton, but when he returned to Sarajevo his people cheered him for bringing peace. On New Year's Eve, three years after Holbrooke spent the night shivering in the Holiday Inn, Sarajevans attended an outdoor concert in front of city hall.

The Bosnian Serbs refused to initial Dayton. During his last long night with Silajdzic, Milosevic betrayed them again and again, and the shock of losing their dream of a Sarajevo crisscrossed with checkpoints was profound. Later they had to sign—Milosevic was still the godfather—but then they set about to foul the deal. Krajisnik exhorted and threatened Serbs into abandoning the city, and grenades were thrown into apartments as their occupants fled. Around the country very few refugees of any group crossed the ethnic boundary lines to resettle in their hometowns. Bosnia remained ethnically cleansed. Serb intransigence and Western weakness kept Karadzic and Mladic safe from the war crimes tribunal for another decade and a half. Elections entrenched all the nationalisms that had brought the war and the corruption that had fed on it, and Bosnian Serb politicians cut the stitches sewn into the Dayton Accords to give Bosnia a chance to heal. With or without war, their thinking remained the same. A fascist project, Silajdzic said, received the imprimatur of the international community. Bosnians with a certain notion of Western values never got over their disillusionment.

The farther we get from the war, the less Dayton is seen as a great thing. People who didn't live through the killing of children and the hunger and cold can easily pick the agreement apart. But diplomats get what they can in the short term. Out of expediency the peace deal created a two-headed monstrosity, with two armies and a weak central government and, within this hybrid entity, a second hybrid entity—the Muslim-Croat federation—that existed mainly in the minds of foreign diplomats. Over time the foreigners moved on—even Holbrooke, after two more years of frequent trips—leaving Bosnia to its fate, which was never to be a normal country. The patient survived but remains deformed. Today the mayor of Srebrenica is a Serb who denies that the genocide took place. Sarajevo is a lovely, beguiling city, but hardly any Serbs or Croats live there, and the Muslims—the young ones—all want to leave.

Maybe this will surprise you, but there are no Richard Holbrooke streets or squares or statues in Sarajevo. Not one thing named after the man most responsible for the fact that people are drinking Turkish coffee at outdoor tables in the Old Town. In Bosnia he's remembered without gratitude, in Serbia with hatred, and in Croatia not at all.

Holbrooke saw Dayton as clearly as anyone, and when he was being honest he acknowledged its flaws. But he couldn't always be honest about Dayton. He cared about Bosnia but he also cared about history, and it was at Dayton that he drove his flag into the ice. You've seen what a struggle it took to reach that altitude—heavy gear, windburn, crevasses, exhaustion. Diplomacy, real diplomacy, is not for the short of breath.

"We are close to our dreams, after a year literally beyond imagination," he wrote to Kati at the end of 1995, "a year in which we have risen to the highest peak, and also faced the nearest of misses." Marriage, Igman, Dayton: he called it "this miracle year."

And recognition came. It arrived that very Tuesday night of the initialing ceremony—Holbrooke reached New York and the Grand Ballroom of the Plaza Hotel just in time to receive the International Rescue Committee's annual Freedom Award and a tremendous standing ovation from the black-tie crowd that suddenly brought home to him what he had just achieved—and it kept pouring in for the next few years. Radio Romania Man of the Year, the Secretary of State's Distinguished Service Award, Humanitarian of the Year Award from the American Jewish Committee, honorary degrees from Georgetown, Brown, the University of Dayton, and too many other honors to name.

He left the government in February 1996 and returned to New York and moved in with Kati and her teenage children at the Beresford. He went back to work on Wall Street, once more with the help of Pete Peterson, though this time around he didn't need as much help. A foreign-owned bank, Credit Suisse First Boston, made him vice-chairman ("I have no administrative or management responsibilities whatsoever," he explained; "it's really a title for status only") and paid him a salary and minimum bonus totaling $1.35 million a year to meet with officials around Europe and East Asia and make the rain fall.

He kept rubbing the legacy of Dayton, shining and polishing it, as if he sensed that over time it would fade. There was his two-part series in *The New Yorker;* his book *To End a War,* which is that unheard-of thing, a gripping diplomatic memoir; a project for an HBO movie based on the book, which mercifully didn't get made; attempts at other Daytons.

When a book by a former NSC official gave Lake more credit than Hol-brooke for the strategy that ended the war, Holbrooke was so enraged that he tried first to have the book blocked from publication and then its author fired by his employer and publisher, the Brookings Institu-tion. Dayton was sacred.

He was now a personage. His son Anthony's friends regarded him with awe. Dinners were held in honor of Holbrooke—dinners "IHO" being a thing that people at his social altitude regularly did to flatter one another. When he began to run for the Nobel Peace Prize, he wrote a strong letter on his own behalf for others to sign, and he could call on an impressive list of friends for recommendations—Elie Wiesel, the Dalai Lama, Kofi Annan, José Ramos-Horta—and he made Oslo a repeat destination and met several times with the secretary of the Norwegian Nobel Committee. He was rumored to be a finalist for a few years, and only when Wiesel told him that he did not fit the profile that the com-mittee was looking for, was not enough of a suffering martyr, that he was too big, too noisy, too American, did Holbrooke understand that the prize Kissinger had won without deserving it would not go to him, who did.

He acquired a higher set of New York friends. Even his cardiologist, Isadore Rosenfeld, was a celebrity—"Doctor to the Stars," including Pam Harriman—with best-selling books and a show on Fox. So was his money manager, Kenneth Starr, whose clients included Tom Brokaw, Carly Simon, and Sylvester Stallone. (And though they all should have seen that a sleaze who would dump his third wife to marry a stripper was unlikely to be an honest custodian of their wealth, greed blinded them and they were stunned when it turned out that Starr was enriching them all off a Ponzi scheme that would send him to prison.) One night Robert De Niro came over to the Beresford so that Holbrooke could vet a screenplay for a political film called *Wag the Dog*. The investor billionaire Henry Kravis and his wife Marie-Josée had the Holbrookes to dinner at their Park Avenue triplex. The hero of Dayton added pres-tige to their table, and Holbrooke in turn was dazzled by their glitter-ing lives, but after Richard and Kati went home the Kravises and their superwealthy friends trashed them for being shameless operators.

Dick Beattie heard the talk and warned Holbrooke that people like that were not his friends, but Holbrooke refused to believe it. Beattie was a top finance lawyer, specializing in leveraged buyouts, who represented Kravis's firm in its epic takeover of RJR Nabisco in 1988. He existed in relation to the Wall Street club as Gelb did to Washington—had all the qualifications but saw through the bullshit and didn't care enough to keep it to himself. In addition to being Holbrooke's attorney, Beattie was also his friend, his real friend. He worried that the gossip of Park Avenue Republicans might hurt Holbrooke's chances of becoming secretary of state. This was the mountain that loomed just behind Dayton.

When Holbrooke left Washington he assured Kati and himself that his ambitions were satisfied. We've been hearing this from him since that night in 1972 when he and Geoffrey Wolff drove from the Spanish coast up to the ski resort near Granada. As usual, Holbrooke was the only one fooled. Kati loved hearing that his happiness with her made him care less about his career, but she still wanted great things for him. What was the point of being with *Richard* Holbrooke? So she became what he'd never had—his climbing partner. They took trips abroad that combined his banking business and unpaid government work with her human rights advocacy and book promotions. He and Kati were harnessed together by thick twelve-millimeter climbing rope. He told her that if he'd married her ten years ago he would already *be* secretary of state.

CLINTON WAS RE-ELECTED on November 5. Politically Bosnia was a success—not a single American casualty in the postwar occupation of the country—and it played a role in Clinton's win by closing a wound that had been hemorrhaging throughout his first term. On Election Day, Warren Christopher announced that he would step down. Holbrooke's name was in the mix for the job that he had wanted since he was twenty. The other contenders were former senator George Mitchell of Maine, Clinton's envoy to the peace talks in Northern Ireland, and Madeleine Albright, the U.N. ambassador.

Two days after the election, Strobe Talbott was at a meeting on Bosnia in the Situation Room when a call came—the president wanted to speak with him. Talbott went to a nearby office phone.

"Where are you?" Clinton asked.

"In the bowels of the White House."

"Hell, come on up. I haven't taken a shower, but we gotta talk. You'll have to deal with me buck naked, but you've dealt with worse."

Talbott had been trying to get fifteen minutes with the president to discuss foreign policy appointments. He went upstairs to the living quarters and found Clinton in sweatpants and T-shirt at his desk in the Treaty Room. Hillary, in her bathrobe, was complaining that they had to attend Warren Christopher's farewell downstairs in twenty minutes. She left to get dressed.

"Fire away," Clinton said.

Talbott took a breath. "My concern here is what will give you the most successful possible second term in foreign policy."

Talbott had been leaning toward Albright—she had done a good job at the United Nations, while Holbrooke's "personality deformations" seemed to rule him out. But Talbott was discouraged by Albright's campaign for the position—her "emotionalism and lack of centeredness"—and Mitchell's support among Republican ex-colleagues in the Senate was tepid at best. As for Holbrooke, their recent conversations had led Talbott to believe that the drive to succeed in the job of his dreams would keep his worst tendencies in check. Talbott was in Clinton's study to make the case for Holbrooke.

"This is about performance," he went on, "this is about ability to deliver. This is about having as much success as possible on the tough issues that will be coming at you. Pound for pound, ounce for ounce, Dick is the most talented, energetic, experienced, able, articulate, broad-gauge foreign policy operative of our generation, maybe of our time. Also a royal pain in the ass. Lots of enemies, lots of detractors. Only subject on which Chris and I disagree. Dick is a big-time example of high value, high maintenance. But worth maintaining because of the unique value. He'd bring home the bacon, over and over."

Clinton replied that he liked and admired Holbrooke but worried about his hunger for the limelight. "He campaigned so hard for the Nobel Prize that that's probably one reason he didn't get it." He asked if Talbott would stay on as deputy secretary to handle Holbrooke. Talbott said that it depended on the wishes of his wife Brooke—he might be able to stick around for another six months.

Clinton moved on to other jobs. "Tony's got to go, you think?"

"Absolutely. That's key. You'll have a dysfunctional national security team as long as he's the surrogate papa."

"Sandy thinks we could keep Tony on for a matter of months, for a kind of decent interval."

"I've told you what I think. Tony would turn the interval into a permanency." Then Talbott suggested Lake for CIA director—though in truth he wasn't sure Lake would even stay in government if Holbrooke became secretary of state.

"Really interesting idea."

"Some of Tony's qualities that have made him not so good at the consensus-building, team-managing side of NSC might serve him and you well at CIA. Secretive, tough—"

"Mean and nasty," Clinton said with admiration.

By now they were in the bathroom. Talbott, whose full name was Nelson Strobridge Talbott III, was a fellow sixties person but far less hang-loose than his boss. He stood by while Clinton shaved, showered, and dressed, starting with midnight-blue jockey shorts.

Talbott returned the conversation to secretary of state and praised Albright. "She's not as smart as Holbrooke—none of us are except maybe you. But Madeleine feels in her guts your vision and your priorities. She's totally loyal, and good in articulating and defending the policy."

Clinton, suddenly closing down, said nothing. Talbott concluded that Albright must be out of the running.

THE MEMORY OF WAITING around after the 1992 election while his calls went unreturned remained so painful that Holbrooke and Kati decided to get away to the ends of the earth. Wisner, the ambassador in New Delhi, had arranged for a few Vietnam friends—Holbrooke, Frankie FitzGerald, Ward Just—to join him with their spouses in the Himalayan kingdom of Bhutan as personal guests of the king. On the morning of November 12, Holbrooke was in the royal guesthouse eight thousand feet above sea level when the phone rang. Al Gore was calling. He and Holbrooke went back to the 1988 presidential campaign, when Holbrooke was an early supporter of his candidacy, and they'd had similar positions on Bosnia. But they weren't close—Gore occupied too high an office, and Holbrooke felt there was an impassable wall between Gore and everyone else, even colleagues he liked.

"Where are you?" the vice president said. "I can't tell you what to do, but if I were you I'd try to get back."

There were only three flights a week out of Bhutan. Holbrooke told the king that he could become an important footnote to history if he flew the Holbrookes to New Delhi on the royal airplane. Within two days Holbrooke was sitting by the fire in the Talbott house in Washington, eating mushroom soup while the Talbotts' border collie snoozed and Strobe prepared Holbrooke for his interviews that evening at the White House.

They didn't talk about foreign policy. Talbott coached Holbrooke on how to handle himself: don't oversell, don't be *solipsistic,* rein yourself in. Holbrooke didn't object. He even confessed some of his sins. Maybe jet lag overwhelmed his defenses—or maybe, in sight of his heart's desire, he came to a sort of epiphany, which he described afterward to Talbott:

> You and others have wondered whether, if I achieved this goal of a lifetime (but not, Strobe, since the age of eleven!) I would change, soften, whatever . . . I think the answer is yes: once the job is there to do, and there are no more personal mountains to climb, the sheer dimensions of the job, its awesome demands, will be the sole focus of my professional life. Moreover, I already feel that simply to have reached the finals has already changed a lot. Having had for years to fight harder just to stay afloat against powerful adversaries sometimes produced actions that left a bad taste or a bad impression. Some of them were very dumb, some were necessary—but all left their mark on me and my associates. There are many things that I wish I had done differently, but the sum of the actions, the good and the bad, produced whatever I am today.

Nowhere in the Holbrooke record does anything come closer to a flash of inward light, as if the blind spot behind his eyes partly cleared. And even these words are hard to see by. Why so many powerful adversaries? Why did his best friend become the main one? That was a dark room he never entered.

And was it true that a job could change his character? Secretary of State Richard C. Holbrooke, finally fixed? I don't think so. We bring ourselves wherever we go, even the inner office on the seventh floor.

The first interview was with Gore. He wanted Holbrooke for the job—that was why he'd tracked him down in Bhutan—but in his know-it-all way he drilled Holbrooke with an oral exam on every region of the world, and Holbrooke, fatigued after four plane flights, ran out of answers around Latin America and sub-Saharan Africa. He felt that he had let Kati and Strobe down, like MacArthur throwing up on the White House steps after a showdown with FDR.

There was no time to worry, because Clinton was next. Holbrooke waited in the Map Room for twenty-five minutes before being summoned upstairs to the Treaty Room. He and Clinton spoke for more than an hour, and it was much friendlier than with Gore. At one point, when the president told him how intensely Talbott was lobbying on his behalf with no regard for his own prospects, Holbrooke got choked up and Clinton had to find him a tissue.

Holbrooke returned to Talbott's house on a high. He was looking ahead to the second term, with Berger as national security advisor instead of Lake, Talbott staying on as Holbrooke's deputy and running the channel between State and the NSC, the two agencies finally signing their own peace treaty after decades of war, everyone working as a team, Holbrooke and Talbott revitalizing the department, alternating weekends in charge to make it easier on their families. He thanked Talbott and told him that he loved him.

Holbrooke and Kati went back to New York to wait.

It took Clinton three weeks to make up his mind.

The president, with Talbott's strong push, was thinking hard about Holbrooke, but he couldn't erase a lingering doubt. He wondered aloud to Gore if Holbrooke was "sufficiently self-aware" to keep his relationships—including with the president—from turning toxic.

Washington, which has an animate and collective mind, considered Madeleine Albright more solid than brilliant, a politically savvy tactician rather than a serious strategist. She had a dramatic life story that she herself didn't know in full. It ran parallel to Kati's—she was born a decade earlier, in 1937, three hundred miles northwest, in Prague, with a pipe-smoking diplomat for a father. The family fled the Nazis in 1938 and the Communists in 1948, and standing up to dictators and appeasers was bred in Madeleine from early on. She was raised Catholic and (like Kati) was never told, perhaps (unlike Kati) did not want to find out, but by the end of 1996 was about to learn that her parents had been born Jewish, and three of her grandparents had perished in the camps.

She came of age in Eisenhower's America and married a moneyed journalist. She followed an upward path in academia (international relations) and politics (Democratic Party) that would have been utterly conventional if she'd been a man. She actually raised her children, unlike Holbrooke, and was left by her husband in midlife. She had a dogged, nearly obtuse optimism, a survival skill in a successful woman of her generation that left her vulnerable to private hurts but armed her for the arduous public struggle.

She had been Holbrooke's closest ally on Bosnia—they were the administration's interventionists. He often championed women in government, but none of them were his peers like Albright. His contempt for her, compounded of sexism and rivalry, was barely concealed. He once jotted his opinion on the back of the menu card at a luncheon she was hosting: "MKA—very articulate, even eloquent on values—weak on process, policy + diplomacy—uneven, unpredictable—charming + mean—insecure—her biography was her career—very strong will."

In the contest to be secretary of state, Albright suffered from the endemic bias in politics: women supported her, men were for someone else. In the past this would have sunk her chances, but not this time.

For more than a year Holbrooke had been cultivating a relationship with Hillary Clinton. In early 1996 he advised her to visit the troops in Bosnia to show the president's support for the peace agreement, and her trip made headlines. He liked her more than he liked Bill—they laughed together, teased each other, and she was, in spite of public appearance, a warmer person than her husband. But Holbrooke was not Hillary's choice. She wanted her husband to be the first president to name a woman as secretary of state, and for reasons fully known only to those inside the marriage, Hillary had a strong hold on Bill, and she leaned on it hard: "Only if you pick Madeleine will you get a person who shares your values, who is an eloquent defender of your foreign policy, and who will make every girl proud."

Clinton might have resisted if he had been able to erase the doubt about Holbrooke.

The call came to the Beresford one day in the first week of December. It was Tom Donilon. "Dick, you didn't get it."

Holbrooke broke the bad news to Kati the way he always did, with no effort to prettify or soothe: "I didn't get it. It's Madeleine." It was unfair, grossly unfair, because Albright was no thinker, she was merely cunning, Clinton had chosen another second-rate secretary of state, and Holbrooke knew Hillary had cost him the job, but he smothered his bitterness until it stopped crying out because Hillary would have a great future and he might be part of it. So he and Kati went to the movies, and she had to express the anguish for both of them.

But he told Talbott, "For the first time in my life I feel old."

HISTORY IS efficiently brutal with our dreams. Dayton wasn't the highest peak after all. It wasn't the Marshall Plan or the opening to China. It solved a nasty problem but it didn't create something new and big. For those who lived through the war, who suffered on the inside or cared on the outside, Bosnia was immense, it was all that mattered. But Holbrooke devoted three years of his life to a small war in an obscure place with no consequences in the long run beyond itself. The disproportion between effort and significance—I respect him for it. *Whatsoever thy hand findeth to do, do it with thy might.* But Dayton did not mark a new path onward and upward in the American story. It was closer to the end of something.

It didn't seem that way at first. It seemed as if Holbrooke might be the author of a new doctrine.

Think of the late nineties, if you're not too young to remember. Microsoft, Tomahawks, *Titanic.* Our economy, military, and culture were unchallenged, apparently unchallengeable. It hasn't been like that before or since. Those years were, you could say, the high-water mark of the American century. But there was no Clinton doctrine. There was barely a Clinton foreign policy, other than the president's boundless confidence in globalization, not much changed since 1993 when Lake replaced "containment" with "enlargement." Everything seemed to be getting better on its own—and if people were killing one another in eastern Congo or the southern Balkans, what did it really have to do with us?

Holbrooke wanted more. He wasn't a grand strategist, but his frenetic public presence made him the embodiment of certain ideas in action. He believed that power brought responsibilities, and if we failed to face them the world's suffering would worsen, and eventually other people's problems would be ours, and if we didn't act no one else would. Not necessarily with force, but with the full weight of American influence. This was the Holbrooke doctrine, vindicated at Dayton. But it didn't come out of government experience, much less analytical rigor. His views, like everyone's, emerged from his nervous system, his amygdala, the core of his character, where America stood for something more than just its own power. He was that rare American in the treetops who actually gave a shit about the dark places of the earth.

Does it sound softhearted and dreamy? Not at all. You could call it an updated version of the liberal internationalism of Roosevelt, Truman, and Kennedy. The enemies were now murky civil wars, second-rank tyrants, mass atrocities, failed states. Kissinger would not have recognized these as subjects of high national interest, but Holbrooke, never a practitioner of pure realpolitik, was alive to the present.

"This is no time for *fin de siècle* malaise," he said in a speech in 1997. "The post–Cold War era demands a thoughtful examination and the design of new tools to meet its challenges—many of them both humanitarian and political. So far into this new, as yet unnamed era, we have only shown a capability to react, which costs dearly in lives and money. Managing chaos is the foreign policy challenge of the 1990s . . . If we were too brash and bold at times during the Cold War era, we are too complacent (or indifferent) and cautious today."

Chaos was an even tougher problem than the Soviet Union, less predictable, more in need of local knowledge and the help of allies. Though the response might or might not include force, it had to be intervention, early and persistent—whereas we Americans like to show up late, in large numbers, impose a quick solution, and then move on. Managing chaos didn't have much of a constituency in the United States. To Republican hawks it turned national security into social work. It didn't fit the anti-war, blame-America model of the left. It violated all the principles of realists in the center. And to the new isolationists on the right, like Jesse Helms, it was practically treasonous.

The argument over how to use America's superpower was mostly with ourselves. We had no rivals. The circumstances were unique. The Dayton Accords placed Russian troops in postwar Bosnia under NATO command—the first and last time that happened. NATO was expanding to the very borders of the former Soviet Union, and Holbrooke brushed off the concerns of people like Kissinger about provoking the old Russian paranoia. What did Russia have to fear from the West? We wanted to include it in the enlarging circle of European democracies, and never mind NATO. One virtue of realpolitik is it gives you a feel for the interests of other people, and Kissinger thought Holbrooke was too much a swaggering American to understand why Russia might imagine it was being encircled. His doctrine risked becoming a kind of liberal imperialism.

Some Europeans—some Americans, too—thought we took the wrong lesson from Bosnia: that America only had to throw its weight around to get results. These skeptics would draw a straight line from Dayton to Iraq, and in Holbrooke they saw the humanitarian face of American hubris. I didn't think so. I thought he represented what was best about us. It looks more complicated now, as you'll see by the end of the story, but I'd still take him over the alternatives.

Pax Americana began to decay at its very height. If you ask me when the long decline began, I might point to 1998. We were flabby, smug, and self-absorbed. Imagine a president careless enough to stumble into his enemies' trap and expend his power on a blue dress. Imagine a superpower so confident of perpetual peace and prosperity that it felt able to waste a whole year on Oval Office cocksucking. Not even Al Qaeda, which blew up two American embassies in East Africa that August, could get our serious attention—Clinton's response, a bunch of Tomahawks, was derided left and right for following the script of De Niro's *Wag the Dog*. The Republicans decided that destroying the president was more urgent than the national interest, and they attacked his every move at home and abroad. Our leaders believed they had the luxury to start tearing one another apart, and they've never stopped. Did any country ever combine so much power with so little responsibility? And slowly, imperceptibly at first, we lost that essential faith in ourselves.

HOLBROOKE NEEDED something to do besides opening doors for Credit Suisse First Boston. In the summer of 1997 he became Clinton's unpaid, one-week-a-month special envoy for Cyprus. The island had been divided between the Turkish north and Greek south since 1974. Holbrooke decided to bring together the leaders of the two communities—each other's friend from college in the early sixties—in a formerly grand hotel, now decaying, on the Green Line in Nicosia. The Americans spruced up an elegant Potemkin room for the meeting, with expensive wines and caviar. The two leaders spent hours reminiscing. Holbrooke knew how to do this—he thought he was getting somewhere. But neither side budged. The Turks wouldn't agree to formal talks until the Greeks recognized the breakaway Turkish republic in the north, which no country except Turkey recognized.

After two or three visits Holbrooke blamed the stalemate on the Turkish leader and left Cyprus to other mediators. Too hard, too little reward. He turned his attention to Kosovo.

The province where Milosevic had launched his career as the leader of Greater Serbia was the unfinished business of the Balkan wars. What started there would end there. When Croatia and Bosnia fell apart, Kosovo went quiet for a few years. At Dayton only the German diplomat

Wolfgang Ischinger had instructions to include Kosovo in the talks, but when he asked about it on the first day, Holbrooke told him that Bosnia would be hard enough. Holbrooke and Milosevic were taking a walk around the base one day when they saw a group of Albanians outside the security fence demonstrating for Kosovo's autonomy. Holbrooke suggested that they go over and speak with the protesters. Milosevic turned him down cold. As far as he was concerned, Kosovo was an internal Serbian affair, none of the world's business.

Dayton taught the Kosovar Albanians that they couldn't expect anything from the West until the conflict reached a crisis. The lesson of Bosnia was that only violence paid. After 1995 the peaceful movement against Serbian repression in Kosovo gave way to armed resistance and demands for independence. By 1998, with guns smuggled across the border from the failed gangster state of Albania, the Kosovo Liberation Army controlled most of the countryside. The insurgents staged attacks against Serbian police and military targets that provoked harsh reprisals against Albanian civilians and were intended to bring Western intervention.

As in Bosnia, the Europeans stood by indifferent or helpless, and the Americans were disengaged and divided. Albright, who felt a personal hatred for Milosevic, wanted to hit Serbia hard. Secretary of Defense William Cohen and the Joint Chiefs wanted to avoid any military involvement. National Security Advisor Berger, more political than his predecessor Tony Lake, fretted over the risks that another Balkan war posed to the president. Clinton was distracted by an investigation into his sexual liaison with a White House intern.

In March 1998, Ibrahim Rugova, the leader of Kosovo's nonviolent opposition, sent a letter to Albright: "I am writing to inform you that I am ready to meet President Slobodan Milosevic, without any preconditions, under the mediation of the United States. I urge you to appoint Mr. Richard Holbrooke as a mediator." The next month, Ischinger (political director in the German foreign ministry) implored Strobe Talbott (still deputy secretary of state) to set Holbrooke loose on Kosovo.

Albright, feeling Holbrooke's hand behind the pressure, hated the idea. "Holbrooke is out of control," she told Talbott. She was a media star, the most famous member of the administration after Clinton, but beneath her black Stetson she was thin-skinned and beset with suspicions. Her distrust of Holbrooke amounted to not unjustified paranoia that he would try to steal Kosovo from her. In May she asked Chris Hill, the American ambassador to Macedonia, to be the mediator in Kosovo. "Chris," Holbrooke implored his favorite protégé, "I need you to tell Madeleine that you need me." In the end, Talbott and Berger persuaded Clinton that Holbrooke's negotiating skill and deep knowledge of Milosevic might keep America out of another Balkan war.

So in mid-May Holbrooke traveled with Hill to Serbia. Milosevic greeted them at his palace as old friends.

"You know what was most important accomplishment of Dayton?" he began. "Americans finally learned what is like to live with Muslims!"

Holbrooke ignored the joke and informed Milosevic that Hill would be the new American envoy for Kosovo.

"Mr. Richard Charles Albert Holbrooke," Milosevic said, leaning forward, "there is no crisis. There are just a few Albanian separatists that the American media is fond of talking to, and our security services are dealing with." Holbrooke tried to break in but Milosevic wouldn't let him. "Mr. Holbrooke, I do not need an envoy. Kosovo is a part of Serbia. It is a *domestic* problem." He added, "But I can say to you that Ambassador Chris is welcome anytime to see me, and can go anywhere he wants in Kosovo."

Kosovo wasn't Bosnia, and Milosevic was no longer the same negotiating partner. He wasn't fun anymore. Demographically, the Serbs in Kosovo—sinking below 10 percent of the population—were doomed, but politically Kosovo was sacred ground, essential to Milosevic's increasingly unpopular hold on power. "Kosovo is more valuable to the Serb people than my neck," he told Holbrooke. Kosovo was also the place where a wider war could break out, pulling in Albania, Macedonia, Greece, and Turkey.

Holbrooke arranged the first meeting between Milosevic and Rugova, but it achieved nothing. In 1995, in Bosnia, diplomacy had been Milosevic's only chance, but in 1998 he used it to stall while his forces rampaged through Kosovo. This war never got Holbrooke's full attention as Bosnia had. Hill was the lead negotiator, and Holbrooke's involvement was sporadic, his command of the issues and people thin. His book was coming out, and he was raising money for the American Academy in Berlin, which was about to get off the ground, and he had to keep Credit Suisse First Boston happy, and too much surplus ambition was distracting him, driving him in too many directions.

"I like Deek," Milosevic told Hill. "But for the sake of career he would eat small children for breakfast."

THE BIGGEST DISTRACTION came in June 1998.

Bill Richardson, the U.N. ambassador, tipped Holbrooke off that he was going to leave that position and become secretary of energy to fill out his résumé and make himself a more attractive running mate for Gore in 2000. Richardson pushed the White House to replace him with Holbrooke. This was a job Holbrooke wouldn't hesitate to take. At the United Nations he could stay in New York with Kati and her kids, get back into the game at cabinet rank, and work on issues all over the globe. He had seen the United Nations fail miserably in Bosnia, but he valued the institution enough to want to fix it, if only to be a better tool of American policy. This time Holbrooke didn't stand around and wait. He called Clinton from Kosovo to report on his trip and added presumptuously that, if offered Richardson's job, he would accept it.

Clinton summoned Holbrooke to Washington on June 11. Just before midnight they met, like the last time, upstairs in the Treaty Room. "I need you desperately," the president said. Holbrooke had read the situation shrewdly. Clinton was dissatisfied with his foreign policy team. Albright was a publicity hound who performed well with a script but wasn't up to the job: "She'll fuck me every time she can." In the year of Monica, Clinton needed to bring in someone heavily credentialed. "I'm putting you in this job because you're big and I want you to scare Madeleine and Sandy, but I also want you to be a team player."

"I've always been a team player," Holbrooke said. "I believe we argue in the huddle and then go out and run the play that's called."

Clinton couldn't resist a little more seduction. "If you do this well, the thing Strobe has long advocated will happen."

Holbrooke asked Clinton for a favor—would he call Kati with the news? She picked up the phone in New York and there was the president, flirting. "Now we'll both be subpoenaed," Clinton told the *really* lovely ex-wife of Peter Jennings, "cuz I'm calling you late at night."

Albright had no choice but to tolerate Holbrooke in her old job.

"It's not my decision," she said flatly when he called. "We've never had a problem when we've worked together." Later, she told her deputy, "He's all yours, Strobe," and she went on to trash Holbrooke's work in Kosovo. "He fucked up there. He's not a genius. He did well in Dayton, but he hasn't distinguished himself in Cyprus and Kosovo."

On June 18, Clinton stood before the cameras in the Rose Garden to announce the nomination. When it was Holbrooke's turn, he spoke about visiting the U.N. construction site with his father and had trouble getting through his remarks.

Trudi, David, and Anthony were there, and as the Holbrookes followed the president along the South Portico colonnade toward the Oval Office for the photo op, Holbrooke leaned toward Anthony and murmured, "The Secret Service turned up an arrest warrant for you." Federal marshals were waiting to seize Anthony as soon as he walked outside the White House gates. "We're working on it."

Anthony had spent four years working with refugees in Thailand, and at the end of 1995 he had come back with a heroin habit. The arrest warrant came after he failed to complete mandatory community service.

Holbrooke was closer to Anthony than to David. They had lived together as New York bachelors, and Anthony's vulnerability and charm had forced his father to take note. David, four years older than Anthony, had seen his parents' divorce through his mother's eyes and grown up pretty much without a father. Holbrooke would take his sons to a Knicks or Yankees game, always the best seats through corporate connections, and impress them with his new friends, like Tom Cruise, who spent three weeks trying to cure Anthony's addiction by recruiting him to Scientology. When Anthony began to pursue art, which became his calling—his first paintings were portraits of his father from news photos—Holbrooke was his biggest supporter, and he always flattered himself that his boys were doing great whether they were or not, and he loved them, but none of this replaced the steady presence in their lives that they needed and he didn't give. After marrying and having children, David told Litty that his father wouldn't recognize his own grandchildren in a toddler lineup.

Kati found Holbrooke's family unbearable. She could hardly stand to spend an hour at a gathering in Scarsdale after the death of Trudi's second husband, Stanley. "We have to stay," Holbrooke told her. "She's my mother." Kati wanted Holbrooke to be close to *her* family, so he used all his patient diplomacy to thaw his chilly and beautiful stepdaughter, Lizzie, who eventually warmed to him, and to charm his aloof father-in-law Endre, who never came around. But Kati made it clear that she didn't want a relationship with Holbrooke's family. He repeated it to his brother in explaining why they rarely saw each other. No, Trudi couldn't ride in their car out to the Hamptons; no, Anthony couldn't stay with them at the Telluride house, even though Lizzie and Chris would be there. Sometimes Holbrooke insisted, but usually he gave in to Kati, and he spent more time with her children than his own.

On the grand piano in the Beresford there were dozens of pictures of Richard and Kati and her children, skiing and doing other glamorous things, and not a single one of Anthony, whose calls Holbrooke took in the bathroom so that Kati wouldn't know they were talking, and whose Post-it notes from their years as roommates ("You are so full of shit. Politics=Diplomacy=B.S.=You," "I suppose leaving half the Grape-fruit Juice out to Spoil is your way of Leading by Example," "Wasn't it Fun? I know you also had a great time. Thanks. Big DAD and Ant Man break New ground on Family Values," "DAD—I cleaned your Room as you Asked—$Please$LeaveUS$") Holbrooke framed and hung in his walk-in closet.

"There are two kinds of people," Holbrooke would tell his sons, "those who like fart jokes and those who don't. We know where the Holbrookes stand." But Kati, who stood on the other side of the fart-joke divide, was the center of his world.

Dick Beattie, Holbrooke's lawyer, fixer, and friend, happened to be at the Rose Garden ceremony. He persuaded the federal marshals not to arrest Anthony when he left the White House. That was the kind of help his father could offer.

THE DAY AFTER the ceremony, someone sent a letter to the State Department's inspector general. "I must bring two matters to your attention which call into question Mr. Holbrooke's suitability for his most recent nomination," the letter began. The first matter was that, immediately after serving as assistant secretary for Europe, Holbrooke had gone to work for a European-owned bank and begun meeting with

top European officials whom he knew from his time as a public servant, sometimes with American ambassadors in tow because he was
still serving as an unpaid advisor to the State Department—wearing
two hats, as they say in government—which, to an outsider, might look
like using American officials to drum up business. The second matter
was that, while serving as assistant secretary, he had intervened in a
contract bid involving the Hungarian government on behalf of Credit
Suisse First Boston just two months before he started talking to the
bank about a job.

The letter was signed "Anon." Four single-spaced pages written with
the detailed knowledge that could only come from a department official. The writer even tipped his hat to Holbrooke's stellar career. If I
knew who Anon. was I'd tell you, but some things just stay buried. The
list of Foreign Service officers with an anti-Holbrooke grudge—you've
met some of them—is far too long to narrow down the suspects. Perhaps Anon. was counting on that.

The Office of the Inspector General was already on Holbrooke's trail
for another matter. As assistant secretary he had lived alone without
paying rent in the fully staffed Georgetown mansion of a rich Clinton
donor named Larry Lawrence, who had been appointed ambassador
to Switzerland in 1993. Lawrence died in 1996, and thanks to a testimo-
nial from Holbrooke he was granted a waiver by the army and buried
at Arlington National Cemetery because of his heroic service in the
merchant marine during World War II—only to be exhumed the next
year and reburied in San Diego because the heroic service turned out to
be fabricated. Holbrooke had failed to include Lawrence's Georgetown
mansion as a gift on his financial disclosure form.

And there were other things, petty things. He was cutting corners,
being careless.

But investment banks hired him because he had great access in
Seoul and Stockholm. Conflicts of interest are normal in the treetops,
where everyone you know can use their influence on your behalf—that's
what it means to be friends. You contribute to my campaign beyond the
legal limit, I give you a plum job for which you're not qualified. You let
me stay rent-free in a Georgetown mansion for eighteen months, I get
you into Arlington for eternity.

Holbrooke and Kati were also given discounted interest rates for large mortgages on their houses in the Hamptons, Connecticut, and Telluride by Countrywide Financial. Its chief, Angelo Mozilo, was cultivating powerful people in Washington with VIP treatment in order to get favorable terms on a business deal with Fannie Mae, whose chief executive, Holbrooke's friend and former partner Jim Johnson, invited Holbrooke to join him as a "Friend of Angelo." Who's going to say no to a sweetheart loan? No one gave it a thought until, a decade later, Countrywide collapsed in the subprime mortgage scandal, and Mozilo became a notorious face of the financial crisis, and his VIP program did its part in making Americans deeply cynical about elites in New York and Washington—even, it wouldn't be stretching things to say, helping pave the way in the next decade for the election of a president who promised to blow everything up.

In mid-July two agents from the Office of the Inspector General spent almost three hours interviewing Holbrooke in Beattie's Midtown law office. Holbrooke handled them beautifully.

"Did you believe that you received a gift from the Lawrences by staying in their home rent-free?" asked Special Agent Brian Hess.

"I'm not sure I understand the question," Holbrooke replied. "It is what it was. I'm an existentialist. They offered me a room in their house. That is a room in a house. Is it a gift? Like a box of chocolates? I don't know, I'd leave that to other people."

It was the summer of "It depends on what the meaning of the word 'is' is." It was a season of investigation, of partisan bloodhounds in hot pursuit of existentialists. A year earlier, the bloodhounds had already run down Tony Lake. After Clinton nominated him to lead the CIA, the Republican chairman of the Senate Intelligence Committee, Richard Shelby of Alabama, began poking into every corner of Lake's life. Shelby obtained Lake's raw FBI files and combed through them for past sins. There was nothing on him except his failure to sell some oil stocks when he was national security advisor, for which he paid a $5,000 fine. But Shelby kept poking, dragging out the confirmation month after month. Clinton tried to talk Lake out of giving up—hugged him in the Oval Office once, twice—but Lake had made up his mind, and he issued a statement: "I have gone through the last three months and more with patience and, I hope, dignity. But I have lost the former and could lose the latter as this political circus continues indefinitely . . . Washington has gone haywire." On that bitter note, at the age of just fifty-seven, Lake ended his career in government.

Holbrooke thought that Albright could have wound down his own investigation if she wanted, but the Clinton administration couldn't afford another fight with Congress, and the investigation kept growing. In the fall of 1998 the inspector general determined that there were grounds to believe Holbrooke had violated federal law. The matter was referred to the Justice Department, which already had its hands full with the Lewinsky matter. Holbrooke would be twisting in the wind for months.

WHAT ELSE COULD he do but go back to Kosovo? Guerrillas with Kalashnikovs, nervous checkpoints, high-stakes talks with Milosevic—nothing else tightened his stomach muscles that way and gave him such a rush.

During the summer and early fall, Serbian forces went on the offensive and hit the Kosovars hard, driving KLA fighters over the border into Albania and creating three hundred thousand refugees. The countryside became a wasteland. Killings by Serbian forces crossed what Berger called the "atrocities threshold," which meant that the United States had to appear to do something.

In early October, over Albright's objections, Holbrooke was dispatched to Belgrade to negotiate a cease-fire. His legal problems followed him. Albright's chief of staff warned Holbrooke, "It's really important to the inspector general's investigation that you be seen as standing shoulder to shoulder with Madeleine." Holbrooke in turn demanded that Albright guarantee his confirmation as a condition for carrying out her instructions on Kosovo.

Holbrooke and Milosevic negotiated not just a cease-fire but Serbian withdrawals to barracks and fourteen hundred unarmed monitors sent across Kosovo to verify compliance. Holbrooke considered it a breakthrough. Albright, who had no faith in Milosevic and wanted U.S. bombers in the sky over Serbia, thought it wouldn't last. She was right—within weeks the cease-fire fell apart. After more Serbian atrocities, NATO—with the new British prime minister Tony Blair, a full-throated humanitarian interventionist, leading the way, and Clinton, trying to get free of the Lewinsky business after his impeachment by the House, stumbling behind—set its course for war.

In February 1999 Albright convened the warring sides for talks outside Paris in the medieval castle at Rambouillet. Her purpose was not so much to pull off her own Dayton as to unite the West against the Serbians. Milosevic remained in Belgrade—he feared arrest on a secret war crimes warrant—while his representatives in France refused to accept a deal that would put foreign forces in Kosovo. The international monitors were withdrawn in preparation for NATO bombing. Holbrooke thought that the rush to war was tactically clumsy, without clear aims or adequate plans for a protracted conflict in Kosovo, escalation around the region, or a postwar occupation force. He wasn't even sure that Wesley Clark, now the supreme commander of NATO, would really pull the trigger. But by now Holbrooke's role was marginal. He called Kosovo "Madeleine's war."

Clinton sent him back to Belgrade to warn the Serbians what was

about to come. On the morning of March 23 he went to see Milosevic
for the last time.

They sat down alone in the huge reception room. There were no
platters of food. Milosevic was grim, fatalistic. Holbrooke asked if he
understood what would happen if the Serbians still refused to sign the
Rambouillet Accords.

"You will bomb us," Milosevic said.

"That's right."

"You are a big and powerful nation. Bomb us if you wish. It is stupid,
because the entire Serb people will unite against you. But we cannot
stop you."

They fell silent. Milosevic walked Holbrooke out to the stairs.

"I wonder if we will ever see each other again," Milosevic said.

Holbrooke couldn't accept the failure of his persuasive powers. He
wanted to stay in Belgrade and keep talking, but Albright told him to
leave that afternoon. The next evening, NATO jets flew their first sor-
ties over Serbia. After several days of bombing Holbrooke called Clark.
"What do you think about a pause?" "Not only no," Clark answered,
"but hell no." Holbrooke reached Milosevic's foreign affairs advisor,
Bojan Bugarcic. "Look, I'm in Budapest," he said. "Tell President Milosevic I'm here if he wants me to come and sign off on what we talked
about." Milosevic refused. He felt betrayed by Holbrooke, and perhaps
he thought that if he held out long enough, he could surrender Kosovo
without paying the ultimate price of being cast out of power by his own
people.

The air war, led by General Clark, was expected to take several days.
It lasted eleven weeks. In the short run Serbians rallied around their
leader, which is what being bombed almost always does. A million Kosovar Albanians, half the population, were driven from their homes.
Holbrooke, uninvolved and in an agonizing career limbo, found little to
admire about the first war in NATO's history. In mid-May he wrote to
himself, "Why, I wonder, would I go through this messy confirmation
process simply for the privilege of spending more time with Madeleine
Albright and the gang that can't bomb straight? I can barely stand being
in the same room with most of these people anymore, and they simply
do not know what they are doing. The moral basis for the war is unas-
sailable, but that is a necessary but not sufficient [*sic*] for success. Yet I

have no choice but to move forward for confirmation, not in order to serve but in order to get vindicated."

The Russians, having blocked approval for the war in the U.N. Security Council, refused to cooperate with the West as they had in Bosnia. But when Blair pushed NATO to prepare for a ground invasion of Kosovo, Milosevic finally realized that the aged and infirm Boris Yeltsin, who was about to step aside for his chosen successor, Vladimir Putin, would not come to his rescue. On June 11, Milosevic gave in. Kosovo became a ward of the United Nations and began its unsteady path to independence. A year later, in the summer of 2000, Milosevic was thrown out of power in a generally peaceful uprising after he tried to steal a presidential election. The next year he was arrested and extradited to the war crimes tribunal in The Hague, where he died in prison in 2006. Karadzic was finally caught in 2008, and Mladic in 2011.

So the decade of the Balkan wars, which were Milosevic's wars, and which made Holbrooke, came to an end.

ONE DAY in late 1998 some unknown person came up to Dick Beattie on the street and handed him an envelope with a second unsigned letter. As soon as Holbrooke dealt with one set of accusations, another sprang up. A lot of people had a more than rooting interest in seeing him go down. And he had made it too easy—like Clinton, he'd been careless. He had to turn over several years of schedules, correspondence, credit card statements, phone logs. The Justice Department investigation went on for months.

Early one morning in late January 1999, while the Senate was trying President Clinton for perjury and obstruction of justice, Beattie met his client in his Midtown law office. Nothing was going to move forward on Holbrooke's nomination unless he gave the investigators something. "Let me plead wrongdoing," Beattie said, "and work out an agreement and pay a fine."

Holbrooke was outraged. "You can't do this to me!"

"If you don't do it, you won't get confirmed. Justice doesn't care about this but they don't know what to do with it."

"It'll ruin my life!"

Holbrooke paced the halls of Simpson Thacher & Bartlett, raving.

But Beattie was a worldly man and knew how these things went—in a week it would be forgotten. Holbrooke relented. While denying any wrongdoing, he paid a $5,000 fine (the exact same amount Lake paid) for bringing the American ambassador in Seoul to the opening of Credit Suisse's first Korean branch within a year of leaving government service. That was all they could pin on him. His legal bill totaled $336,000, though Beattie charged him for just two-thirds.

But that was not the end of it. The Senate Foreign Relations Committee wanted to know about the $3,000 he got from *Time* magazine for an article on Bosnia during the period when he wasn't supposed to benefit from his government work. The committee's chairman, Jesse Helms, kept postponing confirmation hearings while senators held the nomination hostage to their pet fights with the Clinton administration. Mitch McConnell wanted a favorite conservative law professor appointed to the Federal Election Commission. So the permanent American seat on the Security Council remained vacant for an entire year. This was more than just partisan combat—it was a rejection of America's international commitments.

Rumors swirled that the White House was going to cut its losses and find another nominee. By this point someone with more dignity and less tenacity would have bowed out. Holbrooke looked around for a friend in power.

The previous December, he and Kati had thrown a holiday party IHO Hillary Clinton at the Beresford, to show their support at the end of the year of Monica. No Bill—just New York friends, including movie stars who were as flattered by the invitation as the policy types and journalists. Clinton once mentioned in passing that she admired the Salvation Army—Holbrooke hired a Salvation Army band to play Christmas carols for her. So when White House officials made noises about abandoning Holbrooke, he called Hillary at least a dozen times, sometimes late at night, often distraught, urging her to keep the president steady.

"We cannot pull out on Richard Holbrooke," she told her wavering husband. "You've got to stick with him." This was the beginning of their long mutual loyalty.

The hearings started on June 17—the day before the anniversary of Holbrooke's nomination. Among his family members in attendance, he made sure that the three-year-old daughter of David's fiancée, Sarah, was not only present but wearing an adorable blue dress. When Jesse Helms motored into the chamber in his wheelchair, armed with charts intended to embarrass the Clinton administration and a lengthy prepared text that ripped the nominee to pieces, Holbrooke introduced Helms to his family: "This is my son David, his wife, Sarah, and their little daughter, Bebe." And the conservative senator from North Carolina went soft.

In his opening statement, Holbrooke emphasized the crucial role of Congress in making and carrying out U.S. foreign policy. This wasn't just executive branch boilerplate—it was a hard lesson of Vietnam that he had taken to heart, applied under Carter, and again during Bosnia. But the turning point of the hearing came when he started in on the story of his father bringing him to the United Nations and choked up again.

"My father talked to me about his—perhaps I should just submit this for the record. I don't think I am going to be able to read the part about my father."

"We'll get together and talk about my father as well," Helms drawled. "I feel the same way about mine. You are impressing me on this point."

By the end, Helms was telling his staff to take down the charts. He supported the nomination, and in early August the Senate voted overwhelmingly to confirm. Holbrooke would have just seventeen months on the job.

You're Either Going to Win or Fall

I don't know a good way to tell you about those months. There was no single theme but a nonstop blur of purposeful activity, and I'm afraid of leaving you with a highlight film. He couldn't stand to waste twenty seconds in an elevator, let alone a twenty-minute ride across town in his chauffeured car. On the first morning, he tried to fire two employees at the U.S. mission across First Avenue from U.N. headquarters, one for failing to recognize the new ambassador in an elevator. His chief of staff didn't carry out the orders, but the point was made—everyone on their toes all the time.

He compared himself to "a skier in a downhill race just going flat out—you're either going to win or fall." He didn't fall. He got things done that you've probably never heard of—not nearly as dramatic as Dayton, but almost as important. He saved the American position at the United Nations, which amounted to saving the United Nations. He was never more productive, never happier.

It helped that he was in New York, not Washington. He and Kati spent nights at the Beresford instead of in the ambassador's official residence on the forty-second floor of the Waldorf Astoria on the East Side, which they used for entertaining. He carved out his own fiefdom and pursued his own issues, the ones Washington didn't want. If he tried to take on Albright, his superior in the bureaucracy, he couldn't win. That didn't keep him from disparaging her in front of his aides—"We can't have an amateur in that office"—or keep Albright from telling Talbott,

"I hope Gore gets elected, but I'll be damned if Holbrooke is going to succeed me." Their hatred, unlike his and Lake's, was uncontaminated by the dregs of the past. But he was disciplined enough to keep his distance from the State Department and the White House. He avoided the biggest foreign policy issues of Clinton's last year—Iraq's weapons program and the Israeli-Palestinian conflict. Throughout his career he stayed clear of the Middle East, and I'll tell you why: it was too easy to piss off American Jewish organizations and hurt himself on his climb.

In his first week on the job, in early September 1999, there was massive violence in East Timor as militias backed by the Indonesian army went on a rampage against Timorese who had just voted for their independence. Holbrooke got on the phone with the Indonesian foreign minister, whom he'd known during the Carter years when Holbrooke was trying to sell American fighter jets to Indonesia and overlooking its bloody annexation of East Timor. Two decades later, he used his old network to berate and cajole the foreign minister to let East Timor go. He kept the Security Council working through the weekend and got a resolution quickly passed that sent an Australian-led international force to Dili on September 20.

It was the first peacekeeping mission since the disasters of Somalia, Rwanda, and Bosnia, and it showed that the United Nations—with a decent power in the region and American leadership—could stop atrocities and stabilize war-torn countries.

His months at the United Nations came down to two or three things.

The first in time, significance, and difficulty was also the most obscure. The United States, the largest contributor, owed the United Nations around a billion dollars. The back dues, known as "arrears," had been accumulating for years in the Senate, where they were held up by Republicans like Helms, who regarded the United Nations as a sump of wasteful spending and anti-American posturing, a danger to our sovereignty. The Republican Party was headed down the lonesome road away from internationalism and toward America First.

Before he would release the money, Helms wanted draconian reforms at the United Nations—above all, a reduction in U.S. dues. The Helms-Biden bill had passed the Senate, but a lot of members of Congress were eager to see the whole institution go under, and a Republican representative from New Jersey had the legislation paralyzed over funds for family planning in poor countries. Holbrooke's predecessors, Albright and Richardson, had been unable or unwilling to solve the problem and left it for him. By the time he was sworn in, the United States was a few months away from losing its vote in the General Assembly. That would have suited Helms and the America Firsters in Congress fine—they would have just pulled the United States all the way out. And the Clinton administration wasn't eager to go to the mat over U.N. dues just before an election year.

So Holbrooke—whose support for war crimes tribunals and peacekeeping missions embodied the loose approach to national sovereignty that Helms loathed—made it his first order of business to befriend Republicans in Congress. Every week that fall he flew the shuttle down to Washington and buttonholed complete strangers in the Rotunda or on the trolley that ran under the Capitol, listened to their complaints, and told them why the survival of the United Nations was relevant to the people in their district.

In the reception room of Bart Stupak, a conservative Democrat from the Upper Peninsula of Michigan, Holbrooke and his deputy in Washington, Robert Orr, were greeted by a poster that said CHARLTON HESTON IS MY PRESIDENT. Heston was the president of the National Rifle Association.

"Oh my God," Holbrooke whispered to Orr, "where have you brought me?"

Holbrooke sat down with Stupak. "I can see you're a security kind of guy," he began, hard-ass to hard-ass. Stupak was a former cop and state trooper.

"I sure am," Stupak said. "I have militias in my district, and a lot of guns."

"Well, I'm here to talk about our national security with the same kind of passion." The United Nations wasn't about American "values"—it was a tool of hard power to use on behalf of our interests. In nine countries out of ten around the world our influence came through our role at the United Nations, especially with peacekeeping missions. When Stupak mentioned the U.N. effort to limit the global traffic in small arms— the NRA was fighting it like hell—Holbrooke waved away his concern. That was just for show at the General Assembly—what counted was the

Security Council, where we had to protect American interests with our power and our veto.

"I didn't know what to expect when I heard you wanted to see me," Stupak said when Holbrooke had finished, "but I have to say you convinced me."

Holbrooke met one-on-one with more than a hundred members of Congress. Most of them had never sat down with a cabinet member and were flattered by the attention of a diplomatic star. The lucky ones were invited to the dinners IHO some celebrity or other that Holbrooke and Kati regularly hosted at the Waldorf. A few even got to be the guest of honor. In December 1999 the House passed and Clinton signed the Helms-Biden bill.

On January 20, 2000, Holbrooke brought Helms to New York for the honor of addressing the Security Council. And although the owl-eyed old racist and isolationist sat at the famous horseshoe table and denounced the United Nations for daring to tell America whether or not its actions abroad were legitimate, and although the ambassadors listened in stony silence, the effect of his presence was to break the tension. The next day, the Senate Foreign Relations Committee held a hearing on U.N. reform in Midtown Manhattan. Helms chaired it in a blue U.N. baseball cap. By now he was thinking about his place in history. In March he reciprocated by bringing the Security Council to Washington, and in May Kofi Annan, the first black African secretary-general, gave the commencement address at Wingate University in North Carolina, Helms's formerly segregated alma mater.

As a condition for paying the arrears, Helms-Biden required that the American contribution go down from 25 percent to 22 percent of the general budget and from 29 percent to 25 percent of peacekeeping, which would oblige all the other countries to increase their dues, sometimes tripling them. Holbrooke found this nickel-and-diming by the richest country on earth humiliating. "But I'm going to do it, because the United States cannot be the nation that pulls the U.N. apart," he told Sir Jeremy Greenstock, the British ambassador. Holbrooke needed the votes of the entire General Assembly, where resistance was just as fierce as what he'd faced in the Republican Congress. He turned his implacable eye for detail on the 188 other missions at the United Nations, spending time with permanent representatives from small, poor countries like Mauritius who had never met an American ambassador, the geopolitical equivalents of Bart Stupak, learning their sensitivities and their desires. He took a group of African ambassadors to a private viewing of the African collection at the Metropolitan Museum. He got deep into the budget math, walking around with a laminated card in his pocket that showed every country's current and proposed assessment.

On New Year's Eve 2000, during the final vote, Holbrooke kept his colleagues in New York up all night as they conferred with their governments on whether to approve the new budget. Greenstock resisted his instructions to reject the proposed British contribution. "I'm sorry, I've had to deal with Holbrooke on this," he told the undersecretary who was awake at the Foreign Office at four in the morning. "I've done pretty well. We have to accept it." The reforms passed, and the United States began to release the money it owed to the organization that it had created.

Holbrooke—who was too hardheaded to believe in his father's dream, but too idealistic to give up on it—saved the United Nations from the dissolution that would have come with the loss of American leadership. Freud said that the psychoanalyst's job was to transform neurotic misery into common unhappiness. Holbrooke preserved the United Nations' historic role as the organization where the world's major problems can fail to be resolved.

HE NEEDED a larger field of play than lobbying and bean counting in Washington and New York. He found one as large as Africa, where he had never set foot outside the Arab north.

In 1998, Bill Clinton had hailed an "African renaissance" with a new generation of leaders. The announcement came prematurely. By late 1999, brutal wars, started by many of those same leaders, were killing tens of thousands of people on the Ethiopia-Eritrea border, in Sierra Leone, and in eastern Congo, where half a dozen neighboring countries had involved themselves in an ethnic civil war and a scramble for mineral riches. If managing chaos was the foreign policy of the post–Cold War era, Africa looked like a good place to start.

At the beginning of December 1999, Holbrooke led a twelve-day trip—Kati came, along with Senator Russ Feingold and Clinton officials—to ten African countries, including Congo, South Africa, and Zimbabwe. At that pace, Holbrooke couldn't wander off into a pagoda and stare at a monk's charred heart. The more important people become, the less they learn—they don't read as much, they have no time to waste productively, they talk to fewer locals on the receiving end of history. Holbrooke fought this syndrome as much as he could—his gold standard for diplomacy remained his year in the Mekong Delta—but it hit him too.

His purpose was to place the continent's problems in front of the Security Council, especially the war in Congo and the AIDS epidemic, which was destroying the social fabric in every country he visited. In January 2000 it was America's turn to chair the council, and Holbrooke declared it "the month of Africa." He brought heads of state from the warring countries in Congo to New York, and—over the objections of Russia, China, and Kofi Annan—he put AIDS on the Security Council's agenda as a threat to world peace and stability (starting with its spread by U.N. peacekeepers in Africa and elsewhere). He didn't get far trying to end the war in Congo. But the light he shone on AIDS had the best consequences: at the United Nations, where for the first time a health crisis received the collective attention of the world's powers, leading the Security Council to consider other "soft" issues of war and peace, like child soldiers and civilian casualties; and for Holbrooke himself, who, after leaving the U.N. job, became the head of a coalition of multinational businesses in the effort to treat AIDS and popularize HIV testing. He understood ahead of his time that diplomacy would change in the twenty-first century—that it would have more to do with organizing individuals and groups outside of government in complex responses to humanitarian crises than with table talk between men in suits.

Barely a footnote to the story I'm telling you. There isn't even time to describe how he single-handedly blocked the genocidal government of Sudan from taking its expected turn on the Security Council, or how he bludgeoned the United Nations into speeding up the resettlement of East Timorese refugees after the war with Indonesia, or how he tried to get the Chinese to meet with the Dalai Lama and give cultural autonomy to Tibet in exchange for recognition of China's rule (it didn't happen). These are the kinds of things Holbrooke did even when no one was looking.

AT THE UNITED NATIONS he also made an important new enemy.

Bureaucratically, all that stood between him and Africa was a thirty-five-year-old assistant secretary of state named Susan Rice. She was a product of Washington's black intelligentsia, a jock, smart and combative, a protégée of Lake's on the NSC and of Albright's at State, all of which meant that she and Holbrooke were destined to clash. The first time they met, in the summer of 1998, Rice was talking to members of Congress on the Hill when her assistant called to say that the new nominee for the U.N. position was in her sixth-floor office at the State Department and wouldn't leave until she returned. Rice told the assistant to inform Ambassador Holbrooke that she wasn't going to hurry back but he was welcome to wait for her. Which was exactly what he would have done in her place.

She eventually returned to find Holbrooke stretched out on her couch. "I don't like you for beating my record as the youngest regional assistant secretary in history," he said.

He was being charming, in his rough way, but Rice wasn't charmed. She decided right then that he was an arrogant prick. And when, the next year, Holbrooke moved aggressively on African issues, the continent again became a battleground for outside forces. His feel for other people's weaknesses told him that Rice's was Rwanda. She had been the top NSC person on Africa during the genocide and done her small part, along with Lake and Albright, to keep America from lifting a finger to prevent or stop it. This failure haunted Rice, and Holbrooke knew it.

The month of Africa at the start of the new millennium was about the longest month of Rice's life. By summoning African heads of state and her bureau's ambassadors to New York for the Congo talks, Holbrooke was pissing all over her territory. Things got particularly ugly at one meeting in his conference room. The issue was whether U.N. peacekeepers should have a mandate to disarm the Congolese militias, which was Rice's position, or act as monitors, which was Holbrooke's. He stood at the head of the table, condescending to her in front of her ambassadors, suggesting that her judgment was colored by her past fail-ure, and when he said, "I know what it's like to be the youngest regional assistant secretary," it was too much. From her seat near the end of the table she slowly raised her middle finger.

He ignored it and kept talking. After the meeting, Rice called Albright to warn her that she had just flipped off a cabinet member. The secretary congratulated her. In a few years all of this would count.

I can't keep Tony Lake out of this part of the story, either. He was teaching at Georgetown and, having worked on Africa since the late sixties, serving as Clinton's unpaid envoy on Ethiopia and Eritrea. Their border war of trenches and artillery looked like World War I, and it was chewing up soldiers at the same rate. A hundred thousand people died over a parched, famine-stricken frontier town. Weapons poured in from other countries, and American attempts to coax an end to hostilities repeatedly failed.

In early May 2000, the peace talks that Lake was mediating in Algiers reached an impasse over the sequence of steps for implementing a cease-fire. The two countries seemed poised to resume fighting—Ethiopian troops were massing at the border. Lake returned to Washington for consultations just as Holbrooke was traveling around Africa with half a dozen ambassadors from the Security Council. As Holbrooke and his colleagues took off from Kampala for Cairo, they decided to divert their plane to the Horn of Africa to try to head off more fighting and, in Holbrooke's case, teach Lake and Rice how muscular diplomacy was done. Lake knew that if he tried to block Holbrooke's intrusion it would look like another petty chapter in their endless saga. As always, Lake's sense of dignity gave Holbrooke a tactical advantage.

The Clinton administration saw the Eritreans as the main aggres-sors, and Rice was particularly close to Ethiopia's prime minister, Meles Zenawi. Holbrooke believed that this tilt was part of the prob-lem. In their shuttle between Addis Ababa and Asmara, he and his colleagues got Eritrea's president Isaias Afwerki to agree to Ethiopian demands, which put Meles—whose military was spoiling to return to the battlefield—in a corner. Holbrooke argued roughly with the Ethio-pian, as if they were equals: "You misunderstand your position as head of government, Mr. Prime Minister." He left Meles seething.

Within thirty hours of the ambassadors' departure from Addis, the

Ethiopians launched an offensive that went on for two weeks, killing thousands more people, before the war ended in the last days of May.

The offensive was coming anyway, but officials back in Washington concluded that Holbrooke's involvement had triggered it. An email went around the State Department with the subject line "To Start a War." Lake, who received the White House's Samuel Nelson Drew Award for his efforts in the peace talks, vowed never to speak to Holbrooke again.

RICHARD AND KATI WERE never happier than at the United Nations, and never as happy again. They were at last living out their idea of a great couple in the public eye. Their lunches and dinners in suite 42A at the Waldorf Astoria, always in the service of his agenda, became legendary. In the morning they would sit on their bed in the Beresford and arrange the seating chart, moving around guests on Post-it notes—as if, Kati thought, they were two generals arraying troops for battle—in advance of the day's events, taxpayer funded, IHO Mandela, Bono, De Niro, Dikembe Mutombo (there was a strong NBA theme), Paul McCartney, Wes Clark, Barbara Walters, Hillary, Gore (Holbrooke was

paying the vice president extraordinary attention as the 2000 campaign began), Helms, Biden, and the occasional subcommittee chairman from Kentucky. Holbrooke's chef, sous chef, and two protocol officers were nervous wrecks.

One Thanksgiving, Holbrooke's family came to dinner. Kofi Annan and several ambassadors were in attendance, and they went around the table saying what each of them was thankful for. The remarks struck

Andrew as so pious and phony—"having an opportunity to bring peace into the world"—that, when his turn came, he said, "I'm thankful I have such a kind, caring, loving brother." Everyone laughed—even Holbrooke. Then Trudi, who had just lost her second husband and was entering the first stage of Alzheimer's, said, "I have nothing to be thankful for. I'm miserable." No one spoke for some time.

Kati always made the opening toast, but she didn't sit around all day planning courses. Holbrooke was the one who fiddled with his chef's menu to suit his taste, especially dessert—*île flottante,* meringue adrift on vanilla custard. They were partners, and she had her own life. She was writing her sixth book, which would be her most successful to date—about presidential marriages, including the Clintons'—and she had her work raising money for the Committee to Protect Journalists and Human Rights Watch, visiting imprisoned writers abroad, and lecturing foreign dictators on freedom of the press. Richard and Kati were on top of the world.

There was a rumor about an affair, his with a younger woman. It was true. They were at the Beresford doing some work when he moved his face close to hers and said, "I want to kiss you." He didn't wait for an answer—he claimed her in the way of an entitled great man. But the younger woman found him more caring than the other VIPs she knew. They stayed close even during the sexless dry seasons when she was dating someone. The rumor appeared in the tabloids in the summer of 2000, when Holbrooke hoped that he was a few months from becoming Gore's secretary of state. Panicking, he came up with a plan: he and Kati would have lunch in Pete Peterson's booth at the Four Seasons with Peterson and Dick Beattie, under the eyes of their social world. To show that they were happily married. Of course no one noticed or cared.

When Kati picked up the rumor, she handled it with far more sophistication—really, with the savoir faire of the Comtesse de Marton. She made a point of being nice to the younger woman in public by expressing concern for her personal troubles. Kati would not let herself be brought down.

And they were happily married. At least he was, and in his case an affair didn't disprove it. The younger woman merely aroused an appetite in a class where affairs were practically expected. He was still gone on Kati.

But he would not have become Gore's secretary of state even if the Supreme Court hadn't given the presidency to George W. Bush. Gore's foreign policy advisor, Leon Fuerth, told Les Gelb that there was no chance of it "for all the obvious reasons"—too much trouble, too many detractors, underappreciated talent. Gelb argued that Holbrooke had always been loyal to Clinton, but Fuerth was unmoved, and Jim Johnson, who ran Gore's debate prep and transition, confirmed the bad news.

After leaving government Holbrooke took an office at the Council on Foreign Relations and made plans to write another book—a sequel to Kennan's *American Diplomacy 1900–1950*—about diplomacy in the second half of the twentieth century, which was most of the American century, featuring episodes from the career of Richard Holbrooke. But he never got started—he was too restless. Johnson brought him along to another Wall Street firm, this time a merchant bank called Perseus, for a million and a half in salary and bonus, more than Holbrooke had ever made. Beattie tried to warn him off—he considered Frank Pearl, the head of Perseus, a slimy operator—but the money was too enticing. The job came with a secretary, a personal assistant, a car, and a driver who had once chauffeured the police commissioner and still had the NYPD plaque that could get them anywhere fast.

Holbrooke brought in very little business at Perseus. He did his AIDS work and chaired the Asia Society and sat on powerful corporate boards and wrote columns for the *Washington Post* and gave a speech to oligarchs in Kiev for a cool hundred thousand dollars. He was restless, and his restlessness was hard on Kati.

He began to have trouble with his health. Atrial fibrillation—an arrhythmic heartbeat and light-headedness. It happened three times in six years, and each time he had to be cardioverted—doctors applied paddles to his chest and back to deliver an electric shock that felt like a mule's kick, rendering him briefly unconscious, to stop his heart so that it could resume its normal beat. The episodes scared him.

The marriage suffered when he was out of office. Periods of climbing kept their connection taut, but when he was not doing the work he was meant to do, the twelve-millimeter rope started to go slack. They were hardly ever alone together at home, and intimacy died with every night out—restaurants with friends, fund-raisers, dinners IHO someone or other. They were both afraid of standing still under the scrutiny of others and themselves, as if this might show them something they didn't want to see. It was easier to protect each other when his ice-blue eyes were lit as only the work he was meant to do could light them.

In the years between he kept frantically busy, but he couldn't bring them both the excitement of power in high office. His life took up too much space and she always had to fight for her share. He wanted her within reach but could never unplug himself from whatever was distracting him. She began to feel neglected. And this was the essential difference in the ambition that joined them in a chromosomal salute. "What Holbrooke wants attention for is what he's doing, not what he is," Lake once said in a moment of generous insight. "That's a very serious quality and it's his saving grace." What Kati needed was attention for herself—it was as necessary as air.

On three occasions she suggested that he see a shrink to discuss a topic that was too painful for him to talk about with her. The first was his father. The second was Lake, who had ended their friendship, he told her, for no reason at all. But Holbrooke refused to see anyone. "I know what works for me, and I don't want anybody messing with my head," he told her. What worked for him was not to look too deeply into these things.

The third topic that she thought might benefit from professional help was the one that nearly ended their marriage.

By the summer of 2004 she was working on a new book, about her parents and the drama of her early life, which regularly took her to Budapest. The man she met there who became her lover was a Hungarian media executive, rich, handsome, and thoroughly European. She loved speaking her childhood language with him. She loved reading poetry together, and drinking wine in cafés for hours on end, and making love, and basking in his adoring, undivided attention—no cell phone calls—none of which happened with Holbrooke anymore. Kati and her lover spent that summer traveling around Europe in a romantic fever, a state she found irresistible. It made her think of leaving her husband.

One day in August, she and Holbrooke were together at their house in the Hamptons, sitting out on the lawn. "Richard, there's someone—" She started sobbing and couldn't finish. They both cried. He had told her once that if she ever betrayed him he would have to forgive her.

"You got us into this mess," he said, walking away. "Now you have to get us out of it."

That "us"—the flat assertion of a reality that left her no room to fantasize or negotiate—defeated her. She called her lover in Budapest: "I can't do this."

Richard and Kati were driven without speaking back to New York, where they immediately resumed their public life together.

WHEN THE TOWERS FELL on September 11, 2001, Holbrooke was driving out to LaGuardia Airport. Sandy Berger was riding with him— they were going to speak at the same conference in Houston—and the catastrophe unfolding behind them across the East River made the conversation tense and personal.

"When was the last time you saw your son?" Berger asked. And: "Clinton wants to know what happened between you and Tony."

"What did you say?"

"I told him I didn't know."

The flights were canceled, the airport shut down. From a nearby hotel Holbrooke's assistant, Ashley Bommer, got CNN on the phone— so he became one of the first experts to appear on TV, within three hours of the towers falling. He said that the culprit might be Osama bin Laden but that any countries helping the terrorists were equally responsible, and he mentioned Ashley so that her parents wouldn't worry. Berger sounded nervous on the air. He tried to turn the questions away from the Clinton administration's record on terrorism.

Holbrooke actually had no idea what to say about the attacks, other than expressing patriotic support for the Bush administration. The more TV appearances he did the more he felt like a fraud, exploiting the tragedy for his own gain. He fell into a depression. He was out of government at a historic moment, and Al Qaeda was not his thing— terrorism was an intelligence and security matter. How did the attacks fit into the Holbrooke doctrine of American leadership in managing chaos and bringing hope to desperate places?

In October, he used a long-planned speech in Holland to think through a position. The decade following the end of the Cold War had been an "interwar period," and now it was over. September 11 was a shock on the scale of June 28, 1914, and December 7, 1941. For a guide to action in the new era, Holbrooke turned, as he often did, to the Roosevelt and Truman years. Defeating Al Qaeda would require the same level of broad cooperation among democracies. "Today, we must put all our energy into creating the transatlantic community's third great alliance, built around NATO, like the ones we established to fight World War II and the Cold War," he told his Dutch audience. Europe would be essential, and so would the United Nations and other international organizations, but leadership would have to come again from America. Going it alone—the default approach of the Bush administration— would fail, because the United States needed not just allies but legitimacy. The war on terror would be an unconventional war—a war of ideas, in part, like the twilight struggle against communism. The worst mistake would be to make it a war against Islam.

After overthrowing the Taliban, America should apply in Afghanistan the lessons learned in the Balkans. NATO and its partners around the world would have to pour in troops and money to rebuild the country and prevent the return of the terrorists. "As Washington confronts the challenge in Afghanistan," Holbrooke wrote in the spring of 2002, "the question must be asked: What's wrong with nation building? Somewhere along the road from Vietnam to Somalia, this once important part of U.S. national security policy became a dirty word."

The analysis was continuous with the values and ideas of Holbrooke's life. But then it led him into a wrong turn and a fatal case of overreach. After all, we Americans have never been good at managing the internal business of other countries. We're lousy imperialists. We're too chaotic and distracted—too democratic. We don't have the knowledge, the staying power, the public support, the class of elites with the desire and ability to run an empire. And we rarely have the moral standing we imagine. We trick ourselves into thinking we care about human rights when it's convenient. You could point to Germany and Japan as success stories, but those were highly organized societies that we had pulverized for their aggression—they'd lost the right to resist being rebuilt by us. Bosnia and Kosovo were in Europe, which was our turf. East Timor was lucky to have Australia right across the Timor Sea. The main lesson of the nineties—where there's American will there's a way—depended on accidents of history and geography.

President Bush and his advisors had no interest in the lessons of the nineties. They refused to apply them in Afghanistan—"nation building" *was* a dirty word. They quickly turned their sights on Iraq, and they were going it alone. Holbrooke chose to support the war anyway. He believed that Saddam Hussein, with his weapons and his atrocities, posed a much greater threat than Milosevic ever had. In September 2002, Holbrooke went before the Senate Foreign Relations Committee and issued the usual caveats about forming a coalition, going through the United Nations, and having a postwar plan. But he pointed out that the Clinton administration had used force in Bosnia and Kosovo without Security Council resolutions. He downgraded the United Nations' role in Iraq to "desirable but not necessary."

A few friends—his editor at Random House, Joy de Menil; his press secretary at the United Nations, Mary Ellen Glynn—told him that he was making an enormous mistake. But Vietnam had taught him again and again that a soft Democrat was politically doomed. That fall, as Congress debated a war resolution, John Kerry came to dinner at the Beresford. He was thinking of running for president in 2004, and Holbrooke told him point-blank that he had to vote for the resolution if he didn't want to be seen as weak on national security. Holbrooke didn't add that the same was true for himself in his quest to become Kerry's secretary of state.

If that was Holbrooke's main reason for supporting the war, it might have been better to be stupidly, disastrously wrong in a sincerely held belief like some of us. Kerry voted for the resolution and still lost the presidency. And I don't think Kerry would have chosen him anyway. Joe Biden had the inside track to be the next Democratic secretary of state. Holbrooke drove Kerry so crazy with his incessant advice that Kerry's running mate, John Edwards, passed the word for him to stop calling the candidate's cell phone.

1996, 2000, 2004. He kept falling just short of the summit, and the reason was always himself. By the time the next election came around, Iraq was the letter "I" stamped on the foreheads of Democrats like Holbrooke.

HE LIKED HILLARY CLINTON because she was human—vulnerable, funny, warm, and willing to fight when her back was to the wall. She believed in things—her family, her faith, her country. She was conservative that way. As New York's junior senator she joined the Armed Services Committee and served with distinction. She was tougher than her husband, more comfortable with military force—Holbrooke thought she was readier to be commander in chief in 2008 than Bill Clinton had been in 1992. And he just liked her better than Clinton. When Bill started coming to Richard and Kati's solicitous holiday party IHO Hillary, which continued every year for a decade, something was lost—he talked too much and overshadowed his wife.

And Hillary—she enjoyed Holbrooke's company, looked to him for wisdom and experience in foreign policy where she had little of her own, put him in his place when he got to be too much. He had advised her to vote for the war resolution in 2002, and now that it was damaging her chances against Barack Obama in 2008, he advised her to apologize for it. But that wasn't in her makeup.

If there was ever a year for Holbrooke to reach the top, this was it. He staked out his position as Clinton's chief foreign policy advisor early and warned other Democrats to get on the train or get flattened—Obama's people would not be serving in the Hillary Clinton administration. Jeffrey Bader, who worked in the East Asia bureau under Holbrooke during the Carter years, and then in the Clinton White House, signed on with the Obama campaign. "I'm not a great believer in dynasties," he told *Newsweek* in the fall of 2007. Holbrooke saw the quote and called Bader. "I don't know why you're doing this. You're hurting yourself— you ought to be quiet."

"I don't give a shit," Bader shot back. "I'm not going to work for Hillary." When you stood up to Holbrooke he usually backed off.

The next day Bader mentioned the incident to Lake, who let loose a profane torrent of reasons why Holbrooke was impossible to work with. As it happened, Lake was the senior foreign policy advisor on the Obama campaign.

Lake first heard about Obama when he was still an Illinois state senator. Lake had given a speech in Chicago in defense of civil liberties after the September 11 attacks, and an audience member put him in touch with the promising young state senator from the South Side, who enlisted Lake's help on foreign policy, including the war in Iraq, which they both opposed. When Obama was elected to the U.S. Senate and came to Washington in 2005, Lake and his wife (by then he had married an investment banker—she once worked with Holbrooke at Lehman Brothers—and converted to her religion, Judaism) held a small dinner party for Obama and a few foreign policy types, including Susan Rice. When Obama decided to run for president, Lake and Rice took charge of the campaign's foreign policy.

Rice signed up a raft of her colleagues at the Brookings Institution, most of them under fifty, drawn to Obama for his biography, his brilliance, and his opposition to the war. Clinton, Holbrooke, and their team were the old, tired establishment—still fighting the ghosts of Vietnam, which led their judgment or backbone to fail them on the most important issue in a generation. They ought to step aside so that Obama could bring Americans together and remake our place in the world.

Holbrooke was especially disliked among the Obama people for his self-dramatizing ways. Denis McDonough, a top Obama aide, attended a couple of foreign policy lunches in Washington that Holbrooke arranged to build ties to younger people and found him insufferably windy, always pontificating about Vietnam. The harder Holbrooke tried to ingratiate himself, the stonier grew McDonough's long, sunken-eyed face. The problem was generational and temperamental.

So when Obama prevailed that summer in the long attrition of the primaries, it looked very grim for Holbrooke. He had bet everything on a full house and called a hand that turned out to be four of a kind. Not only had his friend, patron, and last best hope lost—the winner was surrounded by his enemies, people who hated him. "Tell him we MIGHT give him the time of day when we win provided he acts better," Susan Rice wrote to Barnett Rubin, an Afghanistan scholar who advised the Obama campaign while working with Holbrooke at the Asia Society. If Obama gave Holbrooke any thought at all, he was disposed against him before he knew him.

Holbrooke had one Obama ally—Samantha Power. They had met when she was a twenty-four-year-old freelance reporter in Bosnia. He took an immediate interest—he must have recognized someone whose energy and ambition and sheer physical presence were near his level. Her book on twentieth-century genocides impressed him, particularly the painful self-examination on Rwanda that she had wrung from Lake: "How did you get him to say these things?" She and Holbrooke were fellow liberal hawks separated by generation, gender, and their position on Iraq. When she went to work for Obama, Holbrooke stayed close. But she lost her political usefulness early in the campaign after telling a Scottish paper that Hillary was "a monster," and Obama had to banish her. When Power got married that summer, Holbrooke's wedding gift was a meeting with Clinton. Power apologized profusely; Clinton accepted coolly. Obama heard about it and said, "Some people give a toaster." Power reported the remark to Holbrooke, who was delighted. He didn't pick up the note of irony—the Obama scorn for naked politics.

Two thousand eight was a Democratic year, but everything was going wrong for Holbrooke. In July he had another episode of atrial fibrillation, the fourth—his heart was jumping around in his chest. In August he endured having no role at the Democratic convention in Denver, just like Harriman at Miami Beach in 1972, watching most of it on his hotel room TV, then flying home halfway through. "It's like a cruise in which there are twice as many passengers as the ship will hold," he wrote in his diary, "you wouldn't want to ever see 90% of them on-shore, and there are no shipboard romances."

Even the financial crisis got personal. In one week in September it wiped out his old firm, Lehman Brothers, and made AIG, the giant insurance company on whose well-compensated board of directors Holbrooke sat, a ward of the United States. Beattie, legal advisor to the board, had seen bankruptcy coming over the summer and persuaded Holbrooke (who had no idea what a credit default swap was) to step down before AIG caused him political damage. When Countrywide Financial collapsed, his name surfaced among the Friends of Angelo who'd gotten VIP treatment. Jim Johnson's reputation was shredded in the Fannie Mae scandal—he no longer ran the place, but its political clout during his years as chairman had created some of the conditions for the crisis—and he had to resign as the head of Obama's search for a running mate. Holbrooke's and Johnson's employer, Perseus, took such large losses in the crash that the soundness of its business came under scrutiny.

Holbrooke was making two to three million a year from banking, boards, and speeches, but he had heavy personal expenses. He and Kati owned nine pieces of property, mortgaged to seven and a half million dollars, and they leased a private plane. With the drop in value of their many houses and their stock portfolio, they were staring at a cash-flow problem. Holbrooke sold the Connecticut house and a piece of land in Telluride.

You can find things to admire and still see the truth cold. A whole class of people in Washington and New York sent other people's children to fight in Afghanistan and Iraq while they found ways to get rich. Now they were caught naked by the ebbing tide.

As Election Day drew near and Obama's victory seemed certain, Holbrooke fell into his old desperate frenzy. He called everyone he could think of. He asked Wes Clark, now retired from the army and campaigning with Obama in the last week of the election, to put in a good word for him. "I'd like to ask one thing of you," Clark told Obama at a rally in Pueblo, Colorado. "Put Richard Holbrooke in your government."

"That's it?" Obama asked. "I've heard a lot of things about Holbrooke."

"He's the best diplomat we've got, and he'll be loyal to you."

Holbrooke even called Toni Lake at her farm in Massachusetts. They hadn't spoken in years, but he asked her to intercede with her ex-husband and tell Tony to stop barring the door. Startled, Toni said that there was nothing she could do. Anyway, by then Lake had receded from the fierce jockeying around Obama. This time he meant it when he said he didn't want a job. Power and Talbott finally told Holbrooke to back off—he was hurting himself.

But Holbrooke's fate didn't just depend on his friends and enemies. He still had a reputation for getting hard things done. Who the hell else had gotten anything done? Obama needed the Democratic establishment—his own bench was thin. Twelve days after the election, on November 16, Holbrooke received a call from transition headquarters. Could he fly to Chicago in the morning? The president-elect wanted to talk to him about a job.

AFGHANISTAN

Everything Is Different—
and Everything Is the Same

I

It seems inevitable now that he would end in Afghanistan. There's a final circular logic to it.

You might remember that he first went there in 1970 when he was working for the Peace Corps. He found the country romantic, beautiful, and at peace. He didn't return for thirty-six years—horrific years.

In the spring of 2006, he went back with Kati. Her nephew Mathieu was working for the United Nations in Kabul and suggested the trip. You can see why it would have appealed to Holbrooke.

Iraq was disintegrating—a war he'd like to have forgotten. He had no desire to see Baghdad for himself. I never met an American, soldier or civilian, who wanted to buy a little villa with a garden on the Tigris River. Iraq was flat and hot and harsh, and every human touch, including ours, made it uglier. But Afghanistan was the good war, provoked by September 11—a war to rid the country of Al Qaeda and the Taliban. By 2006 the Taliban were returning to the Pashtun provinces in the south and east, but Kabul was still safe, a beguiling magnet for expats: the snowy foothills of the Hindu Kush, the mule-drawn carts and white Land Rovers in the muddy roads, the glittery wedding halls, the craft shops on Chicken Street, the British lodges and French restaurants and Lebanese tavernas, the pomegranate juice, the vast suffering, the idealism and opportunism, the gossip.

The scene drew a remarkable cast of foreign characters. There was Rory Stewart, a flamboyant Scotsman in his early thirties, who had tutored Princes William and Harry, served Her Majesty as a diplomat and perhaps a spy, walked across central Asia after September 11, wrote a fine book about it, and then, at the request of Prince Charles and the Afghan president Hamid Karzai, started a foundation to support local craftsmen in restoring the old city of Kabul. There was Michael Semple, an Irishman who wore a long beard and *shalwar kameez* and knew so much that he was suspected of being either MI6 or a Taliban collaborator, when he was just an extremely well-informed analyst. There was Sarah Chayes, the caustic daughter of a Kennedy administration official, who went to Afghanistan for National Public Radio and stayed on to start a soap cooperative for farmers in Kandahar, then to advise U.S. military commanders as a critic of the Karzai government. A certain type of imaginative foreigner fell hard for Afghanistan.

At the beginning of his trip, Holbrooke met the coalition commander, Lieutenant General Karl Eikenberry, who was in the middle of his second tour in Afghanistan. Eikenberry found Holbrooke amazingly opinionated for someone who hadn't set foot in the country since 1970. Holbrooke packed his schedule day and night and grilled everyone he met—farmers, shop owners, journalists, officials. He even met Karzai in the Arg, the presidential palace in central Kabul, and informed him that the ancient minarets Holbrooke had seen in Herat were crumbling because of uncontrolled traffic. Karzai lied about the condition of the minarets, then got on the phone and shouted some orders. A white pigeon flew through the window and the president became distracted trying to chase it out. Holbrooke came away unimpressed.

He stayed just a few days. On his way out, he met Eikenberry again and gave the general a ten-point memo on Afghanistan's various ills—corruption, poppies, bad police training, Pakistani subversion. Eikenberry used the document in his final assessment at the end of his tour. He decided that Holbrooke was the quickest study he'd ever met.

Holbrooke didn't quite fall in love with Afghanistan. He was too American to go native anywhere. The only foreign language he ever learned was French, which he spoke fluently with a heavy New York accent, and when he bought local artifacts it was to give them away as gifts, not to furnish his own houses. He fell for problems, not countries, and it was the problem of Afghanistan that began to consume him. It had everything—geopolitics, beauty, tragedy, hope. He believed that the war would be harder than Americans thought and would go on for a very long time—much longer than Iraq, longer even than Vietnam. Afghanistan would be America's longest war. Al Qaeda was rebuilding itself across the border in Pakistan, a failing state armed with nuclear weapons. The security of those weapons was as intense a concern as the possibility of another terrorist strike at home. Perhaps, in fighting the Taliban in Afghanistan, we were at war with the wrong enemy in the wrong country. But Holbrooke thought this was the region where the history of the present was being made, and where we should put our efforts. We had already abandoned it twice.

THE STORY HAS BEEN told again and again, but it makes me sad and angry every time. It's a story of our folly and waste.

Zahir Shah was overthrown in 1973 by his cousin, Prince Daoud, who established the Republic of Afghanistan. In 1978, Daoud and his family were slaughtered in the Arg by Communist troops. For the next year and a half the coup's leaders killed one another off, until the Soviets tried to impose order by invading on Christmas Eve of 1979.

That was the year political Islam first convulsed the world. In February, an Islamic revolution expelled the shah of Iran and seized power. In April, General Zia ul-Haq of Pakistan hanged the elected prime minister, whom he had overthrown in a coup, then abolished Parliament and began to institute sharia law. In November, hundreds of militant Islamists occupied the Grand Mosque of Mecca for two weeks of bloodletting before surrendering, and then the Saudi king decided to head off the radical tide by imposing even more severe religious strictures—banning cinemas and non-Islamic education, completely segregating the sexes in public life. The next month, in December, the Red Army invaded Afghanistan, provoking a jihad—backed by American and Saudi money, U.S. weapons, and Pakistani intelligence—that continues today.

No event since 1945 changed geopolitics more than the war in Afghanistan. Up to two million Afghans died during the Soviet occupation of the eighties, millions more were maimed, another five or ten million fled to Pakistan and Iran. The Soviets killed so many civilians that it amounted to genocide. The Red Army was forced to limp back across the border in 1989, speeding up the end of the Cold War, and we lost interest in Afghanistan, just as Arab veterans of the jihad were organizing themselves into a global terrorist group called Al Qaeda. In 1992, the mujahedin entered Kabul and turned their guns on one another. The civil war destroyed the capital—you can still see the bullet holes and rubble today, along with the amputees—and Afghanistan fell into banditry.

Out of this chaos rose a movement of religious young Afghans, ethnic Pashtuns schooled in the harsh ideology of Saudi-funded madrassas in Pakistan or the border refugee camps. They called themselves Taliban—"students." In 1994 their army emerged in Kandahar, in southern Afghanistan, led by a one-eyed veteran of the jihad named Mullah Mohammed Omar, and backed—controlled, to some opaque degree—by Pakistan's Directorate of Inter-Services Intelligence, the ISI. The Taliban swept through the country, and by 1996 they had three-quarters of Afghanistan, including Kabul. They were initially welcomed—so were the Khmer Rouge—and replaced the criminality with a form of law and order that amounted to extreme cruelty and ignorance. The strongest of the vanquished warlords withdrew up to the Panjshir Valley and formed a resistance army called the Northern Alliance that did little more than survive.

The Taliban held power for five years of terror. They turned parts of the country over to Osama bin Laden and Al Qaeda, who paid the bills in exchange for shelter while plotting to provoke America into a war with Islam. Then came September 11, 2001. The United States told the Taliban to hand over the perpetrators, but Mullah Omar refused—even at the cost of his own rule.

After the Americans threw out the Taliban and Al Qaeda, it seemed as if the torment of Afghanistan was over. In Bonn that December, a U.N. conference established a *loya jirga,* a national assembly, which chose Hamid Karzai, from a family of Pashtun tribal noblemen, as Afghanistan's interim leader. At the Bush administration's insistence, all Taliban were barred from the new government, with fateful consequences. In 2004 Karzai became the first elected president in the country's history.

He carried himself with a natural, regal grace. He wore a purple-and-green-striped Uzbek silk cape and lambswool karakul hat to symbolize tradition and national unity. He was a brilliant retail politician with a sure touch for bargains that kept important players inside the tent. Like a tribal chief he spent his time receiving people in the Arg over tea and cakes, not governing. He saw power as something to hold, not to use in behalf of a vision for his country. He charmed everyone, Afghan and foreigner, with his openness, listening intently and responding with large, theatrical gestures. Even the occasional twitch that made his left eye squint and the flesh of his cheek jump—nerve damage from an accidental U.S. aerial bombing in late 2001, when Karzai was leading a courageous Pashtun uprising against the Taliban—even this made him sympathetic. He told visitors that Afghans responded above all to sincerity. "The moment an Afghan feels he's being taken for a ride, or that he's being cheated, then he's the worst person to deal with."

But soon, and for the second time, we Americans turned away from Afghanistan—Iraq sucked up all our attention and resources—leaving behind a small number of troops whose mission was to kill terrorists, not provide security. Bush and his defense secretary, Donald Rumsfeld, had no interest in the long, difficult work of building Afghan institutions and training an Afghan army. The writ of Karzai's state was so weak that he became known as the mayor of Kabul. To gain control of the provinces he turned to the same warlords who had laid waste to the country and brought on the Taliban. Among them were his relatives, his brothers. He kept them close through patronage networks, and they fattened off cash from the exploding opium trade and the billions in American dollars for aid projects that seemed to benefit U.S. companies and Afghan bigs more than the dirt-poor ordinary citizens. The lavish mafia villas that arose in Kabul's Sherpur neighborhood, which the locals called Chorpur, Thieves' Town, became the symbol of Karzai's rule.

It wasn't all a waste. Schools and clinics were built, too, and millions of refugees returned, and life improved, especially for women and girls. But the torment hadn't ended. The narco-warlords and corrupt officials, and the American bombings that left so many civilians dead and wounded, disillusioned Afghans who had expected a little safety and justice from the new regime. All this created an opening for the Taliban to return.

They hadn't been defeated, only withdrawn to Pakistan's crowded cities and border mountains, where they were supported by the same ISI that had run the jihad in the eighties and midwifed the Taliban in the nineties. Meanwhile, Al Qaeda was reconstituting itself in Pakistan's tribal region of Waziristan.

The Bush administration didn't care to look too deeply. President Bush saw Karzai and General Pervez Musharraf, the Pakistani dictator, as friends and allies in the war on terror, even as the region started to slip back into chaos.

HOLBROOKE RETURNED in March 2008, in the middle of the Obama-Clinton prizefight. By then the momentum was slipping away from the Afghan government and its Western backers. The Taliban controlled entire districts of Pashtun provinces. Karzai, in spite of his friendly weekly videoconferences with Bush, began to feel that the Americans didn't regard him as an equal partner. He complained bitterly to Condoleezza Rice about the rising number of civilian casualties, including one horrible case of an entire wedding party wiped out by an air strike on a hillside near the Pakistan border. He objected to American crop dusters spraying pesticides on poppy fields in Helmand, without regard for the livelihood of the farmers or the future of the soil and water. But the practices continued.

Karzai began to sound like a nationalist—not an aggressive one like Milosevic, but more like Diem, proud and resentful, with the humiliated anger that a poor man feels toward a rich man whose help he sought. Karzai told visitors that the source of Afghanistan's problem was Pakistan, and since the Americans refused to crush the Taliban there, they must want an endless war in his country for their own strategic reasons. If the United States regarded Afghanistan as a client state rather than a partner, a tool to serve its interests, it would meet the same fate here as the British and the Soviets. His statements became so volatile that Western intelligence agencies speculated that Karzai was mentally unstable, perhaps even on drugs. He hardly ever left the palace for fear of assassination, while the corruption in his regime and his family became rampant—the inner rot that nourished the Taliban.

As a possible next secretary of state, Holbrooke was received again at the Arg. This time he criticized Karzai to his face. "You are responsible for some of the failures of the past few years," he said bluntly.

"What have I done wrong?"

Holbrooke mentioned corruption and Karzai's tolerance of violent warlords. Karzai blamed international aid contracts for the corruption, Bush administration policy for the warlords, and Pakistan for the Taliban. He had a point on all counts. After Holbrooke left, Karzai remarked to his chief of staff that it might be better if Hillary Clinton lost the election.

Holbrooke flew eastward on an aging Russian-made U.N. helicopter to Khost, a provincial capital on a dry plateau at the border with Pakistan. In the 1990s, Osama bin Laden had set up a terrorist training camp near Khost, and in 1998 a few dozen U.S. cruise missiles had just missed killing him there. In the winter of 2001, Osama and his followers had fled over a mountain pass north to Pakistan. Fewer than seven years later, the Taliban again controlled much of the countryside. A few miles east of Khost, over mountains that were greening with early spring rains, was Waziristan, the sanctuary of America's sworn enemies.

Khost wasn't a place many American VIPs visited. It was as close to the ground truth of the war as a potential secretary of state could get.

A Foreign Service officer named Kael Weston had invited Holbrooke to spend the night at the U.S. base on a former Soviet airstrip. Weston was in his mid-thirties, from Colorado. He had spent four years as a political advisor to the marines in the extreme violence of Fallujah, where he came to the conclusion that Iraq was the wrong war. He asked to be posted to Afghanistan, the right war, and in Khost he found more welcoming locals. Weston was a rare American diplomat in the war on terror who didn't live day and night behind blast walls and airlocked doors, chronically on email, sealed off from the country he was supposed to be trying to understand. He wore jeans instead of pressed khakis and spent his time in markets and combat outposts, talking with tribal elders and students, patrolling with American grunts and sharing their risks. He wrote cables back to the State Department criticizing a strategy that relied too heavily on military force and showy aid projects. He thought that the effort in Afghanistan needed to be both more modest and more tenacious than American politicians wanted.

"No one in Washington knows anything about Afghanistan," Holbrooke said when he arrived at the base.

"Don't tell me that," Weston said.

"And what they do know is mostly wrong."

They had met a few months before, in the Midtown Manhattan offices of Perseus, where Holbrooke had shown Weston a black-and-white photograph of himself walking down a street in South Vietnam with his boss, Ambassador Maxwell Taylor. Fifty-eight thousand Americans dead for a mistake. "Why should we care about Afghanistan?" Holbrooke had asked Weston.

There were obvious similarities between Afghanistan and Vietnam, structural ones—rural insurgency, corrupt government, unreliable client, cross-border enemy sanctuary, a muddled and endless war. Weston answered that the difference was strategic. The Vietnamese Communists hadn't posed a threat to the United States—the domino theory turned out to be false. We could walk away from Vietnam. But America had been attacked from the valleys and plains around Khost, and could be attacked again. This was Holbrooke's answer, too, and he added that the vulnerability of Pakistan's nuclear weapons to homegrown terrorists made the strategic stakes all the higher. Afghanistan and Pakistan—Holbrooke had begun to speak of the region as a single organism, "Af-Pak"—would be a major part of his portfolio as Clinton's secretary of state.

Weston introduced Holbrooke to madrassa students, tribal elders, and a handful of former Taliban who had warily come over to the government side. Holbrooke slouched in his chair, hands folded over his belly, and listened as the elders complained about police shakedowns and night raids by U.S. Special Forces. "Not even my brother can enter my house at night," an old man with a white beard said, "but you Americans did not even knock." Afghans were caught between their own predatory government, the heavy-handed foreigners, and the brutal insurgents. Holbrooke asked if the elders wanted the Americans to stay or leave. Without the Americans the Taliban would return to power, they answered, but if the Americans stayed they should build up the country.

Holbrooke's billet that night was the VIP room on base—plywood walls, cheap Afghan rugs, a cot, and a TV with American cable networks. Shoes off, feet propped on a coffee table, he flipped between channels and criticized the pundits and politicians on-screen while peppering Weston with questions about Khost.

"Ambassador, when are you going to visit our other war, Iraq?" Weston asked.

Holbrooke shot him a look. "I see no need to go to Iraq."

Weston reminded him of himself, a lifetime ago in Soc Trang. "At your age I was already an assistant secretary," Holbrooke told him. If Weston wanted to shape American foreign policy, he would need a Washington zip code and State Department badge. But Weston was more like Frank Scotton, who had spent a decade in Vietnam and kept his distance from Washington. It would hurt his career, but Weston was committed to seeing out the war here.

Holbrooke slept in cheap flesh-colored pajamas that looked like something given out by the airline in a plastic bag. He woke early in the morning for his helicopter back to Kabul. As in Sarajevo, twenty-four hours in Khost was enough for him.

He asked for some aspirin. Weston brought him Advil.

"Thanks, but I need aspirin, for here." Holbrooke pointed to his heart.

II

O n the afternoon of November 17, he got thirty minutes with the president-elect at transition headquarters in the Chicago Hilton. He knew, from Strobe Talbott and Tom Donilon, that Obama had already summoned Hillary Clinton four days ago—that Obama's first choice for his secretary of state was his defeated rival. What Holbrooke didn't know was that he was down at number four or five on the short list. Never seriously considered. If Clinton declined, the offer would go to Kerry. It was a sad mercy that he didn't know. Kerry would have been almost as painful as Albright. But Clinton—what could he do? She existed on a higher plane.

At least he was in Chicago. It meant his enemies had failed to stop him—that was already something to savor. In 1992 this meeting didn't happen.

Holbrooke and Obama sat down alone. He presented the president-elect with an inscribed copy of *To End a War*. Predictable, self-serving—a small mistake. Obama was the kind of person who, on meeting you, established his no-bullshit credentials by announcing that he *hadn't* read your book.

Obama addressed Holbrooke as "Dick," the name still used by the former Holbrooke associates on the campaign.

"Would you do me a favor, Mr. President?" Holbrooke said. "It's important to my wife that you call me 'Richard.'"

"Richard."

Holbrooke had just corrected the next president, and in a way that could only be called uxorious. That was a bigger mistake.

Obama moved on with his usual discipline. "You are widely considered the best strategic thinker around. I want your advice and counsel as we go forward. I want you on my team. In fact, you are on my short list. Not the only name—"

"So I've read."

"Don't believe everything you've read. Okay, make your pitch."

And then Holbrooke made his third mistake. He had been a passionate believer in racial equality all his life, and as his eyes filled he told the country's first black president—as he'd already told Obama's close friend and advisor Valerie Jarrett a week ago, when he sought her help over breakfast in New York and the same thing happened in her presence—"You know, you don't have to be African American to cry."

Self-promotion, correction, flattery, emotional display. Nothing extreme—but Obama was one of those rare politicians who thought like a writer, on whom nothing was lost. If Holbrooke had *tried* to repel him in their first minute together he couldn't have done a better job.

He made his pitch. It was the same pitch he had made to Carter in 1976, Gore in 1992, and Clinton in 1996—the one about the basketball team that played well together, about the need to pick people who shared his vision. He warned that a "team of rivals"—the title of a new Lincoln biography that was floating around the Obama transition—could easily slip into dysfunctionality. He described his career and achievements, beginning in Vietnam. As for jobs, one position he didn't want was Middle East envoy. He said that Obama might want to consider him for national security advisor—this seemed to come as a surprise. If he wasn't going to get secretary of state, Hillary would be a great choice.

"She sat right where you're sitting and said the same thing about you," Obama told him.

Toward the end Obama's attention drifted. Holbrooke wondered if he was talking too much. But he thought it went well. He called Gelb immediately after and told him so. Gelb wasn't so sure. The "Richard, not Dick" business made him say, "That's a joke, right?" And it worried Gelb that they hadn't talked about foreign policy at all—only process.

In fact it had not gone well. Holbrooke had no sense of his effect on this intensely focused, opaque man. He couldn't read Obama at all—

not just because Obama could be unreadable, but because Holbrooke couldn't read, not when the text was about him. He flew home believing that he had an outside shot at secretary of state. But he'd been called to Chicago only because he was too big not to be called. The president-elect had no job to offer him. And they would never again be alone together.

AFTER TURNING OBAMA DOWN several times, Clinton finally accepted the position ("my patriotic genes," she told Holbrooke), on the condition that she could name her own staff. Talbott had already suggested Holbrooke as her deputy, and she liked the idea. Holbrooke heard this from Talbott and welcomed it—the position would be his highest rank at State—though he had none of the qualities that Talbott had brought to his seven years on the job: evenhandedness, unselfishness, skill in working with other deputies on the NSC.

On November 20, Holbrooke called Clinton. She told him that he would have been her secretary of state if she'd won (saying so cost her nothing now), and he told her that he would be honored to be her deputy. Her reply was warm but not quite definitive. It took another week of phone calls and leaks and ominous silences and an evening of painful talk at the Talbott house, where he always ended up during a career crisis (but now Strobe's wife Brooke was very ill with cancer), through Thanksgiving in the Hamptons with Kati, before Holbrooke understood that the job would go to someone else.

Denis McDonough, a key member of Obama's small inner circle, and Rahm Emanuel, the Chicago congressman who was going to be chief of staff, argued that the White House needed one of its own under Clinton to keep the State Department from becoming a rival power center. The obvious person was Jim Steinberg—Warren Christopher's director of policy planning—since Steinberg, an Obama favorite, needed to be given something big, having lost the job he'd been semi-promised, national security advisor, to General James Jones, a retired marine four-star and former NATO commander who had been brought in to burnish the young Democratic president's national security credentials and insulate him from military pressure.

This was foreign policy as musical chairs, and Holbrooke was the loser. He fell into a gloom that took him right back to the winter of 1992–93, when no one from Bill Clinton's transition called.

But Hillary Clinton needed him, and at the end of November she proposed a job that seemed to her a perfect match. For months there had been talk in Democratic foreign policy circles of a special envoy for Afghanistan and Pakistan. Holbrooke had been among the first to advance the idea. Since he had made the region his focus, taken trips there as a private citizen, and didn't want the Middle East job— that would go to another figure from the Democratic establishment, George Mitchell—Af-Pak seemed right for Holbrooke, and Holbrooke for Af-Pak.

The idea hadn't even come up with Obama in Chicago. A few days after their meeting, as if he sensed a need to improve his pitch, Holbrooke sent the president-elect a memo titled "The Paradoxes of Pakistan and Afghanistan." It was full of bad news and dire warnings, and the main paradox was this: **"The only reason we went into Afghanistan was because of al-Qaeda—and they are not there anymore.** So our war now is against the enemy which poses no direct security threat to the United States—while our real enemy, al-Qaeda, has sanctuary on the soil of our ally, Pakistan." Our objectives were unclear, our resources inadequate, our partners in both countries unreliable. But we couldn't afford to abandon Afghanistan again, however long and painful the commitment. The objective should not be to defeat the Taliban but to work out a deal between Kabul and Islamabad, with the help of neighboring countries. The new president would need to avoid in Afghanistan the trap that had claimed Johnson in Vietnam and Bush in Iraq. "I believe we must be honest with the American public," Holbrooke wrote. "The most serious error would be to promise results on a specific timetable; the second most serious would be to proclaim progress when it doesn't exist."

I don't know if Obama saw the memo. He wouldn't have liked the lecturing tone, even if he appreciated the hard truths. No one around him was enthusiastic about the idea of having Holbrooke in the administration. McDonough distrusted him, and Rice—Obama's choice for U.N. ambassador, fourteen years younger than Holbrooke in the same job—argued vehemently against him. Donilon, the incoming deputy national security advisor, would be his only powerful friend in the

White House, but Donilon wasn't an Obama insider and had his own
position to worry about. The vice president–elect, Joe Biden, had a
long and contentious relationship with Holbrooke going back to the
seventies. As a politician Biden always had to prove his foreign policy
expertise to Holbrooke, and he felt that he never received credit for his
role in standing up to Milosevic during Bosnia. They were practically
the same age, similarly dominating, agreed on almost everything, and
so naturally they couldn't stand each other.

On December 1, Holbrooke and Clinton spent three and a half
hours together in her suite at Essex House in Manhattan. She told him
that she wanted a strong civilian counterpart to the military effort in
Afghanistan—a diplomat who could match David Petraeus, the four-
star general who commanded U.S. forces across the entire region from
Egypt to Pakistan, which was everywhere Americans were fighting. U.S.
policy, heavily militarized under Bush, needed to be brought back into
balance, with diplomacy and development as equal components. That
would be Holbrooke's mandate.

He laid out his requirements. He would report through her to
the president. He would be a kind of secretary of state for Af-Pak, an
Obama advisor with access to the president outside the normal channels. He would assemble a staff from various departments around the
government—an "interagency team," in the jargon—while raiding talent from State's Bureau of South and Central Asia and hiring outside
experts. He would need a plane to get back and forth to the region. He
couldn't limit himself to Afghanistan and Pakistan—India, the giant
neighbor that shaped and warped Pakistani thinking, would fall into his
portfolio, and so would Iran, whose influence in western Afghanistan
he'd seen firsthand in 2006 in Herat. Solving the conundrum of Af-Pak
would require him to negotiate the dispute between India and Pakistan
over Kashmir and also open talks with the Iranians, the first since the
revolution. But he wouldn't be a "special envoy"—he had done that
already in Cyprus and the Balkans. The French word *envoi* sounded too
light, like a pinstriped pigeon. This time around he would run policy in
Washington as well as diplomacy in the region. He would be the special
representative for Afghanistan and Pakistan—SRAP.

He insisted on these things the way his historical predecessor in such
an undertaking, Blowtorch Bob Komer, had demanded the privileges of

a four-star general at CORDS. Holbrooke was drawing the borders of his empire before Obama's team even knew where the map room was.

He put it all in a memo for Clinton. But his role was still vague, and he came away from their conversation with foreboding. She hadn't insisted on her right to name her number two when Steinberg was imposed on her. She'd told Holbrooke that "Chicago" wasn't yet "comfortable" with him. He saw it as a bad omen—it showed insecurity and weakness. He sensed that she didn't understand the bureaucracy she was about to inherit and hardly trusted anyone. "I am deeply torn about this," he wrote in his diary. "An undefined job is like entering a room in which all the seats are taken, then insisting that everyone move to make room . . . Everyone says I must take this job, and I probably will. But with no great enthusiasm or hope I can make much of it, given its difficulties.—My ability to get something done will depend on H + BO willingness to listen to my views—and I am worried on that score."

It took Clinton two weeks to respond to his memo. "Chicago" kept delaying an answer. She reminded Obama of the conditions with which she'd accepted the job, and he told her that Holbrooke was hers if she wanted him. But he would be Clinton's man, not the president's.

RETURNING TO GOVERNMENT meant a 90 percent pay cut just when he was running into financial trouble. He and Kati had Pete Peterson and his wife over for dinner one night to talk about their finances. "Richard, let's start at the beginning," Peterson (net worth $2.8 billion) said. "What is your net cash flow?" Holbrooke didn't know what that meant. "To simplify, your income minus expenses." Peterson added up the cost of all the mortgages, the private plane and the rest, and subtracted it from Holbrooke's new SRAP salary of $177,000. "You're running a negative cash flow that is very significant," Peterson said. "So let's talk about your liquid net worth."

"What's that?"

Peterson went over the value of Holbrooke's investments. "You're divesting your liquid net worth so rapidly that in four or five years you'll be bankrupt. You're going to be in serious trouble."

"What are you saying to me?"

"I'll make it simple. You need to start selling some of these houses."

The bigger of the two in Telluride was particularly expensive and valuable. Holbrooke's face fell—he loved the Telluride house. But Kati said, "Richard, listen to Pete," and Holbrooke agreed to sell it.

He also had to fill out the sixty-three questions of the Transition Questionnaire—a document of recent vintage designed to deter people who've led interesting lives from going to work for their country lest they embarrass the president. "8. Briefly describe the most controversial matters you have been involved with during the course of your career." "61. Have you had any association with any person, group or business venture that could be used—even unfairly—to impugn or attack your character and qualifications for government service?" Instead of telling the Obama transition team the story I've been telling you, in all its detail, Holbrooke answered 8 with a brief CV and 61 with the word "No."

Question 60 was about the state of his health.

On December 10, he went to see his cardiologist, Izzy Rosenfeld, who was now eighty-two years old. Rosenfeld was known in the field as more of a genius at communication than at medicine. He affected a brilliance that seduced celebrity patients, who donated to his hospital, while relying on a series of more qualified partners to keep them alive. A younger cardiologist named Holly Andersen did most of the work on Holbrooke, but Rosenfeld still saw the patient and wrote up the notes. They were mini-essays: "He's on the verge of taking a big job in government and needs to know about his ability to do long trips and hard work . . . The key, as I have explained to him, is rate control and anticoagulation in someone with paroxysmal fibrillation. Time spent was one hour and 20 minutes discussing all the ramifications of his impending appointment by President Obama and whether he will be able to do it."

At sixty-seven years old Holbrooke weighed around 210 pounds, the heaviest he'd ever been. His blood pressure and heart rate were normal with medication, his lungs clear, his carotids clean, and his abdomen soft. He was on Toprol for blood pressure, Coumadin for clotting, Zetia and Niaspan for cholesterol, aspirin, folic acid, and occasionally Viagra. Every couple of years his heart rate went out of control, he felt dizzy, and he had to be cardioverted. In other words, he was a fairly typical late-middle-aged American man. He told his doctor that he was afraid the strain of the new job might put him at risk. But Rosenfeld pronounced his health excellent for a man his age and cleared him for government service.

He found a place in Georgetown one block from his old roost, the Harriman house. Pam, after burning through 90 percent of her hundred-million-dollar inheritance, had sold the mansion in 1996 to settle the lawsuit brought by Averell's heirs, a few months before she suffered a stroke during her morning laps in the Paris Ritz swimming pool, died, and was buried on the Harrimans' Hudson River estate, in the plot she had chosen by the lake, reunited for eternity with Averell beside the gravestone that said PATRIOT, PUBLIC SERVANT, STATESMAN. But even without the Harrimans there, Holbrooke returned to N Street like a homing pigeon and rented a two-story clapboard townhouse for more than he could afford. He would live there alone. Kati would stay in New York, where she had her friends, her children, her life, and come down to Washington for special occasions—like the Obama inauguration.

On January 20, Holbrooke wrote in his diary: "Good speech, but it lacks the unforgettable phrases of JFK—No one will remember any of his lines, but the occasion is the story. Everyone will remember that—Huge crowds. But Washington looks like a happy police state—Security trumps all other considerations, + sometimes gives our government a semi-fascist look."

On the second full day of Obama's presidency, Holbrooke slipped unnoticed past a large crowd that was waiting at the State Department's main doors to cheer the arrival of Hillary Clinton. He'd once imagined that crowd waiting for Secretary of State Richard C. Holbrooke. Instead of ascending in the secretary's private elevator to Mahogany Row on the seventh floor, he crossed the lobby and disappeared down a linoleum and fluorescent hallway. SRAP would occupy a cramped, charmless first-floor suite next to the cafeteria. This was his fourth tour in the building in four decades, and it would be impossible to get farther away, physically and symbolically, from his heart's desire.

A little before two in the afternoon, Obama arrived for the announcement of the special envoys. The ceremony took place in the Benjamin Franklin Room on the eighth floor, in front of golden drapery and granite columns and a crowd of enthusiastic Foreign Service officers. Both Obama and Biden were there, to signal a renewed emphasis on diplomacy after the militarism of the Bush years, and to show support for

Clinton, the opponent in a recent war that still left raw feelings between staffs, if not principals, of the White House and State Department. Holbrooke stood onstage next to the president, and George Mitchell next to the vice president, while the secretary of state, in a gold-and-brown knitted tunic, already confirmed and sworn in, introduced her special envoys.

When it was Holbrooke's turn, he came to the podium and said, "I thank you for your confidence in offering me this daunting assignment, and all I can do is pledge my best to undertake it." His words were a little off. "I see— Thinking of my early years in the Foreign Service, I see my former roommate in Saigon, John Negroponte, here. We remember those days well. And I hope we will produce a better outcome this time."

Afterward the president met the Holbrooke family. Kati beamed at Obama and told him, "Mr. President, this is more than a job for my husband." There were group photos, and the president talked basketball with David, who was the height of an NBA forward, and everyone went away giddy, as people did after meeting Obama in those early days.

Bringing up Vietnam came naturally. There was no way to avoid it. Holbrooke carried that war around with him like a book he had committed to memory when he was young, and now whole passages were coming back to him.

That night he got an email from Rufus Phillips. Holbrooke's boss at Rural Affairs in Saigon in 1963 was now nearly eighty. He offered congratulations and help. Holbrooke wrote back:

"Rufe—It's worse than the Nam!"

III

When the scope of Holbrooke's ambitions got around Washington, Indian diplomats went crazy. In November, ten Pakistani terrorists had killed 164 people during a three-day assault in Mumbai. They were supported by elements of the ISI, but Pakistan was now resisting India's investigation. In the Indian government's view, Pakistan was part of the problem, while India, the world's largest democracy and a rising power that enjoyed a special relationship with the United States, was part of the solution. If Holbrooke intended to hyphenate India into the Af-Pak mess, and pull the age-old dispute with Pakistan over the Indian territory of Kashmir into his brief, he wouldn't get so much as a visa to Delhi. Holbrooke had to back off. He would try to make it through his job without mentioning what he began calling "the K word." So from the start the idea of a grand bargain—Pakistan demobilizes the Afghan Taliban in exchange for some deal over Kashmir—was taken away.

Iran was tricky, too. Clinton appointed another of her husband's old advisors, Dennis Ross, to be her man on the Persian Gulf, taking the suite right next door to SRAP. This squeezed the western flank of Holbrooke's empire, but he wasn't about to back off. Like India, Iran was inextricable from the problem of Afghanistan. After the overthrow of the Taliban, the United States and Iran had worked together to support the new Afghan government, but Bush's "axis of evil" speech in 2002 killed their short-lived cooperation. Tehran, like Delhi, remained close to the government of Karzai, an important source of aid and stability in western Afghanistan. Iran was also the world's leading market for Afghan opium, which created an enormous number of Iranian drug addicts. On paper, the interests of Iran and the United States seemed to converge in Afghanistan, and Holbrooke wanted to set up a channel to talk.

At a conference on Afghanistan in The Hague, he was seated at the table next to that of the Iranian deputy foreign minister. During lunch, Holbrooke stood up, went over, and introduced himself to everyone at the table until he reached the Iranian.

"I'm Richard Holbrooke. Pleased to meet you." He stuck out his hand. The Iranian, taken aback, had no choice but to shake it. Holbrooke mentioned the similarities he'd seen in the mosques of Herat and Isfahan. He was fluent in discussing architecture as if he knew something about it—icebreaking, trust building. And then: "We must keep in touch." The highest-level contact between the United States and Iran in forty years lasted less than thirty seconds. Clinton later told the press that the encounter had been spontaneous—not quite true; she'd given her approval in advance. The Iranians denied it ever took place. There was no second meeting. "Lesson learned," Holbrooke wrote in his diary: "go slow, prepare."

He wasn't just trying to grab turf, though that was how it looked to his colleagues. He knew that the Taliban could not be defeated on the battlefield, that nation building would be long and inconclusive, and that the road to peace would have to go from the outside in, through Afghanistan's neighbors. The most important neighbor was the nightmare to the east.

PAKISTAN WAS under attack from the virus it had developed in its own laboratory. A homegrown group, the Pakistani Taliban, assassinated the former prime minister Benazir Bhutto in 2007 and blew up the Marriott Hotel in Islamabad in 2008. By the start of the Obama presidency, fighters occupied towns a hundred miles from the capital, where they imposed the usual reign of terror—closing girls' schools, banning videos, destroying Buddhist relics, attacking religious minorities, staging public beatings and executions for un-Islamic behavior. There was other trouble around the country—water shortages, power blackouts, riots, secessionists. Pakistan looked more and more like a failing state. And yet the country seemed paralyzed. Half of Pakistan—its poorer and more traditional citizens—sympathized with the Islamists. The urban elites were weak and distracted, unable to face the enormity of the threat. The civilian politicians were divided and undermined by a military class that held real power and continued to see the great threat—maybe the only threat—as India. There was no vital constituency for taking on the Taliban.

Pakistan's military viewed Afghanistan as an extension of Pakistani interests and a zone of competition with India and other Asian countries. Pakistan could not be secure without a government in Kabul that refused Indian influence and accommodated Pakistan. The Afghan Taliban were a tool to prevent Pakistan from being surrounded by hostile neighbors.

So the "Pak" half of Holbrooke's job required a series of complicated and improbable moves: reassure the Pakistanis that American support was not just short-term and transactional; strengthen the civilian government with huge increases in aid; reduce the military's suspicion of India; bring the neighbors into a regional negotiation; and reorient Pakistan's strategy away from supporting the Taliban. Slowly move Pakistan around to the view that it was more threatened by radical Islamists than by India. American officials talked about the country as an abused child—don't react to the screaming and hitting, just hold her tight. Or a heavily armed desperado who had to be approached with great care: "Put down the gun, take off the suicide vest—we're here as your friend."

Pakistan was the main reason why it was worse than the Nam.

At the end of January, Holbrooke invited the Pakistani ambassador, Husain Haqqani, to lunch. They met in the chandeliered restaurant at the Hay-Adams hotel, hard by the White House—an establishment so famous that no reporter who happened to spot them could imagine they were trying to talk in secret. That was Holbrooke's thinking, anyway, but it produced the kind of Washington theater that the new occupants of the building across Lafayette Square despised.

The next day, Haqqani sent a telegram to Islamabad with an account of their conversation:

"He said that contrary to views expressed in some circles, the US had no ulterior motives regarding Pakistan and had no reason or wish to cause disruption in Pakistan. 'The US will never ask Pakistan to do anything that harms Pakistan's national interest' . . .

"Regarding India he said 'I will deal with India by pretending not to deal with India.' Then he added that India also came within the purview of his brief to the extent that it impinged on Pakistan and Afghanistan's security.

"He asked me if the US could 'be friends with both India and Pakistan at the same time.' I saw this as a rhetorical question and limited myself to a very general 'of course, provided Pakistan's national interests are taken care of.'

"He wondered if President Karzai was the best man to lead Afghanistan under the circumstances and whether alternatives were available. I maintained a diplomatic silence. (Mutual friends have told me that Holbrooke has an incredible memory and, therefore, economy in words with him is the best course.) . . .

"He told me that he had dealt with many complex problems in his diplomatic career but he found our region to be the most challenging. Each actor in the region had a complicated and contending vision of self-identity and had contending expectations which could not be fulfilled without creating a new set of issues and problems."

Haqqani was the author of a highly skeptical book about the Pakistani military, and his official cable left out the heart of the conversation—his warning to Holbrooke not to build up Pakistan's army and intelligence service at the expense of the recently elected government of President Asif Zardari, Benazir Bhutto's widower. In the coming months, Holbrooke and Haqqani would become close friends. They would meet frequently, often outside official settings, and Haqqani would set about to teach Holbrooke how to see through Pakistan's deceptions and self-deceptions.

AS IF BY INSTINCT, he modeled SRAP on Rural Affairs—the freedom and openness, the hostility to bureaucratic convention, the sense of excitement and risk. One day Frank Wisner came in to see what his friend was doing and immediately felt that he could find his way around with his eyes closed. He knew the layout of the entire suite, because they had set up the same thing to run pacification in Saigon. The echo troubled Wisner. Why was Holbrooke replicating a failure?

What Holbrooke called "my shitty office" was at one end of the suite, with a window view of an inner courtyard. On the wall were pictures from Saigon and Dayton, photos signed by Cyrus Vance and Kofi Annan, a framed letter from Nixon after his visit to Bonn in 1994, Holbrooke's obituary for Dean Rusk the same year, a 1995 *Times* front page after the breakthrough at Dayton. On a bookshelf he kept a Vietnam-era Zippo lighter inscribed I LOVE FUCKING THE ARMY, AND THE ARMY LOVES FUCKING ME. Out in the hallway there was a map of Bosnia with proposed boundary lines from some stage of the talks, and a bookcase with volumes on Afghanistan and Pakistan, Kipling's *Kim,* Kati's book on presidential marriages, Clark Clifford's memoirs, and three dozen copies of *To End a War.* The office was decorated as a monument to Holbrooke's career. He was letting his staff know that they were going to be part of history.

Some were rising stars from around the government who jumped at the chance to work for a living link to Kennan and Harriman. Young talent from State, the military, the Pentagon, CIA, FBI, Treasury, Agri-

culture, AID—all were detailed to SRAP and squeezed into rooms 1515 and 1517. Others were not the kind of people who normally wore a government badge around their neck, which was one reason they appealed to Holbrooke. His earliest calls were to Barnett Rubin, a professor at New York University and the leading American expert on Afghanistan, and Vali Nasr, an Iranian-born scholar of political Islam. "Your problem is you care about substance," Holbrooke warned Rubin. "Government is all about process." And he told Nasr, "I want you to learn nothing from government. This place is dead intellectually. It does not produce any ideas—it's all about turf battles and checking the box. Your job is to break through all this. Anybody gives you trouble, come to me." Once their security clearances came through, Nasr would advise Holbrooke on Pakistan and Rubin—who knew Karzai well—on Afghanistan.

And there was Rina Amiri, a young Afghan American with family connections to the king. She worked for the United Nations in Kabul, and then for George Soros's Open Society Institute. One night toward the end of February, she spotted Holbrooke on the last Delta shuttle out of Washington, seated herself in the row behind him, and began to argue a point about the coming Afghan elections.

Holbrooke suddenly said, "You know, I'm building this team."

"I know," Amiri said, "but I'm here to lobby you."

"I'm very efficient. I just turned your lobbying into a job interview." When she continued to resist, Holbrooke raised the pressure: "Do you realize no one will offer you the type of opportunity I'm offering to affect your country?"

Amiri held out for the duration of the flight to New York, but within a month she left her job with Soros and came to work for him.

There were two deputies—Paul Jones, a career Foreign Service officer, and Dan Feldman, a lawyer and Gelb protégé—and a notional organization chart that meant almost nothing. In no time thirty people were working for Holbrooke. Any of them could walk into his office and argue with him. They might get yelled at, but they would be listened to.

Barney Rubin was nine years younger than Holbrooke, and the age difference created a political one. Where Holbrooke was a volunteer in the New Frontier, Rubin was a foot soldier of the New Left, a veteran of Students for a Democratic Society who'd been arrested while protesting Vietnam. His eighty-page FBI file made a security clearance even harder than usual. He was a white-bearded professor with the merry-eyed smile of Jerry Garcia and, Holbrooke noted with concern, a face like Trotsky's. He was critical of the war on terror and skeptical of the habitual American conflation of the Taliban with Al Qaeda. He thought that Holbrooke underestimated America's capacity to do harm in the world. Rubin saw the war in political, not moral, terms, and he rolled his eyes whenever Holbrooke found it necessary to preface any reference to the Taliban with "odious." Rubin believed that peace required a settlement with Taliban leaders. Holbrooke didn't know if this was possible, but he wanted to hear the view.

In early February, while Rubin was waiting for his security clearance, he and Holbrooke met at the Asia Society in New York. Later that week there would be a private dinner with Afghanistan experts in the dining room on the eighth floor of the State Department. Holbrooke coached Rubin on how to conduct himself. He wanted Rubin to argue that America should not encourage Karzai to run for re-election—a position that would put him at odds with the secretary. But if Rubin condescended in any way to Clinton, she wouldn't listen to a thing he said. Holbrooke had noticed Rubin's habit of speaking arrogantly to people he thought knew less than he did.

"Okay, I get it," Rubin said. "Funny, I heard exactly the same thing about you."

"See—that's just what I'm talking about."

Another expert on the guest list was Rory Stewart. He had reached a bare minimalist view of Afghanistan: there was no question to which more troops were the answer. America, Britain, and their NATO allies didn't know how to build an Afghan state or end corruption or navigate the tribal politics of an insurgency. The West could only hope to improve things with modest, carefully targeted aid projects in areas where the foreigners were wanted (like Stewart's own Turquoise Mountain Foundation).

A few nights before the dinner, Holbrooke woke Stewart up with a late phone call.

"I know you think there shouldn't be any more troops sent to Afghanistan," Holbrooke began (he never acknowledged that he was interrupting anyone's sleep). The Obama administration was considering the military's request for twenty-one thousand new troops—it was a certainty they'd be deployed. "What you need to know is they will ask for forty thousand more in August." Holbrooke had just heard this stunning number from Admiral Mike Mullen, chairman of the Joint Chiefs of Staff. "And if you think this is a bad thing, Rory, you need to come out and say it." Holbrooke mentioned a major general in Vietnam who had vehemently disagreed with Westmoreland's call for more troops in 1968 but lacked the nerve to make a compelling case against it. If Stewart didn't speak up, Holbrooke said, he'd be haunted for the rest of his life like that two-star. By now Stewart was sitting on his bed, naked, cell phone pressed to his ear. "This is your moment."

On February 3, two dozen people sat around the secretary's elegant dinner table. The guests were divided about equally between the new administration—Denis McDonough and David Axelrod from the White House; Leon Panetta, the new CIA director—and the experts, among them Sarah Chayes, who had lived in Afghanistan longer than Rory Stewart and arrived with equal certitude at exactly the opposite view. Rubin decided not to say anything about Karzai—with so many people it would surely leak, and Karzai would react negatively.

"I think it's fair to say there's never been such brilliance and talent in this room," Holbrooke announced.

"Richard," Clinton said, "if you're done flattering everyone I think we can get on with the program."

Holbrooke arranged for Stewart to sit next to Clinton. Pumped by Holbrooke's pep talk, he delivered an impassioned speech about Western limitations in Afghanistan. Clinton listened and asked polite questions. Stewart waited for Holbrooke to come in behind him with support, but Holbrooke was silent. Afterward Stewart approached him. "How was that?" Holbrooke gave nothing away.

"Best were Barney Rubin + Sarah Chayes, who really know Af + cordially detest each other," Holbrooke wrote in his diary. "Rory Stewart spoke for all Rudyard Kipling nostalgists everywhere, calling for more Rory-like experts + more respect for the tribes." He wanted Clinton to hear the case against more troops, but on such a sensitive issue he wasn't going to stick his neck out in front of so many important players, none more than his boss. This became Holbrooke's strategy for the rest of the year.

IV

Afghanistan was a bloody ghost from the past, and Pakistan was a sinister hall of mirrors, but the really dangerous theater was Washington.

The day after Inauguration Day, an aide to Donilon drafted Holbrooke's "terms of reference"—government-speak for a job description. But in the chaos of the new administration's first days, no one signed off on a final version. From the beginning there was no clear definition of mandates, overlaps, divisions of labor between SRAP and the NSC. As a result, no one in the White House understood Holbrooke's job.

If he had a counterpart there, it was Douglas Lute, an army lieutenant general who had served as Bush's special assistant on Iraq and Afghanistan, "coordinating" and "implementing" war policy, meaning that he made sure problems were identified and decisions carried out efficiently. Obama's aides wanted to get rid of him as an unreliable holdover, but the new national security advisor, James Jones, persuaded the president that Lute was a loyal soldier. He was kept on the NSC, though demoted to senior director for Afghanistan. When the new team arrived at the White House the day after the inauguration, Lute was already there and had to point out where the coffee machine and restrooms were.

Lute was a midwesterner, a big man with a cheerful, unpretentious manner, comfortable within government structures. He was the kind of official Holbrooke had spent his whole career disregarding. In fact they had crossed paths in 1996, when Holbrooke, a banker again, was sent to pressure Milosevic to keep his end of the Dayton bargain. By then Wes Clark had moved on, and his replacement on Holbrooke's trip was Colonel Lute. When Holbrooke arrived, very late, at Andrews Air Force Base and boarded the C-20, his eyes fell on Lute. "Who are you?" Holbrooke demanded. "I didn't approve you on this flight."

"I can get my bag and leave in five minutes," Lute said.

"No, I don't mean it that way."

Early the next morning in Belgrade there was a knock on Lute's hotel room door. Holbrooke stood there in his bathrobe, barefoot. "Have you got a pair of socks?" He'd forgotten to pack extras, or already sweated through them all. His feet—those instruments of pain and domination, so easily transformed from his own discomfort to that of others. Lute gave him a pair of military-issue dress socks. That was how they met.

Lute was blindsided by Holbrooke's appointment as SRAP—even by the job title. Their offices were bound to be a point of friction if the lines of authority weren't clear. Holbrooke made a habit of walking uninvited into Lute's windowless basement office in the West Wing, leaving the door open behind him, taking off his shoes, and putting his stocking feet up on Lute's desk. He stayed however long he wanted no matter what items on Lute's calendar needed attention that hour. Often these visits came just before a meeting in the Situation Room. Lute's team was responsible for writing the talking points—the three- or four-page agenda, the crown jewels of the NSC—which the president alone got to see the night before. Holbrooke was after any advance intelligence he could get. Lute thought that the feet on his desk showed just how Holbrooke saw him: a useful paper pusher.

Lute repeatedly asked Jones for Holbrooke's terms of reference, but Jones blew him off—they would figure it out as they went along.

Jones was a veteran of Vietnam and Bosnia. He had spent a lot of his marine career in command, including as commandant of the corps itself, and, just before his retirement, in Clark's old job at NATO. He was six four, broad shouldered, a blue-eyed French-speaking John Wayne marine, and he was used to giving orders and having other people carry them out crisply. Now, at sixty-five, he was tasked to be the president's top staffer, a brutal job, swamped in details, on demand every hour of the day. It was too much for him. Holbrooke knew it right away. When

Obama and his foreign policy team gathered in the Madison Room of the State Department on January 22 just before the rollout, Holbrooke noticed that Jones seemed marginal—out of it. Jones spent the weekend after the inauguration at his vacation house on Maryland's Eastern Shore. He looked the part, but he was Obama's first big mistake.

Donilon, Jones's deputy, complained to Holbrooke that Jones read mechanically from his agenda and was slow to understand the subject under discussion. Others thought Jones might be neurologically impaired. It soon became clear that Donilon would have to run the NSC day-to-day, waking up early enough to prepare the president's nine-thirty a.m. brief. Within a few days Donilon was exhausted from doing two jobs.

"You're a brilliant staff person, but now you have to have opinions," Holbrooke told Donilon one day, after going upstairs from Lute's basement warren and barging into Donilon's broom closet next to Jones's corner office. "You can't just spot issues—you need to lead." He was still advising Donilon as if it were the nineties, the way he used to stretch out on Donilon's couch outside Warren Christopher's office and opine for an hour. But things were different now, and Donilon—smart, skillful, and no one to count on under pressure—was going to play it both ways with Holbrooke.

CLINTON WANTED the president to get to know his SRAP, and she brought Holbrooke along to one of her first weekly meetings in the Oval Office. Just the three of them, sitting around the presidential coffee table on furniture left behind by the Bush administration, the décor of a prosperous Dallas living room. Obama was forty-six years old. Six one, Holbrooke's height, but thirty pounds lighter. Even wirier than in pictures. A long face with deep grooves running down either side of his nose, but no gray hair yet. He listened while Holbrooke sketched out a strategy that would involve all the actors in the region—bring India in through a back channel, talk to Iran about Herat and the West, have the Chinese and Saudis work on their ally Pakistan, eventually open up a dialogue with the Taliban. "And we'll have to deceive each of them about what we're willing to do. You've got this big decision on troops and we've got to see what we can get out of these diplomatic—"

Obama cut him off. "We don't do that in this administration." No deception, no lying. Lying was the old way of doing diplomacy. Lies had led to the disaster in Iraq. The Bush administration had besmirched America's reputation around the world, and Obama's mandate was to restore it—end torture, close Guantánamo. The Obama way would be honest and straight.

Holbrooke was sitting forward on a floral cream-and-beige sofa. Clinton saw him thinking, *What the hell are you talking about? How do you think I got Milosevic to the table?* That was her thought as well. He recovered quickly. "I mean," he said, "we've got to figure out what we're going to say and how we're going to say it." But a coolness was now coming from the president—Clinton felt it. The purpose of the meeting, to forge a connection between the two men, had failed.

The public, dazzled by Obama's campaign speeches, his charming banter with Ellen and Oprah, never saw the president his staff was getting to know, the man who walked briskly into the Situation Room, sat down, and said, "Let's get started." He wasted no time on greetings or small talk. He was, Holbrooke thought, the opposite of Bill Clinton—disciplined like a corporate boss, comfortable giving orders, impatient, sometimes cold. Obama had the remoteness of an introvert who didn't pretend affection any more than he'd lie about having read your book. His sense of integrity depended on refusing to backslap. He saved his warmth for the few who really generated it—his family, his old friends. The distance he kept from his advisors gave him a power Clinton never had. Still, Holbrooke wished he'd smile or laugh now and then.

Obama was faced with two foreign quagmires and an economic catastrophe. He was already a historic figure, a democratic prince, the JFK of a new generation. Holbrooke had worked for every Democratic president since Kennedy. He wanted badly to win the trust of this one.

Obama had to make an immediate decision on the military's request for seventeen thousand additional combat troops and four thousand trainers in Afghanistan—necessary for staving off growing chaos in the south and providing security for the Afghan election in August. Holbrooke thought that the president should approve the troops, not just because of the eroding situation in Afghanistan but for political reasons at home. During the campaign, Obama had promised to shift the effort from Iraq to Afghanistan, declaring, "This is a war that we have to win."

Holbrooke also thought that the military was trying to squeeze the new president with deceptive numbers and a rushed decision.

David Petraeus, the commander of Central Command, was the most famous and powerful American general since Vietnam. He was in his mid-fifties, a workout fanatic, lean and slightly hunched from a near-fatal gunshot to the chest during a training accident. His single-mindedness sculpted his face and deprived him of any sense of humor. He had a PhD from Princeton—his dissertation was called "The American Military and the Lessons of Vietnam." He was a genius at press relations, answered reporters' emails within minutes. He made warfare seem intellectually exciting, like an extension of the social sciences. He believed that counterinsurgency could succeed if the military stayed attuned to political pressures.

In the winter of 2009, Petraeus was coming off eighteen months in Iraq during which he had brilliantly applied the ideas of his thesis and of the army's counterinsurgency field manual as revised by him. His strategy of protecting the population and making deals with former enemies helped to pull Iraq back from disintegration and dramatically reduced the violence. It was the first hopeful turn since the start of the war. The surge defied the dismal predictions of Democrats like Obama and Clinton. Republicans wrote Petraeus a blank check, and counterinsurgency became an armed faith. It would take a lot of political courage for Obama to stand up to Petraeus.

One night in January, Clinton invited Holbrooke and Petraeus, who had never met, to the brick mansion she owned near Embassy Row. They sat before her fireplace and talked for two hours about Afghanistan, though Petraeus kept changing the subject to Iraq, which dominated his thinking as much as Vietnam dominated Holbrooke's. Petraeus had Wes Clark's competitiveness but far more shrewdness and self-control. Holbrooke found him more than a match—willful and skilled at evading hard questions. When Holbrooke asked for his objective, Petraeus said vaguely that he wanted to deny Al Qaeda a sanctuary in Afghanistan, which wasn't much of an answer. They got along well, thanks to Clinton's tactful mediation, but afterward Petraeus took to calling Holbrooke "my diplomatic wingman," which annoyed Holbrooke. It suggested how Petraeus saw the relationship between soldiers and civilians. "His job should be to drop the bombs when I tell him to," Holbrooke told his aides. But the military had been winning that fight for a long time—his whole career.

He kept thinking about 1965. That was the year when Johnson, after being elected, increased the number of troops in Vietnam from 23,000 to 184,000. The parallels with 2009 and Obama were uncanny. Holbrooke photocopied and passed around the pages from *Counsel to the President* about Clifford's conversations with LBJ that July. He didn't want Obama to be pressured by Petraeus and the military into the same blind escalation. But the excerpting of his own ghostwritten prose seemed self-aggrandizing to his colleagues and few bothered to read the pages.

"I believe that history, with all its uncertainties, will be written in the next few months," he wrote in his diary.

ON FEBRUARY 13, Holbrooke was in Kabul on his first trip to the region since his appointment. In the Situation Room the president and his advisors were meeting to make a final decision on the troops. Clinton was giving a speech at the Asia Society and had asked Holbrooke to fill in for her. He sat in a darkened room in the U.S. embassy, connected by secure video teleconference to the White House. It was past midnight in Kabul and Holbrooke was tired. When Obama called on him, he began to read from notes he'd written down in a lined copybook.

"Let me speak on Secretary Clinton's behalf, and at her direct instructions, in support of Option 2." This was the option to send seventeen thousand combat troops in one deployment rather than splitting them up into two tranches. "We do so with reluctance, and mindful of the difficulties entailed in any troop deployment. This is a difficult decision, especially at a time when Afghanistan faces a political and constitutional crisis over its own elections that further complicates your decision. As your first decision to send troops overseas and into combat—as opposed to Iraq—this decision lies at the savage intersection of policy, politics, and history."

"Who talks like this?" Obama murmured. He sounded genuinely puzzled. Everyone around the Situation Room table heard him, but Holbrooke, seven thousand miles away, didn't hear and kept going.

"It is in many ways strange to send more American troops into such a potentially chaotic political situation. If we send more troops, of course we deepen our commitment, with no guarantee of success. And the shadow of Vietnam hovers over us."

Obama interrupted him. "Richard, what are you doing? Are you reading something?"

Holbrooke, on-screen, explained that the secretary had wanted to be sure the president heard her views accurately. He continued, "But if we do not send more troops, the chances of both political chaos and Taliban success increase."

"Why are you reading?" Obama insisted.

Holbrooke stopped to explain again. He managed to get through the rest of his notes, which could have been summed up in a couple of lines. But he had lost the president. He didn't understand what he'd done wrong, only that Obama sounded annoyed and ignored him for the rest of the meeting.

It was the worst encounter he'd had with a president since Jimmy Carter chewed him out in South Korea in 1979 over troop withdrawals. He regretted reading his notes aloud. He'd done so in order *not* to ramble on, but it had sounded like a speech or a first draft of his memoirs. A few younger people seated back against the walls found it exciting to hear this old lion talk about savage intersections, but no one around the table wanted to be addressed like that, and when Obama expressed irritation they could only conclude that Holbrooke was already out of favor with the new president. Which meant that nobody had to worry about him. After the meeting, Obama told Jones that he would tolerate Holbrooke in the Situation Room only if he kept his remarks short, and that he wanted to be in Holbrooke's presence as little as possible.

A couple of months later, after a meeting in the Oval Office between Presidents Obama, Karzai, and Zardari—an event orchestrated at great effort by the SRAP team—Holbrooke was lingering to thank Obama when the president asked to speak to him alone. He drew Holbrooke out into the hall and said how much he valued him. Then he added, "I don't like leaks of any sort, and you've done some. They're disruptive."

Donilon and McDonough had complained to Obama about leaks from Holbrooke. He started to defend himself.

"I don't want to hear your reply," Obama said.

"Mr. President, I must reply, since you've made a serious charge which isn't true. If you lose confidence in me, I can't function effectively."

"I have confidence in you," Obama said and walked away. Holbrooke was left shaking.

He didn't tell Kati—she would get so mad that she'd tell someone else and the story would leak. Instead he took his bitterness to Donilon, who told him not to worry—the president did the same to him and others. Obama sometimes stuck a finger in Donilon's chest when he was blaming him for something. But in fact Obama had a distaste for Holbrooke, almost a physical repulsion that made him go cold. At a White House reception during the week of Karzai's and Zardari's visit, Holbrooke was laying the flattery on so thick—"Mr. President, that was a brilliant speech"—that Obama's body language conveyed open contempt.

And yet Holbrooke left most of their encounters feeling what he had felt in Chicago: *That went well*. On the way out of the White House he'd tell Jake Sullivan, Clinton's aide, "Jake, that was fantastic," and Sullivan, who had seen colleagues rolling their eyes, had to set the much older man straight: "No, we really have our work cut out for us, they weren't convinced at all."

Sullivan was in his early thirties, from Minnesota. He was sincere, effective, and a rare Clinton person who was popular at the White House, which required him to devote a lot of time to repairing damage created by Holbrooke. Obama reminded Sullivan of his Yale law professors—he wanted a logical, linear presentation of the case before him. That was Sullivan's way of thinking, too, but he was also one of the younger officials who admired Holbrooke. He imagined Holbrooke as a diplomat from a foreign country—the past—who thought he was speaking eloquently when he was barely fluent in the local language.

Sullivan was one of Les Gelb's many protégés spread around the administration's national security archipelago. The stories about Obama and Holbrooke got back to Gelb, and he tried to help his friend.

"Stop the ass-kissing." Gelb was the only one who talked to Holbrooke like that.

"I'm not ass-kissing. If he says something really smart, why can't I compliment him?"

"Dick, just stop, don't do it. I know Obama hates it."

"Who told you that?"

"People in the meeting. I'm not going to tell you who told me, but I wouldn't say it to you unless I knew it for an outright fact. Stop it."

Holbrooke didn't know what Gelb was talking about. He expected to be one of the president's main advisors. He asked Donilon to set up a meeting with Obama, but Donilon angrily refused—that wasn't how the NSC worked. Late one night in March he called up Ben Rhodes, the president's foreign policy speechwriter, who was at home after finishing a speech on Afghanistan that Obama was to give the next day.

"Ben, I'm here at Café Milano with David Petraeus. We have some edits to your speech." Over the loud background noise of a Washington power restaurant, Holbrooke dictated the edits, which made U.S. goals for improvements in Afghan governance more ambitious. "Are you going to take them?"

"Yeah, I'll take most of them, but the president has the speech now and I don't know what he's going to do with it."

"You *must* take these edits. They're from me and David Petraeus."

Rhodes was a former aspiring novelist who once might have been pleased by a phone call from Richard Holbrooke, but intrusions like this—Holbrooke assuming he had a privileged relationship with the president, like Harriman's with Kennedy or Clifford's with Johnson—were driving Rhodes toward the dimmer view taken by his friend Denis McDonough. Obama ignored most of Holbrooke's changes.

Government had grown specialized, compartmentalized, and that suited Obama, who was a stickler for orderly process—a technocrat disguised as a visionary. But Holbrooke required a sense of drama in heightened language to make the work come alive. He wanted SRAP's weekly memos to the president crafted in textured sentences, and when his aides wrote bureaucratic prose he dressed them down and forced multiple revisions. Obama, who also loved good writing, hated Holbrooke's memos and asked Donilon to rewrite them first so that he could understand what Holbrooke was trying to say without the flourishes and flattery.

Maybe Holbrooke lost some edge in the years out of service—all the dinners IHO some glittering new friend. Maybe part of the trouble was having become a personage. When he returned to action he didn't stop to survey the terrain, assess the friendlies and enemies, take stock of his equipment and ability. He didn't see what a steep climb this last mountain would be. And even when he finally accepted that the president disliked him ("Obama has ice water running in his veins," he told the younger woman who had been his lover), he didn't know why or what to do. He couldn't change the character of a long life in which he'd always been his immovable self. He didn't even have the insight to adjust his tactics. So he began to panic, but panic only led him to try harder and make things worse.

I CAN'T HELP thinking the heart of the matter was Vietnam. Holbrooke brought it up all the time. He couldn't resist. He passed around copies of a book he'd recently reviewed, *Lessons in Disaster,* about McGeorge Bundy and the fatally flawed decisions that led to escalation. He invoked the critical months of 1965 so portentously that Obama once asked him, "Is that the way people used to talk in the Johnson administration?" It wasn't just that Holbrooke was becoming a Vietnam bore, a sodden old vet staggering out of the triple-canopy jungle to grab strangers by the shirtfront and make them listen to his harrowing tale. Obama actually didn't want to hear about Vietnam. He told his young aides that it wasn't relevant, and they agreed: Vietnam was ancient history. Obama was three when Clifford warned Johnson not to send ground troops. McDonough and Rhodes were years from being born.

You could understand the response. What was Obama supposed to do with the analogy? It didn't tell him how many more troops could make a difference in Helmand province. It told him that his presidency might be destroyed by this war. It was the note of doom in the Situation Room. It turned Holbrooke into a lecturer, condescending to the less experienced man, and that was as intolerable to Obama as flattery. He liked young, smart, ultra-loyal staffers. He didn't like big competitive personalities.

The divide between them began with temperament, widened with generation, and ended in outlook. Obama—half Kenyan, raised in Indonesia, Pakistani friends in college—saw himself as the first president who understood the United States from the outside in. He grasped the limits to American power and knew that not every problem had an American solution. The Bush administration, and Clinton's before it, had fallen prey to the hubris of a lone superpower. Then came the Iraq War and the economic collapse, and a reckoning required us to sober up.

Obama wouldn't say so, but his task was to manage our decline, which meant using power wisely. He embodied—his long slender fingers pressed skeptically against his cheek as he listened from the head of the table in the Situation Room—the very opposite of the baggy grandiosity that thought we could do anything and the craven fear of being called weak for not trying. My guess is Obama wasn't thinking of the Berlin airlift or Dayton, only of the impulses that sank America in Vietnam and Iraq. The president and his aides believed these were Holbrooke's impulses too, when in fact he was only saying, *Be careful. It could happen to you.* Obama didn't want to hear it—couldn't hear it, because the speaker kept distracting him with theatrics and bombast worthy of LBJ himself.

So Obama told Jones, and Jones told Clinton, and Clinton told Holbrooke: stop it with Vietnam. "They don't think they have anything to learn from Vietnam," she said.

"They're going to make the same mistakes!"

Holbrooke confessed to Gelb that even Hillary wasn't interested.

He tried to stop, but it was impossible. How could he not be haunted? There was nothing new under the sun. Somehow, after a half-century excursion across the heights of American greatness, we had returned to the exact same place. All the questions in Afghanistan had been the questions in Vietnam. Could we transform their society? If not, could we still win the war? Did our very effort make it less likely? What leverage did we have? Should we get rid of their leader? Could we talk our way out?

It is beyond ironic that 40+ years later, we are back in Vietnam. Of course, everything is different—and everything is the same. And somehow, I am back in the middle of it, the only senior official who really lived it. I had not thought much about VN for years, now it comes back every day. Every program has its prior incarnation—mostly unsuccessful. Yet the 9/11 difference is also there. The V Cong + the North Vietnamese posed no threat to the US . . . Gates will be in same spot as McNamara, Biden will play George Ball, and I—well,

I think we must recognize that military success is not possible, + we must seek a negotiation. But with who? The Taliban are not Hanoi, + their alliance with Al Qaeda is a deal-breaker.

Here was the paradox: he knew from Vietnam that what we were doing in Afghanistan wouldn't work—but he thought he could do it anyway. He was speaking with Wisner regularly and Gelb daily, sometimes several times a day. They heard him out, expressed their doubts, and encouraged him to press on. They drove him deeper into the paradox because, knowing both Vietnam and Holbrooke, they thought the same thing: it was impossible, but he might succeed. Because if not Holbrooke, who?

And there was something else. If he applied the real lesson of Vietnam—"*Don't*"—he would be out of a job. And then who would he be?

Over time he learned to save Vietnam for his staff. He got Rufus Phillips to tell them about Rural Affairs and Lionel Rosenblatt to talk about CORDS. One day, as he sat through another White House meeting on Afghanistan, listening to another optimistic military briefing, a quote surfaced from the deep past, and he scribbled it down on a scrap of paper and took it back to the office to show his young aides, who of course had no idea where it came from:

"How can we lose when we're so sincere?"

V

Holbrooke believed that the war would be lost if Karzai remained in the Arg for another five years. Along with civilian casualties and the sanctuary in Pakistan, his government's corruption was the Taliban's best weapon. Karzai believed that Afghanistan was the battleground of a new Great Game, an imperial grab for land and resources, with America and China the strategic competitors in place of nineteenth-century Britain and Russia. He talked wildly about going to the mountains and joining his "brothers," the insurgents. He was increasingly unpopular among Afghans, including his fellow Pashtuns, as the promise of 2002 dimmed in the rising blood tide.

One lesson Holbrooke took from 1963 was that America shouldn't choose other countries' leaders—not through coups and assassinations anyway. But there were other ways to get rid of Karzai. Holbrooke's first priority as SRAP was to prevent him from winning re-election in August. He didn't try to hide the fact—he was extraordinarily indiscreet about it. Indiscretion seemed to be the only consistent tactic in his approach to Karzai.

Just after his appointment, Holbrooke told Zalmay Khalilzad, the Afghan-American diplomat who'd been ambassador in Kabul during Karzai's early years and was quite close to the president, "I'm going to make his life a living hell." Khalilzad warned him to be careful saying such things—what if he was stuck with Karzai? The comment must have both tantalized and alarmed Khalilzad, who was exploring a run for the

Afghan presidency himself, but who also thought that you shouldn't put a gun to a king's head unless you damn well intended to pull the trigger.

Holbrooke was right about Karzai—but he had no strategy, and no one else in Washington had the clarity or courage to back him. He was making it up as he went along, with no authority in official policy. He calculated that if enough candidates, especially Pashtuns, entered the race, they would run up the anti-Karzai vote, deprive him of a majority, and force a second round in which the opposition would unite around a single candidate, who would go on to win. This was wishful thinking based on no analysis of voting data or even conversations with Afghan insiders, most of whom expected Karzai to win outright because he had the power of the presidency and there was no one who could beat him.

Holbrooke encouraged so many Afghan politicians to enter the race that Ahmad Zia Massoud, the first vice president, lamented, "I must be the only person in Kabul whom Holbrooke has not invited to challenge Karzai for the presidency." Holbrooke claimed that an open and competitive race would be good for Afghan democracy—America wasn't choosing sides, just seeking a level playing field. But Afghans took his efforts to mean that omnipotent America intended for someone other than Karzai to win. Each potential candidate assumed that he would get American support and was disappointed when it turned out not to be true. An aspect of Afghans' fierce independence was that every last one of them seemed to think he would make the best president and would win if he ran.

Holbrooke's maneuvers enraged Karzai, who knew just how to use a foreigner's clumsy interference in Afghan politics.

Holbrooke's main source of insight into Karzai was the British ambassador, Sir Sherard Cowper-Coles, who had been in Kabul for two years and saw the Afghan president almost every day. To keep up with the Americans, Foreign Secretary David Miliband was about to appoint Cowper-Coles as the British Holbrooke. In his diary, Holbrooke called him "my semi-neo-colonial UK counterpart, smart + supportive + cunning + not entirely trustworthy." Holbrooke enjoyed mocking him for belonging to Brooks's, a posh private club in Piccadilly, where they were seated at the best corner table, to Holbrooke's obvious pleasure.

The British, who had thousands of soldiers fighting in southern Afghanistan, believed that a military strategy without a political strategy—plunging ahead with another election, more troops, more money, without finding a way to improve governance out in the districts and involve neighboring countries in a regional solution—would lead to disaster. Holbrooke was sympathetic to this view. When he and Cowper-Coles sat down with Clinton and Miliband in the foreign secretary's vast office overlooking Horse Guards Parade, Cowper-Coles began describing Karzai's complex personality. He prescribed a delicate daily mix of "public respect and private tough love" as the best way to handle Karzai. Holbrooke had already violated just about every word of the prescription.

Clinton suddenly asked, "Is he gay?"

"Madam Secretary, he's bisexual," Cowper-Coles answered at once. "He has a crush on his minister of mines."

Cowper-Coles had a semi-neocolonial idea for what to do with Karzai during the election year. Instead of trying to get rid of him, kick him upstairs—give him the title last held by Zahir Shah, make him "the Father of the Nation," presiding over a *loya jirga* that would seek national reconciliation regardless of election results. Maybe not even have an election. That might be just the way to appeal to Karzai's sense of his own destiny.

Snow was falling hard when Holbrooke flew into Kabul late one night in February for his first official meeting with Karzai. Two days before, the Taliban had carried out a bloody series of attacks on government targets across the capital, and everyone was rattled. Holbrooke slept at the embassy residence, in the diplomatic quarter that every year looked more like Baghdad's Green Zone, layers within layers of blast walls and razor wire. In the morning the senior U.N. official in Kabul, Kai Eide, a Norwegian diplomat, came to the embassy for breakfast. Holbrooke didn't care for Eide, or for the American ambassador, William Wood, nicknamed "Chemical Bill" because of his enthusiasm for spraying poppy fields with herbicides—a practice Holbrooke found completely counterproductive and vowed to end. Holbrooke was pushing Wood out and had already found his replacement—Karl Eikenberry, the general whom Holbrooke had annoyed and impressed in Kabul back in 2006. But Holbrooke had no control over Eide.

As soon as they sat down in Wood's living room, Holbrooke asked Eide, "When does your contract expire?" It was a tactless question at best.

"I've just renewed it for another year."

Holbrooke took this in. "I understand you're an old friend of Peter Galbraith." Eide and Galbraith had known each other in Zagreb during the Balkan wars, where Eide had introduced Galbraith to a Norwegian U.N. worker who became his wife. Holbrooke wanted Galbraith for the job of Eide's deputy in Kabul, where he could act as Holbrooke's man. Eide didn't think that Galbraith would make a good number two— nor did Galbraith, who thought he should be number one—but Holbrooke obviously had the fix in with Eide's boss, Secretary-General Ban Ki-moon.

Then Holbrooke brought up Karzai. Everyone agreed that he couldn't stay on, he said, but no one knew who should replace him or how to do it. "Who would be the best candidate?" He asked about Hanif Atmar, the minister of interior and the most impressive member of Karzai's cabinet. "I'm going to call him."

"Don't do that," Eide said. "Karzai will know immediately."

But the next day Holbrooke met with Atmar, a former Communist who had lost a leg fighting against the mujahedin in the 1980s. Atmar politely declined the invitation of disloyalty. By the time Holbrooke went to see the president, Karzai knew what he was up against.

On February 14 they met in Karzai's small, book-lined office on the second floor of the Arg. They hadn't seen each other in a year and mutual hostility had been building the whole time. "I'm a friend of the United States," Karzai said, "but an angry friend, a friend who has been hurt."

Holbrooke floated the British proposal—only he presented it as "Miliband and Cowper-Coles want to get rid of you." Karzai, who believed some wild conspiracy theories about British plots in Afghanistan, later told Cowper-Coles that he didn't believe Holbrooke. He knew who really wanted to get rid of him. It was indiscreet at best, maybe even treacherous, for Holbrooke to hang his British counterpart out to dry like that, but Cowper-Coles didn't hold it against him for long. He had a bit of a crush on Holbrooke, a diplomatic crush, and he spent the rest of the year and the next chasing Holbrooke around the world, from meeting to meeting, trying to hold his flickering attention for thirty seconds in order to solve Afghanistan together, and generally being ignored.

After Holbrooke's departure from Kabul, Karzai summoned Eide to the palace. "He is after you and he is after me," Karzai said.

THE REFORMERS AMONG Karzai's advisors wanted the president to step aside. They thought that a carefully orchestrated campaign of gentle persuasion by Holbrooke, other diplomats, and key Afghans might ease Karzai out of the Arg and into the role of a father figure who had moved Afghanistan toward a brighter future. And they all watched Holbrooke's efforts with growing dismay. Everything he did seemed to strengthen the president's hand.

In the incestuous world of Afghan politics, the details of Holbrooke's visits—he came to Kabul every six or eight weeks and was careless about speaking on unsecure cell phones—flew around the capital. How his tone and posture conveyed aggression—he even displayed the soles of his feet! How he told Karzai to fire his half brother, Ahmed Wali Karzai, the main power broker in Kandahar, a man steeped in corruption and drug trafficking as well as being on the CIA payroll. But the Karzai family had been running Kandahar for hundreds of years, the reformers explained to Holbrooke. The president's base was there. How could he just get rid of his brother?

Afghans knew Holbrooke's history in the Balkans. They warned him that Afghanistan was different. Intimidation and bullying and dick-swinging—the common notion of Holbrooke's success with Milosevic—wouldn't work here. If you cornered an Afghan he would have no choice but to fight. There was a large supply of proverbs on this score, such as "You cannot get an Afghan to heaven with you by force, but by friendship you can take him to hell." Rina Amiri, the Afghan American on Holbrooke's staff, told him, "We Afghans will self-destruct before we give up our pride and honor. That's what you need to understand about us. It's our strength and our tragedy."

The effect of Holbrooke's anti-Karzai campaign was to offend Afghan sensibilities and rally Pashtun support around the president. If Karzai won in August, some Afghan politicians thought, it would be partly Holbrooke's fault.

By spring Holbrooke realized that he wouldn't be able to keep Karzai out of the race. He sat on the lawn of the embassy compound with the *Times*'s Dexter Filkins and, off the record, admitted defeat.

"The problem with this whole goddam thing is Karzai. His government is so corrupt—we're going to lose if we can't change it. He's been in power too long and this is what happens. When I got this job my first order of business was to make sure he didn't run for re-election. It didn't work—my effort failed. I tried—I even went to the president. He didn't really listen, amid the inevitable distractions of a new administration. Nobody's up to speed, nobody knows the background, all the jobs are vacant. But I'm up to speed."

HE FOUND OTHER WAYS than politics to get the civilian side involved—in the language of his youth, to ramp up "the other war." He pushed his staff to come up with plans for agriculture, prison reform, health and education, counter-narcotics, information warfare. The Obama administration was increasing spending in both Afghanistan and Pakistan by billions of dollars, and Holbrooke took over all the contracts, which created huge bottlenecks at his office. He wanted aid officials working alongside Afghans in the field, like in Rural Affairs under Rufus Phillips, instead of reviewing proposals and writing cables in the Green Zone. He tore up some contracts and rewrote others to push the money to local governments and villagers rather than American companies. "Nation building" was just as dirty a word for Obama as for Bush, but that's what this was, even by the latest euphemism: "fully integrated civil-military effort."

Holbrooke had done it all in Vietnam, and it had failed. Yet he threw himself into Komer's old role of pacification czar with an energy that sometimes resembled the panic of an animal trying to escape from a trap. In the first half of 2009—always obliged to ask the White House for approval of his trips and then chisel a Pentagon C-20—he flew to Islamabad five times, Kabul four, and thirteen other world capitals from Riyadh to Tokyo. The monthly travel to the ends of the earth and back, the hundreds of White House meetings, the weekend sprints up to New York—he complained constantly of exhaustion. He was always arriving late and leaving early, always on his phone or BlackBerry, reading a newspaper while someone was briefing him, walking out of meetings to take calls that always seemed to come from "the secretary," even when his aides suspected it was Kati. No one was spared his inattention—not cabinet members, not even Petraeus, who began to think Holbrooke suffered from attention deficit disorder. He read his newspaper in the Situation Room, he answered his phone in Clinton's office. "You have to put your phone away," she told him sharply—it was forbidden to bring an electronic device into the secretary's suite. Only Obama, who didn't want it, had his full attention.

He hadn't lost his huge appetite for details, his need to understand from the ground up. He flew to Helmand province, the heart of the insurgency and the opium trade, where he quizzed the governor on the export of wheat and whether farmers could be induced to grow pomegranates instead of poppies. He bore deep into the subject of cold-storage facilities in Wardak. His colleagues in the Situation Room couldn't understand why he went on about Afghan agriculture. Defense Secretary Robert Gates, who came from Kansas, scoffed at his instant expertise. Others thought that the war's intractability was making him flit from idea to idea in a manic state. But everything in Afghanistan—including the next White House debate over troops and strategy, including the possibility of a political settlement—was on hold for the election. So Holbrooke's hand looked for something else to do with his might, and it found pomegranates.

KARL EIKENBERRY, Holbrooke's pick as ambassador, was an awkward man, and rigid about rank and rules—he had spent his life in the army—but a subtle and unorthodox thinker. He not only knew Afghanistan from his military tours of duty, he cared about the people—was recognized on the streets of Kabul, often traveled to villages and walked through markets, even gave blood alongside his wife after a suicide bombing—and Afghans appreciated it. He once fell into a conversation about Osama bin Laden with a Kabul auto mechanic. "Maybe one day you'll get bin Laden," the mechanic said, "but remember, there are a hundred bin Ladens in Afghanistan and they're all in the government."

Eikenberry saw problems that short-term Americans might have thought fixable but he knew were firmly entrenched: low morale and high attrition in the Afghan army; chronic corruption and incapacity in the government; Pakistani treachery that allowed the Taliban to withstand whatever NATO threw at them. As a commander he had come to believe that the only hope was to give Afghans ownership of the fight. As a retired general he was uniquely qualified to cast a skeptical eye on American military strategy.

When Eikenberry came to Washington for his confirmation in April 2009, he had a beer with Petraeus at the Four Seasons Hotel.

"Karl, your biggest problem as ambassador will not be Hamid Karzai," Petraeus said. "It will be Richard Holbrooke."

Eikenberry laughed uneasily. "What do you mean?"

"Mark my words."

It took a few months for Eikenberry to understand what Petraeus meant.

In late July, Holbrooke and Eikenberry met Karzai for lunch at the Arg. There was none of the casual mafia intimacy of meals in Milosevic's palace. A dozen Americans faced Karzai and his cabinet across a long table in the first-floor banquet room where troops had slaughtered President Daoud Khan and his family during the 1978 Communist coup. Karzai, in a black jacket and white tunic buttoned to the throat, was jumpy and theatrical, and the steady underwater pressure of Holbrooke's voice made him jumpier.

Karzai feared that much of his Pashtun base would be unable to vote—the Taliban were threatening to cut off voters' ink-stained fingers, and there were hundreds of polling places in areas too remote or too violent to operate. "I am concerned that more than twenty percent of the Pashtuns will be disenfranchised," he began.

Atmar, his interior minister, announced that the number of lost Pashtun votes might be as high as 30 or 40 percent.

"More than thirty to forty percent—this is even worse than I thought!" Karzai said with elaborate surprise, as if he was hearing it for the first time. In fact, he had told Atmar before lunch that the 20 percent figure Atmar had earlier given to the Americans was too low.

Holbrooke gazed evenly across the table at Karzai. "Since your poll numbers are higher than anyone else's, what do you want to do about it?"

Atmar proposed sending additional troops to high-risk areas and asking the Pakistanis to communicate to their Taliban contacts not to disrupt the election.

"We can't count on that," Karzai said darkly.

"You can't have a surprise on August twentieth that eight hundred sites couldn't open," Eikenberry said. "You need to bring it out now. Truth is the best—tell the Afghan people the truth, that we can't have the election as planned in some places and we need the help of our Pakistani friends."

"I began my career in Vietnam," Holbrooke said, "where they had elections during the war but the elections were fake. This one is real. You're worried about one set of issues, which is the effect on the Pashtun people."

"And the aftermath of the elections, the effect on Al Qaeda and the Taliban. We've done an analysis." Karzai turned to his intelligence chief, Saleh, who declared that large-scale disenfranchisement would allow the Taliban to claim the political initiative and the support of the people.

"Absolutely, that's the main point," Karzai said. "They will claim control of the people."

"And the territory," Saleh added.

"And the territory."

Karzai's eyes shifted around the table as his jaw muscles worked his food. He spoke like a stage king stirring himself up against a plot to steal his throne. Holbrooke knew that this performance was a way for Karzai to contest the results if they went against him. It could also justify vote fraud, Karzai's insurance against a Western plot to get rid of him.

Holbrooke changed the subject. "Whenever international forces have driven out the Taliban in Helmand the last few weeks, there has been no effort to bring in administrative structures of your government."

"Has this been done in coordination with our government?"

"I think this is a huge issue for you," Holbrooke persisted. "If the military goes into new districts we know they'll be successful militarily, but the people ask why there's no government follow-up. We know it's hard to get people in, but we beg the government—because this isn't waiting for the elections—to sit down with NATO and the embassy to work out a quick-reaction administrative effort to bring the districts health, schools, and, above all, justice. This is the most critical."

Karzai nodded and said nothing. The lunch soon ended. He was the unreliable client whose very weakness was his strength over his rich and powerful sponsor. The Americans had the F-16s and the agronomists, but Karzai had the leverage, and he wanted another five years of it.

As August 20 approached, an atmosphere of crisis seized Kabul. Rina Amiri urged Holbrooke to stay out of Afghanistan for the election. So did Eikenberry and Cowper-Coles. The situation would be supercharged and he might say something to set off an explosion. But Holbrooke wouldn't miss it.

ELECTION DAY WAS the most violent in fifteen years. Fear and disillusionment drove voter turnout down to the low 30s, far below previous elections—in some districts as low as 5 or 10 percent, with hardly a single woman daring to come out. And vote fraud was historic, on an industrial scale.

Holbrooke toured polling places and gave an uncharacteristically bland statement of satisfaction with the Afghan democratic process. The next morning, he went to see Ashraf Ghani, one of the prominent candidates, at his house in western Kabul. Ghani recited numerous cases of ballot stuffing—whole tablets of ballot sheets with every one premarked for Karzai. Next Holbrooke went with Eikenberry, Amiri, and Barney Rubin to the heavily guarded U.N. compound, known as

Palace 7, just outside the Green Zone. Kai Eide was there with Peter Galbraith. Holbrooke argued that Karzai could not be allowed to claim victory. Amiri thought that it was even possible Abdullah Abdullah, Karzai's main challenger, had won the first round. Given the level of reported fraud, Holbrooke said, the international community needed to insist on a second round.

"Dick, don't say this to Karzai," Eide said. "You have to understand that he sees you as someone who wants to get rid of him."

Holbrooke had written off Eide as the last foreign defender of an indefensible regime. "I'm on good terms with Karzai now," Holbrooke said. "I can handle him."

Back at the embassy, shortly before noon, Holbrooke got on a conference call with his fellow SRAPs—by now thirty countries had appointed their own Holbrookes. The world could live with vote stealing in Afghanistan, he said, but "this is a completely unacceptable level of fraud." Karzai was already declaring victory; the other candidates were disputing the results. Holbrooke repeated what he'd told Eide about the need for a second round of voting.

He was speaking on his cell phone, on an open line. The intelligence services of several countries, including Afghanistan's, were listening in. News of the call reached Karzai within minutes. What he heard was that Holbrooke was conspiring with other foreigners to steal his victory. Karzai believed that the Americans were actually tampering with ballots. When Holbrooke arrived at the Arg at twelve-thirty, the president was already seething.

They sat down for lunch in the same murder-haunted banquet room. It was a smaller group this time, four or five on each side. Holbrooke didn't sense Karzai's brittle mood. Thirty minutes into the meal, he said, "Mr. President, may I ask a difficult question? If the Independent Election Commission finds that no one got to fifty percent, will you accept a second round?"

Eikenberry and his deputy, Frank Ricciardone, gasped. Holbrooke was challenging Karzai in front of his own people, calling him a liar.

"Of course." Karzai, already strung like a bow, tightened more. "But why are you asking this? No one believes that there will be a second round, no one. Who would believe that?"

Holbrooke said that it was a hypothetical question.

"I understand what you are doing," Karzai said.

"Are you suggesting that we're pushing for some specific result? Because we're not." Holbrooke added, "We have heard there's been massive fraud."

"Where have you heard that?"

"The whole city is talking about it."

"Who are you speaking to?"

"I saw Ashraf Ghani this morning."

"So, you are speaking for Ghani!"

There was a silence.

"You, sir, are a guest in our country and may leave." Karzai was gripping the table. "Thank you for coming, Mr. Holbrooke."

Holbrooke stayed in his seat. He didn't want to walk out this way. "Thank you for inviting me."

"Thank you for coming."

"Thank you for inviting me."

Karzai and Holbrooke stared at each other. Another excruciating silence, almost a full minute. Then Karzai stood up and went around the table shaking hands. Fruit and tea had not yet been served.

Holbrooke knew he'd made a grave error. At the embassy he tried to conceal the extent of the mess from Amiri and Rubin, but his face told the story. Amiri was furious: "This is exactly what I was afraid of! You completely mucked things up."

"I'm going to fix this," he said.

Holbrooke didn't want the news to get back to Washington. He scrubbed the embassy's cables and sent reporters to Ricciardone for a prettied-up account of the lunch. Ricciardone was a veteran diplomat who had served as ambassador in several countries, most recently Egypt. Holbrooke had persuaded him to come to Kabul as Eikenberry's "deputy ambassador," a more exalted title than the usual deputy chief of mission and one that hadn't been used, Holbrooke told him, since 1965, when William Porter served under Henry Cabot Lodge. Ricciardone had the sense that Holbrooke was consciously re-creating the old Saigon embassy and trying to make the story come out differently. Holbrooke put him in mind of the late-career Reggie Jackson—still fun to watch, you still hoped for a home run, every now and then he smacked a long one, but far more often he struck out. Holbrooke had needlessly provoked Karzai without knowing his next move.

"I can't spin this," Ricciardone told Holbrooke. Rather than lying to the press, he refused to be interviewed. Before long the White House heard what had happened.

That evening, Eikenberry returned to the Arg to undo the damage, and after an hour Karzai calmed down. But it was too late.

It took another two months for the election disaster to play out. At the U.N. mission, Eide tried to minimize the fraud, but Galbraith leaked the details to the press: it was so vast that in Kandahar fifteen times more ballots were counted for Karzai than the total actually cast. With the international community apparently ready to bless a stolen election, Galbraith came up with a plan to get rid of Karzai, by having Biden persuade Obama to gather support among the allies for an interim Afghan president until a new election could be held in the spring of 2010. The scheme sounded like an American-engineered coup that justified Karzai's wildest paranoid theories. Eide had Galbraith fired for insubordination. Holbrooke, who was now resigned to Karzai's re-election, had nothing to do with Galbraith's plot, but because he had installed Galbraith in Kabul he was further tainted by it.

The final vote count had Karzai a few tenths of a point below fifty. As far as the diplomats were concerned, this was the worst possible outcome—a rigged election and no winner. Karzai, feeling that foreign powers had conspired to keep him from a clear victory, resisted a runoff that he would very likely win. Holbrooke absented himself from Kabul, and Senator John Kerry took his place. With a patience and tact that Holbrooke had not managed, Kerry tried to persuade Karzai to acknowledge that he hadn't won the first round and then, rather than going to a second round that would probably result in even more fraud and more bloodshed, appoint Abdullah as his chief executive. Karzai conceded on the first round but refused to share power. A week before the November 7 runoff Abdullah withdrew, saying that a fair election was impossible. In late November, Karzai was inaugurated for a second term in the Arg. But he had been humiliated, and he would never forgive it.

Afghanistan and America were stuck with five more years of him—

certain to be volatile, perhaps catastrophic years. Holbrooke tried to patch things up. "Tell your president I love him," he entreated Saleh, the intelligence chief. When Zalmay Rassoul, the foreign minister, called Amiri after the inauguration to say that his president was willing to work with her boss, Holbrooke was overjoyed. "That's great! Get it in an email to me so I can show it to the secretary. We're going to send this to the seventh floor." But Karzai sensed Holbrooke's vulnerability in Washington and moved to exploit it, playing him off against more amenable Americans, such as Gates and Clinton, who saw Karzai as weak and conniving but not venal and thought that encouragement could bring him around.

Holbrooke was now persona non grata in Kabul. Karzai asked Eikenberry to keep him away, and Eikenberry was happy to comply. The gaps between Holbrooke's trips grew longer. Obama did nothing to stand behind our man in Af-Pak.

VI

The biggest threat to him came from the rear. The White House view was that Holbrooke, who waved a gun in Karzai's face and failed to shoot, had gone rogue and then screwed up the election. And other dangers were gathering. In September an article on him appeared in *The New Yorker*. Not a particularly good one, since the writer didn't realize how perilous Holbrooke's standing was in both Washington and Kabul. The piece was too close to Holbrooke's view of himself, which created a major problem for its subject, confirming every dark thought in Obama's inner circle about Holbrooke the shameless self-promoter. During fact-checking he began to sense intense unhappiness from the White House. Only one member of the Obama administration was allowed this kind of press. At the last minute he declined to sit for a portrait. He claimed that he'd thought the piece was to be about Af-Pak, not him, even though he'd made old friends available for interviews. His appetites were always stronger than his fears.

The president asked his advisors, "Who's going to talk to Holbrooke?" The assignment went to Denis McDonough. Every president needs a loyalist who doesn't care what anyone else thinks as long as the boss has his back, which gives his actions a higher blessing than ordinary morality. McDonough had been a student at Georgetown's School of Foreign Service when Holbrooke was negotiating peace in Bosnia. But he summoned Holbrooke to the White House and subjected him to a finger-pointing rebuke. Winning the trust of the president is a priceless achievement no matter what else you haven't done, sending outsized power straight to your head.

By now Eikenberry was also fed up with Holbrooke. The SRAP still descended on the Kabul embassy every month like Lear with his hundred knights and horses. The number of U.S. civilian officials in Afghanistan was ballooning from several hundred to a thousand, the largest number in any country, and there was hardly any available space on the compound, but Holbrooke's retinue had to be housed, fed, and scheduled. Once, when Eikenberry's number three, an ambassador named Jim Keith—there were five ambassadors at the embassy—told Holbrooke that a certain request was impossible, Holbrooke said, "So, Jim, what are you doing for your next assignment?" He even insisted on changing the configuration of desks in the embassy office. He called Eikenberry in the middle of official dinners and at every hour of the Kabul night, and the calls dragged on for more than an hour as Holbrooke made the ambassador the recipient of whatever his preoccupation of the moment might be, while Eikenberry held the phone away from his ear and finally begged off in order to return to his guests or get some sleep.

The treatment offended Eikenberry's sense of order and, even more, his pride. He took to calling Holbrooke "the Sun King." He delayed clearance for members of Holbrooke's team, limited the entourage to half a dozen, and restricted their travels in-country. Ashley Bommer, now Holbrooke's communications chief, was temporarily banned from Afghanistan after she left the embassy without permission to meet with Afghans. Rina Amiri had dozens of contacts around Kabul—her family was related by marriage to Karzai's—but Eikenberry forced her to work through his political section, which meant that she couldn't talk to important people who would tell her things they kept from other Americans. Amiri decided that the U.S. government outdid the Afghans in pettiness. Meanwhile, Americans were dying in the mountains and fields.

After the election, Holbrooke told Eikenberry that the White House wanted the ambassador to present Karzai with a list of five objectives for his second term. The demand made Eikenberry suspicious.

"Dick, who in the White House gave you this instruction?"

"Are you saying you don't believe me?"

"No, but who gave you this?"

"Are you saying I'm lying?"

"I'm saying within a minute of my leaving Karzai's office it will be all over Kabul that we're trying to run his second term, and he'll use it brilliantly against us. We need to have it in writing, in a cable."

"Goddam you, son of a bitch, you don't trust me."

Eikenberry finally told Ricciardone that he couldn't take it anymore—the bullying, the lying, the abuse of embassy staff. It had to be him or Holbrooke. He took his complaints to his close friend at the White House, Doug Lute. "Tell Jones," Lute said. "He's coming out there. I can't fire Richard Holbrooke—tell Jones." A trio of generals, ten stars among them, friends from the same exclusive fraternity, all aggrieved by Holbrooke. They set about to get rid of him.

"NONE OF US can understand why you are here," Amrullah Saleh once said to Eikenberry over dinner. "Karzai thinks you are here for reasons you haven't told him yet"—geopolitics, resources, maybe Christian proselytizing. None of them made sense to Saleh. "But why don't *you* know? You should have a better idea than you do." The muddle of American thinking offended the sharp mind of the young Afghan intelligence chief. After eight years, we were still trying to explain the war to ourselves.

In the fall of 2009, Obama faced another decision on troops. His new commander in Afghanistan, General Stanley McChrystal—with the support of Petraeus at Central Command and Chairman Mullen at the Pentagon—was asking for forty thousand on top of the earlier twenty-one thousand, which would put the total at more than one hundred thousand. McChrystal had been in Afghanistan since June, traveling around the country, learning the state of the war, and he had come to a conclusion: without a surge, Afghanistan would go into a "death spiral." McChrystal's troop request had leaked, and Obama and his advisors felt boxed in again by the military.

Gelb, who had known McChrystal at the Council on Foreign Relations, was asked by a reporter to describe him. "I think of no body fat," Gelb said. McChrystal was a general in the intense Petraeus mold—four hours of sleep a night, one meal a day, audiobooks during kick-ass workouts. On Holbrooke's recommendation, he listened to Stanley Karnow's *Vietnam: A History* during his early morning runs around the NATO base in Kabul. McChrystal was more of a political innocent than Petraeus, not nearly as shrewd about publicity. There was an earnest, self-improving drive in him, combined with a lethal dedication to finding and killing Al Qaeda members when he was running special operations in Iraq. His credo in Afghanistan was no civilian casualties, and through his strenuous efforts the number came down. McChrystal was the best of the army. Karzai loved him and tried to use him against Eikenberry and Holbrooke.

Over ten weeks in the fall of 2009, between countless meetings of the principals and deputies committees, Obama presided at no fewer than nine sessions of his National Security Council, two or three hours at a time. In his diary Holbrooke once called the Situation Room "a room that, to me, symbolizes the problem; a windowless below-ground room in which the distance from real knowledge to people is at its very greatest—very high-ranking people who know very little make grand (or not so grand) decisions, or maybe (as in the Clinton years so often) no decisions at all." Lute had run an Afghanistan strategy review in the last months of the Bush administration, and there had been another in Obama's first weeks in office, and here they were again, this time a marathon review—a sure sign of a troubled war, like the many factfinding missions Kennedy sent to South Vietnam, or Johnson's constant reorganizing of pacification.

The discussion ran up against the fundamental contradictions of the war. Obama knew them as well as anyone. Around and around they went in the Situation Room as the weeks dragged on and Obama, crisp and lawyerly, listened and asked hard questions.

Let's get started.

Why are we in Afghanistan?

Because Al Qaeda attacked us from Afghanistan. Our objective is to prevent another attack, and ultimately to destroy Al Qaeda.

But Al Qaeda is in Pakistan.

If the Taliban take power again in Afghanistan, Al Qaeda could regain its safe haven there.

But Al Qaeda already has a safe haven in western Pakistan—not to mention in Somalia and Yemen and the African Sahel. Why do we need a hundred thousand troops and a counterinsurgency campaign in Afghanistan to go after one hundred Al Qaeda members in the tribal areas of Pakistan?

Pakistan, our supposed ally, is actually supporting our enemies. The Pakistanis won't stand for American troops on their soil. All we can do is covert ops, intelligence collection, drone strikes in the tribal areas against militants, some of whom are attacking Pakistani targets—even that is very unpopular.

What do we really know about the Taliban? Are we sure they will allow Al Qaeda back into Afghanistan?

No, but they refuse to renounce Al Qaeda.

Why not do what Biden is calling for—drones and a few thousand Special Forces and spies going after the hard-core bad guys—a counterterrorism campaign?

That's what we've been trying since 2001, and it hasn't worked. Only counterinsurgency will give the Afghan government the breathing space to win the support of the people and gain strength until it can defend itself.

But classic counterinsurgency requires hundreds of thousands of troops.

So we'll limit ourselves to protecting population centers and key lines of communication—the oil spot—until the Afghan army gets bigger and better.

What if the enemy keeps getting bigger and better?

We might need to send more troops in a year or two.

What if our presence *makes* it bigger and better?

We'll begin to transfer responsibility to the Afghan government in two to three years.

What if Karzai wants us to stick around for the fat contracts and the combat brigades while his government continues to prey on the people? Counterinsurgency can only succeed with a reliable partner, and the election did Karzai's legitimacy great harm. What if the Afghan government lacks the ability or will to win the support of the people?

There's no good answer.

And what if the Pakistani military will never change its strategy?

There's no good answer.

Holbrooke sat at the far end of the table, next to Petraeus with his four stars, and took notes. Among his notes were private interjections. When McChrystal showed a slide that changed his definition of the American goal from "defeat the Taliban" to "the Taliban-led insurgency no longer poses an existential threat to the government of Afghanistan," without changing the number of troops, Holbrooke wrote: "Wow! Words can be used to mean whatever we want them to mean." Rice proposed joint U.S.-China aid programs in Pakistan: "NONSENSE." Gates argued that civilian aid to Pakistan might cause a backlash against the United States: "THIS IS NONSENSE!" Biden said that every one of Pakistan's interests was also America's interest: "HUH?"

He kept the caustic skepticism to himself. He no longer gave speeches or read from notes. He complimented the president less often. He spoke very little, and when he did, it was on subjects that were part of his job but peripheral to the main discussion—agriculture and police corruption. He advocated for the civilian surge—the State Department's plan to recruit more than a thousand American experts and deploy them to Afghanistan's cities and districts. The civilian surge gave Holbrooke a place at the table and credibility with the generals, who were always complaining that the civilian effort lagged behind. So at the White House he was careful not to say what he really thought—but back at the office, when his advisor on aid, Sepideh Keyvanshad, who did not believe that more was better in Afghanistan, asked him, "Why are we sending all these people? It won't make any difference," Holbrooke shot back, "You don't think I know that?"

During meetings on Bosnia, Holbrooke had said whatever he believed—hadn't hesitated to contradict his boss Warren Christopher, or even President Clinton, when he thought they were wrong. Now, in the forty-seventh year of his career, he grew careful. He felt that he didn't have the standing with President Obama to go up against the military, least of all the famous general sitting just to his left. He had no supporters in the room except Clinton, and because he was wounded, and his need for her was existential, he couldn't allow a glimmer of light or a breath of air between them. And she was with the generals and with Gates, her closest colleague in the administration.

As a result, almost no one knew what Holbrooke thought of the surge. He kept it from his colleagues and his staff. In Kabul, when

Eikenberry and Ricciardone expressed skepticism about McChrystal's request, Holbrooke's reply was deliberately ambiguous: "Karl, it's going to happen." He crossed two fingers and said, "Hillary and I are like this," and he never reported their views back to her.

In early November, at the urging of Biden, Jones, and Lute, who were similarly skeptical, Eikenberry put his five years of experience in Afghanistan into a pair of "eyes only" cables. He, Ricciardone, and two aides pulled an all-nighter at the embassy, eating pizza and drinking beer, and constructed a powerful argument against the surge: Karzai would never be an adequate partner; more troops, while improving security in places like Kandahar, would have the long-term effect of deepening the Afghan government's corruption and dependency; counterinsurgency couldn't succeed as long as Pakistan provided a sanctuary for the Taliban. The cables, which eventually leaked to the *Times*, lit a few sticks of policy dynamite under the generals' plans and enraged both McChrystal, who had been kept in the dark by Eikenberry, and Petraeus, who thought the ambassador was grandstanding for history.

Clinton regarded the cables as a betrayal from within her department, and her relationship with Eikenberry never recovered. She wanted no dissent from her own position. When Holbrooke told her that General "Hoss" Cartwright, vice-chairman of the Joint Chiefs, had expressed disagreement with McChrystal's request, she replied, "That's outrageous." She had always been a hawkish Democrat—"You'd be surprised how conservative she can be," Holbrooke once told Barney Rubin. He found her frustratingly complicated—at once closed off and candid, secretive and indiscreet, lacking a strategic intelligence to temper her political instinct, which now told her that denying the wartime request of a field commander who would later blame failure on the civilians did not seem like a good career move.

The truth is, Holbrooke could have written almost every word in Eikenberry's cables. He had written his own version a month before.

ON COLUMBUS DAY WEEKEND in the Hamptons he stayed up one night till four a.m. drafting a nine-page memo for Clinton. He rewrote it several times in the following days, still not satisfied. Reading it takes

me straight back forty years to the memo he wrote for Johnson in the
fall of 1967, the one about Napoleon's Russia campaign. It has the same
clarity, the same ice-blue gaze at a difficult reality.

> Like you, I believe in the possibilities of American leadership, and
> I am not a pessimist by nature. I hope my judgments are wrong. In
> 1965, over the course of a week, LBJ had the same kind of discussions
> we are having now, but came up with the wrong answers. In 2002–3
> George W. Bush never even really consulted his own Secretary of
> State before committing himself to the Iraq war. Now it is our turn,
> and Barack Obama deserves credit for having lengthy discussions and
> listening to everyone before making his decisions. But the parameters
> of the debate have been defined almost entirely by the military, and
> I do not believe the full political, regional, and global implications of
> McChrystal's requests have been adequately discussed.

Holbrooke believed that counterinsurgency would never succeed
in Afghanistan. Historically it had worked in colonial wars, where
it required a lot of coercion—the Philippines, Malaya, and French
Morocco, the birthplace, he told Clinton, of the term "oil spot," the
strategy he'd first heard in Bac Lieu in 1963, and which McChrystal was
reviving at their NSC meetings. It only worked where the enemy had no
cross-border sanctuary. In Iraq, Petraeus's counterinsurgency strategy
had depended on specific political developments in the Sunni and Shia
communities. The analogy for Afghanistan was none of these. It was
Vietnam, the war that had been barred from discussion.

Rather than securing the Afghan population, a hundred thousand
American troops would only confirm the Taliban narrative of an infidel
army of occupation supporting a puppet government. Everyone said
that this was a political war, but Holbrooke pointed out that the review
had ignored politics—the election disaster, the cancer of corruption,
Karzai's illegitimacy. The discussions had focused almost entirely on
troop numbers—but what kind of government would tens of thousands
of new troops be sent to support? "The current government does not
have sufficient legitimacy and appeal to motivate hundreds of thousands of Afghans to die for it," he wrote. "While a substantial portion
of the Afghan population is strongly motivated to fight the TB, their

principal motivation is usually ethnic and tribal, not any commitment to the values supposedly represented by the government in Kabul."

And then there was Pakistan. The NSC had held a three-hour meeting on Pakistan on October 7, and they'd agreed on an all-out effort to move Pakistan away from its militant clients through some combination of aid money and coercive goodwill. But this fell short of a strategy. General Pasha, head of the ISI, had come out against more American troops, which dampened any hope for Pakistani cooperation. "We simply cannot succeed without the full participation of Pakistan in our efforts," Holbrooke wrote.

He wasn't arguing against sending more troops—not in a memo to Clinton, anyway. (He told Gelb privately that if it were up to him they'd send just forty-five hundred advisors, but he couldn't tell Hillary that, not even discreetly.) An American withdrawal from Afghanistan would "set off a cycle of uncontrollable events that could seriously damage our most vital interests." It was a kind of soft domino theory—not that neighboring governments would topple one after another, but the whole region stretching from the Middle East to India, with nuclear weapons and numerous insurgencies and jihadi groups, would be destabilized. Instead of a way out, Holbrooke was seeking a policy that allowed us to stay.

Americans didn't want to hear this, and neither did Obama, but we needed to be long-distance runners in Afghanistan. That was why Holbrooke kept saying it would be our longest war. A big surge promised too much, to both Americans and Afghans, and would soon play out in predictable ways, with calls for yet more troops or a rapid departure. A more modest number—Holbrooke settled on twenty to twenty-five thousand, just one combat brigade and the rest trainers and advisors to the Afghan army—would hold off the Taliban and the American public while giving a new political strategy time to work. "And time, the commodity we need most to succeed, is in the shortest supply." More time—that had been the theme of his Napoleon-in-Russia memo, too.

What would a political strategy look like? That part wasn't clear—solutions for Afghanistan were never as persuasive as critiques. Holbrooke included a brief, vague paragraph on "Reintegration and Reconciliation"—"the biggest missing piece of our policy." Reintegration meant bringing in low-level Taliban defectors. Reconciliation meant talking to the Taliban leadership. That was what he'd hired Barney Rubin to look into, and Rubin was turning up some interesting leads. But Clinton didn't want to hear of peace talks, and neither did the military, and neither did the White House. Talking to the enemy—the only way to end the war—was never part of the strategy review.

On the morning of October 26 he sat down with Clinton for an hour in the secretary's large reception room outside her private study on the seventh floor, beside a window looking out on the Lincoln Memorial. He sketched his views and gave her two pages of talking points based on the memo. She scanned them. "Too cute by half," she said of his idea for twenty thousand troops. Then she left for a meeting in the Oval Office with Gates, Obama, and his White House advisors, where she stuck to her position in favor of McChrystal's forty thousand. "She went to the hard side of Gates," Donilon told Holbrooke, adding that Obama had lost respect for Clinton. He needed her help in resisting the generals, but her advice seemed driven by politics.

Neither Holbrooke nor his boss ever brought his ideas to the president and the NSC. Holbrooke confided them privately to Donilon and Axelrod, hoping that one of them would pass them on to Obama, but that didn't matter. Throughout the ten weeks of the review that fall he never said what he really believed where it counted most, in the Situation Room. As far as his colleagues were concerned, Holbrooke supported the surge.

On November 19, along with eight hundred other dignitaries from around the world, he sat through the farce of Karzai's inauguration in Kabul, next to Eikenberry in the third row. Four nights later, on November 23, the NSC held its final meeting on the troop request.

"We have spent almost a year waiting for the Afghan election to be over, and it is time to move forward," Clinton said. "If we do not commit to this, we know the outcome. It will be tough. It may not work. There will be daily consequences. But it must not be half-hearted. Let's get on with it." She pounded her fist on the Situation Room table. "This is in our national interest. We must do this."

Afterward, around eleven that night, Holbrooke was on the phone with Clinton when a call broke in from the White House operator. "The President of the United States wishes to speak with Ambassador Holbrooke."

Obama came on the line. "Richard, I failed to call on you at the end. What is your view?"

Holbrooke overcame his surprise and gave the president his view that everything depended on Pakistan and the training of the Afghan army. He had been so quiet that Obama didn't know what he thought.

ON DECEMBER 1, in a speech before cadets at West Point, and keenly aware that his audience included future casualties of the war, the president announced that he would send thirty-three thousand more troops to Afghanistan. In the same sentence he added that the first withdrawals would begin in the summer of 2011. McChrystal would have eighteen more months to show that counterinsurgency could work, and then the Afghans would begin to take over responsibility. Obama could have called it "Afghanization," except that would remind people of "Vietnamization." He was sending the troops on a mission about which he'd shown persistent skepticism. The uncharitable view was that his objective was to demonstrate failure and get Afghanistan behind him.

After ten weeks of intense discussions, the president distrusted his generals and was cool toward Mullen, his top military advisor. Some of the generals despised the civilians, though only McChrystal was naïve enough to show it. Gates resented the White House advisors for fighting off the military's attempt to buffalo the president. The NSC staff was engaged in a war of leaks with the Pentagon and a covert war with SRAP. Obama was disappointed in Clinton, and Clinton was furious at the White House. Eikenberry had alienated Clinton, McChrystal, Petraeus, and Gates. Jones and his deputy, Donilon, hated each other. Most of Jones's staff thought their boss was incompetent.

And Holbrooke? Holbrooke had Clinton, had her for dear life. And he had Mullen—their friendship survived disagreement over McChrystal's forty thousand because of the two things they shared, love of musical theater and loyalty to Clinton. But that was it. By the end of 2009 he was almost completely isolated. Everyone seemed to recognize it except him.

With the Afghan election and the strategy review out of the way, his enemies moved in for the kill.

At the end of the year Jones had Lute and his staff put together a file on Holbrooke's sins—the fallout from Karzai's re-election, Eikenberry's reports on Holbrooke's behavior in Kabul, the article in *The New Yorker*.

One morning in January 2010, Obama was receiving his usual daily briefing in the Oval Office when he suddenly asked, "Is there anyone here who thinks Richard Holbrooke is adding value to our efforts in the region?" Neither Biden, Jones, Donilon, Emanuel, nor John Brennan, the homeland security advisor, said a word in Holbrooke's favor. After a pause Jones raised his hand and asked if the president wanted him to relieve Holbrooke of his duties. "Yeah, that would be helpful," Obama said. "But be sure to tell Hillary I'm not saying he should leave the State Department if she can find another job for him. But it's time for a change."

Jones told Clinton of the president's decision, and she nodded and said that she would carry it out. But January turned to February and nothing happened. When Jones called Clinton to remind her, she said that she was having a hard time finding another job for Holbrooke. In early February, Jones went to Kabul and commiserated with Eikenberry. Holbrooke would soon be gone, he told the ambassador, and he said the same thing to Kai Eide. Two weeks later, Holbrooke swept into Kabul again. Eikenberry complained to Jones and Lute, and on February 23 Jones wrote him a letter:

> I'm sorry that you had to endure a "farewell tour" once again; I can assure you that it will be the last as there can be no doubt as to our boss's intent any longer, and it has [to] be reissued clearly.

The letter went out as an unclassified cable via diplomatic pouch rather than a private communication, which meant that dozens of people around the State Department received copies. Holbrooke got his on March 16, but he didn't grasp the meaning until Ricciardone, who also received the letter, warned him by email of "yet another nastiness . . . it makes unnamed but unmistakable and negative reference to you . . . Obviously, it is likely to leak and bring discredit on everyone. I am so sorry, for all of us." Ricciardone had been at Eikenberry's side for almost a year and seen enough of Holbrooke's high-handedness—had once received a chewing out right in front of a reporter—that what he felt on Holbrooke's behalf was less outrage than sadness.

Holbrooke saw Jones's letter as the smoking gun of a conspiracy centered in the Kabul embassy, and the betrayal stung him. Eikenberry and Ricciardone had their jobs thanks to him. He couldn't understand why they had turned on him.

Two days later, Jones asked Holbrooke to come see him at five that afternoon.

They sat down together in the national security advisor's spacious corner office where, in 1993, Holbrooke had argued about Bosnia over lunch with Tony Lake. Jones started out with small talk, but beneath his Semper Fi charm and apparent checked-outness, Holbrooke sensed something dangerous—a tough old marine's refusal to retreat if it came down to one of them or the other.

"SRAP is not working," Jones said, getting to the point. "The president has made a decision. He told Hillary to do this in January but she didn't. Now I am. She has to make a transition. You're free to go out and write a book about how stupid we all are." Jones added that Obama wanted to send him off honorably, with accolades.

The color had drained from Holbrooke's face. "Well, this is a fine way to end my career." He spent several minutes describing his long record of achievement and what a terrible legacy would come from being fired in this way. Finally Jones cut him off.

"Richard, this isn't about you, it's about the country and the president. We all serve at his pleasure. I'll be leaving after two years."

Holbrooke said that Jones had no idea what SRAP even did. "What do you mean by 'transition'?"

"That's up to Hillary."

"So you're firing me?"

"Oh, no. She must work out a transition."

"To what?"

"That's up to her and you."

Holbrooke tried to calm down as Jones recited the charges. The president's special representative was practically persona non grata throughout the Af-Pak region. The Indians didn't want him coming to Delhi, General Kayani didn't want to have dinner with him in Islamabad, Karzai and Eikenberry didn't want him in Kabul at all.

"We did a three-sixty on you," Jones said. "No one can get along with you."

Biden had once said exactly the same thing when Gelb visited the White House: "What the fuck are you going to do about your friend Holbrooke? He's such a pain in the ass—nobody can stand him. I can't stand him." Gelb replied that Holbrooke was the very best they had. Biden didn't disagree—it was just that everyone hated him.

"No one?" Holbrooke asked Jones. "What about Mullen?"

"He is a solitary exception."

"Gates?"

"I would rather not comment."

"Petraeus?"

"I would rather not comment."

"McChrystal?"

"I would rather not comment."

"Donilon?"

"I will not reveal what was said."

It lasted forty-five minutes. At the end, somehow, they shook hands. "After I talk to Hillary, I want to see the president," Holbrooke said.

"I'll tell him."

Holbrooke went next door to the deputy national security advisor's broom closet, but Donilon wasn't there. He walked outside the building.

They talked about the White House as if it were a collective person— "The White House thinks," "the White House is unhappy"—the way "the palace" gave every courtier the authority of the king. The West Wing was the most unimpressive collection of burrows and tunnels from which an empire ever tried to impose its will on the world, but the commissars in that building, all puffed up with their proximity to power, turned the most senior people at State into peons. McGeorge Bundy, never mind his second deputy, if he had one, couldn't have done that to Averell Harriman.

On West Executive Avenue the black limousines were waiting for their VIP passengers. But he had come on foot, and he started walking toward the gate. The evening was clear and warm. The March sun was beginning to set behind the Eisenhower Executive Office Building. I'm not sure he had ever been so alone.

But he could not be alone, and he turned around and went back inside and walked down the narrow corridor to David Axelrod's office, right next door to the president's private dining room. Holbrooke no longer knew if Donilon was his friend, but he thought that Axelrod might be, and he hoped that at some point Axelrod could get him in to see the president. They went out to dinner every few months, and Axelrod enjoyed the theater of it all, Holbrooke's appetite for politics and history, but the flattery made him uncomfortable. Gelb warned Holbrooke that Axelrod was not his friend—he had no friends in the White House. The White House didn't like him.

Axelrod's young assistant, Eric Lesser, said that Axelrod was out. Holbrooke sat in the cramped office and waited. When Axelrod returned, Holbrooke told him what Jones had done. He tried to claim the high ground—this would hurt the administration and the war effort—but he couldn't help adding, "Jones doesn't know who he's dealing with." It all came as a surprise to Axelrod. He said that he would call Holbrooke in the morning.

On his way out, Holbrooke looked for Donilon again, but he still wasn't there.

He called his closest aides—Ashley Bommer and Rosemarie Pauli, his chief of staff, both of whom had worked for him for years—and told them to meet him at his N Street townhouse, where no one else on the staff would hear that he was about to be fired. It was a house he barely lived in—there was nothing in the fridge except maybe a piece of moldy cheese and a carton of expired milk. Without Kati around he had returned to his bachelor habits, eating dinner at Strobe's house or with Samantha and her husband at Cafe Milano, or junk food at his desk, staying at the office till midnight, going to the movies in Georgetown with his friend Husain Haqqani, the Pakistani ambassador, calling his aides at any hour of the weekend to bring over a charger for his Black-Berry or locate his passport.

"Does Hillary know?" Bommer asked.

"They're in Russia," Holbrooke said.

"Let's call Jake. They're up at all hours."

It was two in the morning in Moscow. Sullivan waited until Clinton was awake to tell her. She was both angry and amused at Jones's methods. She told Holbrooke to do nothing until she got back.

Later that night Donilon called. Jones was "an idiot," he said—he did this kind of thing all the time—Holbrooke should just ignore him. Donilon denied having said anything bad to Jones, but his tone was lukewarm and Holbrooke didn't believe him, much as he wanted to, especially when Donilon asked how long he planned to stay in the job. The truth was that Donilon was fed up with Holbrooke, too. He sometimes told Sullivan that they couldn't keep covering for Holbrooke, he wasn't on his game, this was no longer the Holbrooke of the Bosnia years.

Only Clinton could save him. She was determined to do it, because she was loyal, she needed Holbrooke, and the attack was aimed at her as well.

Bommer and Sullivan put together a set of talking points on SRAP's achievements, an answer to Lute's dossier of misdeeds, for the secretary to take to Obama. Clinton told Holbrooke to stop talking to people and let her handle it. "This is going to be an uphill struggle," she said, before heading to the White House on the morning of March 26.

Obama told Clinton that he had nothing personally against Holbrooke, but he was disruptive—the same word Obama had used to Holbrooke's face. Both Eikenberry and McChrystal had told the president at the end of the strategy review that Holbrooke not only caused problems, he was no longer even useful in Afghanistan. "So," Obama asked her, "why are you so resistant to making a change?"

The problem wasn't Holbrooke, Clinton said, it was Eikenberry's hypersensitivity and Jones's hostility. She let Obama know all that Holbrooke and his team were doing. The president could fire him, but it would be over his secretary of state's objection.

"Okay, let's give it three more months and see where we are," Obama said.

Clinton and Holbrooke agreed not to tell anyone about the looming execution and its stay. He never let on to his staff, didn't even tell Kati. "Anyway, in my bones I don't think it will happen. And, if it does, I am fully prepared for it. I have my friends, my life, and I know I have done a good job even while having doubts about the strategy, doubts I have expressed. (I will not end up like McNamara, who, by failing to speak up when he had concluded the war was lost, wrote his own epitaph—forever.)"

So he told his diary the day Clinton saved his neck. Whistling past the graveyard on every count.

VII

Everything seemed to come apart that last week of March. Obama—who had just scored the biggest success of his presidency with the passage of a health care bill—took his first trip to Kabul without informing his Af-Pak advisor, because his Af-Pak advisor was not included on the trip, because the president had no confidence in his Af-Pak advisor. Holbrooke barely protested this humiliation. He had to keep working with people who'd tried to destroy him.

At the end of the month, Dr. Rosenfeld called to tell him that a scan had shown three of his four coronary arteries were severely blocked, as much as 75 percent. He would need to undergo an angiogram—a stent might be necessary, maybe even bypass surgery. He went up to New York to see Rosenfeld and Andersen. "Is this job going to kill me?" he asked. The doctors had never seen him so worried, and they spent almost two hours talking about how to keep the risk factors down.

But it had been a false positive. In early April the angiogram at New York Hospital showed that the blockage was no more than 40 percent. At the same time, an aortogram—a radiograph of the body's main artery, which curves like a cane from the top of the heart down to the abdomen and then divides into the legs—revealed that Holbrooke had an ascending aortic aneurysm, a dilation of the root of the aorta where it emerged from the left ventricle. The normal size was around 4 centimeters. Holbrooke's was 4.5. Surgery was indicated at 5.0, but some people's aortic root remained at 4.9 centimeters for years. It was something to watch—he would need to come back in November, six months from now, for another exam. Holbrooke got up from the gurney and immediately flew halfway around the world.

He tried to hide from his staff how embattled he was, but they knew anyway. None of them deserted SRAP to return to their old jobs. Their devotion to Holbrooke went beyond almost anything you normally find in the annals of our rigid, self-centered bureaucracy. It was like the loyalty of young players toward their aging, intense, big-hearted coach.

He plucked junior officials out of obscurity and gave them chances far above their station that could change their career. He told Shamila Chaudhary, who worked on the Pakistan desk, to accompany him to a briefing in Clinton's reception room, and when Clinton asked if Chaudhary had anything to add to the discussion, she said, "I think we should talk to Nawaz Sharif." Sharif was the leader of a conservative Pakistani party, and American policy was not to deal with the opposition.

"Doesn't Sharif talk to the Taliban?" Clinton asked.

"Which Pakistani politician doesn't talk to the Taliban?" Chaudhary replied. Everyone laughed. Clinton was surprised and pleased, and Holbrooke gave Chaudhary a thumbs-up. The next day she was promoted. But when she hesitated to take on a project Holbrooke offered, he told her, "I made you and I can end you," and she wept in his office until he begged, "Oh my god, why are you doing this to me? Please stop."

He yelled less often than in the past but he rode them hard, criticized their thinking habits, their prose style. When a particularly turgid memo crossed his desk he called everyone into his office and handed out copies of Orwell's essay "Politics and the English Language." "Don't begin sentences with the passive voice," he commanded. "Say 'I believe,' not 'It is believed.'"

His aides saw his feelings, his wounds, and grew protective of him. He took a keen interest in their careers and lives, who was dating whom. He told Sepideh Keyvanshad, his aid advisor, who was going through a divorce while raising two children, to leave the office at five o'clock, but he worked others deep into the night. One afternoon he asked Vali Nasr to stay late to draft a memo. Nasr took out his phone to tell his son that he would need to find another ride home from his soccer game. Holbrooke said something about the importance of fatherhood and jot-

ted down a note on his own letterhead for Amir Nasr: "This is to excuse
your father Vali for his failure to pick you up after the soccer game
today, but he was helping me write a memo that could save the world."

He believed he'd assembled the best group in the entire government,
and he took every chance to introduce them all by name before important audiences at the Council on Foreign Relations and Brookings. They
were his last achievement.

The rare weekends that brought Kati to Washington were a relief to
his staff, because he left them alone and arrived at the office on Monday
morning looking better. He got nervous before her visits and wanted
everything just right. His aides thought he was a little afraid of her,
which puzzled them since Holbrooke wasn't afraid of anyone. He talked
about her constantly, showed off her picture—"Isn't she beautiful?"—
and asked others to get her to visit more often. When she came down for
the White House Correspondents' Dinner, Holbrooke took her out with
Husain Haqqani to the Bloomberg after-party. "You know, it's really
fun to go to the movies with Richard," Haqqani told her, at Holbrooke's
prior request, "but it would be more fun to have you with us. Washington isn't such a bad town."

"I'll try to come down more often," she said, but she disliked Washington and more often never happened. Some of his aides believed that
she had abandoned him when he needed her most.

Her latest book, the one about her parents and the drama of their
life in Budapest, was called *Enemies of the People*. It got the best reviews
of any of her books and was nominated for a big prize. Just as his career
was running into turbulence hers was taking off. She had always wanted
the recognition her husbands had, and Holbrooke went out of his way to
make room for her dilating life. He raced to catch the last Friday night
shuttle up to LaGuardia, drove out to the Hamptons for the weekend
though he didn't like the beach or the social scene, then boarded the
Monday morning shuttle down to Reagan National carrying her pink
tiered strapless evening dress for that night's dinner at the Jordanian
ambassador's residence IHO them both.

She was going to teach at a university in Jerusalem starting in January 2011, and the thought made him miserable. "I need her," he complained to his old friend Sally Quinn, who regularly had him over to
dinner at her Georgetown mansion.

Perhaps it was loneliness, and not just vanity, that led him to spend so many Sunday mornings at the house of Bob Woodward, justifying himself for hours and hours while Woodward ran his tape recorder for a book he was writing on Obama and Afghanistan. Holbrooke told friends, even those who didn't ask, that he hadn't spoken to Woodward, would never do that, only the foolish or disloyal would do it. When Gelb said of people they both knew, "You really have to be an idiot thinking you can talk to Woodward and he's not going to fuck you anyway," Holbrooke said, "Absolutely," and he continued to say it after the book was published with deeply hurtful quotes about him from colleagues, and—worse still—few quotes of his own, because Woodward judged him not important enough.

AFTER 2009 Afghanistan was pretty much closed to Holbrooke. Karzai didn't want him, and Obama allowed Karzai to pick among American envoys. The surge was under way and the military was in the saddle, driving U.S. policy. So in 2010 Holbrooke had to look for another way to do his job. He let wheat and pomegranates go, and he became a diplomat again. There had never been a political strategy for this war—never—and he set about to find one. The road led through Pakistan.

At the beginning of the year he jotted down some cryptic notes on the back of an official document:

<u>Possible Process:</u>
1) Stan puts pressure on TB
2) US-Pak start talks aimed at getting them to push TB toward dialogue
3) US-Af talks to give them assurances, + encourage them to open dialogue
4) US-India talks to keep them informed, get them to help by: XYZ (No ref to Kashmir!)
5) _____ talks with Iran
6) US outreach to other neighbors (PRC, 3 'Stans)
7) Indirect contacts with TB, conducted with HK, Pakmil, Saudis etc.

Something like this sequence had been in his mind for months, but he had never written it down and never discussed it in any depth. It became the outline of his strategy for trying to end the war. But there were obstacles at every step—in Afghanistan, in Pakistan, in India, with the Taliban, and inside the U.S. government.

Holbrooke made fifteen trips to Pakistan, one every six weeks. He would land in Islamabad sometime after midnight, sleep three hours, and then meetings, meetings, meetings. There was always a crisis. Hundreds of thousands of refugees fleeing army operations against the Pakistani Taliban in the Swat Valley; followers of Nawaz Sharif filling the streets to protest Zardari's dismissal of the chief justice of the Supreme Court; power shortages and riots in the south; rumors of an impending coup; a fifth of the country under floodwaters. Officials at SRAP debated whether Pakistan was a failed or a failing state.

In President House he sat down with Zardari—wire-rim glasses and a weak gray mustache, short and quick-witted—who surrounded himself with pictures of Benazir Bhutto.

"What have you been doing?" Zardari began, as if they were old buddies.

"All I do is work."

"You were working in Italy. You were working on the beach."

"I *was* in Italy. You're very well informed." Holbrooke laughed. "Things get a little better every time I come."

"It's the karma. You bring good stars to us. We believe in that, we Eastern people."

Zardari was from a landowning family in Sindh. Feudal origins and his late wife's political career had put his net worth close to two billion dollars. The palace guards wore colonial-era uniforms, the courtiers bowed deep. This was not a country where everyone believed he should be president.

"We need some Marshall Plan," Zardari went on. "Because of thirty years of security being our mindset, it has all depressed our capabilities. Ambassador Holbrooke, you can help us move from the extreme mindset to a civilized discussion with the world."

Holbrooke was popular with civilians in Pakistan. He sat for hours while Zardari talked about his grief for Benazir, and the ISI listened

on devices installed in the president's office. He spent time with the refugees from Swat in their broiling tents, and Pakistanis asked why their own leaders didn't do the same. He toured the flood zone and secured hundreds of millions of dollars for relief, while Zardari stayed at his château in Normandy. He held roundtables with the unbridled Pakistani press, groups of women and students, Pashtuns who braved travel to the capital from the tribal areas.

Holbrooke was pursuing a hold-the-abused-child-close approach. He believed that the U.S.-Pakistan relationship had always been transactional—money and weapons in exchange for support against Communists and terrorists—leading to short-term deals and repeated betrayals, creating deep distrust on both sides. He wanted to build an enduring relationship, and he was willing to invest a lot of personal time and U.S. Treasury funds to do it, kissing the ass of members of Parliament who had bought their seats with a family inheritance. He considered Zardari a terrible president if an enjoyable schmoozer, but he wanted to show support for Pakistan's elected leaders. They might be divisive and corrupt, but at least they had no ties to the terrorists who were destabilizing the region and threatening the United States.

There were two separate American policies in Pakistan: one above the waterline, visible to the public, made up of aid packages and bilateral meetings; and one below the waterline, the undercover spies and secret drones whose business was to keep America safe. The overwhelming interest of the U.S. government, including the president, was below the waterline, especially after a terrorist trained by the Pakistani Taliban tried to detonate a car bomb in Times Square. When Obama sent off a new ambassador to Islamabad, his only instruction was to make sure no major attack on the homeland came from Pakistani soil. While the Pentagon ran the policy in Afghanistan, it was the CIA in Pakistan. The diplomats pulled up the rear.

Pakistan's generals, not its politicians, defined the national interest. General Ashfaq Kayani, the chief of army staff, and General Shuja Pasha, head of the ISI, were Punjabis from the lower middle class. The military offered a path upward to hardworking Pakistanis like them, and it taught them to despise the civilian politicians as privileged, selfish, undisciplined. Kayani was a chain-smoking golfer with a strategic mind that remained stuck in the 1950s, when the existential threat to Pakistan came from India. He had studied at Fort Leavenworth and admired the U.S. armed forces. He had all the time in the world for his American counterpart, Admiral Mullen, who made twenty-seven trips to Pakistan as chairman of the Joint Chiefs and always dined alone with Kayani at his house in Rawalpindi, the cantonment city next to Islamabad, patiently trying to understand what Pakistan wanted from the United States. Kayani had less interest in seeing Holbrooke.

When Holbrooke first met Kayani and Pasha in Islamabad in February 2009, he asked them for help in finding the American journalist David Rohde.

Over the years, when Holbrooke saw Rohde at parties and events, he could be a bit cruel, reminding Rohde of his capture by Bosnian Serbs during the Dayton conference as if it showed only stupidity, and not courage, too. In the summer of 2008 they both attended Samantha Power's wedding in Ireland, and when Holbrooke heard that Rohde was about to go to Afghanistan to finish a book on the war, he told him not to do anything reckless again. But in November, Rohde and his interpreter and driver were taken hostage by a Taliban commander they'd gone to interview outside Kabul.

The Pakistanis told Holbrooke that they had no idea where David Rohde was. Pasha suggested that he was still in Afghanistan. In fact, Rohde was in Waziristan, the Pakistani tribal area where the Haqqani family (no relation to Ambassador Haqqani) had its headquarters. The Haqqani network was a hard-line Taliban group that operated through-out eastern Afghanistan and carried out attacks and suicide bombings in Kabul. U.S. intelligence had clear evidence that the Haqqanis took direction and support from the ISI. In 1995, Holbrooke had sprung Rohde from the Bosnian Serbs with a simple ultimatum to an adversary who had been sanctioned and bombed to the table. This time he was dealing with a supposed ally, a recipient of massive American aid, who smiled and lit another cigarette and lied.

The ISI passed a report of the conversation with Holbrooke to Sira-juddin Haqqani, son of the network's leader, who was holding Rohde. The report raised the terrorists' estimation of their captive's value to the U.S. government. Now the Haqqanis wanted to negotiate directly with Rohde's good friend Richard Holbrooke.

Holbrooke returned from Islamabad and told Ambassador Haqqani about his talk with Kayani and Pasha. "Your army wants a balance of power with India," Holbrooke said. "The civilians want more money for economic development. What if we offer both of them what they want?"

"That's a great formula," Haqqani replied. "But what if the army doesn't just want to be able to defend against India—because, is there a real threat? What if what they want is pride and prestige equal to that of India? Look at the record."

Haqqani—who was distrusted in both Washington and Islamabad—began a campaign to educate Holbrooke in Pakistani reality. The lessons began in the SRAP office during working hours but continued evenings and weekends at Georgetown restaurants and movie theaters and ice cream parlors, where Haqqani always paid. When Holbrooke asked why the Foreign Ministry was holding up visas for American undercover operatives who could help track terrorists, Haqqani told him that the ISI didn't want the United States to know Pakistan too well. Haqqani once heard Pasha say, "You civilians are wrong—there is no way Holbrooke has our interests at heart. He's a Jew." Haqqani explained to Holbrooke that the Pakistani military was deceiving itself as well as America—imagining an Indian menace in order to justify the outsized power and budget it had claimed ever since the founding of the state. Why would the generals cut a deal over the Taliban that would only deflate their significance by reducing tensions with India? Holbrooke's effort to change Pakistan's perception of its national interest was doomed, because the perception was based on delusions.

As for Pakistan's politicians, they would always promise things they couldn't deliver because they didn't have the popular standing at home. The public was divided on violent Islamists but nearly united in its strident anti-Americanism, which no amount of flood relief could change. But the promises kept coming along with the deceptions, because the generals and the politicians needed the Americans. It was like theater, Haqqani said. The whole region was a theater in which everyone understood their part, except the Americans.

These lessons were delivered below the waterline. They bore no resemblance to the ambassador's official cables to the foreign secretary in Islamabad after his formal meetings with Holbrooke, in which he echoed the Pakistani military's suspicion of every American move. His cables were part of the theater.

Holbrooke's labors were gargantuan. The contemplation of them wears me out. Repeated trips to Islamabad, strategic dialogues in Washington, donor meetings in Tokyo and Madrid, the bilats, the trilats, the fifth draft of the thirty-seventh memo, the sheer output of words—in pursuit of a chimera. All the while knowing what he was dealing with—all the while thinking he could do it anyway, with another memo, another meeting . . .

One evening he was sitting in Haqqani's library when the ambassador took a copy of *To End a War* off the shelf. He opened the book and read aloud a description of the Balkan presidents at Dayton—their selfishness, their lack of concern for the lives of their people.

"Do you feel that you're dealing with a similar situation now?" Haqqani asked.

"God, I'd forgotten about that," Holbrooke said. "Maybe it's true."

Haqqani asked what Holbrooke was hoping to achieve.

"I am trying to get the Pakistani military to be incrementally less deceitful toward the United States."

VIII

The other part of a political strategy went through the Taliban.
Talking to the enemy was an unwelcome idea almost everywhere in the U.S. government. The White House was uneasy about any contacts with a group that had not renounced its ties to Al Qaeda. The CIA believed that Taliban leaders didn't want a settlement because they thought they were winning, and American analysts in Kabul told Barney Rubin that higher-ups edited out any mention of Taliban interest in talks. The military, and above all Petraeus, thought it was much too soon to negotiate in 2009, or even 2010—the surge needed time to punish the enemy first. In Iraq, Petraeus had bought off Sunni insurgents from the bottom upward—he wanted to pursue the same strategy in Afghanistan. Clinton stayed close to the military view, and she was also concerned about her global reputation as a champion of women's rights.

Throughout 2009 Holbrooke never brought up peace talks at White House meetings, or even with his staff other than Rubin and one or two others. The euphemism they used was "reconciliation," which Holbrooke further neutered to "threat reduction." He held Rubin's memos back from just about all their colleagues. "Remember," he told Rubin, who was as naïve in the ways of the U.S. government as he was sophisticated in the politics of Afghanistan, "your main problem is not the Taliban, but the CIA and Denis McDonough." During the 2008 campaign Rubin had to resign as an Obama advisor after the *Times* described his efforts to develop channels to the Taliban. Throughout the administration's first year he was kept out of the White House.

Holbrooke was skeptical, too. He—we—knew almost nothing about the Taliban. Who were they? What did they want? Did they follow a chain of command, or had they become a collection of semi-autonomous local groups, some radical Islamists, some Pashtun nationalists, some just criminals? Were they the same barbarians who had tryannized Afghanistan in the 1990s and allowed it to become a staging ground for global terrorists? They still showed the same cruelty—the vast majority of civilian casualties were victims of Taliban bombings. Holbrooke insisted on hearing the view of Rina Amiri, who spoke of the millions of Afghans—women, ethnic and religious minorities, educated urbanites—who opposed any deal that would give the Taliban a share of power. But he also sent Rubin out to test the possibilities in secret.

At the beginning of 2009, Qayum Karzai, the president's brother, introduced Rubin to a Saudi lawyer named Mansour bin Saleh, a former mujahid in Afghanistan in the eighties and the Balkans in the nineties, who was now close to the Saudi minister of intelligence. Mansour and Qayum had gone to Kandahar and met with a Talib who had direct connections to the Quetta Shura across the border in Pakistan, the Taliban high council around Mullah Omar. The Quetta Shura had just formed a political commission. It turned out that a few senior Taliban wanted to talk to the Americans away from the eyes of their ISI masters.

Rubin learned all this from Mansour on a trip to Saudi Arabia in the spring of 2009. When he returned to Washington he wrote up a memo for Holbrooke. "RCH should visit Riyadh as soon as possible . . . Need to create a public 'address' for the Taliban to facilitate talks. The Saudis can do this in Riyadh or Mecca. This is the address, free of Pakistani pressure or al-Qaida threats, that will be able to dissociate Taliban from al-Qaida . . . The address for the Taliban can be created only with the full support of the US . . . The US should signal support by releasing Afghans from detention."

Holbrooke read the memo on the shuttle to New York—he got Rubin a seat next to him in first class—and said, "If this works, it's the only way we're going to get out."

Rubin arranged for Holbrooke to meet Mansour in the VIP lounge at the Dubai airport. Holbrooke, en route from Abu Dhabi, had only thirty minutes, part of which he spent on the phone and in the bathroom.

"Excellency, don't trust the Pakistanis," Mansour told Holbrooke. "You should handle everything yourselves. Listen to them, but don't trust. Take the sunglasses away from your eyes and look at everything clearly. If you take care of the peace process yourselves, everyone in the region will appreciate it. This will change all the mess in the Islamic world. Now they all hate you."

Holbrooke had trouble with Mansour's heavy accent and nervous mumble. "So you claim to have contact with the Taliban?" he broke in.

"Yes."

"Well, if you're talking to them, do something about David Rohde." He wrote the name on a scrap of newspaper and gave it to Mansour, testing his bona fides. "This is a good friend of mine and he's a hostage of the Taliban. He has a family. Can you do something?"

Mansour said that he would try.

On the flight back to the United States, Holbrooke, in his flesh-colored sleep suit, and Rubin stood talking in the galley between first class and business. "I couldn't understand a word that guy was saying," Holbrooke said. "Is he one of those guys you have to sit around and drink tea with for hours?"

"I'm afraid so."

"Well, I don't do that. You do it."

Mansour knew a crooked Afghan businessman who had spent ten years in a New York prison for heroin smuggling, and who maintained contacts on all sides of the Afghan war. The businessman got in touch with the kidnappers, and they soon released a video of Rohde trying to reassure his family. This gave Mansour some credibility. The kidnappers demanded fifteen million dollars to ransom a friend of Richard Holbrooke's. The businessman and the Saudis tried to negotiate the figure down to five million. But one night in June 2009, after seven months of hellish captivity, Rohde and his interpreter escaped by climbing over the safe house wall on a pilfered length of rope and presenting themselves at a nearby Pakistani base. They were flown to the American base at Bagram, outside Kabul, where the first call Rohde received was from Holbrooke.

"I apologize," Rohde said at once, and he braced for Holbrooke's withering scorn.

"God, it's so good to hear your voice," Holbrooke said.

Rubin continued to pursue the Saudi path to the Taliban. In August, Mansour summoned him back to Dubai, where he told Rubin that he had recently received a letter and two calls from Taliban representatives. Mullah Omar had just appointed a new political commissioner to represent the Quetta Shura in negotiations. His name was Tayeb Agha. He was related to Omar by marriage and had served as the commander of the faithful's personal secretary in Kandahar during the waning years of Taliban rule. He was now in his late thirties, dark and slender, with a melancholy demeanor. When Mansour met Tayeb Agha, he told him that the Americans would stay in Afghanistan for twenty years if necessary, which made talking inevitable: "The U.S. does not want to lose, and the Taliban do not want to lose. Both want a way out in which they do not lose."

Rubin wrote to tell Holbrooke that they now had an interlocutor with a name. Unfortunately, Tayeb Agha was also a Taliban fundraiser—just then he was in Jeddah making the rounds of private Saudi sources. The Americans would have to take him off their sanctions list before they could talk to him. Freeing its prisoners and delisting its leaders were the first Taliban priorities for any negotiation.

Holbrooke wanted to keep the new channel for himself rather than letting the CIA take it over. He told colleagues that negotiating Afghanistan, with its many sides and murky relationships, would be "tougher than Vietnam or Bosnia." Rubin once joked that they should lower their sights from winning the Nobel Peace Prize to not becoming subjects of a film like *The Fog of War*, Errol Morris's anatomy of Robert McNamara. Holbrooke had enough sense of humor to laugh.

Tayeb Agha refused the Saudi demand that the Taliban break with Al Qaeda and meet with Karzai. "We will never sit with Karzai until he pledges loyalty to Mullah Omar," Tayeb Agha declared. He was sent packing from the kingdom and landed in Doha, Qatar, where the Taliban set up their first political office.

But for the rest of 2009 nothing happened. First came the disastrous Afghan election, and then the endless review of McChrystal's troop request, and then the surge. Political strategy was not on the Situation Room table, and Holbrooke didn't put it there. "I am *so* disappointed in this administration," Rubin said to him one night. Obama and his advisors were unwilling to consider any approach except the military one that they clearly doubted would work—as if talking with the enemy would cost the president too much of his limited capital.

HOLBROOKE KNEW from Vietnam and Bosnia that negotiations had to be timed to battlefield realities. In Vietnam, Nixon had delayed serious talks while unilaterally withdrawing hundreds of thousands of troops, which weakened Kissinger's hand with the North Vietnamese in Paris (Lake had warned Kissinger of this). "By the time they cut the final deal in later 197[2], the two men were like the losers in a strip poker game, naked," Holbrooke wrote in early 2010 in a memo to Clinton. In Bosnia, Holbrooke allowed the Muslim-Croat offensive to continue until the map gave him maximum leverage with the Serbs at Dayton. If Obama waited to talk until the surge troops began to leave in mid-2011, then he would repeat Nixon's and Kissinger's mistake.

In the spring of 2010, Holbrooke and Lute became unlikely partners. Their offices, SRAP and the NSC, both wanted to pursue negotiations while the surge continued. In April, Obama finally gave the go-ahead, and Lute began to chair what was called the Conflict Resolution Cell—a group of officials from different agencies who met weekly in a small, secure conference room just off the Situation Room. The group got rid of a Bush administration order that had blacklisted Taliban leaders until they surrendered, and it turned the order's three preconditions for talks into the end goals of talks: the Taliban should stop fighting, renounce Al Qaeda, and accept the Afghan constitution.

In May, Vikram Singh, a Pentagon civilian whom Holbrooke had recruited for SRAP, and Chris Kolenda, an army colonel, took these ideas to McChrystal. The military had opposed talking with the Taliban in the middle of the surge, but the three-hour briefing in the Pentagon basement convinced the general that a political strategy had the best chance of success at the point of greatest troop strength, when military pressure could reward cooperative elements of the Taliban and punish the irreconcilables. McChrystal's support for talks would make it easier to bring around the president and his advisors. "If Stan is for it," Holbrooke told Singh, "then we won't be the diplomats who ruined the war."

The Conflict Resolution Cell looked for leads to Taliban counterparts. They assembled a list of fifteen names, and Tayeb Agha's went to the top. He was closely connected to Mullah Omar, he was outside Pakistan, and—Holbrooke had recently learned—the Germans, convinced of his credibility, were now talking to him as well. Holbrooke thought that Tayeb Agha's identity was so sensitive that he needed a code name. He proposed "A-Rod," after the Yankee third baseman. This struck Lute as more Holbrooke bullshit, but he said, "If you must."

Holbrooke assumed that he would eventually be the one to negotiate. He sometimes said that there would be no Dayton for Afghanistan, but don't you think that in quiet moments he allowed himself to imagine a round table in a gilded hall in some Arab principality, with Karzai in his purple cape, Kayani in his khaki uniform, a bearded mullah in a black turban, and himself in a suit? He still aspired to be the diplomat who ended America's longest war. It would secure his place among the great men.

Lute had a different idea. Everyone agreed that the Afghan government would nominally take the lead, but Holbrooke had burned his bridges with Karzai. And since the Americans were combatants in Afghanistan, shouldn't a non-American lead the negotiations? Lute proposed the elderly Algerian diplomat Lakhdar Brahimi, who had chaired the U.N. conference in Bonn in 2001. Hillary Clinton immediately shot down the idea: "We don't outsource our diplomacy." An American would be in the lead.

But when Holbrooke told her that he would need diplomatic help once negotiations began, she replied coolly that it wasn't at all certain he would be doing the talking. Holbrooke was stunned. There were limits to what she would do for him.

IN JUNE, *Rolling Stone* published "The Runaway General," an article by Michael Hastings that quoted McChrystal and his inner circle talking about civilian leaders—Biden, Jones, Eikenberry, even Obama—with arrogant derision. Holbrooke came in for brutal treatment. "The boss says he's like a wounded animal," someone on McChrystal's staff said.

"Holbrooke keeps hearing rumors that he's going to get fired, so that makes him dangerous." The image was vivid and accurate. "He's a brilliant guy, but he just comes in, pulls on a lever, whatever he can grasp on to." McChrystal was seen groaning over yet another Holbrooke email and cramming his BlackBerry back in his pocket: "I don't even want to open it."

When the piece appeared, Holbrooke and McChrystal were both in Kabul. Holbrooke had just flown up that night from Helmand, where his V-22 Osprey took gunfire as it landed at the marine base in Marja, then two suicide bombs exploded a few hundred yards from his vehicle as he was driven to meet a village chief. Holbrooke, in his Yankees cap, was casual throughout, which might have impressed even the men around McChrystal.

In the middle of the night, the phone in Holbrooke's room at the embassy residence woke him up. It was McChrystal. Holbrooke immediately thought that either Karzai had been killed or the Green Zone was under attack.

"Sir, I want to apologize," McChrystal began.

"What for?"

"There's an article coming out in *Rolling Stone* about me that says some bad stuff about you."

"So what?"

"Well, it's going to cause a firestorm, and I wanted to tell you. It's my fault and I owe you an apology. I have offered the secretary of defense my resignation."

"Well, we all take hits in the press." Holbrooke was beginning to imagine how bad the stuff was. "Don't worry about me, Stan. Whatever it says, I've had worse. And it won't affect my respect and friendship for you."

After they hung up, Holbrooke wrote McChrystal an email that the general might have been pleased to open:

> I am lying here only a few hundred meters from you at 3am, thinking about the call you just made to me. And here is what I want to say, before I have seen this article: Whatever it says about you or your staff or me or anyone else, the article will have no effect on the mission

we are jointly embarked on. Nor will it affect my feelings for you . . . I assume and hope, of course, that your offer to SecDef was rejected on the spot. Your friend, Richard

Gates, along with Mullen and Clinton, wanted McChrystal to stay on. But the president, with Biden snarling in his ear, fired him for insubordinate conduct, which ended his career. Obama replaced McChrystal with Petraeus, to whom Holbrooke immediately wrote: "I feel awful for Stan, whom I spent much time with on his last 2 days in Kandahar and Kabul. But this feels right to me."

Petraeus imposed his iron will on the war, bringing full-spectrum counterinsurgency with a lethal edge. The civilians were squeezed out and then blamed for not holding up their end. With McChrystal gone, the military command in Afghanistan lost interest in talking to the enemy. When Holbrooke brought up the subject, Petraeus dismissed it: "That's a fifteen-second conversation." At one point the general tried to take over negotiations in order to smother them: he revealed to reporters that NATO was providing safe conduct from Quetta on its own aircraft for a Taliban leader to meet Karzai at the Arg. Holbrooke was outraged—if a civilian leaked such a thing he'd be fired.

Then came some startling news. Holbrooke was giving a press briefing at the Kabul embassy when he spotted the *Times*'s Dexter Filkins, who had figured out that the Talib in question was Mullah Akhtar Mansour, the number two in the Quetta Shura. Throughout the briefing Holbrooke conspicuously ignored Filkins's raised hand. Toward the end, an aide handed Filkins a note from Holbrooke: "Would you have a minute to talk confidentially?"

As Filkins was leaving the room with the other reporters, the aide grabbed him and shoved him into a nearby men's room.

Holbrooke was standing at a urinal with his back to the door. "Are we alone?"

"I think so."

"Check the stalls."

Filkins looked under the stalls. "Richard, I think we're alone."

"You know that Taliban guy you've been writing about? The guy we're talking to isn't him."

"What do you mean?"

"Our guy is a total fraud." Holbrooke was still urinating. "He's a shop owner in Quetta. And we gave him a lot of money"—$250,000 in cash.

"Didn't you check his identity?"

"We did. We thought he checked out." No one seemed to know what Mullah Mansour looked like, except an Afghan at the border who pointed out the impostor. "The whole thing is a total farce." Holbrooke zipped his pants and flushed. "There's nothing to be redeemed from this." He opened the bathroom door and pushed Filkins into the hall. "And if you tell anyone where you got this, I'll never speak to you again."

"THE INSURGENTS WIN in a guerrilla war if they don't lose," Holbrooke wrote in a memo to Clinton in September. "We cannot convince Pakistan to make its strategic interests symmetrical with ours because of its obsession with India and the military domination of its strategic policies. For these reasons, we should explore whether there is a basis for a political settlement with the Taliban that falls within our red lines. Nothing is less appealing than the idea of dealing with the Taliban, but it would be irresponsible to continue to ignore this area."

Clinton was ready to support the idea. With Obama's approval, Holbrooke's deputy Frank Ruggiero would have a first meeting in Munich with Tayeb Agha and the German diplomat Michael Steiner, who had been with Holbrooke at Dayton. The Taliban path was beginning to open up. But Holbrooke had begun to think it wouldn't lead all the way to an end to the war. The fighting would go on unless something changed outside Afghanistan, in the region. The United States needed a regional strategy.

The Rubik's cube was so complex. Karzai was playing the United States and Pakistan against each other, talking to both, trusting neither. The northerners in his government were anxious about any concessions to either the Taliban or the ISI. India would only talk to Pakistan without a third party, and never about Kashmir, but Pakistan wanted the United States in the middle of its standoff with its hated neighbor. China, Pakistan's ally, was uninvolved politically while seeking economic advantage in Afghanistan and Pakistan. Iran was a Karzai ally that also gave money to the Taliban. The Saudis were offering their good offices for peace in Afghanistan but feared antagonizing Pakistan. Any solution had to involve all of these actors in the right alignment of interests.

Holbrooke thought that India and Pakistan might have a dialogue if it was limited to Afghanistan. There were subtle signs of change coming from Pakistan. Kayani had written a fifteen-page white paper, his third in a year, and given it to Obama and a few other Americans. It suggested that Pakistan now saw the Taliban as part of a regional problem: "Peace in Pakistan will only be possible if Afghanistan is peaceful. An early end to conflict in Afghanistan is one of Pakistan's key strategic interests . . . The United States and Pakistan wish to see Afghanistan free of extremist and radical forces."

Holbrooke thought if India and Pakistan came to understand that their common problem—"extremist and radical forces"—was more serious than what divided them, they could choke off the oxygen that fed the war by applying pressure on both sides. He put his thoughts into a memo for Clinton. The audience he most wanted remained unavailable.

He had been alone with Obama once, in Chicago, and never again. He knew that the president didn't like or trust him, but he thought that fifteen minutes together, uninterrupted by anyone else, might be enough to show how useful he could be. He wanted Obama at least to hear these ideas. Sooner or later—he never stopped believing this—the president would have to come for him. He kept trying to see Valerie Jarrett, Obama's close friend and advisor, but she always rescheduled and they never met. He tried to get an appointment to the president through Axelrod, but Axelrod had stopped returning his calls. So he went through Axelrod's young assistant, but he couldn't even get Eric Lesser, who looked like a college sophomore, to reply.

One day Lesser was using the men's room in the West Wing basement, around the corner from the Situation Room, when he glanced to his right and saw Holbrooke standing at the next urinal.

"Eric, I'm very, very disappointed."

Lesser said nothing as they stood side by side.

"I'm just very, very disappointed. I called you, I reached out about setting up a meeting, and I've heard nothing back."

The tone suggested a personal hurt, as if Lesser had betrayed their friendship.

"I'm sorry, Ambassador Holbrooke. I'll email with you, I'll talk to David, and as soon as we can set something up I'll get back to you."

Lesser fled.

Friends who saw Holbrooke that fall knew there was something wrong. He was eating badly, not exercising, not sleeping enough. His belly was distended and his face flushed from jawline to scalp. One night, at the embassy residence in Kabul, he had his bare feet up and Eikenberry noticed that his ankles were badly swollen. "Dick, your feet," Eikenberry said, "they're red and puffy."

"It's a problem I have."

"It's dangerous. I'm having the embassy doctor come look at you."

Walking the short flight of stairs up to his bedroom on N Street left him wheezing. Wisner noticed one night when Holbrooke asked him to come back to the house because he didn't want to be alone. Wisner expressed concern, and Holbrooke said that he'd see his doctor, but he missed the six-month follow-up appointment in November for his aortic aneurysm. Soon after, Holbrooke and Wisner were having their ritual annual dinner at Wisner's Washington club, the Metropolitan, where they always ordered congressional bean soup, two dozen cherry-stone clams, green salad, and rice pudding, and Wisner always paid. Holbrooke was eating too fast and greedily, and on its way to his mouth the edge of a clamshell scratched the tip of his nose. A jet of blood began spurting out, so much blood that Holbrooke needed two cloth napkins to absorb the flow. He was still on Coumadin, an anti-coagulant. Wisner was horrified.

"What are you doing this for?" Wisner said. "Get the fuck out."

"I will, I will."

Wisner made him promise he'd be gone by the end of the year. They both knew Holbrooke had no intention of keeping his promise. It was the same with Gelb. He and Holbrooke spoke by phone several times a day—Holbrooke was always the one to call and talk over the drama of the moment—and when Gelb urged him to quit, since there was nothing left to stay for except more pain and humiliation, Holbrooke would say that he'd start thinking about an exit plan in six months but he couldn't leave yet, he could still get things done, at least he had to outlast Jones.

He crashed meetings in Clinton's office to which he wasn't invited, and her young aides had to ease him out. He asked the Pakistani foreign minister to tell her what a good job he was doing. There was something frantic about him—he didn't know what he would do next. He confided to Vincent Mai, his pal from Lehman days, that Perseus wouldn't take him back. This time around no one on Wall Street was going to hire Holbrooke for his name and connections. "Certainly someone will want to have you on their letterhead," Mai said, and he offered to bring Holbrooke on at his investment firm, the act of a friend.

He could write a book—he always planned on writing another book. But there was no path higher. The Obama years might very well be the end of his climb. He couldn't bear for it to end like this.

After Kati's affair with the Hungarian in 2004 he'd begun seeing a woman in Germany. She was middle-aged, divorced, wealthy, warm-hearted. His visits to Germany multiplied year by year. On trips to Afghanistan the SRAP's C-20 stopped over for rest and refueling in Munich, the only destination where he made his assistants stay on a separate floor or in a different hotel. A city known for its beer halls and soccer club always got a thrilling exclamation point in his diary, and on his magenta-colored Nokia slide phone—which his aides called his "Candy phone," imagining that he was having an affair with a girl by that name—he kept a picture of the woman in her bathrobe. She made him happy, but she wasn't an alternative to his marriage.

Once he quit, he and Kati would live together again in New York. It wouldn't be easy. The balance of power would flow in her direction. There was still no one else either of them would rather talk to, but she was often annoyed with him. "Vacation with K, but, alas, each day there is at least one argument," he wrote on a trip through the Po Valley. "Wish K were happier with me, but I suppose I recognize it's partly my fault."

David once asked his father why he didn't leave after Kati's affair. "I don't want to start over," Holbrooke said. "I've been married three times. I love her and I want to make it work." But that fall he told a few friends that he didn't know if the marriage would survive. Yet he still loved her, needed her—more than she needed him.

Toward the end of 2010 he returned more and more to the past. He spent several days working on a speech for a State Department event on the opening of the Vietnam War archives. He attended a dinner with Rufus Phillips and other surviving Saigon hands on the ninetieth birthday of one of them. When *Foreign Policy* celebrated its fortieth anniversary, he was there to receive an award and give a speech recalling his years as editor. These occasions were much more than duties. They awoke his deepest feelings.

I want you to hear his voice one more time. Each time it's the same because he never changes. The same crystal brilliance, the same inward occlusion, the blind spot growing bigger with the pressure of these last months. And each time it's different because of history, his own and the country's. The pitch is lower than in the past, the words come from his throat more than his nose, he keeps coughing as if speaking is an effort—as if the underwater current has reversed course and now the relentless pressure of that voice is bearing down on *him,* cajoling, bullying, needling him, saying, "Don't stop now. Why would you stop? You're almost there."

IX

Today was a difficult day because I woke up in the morning feeling quite uncomfortable and realized I was back in atrial fibrillation. So I left New York, did not tell Kati till I got to Washington and had it confirmed. When I landed in Washington I went directly to the White House for a meeting of the non-group that discusses intelligence matters. We discussed some of the most sensitive issues involved in our efforts in Pakistan and Afghanistan—what to do about the Haqqani group, what we should do if there's an attack on the United States from Pakistani soil. After that meeting, I went directly out to Sibley Hospital and spent much of the early afternoon out there getting my blood tested and preparing for the electro-conversion tomorrow.

One can just feel the growing tension and pressure in every direction. I certainly can feel it, and I just have a feeling it's just going to explode once we get past the summer holidays. More and more people are saying the war isn't going well. Zardari has just announced publicly that we were losing, in London—that wasn't helpful. He damaged himself greatly by staying in Europe apparently promoting his son's political career while Pakistan faced the worst floods in its modern history.

Just a thought, a memory from the past. I remember once sitting with Averell Harriman in Paris when he was getting too many instructions on the Vietnam peace talks. This would have been in late

1968, probably the fall, and he said rather frustratedly that in 1942–43 FDR had sent him to Moscow with Churchill with the simplest instruction: go with Churchill and explain to Stalin why we can't open a second front yet. And now, he said, he was getting overly instructed by the likes of Walt Rostow. I was reminded of this today because I found myself telling old war stories to my young team in the middle of a meeting on something else, and I turned to one of my team, Shannon Darcy, a nice young thirty-one-year-old AID person—we'd assigned her something to write—and I said, "Can you write well?" and she said, "I do my best," and somebody else said, "But Holbrooke will edit it for you a lot." I found myself telling the story about how the first article I'd ever edited for *Foreign Policy* was the article with George F. Kennan in 1972, and I suddenly found myself telling these people, who probably were bored to death by this old story, that the first person I ever edited was George Kennan, and he was uneditable because he wrote so perfectly, the best writer ever to work in that building. And now I was editing Shannon Darcy.

We presented Hillary with three papers. One, written by Rina Amiri and rewritten extensively by me, was the first road map I'd found for a way to integrate the women's issue with the negotiating track by making it a central part. This may face some opposition at the White House but it's the right way to go and I think it was a tremendous step forward. Working deeply and in detail with Rina, we recast a traditional advocacy memo into a new political strategy in which if there's ever a negotiation of any sort on the political future, women's issues take a central place, because otherwise there's no domestic support for supporting Afghanistan afterwards anyway, and because it's the right thing to do.

Then, even more important, we began an aggressive advocacy of sending an American to meet with the most important channel that we've ever had to the Taliban, the man I call "A-Rod." The only absolutely clear channel to Mullah Omar that exists. And finally we have an advocacy paper on opening up a channel to Iran. So everything's in place at the same time.

Early in the day I talked to Hillary and told her I thought we were at the crunch point, and it would be morally inexplicable if we delayed any further discussions if we had an opportunity to talk to the Taliban.

Petraeus is strongly opposing all this. He says it's too early and he wants to do it only when he says the time is right, which he says will be next year, by which time he'll have had more military success. Frankly I just don't believe him. I think the situation will still be an ambiguous muddle, with elements of progress and elements of retrogression. But above all, there won't be enough time to achieve what he calls classic counterinsurgency, which in any case is a theory I've always doubted.

What's interesting about this is that these are the things we've advocated doing in a methodical way since last year when we were blocked by a combination of opposition from certain aspects of the U.S. government and passivity from others. And suddenly everybody has gotten excited about this all at once.

The chances of being able to pull this off are very small, but the effort has to be undertaken and finally the president is focused on it. The final memo, which Hillary will hand to the president today, is one that I think is pretty good. Maybe we'll look back on it as one of the most important memos we ever wrote, but that remains to be seen.

Flashback: Early last year, 2009, in some of the early NSC meetings with the president, I referred to Vietnam and was told by Tom Donilon and Hillary both that the president did not want any references to Vietnam. That they did not apply, they didn't like them, it concerned them. I was very struck by this, since I thought there were obviously relevant issues.

It just struck me that this is the forty-second anniversary of the Soviet invasion of Czechoslovakia. It happened during the Democratic Convention in 1968. I remember Dean Rusk was testifying before the Platform Committee, I think, and I remember when the news came in he was so shocked by it.

The number one issue during my attempt at vacation has been the Pakistani floods. I think we've been moderately successful in raising the profile of it by relentless harassing of journalists and government officials. The White House initially paid it almost no attention, the president issued a meaningless statement, but Hillary understood it from the beginning and I did massive media. We've now put about $150 million into the kitty, and more to come, but the dimensions of it keep growing, an area larger than the size of Italy is apparently under water, 20 million people affected. Cholera, failures in the electrical grid, destruction of the cotton crop, which will destroy the textile industry. The country is facing a series of problems which are hard to fathom.

Yesterday Kati and I went to the final performance of the revival of *South Pacific* at Lincoln Center with Frank Rich and Alex Witchell and Linda Janklow. A fantastic production, which I found immensely moving. Men were crying, myself included. I tried to understand why that show had such an enormous emotional impact on us. For me it was the combination of the beauty of the show and its music, and the capturing in that show of so many moments in American history, the show itself opening in New York at the height of New York's greatness, 1949, the theme—Americans at war in a distant land or islands in the South Pacific—the sense of loss of American optimism and our feeling that we could do anything. The contrast with today—it was very powerful, and I kept thinking of where we were today, our nation, our lack of confidence in our own ability to lead compared to where we were in 1949 when it came out, evoking an era only five years or seven years earlier, when we had gone to the most distant corners of the globe and saved civilization.

KABUL BANK, Afghanistan's biggest bank, appears to amount to little more than a giant Ponzi scheme, with most of the money having been given to its own owners without any interest. If it's true it would be a staggering piece of criminal action and would have enormous repercussions. I called Hillary—she was very good on every issue, but the one she was most upset about of course was the Kabul Bank. She saw immediately that it could be catastrophic, and we talked about ways to minimize the damage. On the reconciliation channels, she urged me to show that we've been on top of this issue for over a year. She wanted me to collect all these memos, which is a physical impossibility, because she keeps saying they're going to look for anything to avoid letting you do this.

I saw Biden alone. When I mentioned the women's issue, Biden erupted. Almost rising from his chair, he said, "I am not sending my boy back there to risk his life on behalf of women's rights, it just won't work, that's not what they're there for." I said, "Joe, I agree with you, we're not there for that but it has the following content," and I tried to outline to him the position Hillary and I had taken. He thought it was bullshit, and this spiraled into a much larger discussion concerning the whole course of what would happen, and this was quite extraordinary. Joe took the position, plain and simple, that we have to get out of Afghanistan. I reminded him that the president and Hillary and indeed, I think, Joe himself had talked about a residual presence like Iraq, which he said he'd been working on most of the last year, that we would need congressional appropriations to train the army and the police and give economic assistance, we wouldn't get any of that if women were sent back to the black years and the dark ages. He said it ain't going to happen, he said I don't understand politics, he said we're facing a debacle politically, he said we're going to lose the presidency in 2012 if unemployment remains high, and Afghanistan was the other issue that could pull us down and we have to be on our way out, that we had to do what we did in Vietnam.

This shocked me and I commented immediately that I thought we had a certain obligation to the people who had trusted us. He said, "Fuck that, we don't have to worry about that. We did it in Vietnam, Nixon and Kissinger got away with it." I said, "But there are larger strategic consequences here," and he said, "What are they?" and I tried to outline them. He clearly thought I was mouthing some kind of right-wing crap, and it got quite intense.

I said I thought I had been successful in moving Hillary very much in the direction where he was over the last year. He replied that that may be true but why hadn't I spoken up in the meetings with the president more? I said, "Look, I can't speak up in those meetings to tell him some of the things I believe, for example that counterinsurgency won't work, not because Hillary doesn't agree with me, although she doesn't, but because I can't take issue with Petraeus, Mullen, and, in those days, McChrystal and Gates in front of the president without compromising my ability to work directly with them on a day-to-day basis to implement counterinsurgency." Even if I don't believe in it, it's the presidential policy and I said I felt I had to do it.

Even though the chances of success in any kind of dialogue with the Taliban are very small—I put it at 10 to 20 percent—it would be irresponsible of us not to try given the fact that there's no military solution to the war and given the fact that we are in a harsh spiral right now, a declining relationship with Karzai and at home. The bottom is falling out of this policy as we speak, and everybody knows it. The only way to deal with it, in my view, is to seek a political solution. Petraeus, on the other hand, believes deeply that classic counterinsurgency is the answer. By classic counterinsurgency he means what he wrote about in his doctrine. I don't believe it will work here any more than it did in other places. They can talk about the Algerian or Moroccan or Malaysian or Philippine models all they want, but it won't work here because of the sanctuary that is Pakistan, and because of the incompetence of the government, because we don't have enough resources and we don't have enough time, and because the president is going to start drawing down troops next year. Petraeus is gambling that his brilliance—and he's undeniably brilliant—will trigger an outcome which will decimate the enemy, and then they will in effect fade away. Highly unlikely.

Petraeus has changed, mainly for the worse. Time is short for him. July 2011 looms just ahead. His normal intensity has been supplanted by a nearly demonic style, and he no longer listens much to other people unless protocol or short-term self-interest requires it. If his interlocutor is another American not in his chain of command, his lack of patience when he isn't speaking is palpable. At one level, I have real sympathy for him. He knows that every moment counts. He has to produce, and, like most great commanders, including his favorite, Ulysses S. Grant, he is totally convinced of his own correctness and destiny. His own personal story—the near-death training accident, his memorable struggles with senior officers who despised him, his apparent success in Iraq when few believed it possible—has enhanced a near-mythic persona. He is surrounded by his team of fanatically loyal aides, like almost all four-stars, but his team is quietly efficient, unlike McChrystal's group of cocky and contemptuous cowboys, who thought they were a high priesthood of shadow warriors saving our nation from itself.

Despite his vast talents, in fact, he has lousy instincts outside his own narrow fields of military affairs and self-promotion. His single-mindedness, his lack of genuine interest in other issues, and his coldness are sometimes chilling. Mullen dislikes him but now has to support him. Lute deeply dislikes him and thinks he is driving us in a direction contrary to the agreed strategy. This is a judgment I understand but don't fully share. "He is trying to do nation building," says Lute, but what is "COIN" if not nation building? The real problem is whether Petraeus' strategy will work, and at what cost. His dynamism is clearly hurting the Taliban, as evidenced by the growing number of enemy who are reaching out to cut deals at the provincial level. Ironically, however, it is not his population-securing efforts that have produced these results so much as the incredible effect of his "night raids" (not all of which are at night). In the last ninety days, he says, over 1500 Special Forces actions, battle tempo unmatched in the history of warfare! So where is the problem, if there is one? In a word, sustainability. Or in another word, transferability.

When I went up to see Axelrod, I said as I was leaving, "David, I know you don't want to hear this again from me, but the president is the only person in the Administration at a high level who I haven't ever given my views to directly and candidly, and I hope we can correct that." He just nodded. This has been my greatest frustration, though I do not believe that if I saw him I would actually make a difference. At least, however, I would have fulfilled my obligation to him.

The question constantly arises—I ask it of myself, friends ask me— how long do you want to do this? My answer is simple: as long as I can make a difference. We're now embarked on the most difficult period in terms of formulation of policy. Since last year, we're shaping the policy, as I wrote Hillary in my memo last week, in ways that will determine the rest of the course of the war. It's the president's last chance to turn away from the problems that are faced. We are going to try to get them to make one effort at what we call reconciliation. That's really a euphemism for seeing if there's the basis for a political settlement with the odious Taliban. But since a military victory is impossible, we have to make that search.

I'M IN ISLAMABAD after two grueling days in the southern part of Afghanistan and Sindh, visiting the flood areas. Hard to imagine a more overwhelming sight. The refugees themselves are in bad shape, but I've seen worse in refugee camps in Angola and Cambodia and even Bosnia. But what makes this so extraordinary is the endless display of areas under water, people clinging to not even shelter but just clinging to the dikes, as close to their land as possible, scattered all across the landscape of southern Sindh. We went to Thatta Wednesday the 15th and saw this vast display of people clinging to survival. They're resilient and they're tough.

As we helicoptered out of Karachi on Wednesday morning after having flown in from Dubai, where we spent the night, we started seeing patches which were under water, and then as we got further north of Karachi just endless inland sea, with trees occasionally popping up through the water, an occasional spot of land, and on the dikes and raised areas people in tents just huddled along the roads. Finally we reached Thatta and went to a refugee camp run by the army. People were in tents in a tremendously hot area. They had nothing except most of them had brought the bed frames out with them. No information, no knowledge of what was going on. When we talked to them they all wanted to go home, of course. They were not critical of the government, but the government was with us—there was a general with us and the district commissioner, a very good man who seemed very genuinely concerned about the situation. I gave him $100 to use in any way he saw fit because I just couldn't imagine leaving without leaving something behind.

Most important meeting in long term was the one with Kayani, where for the first time I broached the subject on a hypothetical basis of contact with the Taliban. Kayani is a critical figure in American foreign policy, and a very enigmatic one. Obviously extremely smart, with a real strategic sense, disciplined, talks with a kind of a mumbly, slurry accent, which makes him a little bit hard to follow and that requires one to concentrate very closely. When I first met him we always met him in the GHQ headquarters in uniform, but early this year he began to meet me in civilian clothes at his house, a very calibrated sign of respect. He's usually accompanied, and was last night, by his sidekick General Pasha, the head of the ISI. Pasha, in his first meeting with Hillary in February of last year, introduced himself as the head of the world's most notorious spy service. Which shows of course that he has a very good sense of humor. What makes dealing with these two men so complicated is that their buy-in to our policies is absolutely critical but they don't really trust us or agree with us and they don't always tell us everything they're doing. It is one of the eternal complexities of our foreign policy that the CIA's main counterpart organization in this part of the world is also the one with ties to America's enemies. We support them, we work with them, we exchange information, we give them money and technical assistance, they collaborate with us when they feel like it and don't when they don't feel like it. All of this was on exhibit last night at dinner.

I posed the question to them of what they really want, and they posed it back to me—what are your intentions in Afghanistan? I said, "You've asked us many times and I thought we had answered the question, but we will try to do it again." This time, I moved the ball forward somewhat by telling them that I wanted to discuss the issue of reconciliation, meaning of course whether or not we should talk to the Taliban and if so under what circumstances. I said I wanted to talk entirely hypothetically because no decisions have been made. This is technically true although we're clearly moving towards the President checking the box to authorize an outreach to the Taliban.

The Pakistani position was essentially contradictory in three ways. On one hand, they said that all contacts with the Taliban should be led by Karzai and we should be in the background. That's standard U.S. policy as well. Secondly, they said nonetheless we should work directly to try to negotiate with the Haqqani group, to which I replied, "How can we talk with the Haqqani group? They're nihilists allied with Al Qaeda, they don't stand for anything, and they're the most dangerous people in the area." To which, with a slight tone of pride—it seemed to me almost to be pride—Pasha said, "Yes, they are the best." Of course historians of the conflict know the Haqqani group was established by the CIA and the Pakistanis in the 1980s by Reagan as part of our anti-Soviet policy, the very policy which has come back and bitten us so disastrously after 9/11. The third contradictory point from the Pakistanis was—even having told us we should talk to Haqqani—they said they don't know how to get in touch with them. Now, nobody in the CIA or the US government believes that. So there we are, caught in a triple contradiction of Pakistani attitudes, necessarily being polite.

What is clear is that something is afoot. It looks to me like the

Taliban are starting some kind of diplomatic charm offensive, or at least intensifying one that's been going on for a while, and that their proximate goal is to set up an international presence, probably in Saudi Arabia, a place where they can have access to the international community out from under the thumb, pressure, and rather distrustful eye of the Pakistani intelligence services. What is less clear is whether or not the Pakistanis will let them do anything. And what is even less clear is what the terms of any agreement with the Taliban would be. I pressed Barney Rubin on this today when we had a lunch alone on Lexington Avenue, and even he, the eternal optimist on what can be done with the Taliban, was uncertain.

Yesterday the *Wall Street Journal* broke the story which we'd been most dreading: the Justice Department is investigating Karzai's older brother, Mahmoud Karzai, who is the business leader of the family. The Karzai family, I should note, is organized very much like the Corleone family in *The Godfather,* with one person who's the businessman, one who's the drug dealer, one who runs restaurants, and one who's the president—and just the dream that Don Corleone had for his family. Of course it didn't work for the Godfather and his family, and it doesn't look like it's working well here either.

THE WOODWARD BOOK CONTINUES to astonish everybody who looks at it. Not that it's a good book—on the contrary, it's a very poor book in terms of explaining how policy is made. It's full of meaningless and trivial little factoids and anecdotes that are irrelevant to the larger theme. Woodward would argue that those illustrate the personality of the president, and in that sense he's right. But he doesn't have the ability to distinguish between what matters and what doesn't matter, and because he writes as he gets the information, the information is out of context. A minor dispute that was resolved quickly but with great intensity might take precedence over a major policy dispute which is resolved in a different, more orderly way. But the real shocker of the book is the self-indulgent, undisciplined performance of the White House. Tom Donilon told me today that he didn't think Jim Jones would last another seventy-two hours because Jones was the main leaker in the book. While I won't lament Jim Jones's departure, since he had tried to force me out of the government, I will welcome his departure ahead of me. On the other hand, he is far from the only leaker. General Lute is a major source. I feel embarrassed now to be part of an administration whose performance is this bad and that is so undisciplined and so self-righteous and arrogant.

Jim Jones was fired today, rather brutally, and Tom Donilon replaced him. This obviously removed from the government the person who made the most active attempt to destroy me, and he's replaced by the person who's my closest friend in the White House, although anyone who's worked with Tom knows quite well you can't really rely on him in the end because of his inherent weaknesses. But he's grown a lot, he's the best person for the job, and it's the best outcome for us.

Jones was fired by receiving a phone call from Denis McDonough around seven-fifteen in the evening at the USO gala, the annual gala— that's the charity he loves most, and he probably was in all his fine regalia as a marine in black tie when he got the call. I learned this this morning from Admiral Mullen while I was over there having a private talk about the negotiating tracks. Even though Mullen thought Jones had to go, he also thought the way it was handled was shabby. The military code was violated and forty years of service were treated like shit by a man they consider a junior kid, a punk. They have no respect for McDonough in the military, and they have their reasons. Once again, the coldness, almost deliberate cruelty, of the White House is on exhibit. It's a recurring theme, and while no one can attribute it directly to the President, it obviously emanates from a style which he doesn't object to at all.

TUESDAY NIGHT, November 2, election night. It seems to me, looking back on the last two years, that Obama won based on a brilliant campaign which was premised on his biography as the promise of what could happen in America. He was very skillful at it, and once he won he abandoned that, retreated into tactical decisions with no coherence or soaring aspirations except health care. He also did some very good things, impressive achievements, which he couldn't present as part of the achievement of his promise, and he got out-maneuvered by the Republicans. At the core of it I think is the strange sense that Obama thinks he's better than most Americans, and he doesn't reach out to them the way Clinton does. I know there are flaws in this analysis and I can see them as I say it, but I just feel he's so detached and people sense that. Gore and Carter had the same flaws. Clinton did not, Reagan did not. They reached out to people, and when they got into trouble that helped them.

Thinking about the election, thinking about two years, I'm left with a fundamental and disturbing conclusion. Barack Obama is brilliant and impressive, his biography is powerful, and he ran a pitch-perfect campaign during 2008. But, having said that, one must also conclude on the basis of the first two years that he was not ready to be President. Most presidents have stumbled in the early part of their presidency recently—it happened to Clinton in '93, Reagan in '81, Carter in '77, and Bush of course in 2001 until 9/11, which prevented him from being a one-term president. So in that sense Obama's not unique. But his lack of experience at government was greatest of any president in our lifetime—no one had had less experience, and it showed. He simply wasn't ready, and now he has to pull himself back together, change his style, open up, communicate more, think more strategically, gain more control over the levers of government and persuasion, and show leadership. If he does, he'll win a second term, as Clinton and Reagan did after similar debacles in their first midterm. If not, it's going to be Jimmy Carter, George Bush Senior all over again for him, a one-term presidency.

The most interesting event of the day was one hour with Donilon, in his new office as NSA. He was more relaxed than he used to be. He no longer has to fight off a war with his immediate boss. I began by saying that I'd entered this room many times and I'd known every NSA since McGeorge Bundy, and that since 1977 when Kissinger had left that room that I was now in, there'd been a peculiar thing that had occurred. I said that I thought Kissinger had left some kind of chemical in the paint and that it had infected all of Kissinger's successors, so that people became Sandy Kissinger and Tony Kissinger and Brent Kissinger, Bud McFarland Kissinger. I noted that one person had tried to commit suicide out of the job, another had gone to jail, several had had crackups in the job, and I urged him not to be Tom Kissinger but just Tom Donilon.

As I started to leave I mentioned the Woodward book, and this caused an eruption by Tom, who said that he would not ever speak to Woodward again. I said, "But your wife and his wife are close friends." He said, "Not anymore." Tom's reaction seemed strange to me, given the fact that there's only one comment in the book that was negative and that was a comment about Tom by Gates, which Gates denies having said and in any case was inconsequential. But the more likely explanation was that Tom was a source for the book and that Woodward burned him. Tom claims not to have opened the book, which I find unlikely given his anger at it.

This, however, launched Tom into a diatribe against Jim Jones. Tom offered the suggestion that Jones was the worst NSA ever and that he was simply a clown. I can't disagree. Tom's hatred of Jones is justified, although his odd double standard about how it affects him and how it affects me is sort of characteristic.

THE PRESIDENT IS apparently airborne on his way to Kabul, which I discovered last night by piecing little details together—particularly Doug Lute's failure to show up at the dinner we were co-hosting together for the internationals, sending his deputy Colonel Tien, who said to me, rather tonelessly, "Doug is with the President." I said, "You mean they're in the air." He said, "I cannot answer that." I said, "Okay, don't answer it. But tell me he's not." And Tien, trying to signal without saying, said, "I cannot answer it." I can't pretend I'm happy that the trip has gone ahead without me. The last one I didn't care much about, the short one in April, which was a farce, but this one is more consequential and I think I should have been asked on it, and I will have to spend the day pretending it was a routine thing. But, anyway.

Kati suggested I call the book I'll eventually write *Outsider,* as an ironic reference. Of course that's just an idea but it has its merits this morning, particularly with a subtitle like *Outsider: The Inside Story of the Obama Administration in Afghanistan.*

My Indian counterpart, S. K. Lambah, came here at my invitation to test a new idea that I had come up with, which would be to see if we could get the Indians and the Pakistanis to agree to talk to each other, but only about Afghanistan, not their bilateral issues. Frank Wisner had predicted this would fail, but we got it put together. Today Lambah went in to see Hillary Clinton. He did extremely well with her. At my suggestion she saw him alone for a while in her big ornate room, her legs occasionally tucked under her, which means she's feeling quite informal, after we threw everyone else out and it went down to she, S. K. Lambah, and myself. She liked the idea very much.

S. K. Lambah and I saw each other privately later in the day at his hotel. He was very enthusiastic. I'm going to have breakfast with Ambassador Haqqani in the morning, and then we're launching a very, highly difficult process to see if we can get India and Pakistan to be willing to talk to each other if the talk is restricted just to Afghanistan. So that's the essence of it, and we will see what happens next.

End of Tuesday, December 7.

X

The next morning, Holbrooke met Haqqani for breakfast at the Four Seasons. He told the Pakistani ambassador that S. K. Lambah, a veteran Indian diplomat, was in town and had responded favorably to the idea of an India-Pakistan dialogue on Afghanistan. Haqqani reported this back in his telegram to Islamabad, and he advised a noncommittal Pakistani response, holding the idea in reserve as an option to rein in Indian ambitions.

But, below the waterline, he told Holbrooke that Pakistan would never let go of Afghanistan. "How long are you going to go on?" Haqqani asked. "I'm done."

"As long as I can make a difference. We can't quit." Holbrooke said that the whole world wanted to know what motivated Pakistan's military. "I wonder if they know themselves. Maybe I've come close to understanding that their interests are commercial. Maybe we can come up with some commercial deal that will pressure them."

"Try," Haqqani said. "But very frankly, when somebody has an entire country, why should they be satisfied with some commercial interests?"

After breakfast, Holbrooke met Lambah at his hotel. Lambah was just as skeptical as Haqqani. He was willing to take the idea back to Delhi, but he had little confidence that Pakistan would change, even after Holbrooke showed him Kayani's latest white paper. Pakistan had never had any desire to talk about Afghanistan with India—it regarded

Afghanistan as one of its dominions. Holbrooke's optimism had the smell of desperation.

They left for separate airports, Lambah back to India, Holbrooke to New York. He had time to make one of his daily calls to Gelb.

Gelb, who had better sources around the administration than Holbrooke, had heard that another move was afoot to get rid of him. They left him off Obama's trip to Afghanistan, they kept him from the NATO summit in Lisbon, they excluded him from the latest strategy review. Holbrooke was worried about Donilon, and he feared even Clinton was tired of fighting for him.

"I'm trying to see the president," Holbrooke told Gelb. They never bothered with greetings.

"I don't think it's going to happen."

"I'm trying to see Axelrod but he hasn't returned my call. Do you have any idea what's going on?"

"As I've told you all along, he's not your friend. You keep telling me he's your friend and he's giving you good advice. He's not your friend. My guess, though I don't know for sure, is he's one of the people who's blocking you from seeing Obama."

Holbrooke was silent for a moment. Then he moved on to the Indians and the Pakistanis and began describing the latest promising developments.

"Bullshit," Gelb said. "They always tell the Americans they agree with us and they never deliver, and Kayani's not going to deliver on this."

"I can tell whether they're serious or not."

"I know, you were there. I don't believe it. Their track record is they never deliver on this because they don't see their interest the way we see their interest. Their first and second priority is to fuck India."

When Holbrooke arrived at the Beresford he was exhausted. Kati had never seen him so pale. She told him to lie down and rest, but he said—almost sobbed—"I don't want to rest. I want to talk to you." He couldn't stop fretting about the wallet he'd recently lost, and with it the scrap of pink embassy message paper on which he'd written Kati's sister's phone number in Paris in 1993. He had kept it ever since. Losing it was anguish.

But there wasn't time to talk. They had three parties that evening: a book launch for *A Rope and a Prayer,* David Rohde and his wife

Kristen's story of the kidnapping ordeal; a party for the financier Felix Rohatyn's autobiography; and a farewell party for their friend Jim Hoge, who was retiring as editor of *Foreign Affairs*. This last, a dinner at the Four Seasons hosted by the Petersons, was the kind of event that brought out New York's aristocracy of success, now fading into irrelevance—the bankers, journalists, TV personalities, and foreign policy types he called his "real friends" when he was feeling wounded by Washington.

The dinner was in the private dining room upstairs. In the crowd on the staircase Wisner and his fiancée were a couple of steps behind Kati and Holbrooke, who turned to greet them. Wisner started to say something about Holbrooke's idea for India and Pakistan—that it might work if he tried to—

Wisner saw Holbrooke's face drop into a frown, and he saw Kati looking hard at her husband, and he stopped talking.

During dinner Holbrooke left his table and went up to Gelb and pulled him over to an empty table. He was shaking with emotion.

"Kati and I just had a terrible fight."

But then a *Wall Street Journal* photographer approached the two old friends for a picture. They posed with index fingers raised as if they were arguing about Afghanistan and Pakistan, except they were both smiling. From the jawline up Holbrooke's face was mottled red, his eyes dim with fatigue, his belly swollen over his belt. "Let's talk tomorrow," he said. They went back to their tables.

After dinner Holbrooke asked Wisner to stay with him on N Street the following night. Wisner declined—he would be staying at the Metropolitan Club.

In the morning Holbrooke flew back to Washington. On the way to the airport he got a call from Dick Beattie. Beattie's wife had seen Holbrooke at the party and told her husband that Holbrooke was going to die of a heart attack—his color, his weight, everything about him looked terrible. Beattie wanted Holbrooke to see his cardiologist—he didn't trust Dr. Rosenfeld. Holbrooke mentioned the fight with Kati. He was still furious with her, but also ashamed of how he had responded. They had said harsh things.

At the State Department cafeteria he had lunch with Susan Glasser, the editor of *Foreign Policy,* and consumed her California roll along with his sushi. She left him with the award from the fortieth anniversary party that had delighted him but that he'd forgotten to take home, a Lucite replica of the magazine's first issue with his article "The Machine That Fails" listed on the cover. He worked late at his desk, and an aide caught him devouring fistfuls of chocolate-covered espresso beans from a gift basket that a group of Pakistani-Americans had sent for the Islamic New Year. The aide took them away.

He went home to N Street and changed into jeans and a powder-blue sweater before going out to 1789, a Georgetown restaurant in an old Federal building, with a fireplace and exposed ceiling joists. He had an eight o'clock dinner with Michael Abramowitz, the son of his friend Mort Abramowitz, who was really his former friend ever since they had fought over Kosovo. Holbrooke was tired, subdued, but catching up on the Abramowitz family lifted his mood, because they belonged to his past. He didn't want to talk about his work, except to suggest that it was a grind but what could you do when the president asked you to take on the country's most important challenge?

What he wanted to talk about was Kati. That she was a brilliant writer, that she had written two books with Holocaust themes (Michael was an official at the Holocaust museum), that she discovered she was Jewish only later in life, that her father had been a cold man, that Peter Jennings had wanted her to quit working at ABC after they married. Only Holbrooke fully appreciated her. He didn't want to stop talking about Kati. Perhaps it made him feel closer to her. They hadn't spoken since the fight.

Abramowitz drove him back to N Street. On the way, Holbrooke said that he and Kati were losing money by the hundreds of thousands of dollars every year he stayed in government.

When he got home, it was ten-thirty. He called Wisner at his club and asked him to come over. "I really want to see you. I need to talk to you about what happened last night."

"I can't do it. I just got back to my room. It's late."

"What you said about my idea—I've never discussed it with Kati, and she has been on a full-scale anger offensive, attacking me, criticizing me. We had one of the worst fights of our marriage."

"Oh, shit. I'm sorry. It was completely inadvertent."

"I know you didn't mean it, but she's very angry that I told you and not her. I'm trying to package this and take it to the president, and Kati likes to talk too much—I can't trust her with anything I'm working on. So we had this big fight, and we haven't spoken since." Their marriage, he said, was in deep trouble.

He stayed up late. He called the younger woman who had been his lover, and when she didn't pick up he said to her voicemail, "You've forgotten me. I'm heartbroken." A message came from his secretary, Donna Dejban: Axelrod would see him at the White House at nine in the morning. He watched Stephen Colbert and made phone calls and wrote emails until well past midnight.

FRIDAY, DECEMBER 10. He woke up tired and anxious. At seven-thirty he called his deputy, Frank Ruggiero. Ruggiero was scheduled to brief Clinton at ten that morning about his encounter in Munich with Tayeb Agha, which had laid the groundwork for more talks. Holbrooke kept him on the phone for an hour, talking about whatever was on his mind, reminiscing about old Washington people. He asked whether Ruggiero knew why Axelrod wanted to see him on such short notice, as if the meeting might be bad news—as if Axelrod might be about to fire him.

He made a quick call to Kati. There wasn't time to discuss what had happened between them and repair the damage. They laughed about a news story—India's ambassador, a woman they both disliked, had been outraged by an airport pat down in Mississippi. "It feels so good to laugh," Holbrooke said. But on the drive to the White House he was agitated.

He arrived out of breath, pasty-faced and sweating. Axelrod thought he looked awful.

"I'm going to tell you something that only five people in the world know about," Holbrooke began. It was the kind of windup that annoyed the Obama crowd, but Axelrod listened politely as Holbrooke told him about Tayeb Agha, the channel to Mullah Omar, the need for a political settlement. He seemed less focused than usual, as if something was bothering him. At one point he fell into such a bad coughing fit that Axelrod told Lesser to get a glass of water.

"I need to talk to the president," Holbrooke said. "I'm not sure he knows everything he needs to know."

Axelrod made it clear that he wouldn't go around the NSC. Had Holbrooke talked to Donilon and McDonough?

Holbrooke said that they were the ones blocking his path. "I know the president doesn't like me."

Axelrod didn't deny it—he would have lost all credibility. "I'm sure he appreciates your efforts, but you need to present your thoughts in a productive way." Not advice for how to talk to Obama, but explanation for why he would never get to.

Suddenly Holbrooke looked at his watch. "I've gotta go to a meeting with Hillary." He rushed out of the White House, and Lesser followed to escort him to his car on West Executive Avenue. Axelrod was leaving at the end of the year to work on the president's re-election, and Lesser would leave too, and as they walked together Holbrooke mastered his disappointment enough to offer him a job at SRAP. Lesser was going to law school, but he was grateful.

On the ride to the State Department Holbrooke called Gelb. "I saw him. It doesn't look like it's going to work out." Gelb had no idea of an Axelrod meeting, but he knew immediately what Holbrooke meant.

He took the elevator up to the seventh floor.

Rushed down the hallway, past the Operations Center, where his call from Sarajevo came in on the day of Igman. Past Gelb's old office, Lake's old office.

Into the mahogany corridor of the secretary's suite. The official portrait of Dean Rusk watching him from the wall opposite the door, baggy eyed, unsmiling—the reluctant father who had made him a diplomat if anyone had.

Rushed past Clinton's executive secretary, Steve Mull.

"How are you, Ambassador?"

"Worst day ever. And now I'm late for Hillary."

Into the secretary's outer office, where he used to loiter with Wisner and Tarnoff, hoping to catch sight of Cyrus Vance. Dropped his coat on a chair for Claire Coleman, Clinton's assistant, to hang up in the tiny closet within the doorjamb. Into the secretary's vast reception room where he and S. K. Lambah had met with Clinton three days ago. Where he had once met with Albright, and Christopher, and Vance, and, when he was only twenty, Rusk. Where he had always dreamed of receiving important visitors like himself.

There was a Christmas tree in a far corner of the room. Paintings of Washington, Madison, and John Quincy Adams on the walls. An enormous Persian rug across the floor. Blue-and-pink drapes with a design called "the Four Continents," based on ones Ben Franklin had brought back from France in 1799. Clinton was sitting on her couch beneath the window that looked out on the Lincoln Memorial. Jake Sullivan sat to her left on the couch. Ruggiero sat to Sullivan's left in an armchair.

Holbrooke was fifteen minutes late—the meeting was almost over. He sat down in the armchair to Clinton's right. "I just came from seeing Axelrod. It was very interesting." He began to talk about the historic importance of negotiating with the Taliban, why this would be more difficult than Vietnam and Bosnia. It was the kind of speech that had long since lost Obama.

"Come on, Richard," Sullivan said, "everyone understands your point so let's keep on track."

Ruggiero continued briefing the secretary for her meeting at the White House.

Holbrooke started to say something.

"Oh my God, Richard, what's happening?"

Clinton was looking at his face. It had turned a color that never appears in a human face, so furiously red it was cartoonish. Holbrooke stood up.

"I don't know." He looked bewildered—not in pain, but as if he had received a tremendous surprise. "I don't feel good. Something horrible is happening."

"Let's get you down to the medical office right away."

"No, I'll wait."

"Go right now. Claire is going to take you down to the nurse."

Ruggiero and Sullivan walked Holbrooke to the secretary's private elevator while he barked instructions—"I'm fine, Claire can take me. Get back to briefing Hillary so Frank can move ahead."

Coleman took him down to the first floor. Left, left again, past room 1515, his shitty office. Downstairs to the basement, a labyrinth of white corridors, linoleum floors, low ceiling tiles. Donna Dejban, his secretary, caught up with them. A few feet from Medical Services he collapsed against the wall.

"My legs! Something's wrong!"

Dejban and Coleman helped him inside the clinic. "Don't call Kati, don't call Kati," he kept telling Dejban.

"My phone doesn't work down here," Dejban said. "I'm going to have to call her when we know more."

The nurses laid him on a gurney. They took off his coat and tie and shirt, and they covered his big trunk with a gown. His face was ashen below and crimson above. He was screaming in pain. The ambulance was taking forever.

"Where's my staff? Where's the ambulance?"

His deputies, Ruggiero and Dan Feldman, came in along with his body man, Chris LaVine. "I'll go with you," Ruggiero said.

"Dan, stay with me," Holbrooke said. Feldman had been with him the whole two years. He was the closest thing available to a son.

They wheeled Holbrooke through the loading dock out into the winter air of the sidewalk on Twenty-first Street. He pulled the sheet over his face. "This is the end of my career. It's never going to be the same again." They waited in the cold for another ten minutes until the ambulance pulled up.

Feldman got in back with Holbrooke and LaVine in front with the driver. The ambulance sped down Twenty-first Street and turned left on C Street and left again on Virginia Avenue, toward Georgetown, where almost everyone he once knew was dead.

His chief of staff had directed the ambulance to Sibley Memorial Hospital, out past the house on Nebraska Avenue that he had shared with Litty. But his aides thought he might not make it that far and told the driver to turn up Twenty-third Street to George Washington Hospital, ten minutes closer than Sibley.

"We should call Kati," Feldman said.

LaVine dialed on his BlackBerry, and when Kati answered he told her, "I'm here with Richard. We're in an ambulance. Let me put him on." He gave the phone to Holbrooke.

"I feel a pain I've never felt," Holbrooke said. It was the flat, lifeless voice of the call he'd made to her after the accident on Mount Igman. "I have no feeling in my legs."

Kati was at the Beresford, just back from the gym and still in her workout clothes. She said she was coming. The call was brief.

Holbrooke complained about his treatment—no doctor, just nurses, and the ambulance had taken twenty minutes. "Tell Hillary the medical staff are terrible."

Feldman began taking notes on the back of a credit card receipt from a Chinese restaurant.

"Call my kids—tell them how much I love them. Tell David and Lizzie to come down. Call Anthony"—he was in Germany—"he doesn't have to come. Tell Chris he can come down if he wants. This is the best staff ever. Make sure you let everyone know that."

The pain in his chest was terrible. Feldman was trying to hold Holbrooke's hand and take notes.

"You're going to have a great career. Everyone likes you. Your kids are great. Spend more time with your family. Don't let me die here."

"I won't. We're getting to the hospital."

"What's happening? There's no flow. My ass, my legs—I can't feel anything. Maybe it's a clot." He was in a panic. "Don't let me die alone. I want to die at home with my family. I have so much to do."

Hillary Clinton's doctor, Jehan El-Bayoumi, worked at George Washington and heard from a Clinton aide that an important person was coming their way. A young cardiologist named Monica Mukherjee met the ambulance at the doors and led the gurney through the emergency room to radiology.

Holbrooke was screaming in pain. Mukherjee tried to settle him down for the CT scan. She could already tell that his aorta had torn. She didn't know who he was but he seemed gigantic to her, much too long for the gurney. His enormous feet almost fell off the end. No blood was reaching those feet and their distress was now extreme.

Feldman stepped away to call the doctors in New York.

"Where's Dan," Holbrooke demanded, "where's Dan?"

"You have to calm down," Mukherjee told him.

The scan showed a Type A aortic dissection, meaning straight to surgery. In the secretary of state's office the force of his heart pounding blood under immense pressure through the stressed and weakened aneurysm had torn a hole in the aorta's inner layer, and as blood streamed between the layers the torn flaps blocked the flow to the spinal arteries, and his lower half was cut off.

Mukherjee called the hospital's chief cardiac surgeon, who was fifteen minutes away. "You need to come right now. It's a VIP."

"Who is it?"

"His name is Holbrooke."

He was wheeled into the triage trauma bay and a curtain was drawn around the gurney. Feldman was on his left side, holding his hand, and LaVine was at the foot of the bed. Mukherjee was trying to get a catheter into his right wrist to monitor blood pressure, but he was in such turmoil that she couldn't do it. His skin was cold and clammy and he looked as if he was about to pass out, but Mukherjee was struck by how he dominated the room—not just his size but his sheer presence, the light in his ice-blue eyes.

She was still struggling with the IV. "This may hurt."

"It's a good thing you're beautiful, Doctor," Holbrooke told her.

El-Bayoumi and others were now in the room. His blood pressure was spiking and the pulse in his legs was dying but he wouldn't stop talking, giving orders to Feldman, who was still taking notes, as if this were a staff meeting.

"I love so many people. Tell Les I love him. Call Frank and Strobe. Call Jim Johnson. Thank Claire for me. Tell Rosemarie. Tell Hillary what's happened. Tell Eric Lesser in Axelrod's office. Tell Ash I love her and to come over. Make sure you're recording my every witticism."

Mukherjee turned to El-Bayoumi. "Whatever you can do to calm him down."

"I want you to close your eyes and relax," El-Bayoumi said. "Pretend you're at the beach."

He closed his eyes. "I hate the beach."

"Okay, what do you like?"

He opened them and looked at Mukherjee. "I like beautiful women."

Mukherjee was getting a little annoyed. El-Bayoumi told him again to relax.

"I can't relax. I'm in charge of Afghanistan and Pakistan."

"And Iraq?"

"No, I don't care about Iraq. I'm trying to bring peace to Afghanistan."

"Just relax," El-Bayoumi said. "Let me worry about Afghanistan."

"Fine. You end the war."

He was handed consent forms to sign but was in too much pain to read them. "I have a problem with the second clause," he said, putting on. He signed.

They wheeled him to the elevator and took him up to the second floor. He kept instructing Feldman.

"Tell Mort Janklow. No, wait till the operation is over, and don't release a press statement till it's over."

In the intensive care unit the surgeon introduced himself. "Mr. Holbrooke, I am Dr. Farzad Najam, the cardiac surgeon here."

"Any Indian-American doctor is okay with me," Holbrooke said. Still putting on. Najam and Mukherjee exchanged a look. Najam was a Pakistani American, from Lahore. He knew about Holbrooke's work. "Just tell me it's going to be okay."

"Mr. Holbrooke, you have an acute aortic dissection—the aorta has ripped. It's a surgical emergency and we need to take you to the operating room." Najam would have to cut through the breastbone, put him on a bypass pump, and replace the aorta and perhaps the valve.

"What are you going to put in its place? A mechanical thing? Get me anything you need—part of a pig's heart, part of Dan's heart."

Hospital staff were removing Holbrooke's watch, his wedding ring, his State Department pass, and giving them to Feldman.

"This is a very high-risk operation," Najam said. "The risks of death are significant. Fifty percent or greater."

Holbrooke heard this and became calmer. "I like you," he said. "I know you're not bullshitting me. If my life is saved I know it's because I'm here."

The performance that carried him through the fear and pain fell away. The continuous effort of action that never let up even in the final extremity suddenly ceased. For the first and last time the ice-blue eyes filled with a resolve to see the truth about himself and did not look away.

He was holding Feldman and Mukherjee by the hand. He squeezed.

"Call Kati."

That was the end. Twenty hours of surgery, massive bleeding because of the Coumadin, his aorta shredding down to his pelvis. He never woke up. On Monday evening, December 13, his heart gave out. Hillary Clinton broke the news to his staff in the lobby of the hospital where they had kept a vigil, and they wept in her arms. She took them to the Ritz-Carlton and they sat in the bar and told stories about him into the night.

When a king dies the grieving gets competitive, as if the greatness of the departed might be transferred to those who are seen to mourn him most. This happened with Holbrooke, who never sat on the throne but aroused a similar response. There was a curious scramble to have been close to him, and many of the competitors were far kinder once he was gone than while he was here. Karzai phoned Kati with his deep dismay. A pink-flowered "Feel Better Soon" Hallmark card, from "Lt Gen Ahmed Shuja Pasha, Director General, Inter Services Intelligence," arrived after Holbrooke's death. The memorial service at the Kennedy Center Opera House was like a state funeral. Zardari was there from Pakistan, and generals, diplomats, bankers, journalists, Carl Bildt, Dikembe Mutombo, Albright, Biden, the White House staffers who had tied him down like Gulliver, and Litty, and the woman from Germany. Renée Fleming sang "Ave Maria." Fake palm trees from the set of *South Pacific*, playing at the Kennedy Center, were onstage, and so—seated alongside Kati, David, Anthony, and the other eulogists—were Hillary and Bill Clinton and Barack Obama.

"Richard was a very good husband," Kati said.

"Never, never forget Dick's fragility, his vulnerability," Les Gelb said.

"I could never understand people who didn't appreciate him," Bill Clinton said. "Most of the people who didn't were not nearly as good at *doing*."

"God bless you, my friend," Hillary Clinton said.

Obama sat for the entire two hours, a form of respect or penance. When his turn came he praised his late humiliated SRAP in abstract, secondhand terms, and quoted Matthew Arnold's poem "The Buried Life," an odd choice since it's about the quest for an inner life—one mountain the deceased never wanted to climb.

Privately, Obama expressed exasperation with the notion going around that he had killed Richard Holbrooke.

COULD HOLBROOKE HAVE SOLVED Afghanistan? I don't think so. The best ideas are useless without the ability to bring them into the world. He had lost an essential knack for persuasion. And perhaps by the time Holbrooke got there Afghanistan had already become one of those terrible things that have to be done but can't be done. Still, if Obama thought it was worth sending sixty thousand troops, it was also worth mastering his dislike of his long-winded special representative and using Holbrooke's fading powers to help end the war. Afghanistan never mattered enough.

By the end he was living in each chapter of his life simultaneously— Kennedy and Obama, Vietnam and Bosnia and Afghanistan—as if he were floating in a single body of water whose temperature varied from place to place and depth to depth. All that accumulated experience— we Americans don't want it. We're almost embarrassed by it, except when we're burying it. So we forget our mistakes or recoil from them, we swing wildly between superhuman exertion and sullen withdrawal, always looking for the answers in our own goodness and wisdom instead of where they lie, out in the world, and in history. I'm amazed we came through our half century on top as well as we did. Now it's over.

There were other ceremonies in other cities. In New York the same mix of those who loved and detested him filled the seats at the U.N. General Assembly. Samantha Power and Susan Rice made a late entrance together. And alone in the balcony sat Tony Lake.

He was seventy-one and wore a gray beard. He had walked half a block from the offices of UNICEF, where, thanks to Obama and Rice, he was in charge of trying to save the world's children, from Syria to Burma—a job for which he was superbly suited and in which he would be finally happy. He had come to see off his old friend and enemy, and being here made him feel, as he often felt, conflicted. He didn't want to create a stir, but he wanted to pay his respects. If not to Dick Holbrooke, at least to the past they had shared. Then Lake slipped out unnoticed.

THERE WAS SOMETHING restless about Holbrooke in absentia. He had disappeared so abruptly from a world in which his presence had caused such commotion. Nothing was settled by his death—everything was up for grabs.

Kati asked Hillary Clinton and Admiral Mullen to get him buried at Arlington. It would require a waiver from the secretary of the army since Holbrooke had never served in the military. Clinton and Mullen wrote letters, and Mullen pushed hard inside the Pentagon, but the resistance from Petraeus and General John Kelly, Gates's military assistant, was too much. Holbrooke had served his country on and off for five decades and died in action, but there was no room for him in the national cemetery.

His very ashes were restless. They kicked around unburied for years. First at the crematorium, because Kati was too undone to claim them, and then for months at the house of his chief of staff, until she brought them in a colorful macramé bag to a Georgetown book party where she knew that Kati would be a guest, and Kati took the ashes up to her new Manhattan apartment, where she kept them for several more years.

She transmuted her loss into a campaign of interviews and speeches and op-eds. She spoke for her late husband's legacy in Berlin and Srebrenica and Dayton. She denounced Obama. She wrote a book about her marriages and recalled a last loving phone conversation just before Holbrooke's collapse, though not the fight that preceded it. When David set out to make a film about the father he had never known well, Kati tried to stop him, and they quarreled over who would speak for Holbrooke's memory. In widowhood she became as relentless an advocate on his behalf as he had ever been in life.

He was finally buried in the fall of 2015, in a cemetery out in the Hamptons, under a gravestone that says:

RICHARD C.
HOLBROOKE
APR. 24, 1941
DEC. 13, 2010
STATESMAN
HUMANITARIAN
PATRIOT

As I watched all this, at the remove of those lesser friends in general admission seating, I felt that the restlessness had something to do with his being almost great. If he had climbed to the height that he and his admirers hoped for, his death would have been followed by honored burial in the fixed and serene place that history reserved for him. If he had been like most of us, grief and memory would have stayed private. But in that unfinished space between, where the souls of the almost great clamor to be recognized, he was still struggling, striving, yearning for more.

That's all I have to tell you. I've gone on longer than I meant to. There was too much to say, and I still can't get his voice out of my head. One day I know it will start to fade, along with his memory, along with the idea of a life lived as if the world needed an American hand to help set things right. By this point you're familiar with its every failing. But now that Holbrooke is gone, and we're getting to know the alternatives, don't you, too, feel some regret? History is cruel that way. He loved it all the same.

Note on Sources

The primary sources for this book are the Holbrooke Papers (to be housed at Princeton University's Seeley G. Mudd Manuscript Library) and the author's interviews with nearly two hundred fifty people. Those interviews took place in the United States and nine other countries, including Vietnam, Bosnia, Serbia, Croatia, and Afghanistan. The interviews were conducted on background, meaning that the author could use the information without any attribution. Therefore, although the interviews provided a great deal of material for the book, these notes do not include them as sources. For example, the description of Saigon at the start of the Vietnam section is drawn from interviews with many people who were there, as well as from the books and other sources mentioned in the notes; the account of the accident on Mt. Igman in the Bosnia section is based on interviews with those personally involved, as well as on the U.N. investigation report; scenes at the Obama White House in the Afghanistan section are drawn from interviews with numerous former officials, as well as from the Holbrooke Papers and other written sources. Names of those interviewed are listed below, with the author's gratitude.

Hassan Abbas, Michael Abramowitz, Morton Abramowitz, Christiane Amanpour, Rina Amiri, Dejan Anastasijevic, Holly Andersen, Michael Armacost, Ken Auletta, David Axelrod, Jeffrey Bader, Randall Banky, Peter Bass, Richard Beattie, Edina Becirevic, Elizabeth Becker, Richard Bernstein, Carl Bildt, Avis Bohlen, Ashley Bommer, Lakhdar Brahimi, Marie Brenner, Kevin Buckley, Bojan Bugarcic, John Fisher Burns, Gahl Hodges Burt, Robert Campagna, Aida Cerkez, Shamila N. Chaudhary, Derek Chollet, Zoran Cirjakowicz, Wesley Clark, Hillary Rodham Clinton, Richard Cohen, Roger Cohen, Summer Coish, Steve Coll, Sherard Cowper-Coles, James B. Cunningham, Pete Dawkins, Muhammad Omar Dawudzai, Donna Dejban, Joy de Menil, John Dempsey, Sasa Djogovic, Tom Donilon, Peter Duchin, David Dunn, R. P. Eddy, Kai Eide, Karl Eikenberry, Jehan El-Bayoumi, Lawrence P. Farrell, Jr., Ronan Farrow, Dan Feldman, Burt Field, Dexter Filkins, Jon Finer, Frances FitzGerald, Sylvana Foa, Stefanie Frease, Dervo Gadzo, Peter W. Galbraith, Bob Gallucci, Ejup Ganic, Judy Gelb, Les Gelb, Daniel Gerstein, Susan Glasser, Mary Ellen Glynn, Philip Goldberg, Mary Beth Goodman, Mate Granic, Jeremy Greenstock, David Greenway, Eliza Griswold, Claudia

Grose, Peter Grose, Mirza Hajric, Husain Haqqani, Paul Hare, Peter Hargraves, Stephen Heintz, Christopher Hill, James Hoge, Andrew Holbrooke, Anthony Holbrooke, Blythe Babyak Holbrooke, David Holbrooke, Litty Holbrooke, Martin Indyk, Wolfgang Ischinger, Susannah Jacob, Ali Jalali, Michael Janeway, Morton L. Janklow, Elizabeth Jennings, James A. Johnson, James Jones, Paul W. Jones, Ward Just, Robert G. Kaiser, Marty Kaplan, Hamid Karzai, Nicholas deB. Katzenbach, James Keith, Donald L. Kerrick, Sepideh Keyvanshad, Zalmay Khalilzad, Ann Kinney, Gilbert Kinney, Henry Kissinger, Fawzia Koofi, John C. Kornblum, Momcilo Krajisnik, Norm Kurz, Mark Lagon, Anthony Lake, Antonia Lake, S. K. Lambah, Chris LaVine, Vladimir Lehovich, Eric Lesser, Jonathan Levitsky, Jean-David Levitte, Mark Lippert, Jawad Ludin, Douglas Lute, Mark Lynch, Vincent Mai, Gail Malcolm, Mark Malloch-Brown, Kati Marton, Veran Matic, Denis McDonough, George McDowell, John Menzies, David Miliband, Tom Miller, Anne Milliken, Ivan Misetic, Saad Mohseni, Roger Morris, Nader Mousavizadeh, Monica Mukherjee, Steve Mull, Mike Mullen, Cameron Munter, Farzad Najam, William Nash, Vali Nasr, Shuja Nawaz, John Negroponte, Pauline Neville-Jones, Thu Ha Nguyen, John W. Nicholson, Jr., Rod Nordland, Suzanne Nossel, Morgan O'Brien, Robert Orr, Peter Osnos, James Pardew, Anne Patterson, Peter Peterson, David Petraeus, Annie Pforzheimer, Barbara Phillips, Rufus Phillips, Nicholas Platt, Richard Plepler, Jelani Popal, Samantha Power, John Prendergast, Kenneth Quinn, Sally Quinn, Ahmed Rashid, Zalmai Rassoul, Saskia Reilly, Chris Reimann, David Remnick, Ben Rhodes, Francis J. Ricciardone, Enver Robelli, Robbie Robinson, David Rohde, Lionel Rosenblatt, Peter R. Rosenblatt, Jack Rosenthal, James Rosenthal, Barnett Rubin, Frank Ruggiero, Muhamed Sacirbey, Nikola Sainovic, Amrullah Saleh, Mansour bin Saleh, Tom Schick, Douglas Schoen, Frank Scotton, Daniel Serwer, Maureen Shea, Maria Sheehan, Neil Sheehan, Haris Silajdzic, John Silson, Vikram J. Singh, Vesna Skare-Ozbalt, E. Benjamin Skinner, Edie Smith, Gary Smith, Scott Smith, Peter J. Solomon, Matthew Spence, Jovica Stanisic, James Steinberg, Michael Steiner, Jim Sterba, Fritz Stern, Rory Stewart, Howard Stringer, Jake Sullivan, Mona Sutphen, Strobe Talbott, Peter Tarnoff, Alex Their, James Townsend, Milo Vasic, Alexander Vershbow, Karl von der Heyden, Barbara von Schreiber, Jenonne Walker, Volney F. Warner, Kael Weston, Maureen White, Leon Wieseltier, Frank Wisner, Peter Wittig, Geoffrey Wolff, Priscilla Wolff, Tobias Wolff

Notes

PROLOGUE

3   Saying, "I feel": Richard Holbrooke (hereafter cited as RH), Afghanistan audio diary, September 14, 2010, Holbrooke Papers (hereafter cited as HP).

4   Once, in the 1980s: Leon Wieseltier, "Richard," *The New Republic*, December 14, 2010, https://www.thenewrepublic.com.

7   In one of his letters: Joseph Conrad, *The Collected Letters of Joseph Conrad,* vol. 2 (Cambridge: Cambridge University Press, 1986), 349.

8   "For me it was": RH, Afghanistan audio diary, August 23, 2010, HP.

9   This was what Les: Leslie H. Gelb, "Leslie H. Gelb on the Late Richard Holbrooke's Contributions to Foreign Policy," *The Daily Beast,* January 02, 2011, https://www.thedailybeast.com.

DREAMS SO FAR AWAY

11   His name was Abraham: For background on RH's parents, letters, photographs, passports, other official documents, and an audio recording were provided to the author by Andrew Holbrooke.

11   He was born in 1912: Trudi Kearl to Anthony Holbrooke, March 28, 1994, HP.

12   "After the war the Americans": Sami Moos to Rudolf Saenger, February 5, 1916, HP.

12   Later, Sami Moos: Trudi Kearl to Anthony Holbrooke, March 28, 1994, HP.

13   "Is Nasser another Hitler?": RH to Dan Holbrooke, August 2, 1956, HP.

13   "I am going to send Andy": RH to Trudi Holbrooke, August 2, 1956, HP.

13   That year, Dan had received: Isamu Noguchi to Dan Holbrooke, undated 1950. Provided to the author by Andrew Holbrooke.

14   Forty-one years later, in 1998: "USA: Richardson and Holbrooke Head for New Posts Update," Associated Press Video Archive, March 18, 1998, https://www.aparchive.com.

15   But when, in the spring of 1958: RH interviewed by Richard Rusk, March 1985,

Dean Rusk Oral History Collection, Richard B. Russell Library for Political Research and Studies, University of Georgia Libraries, Athens, http://purl.libs .uga.edu.

15 The previous May: RH in Michael J. Berland and Douglas E. Schoen, eds., *What Makes You Tick? How Successful People Do It—and What You Can Learn from Them* (New York: HarperCollins, 2009), 159; E. Benjamin Skinner, "Reporting Truth to Power," in *The Unquiet American,* ed. Derek Chollet and Samantha Power (New York: PublicAffairs, 2011), 48–51.

16 Once, the college student: RH, untitled paper for History 174 course at Brown University, May 14, 1962, HP.

17 "the first calamity": Fritz Stern, *Einstein's German World* (Princeton, N.J.: Princeton University Press, 1999), 199.

17 He "had a beautiful dream": RH, untitled paper for History 174 course at Brown University, May 14, 1962, HP.

18 "With warm congratulations": RH to Litty Holbrooke, undated, HP.

HOW CAN WE LOSE WHEN WE'RE SO SINCERE?

21 "Boys, take off": Rufus Phillips, *Why Vietnam Matters: An Eyewitness Account of Lessons Not Learned* (Annapolis, Md.: Naval Institute Press, 2008), 161; RH, untitled memoir on early days in Vietnam, September 12, 1969, HP.

22 But in the summer of 1963: Harry Maurer, ed., *Strange Ground: An Oral History of Americans in Vietnam, 1945–1975* (New York: Avon Books, 1989), 101.

22 Everyone went home for noon siesta: Anne E. Blair, *Lodge in Vietnam: A Patriot Abroad* (New Haven, Conn.: Yale University Press, 1995), 8.

22 "Private clubs in Saigon": Malcolm W. Browne, "Saigon AP Bureau Handbook," January 25, 1963, PBS, *Reporting America at War,* https://www.pbs.org.

24 On his final exam: Vladimir Lehovich interviewed by Charles Stuart Kennedy, 1998, Association for Diplomatic Studies and Training (hereafter cited as ADST), Arlington, Va., https://www.adst.org; Vladimir Lehovich Foreign Service Institute Evaluation Form, undated. Provided to the author by Vladimir Lehovich.

24 He declared his intention: RH to Litty Holbrooke, November 5, 1962, HP.

24 Holbrooke and a few classmates: Script for "Modernizing at the Mekong," undated, HP.

25 He went to Vietnam thinking: RH to Litty Holbrooke, November 9, 1962, HP.

25 That story isn't my concern: Among the best books in English on the American experience of the Vietnam War are Fredrik Logevall's *Choosing War* and *Embers of War,* Neil Sheehan's *A Bright Shining Lie,* David Halberstam's *The Best and the Brightest,* Frances FitzGerald's *Fire in the Lake,* Stanley Karnow's *Vietnam: A History,* and the Library of America's two-volume *Reporting Vietnam.* Among the most useful books on the early years of the war are David Halberstam's *The Making of a Quagmire,* John Mecklin's *Mission in Torment,* Robert Shaplen's *The Lost Revolution,* William Prochnau's *Once Upon a Distant War,* Rufus Phillips's *Why Vietnam Matters,* Frank Scotton's *Uphill Battle,* and Max Boot's *The Road Not Taken.*

26 "Do what you did": Jonathan Nashel, *Edward Lansdale's Cold War* (Amherst: University of Massachusetts Press, 2005), 1.

26 He created his own: Fredrik Logevall, *Embers of War: The Fall of an Empire and the Making of America's Vietnam* (New York: Random House Trade Paperbacks, 2014), 635.

28 Lansdale came up with: Cecil B. Currey, *Edward Lansdale: The Unquiet American* (Boston: Houghton Mifflin, 1988), 278.

28 Kennedy called Lansdale: David C. Martin, *Wilderness of Mirrors* (New York: HarperCollins, 1980), 128.

28 Lansdale also had detractors: Max Boot, *The Road Not Taken: Edward Lansdale and the American Tragedy in Vietnam* (New York: Liveright Publishing Corporation, 2018), 366–80.

30 The Rural Affairs handbook: Phillips, *Why Vietnam Matters*, 130.

30 Perhaps they make you think of: Graham Greene, *The Quiet American* (New York: Viking Paperback, 1996), 60.

30 I always thought Orwell: George Orwell, "Review of *The Heart of the Matter* by Graham Greene," in *All Art Is Propaganda: Critical Essays,* ed. George Packer (New York: Harcourt, Inc., 2008), 348.

31 "We used to sit": Logevall, *Embers of War,* 708.

31 Holbrooke disposed: RH to Litty Holbrooke, October 5, 1962, HP.

31 Years later, Holbrooke asked: RH interviewed by Neil Sheehan, May 29, 1976, Library of Congress, Recorded Sound Reference Center, RYB 6803-4, Washington, D.C.

32 "The fight that the Negro": RH to Andrew Holbrooke, August 6, 1963, HP.

33 An old monk named Thich Quang Duc: Malcolm Browne interviewed by Brian Lamb, "Red Socks and Muddy Boots," C-Span, September 26, 1993, https://www.c-span.org.

34 "Jesus Christ!": William Prochnau, *Once Upon a Distant War* (New York: Vintage Books, 1996), 308.

34 At the end of Holbrooke's first day: RH, untitled memoir on early days in Vietnam, September 12, 1969, HP.

34 On his second day: RH, untitled memoir on George Melvin, undated, HP.

36 "The terrible truth": RH, untitled memoir on trip to Vietnam, February 22–23, 2003, HP.

36 In Nha Trang: RH to Andrew Holbrooke, August 6, 1963, HP.

37 But the VC kept overrunning them: RH to Litty Holbrooke, August 20, 1963, HP.

37 Inside, David Halberstam: Prochnau, *Once Upon a Distant War,* 228.

38 "I'm not that kind of general": David Halberstam, *The Best and the Brightest* (New York: Ballantine Books, 1993), 184.

38 In late 1961, Rusk cabled: "Telegram from the Department of State to the Embassy in Vietnam," November 28, 1961, Foreign Relations of the United States (hereafter cited as FRUS), 1961–1963, Volume I, Vietnam, 1961, Document 288.

39 Nolting once asked François Sully: Prochnau, *Once Upon a Distant War,* 50.

39 Nolting threw Halberstam: Prochnau, *Once Upon a Distant War,* 172.

40 "the young commandos": RH to Litty Holbrooke, October 15, 1963, HP.

40 They took Holbrooke to dinner: Neil Sheehan, *A Bright Shining Lie: John Paul Vann and America in Vietnam* (New York: Random House, 1988), 350–51; RH, untitled memoir on trip to Vietnam, February 22–23, 2003, HP; RH interviewed by Neil Sheehan, May 29, 1976, Library of Congress, Recorded Sound Reference Center, RYB 6803-4, Washington, D.C.

43   On Election Eve in 1960: Antonia Lake and Anthony Lake, "Coming of Age Through Vietnam," *New York Times Magazine*, July 20, 1975, 9.

47   Shortly after midnight, truckloads: Prochnau, *Once Upon A Distant War*, 366–70.

48   "Dave is really high": RH to Litty Holbrooke, August 23, 1963, HP.

49   Henry Cabot Lodge Jr. had arrived: Blair, *Lodge in Vietnam*, 37.

49   "Now let's do some play-acting": RH to Litty Holbrooke, August 23, 1963, HP.

50   He might have been an American puppet: Maurer, ed., *Strange Ground*, 80.

50   Three days after the pagoda raids: RH to Litty Holbrooke, August 24, 1963, HP.

50   Dunn told Phillips: Phillips, *Why Vietnam Matters*, 165.

51   "We are in this thing": RH to Litty Holbrooke, August 24, 1963, HP.

51   That same night of Saturday, August 24: Richard Reeves, *President Kennedy: Profile of Power* (New York: Simon & Schuster, 1993), 560–68.

51   The cable told Lodge: "Telegram from the Department of State to the Embassy in Vietnam," August 24, 1963, FRUS, 1961–1963, Volume III, Vietnam, January–August 1963, Document 281.

52   The next day, Lodge wrote back: Blair, *Lodge in Vietnam*, 43–44.

52   "My god! My government's coming apart": Richard Reeves, *President Kennedy*, 565–67.

52   "It is difficult indeed": William Colby, *Lost Victory: A Firsthand Account of America's Sixteen-Year Involvement in Vietnam* (New York: Contemporary Books, 1989), 138.

52   And Lodge—who had been: Phillips, *Why Vietnam Matters*, 168–9.

53   On August 28 he cabled: Blair, *Lodge in Vietnam*, 45.

53   "It is coming to": RH to Litty Holbrooke, August, 25, 1963, HP.

54   "I'd like to have a province": RH interviewed by Neil Sheehan, May 29, 1976, Library of Congress, Recorded Sound Reference Center, RYB 6803–4, Washington, D.C.

55   It was almost all the way: Maurer, ed., *Strange Ground*, 109.

55   There were 324 of them: RH in Kim Willenson, ed., *The Bad War: An Oral History of the Vietnam War* (New York: Newsweek, 1987), 107–8.

56   The American military advisors had: RH to Litty Holbrooke, October 16, 1963, HP.

57   "I wish I could tell it all": This narrative is composed of excerpts from letters RH wrote to Litty Holbrooke on September 3, 1963; September 15, 1963; September 17, 1963; September 19, 1963; September 28, 1963; October 3, 1963; October 9, 1963; October 25, 1963; October 27–29, 1963; November 10, 1963; December 7–8, 1963; December 17, 1963; February 25, 1964; March 10, 1964; March 11, 1964; March 24, 1964; and March 27, 1964; and to David Rusk on November 8, 1963; December 11, 1963; and January 31, 1964, HP. The letters have been very lightly edited for clarity.

71   He had been called: Phillips, *Why Vietnam Matters*, 179–87; Rufus Phillips interviewed by Charles Stuart Kennedy, 1998, ADST, Arlington, Va., https://www.adst.org.

73   Phillips returned to Saigon: Phillips, *Why Vietnam Matters*, 198–201.

74   On Friday, November 1: RH to Litty Holbrooke, November 2, 1963, HP.

74   The slogan Holbrooke devised: Rufus Phillips, "The Story of a School," memorandum to the Committee on Province Rehabilitation, November 23, 1963, HP.

75   And after Lodge, upon finishing his lunch: Henry Cabot Lodge interview, 1979,

Vietnam: A Television History, America's Mandarin (1954–1963), WGBH Media Library & Archives, Boston, https://www.openvault.wgbh.org/.

75 "I would like you to know": Blair, *Lodge in Vietnam*, 69.

76 "I feel we must": "Listening in: JFK on Vietnam (November 4, 1963)," November 4, 1963, John F. Kennedy Library, https://www.youtube.com.

77 At the Tu Do nightclub: Maurer, ed., *Strange Ground,* 103.

77 "I think things are looking up": RH to Litty Holbrooke, November 5, 1963, HP.

78 Halberstam's tour: RH to Litty Holbrooke, December 3–6, 1963, HP.

78 Years later, Holbrooke would describe: RH interviewed by Neil Sheehan, May 29, 1976, Library of Congress, Recorded Sound Reference Center, RYB 6803-4, Washington, D.C.

79 Seventy kilometers south: Jack Cushman interviewed by Robert Mages, 2013, West Point Oral History Collection, Volume Three, West Point, New York, https://www.west-point.org.

80 "While Diem definitely": RH to David Rusk, January 31, 1964, HP.

80 Cushman was scheduled: Jack Cushman, "Reflections on Vietnam, 1963–64: Trying to Talk to Gen. Westmoreland about COIN," *Foreign Policy,* January 6, 2012, https://www.foreignpolicy.com.

80 A top official at State: David Halberstam, *War in a Time of Peace: Bush, Clinton, and the Generals* (New York: Touchstone, 2002), 182.

81 Joe Alsop's laundry: RH, untitled memoir on trip to Vietnam, February 22–23, 2003, HP.

81 There was a *Peanuts* cartoon: Charles Schulz, *Peanuts,* April 6, 1963.

82 "The best weapon for killing": Prochnau, *Once Upon a Distant War,* 162.

83 Lake's parents owned: James Thurber cartoon, *The New Yorker,* June 18, 1938.

85 These women, Holbrooke later confessed: RH, untitled memoir on trip to Vietnam, February 22–23, 2003, HP.

85 The older Asia hands: RH, untitled memoir on trip to Vietnam, February 22–23, 2003, HP.

86 "I have the theory": Maurer, ed., *Strange Ground,* 474.

86 "I not only don't wanna": RH, untitled memoir on trip to Vietnam, February 22–23, 2003, HP.

86 "the greatest crisis": RH to Litty Holbrooke, October 2, 1962, HP.

86 "darlingbabyhoneylamb": RH to Litty Holbrooke, November 27, 1962, HP.

87 And so, a week: Litty Holbrooke to RH, October 7, 1962. Provided to the author by Litty Holbrooke.

87 "It seems to me": RH to Litty Holbrooke, October 9, 1962, HP.

88 "It's fine for you": Litty Holbrooke to RH, October 14, 1962. Provided to the author by Litty Holbrooke.

89 "Either never never": RH to Litty Holbrooke, October 10, 1962, HP.

89 "I'm afraid that letter": Litty Holbrooke to RH, October 14, 1962. Provided to the author by Litty Holbrooke.

89 "Thank you for saying": RH to Litty Holbrooke, October 18, 1962, HP.

90 "By the time this letter": RH to Litty Holbrooke, February 19, 1964, HP.

91 "I got a nice letter": RH to Litty Holbrooke, March 16, 1964, HP.

91 "Oh darling, I am": RH to Litty Holbrooke, April 20, 1964, HP.

91 "Well, darling": RH to Litty Holbrooke, May 18, 1964, HP.

92   "If I figure right": RH to Litty Holbrooke, May 24, 1964, HP.

92   Toni helped Litty: Litty Holbrooke to parents, June 17, 1964. Provided to the author by Litty Holbrooke.

92   That afternoon in the Lakes' tropical garden: RH to Litty Holbrooke's parents, July 1, 1964. Provided to the author by Litty Holbrooke.

95   In 1961, Kennedy had signed: Blair, *Lodge in Vietnam*, 19.

95   "To one brought up": RH to Dean Rusk, June 16, 1964, HP.

96   Nineteen sixty-four: Fredrik Logevall, *Choosing War: The Lost Chance for Peace and the Escalation of War in Vietnam* (Berkeley: University of California Press, 1999), 108.

96   Holbrooke's tour was: RH interviewed by Neil Sheehan, May 29, 1976, Library of Congress, Recorded Sound Reference Center, RYB 6803–4, Washington, D.C.

97   Toni would push the baby: Lake and Lake, "Coming of Age Through Vietnam," 24.

98   On January 23: "Viet Mob Burns 5000 Books," *Boston Globe*, January 24, 1965, 1.

100   On February 6: RH, "The Smartest Man in the Room," *Harper's Magazine*, June 1975; RH, "The Doves Were Right," *New York Times Book Review*, November 30, 2008.

100   Since the United States had been hoping: Logevall, *Choosing War*, 324.

100   Toni Lake and her baby: Lake and Lake, "Coming of Age Through Vietnam," 24.

101   But in a classified cable: "Telegram from the Embassy in Vietnam to the Department of State," February 1, 1965, FRUS, 1964–1968, Volume II, Vietnam, January–June 1965, Document 54.

102   Holbrooke's friend John Negroponte: RH to Anthony and Antonia Lake, October 29, 1965, HP.

102   "The atmosphere in Saigon": RH, untitled memoir of New Year's Eve party, February 27, 1970, HP.

103   "You can't be a good counterinsurgent": RH to Robert Komer, memorandum, "Vietnam Trip Report: October 26–November 18, 1966," December 1, 1966, HP.

103   Holbrooke once flew out: Willenson, ed., *The Bad War*, 147; RH, untitled memoir on trip to Vietnam, 1992, HP.

103   In the fall of 1965: RH, "Pushing Sand," *The New Republic*, May 3, 1975.

104   A few months later, Holbrooke: RH, "An Unimportant Incident," undated, HP; RH to Philip Habib, "Impressions of 1st Infantry Division," memorandum, December 16, 1965, HP.

105   One day in early December 1965: RH, untitled memoir on New Year's Eve party, February 27, 1970, HP.

107   "The pressure on people": RH to David Rusk, March, 11, 1966, HP.

107   "EL has made one bad mistake": RH to Anthony Lake and Antonia Lake, October 29, 1965, HP.

108   Holbrooke spread the word: Stanley Karnow, "Legend of Lansdale's Miracles Badly Tarnished in Vietnam," *Washington Post*, February 25, 1966, A1.

109   "in due course": Frank Wisner to RH, September 2, 1966, HP.

110   A few days later: R. W. Apple, "U.S. Study Calls a Night Army Essential for Victory in Vietnam," *New York Times*, August 6, 1967, 6.

110   Frank, he thought: RH, notes for Frank Wisner's sixtieth birthday speech, July 19, 1998, HP.

110   "You have a brilliant future": RH in Berland and Schoen, eds., *What Makes You Tick?*, 162.

112 "I've been reading": Willenson, ed., *The Bad War*, 148; RH in Berland and Schoen, eds., *What Makes You Tick?*, 162–63.

114 Johnson wanted quick results: Richard A. Hunt, *Pacification: The American Struggle for Vietnam's Hearts and Minds* (Boulder, Colo.: Westview Press, 1995), 71.

114 In May 1967: Frank Leith Jones, *Blowtorch: Robert Komer, Vietnam, and American Cold War Strategy* (Annapolis, Md.: Naval Institute Press, 2013), 137–38.

115 "It's the end": RH to Litty Holbrooke, May 10, 1967, HP.

115 One night, over dinner: John J. Helble interviewed by Thomas F. Conlon, 1998, ADST, Arlington, Va., https://www.adst.org.

117 "Sit down," Joe Alsop growled: RH interviewed by E. Benjamin Skinner, August 21, 2002, HP.

118 One night at Polly Wisner's: Geoffrey Wolff, "Extravagant Laughter," *Berlin Journal* 20 (Spring 2011), 8.

118 Bobby became Holbrooke's political hero: RH in Berland and Schoen, eds., *What Makes You Tick?*, 164.

118 After RFK's assassination: RH to Ethel Kennedy, June 8, 1968, HP.

119 In the summer of 1966: RH, untitled memoir on meeting Averell Harriman, undated, HP.

120 The war was making him sick: Lake and Lake, "Coming of Age Through Vietnam," 24.

121 At the beginning of 1967: James Rosenthal to Anthony Lake, January 5, 1967, Box 4, Folder 1, Anthony Lake Manuscript Collection, Library of Congress, Washington, D.C.

122 Toni had become a dove: Lake and Lake, "Coming of Age Through Vietnam," 23.

122 An Asia hand during the Vietnam years: James Thomson, "How Could Vietnam Happen? An Autopsy," *Atlantic Monthly*, April 1968.

123 To keep him in the Foreign Service: Nicholas deB. Katzenbach, *Some of It Was Fun: Working with RFK and LBJ* (New York: W. W. Norton & Company, 2008), 254.

125 Gelb had just been handed: A. J. Langguth, *Our Vietnam: The War 1954–1975* (New York: Simon & Schuster, 2000), 539.

127 "We have concentrated": *The Pentagon Papers*, Senator Gravel Edition, vol. 2 (Boston: Beacon Press, 1972), 622.

128 It wasn't welcome: "Analyst Assigned to Compile Pentagon Papers Discusses Their Release," All Things Considered, National Public Radio, June 14, 2011, https://www.npr.org.

128 On that evening of November 1: Walter Isaacson and Evan Thomas, *The Wise Men: Six Friends and the World They Made* (New York: Simon & Schuster, 1986), 678–80.

128 He thought the briefing: Katzenbach, *Some of It Was Fun*, 268.

129 Holbrooke thought so: "Memo from Undersecretary of State (Katzenbach) to Johnson," November 16, 1967, FRUS, 1964–1968, Volume V, 1967, Document 401.

130 No word came back: Katzenbach, *Some of It Was Fun*, 268–69.

130 For Rusk, it was always the early spring: Dean Rusk to RH, September 26, 1985, HP.

131 Things hadn't been the same: RH interviewed by Richard Rusk, March 1985, Dean Rusk Oral History Collection, Richard B. Russell Library for Political Research and Studies, University of Georgia Libraries, Athens, http://purl.libs.uga.edu.

131 In December 1967: Philip Geyelin to Katharine Graham, December 20, 1967, Box 74, Folder 7, Philip Geyelin Manuscript Collection, Library of Congress, Washington, D.C.

132 "I absolutely refused": RH to Dean Rusk, August 26, 1985, HP.

133 There was panic: Willenson, ed., *The Bad War*, 149–50.

134 Holbrooke found Westmoreland: Stanley Karnow, *Vietnam: A History* (New York: Penguin Books, 1984), 562.

134 Ten days after Tet: RH interviewed by Neil Sheehan, May 29, 1976, Library of Congress, Recorded Sound Reference Center, RYB 6803–4, Washington, D.C.

135 At the Pentagon, Clifford began: Clark Clifford with RH, *Counsel to the President* (New York: Anchor Books, 1992), 492.

135 "Who poisoned the well?": Clifford with RH, *Counsel to the President*, 518.

135 But there were two versions: George Packer, "From the Vietnam Archive," *The New Yorker*, August 12, 2008, https://www.newyorker.com; Clifford with RH, *Counsel to the President*, 521.

136 Later, Holbrooke imagined telling Johnson: Willenson, ed., *The Bad War*, 150.

136 On April 3: Clifford with RH, *Counsel to the President*, 529.

136 Rusk, still loyal: Clifford with RH, *Counsel to the President*, 537.

136 Holbrooke attended the French Open: RH to Litty Holbrooke, June 4, 1968, HP.

137 Harriman told Holbrooke: RH, Afghanistan audio diary, August 4, 2010, HP.

137 Summer turned to fall: Averell Harriman, "Memorandum Prepared by Ambassador at Large Harriman," December 14, 1968, FRUS, 1964–1968, Volume VII, Vietnam, September 1968–January 1969, Document 255.

137 But before anything could happen: John A. Farrell, "Nixon's Vietnam Treachery," *New York Times*, December 31, 2016, https://nytimes.com; Clark Clifford with RH, *Counsel to the President*, 581–84.

137 The only outsider: Walter Isaacson, *Kissinger: A Biography* (New York: Simon & Schuster, 1992), 129–34.

138 He called to warn Nixon: Farrell, "Nixon's Vietnam Treachery," https://nytimes.com.

138 "Henry, I don't want a job": RH in Berland and Schoen, eds., *What Makes You Tick?*, 165.

139 Lake was going back in: Lake and Lake, "Coming of Age Through Vietnam," 24.

139 Holbrooke, on his way out: RH to Anthony Lake, May 6, 1969, and June 21, 1969, HP.

HOW DOES HE DO IT?

141 So he read Vonnegut's: RH, 1970 diary, HP.

142 Lake discovered that the transcripts: Jason DeParle, "The Man Inside Bill Clinton's Foreign Policy," *New York Times Magazine*, August 20, 1995.

143 "Tony, I knew what you were going to say": Clara Bingham, ed., *Witness to the Revolution* (New York: Random House Trade Paperbacks, Reprint Edition, 2017), 347.

143 Kissinger justified it: Folder 9/19: Wiretaps, Nixon Grand Jury Records, Watergate Special Prosecution Force, National Archives, College Park, Md., https://www.archives.gov.

143 "Just gobs and gobs": Seymour M. Hersh, "Kissinger and Nixon in the White House," *Atlantic Monthly,* May 1982.

143 "Their country in the world": RH to Charles Bohlen, October 21, 1969, HP.

144 He didn't understand the conversation: Kim Willenson, ed., *The Bad War* (New York: Newsweek, 1987), 274.

145 To Holbrooke, Watergate: RH to Phil Habib, August 6, 1973, HP.

145 "the triggering mechanism": Willenson, ed., *The Bad War,* 275.

145 "I wish I had half a dozen Holbrookes": "Department of State Evaluation Form: Richard Holbrooke," March 13, 1972, HP.

145 "Please send me": Litty Holbrooke to parents, March 22, 1971. Provided to the author by Litty Holbrooke.

146 "John just died": RH in Michael J. Berland and Douglas E. Schoen, eds., *What Makes You Tick? How Successful People Do It—and What You Can Learn from Them* (New York: HarperCollins, 2009), 166.

146 "Right now I am so depressed": RH to Litty Holbrooke, November 10, 1971, HP.

146 "He loved the Foreign Service": RH, eulogy for John Campbell, undated, HP.

148 "Since my life depends on yours": Litty Holbrooke to RH, December 13, 1971. Provided to the author by Litty Holbrooke.

149 "When Daddy comes": Litty Holbrooke to RH, February 7, 1972. Provided to the author by Litty Holbrooke.

153 Pamela wasn't quite beautiful: Kitty Kelley, "The Courtesan and the Consort," New York Social Diary, December 30, 2016, https://www.newyorksocialdiary .com.

154 eating steaks purchased: Christopher Ogden, *Life of the Party: The Biography of Pamela Digby Churchill Hayward Harriman* (New York: Little, Brown and Company, 1994), 174.

156 "It was lost in the rice paddies": Willenson, ed., *The Bad War,* 266.

156 "The Machine That Fails": RH, "The Machine That Fails," *Foreign Policy* 1, Winter 1970–71.

156 "A Little Lying": RH, "A Little Lying Goes a Long Way," *The New York Times,* September 10, 1971.

156 "Relentless Patterns": RH, "Relentless Patterns to Our Vietnam Nightmare," *Washington Post,* May 15, 1972.

156 "Dissent took unusual courage": Anthony Lake, ed., *The Legacy of Vietnam* (New York: Council on Foreign Relations, 1976), 161–62.

156 Gelb, who had gone to work: Leslie H. Gelb, "The Irony of Vietnam: The System Worked," *Foreign Policy* 3, Summer 1971.

157 John Negroponte, who remained: Tad Szulc, "Behind the Vietnam Cease-Fire Agreement," *Foreign Policy* 15, Summer 1974.

157 "We remember, more clearly": Anthony Lake and Roger Morris, "The Human Reality of Realpolitik," *Foreign Policy* 4, Autumn 1971.

161 They once walked into a party: Tom Bethell, "The Making of Richard Holbrooke," *The Washingtonian,* February 1980.

162 On a trip to Berlin: RH to Gail Malcolm, November 1975. Provided to the author by Gail Malcolm.

162 The end materialized: RH, 1975 diary, September 29, 1975, HP.

SWALLOW HARD

166 "It was the most curious mixture": RH, "Pushing Sand," *The New Republic,* May 3, 1975.

166 "He is the most successful diplomat": RH, "Kissinger: A Hero, Perhaps, But Not a Model," *Boston Globe,* September 15, 1974.

166 In private he called Kissinger: RH interviewed by E. Benjamin Skinner, August 21, 2002, HP.

166 "We want a decent": Henry Kissinger, Polo I briefing book, July 1971, 62, https://www.scribd.com.

167 "there's nothing decent": RH interviewed by Neil Sheehan, May 29, 1976, Library of Congress, Recorded Sound Reference Center, RYB 6803-4, Washington, D.C.

167 "I am an expert on Holbrooke": "Memorandum of Conversation," November 4, 1976, FRUS, 1969–1976, Volume XXXVIII, Part 2, Organization and Management of Foreign Policy; Public Diplomacy, 1973–1976, Document 216.

167 In the new era, with new and better leadership: RH, "Escaping the Domino Trap," *New York Times Magazine,* September 7, 1975.

167 "We still possess": RH, "A Sense of Drift, a Time for Calm," *Foreign Policy* 23, Summer 1976.

168 He was on the board: RH to Samuel Huntington, May 11, 1973, HP.

169 Two months later, he helped: RH, "Jimmy Carter: A Personal View," *Newsweek,* July 26, 1976.

169 Holbrooke became one of Carter's main conduits: Patrick Tyler, *A Great Wall: Six Presidents and China* (New York: PublicAffairs, 2000), 231.

169 After getting one of these memos: Jimmy Carter to RH, May 9, 1976, HP.

169 "If there is anything of value": RH to Jimmy Carter, memorandum, undated, HP.

169 "Your performance was impeccable": Jimmy Carter to RH, memorandum, November 15, 1976, HP.

169 On Thanksgiving, Carter called: The conversation is recounted in RH interviewed by E. Benjamin Skinner, audio, September 6, 2002, HP; Nayan Chanda, *Brother Enemy: The War After the War* (New York: Collier Books, 1986), 145–46; and Tyler, *A Great Wall,* 234–35.

171 "That's great news": RH interviewed by E. Benjamin Skinner, audio, September 6, 2002, HP.

172 "1976—I did not see JC clearly": RH, 1980 memoranda book, December 12, 1980, HP.

172 Holbrooke told his new special assistant: Kenneth Quinn oral history for the ADST, unpublished. Provided to the author by Kenneth Quinn.

172 His mother was there: Carol C. Laise to Cyrus Vance, memorandum, "Swearing-in of Richard C. Holbrooke 4:30 p.m., Thursday, March 31, 1977," undated, HP.

173 As Helble watched: William Andreas Brown interviewed by Charles Stuart Kennedy, 1998, ADST, Arlington, Va., https://www.adst.org; John J. Helble interviewed by Thomas F. Conlon, 1998, ADST, Arlington, Va., https://www.adst.org.

174 "This office exclusively schedules": Elva Morgan to RH, memorandum, June 7, 1978, HP.

175 Since the Republican administration: Kenneth Quinn oral history for the ADST, unpublished.

175 He gave his staff: Harry E. T. Thayer interviewed by Charles Stuart Kennedy, 1998, ADST, Arlington, Va., https://adst.org.

176 Vance believed that: Chanda, *Brother Enemy*, 145–46.

177 The two sides met: Flora Lewis, "U.S. Won't Bar Hanoi from U.N.; Vietnam to Press Hunt for Missing," *New York Times*, May 5, 1977.

177 As Holbrooke sat: RH interviewed by E. Benjamin Skinner, August 21, 2002, HP.

177 Once, on an official trip to Japan: Nicholas Platt, *China Boys: How Relations with the PRC Began and Grew* (Washington, D.C.: New Academia Publishing/VELLUM Books, 2010), 240; Kenneth Quinn oral history for the ADST, unpublished.

177 Phan Hien produced: Chanda, *Brother Enemy*, 152.

177 Holbrooke considered the secret letter: RH interviewed by E. Benjamin Skinner, August 21, 2002, HP.

178 At the second meeting: Chanda, *Brother Enemy*, 152; Kenneth Quinn oral history for the ADST, unpublished.

178 "You understand, Mr. Minister": RH interviewed by E. Benjamin Skinner, August 21, 2002, HP.

178 Holbrooke reminded Phan Hien: Gareth Porter, "U.S. and Vietnam: Prisoners of the Past," *Washington Post*, July 3, 1977.

179 He considered the State Department: Zbigniew Brzezinski, *Power and Principle: Memoirs of the National Security Adviser, 1977–1981* (New York: Farrar, Straus, and Giroux, 1983), 228.

179 "I cannot help suspecting": "Memorandum from the President's Assistant for National Security Affairs (Brzezinski) to President Carter," October 13, 1978, FRUS, 1977–1980, Volume XIII, China, Document 143.

179 Brzezinski considered Vance: Brzezinski, *Power and Principle*, 43.

180 Back in Washington, Holbrooke, Lake: I. M. Destler, Leslie H. Gelb, and Anthony Lake, *Our Own Worst Enemy: The Unmaking of American Foreign Policy* (New York: Simon & Schuster, 1985), 96.

180 Vance didn't want to hear it: Tyler, *A Great Wall*, 238.

180 When a story in *Time*: Destler, Gelb, and Lake, *Our Own Worst Enemy*, 96.

181 Holbrooke and Oksenberg shared: Tyler, *A Great Wall*, 236.

182 The Communist Party had just finished: Cyrus Vance, *Hard Choices: Critical Years in America's Foreign Policy* (New York: Simon & Schuster, 1983), 80; RH, untitled book proposal, November 11, 1980, HP.

182 (When Blythe first laid eyes): RH, untitled book proposal, November 11, 1980, HP.

182 "You know I am": Vance, *Hard Choices*, 82.

183 Holbrooke couldn't tell: RH, untitled book proposal, November 11, 1980, HP.

183 "Policy is not a dry": RH, untitled book proposal, November 11, 1980, HP.

184 "I have never heard": Tyler, *A Great Wall*, 252.

184 The humiliation continued: This account of Brzezinski's and Holbrooke's trip to China is largely drawn from Tyler's *A Great Wall*, 252–56.

184 On the flight over: William H. Gleysteen Jr. interviewed by Thomas Stern, 2000, ADST, Arlington, Va., https://www.adst.org.

186 He rushed up the aisle: Tyler, *A Great Wall*, 256; William H. Gleysteen, Jr. interviewed by Thomas Stern, 2000, ADST, Arlington, Va., https://www.adst.org.

186 "You need to choose": "Memorandum from the President's Assistant for National Security Affairs (Brzezinski) to President Carter," July 7, 1978, FRUS, 1977–1980, Volume XIII, China, Document 126.

187 "So the ball is in our court": Transcript of meeting between Nguyen Co Thach and Richard Holbrooke, September 22, 1978, NLC-26-32-2-6-9, Jimmy Carter Presidential Library.

187 "His adrenaline obviously flowing": Michael Oksenberg to Zbigniew Brzezinski, memorandum, "Dick Holbrooke's Conversation with the Vietnamese," September 22, 1978, NLC-26-32-1-5-1, Jimmy Carter Presidential Library.

187 Holbrooke collected his papers: Chanda, *Brother Enemy*, 265.

187 "We will tell you": "Thach Holbrooke Meeting on Vietnam," memorandum, September 27, 1978, NLC-26-32-2-7-8, Jimmy Carter Presidential Library.

188 In the meantime, each side: Chanda, *Brother Enemy*, 282.

189 On October 11, Carter: Jimmy Carter, *Keeping Faith: Memoirs of a President* (New York: Bantam Books, 1982), 195.

189 Brzezinski and Woodcock persuaded: Chanda, *Brother Enemy*, 289–90; Tyler, *A Great Wall*, 258.

189 Then he heard some very bad news: Chanda, *Brother Enemy*, 294; RH interviewed by E. Benjamin Skinner, August 27, 2002, HP.

190 In their syndicated column: Rowland Evans and Robert Novak, "A Case of Soviet Disinformation," *Washington Post*, November 13, 1978.

190 Holbrooke stuck by the lie: RH interviewed by E. Benjamin Skinner, August 27, 2002, HP.

191 The next day, Woodcock and Deng: This account of the events leading to the normalization announcement on December 15, 1978, is largely drawn from Tyler's *A Great Wall*, 264–71.

191 When the cables came: "Memorandum from Michel Oksenberg to the President's Assistant for National Security Affairs (Brzezinski)," December 19, 1980, FRUS, 1977–1980, Volume XIII, China, Document 327.

191 As the day wore on: RH, untitled memoir, July 4, 1981, HP; Vance, *Hard Choices*, 118.

192 A week later, in Moscow: Vance, *Hard Choices*, 110–11.

193 But Holbrooke thought that Vance: RH, untitled memoir, July 4, 1981, HP.

193 At the end of 1980: RH, 1980 memoranda book, December 10, 1980, HP.

193 Brzezinski later called Deng's attitude: Brzezinski, *Power and Principle*, 25.

193 Deng's sixteen-day "lesson": Chanda, *Brother Enemy*, 356–61.

194 In early 1974: Quinn, airgram, "The Khmer Krahom Program to Create a Communist Society in Southern Cambodia," February 20, 1974. Provided to the author by Kenneth Quinn.

195 "The new government seeks": RH, testimony to House Subcommittee on International Organizations, U.S. House of Representatives, July 26, 1977, Washington, D.C., HP.

195 "Do we sit on the sidelines": William Shawcross, *The Quality of Mercy: Cambodia, Holocaust and Modern Conscience* (New York: Touchstone, 1984), 68.

196 Human rights was Jimmy Carter's: Robert B. Oakley interviewed by Charles Stuart Kennedy and Thomas Stern, 1999, ADST, Arlington, Va., https://www.adst.org.

196 In April 1977: Raymond Bonner, *Waltzing with a Dictator: The Marcoses and the Making of American Policy* (New York: Vintage Books, 1988), 191; "Holbrooke Discussions with President and Mrs. Marcos," telegram, April 20, 1977, NLC-26-39-5-4-1, Jimmy Carter Presidential Library.

197 They fell into shouting matches: Bonner, *Waltzing with a Dictator*, 231.

198 Over Holbrooke's objections: Morton I. Abramowitz interviewed by Thomas Stern, 2009, ADST, Arlington, Va., https://www.adst.org.

198 The night before the vote: Vance, *Hard Choices*, 127.

198 Holbrooke called the decision: Bonner, *Waltzing with a Dictator*, 187.

202 "The motivation is simple": RH, testimony to House Subcommittee on Immigration, Citizenship, and International Law, U.S. House of Representatives, August 4, 1977, Washington, D.C., HP.

202 Holbrooke found this airless: RH, "Conscience and Catastrophe," *The New Republic*, July 30, 1984.

202 "Are you telling me": Walter Mondale, *The Good Fight: A Life in Liberal Politics* (New York: Scribner, 2010), 213.

202 "I didn't like the mission": Mondale, *The Good Fight*, 215–16.

204 A young British U.N. worker: Shawcross, *The Quality of Mercy*, 176.

204 Many of them were skeptical: Shawcross, *The Quality of Mercy*, 325.

205 "Create a photo opportunity!": Shawcross, *The Quality of Mercy*, 189.

205 "It's like nothing": Henry Kamm, "Mrs. Carter Visits Thai Camp: 'It's Like Nothing I've Seen,'" *New York Times*, November 10, 1979.

205 By 1982 the United States: Shawcross, *The Quality of Mercy*, 94.

SINCE I AM NOW HOPELESS

207 "Clifford—Dems coasting": RH, 1980 memoranda book, December 2, 1980, HP.

207 By the second week: RH, untitled book proposal, November 11, 1980, HP.

207 A. M. Rosenthal: RH in Michael J. Berland and Douglas E. Schoen, eds., *What Makes You Tick? How Successful People Do It—and What You Can Learn from Them* (New York: HarperCollins, 2009), 167.

207 "In journalism I was regarded": RH, 1980 memoranda book, January 8, 1981, HP.

207 In his notebook: RH, 1980 memoranda book, December 19, 1980, HP.

207 Two weeks after Carter's defeat: RH to Pete Peterson, March 19, 1985, HP.

208 But in January a senior banker: RH, 1980 memoranda book, January 7, 1981, HP; RH to Barbara E. Gregory, July 1, 1981, HP.

209 "Dear Mr. Crown": RH to Lester Crown, February 12, 1981, HP.

209 Holbrooke advised Philip Knight: RH to Philip Knight, March 1, 1982, HP.

209 But the work smelled: RH in Berland and Schoen, eds., *What Makes You Tick?*, 167.

209 "Nice house": RH to Pamela Harriman, July 31, 1986, HP.

209 He already knew: Sally Bedell Smith, *Reflected Glory: The Life of Pamela Churchill Harriman* (New York: Simon & Schuster, 1996), 287.

210 "Money doesn't interest me": RH in Berland and Schoen, eds., *What Makes You Tick?*, 168.

210 "A liberal foreign policy": RH to Gary Hart, May 23, 1985, HP.

211 He called for human rights: RH, testimony to House Subcommittee on East Asian and Pacific Affairs, U.S. House of Representatives, August 10, 1982, Washington, D.C., HP.

211 "As Commander-in-Chief": RH to Walter Mondale, November 16, 1982, HP.

212 It struck CBS veterans: Sheila Weller, *The News Sorority* (New York: Penguin Books, 2014), 132–33.

212 She called up every official: Diane Sawyer interviewed by David Holbrooke. Provided to the author by David Holbrooke.

213 "DS—calm?": RH, 1980 memoranda book, January 12, 1981, February 13, 1981, HP.

213 "Did you observe": RH and Diane Sawyer, "Diary: Trip to Tibet," unpublished, June 8, 1983, HP.

213 He pushed her: Diane Sawyer interviewed by David Holbrooke.

215 "You're my hero": Joan Juliet Buck, "Live Mike," Vanity Fair, June 1994.

216 "Now that he is divorced": Liz Smith, "Society Today," New York Daily News, October 1, 1987.

216 "My friends": RH to Liz Smith, October 7, 1987, HP.

217 Holbrooke wrote Pam: RH to Pamela Harriman, July 31, 1986, HP.

217 Only two or three family members: Christopher Ogden, Life of the Party (New York: Little, Brown and Company, 1994), 406–7; Smith, Reflected Glory, 316–17.

218 She started her own: Ogden, Life of the Party, 392–96.

218 his calls to her office: Ogden, Life of the Party, 428.

218 she sometimes taped: Smith, Reflected Glory, 346.

219 "There is, at times": RH, notes, August 4, 1988, HP.

220 Ever since the acquisition: RH, notes, September 28–29, 1988, HP.

222 The bank's mahogany-paneled premises: Douglas Frantz and David McKean, Friends in High Places: The Rise and Fall of Clark Clifford (New York: Little, Brown and Company, 1995), 324–25.

222 Over lunch, Clifford: RH, notes, October 27, 1987.

223 In July 1965: Clark Clifford with RH, Counsel to the President (New York: Anchor Books, 1992), 419–20.

223 In his Senate office, Kennedy: RH, notes, June 4, 1988, HP; David Pietrusza, 1960: LBJ vs. JFK vs. Nixon (New York: Union Square Press, 2008), 148–49; Michael O'Brien, John F. Kennedy: A Biography (New York: Thomas Dunne Books, 2005), 440–42; Seymour M. Hersh, The Dark Side of Camelot (New York: Little, Brown and Company, 1997), 106–10. The Holbrooke Papers include RH's audio recordings of his interviews with Clifford, but the story of Pam Turnure is not on them.

224 When Holbrooke interviewed Marny Clifford: RH, interview notes with Marny Clifford for Counsel to the President, March 7, 1988, HP.

225 "Onboard was a group": Clifford with RH, Counsel to the President, 36.

226 (First American got): Clifford with RH, Counsel to the President, 268.

226 a man so consumed: Frantz and McKean, Friends in High Places, 372.

226 Pam Harriman threw a party: Frantz and McKean, Friends in High Places, 362–3.

226 He and his partner: Frantz and McKean, Friends in High Places, 334.

226 "I have a choice": Neil A. Lewis, "Washington at Work: Clark Clifford, Symbol of the Permanent Capital, Is Faced with a Dilemma," New York Times, April 5, 1991.

227 "become a pariah": RH, notes, January 30, 1992, HP.

227 She blamed her old friend: Smith, Reflected Glory, 423.

227 "I have spent too little time": RH, notes, May 6, 1988, HP.

228 After a prolonged struggle: Nicholas von Hoffman, "Bland Ambition," Spy, May 1990.

228 Holbrooke tried to help: RH to Marie Brenner, June 28, 1988, HP.

229 "In the long run": RH, notes, July 9, 1988, HP.

229 "Ahead of us lies": RH, notes, August 7, 1991, HP.

233 Every four years, Democrats refought Vietnam: Derek Chollet and James Gold-geier, *America Between the Wars* (New York: PublicAffairs, 2008), 30.

233 After dinner, Lake got ten minutes: Jason DeParle, "The Man Inside Bill Clinton's Foreign Policy," *New York Times Magazine,* August 20, 1995.

234 The speech blamed Bush: Chollet and Goldgeier, *America Between the Wars,* 37–38.

234 "What's the matter?": David Halberstam, *War in a Time of Peace* (New York: Touchstone, 2002), 157.

235 Clinton called for air strikes: Andrew Rosenthal, "Clinton Attacked on Foreign Policy," *New York Times,* July 28, 1992.

235 "Great campaign": RH, notes, November 23, 1992, HP.

236 Strobe Talbott, an old Clinton friend: Strobe Talbott diary, November 19, 1992. Provided to the author by Strobe Talbott.

THEY'LL COME FOR ME

241 "The damn thing": RH, December 1992 diary, December 29, 1992, HP.

241 Following careful plans: Laura Silber and Allan Little, *The Death of Yugoslavia* (New York: Penguin Books, 1995), 244–45.

242 On an earlier trip to Bosnia: RH, *To End a War* (New York: Random House, 1998), 37–38; RH, December 1992 diary, December 29, 1992, HP.

242 There was a factory worker: RH, December 1992 diary, undated, HP.

243 As Holbrooke started to leave: RH, "Endpaper: Workbook; With Broken Glass," *New York Times Magazine,* April 25, 1993; Richard Holbrooke interviewed by Charlie Rose, *Charlie Rose,* PBS, January 4, 1993, https://www.charlierose.com.

246 By the time of Bosnia: United Nations High Commissioner for Refugees, "The State of the World's Refugees: The Challenge of Protection," The UN Refugee Agency, January 1, 1993, https://www.unhcr.org.

246 He returned with a sack: Christiane Amanpour, "Scream Bloody Murder," CNN, 2008, https://www.cnn.com.

247 Kiseljak was the beginning: Silber and Little, *The Death of Yugoslavia,* 296.

247 By the time a small sack of potatoes: John F. Burns, "At a Lunch in Sarajevo, Muslims Try to Fathom the Hatred," *New York Times,* January 3, 1993.

247 The airport was under U.N. control: "A Sarajevo Diary—From Bad to Worse," Channel 4, 1993, https://www.youtube.com.

248 As the convoy arrived: Burns, "At a Lunch in Sarajevo, Muslims Try to Fathom the Hatred"; Peter Maass, *Love Thy Neighbor: A Story of War* (New York: Knopf, 1996), 175–82; Kevin Sullivan, "U.N. Secretary-General Boutros Boutros-Ghali paid a New Year's Eve . . . ," UPI, December 31, 1992.

248 Children were picking through a garbage pile: RH, "The New Sarajevo," *Travel + Leisure,* May 7, 2009.

249 As casually as if: RH to Joseph Lelyveld, January 7, 1993, HP.

249 Snow was falling over the city: "A Sarajevo Diary—From Bad to Worse."

249 A reporter for *Oslobodenje*: Hamza Baksic, *Sarajevo Is No More* (online: self-published, 1995), 8, https://www.scribd.com.

249 In a small, crowded apartment: Burns, "At a Lunch in Sarajevo, Muslims Try to Fathom the Hatred."

250 Burns went up the river: John F. Burns, "The Death of a City: Elegy for Sarajevo—A Special Report; A People Under Artillery Fire Manage to Retain Humanity," *New York Times*, June 8, 1992.

250 Burns had interviewed: John F. Burns, "Some Serbian Gunners Shell Their Own Sarajevo Homes," *New York Times*, December 27, 1992.

251 "FROM THIS PLACE": David Binder, *Fare Well, Illyria* (Herndon, Va.: CEU Press, 2013), 36.

251 "You'll see something": RH, "The New Sarajevo."

252 A group of friends: Burns, "At a Lunch in Sarajevo, Muslims Try to Fathom the Hatred."

252 "If I don't make my views known": RH, *To End a War*, 50.

254 President Alija Izetbegovic of Bosnia: Alija Izetbegovic, *Inescapable Questions: Autobiographical Notes* (Markfield, Leicestershire, U.K.: The Islamic Foundation, 2003), 4.

255 the forbidden flag of Serb nationalism: "Serb" and "Croat" are used throughout to refer to the ethnic groups and "Serbian" and "Croatian" to the territories.

258 Hundreds of men: Silber and Little, *The Death of Yugoslavia*, 180.

258 By the end of the year half a million Croats: Silber and Little, *The Death of Yugoslavia*, 198.

258 In the summer of 1991: Silber and Little, *The Death of Yugoslavia*, 150–51.

259 "Even though the Muslims": Silber and Little, *The Death of Yugoslavia*, 208.

259 In 1989, an Englishman: "A Sarajevo Diary—From Bad to Worse."

259 In the mid-eighties: Dusko Doder and Louise Branson, *Milosevic: Portrait of a Tyrant* (New York: The Free Press, 1999), 115.

260 In the fall of 1991: Silber and Little, *The Death of Yugoslavia*, 215.

260 Milosevic secretly ordered: Doder and Branson, *Milosevic*, 117–18.

261 "Don't get bogged down": George H. W. Bush interviewed by Brian Gallagher, Editorial Board meeting: *USA Today*, August 4, 1992, https://www.c-span.org.

262 Two nights after getting back: Richard Holbrooke interviewed by Charlie Rose, *Charlie Rose*.

263 Holbrooke drafted a memo: RH, *To End a War*, 50; RH, memorandum for the record, January 3, 1993, HP.

264 A few weeks after sending the memo: RH, *To End a War*, 53.

264 The smoke drifted: Anthony Lake interviewed by Chris Bury, *Frontline*, "The Clinton Years," PBS, September 2000, https://www.pbs.org.

264 Kissinger told people: David J. Rothkopf, *Running the World: The Inside Story of the National Security Council* (New York: PublicAffairs, 2005), 310.

264 In February, Holbrooke invited himself: RH, *To End a War*, 54.

264 Muslim refugees crowded: Mark Danner, *Stripping Bare the Body: Politics Violence War* (New York: Nation Books, 2009), 178.

264 all humanitarian relief blocked: Silber and Little, *The Death of Yugoslavia*, 266.

266 Powell warned that any American involvement: Rothkopf, *Running the World*, 325.

266 He'd roll his eyes: Rothkopf, *Running the World*, 322.

267 Clinton's pollster: Elizabeth Drew, *On the Edge: The Clinton Presidency* (New York: Touchstone, 1995), 150.

268 That was the message: Taylor Branch, *The Clinton Tapes: Wrestling History with the President* (New York: Simon & Schuster, 2009), 10.

269 In the Oval Office on May 6: Drew, *On the Edge,* 157.
269 Foreign Service officers were resigning: Drew, *On the Edge,* 143.
269 He described his philosophy: Thomas L. Friedman, "Clinton's Foreign Policy: Top Adviser Speaks Up," *New York Times,* October 31, 1993.
269 Holbrooke thought that it was in Lake's character: Rothkopf, *Running the World,* 366.
270 "Must be engaged": RH, notes, December 1, 1993, HP.
270 Then Walter Mondale: Strobe Talbott diary, January 17, 1993.
271 Holbrooke grabbed the early edition: Elaine Sciolino, "Some Friends Fret as Clinton Is Slow in Choosing Envoys," *New York Times,* June 4, 1993.
271 "The bad news": RH, *To End a War,* 55.
272 "Tell me what's wrong": Craig R. Whitney, "Bonn Journal; What's an Asia Hand Doing in Germany? Plenty!," *New York Times,* January 25, 1994.
272 "2215: Upon arrival": Schedule of the ambassador for Bonn, undated, HP.
272 The arrival of the Clintons: RH, Bosnia audio diary, July 10, 1994, HP.
275 In the morning Holbrooke pulled up: Regional Security Office memorandum, September 1993, HP.
275 He saw her slouching: Kati Marton, *Paris: A Love Story* (New York: Simon & Schuster, 2012), 115; RH to Kati Marton, January 25, 1994. Provided to the author by Kati Marton.
275 "Just imagine the pilgrims'": Marton, *Paris: A Love Story,* 117.
276 At the hotel in Tours: RH, "KATI KATCHWORDS," undated notes. Provided to the author by Kati Marton.
276 "Wait a second": RH, "KATI KATCHWORDS."
276 She said that he might be intimidated: RH to Kati Marton, January 25, 1994.
276 "Do you know that I cried": RH, "KATI KATCHWORDS."
276 Pam had no time: Marton, *Paris: A Love Story,* 118.
276 Holbrooke drove Kati: RH to Kati Marton, January 25, 1994.
277 "Trenchant—To me": RH to Kati Marton, January 16, 1994. Provided to the author by Kati Marton.
277 He let her know that: RH to Kati Marton, February 11, 1994, June 14, 1994, February 5, 1994. Provided to the author by Kati Marton.
278 "I awoke this morning": RH to Kati Marton, January 21, 1994. Provided to the author by Kati Marton.
280 Her father's debonair style: Marton, *Paris: A Love Story,* 67.
280 a woman in Budapest told her: Kati Marton, *Enemies of the People: My Family's Journey to America* (New York: Simon & Schuster, 2009), 12.
281 "You will never understand": Marton, *Enemies of the People,* 13.
282 "the idea of our couple": Kati Marton to RH, February 15, 1994. Provided to the author by Kati Marton.
282 "T.—I want": RH to Kati Marton, June 14, 1994.
283 A few months later Lake drafted: Anthony Lake, untitled resignation letter, undated, Box 48, Folder 2, Anthony Lake Papers, Library of Congress, Washington, D.C.
286 Lake began to feel: Anthony Lake interviewed by Chris Bury, *Frontline,* "The Clinton Years," PBS, September 2000, https://www.pbs.org; Anthony Lake, *6 Nightmares: Real Threats in a Dangerous World and How America Can Meet Them* (New York: Little, Brown and Company, 2000), 146.

286   Berger, Lake's deputy: Madeleine K. Albright Oral History, Presidential Oral Histories, Miller Center, University of Virginia, https://www.millercenter.org.

287   A single harmless word: Leslie H. Gelb, "Foreign Affairs; Where's Bill?," *New York Times*, March 11, 1993.

288   In the middle of May 1994: RH, Bosnia audio diary, May 12, 1994, HP.

289   Christopher had the impression: RH, Bosnia audio diary, June 7, 1994, HP.

290   It took another two weeks: RH, Bosnia audio diary, June 12, June 13, 1994, HP.

290   "Mr. Holbrooke, reached by telephone": Elaine Sciolino, "Christopher and Lake Shuffle Their Staffs," *New York Times*, June 14, 1994.

292   "This has been a very bad day": This narrative is composed of excerpts of entries from RH's Bosnia audio diary dated January 10, 1994; March 28, 1994; April 9, 1994; April 19, 1994; April 20, 1994; June 7, 1994; July 9, 1994; September 3, 1994; October 2, 1994; November 8, 1994; November 22, 1994; November 27, 1994; February 13, 1995; March 2, 1995; March 16, 1995; April 24, 1995; April 28, 1995; and May 22, 1995, HP.

306   Lake thought of Lord Nelson: Anthony Lake Oral History, Presidential Oral Histories, Miller Center, University of Virginia, https://www.millercenter.org.

307   "I think he is satisfied": Peter Galbraith diary, May 19, 1995, Peter Galbraith Papers, National Defense University, Washington, D.C. The author was granted permission by Peter Galbraith to use the collection.

307   "The lambs of Serbia": Robert Frasure from U.S. Embassy in Belgrade, cable, May 22, 1995, HP.

308   Holbrooke, at the ambassador's house: RH, *To End a War*, 64; Tim Weiner, "Clinton's Balkan Envoy Finds Himself Shut Out," *New York Times*, August 12, 1995.

309   "America, a European Power": RH, "America, A European Power," *Foreign Affairs*, March/April 1995.

309   Once he had to wait: Christopher Hill, *Outpost: Life on the Frontlines of American Diplomacy* (New York: Simon & Schuster, 2014), 76.

310   After Thanksgiving, he sent: Anthony Lake to Bill Clinton, "Bosnia Policy After the Fall of Bihac," memorandum, November 27, 1994, https://www.cia.gov.

310   You can read about: Lake, *6 Nightmares*; Ivo H. Daalder, *Getting to Dayton: The Making of America's Bosnia Policy* (Washington, D.C.: Brookings Institution Press, 2000); Rothkopf, *Running the World*; Carl Bildt, *Peace Journey: The Struggle for Peace in Bosnia* (London: Weidenfeld & Nicolson, 1998); Derek Chollet, *The Road to the Dayton Accords: A Study of American Statecraft* (New York: Palgrave Macmillan, 2005); Bob Woodward, *The Choice: How Bill Clinton Won* (New York: Simon & Schuster, 1996); David Halberstam, *War in a Time of Peace* (New York: Touchstone, 2002); Nancy Soderberg, *The Superpower Myth: The Use and Misuse of American Might* (Hoboken, N.J.: John Wiley & Sons, Inc., 2005).

310   One day in June he went: Jason DeParle, "The Man Inside Bill Clinton's Foreign Policy," *New York Times Magazine*, August 20, 1995.

310   "Mr. President, tell me": Woodward, *The Choice*, 258.

311   I'm sure he had: George Stephanopolous, *All Too Human: A Political Education* (New York: Little, Brown and Company, 1999), 382.

311   "I'm getting creamed": Halberstam, *War in a Time of Peace*, 317.

312   Chin jutting out: "Ratko Mladic—Srebrenica Fontana Hotel 1—July 11, 1995," YouTube, https://www.youtube.com.

313   His boss in New York: Samantha Power, *"A Problem From Hell": America in the Age of Genocide* (New York: Basic Books, 2002), 403.

314   If more officials: Power, *"A Problem From Hell,"* 410.

314   "Our position is unsustainable": Woodward, *The Choice,* 262.

314   But he remained strangely detached: RH, Bosnia audio diary, June 20, 1995, June 27, 1995, HP.

315   Every agency contributed: Daalder, *Getting to Dayton,* 102.

315   "We should bust our ass": Woodward, *The Choice,* 265–66; Stephanopolous, *All Too Human,* 383–84.

316   Instead of Holbrooke: Chollet, *The Road to the Dayton Accords,* 42.

316   Albright suggested: Daalder, *Getting to Dayton,* 115.

317   Holbrooke was already talking: State Department Office of Inspector General interview with RH, transcript, July 14, 1998, HP.

318   Lake's talks were: Weiner, "Clinton's Balkan Envoy Finds Himself Shut Out."

318   When Christopher, who kept himself: Strobe Talbott diary, August 12, 1995.

318   Sandy Berger called Lake: Daalder, *Getting to Dayton,* 116.

318   Lake gave Holbrooke: Chollet, *The Road to the Dayton Accords,* 43.

319   The idea had been: Daalder, *Getting to Dayton,* 116; Peter Tarnoff interviewed by Derek Chollet, Dayton Oral History Project, October 23, 1996, https://www.foia .state.gov.

319   "After Srebrenica": RH, *To End a War,* 75.

319   "We shouldn't let expectations": Chollet, *The Road to the Dayton Accords,* 45; RH, "The Road to Sarajevo," *The New Yorker,* October 21 and 28, 1996.

319   "Oh, at least fifty percent": RH, Bosnia audio diary, August 23, 1995, HP.

319   "I'm going to be with you": Roger Cohen, *Hearts Grown Brutal: Sagas of Sarajevo* (New York: Random House, 1998), 448–49; RH, *To End a War,* 74–75.

322   "Over the last three years": Chollet, *The Road to the Dayton Accords,* 21.

322   One day, Frasure: Hill, *Outpost,* 78. Hill changed "Clinton Brigade" to "Inter-agency Brigade" in the book.

322   Each middle-aged: Bildt, *Peace Journey,* 90; RH, *To End a War,* 8.

323   In November 1994: Peter Galbraith diary, November 15, 1994, Peter Galbraith Papers.

323   Over Croatian shellfish: Peter Galbraith diary, November 15, 1994. Peter Galbraith Papers.

324   So he got off the plane: Raymond Bonner, "Minister Says New U.S. Plan Lets Bosnia Keep Enclave," *New York Times,* August 16, 1995.

325   He regarded his two counterparts: Peter Galbraith interviewed by Charles Stuart Kennedy, 1999, ADST, Arlington, Va., https://www.adst.org.

326   Frasure wrote a note: RH, *To End a War,* 73.

327   Along the streets: Peter Galbraith diary, August 2, 1995. Peter Galbraith Papers.

327   When they sat down: "Serbia—Holbrooke Meets Milosevic in Belgrade," August 17, 1995, AP Archive, https://www.aparchive.com.

328   A Serb psychologist: Doder and Branson, *Milosevic,* 138.

328   Milosevic drank like: Rudy Perina interviewed by Christopher Hoh and Steve Engel, Dayton Oral History Project, July 19, 1996, https://www.foia.state.gov.

328   though in fact he'd spent: Doder and Branson, *Milosevic,* 64.

328   He found Holbrooke: Bildt, *Peace Journey,* 86.

329   "Frankly, no": Rudy Perina interviewed by Christopher Hoh and Steve Engel, Dayton Oral History Project, July 19, 1996, https://www.foia.state.gov.

332   On the morning of August 19: The first story of the accident on Mount Igman is a compressed version of the accounts in Holbrooke's *To End a War*, pp. 10–13, and *A Time to Lead: For Duty, Honor and Country* by Wesley K. Clark with Tom Carhart (New York: St. Martin's Press, 2007), pp. 180–82. The second story is based on the author's interviews with surviving participants, American and Bosnian; a daylong visit to the site; and numerous documents provided to the author, including entries from the contemporaneous diary of Ambassador John Menzies; the personal notebook of Lieutenant Colonel Randall Banky, with notes taken during and immediately after the incident; a narrative written by Banky at the end of August 1995 in support of the nomination of Staff Sergeant David Respass (now deceased) for a Soldier's Medal; a letter from Banky to Holbrooke, written on April 13, 1999, which Banky gave to Holbrooke when they met in Minneapolis and was filed in the Holbrooke Papers; and, most important, the eighty-eight-page official United Nations Protection Force Military Police Report on the accident, completed in Sarajevo on September 1, 1995, which includes maps, sketches, photographs, medical certificates, and statements by Banky, Respass, nine French soldiers, and two Bosnian soldiers. The U.N. report was never made public by the U.S. government or any other institution—it was essentially suppressed—but a copy was given to the author by a former State Department official. (The author's requests for U.S. government documents on the Igman incident, and on most other chapters of Holbrooke's career, were thwarted by the FOIA process, which has become dysfunctional.) These interviews and documents contradict aspects of the published accounts, while correcting the record on the role of little-known participants, particularly Banky.

338   two or three kilometers ahead: The use of metric in the rest of this account is based on the U.N. report and Banky's statement and recollections.

346   Kruzel's family was: Strobe Talbott diary, August 19, 1995.

346   It fell upon Tony: Lake, *6 Nightmares*, 161.

349   "Man, I'm sorry": Strobe Talbott diary, August 19, 1995.

350   Holbrooke didn't want to get on: RH, Bosnia audio diary, August 23, 1995, HP.

351   "He's a great admirer": Hill, *Outpost*, 85.

351   Her loss was still: RH, *To End a War*, 89.

351   "How can you do this": Hill, *Outpost*, 82.

352   There was a VIP compartment: James Pardew diary, August 29, 1995. Provided to the author by James Pardew.

352   Of the three Balkan leaders: RH to Generals Joulwan and Smith, December 9, 1995, HP.

352   After seeing so much suffering: RH, *To End a War*, 97.

352   "Mr. President, you are": Izetbegovic, *Inescapable Questions*, 271.

354   "And Averell would have been so proud": RH, *To End a War*, 95.

355   Neighbors of the embassy driver: Strobe Talbott diary, August 31, 1995.

355   Holbrooke thought there was: RH, *To End a War*, 104–5.

355   When the white-jacketed waiter: Hill, *Outpost*, 87.

356   "I wish Bob were here": Hill, *Outpost*, 89; RH, *To End a War*, 105–6.

356   The talking and eating: James W. Pardew, *Peacemakers: American Leadership*

and the End of Genocide in the Balkans (Lexington: University Press of Kentucky, 2017), 39.

356 He would step out: Hill, *Outpost,* 89–90.

356 When Milosevic finally: James Pardew diary, August 30, 1995; Pardew, *Peacemakers,* 42.

357 "Hey, man": Leslie H. Gelb interviewed by David Holbrooke. Provided to the author by David Holbrooke.

358 Pardew wondered if Holbrooke's ego: Pardew, *Peacemakers,* 40.

358 "We have no one else": James Pardew diary, September 2, 1995.

360 Izetbegovic replied: Izetbegovic, *Inescapable Questions,* 270–71; RH, *To End a War,* 130–31.

360 Afterward, in the early hours: RH, *To End a War,* 132.

361 I can hear it telling: RH, *To End a War,* 151.

361 Telling the press: Hill, *Outpost,* 90.

361 Telling Izetbegovic: RH, *To End a War,* 197.

361 Telling Pardew: Pardew, *Peacemakers,* 48.

361 "They say that diplomacy": Izetbegovic, *Inescapable Questions,* 271.

363 To give himself courage: RH, Bosnia audio diary, September 14, 1995, HP.

363 Holbrooke was determined: RH, Bosnia audio diary, September 14, 1995, HP; RH, *To End a War,* 149.

364 Of his former bosses: Robert A. Pratt, *Selma's Bloody Sunday: Protest, Voting Rights, and the Struggle for Racial Equality* (Baltimore: Johns Hopkins University Press, 2016), 110.

365 The Serbs signed: Hill, *Outpost,* 105–7; Pardew, *Peacemakers,* 56–61; RH, *To End a War,* 147–52; James Pardew diary, September 13, 1995.

365 But when Holbrooke walked outside: Hill, *Outpost,* 109; RH, *To End a War,* 163.

365 Milosevic begged: RH interviewed by Christopher Hoh and Steve Engel, Dayton Oral History Project, June 18, 1996, https://www.foia.state.gov.

370 Izetbegovic hated to negotiate: Izetbegovic, *Inescapable Questions,* 289–90.

370 He slept badly: Izetbegovic, *Inescapable Questions,* 309.

370 But at Packy's: RH, Dayton diary, November 1, 1995, HP.

371 He went shopping at a mall: Laura Silber and Allan Little, *The Death of Yugoslavia* (New York: Penguin Books, 1995), 372.

371 It didn't go any better: RH, Dayton diary, November 1, 1995, HP; RH, *To End a War,* 238.

371 "You're going to sit": RH, Dayton diary, November 1, 1995, HP.

372 "We always admired": RH, *To End a War,* 245.

372 "The most difficult thing": RH, Dayton diary, November 4, 1995, HP.

373 "You would do all this": RH, *To End a War,* 243.

373 "It's increasingly unlikely": RH, Dayton diary, November 9, 1995, HP.

374 "Saturday, Sunday, Monday": RH, Dayton diary, November 10, 1995, HP.

374 On Saturday, November 11: RH, Dayton diary, November 11, 1995, HP; RH, *To End a War,* 267–68.

374 This was one of his tricks: RH, *To End a War,* 279–80.

375 Even Izetbegovic: Izetbegovic, *Inescapable Questions,* 299.

375 Milosevic presented the Serb map: RH, Dayton diary, November 12, 1995, HP.

375 The Bosnian map was: Bildt, *Peace Journey,* 139–40.

375   The Bosnians now: RH interviewed by Christopher Hoh and Steve Engel, Dayton Oral History Project, June 18, 1996, https://www.foia.state.gov.

375   The Frasure, Kruzel: RH, *To End a War*, 269; RH, Dayton Diary, November 12, 1995, HP.

376   Over dinner one night: RH, Dayton diary, November 12, 1995, HP.

376   She was thinking of writing: "Classified Information Nondisclosure Agreement," December 3, 1995, HP.

376   On Wednesday night: RH, *To End a War*, 279.

377   Holbrooke crossed the floor: RH, *To End a War*, 280–81.

378   He told Holbrooke that back: Warren Christopher, *Chances of a Lifetime* (New York: Scribner, 2001), 267.

380   As Lake and Holbrooke walked: RH, *To End a War*, 282.

380   "Endgame personal": RH, *To End a War*, 289.

380   Bildt thought that: Bildt, *Peace Journey*, 146.

381   "Sarajevo must be": RH, *To End a War*, 291.

381   "You deserve Sarajevo": Silber and Little, *The Death of Yugoslavia*, 374.

382   "You tricked me": RH, *To End a War*, 295.

383   "This is going to ruin": Silber and Little, *The Death of Yugoslavia*, 373.

383   Around three-thirty a.m.: RH, *To End a War*, 299–300.

383   Izetbegovic was staring: Izetbegovic, *Inescapable Questions*, 325.

384   Earlier that night, Izetbegovic: Silber and Little, *The Death of Yugoslavia*, 375.

384   That night Christopher went: Bildt, *Peace Journey*, 157; Christopher, *Chances of a Lifetime*, 265.

384   With the knowledge: Izetbegovic, *Inescapable Questions*, 326.

385   The Balkan leaders were all crazy: Bildt, *Peace Journey*, 155.

385   He suspected they: Bildt, *Peace Journey*, 128.

385   "Give me something": Bildt, *Peace Journey*, 155.

385   "You can't let this happen": RH, *To End a War*, 306.

386   Holbrooke was desperate: Peter Galbraith diary, November 1995. Peter Galbraith Papers.

386   "It is not a viable contract": RH, *To End a War*, 308–9.

386   Izetbegovic experienced: Izetbegovic, *Inescapable Questions*, 326.

386   To Silajdzic he looked: "The Death of Yugoslavia, Part 6: Pax Americana," BBC, https://www.youtube.com.

WE ARE CLOSE TO OUR DREAMS

387   "Persistence": RH in Martyn Lewis, *Reflections on Success* (London: Queen Anne Press, 1997), 1.

389   Holbrooke saw Dayton: RH in Lewis, *Reflections on Success*, 10.

389   "We are close": RH to Kati Marton, December 13, 1995. Provided to the author by Kati Marton.

389   ("I have no administrative"): Office of Inspector General interview with RH, transcript, July 14, 1998, HP.

391   Two days after the election: Strobe Talbott diary, November 7, 1996.

393   Then Talbott suggested Lake for CIA: Strobe Talbott diary, November 11, 1996.

394   Within two days Holbrooke: Strobe Talbott diary, November 14, 1996.

394 "You and others have wondered": RH to Strobe Talbott, November 16, 1996, HP.

395 The first interview was with Gore: RH to Strobe Talbott, November 16, 1996, HP; Strobe Talbott diary, November 16, 1996.

395 He was looking ahead: RH to Strobe Talbott, November 16, 1996, HP.

395 He wondered aloud: Strobe Talbott diary, November 16, 1996.

396 "MKA—very articulate": RH, menu card from luncheon by secretary of state, Conrad Suite, New York, September 11, 2000, HP.

397 "Only if you pick": Madeleine Albright, *Madam Secretary: A Memoir* (New York: Miramax Books, 2003), 220.

398 "This is no time": RH, "Humanitarian Disasters: Forging a New Policy of Prevention," speech draft, January 13, 1997, HP.

401 "I am writing to inform you": Ibrahim Rugova to Madeleine Albright, March 16, 1998, HP.

401 "Holbrooke is out of control": Strobe Talbott diary, March 1998.

402 "You know what was": Christopher Hill, *Outpost: Life on the Frontlines of American Diplomacy* (New York: Simon & Schuster, 2014), 127.

402 "Kosovo is more valuable": RH memorandum to Madeleine Albright and Sandy Berger, July 10, 1998, HP.

403 "I like Deek": Hill, *Outpost,* 133.

403 "I need you desperately": Strobe Talbott diary, June 11, 1998; RH interviewed by Derek Chollet, March 26, 2000, HP.

404 "It's not my": Strobe Talbott diary, June 11, 1998.

404 Later, she told: Strobe Talbott diary, June 18, 1998.

405 whose Post-it notes: Provided to the author by Anthony Holbrooke.

405 "I must bring": Anonymous to State Department Office of Inspector General, June 18, 1998, HP.

406 Holbrooke and Kati were: "Friends of Angelo: Countrywide's Systematic and Successful Effort to Buy Influence and Block Reform," staff report, U.S. House of Representatives, 111th Congress Committee on Oversight and Government Reform, March 19, 2009, Washington, D.C., https://www.oversight.house.gov.

407 "Did you believe": Office of Inspector General interview with RH, transcript, July 14, 1998, HP.

407 "I have gone through": "Anthony Lake's Letter of Withdrawal," *PBS NewsHour,* March 18, 1997, https://www.pbs.org.

409 Killings by Serbian forces crossed: Ivo H. Daalder and Michael E. O'Hanlon, *Winning Ugly: NATO's War to Save Kosovo* (Washington, D.C.: Brookings Institution Press, 2000), 43.

409 In early October: Strobe Talbott diary, October 3, 1998.

409 His legal problems: Strobe Talbott diary, October 7, 1998.

409 Holbrooke in turn demanded that: Strobe Talbott diary, February 28, 1999.

409 Holbrooke thought that the rush: RH to Strobe Talbott, unsent, May 16, 1999, HP.

409 He wasn't even sure: RH to Madeleine Albright and Sandy Berger, memorandum, May 12, 1999, HP.

410 "You will bomb us": David Rothkopf, *Running the World: The Inside Story of the National Security Council* (New York: PublicAffairs, 2005), 378; Hill, *Outpost,* 156.

410 He wanted to stay in Belgrade: Strobe Talbott diary, March 22, 1999.

410 "Why, I wonder": RH, notes, May 12, 1999, HP.

412 His legal bill: Richard Beattie to RH, March 26, 1999, HP.

413 "My father talked": RH, testimony to Senate Committee on Foreign Relations, U.S. Senate, June 17, 1999, Washington, D.C., HP.

YOU'RE EITHER GOING TO WIN OR FALL

414 He compared himself: James Traub, "Holbrooke's Campaign," *New York Times Magazine*, March 26, 2000.

415 "I hope Gore": Strobe Talbott diary, February 28, 2000.

416 Every week that fall: RH interviewed by Derek Chollet, March 26, 2000, HP; James Traub, "Holbrooke in Turtle Bay," in *The Unquiet American*, ed. Derek Chollet and Samantha Power (New York: PublicAffairs, 2011), 242–43.

417 Holbrooke met one-on-one: RH interviewed by Derek Chollet, March 26, 2000, HP.

417 Holbrooke found this nickel-and-diming: RH interviewed by Derek Chollet, June 20, 2000, HP.

418 He got deep into the budget: Traub, "Holbrooke in Turtle Bay," 247.

419 At the beginning of December 1999: Confidential cable from the secretary of state, "Summary of Ambassador Holbrooke's December 1–12 Trip to Africa," December 21, 1999, HP.

421 In early May 2000: Justin Pearce, "Diplomats Fail to Bridge the Gap," BBC News, May 12, 2000, https://www.news.bbc.co.uk; Jane Perlez, "U.S. Did Little to Deter Buildup as Ethiopia and Eritrea Prepared for War," *New York Times*, May 22, 2000.

425 a speech to oligarchs: Viktor Pinchuk, Interpipe Group, to Sonya Giacobbe, Greater Talent Network, June 8, 2004, HP.

426 "What Holbrooke wants": Roger Cohen, *Hearts Grown Brutal: Sagas of Sarajevo* (New York: Random House, 1998), 449.

427 He said that the culprit: "CNN 9-11-2001 Live Coverage 8:46.32 A.M E.T—5.00 P.M E.T," YouTube, 4:17:26, https://www.youtube.com.

427 The more TV appearances: RH, "Notes on the First Two Weeks After September 11, 2001," September 14, 2001, HP.

428 In October, he used: RH, "After September 11: Creating the Third Transatlantic Alliance," speech draft, October 9, 2001, HP.

428 After overthrowing the Taliban: RH, "Letters to the Editor: Long-Term Dangers in Afghanistan," *Wall Street Journal*, March 29, 2002.

428 "As Washington confronts": RH, "Rebuilding Nations in Crisis," *Washington Post*, April 1, 2002.

429 Holbrooke chose to support: RH, testimony to Senate Committee on Foreign Relations, U.S. Senate, September 25, 2002, Washington, D.C., HP.

430 And he just liked her better: RH interviewed by the author, December 2007.

430 "I'm not a great believer": Michael Hirsh, "Battle for the Best and Brightest," *Newsweek*, September 5, 2007.

431 "Tell him we MIGHT": Barnett Rubin, unpublished book manuscript, chapter 1. Provided to the author by Barnett Rubin.

432 When Power got married: RH, Afghanistan written diary, August 6, 2008, HP.

432 In July he had another episode: RH, Afghanistan written diary, July 23, 2008, HP.

432 "It's like a cruise": RH, Afghanistan written diary, August 27, 2008, HP.

433 He and Kati owned: "Questionnaire for National Security Positions," U.S. Office of Personnel Management, January 6, 2009, HP.

EVERYTHING IS DIFFERENT—AND EVERYTHING IS THE SAME

438 A white pigeon: Joshua Partlow, *A Kingdom of Their Own: The Family Karzai and the Afghan Disaster* (New York: Knopf, 2016), 20.

438 On his way out: RH, notes, undated, HP.

439 The story has been told: Among the best books in English on the Afghan wars are Steve Coll's *Ghost Wars: The Secret History of the CIA, Afghanistan, and Bin Laden from the Soviet Invasion to September 10, 2001* (New York: Penguin Press, 2004) and *Directorate S: The CIA and America's Secret Wars in Afghanistan and Pakistan* (New York: Penguin Press, 2018), Anand Gopal's *No Good Men Among the Living* (New York: Metropolitan Books, 2014), Dexter Filkins's *The Forever War* (New York: Knopf, 2008), Ahmed Rashid's *Taliban: Militant Islam, Oil and Fundamentalism in Central Asia* (New Haven, Conn.: Yale University Press, 2000) and *Descent into Chaos: The United States and the Failure of Nation Building in Pakistan, Afghanistan, and Central Asia* (New York: Viking, 2008), Sarah Chayes's *The Punishment of Virtue: Inside Afghanistan After the Taliban* (New York: Penguin Press, 2006), Hassan Abbas's *The Taliban Revival: Violence and Extremism on the Afghanistan-Pakistan Frontier* (New Haven, Conn.: Yale Univeristy Press, 2014), Barnett Rubin's *Afghanistan from the Cold War Through the War on Terror* (Oxford: Oxford University Press, 2013), Abdul Salam Zaeef's *My Life with the Taliban* (London: Hurst, 2011), J. Kael Weston's *The Mirror Test: America at War in Iraq and Afghanistan* (New York: Alfred A. Knopf, 2016), and Rajiv Chandrasekaran's *Little America: The War Within the War for Afghanistan* (New York: Vintage Books, 2012).

443 A Foreign Service officer named: Weston, *The Mirror Test*, 270–78; RH, "The Longest War," *Washington Post*, March 31, 2008.

446 On the afternoon of November 17: RH, Afghanistan written diary, November 17, 2008, HP; RH interviewed by the author, July 27, 2009.

446 Obama was the kind of person: The author had this experience in a 2006 interview with Senator Obama.

448 ("my patriotic genes"): RH, Afghanistan written diary, November 28, 2008, HP.

448 On November 20, Holbrooke: RH, Afghanistan written diary, November 28, 2008, HP.

449 A few days after their meeting: RH to Barack Obama, "The Paradoxes of Pakistan and Afghanistan," November 21, 2008, HP.

450 He laid out his requirements: RH interviewed by the author, June 15, 2009.

451 "I am deeply torn": RH, Afghanistan written diary, December 18, 2008, HP.

452 "8. Briefly describe": "Questionnaire for National Security Positions," U.S. Office of Personnel Management, January 6, 2009, HP.

452 "He's on the verge": Isadore Rosenfeld, RH medical records, December 10, 2008. Provided to the author by Dr. Holly Andersen.

452 But Rosenfeld pronounced: "Questionnaire for National Security Positions," U.S. Office of Personnel Management, January 6, 2009, HP.

453 "Good speech, but": RH, Afghanistan written diary, January 20, 2009, HP.

454 When it was Holbrooke's turn: "President Obama Delivers Remarks to State Department Employees," CQ Transcriptions, *Washington Post,* January 22, 2009.

456 "Lesson learned": RH, Afghanistan written diary, March 31, 2009, HP.

457 The next day, Haqqani: Husain Haqqani cables to Pakistan's foreign secretary, January 30, 2009. Provided to the author.

459 On a bookshelf: Marvin Kalb and Deborah Kalb, *Haunting Legacy: Vietnam and the American Presidency from Ford to Obama* (Washington, D.C.: Brookings Institution Press, 2011), 265.

460 "Your problem is": Barnett Rubin, unpublished book manuscript, chapter 1.1.

460 And he told Nasr: Vali Nasr, "The Inside Story of How the White House Let Diplomacy Fail in Afghanistan," *Foreign Policy,* March 4, 2013, https://www .foreignpolicy.com.

461 Holbrooke coached Rubin: Barnett Rubin, unpublished book manuscript, chapter 2; Barnett Rubin to Kati Marton, January 18, 2011. Provided to the author by Barnett Rubin.

462 Holbrooke had just heard: Burt Field notebooks, January 27, 2009. Provided to the author by Burt Field.

462 "Best were Barney": RH, Afghanistan written diary, February 11, 2009, HP.

465 Obama and his foreign policy team gathered: RH, Afghanistan written diary, January 22, 2009, HP.

465 Donilon, Jones's deputy: RH, Afghanistan written diary, January 26, 2009, HP.

466 He wasted no time: RH, Afghanistan written diary, February 23, 2009, HP.

466 "This is a war": "Obama's Remarks on Iraq and Afghanistan," *New York Times,* July 15, 2008.

467 "His job should be": Chandrasekaran, *Little America,* 247.

468 "I believe that history": RH, Afghanistan written diary, January 22, 2009, HP.

468 "Let me speak": RH, Afghanistan written diary, February 13, 2009, HP.

469 Then he added, "I don't like leaks": RH, Afghanistan written diary, May 11, 2009, HP.

470 Obama sometimes stuck a finger: RH, Afghanistan written diary, November 5, 2009, HP.

473 "It is beyond ironic": RH, Afghanistan written diary, July 29, 2009, September 7–8, 2009, HP.

476 He calculated that: Sherard Cowper-Coles, memorandum, "CONFIDENTIAL: CONVERSATION WITH KARZAI 14 MARCH," March 14, 2009, HP.

476 Holbrooke encouraged so many: Kai Eide, *Power Struggle Over Afghanistan* (New York: Skyhorse Publishing, 2012), 128.

477 In his diary, Holbrooke called him: RH, Afghanistan written diary, March 12, 2009, HP.

477 He prescribed a delicate daily mix: Sherard Cowper-Coles, *Cables from Kabul: The Inside Story of the West's Afghanistan Campaign* (London: HarperPress, 2011), 157, 221.

478 As soon as they sat: Eide, *Power Struggle Over Afghanistan,* 125–27; Scott Smith diary, February 13, 2009. Provided to the author by Scott Smith.

479 "I'm a friend": RH, untitled note from meeting with Karzai, undated, HP.

479 Holbrooke floated: Cowper-Coles, *Cables from Kabul,* 210.

479 How he told Karzai: RH, Afghanistan written diary, April 9, 2009, HP.

481 He flew to Helmand: The author attended the meeting.

482 In late July, Holbrooke and Eikenberry: The author attended the lunch.

484 So did Eikenberry: Cowper-Coles, *Cables from Kabul,* 234.

485 They sat down for lunch: RH, Afghanistan written diary, September 7–8, 2009, HP.

489 In September an article: George Packer, "The Last Mission," *The New Yorker,* September 28, 2009.

489 But he summoned Holbrooke: James Mann, *The Obamians: The Struggle Inside the White House to Redefine American Power* (New York: Penguin Books, 2012), 234.

491 "I think of no body fat": Elisabeth Bumiller and Mark Mazzetti, "A General Steps from the Shadows," *New York Times,* May 13, 2009.

492 In his diary Holbrooke once called the Situation Room: RH, Afghanistan written diary, March 12, 2009, HP.

494 Among his notes: RH, notes from National Security Council meetings, October 7, 2009, October 9, 2009, HP.

494 Now, in the forty-seventh year: RH, notes from Kabul, June 20, 2010, HP.

495 "That's outrageous": RH, Afghanistan written diary, October 18, 2009, HP.

495 He found her frustratingly complicated: RH, Afghanistan written diary, January 29, 2010, HP.

496 "Like you, I believe": RH to Hillary Clinton, "Suggested Policy for Afghanistan," memorandum, October 12, 2009, HP.

498 "Too cute by half": RH to Hillary Clinton, "The Proposal," talking points, October 26, 2009, HP.

498 "She went to the hard side": RH, Afghanistan written diary, October 27, 2009, November 16, 2009, HP.

498 "We have spent almost": RH, notes from National Security Council meeting, November 23, 2009, HP.

498 Afterward, around eleven: RH, Afghanistan written diary, November 23, 2009, HP.

500 "I'm sorry that you had to endure": James Jones to Karl Eikenberry, February 23, 2010, HP.

500 Holbrooke got his on March 16: Frank Ricciardone to RH, March 16, 2010, HP.

503 Jones was "an idiot": RH, Afghanistan written diary, March 18, 2010, HP.

504 Obama told Clinton: RH, Afghanistan written diary, March 26, 2010, HP; RH, notes, March 26, 2010, HP.

504 "Anyway, in my bones": RH, Afghanistan written diary, April 12–13, 2010, HP.

507 "This is to excuse your father": RH, note to Amir Nasr, November 3, 2010. Provided to the author by Vali Nasr.

508 Possible Process: RH, "David Miliband Dinner—UK EMB/KABUL," notes, January 16, 2010, HP.

509 In President House: The author attended the meeting.

514 "Remember," he told Rubin: Barnett Rubin, spreadsheet of dates with RH, August 12, 2009. Provided to the author by Barnett Rubin.

515 "RCH should visit Riyadh": Barnett Rubin, "Visit to Riyadh, Saudi Arabia, 13–15 April 2009," memorandum, undated, HP.

517 In August, Mansour summoned him: Coll, *Directorate S,* 416–18.

517 He was related to Omar: Coll, *Directorate S,* 446.

517 He told colleagues: Coll, *Directorate S,* 423.

518 "By the time they cut": Coll, *Directorate S,* 432.

518 If Obama waited: RH interviewed by Steve Coll, February 27, 2010. Provided to the author by Steve Coll.

519 "The boss says": Michael Hastings, "The Runaway General," *Rolling Stone,* June 22, 2010, https://www.rollingstone.com.

520 "Sir, I want to apologize": RH, notes, June 20, 2010, HP.

520 "I am lying here": RH to Stanley McChrystal, June 22, 2010, HP.

521 "I feel awful": RH to David Petraeus, June 23, 2010, HP.

522 $250,000 in cash: RH, Afghanistan audio diary, date unknown, HP.

522 "The insurgents win": RH to Hillary Clinton, "At the Crossroads," memorandum, September 10, 2010, HP.

523 Kayani had written: Coll, *Directorate S,* 502.

525 "Vacation with K": RH, Afghanistan written diary, June 30, 2009, HP.

527 "Today was a difficult day": This narrative is composed of excerpts of entries from RH's Afghanistan audio diary dated August 2, 2010; August 4, 2010; August 5–6, 2010; August 7, 2010; August 9, 2010; August 11, 2010; August 20, 2010; August 23, 2010; August 24, 2010; August 27, 2010; September 14, 2010; September 17, 2010; September 18, 2010; September 22, 2010; September 28, 2010; October 8, 2010; November 2, 2010; November 4, 2010; November 17, 2010; December 3, 2010; and December 7, 2010, HP.

532 Petraeus has changed: RH, notes, October 28, 2010, HP.

541 Haqqani reported this: Husain Haqqani cables to Pakistan's foreign secretary, November 24, 2010, December 8, 2010.

541 "I wonder if they know": Husain Haqqani, *Magnificent Delusions: Pakistan, the United States, and an Epic History of Misunderstanding* (New York: PublicAffairs, 2013), 344.

544 Holbrooke was tired, subdued: Michael Abramowitz, "Holbrooke Dinner, Dec 9, 2010," memorandum. Provided to the author by Michael Abramowitz.

EPILOGUE

553 A pink-flowered: Shuja Pasha, Hallmark card, undated, HP.

553 The memorial service: "Ambassador Richard Holbrooke Memorial Service," C-SPAN, January 14, 2011, https://www.c-span.org.

554 as if he were floating: The image was suggested by Cameron Munter, former U.S. ambassador to Pakistan.

Acknowledgments

My first thanks go to Kati Marton, who, a month after her husband's death, entrusted me with his papers, gave me the exclusive right to quote from them, encouraged others to provide help, and imposed no conditions whatsoever, except that I write the best book I could. It wouldn't exist without her faith and generosity.

Thanks to Christian Kerr, my research assistant and indispensable partner in discovering, organizing, and understanding the vast record of Richard Holbrooke's life.

To those who shared diaries, letters, notes, photographs, videos, and other personal material: Michael Abramowitz, Holly Andersen, Randall Banky, Richard Beattie, Ashley Bommer, Steve Coll, John Dempsey, Dan Feldman, Burt Field, Peter Galbraith, Andrew Holbrooke, Anthony Holbrooke, Litty Holbrooke, Vladimir Lehovich, Gail Malcolm, John Menzies, Vali Nasr, Don North, James Pardew, Kenneth Quinn, Saskia Reilly, Barnett Rubin, Scott Smith, Strobe Talbott, Frank Wisner, and especially David Holbrooke.

To Aida Cerkez and Sasa Halulic in Bosnia, Jovana Gligorijevic and Bratislav Grubacic in Serbia, Thu Ha Nguyen in Vietnam, Ruhullah Khapalwak, Rod Nordland, and SEPAR International in Afghanistan, and John McCance at Wright-Patterson Air Force Base in Dayton for vital assistance on the road.

To the American Academy in Berlin, the Dorothy and Lewis B. Cullman Center for Scholars and Writers, the New America Foundation, the Whiting Foundation, and their staffs for generous fellowships that helped support four years of research and writing.

To David Remnick and Daniel Zalewski of *The New Yorker* for giving me the chance to learn my trade from the best. And to Rozina Ali for her acumen with facts.

To those discerning friends who took time to read all or part of the manuscript and improved it with their advice: Daniel Bergner, Roger Cohen, Dexter Filkins, Jonathan Galassi, Eliza Griswold, Gordon Harvey, Larissa MacFarquhar, David Remnick, David Rohde, Vikram Singh, Amy Waldman, and Daniel Zalewski.

To Sarah Chalfant of the Wylie Agency for her keen and tireless support.

To Sonny Mehta of Alfred A. Knopf, who took the book on before I knew how to explain it; to Andrew Miller, whose editorial intelligence and friendship kept faith with it even when the author didn't; and to Zakiya Harris, Erinn Hartman, Maria Massey, and Tyler Comrie, who helped bring it into the world.

To my mother, Nancy Packer, who gave me my first, most arduous, and most important education in the art of writing.

To Charlie and Julia, shining lights in dark times; and to Laura, my best reader and friend, my touchstone and heart's desire: there are no words for what I owe you, only love.

LIST OF ILLUSTRATIONS

Index

Page references in *italics* indicate images.
RH indicates Richard Holbrooke.